Adversarial Machine Learning

Written by leading researchers, this complete introduction brings together all the theory and tools needed for building robust machine learning in adversarial environments. Discover how machine learning systems can adapt when an adversary actively poisons data to manipulate statistical inference, learn the latest practical techniques for investigating system security and performing robust data analysis, and gain insight into new approaches for designing effective countermeasures against the latest wave of cyberattacks. Privacy-preserving mechanisms and near-optimal evasion of classifiers are discussed in detail, and in-depth case studies on email spam and network security highlight successful attacks on traditional machine learning algorithms. Providing a thorough overview of the current state of the art in the field and possible future directions, this groundbreaking work is essential reading for researchers, practitioners, and students in computer security and machine learning and for those wanting to learn about the next stage of the cybersecurity arms race.

Anthony D. Joseph is a Chancellor's Professor in the Department of Electrical Engineering and Computer Sciences at the University of California, Berkeley. He was formerly the Director of Intel Labs Berkeley.

Blaine Nelson is a Software Engineer in the Counter-Abuse Technology (CAT) team at Google. He previously worked at the University of Potsdam and the University of Tübingen.

Benjamin I. P. Rubinstein is an Associate Professor in Computing and Information Systems at the University of Melbourne. He has previously worked at Microsoft Research, Google Research, Yahoo! Research, Intel Labs Berkeley, and IBM Research.

J. D. Tygar is a Professor at the University of California, Berkeley, and he has worked widely in the field of computer security. At Berkeley, he holds appointments in both the Department of Electrical Engineering and Computer Sciences and the School of Information.

"Data Science practitioners tend to be unaware of how easy it is for adversaries to manipulate and misuse adaptive machine learning systems. This book demonstrates the severity of the problem by providing a taxonomy of attacks and studies of adversarial learning. It analyzes older attacks as well as recently discovered surprising weaknesses in deep learning systems. A variety of defenses are discussed for different learning systems and attack types that could help researchers and developers design systems that are more robust to attacks."

Richard Lippmann, *Lincoln Laboratory, MIT*

"This is a timely book. Right time and right book, written with an authoritative but inclusive style. Machine learning is becoming ubiquitous. But for people to trust it, they first need to understand how reliable it is."

Fabio Roli, *University of Cagliari*

Adversarial Machine Learning

ANTHONY D. JOSEPH
University of California, Berkeley

BLAINE NELSON
Google

BENJAMIN I. P. RUBINSTEIN
University of Melbourne

J. D. TYGAR
University of California, Berkeley

CAMBRIDGE
UNIVERSITY PRESS

CAMBRIDGE
UNIVERSITY PRESS

University Printing House, Cambridge CB2 8BS, United Kingdom

One Liberty Plaza, 20th Floor, New York, NY 10006, USA

477 Williamstown Road, Port Melbourne, VIC 3207, Australia

314–321, 3rd Floor, Plot 3, Splendor Forum, Jasola District Centre,
New Delhi - 110025, India

79 Anson Road, #06-04/06, Singapore 079906

Cambridge University Press is part of the University of Cambridge.

It furthers the University's mission by disseminating knowledge in the pursuit of
education, learning and research at the highest international levels of excellence.

www.cambridge.org
Information on this title: www.cambridge.org/9781107043466
DOI:10.1017/9781107338548

© Cambridge University Press 2019

First published 2019

Printed and bound in Great Britain by Clays Ltd, Elcograf S.p.A.

A catalogue record for this publication is available from the British Library

Library of Congress Cataloging-in-Publication data
Names: Joseph, Anthony D., author. | Nelson, Blaine, author. | Rubinstein, Benjamin I. P., author. |
Tygar, J. D., author.
Title: Adversarial machine learning / Anthony D. Joseph, University of California, Berkeley, Blaine Nelson,
Google, Benjamin I.P. Rubinstein, University of Melbourne, J.D. Tygar, University of California, Berkeley.
Description: Cambridge, United Kingdom ; New York, NY : Cambridge University Press, 2019. |
Includes bibliographical references and index.
Identifiers: LCCN 2017026016 | ISBN 9781107043466 (hardback)
Subjects: LCSH: Machine learning. | Computer security. | BISAC: COMPUTERS / Security / General.
Classification: LCC Q325.5 .J69   2017 | DDC 006.3/1 – dc23
LC record available at https://lccn.loc.gov/2017026016

ISBN 978-1-107-04346-6 Hardback

Contents

Symbols

$A\,(\,\cdot\,)$: The adversary's cost function on $\mathcal{X}$ (see Section 8.1.1). See 203–209, 211, 212, 214, 216, 219–221, 228, 231, 234, 235

$\mathbb{D}$: A set of data points (see also: dataset). See 23–26, 183

   N : The number of data points in the training dataset used by a learning algorithm; i.e., $N \triangleq \left|\mathbb{D}^{(\text{train})}\right|$. See 21, 23, 25–27, 36, 38–40, 46, 47, 50, 54, 56, 183, 184, 256

   $\mathbb{D}^{(\text{train})}$: A dataset used by a training algorithm to construct or select a classifier (see also: dataset). See 21, 25, 26, 36, 39, 40, 48, 50, 107, 120, 128

   $\mathbb{D}^{(\text{eval})}$: A dataset used to evaluate a classifier (see also: dataset). See 21, 22, 25, 27, 36, 39, 40, 46, 48, 50, 51, 128

$\triangleq$: Symbol used to provide a definition. See 23, 24, 26, 57, 58, 60, 107, 108, 137, 139, 141, 142, 149, 153, 204, 206, 256–259, 265, 276, 278, 279, 281, 282

$\epsilon\text{-}IMAC$: The set of objects in $\mathcal{X}_f^-$ within a cost of $1 + \epsilon$ of the MAC, or any of the members of this set (see also: $MAC\,(f, A)$). See 204–206, 209–214, 216, 219–221, 225, 229, 231–235, 237, 251

$f\,(\,\cdot\,)$: The classifier function or hypothesis learned by a training procedure $H^{(N)}$ from the dataset $\mathbb{D}^{(\text{train})}$ (see also: classifier). See 21, 24–27, 39, 40, 48–51, 54, 71, 74, 102, 120, 139, 174, 176–183, 189, 195, 196, 202–207, 209, 210, 212, 215, 217–220, 234–237, 251

L_ϵ : The number of steps required by a binary search to achieve ϵ-optimality (see Section 8.1.3). See 205, 210–212, 214–218, 220, 221, 225, 228, 232

$MAC\,(f, A)$: The largest lower bound on the adversary's cost A over $\mathcal{X}_f^-$ (see also: Equation 8.2). See 204, 206, 207, 210, 212–214, 216, 219, 221, 229, 230, 234, 235

$\mathfrak{N}$: The set of natural numbers, $\{1, 2, 3, \ldots\}$. See 77–79, 81, 83, 88, 137, 256, 257, 276

$\mathfrak{N}_0$: The set of all whole numbers, $\{0, 1, 2, \ldots\}$. See 73, 77–79, 81, 82, 86, 256

$\|\cdot\|$: A non-negative function defined on a vector space that is positive homogeneous and obeys the triangle inequality (see also: norm). See 145, 147, 149, 152, 153, 203, 226, 227, 257

ℓ_p $(p > 0)$: A norm on a multidimensional real-value space defined in Appendix A.1 by Equation (A.1) and denoted by $\| \cdot \|_p$. See 11, 18, 200, 203, 204, 208, 210–214, 216–218, 220, 221, 223, 225–234, 244, 245, 260, 261, 264, 265

$m_{\mathbb{C}}$ ($\cdot$) : A function that defines a distance metric for a convex set $\mathbb{C}$ relative to some central element $\mathbf{x}^{(c)}$ in the interior of $\mathbb{C}$ (see also: Minkowski metric). See 210, 211

$N^{(h)}$: The total number of ham messages in the training dataset. See 107, 108, 111, 277–280

$n_j^{(h)}$: The number of occurences of the jth token in training ham messages. See 107, 108, 111, 277–280

$N^{(s)}$: The total number of spam messages in the training dataset. See 107, 108, 111, 119, 277–280

$n_j^{(s)}$: The number of occurrences of the jth token in training spam messages. See 107, 108, 111, 119, 277–280

$\mathbf{Q}$: The matrix of network flow data. See 137, 138, 152

$\mathbf{R}$: The routing matrix that describes the links used to route each OD flow. See 138, 142, 152

$\Re$: The set of all real numbers. See 23–25, 27, 142, 256–259
  $\Re_{0+}$: The set of all real numbers greater than or equal to zero. See 26, 203, 211, 256, 276
  $\Re_{+}$: The set of all real numbers greater than zero. See 27, 216, 256, 257
  $\Re^D$: The D-dimensional real-valued space. See 24, 139, 142, 143, 147, 202, 216, 226, 257, 259

$\mathbf{x}$: A data point from the input space $\mathcal{X}$ (see also data point). See 22–24, 138, 139, 141, 145, 147, 148, 200, 203–206, 208–211, 213, 223, 224, 226, 255
  $\mathbf{x}^A$: A (malicious) data point that the adversary would like to sneak past the detector. See 70, 203–206, 209–215, 217, 218, 221–223, 225, 226, 231, 233–235, 261, 264, 265

$\mathcal{X}$: The input space of the data (see also: input space). See 22–25, 49, 202, 203, 206, 208, 210, 211, 224, 233, 235, 236, 259, 260
  D : The dimensionality of the input space $\mathcal{X}$. See 22, 23, 202–205, 212–218, 220, 223–232, 235, 237, 259
  $\mathcal{X}_f^-$: The negative class for the deterministic classifier f (see also: negative class). See 203–206, 208, 210–213, 219, 221–224, 226, 231, 233, 235, 236
  $\mathcal{X}_f^+$: The positive class for the deterministic classifier f (see also: positive class). See 203, 205, 210–214, 216, 218, 233, 234

y : A label from the response space $\mathcal{Y}$ (see also: label). See 23, 26, 27, 107

$\mathcal{Y}$: The response space of the data (see also response space). See 23–27, 59, 203

$\mathfrak{Z}$: The set of all integers. See 23, 256, 258

Acknowledgments

We gratefully acknowledge the contributions and assistance of our colleagues in making this book possible, who include but are not limited to Sadia Afroz, Scott Alfeld, Tansu Alpcan, Rekha Bachwani, Marco Barreno, Adam Barth, Peter Bartlett, Battista Biggio, Chris Cai, Fuching Jack Chi, David Fifield, Laurent El Ghaoui, Barbara Goto, Rachel Greenstadt, Yi Han, Ling Huang, Michael Jordan, Alex Kantchelian, Hideaki Kawabata, Marius Kloft, Pavel Laskov, Shing-hon Lau, Chris Leckie, Steven Lee, Justin Ma, Steve Martin, Brad Miller, Satish Rao, Fabio Roli, Udam Saini, Tobias Scheffer, Russell Sears, Anil Sewani, Arunesh Sinha, Dawn Song, Nedim Šrndić, Charles Sutton, Nina Taft, Anthony Tran, Michael Tschantz, Kai Xai, Takumi Yamamoto, and Qi Zhong. We additionally thank Matthias Bussas and Marius Kloft for their careful proofreading of Chapter 4 and the staff at Cambridge University Press including Heather Brolly and Julie Lancashire for their help in preparing this manuscript. We would also like to thank the many colleagues with whom we have had fruitful discussions at the Dagstuhl Perspectives Workshop on Machine Learning Methods for Computer Security (Joseph, Laskov, Roli, Tygar, & Nelson 2013) and at the ACM Workshop on Artificial Intelligence and Security (AISec) and other workshops and conferences.

The authors are currently at the University of California, Berkeley, the University of Melbourne, and Google. We thank these institutions. While we were writing this book, some of the authors were at Universität Tübingen, Universität Potsdam, Università di Cagliari, IBM Research, and Microsoft Research, and we also thank those institutions. We offer special thanks to our support staff, including Angie Abbatecola, Kattt Atchley, Carlyn Chinen, Barbara Goto, Damon Hinson, Michaela Iglesia, Shane Knapp, Jey Kottalam, Jon Kuroda, Lena Lau-Stewart, Christian Legg, and Boban Zarkovich.

We are grateful for the financial sponsors of this research. We received U.S. government funding from the Air Force Office of Scientific Research, Homeland Security Advanced Research Projects Agency, National Science Foundation, and State Department DRL, and in some cases through UC Berkeley laboratories (DETERlab and TRUST). Some authors received additional support from the Alexander von Humboldt Foundation, the Australian Research Council (DE160100584), the Center for Long-Term Cybersecurity, the Future of Life Institute, Oak Ridge National Laboratory, and the Open Technology Fund. The opinions expressed in this book are solely those of the authors and do not necessarily reflect the views of any funder.

The authors could not have written this book without the support, encouragement, and patience of their friends and families.

Part I

Overview of Adversarial Machine Learning

1   Introduction

Machine learning has become a prevalent tool in many computing applications. With the rise of machine learning techniques, however, comes a concomitant risk. Adversaries may attempt to exploit a learning mechanism either to cause it to misbehave or to extract or misuse information.

This book introduces the problem of secure machine learning; more specifically, it looks at learning mechanisms in adversarial environments. We show how adversaries can effectively exploit existing learning algorithms and discuss new learning algorithms that are resistant to attack. We also show lower bounds on the complexity of extracting information from certain kinds of classifiers by probing. These lower bound results mean that any learning mechanism must use classifiers of a certain complexity or potentially be vulnerable to adversaries who are determined to evade the classifiers. Training data privacy is an important special case of this phenomenon. We demonstrate that while accurate statistical models can be released that reveal nothing significant about individual training data, fundamental limits prevent simultaneous guarantees of strong privacy and accuracy.

One potential concern with learning algorithms is that they may introduce a security fault into systems that employ them. The key strengths of learning approaches are their adaptability and ability to infer patterns that can be used for predictions and decision making. However, these advantages of machine learning can potentially be subverted by adversarial manipulation of the knowledge and evidence provided to the learner. This exposes applications that use machine learning techniques to a new class of security vulnerability; i.e., learners are susceptible to a novel class of attacks that can cause the learner to disrupt the system it was intended to benefit. In this book we investigate the behavior of learning systems that are placed under threat in security-sensitive domains. We will demonstrate that learning algorithms are vulnerable to a myriad of attacks that can transform the learner into a liability for the system they are intended to aid, but that by critically analyzing potential security threats, the extent of these threats can be assessed and proper learning methods can be selected to minimize the adversary's impact and prevent system failures.

We investigate both the practical and theoretical aspects of applying machine learning to security domains in five main foci: a taxonomy for qualifying the security vulnerabilities of a learner, two novel practical attacks and countermeasure case studies, an algorithm for provable privacy-preserving learning, and methods for evading detection by a classifier. We present a framework for identifying and analyzing threats to learners and use it to systematically explore the vulnerabilities of several proposed learning systems. For these systems, we identify real-world threats, analyze their potential impact, and study learning techniques that significantly diminish their effect. Further, we discuss models for privacy-preserving learning and evasion of classifiers and use those models to defend against, and analyze, classifier vulnerabilities. In doing so, we provide practitioners with guidelines to identify potential vulnerabilities and demonstrate improved learning techniques that are resilient to attacks. Our research focuses on learning tasks in virus, spam, and network anomaly detection, but also is broadly applicable across many systems and security domains and has momentous implications for any system that incorporates learning. In the remainder of this chapter, we further motivate the need for a security analysis of machine learning algorithms and provide a brief history of the work that led us to this research and the lessons learned from it.

Our work has wide applicability. While learning techniques are already common for tasks such as natural language processing (cf. Jurafsky & Martin 2008), face detection (cf. Zhao, Chellappa, Phillips, & Rosenfeld 2003), and handwriting recognition (cf. Plamondon & Srihari 2000), they also have potentially far-reaching utility for many applications in security, networking, and large-scale systems as a vital tool for data analysis and autonomic decision making. As suggested by Mitchell (2006), learning approaches are particularly well suited to domains where either the application *i*) is too complex to be designed manually or *ii*) needs to dynamically evolve. Many of the challenges faced in modern enterprise systems meet these criteria and stand to benefit from agile learning algorithms able to infer hidden patterns in large complicated datasets, adapt to new behaviors, and provide statistical soundness to decision-making processes. Indeed, learning components have been proposed for tasks such as performance modeling (e.g., Bodík, Fox, Franklin, Jordan, & Patterson 2010; Bodík, Griffith, Sutton, Fox, Jordan, & Patterson 2009; Xu, Bodík, & Patterson 2004), enterprise-level network fault diagnosis (e.g., Bahl, Chandra, Greenberg, Kandula, Maltz, & Zhang 2007; Cheng, Afanasyev, Verkaik, Benkö, Chiang, Snoeren, Savage, & Voelker 2007; Kandula, Chandra, & Katabi 2008), and spam detection (e.g., Meyer & Whateley 2004; Segal, Crawford, Kephart, & Leiba 2004).

1.1   Motivation

Machine learning techniques are being applied to a growing number of systems and networking problems, a tendency that can be attributed to two emerging trends. First, learning techniques have proven to be exceedingly successful at finding patterns in data-rich domains and have provided statistically grounded techniques applicable to a wide variety of settings. In rapidly changing environments, machine learning techniques are considerably advantageous over handcrafted rules and other approaches because they can infer hidden patterns in data, they can adapt quickly to new signals and behaviors, and they can provide statistical soundness to a decision-making process. Second, the need to protect systems against malicious adversaries continues to increase across systems and networking applications. Rising levels of hostile behavior have plagued many application domains including email, web search, pay-per-click advertisements, file sharing, instant messaging, and mobile phone communications. The task of detecting (and subsequently preventing) such malicious activity is broadly known as the malfeasance detection problem, and it includes spam, fraud, intrusion, and virus detection. In such problem domains, machine learning techniques are arguably necessary because they provide the ability for a system to respond more readily to evolving real-world data, both hostile and benign, and to learn to identify or possibly even prevent undesirable activities.

In the malfeasance detection problem, machine learning techniques are proving themselves to be an invaluable tool to maintain system security. From spam filtering to malware detection to fast attack response and many other applications, machine learning is quickly becoming a useful tool for computer security. For example, network intrusion detection systems (NIDSs) monitor network traffic to detect abnormal activities such as attempts to infiltrate or hijack hosts on the network. The traditional approach to designing an NIDS relies on an expert to codify rules defining normal behavior and intrusions (e.g., Paxson 1999). Because this approach often fails to detect novel intrusions, a number of researchers have proposed incorporating machine learning techniques into intrusion detection systems (e.g., Mahoney & Chan 2002; Lazarevic, Ertöz, Kumar, Ozgur, & Srivastava 2003; Mukkamala, Janoski, & Sung 2002; Eskin, Arnold, Prerau, Portnoy, & Stolfo 2002). Machine learning techniques offer the benefit of detecting novel patterns in traffic—which presumably represent attack traffic—by being trained on examples of innocuous (known good) and malicious (known bad) traffic data. Learning approaches to malfeasance detection have also played a prominent role in modern spam filtering (e.g., Meyer & Whateley 2004; Segal et al. 2004) and have been proposed as elements in virus and worm detectors (e.g., Newsome, Karp, & Song 2005; Stolfo, Hershkop, Wang, Nimeskern, & Hu 2003; Stolfo, Li, Hershkop, Wang, Hu, & Nimeskern 2006), host-based intrusion detection systems (HIDSs) (e.g., Forrest, Hofmeyr, Somayaji, & Longstaff 1996; Hofmeyr, Forrest, & Somayaji 1998; Mutz, Valeur, Vigna, & Kruegel 2006; Somayaji & Forrest 2000; Warrender, Forrest, & Pearlmutter 1999), and some forms of fraud detection (cf. Bolton & Hand 2002). These systems utilize a wide variety of machine learning techniques including clustering, Bayesian inference, spectral analysis, and maximum-margin classification that have been demonstrated to perform well for these diverse dynamical domains. However, many such techniques also are susceptible to attacks against their learning mechanism, which jeopardize learning systems used in any adversarial setting.

However, while there is an increasing need for learning algorithms to address problems like malfeasance detection, incorporating machine learning into a system must be done carefully to prevent the learning component itself from becoming a means for attack. The concern is that, in security-sensitive domains, learning techniques may expose a system to the threat that an adversary can maliciously exploit vulnerabilities that are unique to learning. Pursuing these exploits is particularly incentivized when learning techniques act as countermeasures against cybercrime threats; e.g., in malfeasance detection. With growing financial incentives to engage in cybercrime inviting ever more sophisticated adversaries, attacks against learners present a lucrative new means to disrupt the operations of or otherwise damage enterprise systems. This makes assessing the vulnerability of learning systems an essential problem to address to make learning methods effective and trustworthy in security-sensitive domains.

The essence of this threat comes from the ability of an adversary to adapt against the learning process. A well-informed adversary can alter its approach based on knowledge of the learner's shortcomings or mislead it by cleverly crafting data to corrupt or deceive the learning process; e.g., spammers regularly adapt their messages to thwart or evade spam detectors. In this way, malicious users can subvert the learning process to disrupt a service or perhaps even compromise an entire system. In fact, a growing body of literature, which we discuss in detail in Chapter 3, shows that attackers can indeed successfully attack machine learning systems in a variety of application domains including automatic signature generation (Chung & Mok 2006, 2007; Newsome, Karp, & Song 2006), intrusion detection systems (Fogla & Lee 2006; Tan, Killourhy, & Maxion 2002), and email spam filtering (Lowd & Meek 2005*b*; Wittel & Wu 2004). It is imperative to ensure that learning is successful despite such attacks—in other words, to achieve *secure learning*.

The primary vulnerability in learners that attackers can exploit lies in the assumptions made about the learners' data. Many common learning algorithms assume that their training and evaluation data come from a natural or well-behaved distribution that remains stationary over time, or at worst, drifts gradually in a benign way. However, these assumptions are perilous in a security-sensitive domain—settings where a patient adversary has motive and the capability to alter the data used by the learner for training or prediction. In such a domain, learners can be manipulated by an intelligent adversary capable of cleverly violating the learners' assumptions for their own gains, making learning and adaptability into potential liabilities for the system rather than benefits. We analyze how learners behave in these settings and we explore alternative methods that can bolster resilience against an adversary.

We consider several potential dangers posed to a learning system. The principal threat is that an attacker can exploit the adaptive nature of a machine learning system to mistrain it and cause it to fail. Failure includes causing the learning system to produce classification errors: if it misidentifies a hostile instance as benign, then the hostile instance is erroneously permitted through the security barrier; if it misidentifies a benign instance as hostile, then a permissible instance is erroneously rejected and normal user activity is interrupted. The adversarial opponent has the potential ability to design training data to cause a learning system to mistakenly make decisions that will misidentify instances and degrade the overall system. If the system's performance sufficiently degrades, users will lose confidence in it and abandon it, or its failures may even significantly compromise the integrity of the system. A second threat is that the learner will reveal secrets about its training data and thereby compromise its data's privacy. In this case, the failure concerns the amount of information inadvertently leaked by the learner, rather than being a direct consequence of the decisions it makes. Learning algorithms necessarily reveal some information about their training data to make accurate predictions, which could potentially lead to a breach of privacy, again eroding the confidence of users. These threats raise several questions. *What techniques can a patient adversary use to mistrain or evade a learning system or compromise data privacy?* and *How can system designers assess the vulnerability of their system to vigilantly incorporate trustworthy learning methods?* We provide a framework for a system designer to thoroughly assess these threats and demonstrate how it can be applied to evaluate real-world systems.

Developing robust learning and decision-making processes is of interest in its own right, but for security practitioners, it is especially important. To effectively apply machine learning as a general tool for reliable decision making in computer systems, it is necessary to investigate how these learning techniques perform when exposed to adversarial conditions. Without an in-depth understanding of the performance of these algorithms in an adversarial setting, the systems will not be trusted and will fail to garner wider adoption. Worse yet, a vulnerable system could be exploited and discourage practitioners from using machine learning in the future. Hence, it is essential for security practitioners to analyze the risks associated with learning algorithms and select techniques that adequately minimize these risks. When a learning algorithm performs well under a realistic adversarial setting, it is an algorithm for secure learning. Of course, whether an algorithm's performance is acceptable is a highly subjective judgment that depends both on the constraints placed on the adversary and on the job the algorithm is tasked with performing. This raises two fundamental questions: *What are the relevant security criteria necessary to evaluate the security of a learner in a particular adversarial environment?* and *Are there machine learning techniques capable of satisfying the security requirements of a given problem domain, and how can such a learner be designed or selected?* We demonstrate how learning systems can be systematically assessed and how learning techniques can be selected to diminish the potential impact of an adversary.

We now present four high-level examples (1.1 to 1.4) that describe different attacks against a learning system. Each of these examples is a preview of the in-depth case studies that we will comprehensively analyze in Chapters 5, 6, 7, and 8. In each synopsis we motivate the learning task and the goal of the adversary; we then briefly describe plausible attacks that align with these goals.

Example 1.1 (Spam Filter and Data Sanitization)

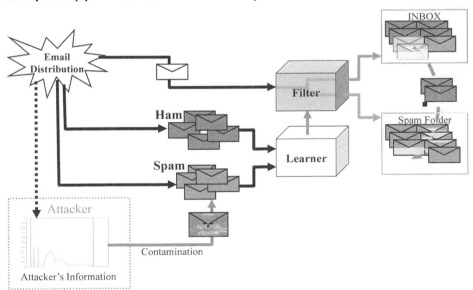

Email spam filtering is one of the most well-known applications of machine learning. In this problem, a set of known good email (ham) and unwanted email (spam) messages is used to train a spam filter. The learning algorithm identifies relevant characteristics that distinguish spam from ham (e.g., tokens such as "Viagra," "Cialis," and "Rolex" or envelope-based features) and constructs a classifier that combines observed evidence of spam to make a decision about whether a newly received message is spam or ham.

Spam filters have proven to be successful at correctly identifying and removing spam messages from a user's regular messages. This has inspired spammers to regularly attempt to evade detection by obfuscating their spam messages to confuse common filters. However, spammers can also corrupt the learning mechanism. As depicted in the diagram above, a spammer can use information about the email distribution to construct clever *attack spam* messages that, when trained on, will cause the spam filter to misclassify the user's desired messages as spam. Ultimately, this spammer's goal is to cause the filter to become so unreliable that the user can no longer trust that its filter has accurately classified the messages and must sort through spam to ensure that important messages are not erroneously filtered.

In Chapter 5, we demonstrate several variants of this attack based on different goals for the spammer and different amounts of information available to it. We show that this attack can be quite effective: if a relatively small number of attack spam messages are trained on, then the accuracy of the filter is significantly reduced. However, we also show that a simple data sanitization technique designed to detect deleterious messages is effective in preventing many of these attacks. In this case, the attacker's success depends primarily on the scope of its goal to disrupt the user's email.

Example 1.2 (Network Anomaly Detector)

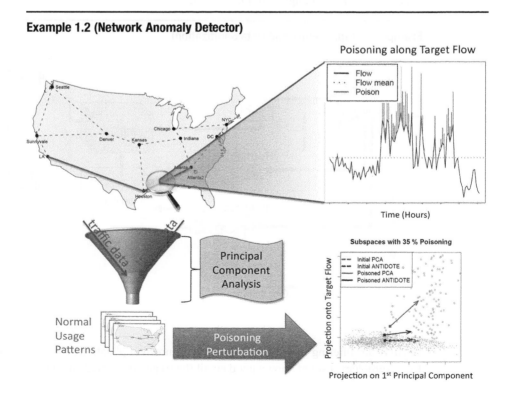

Machine learning techniques have also been proposed by Lakhina, Crovella, and Diot (2004*b*) for detecting network volume anomalies such as denial-of-service (DoS) attacks. Their proposal uses a learning technique known as principal component analysis (PCA) to model normal traffic patterns so as to identify anomalous activity in the network. We demonstrate that this technique is also susceptible to contamination.

As depicted in the above diagram, PCA is first used to extract patterns from traffic observed in a backbone communications network to construct a normal model. This model is subsequently used to detect DoS attacks. An adversary determined to launch a DoS attack must first evade this detector. A crafty adversary can successfully evade detection by mistraining the detector. The attacker can systematically inject chaff traffic that is designed to make its target flow align with the normal model—this chaff (depicted in the top-right figure) is added along the target flow to increase its variance. The resulting perturbed model (see the bottom-right figure) is unable to detect DoS attacks along the target flow.

We explore attacks against the PCA-based detector in Chapter 6 based on different sources of information available to the adversary. Attacks against PCA prove to be effective—they successfully increase its rate of misdetection eight- to tenfold. We also explore an alternative robust statistics-based detection approach called ANTIDOTE designed to be more resilient to chaff. The evasion success rate for the same attacks against ANTIDOTE is roughly halved compared to the PCA-based approach. However, resilience to poisoning comes at a price—ANTIDOTE is less effective on nonpoisoned data than is the original detector.

Example 1.3 (Privacy-Preserving Learning)

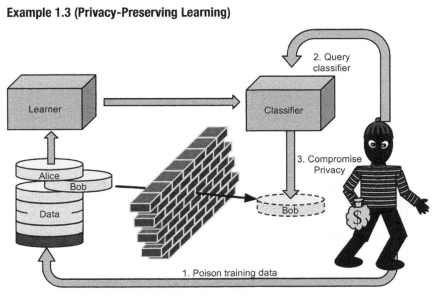

Privacy is another important facet for learning practitioners to consider. In many situations, a practitioner may want to employ a learning algorithm on privileged data to subsequently provide a public utility without compromising data privacy. For example, a hospital may want to use private medical records to construct a classifier that can identify likely H1N1 swine flu patients, and they may want to share that classifier with the general public in the form of a self-assessment tool (Microsoft 2009). However, in providing this classifier, the health care provider must not expose privileged information from its records. As such, it requires strong guarantees that the classifier will not compromise the privacy of its training data.

Learning algorithms pose a risk to privacy because the behavior of the learner is a reflection of its data and hence may reveal the underlying secrets contained within. Fundamentally, a learning algorithm produces a summary of data it was trained on based on the patterns it gleans from that data. This summary reveals aggregate information about the data and can potentially be exploited by an adversary to violate a specific datum's privacy. It is possible that a clever adversary could contaminate the learner's data or query the learner to eventually infer private data.

Privacy-preserving learning is a field within learning, statistical databases, and theory that studies the privacy properties of learning algorithms and seeks to develop learning algorithms with strong privacy guarantees (cf. Dwork 2010). In Chapter 7, we explore a model that provides strong privacy-preserving guarantees and develop a privacy-preserving support vector machine within that model. Further, we explore the limits of privacy-preserving learning that demonstrate the fundamental tradeoff between accuracy and privacy preservation.

Example 1.4 (Near-Optimal Evasion)

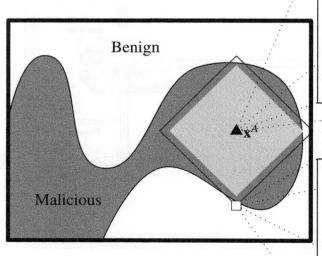

In addition to misleading learning algorithms, attackers also have an interest in evading detectors by making their miscreant activity undetectable. As previously mentioned in Example 1.1, this practice is already common in the spam filtering domain where spammers attempt to evade the filter by *i*) obfuscating words indicative of spam to human-recognizable misspellings; e.g., "Viagra" to "V1@gra" or "Cialis" to "Gia|is," *ii*) using HTML to make an unrendered message difficult to parse, *iii*) adding words or text from other sources unrelated to the spam, and *iv*) embedding images that display a spam message. All of these techniques can be used to evade spam filters, but they also are costly for the spammer—altering its spam can make the message less profitable because the distortions reduce the message's legibility or its accessibility. In evading the filter, the spammer would like to minimally modify its messages, but for a dynamically learned filter, the spammer does not know the learned filtering rules. Instead, the spammer constructs test spams for probing the filter and refining modifications according to some cost function. This raises the following question: *How difficult is it for the spammer to optimally evade the filter by querying it?*

The near-optimal evasion problem, which we examine in Chapter 8, formalizes this question in terms of the query complexity required by the spammer to evade a particular family of classifiers. We study the broad family of convex-inducing classifiers and show that there are efficient algorithms for near-optimal evasion under certain ℓ_p cost functions.

1.2   A Principled Approach to Secure Learning

In this book, we analyze four separate security problems for machine learning systems. In each, we first specify the threat model posed, subsequently analyze the threat's impact, and, where appropriate, propose defenses against the threat. It is a well-established practice in computer security that evaluating a system involves a continual process of, first, determining classes of attacks on the system; second, evaluating the resilience of the system against those attacks; and third, strengthening the system against those classes of attacks. Within each of the security problems we consider, we follow exactly this model to evaluate the vulnerabilities of learning algorithms.

To assess the vulnerabilities of learning systems, our approach builds on many well-established principles from traditional computer security. Generally speaking, computer security is concerned with quantifying, managing, and reducing the risks associated with computer systems and their usage. Traditional topics in security include cryptography, authentication, secure channels, covert channels, defensive programming practices, static code analysis, network security, and operating system security; traditional (code-based) vulnerabilities include buffer overflows, format string vulnerabilities, cross application scripting, code injection attacks, and privilege escalation. Unlike classical security settings, attacks against a learning system exploit the adaptive nature of the learning system. Not only can the adversary exploit existing flaws in the learner, it can also mislead the learner to create new vulnerabilities. Nonetheless, classical security principles are still applicable for analyzing machine learning algorithms. In particular, the principles of *proactively studying attacks*, *Kerckhoffs' Principle*, *conservative design*, and *formal threat modeling* are the foundations of our approach.

Proactive Analysis

The first guideline of computer security is to conduct proactive studies to anticipate potential attacks before a system is deployed or widely used. Analysis of and open debate about the security of a system provide a level of confidence in it. Further, if vulnerabilities are successfully identified before deployment, the system's design can be preemptively repaired, thereby reducing the chance that costly patches, rewrites, or recalls of a flawed system will be necessary after its deployment. Finally, revelations of security flaws in a deployed system erode users' confidence in it and can lead to costly damages, which may have been avoidable had the system been adequately vetted. In this book we advocate a proactive approach to the security of learning systems. For the already existing systems that we analyze, we seek to identify their vulnerabilities and raise awareness about them before the system is damaged or compromised by an unscrupulous adversary. Further, we not only expose vulnerabilities but we also offer alternative systems that thwart their exploits or mitigate their effect. Lastly, we provide general guidelines to system designers to aid them in analyzing the vulnerabilities of a proposed learning system so that learning can be deployed as an effective and reliable component even in critical systems.

Kerckhoffs' Principle

The second guideline often referred to as *Kerckhoffs' Principle* (Kerckhoffs 1883) is that the security of a system should not rely on unrealistic expectations of secrecy. An over-dependence on secrets to provide security is dangerous because if these secrets are exposed the security of the system is immediately compromised. Ideally, secure systems should make minimal assumptions about what can realistically be kept secret from a potential attacker. The field of cryptography has embraced this general principle by demanding open algorithms that only require a secret *key* to provide security or privacy. We apply this principle to analyzing machine learning systems primarily by assuming that the adversary is aware of the learning algorithm and can obtain some degree of information about the data used to train the learner. However, determining the appropriate degree of secrecy that is feasible for secure machine learning systems is a difficult question, which we discuss further in Chapter 9. In each of the chapters of this book, we consider various levels of information that the adversary potentially obtains and assess how the adversary can best utilize this information to achieve its objective against the learner. In doing so, we demonstrate the impact of different levels of threat and show the value an adversary obtains from a particular source of information.

Conservative Design

The third foundational principle we apply is that the design and analysis of a system should avoid unnecessary or unreasonable assumptions about and limitations on the adversary. If designers fail to anticipate the capabilities of an adversary, under-estimate the attacker's tenacity, or misunderstand the resources and information at its disposal, major security compromises can occur. Instead, by assuming the adversary has the broadest possible powers, one can understand the worst-case threat posed by an adversary, and users are less likely to be surprised by an attack by some unan-ticipated adversary. Conversely, however, analyzing the capabilities of an omnipo-tent limitless adversary reveals little about a learning system's behavior against real-istic constrained attackers and may lead to an unnecessarily bleak outlook on the security of a system. Instead, while we also consider worst-case adversaries, our approach focuses on constructing an appropriate threat model to quantify the relation-ship between the adversary's effort and its effect on the system under a variety of threat levels.

Threat Modeling

Finally, to analyze the vulnerabilities of machine learning systems, we follow the typical security practice of constructing a formal (attacker-centric) threat model to analyze a learning system's vulnerabilities. As stated by Denning & Denning (1979),

No mechanism is perfectly secure. A good mechanism reduces the risk of compromise to an acceptable level.

Under the approach we advocate, a system analyst constructs a threat model of a learn-ing system to analyze the potential risks against it. This threat model describes each potential adversary in terms of its incentives, objectives, resources, and capabilities. The threat model allows the analyst to quantify the degree of security; that is, the level of security expected against potential adversaries in terms of the damage that can be inflicted and the feasibility of such an attack. Ultimately, this characterizes the security of the system, helps to identify its weaknesses, and provides a mechanism to compare the security of different proposals.

To construct a threat model for a particular learning system, first the analyst quan-tifies the security setting and objectives of that system to develop criteria to measure success and quantify the level of security offered. Formalizing the risks and objec-tives allows the analyst to identify potential limitations of the system and potential attacks and focuses this analysis on immediate threats, so as to avoid wasting effort protecting against nonexistent or ancillary threats. Next the analyst identifies poten-tial adversarial incentives, objectives, resources, capabilities, and limitations. By exam-ining the nature of anticipated adversaries and their goals, the analyst can quantify the effort required by the adversary to achieve a particular objective. Based on this threat model, the analyst can then analyze the security of the system and construct appropriate defenses against realistic forms of attack. Formal analysis provides a rig-orous approach to security. Additionally, by formalizing the threats and security of a system, other analysts can critique assumptions made by the analyst and suggest potential flaws in the system's design. This open process tends to improve a system's security.

1.3   Chronology of Secure Learning

The discipline of secure learning has emerged as an important field of study from a series of important developments within the fields of artificial intelligence and computer security primarily in the last two decades. Contributions that led to the formation of secure learning, however, originated with influential works from both disciplines dating decades earlier. While many of these developments addressed separate problems within these otherwise distinct communities, they share some common themes that converged as many security problems began to require adaptive approaches and as the vulnerability of learning techniques to malicious data became apparent. Together these trends formed a basis for the field of secure learning that has since coalesced. Here we provide a chronology of the major events that contributed to this development to better understand the context and motivations for secure learning. While this is not meant to be a complete history of all the significant work that forms the foundation of secure learning, this brief chronology provides a few highlights from the fields of computer security and artificial intelligence that contributed to the formation of secure learning as a discipline. See Chapter 3 for additional discussion of the secure learning framework and the organization of research in the field.

1940s Wartime cryptanalysis: Using computers, many of the Axis Powers' crypto-ciphers are broken. Claude Shannon publishes declassified material in his paper, "Communication Theory of Secrecy Systems," which shows that any theoretically unbreakable crypto-system has the same requirements as a one-time pad (Shannon 1949). The standards developed for crypto-systems later serve as a model for standards of computer security.

1940s and 1950s Foundation of artificial intelligence: With the advent of early computing machines, researchers began investigating artificial intelligence. Famously, in 1950 Turing publishes Computing Machinery and Intelligence and introduces the famous *Turing Test* for determining whether a machine can demonstrate intelligence (Turing 1950).

1960s and 1970s Foundation of robust statistics: While the history of robust statistics dates back to the origins of statistics, the first formal methods in this area arose in the 1960s and 1970s. The principal texts summarizing this work are Huber (1981) and Hampel, Ronchetti, Rousseeuw, and Stahel (1986), which present two different approaches to robust statistics: the minimax approach and the approach based on the influence function, respectively.

Late 1970s Advent of public-key cryptography: First proposed by Whitfield Diffie and Martin Hellman in 1976, public-key cryptography revolutionized cryptography (Diffie & Hellman 1976). Ronald Rivest, Adi Shamir, and Len Adleman, in 1978, introduce the RSA public-key system (Rivest, Shamir, & Adleman 1978).

1979 Denning & Denning publish "Data Security": In this seminal paper, Dorothy and Peter Denning introduce four different forms of safeguards for data: access controls, flow controls, inference controls, and encryption (Denning

& Denning 1979). With inference controls, they address the need for guarding against information leaks in database aggregation procedures, a topic that precedes the broader notion of privacy-preserving learning.

1984 Introduction of PAC learning framework: Valiant introduces probably approximately correct (PAC) learning as a framework for studying the ability of learning algorithms to learn a particular concept given instances exemplifying it (Valiant 1984). Importantly, the PAC framework ties learning theory to hypothesis complexity theory, and belongs in the area of empirical process theory within mathematical statistics.

1990s Polymorphic viruses are developed: Computer viruses begin using encryption, code obfuscation, and polymorphism to avoid detection (Chen & Robert 2004). These stealthy viruses are engineered to thwart signature-based antivirus detectors, making it increasingly difficult to identify malicious code via signatures.

1993 Kearns and Li study learning under malicious errors: Using the PAC model, Kearns and Li (1993) investigate the feasibility of learning with worst-case errors in the training data in their paper, "Learning in the Presence of Malicious Errors."

1996 First commercial Bayesian spam filters: The iFile program written by Jason Rennie is credited as the first mail program that incorporated the probabilistic approach to spam filtering that is popularly known as *Bayesian filtering*. The first research paper on Bayesian methods for spam filtering was published by Sahami, Dumais, Heckerman, and Horvitz (1998).

1999–2004 Emergence of fast-spreading computer worms: Capitalizing on the spread of the Internet, computer worms including Melissa, ILOVEYOU, Code Red, Nimda, Klez, Slammer, Blaster, Sobig, MyDoom, and Netsky quickly infect vulnerable hosts and cause widespread damage to computer and network resources (Chen & Robert 2004). These prolific and damaging worms highlight the need for fast adaptive detection systems.

2002 Paul Graham's approach to spam filtering: In his essay, "A Plan for Spam," Paul Graham refined and popularized the so-called Bayesian methods for spam filtering (Graham 2002). The basic technique he introduced is still employed today in many spam filters, including SpamBayes, BogoFilter, and the learning component of the Apache SpamAssassin filter (Apa n.d.).

August 2006 AOL search data leak: AOL Research releases 20 million search keywords of 650,000 users over a three-month period, which were anonymized by replacing names with a unique key. The *New York Times* and other organizations denonymized these users by cross-referencing public information (Barbaro & Zeller 2006). This led to a class action lawsuit against AOL.

2006 Differential privacy proposed: With the development of differential privacy (Dwork, McSherry, Nissim, & Smith 2006), learning while strongly preserving privacy was set on a firm footing.

January 2007 Storm worm discovered: This malware spreads through a Trojan horse and creates a network of compromised machines called a *botnet*—Storm was one of the first botnets discovered (cf. Holz, Steiner, Dahl, Biersack, & Freiling 2008). Botnets have been used for a variety of malicious purposes including sending spam, distributed denial-of-service (DDos) attacks, and cybertheft, significantly facilitating these abusive activities.

December 2007 NIPS Workshop on Machine Learning in Adversarial Environments for Computer Security: The first formal workshop to address the role of machine learning as a tool for computer security was held in conjunction with the conference on Advances in Neural Information Processing Systems (NIPS). This workshop, organized by Richard Lippmann and Pavel Laskov, brought together researchers from both fields and led later to a special issue on this topic in the journal, *Machine Learning* (Laskov & Lippmann 2010).

October 2008–November 2016 CCS Workshop on Security and Artificial Intelligence: The longest running workshop organized to address uses of artificial intelligence within computer security was first held in 2008. This first workshop was organized by Dirk Balfanz and Jessica Staddon and held in conjunction with the ACM Conference on Computer and Communications Security (CCS) and continues to meet annually through the time of this writing in 2016 (Balfanz & Staddon 2008, 2009; Greenstadt 2010; Cárdenas, Greenstadt, & Rubinstein 2011; Cárdenas, Nelson, & Rubinstein 2012; Nelson, Dimitrakakis, & Shi 2013; Dimitrakakis, Mitrokotsa, & Rubinstein 2014; Dimitrakakis, Mitrokotsa, & Sinha 2015; Freeman, Mitrokotsa, & Sinha 2016).

December 2009 Netflix privacy breach: A class action lawsuit is brought against Netflix, Inc., for releasing private information of about 500,000 customers in a movie rating contest for machine learning. Researchers were able to deanonymize the disclosed users by cross-referencing their ratings with those on IMDB (Narayanan & Shmatikov 2008).

September 2010 Workshop on Privacy and Security issues in Data Mining and Machine Learning (PSDML): The PSDML workshop is held in conjunction with the ECML/PKDD conference (Dimitrakakis, Gkoulalas-Divanis, Mitrokotsa, Verykios, & Saygin 2011). This workshop provides machine learning researchers with a forum for discussion of privacy and security applications.

September 2012 Dagstuhl Perspectives Workshop: Machine Learning Methods for Computer Security: A workshop is convened in Schloss Dagstuhl, Germany, to bring together leading researchers from both the computer security and machine learning communities to discuss challenges and future research directions for adversarial learning and learning-based security techniques and to foster a common community Joseph et al. (2013).

June 2014 Workshop on Learning, Security, and Privacy: Held in conjunction with the International Conference on Machine Learning (ICML), this workshop provides a new venue for machine learning researchers to address problems with security and privacy considerations (Dimitrakakis, Laskov, Lowd, Rubinstein, & Shi 2014).

February 2016 Workshop on Artificial Intelligence for Cyber Security (AICS):
The AICS workshop, organized by groups from MIT Lincoln Labs and the
University of Southern California, is held in conjunction with the premier AI
conference AAAI (Martinez, Streilein, Carter, & Sinha 2016). The workshop
brings together members of the network security, security games, and learning
communities.

1.4   Overview

In this book, we present a systematic approach for identifying and analyzing threats to a
machine learning system. We examine a number of real-world learning systems, assess
their vulnerabilities, demonstrate real-world attacks on their learning mechanism, and
propose defenses that can successfully mitigate the effectiveness of such attacks. In
doing so, we provide a systematic methodology for assessing a learner's vulnerability
and developing defenses to strengthen its system against such threats. Additionally, we
also examine and answer theoretical questions regarding the limits of adversarial contamination, privacy-preserving learning, and classifier evasion.

This text is organized into four parts. In the first part, we present the background and
foundational materials that form the basis of our approach. In Chapter 2, we present a
synopsis of machine learning and introduce our notation. Then in Chapter 3, we introduce a framework for assessing the security properties of learning agents, present the
taxonomy of attacks against learners, and categorize and discuss the prior work within
the context of this framework. We identify different classes of attacks on machine learning systems and show that there are at least three interesting dimensions on which to
qualify threats to a learning system. Further, we cast secure learning as a game between
an *attacker* and a *defender*. The taxonomy determines the structure of this game and cost
model for our players. Based on this framework, the remainder of the text is organized
according to different vulnerabilities in learning systems.

In the second part of the book, we explore attacks in which the attacker actively
interferes with learning by maliciously tampering with the learner's training data. In
Chapter 4, we investigate how an attacker could poison a hypersphere-based anomaly
detector through an iterative attack. For several different attack scenarios, we quantify
the effort required by an attacker to achieve a successful poisoning result in terms of the
amount of data the attacker must control and the number of required attack iterations.
We provide bounds on the difficulty of the problem for the attacker under a number of
different attack and retraining scenarios and discuss how these results affect the attack's
feasibility.

We next provide two real-world case studies of practical learning systems, and for
both, we use our framework to methodically explore potential threats to these systems;
finally we suggest corresponding defenses that counter or mitigate the effects of the
attacks. The first learning system is a spam filter called SpamBayes that we investigate

in Chapter 5. We show that this spam filter is highly vulnerable to adversarial contamination of its training data. In particular, we show how an attacker can construct highly effective attack messages that, once injected into the learner's training set, cause Spam-Bayes to subsequently misclassify many normal messages as spam. However, we also propose a data sanitization defense that is able to successfully detect and remove attack messages based on the estimated damage the message causes. This defense effectively eliminates most attack messages and only has a minimal impact on the filter's performance. The second learning system we analyze is a network anomaly detection system in which a PCA-based subspace estimation technique is used to identify network-wide DoS attacks in a backbone communication network. In Chapter 6, we study a class of data poisoning strategies against this PCA-based anomaly detector. The goal of the adversary in this system is to evade detection, and to do so, it contaminates the learner's training data by gradually perturbing the network traffic used to train the detector. Again, we show that this class of algorithms is highly susceptible to poisoning methods. To combat our attacks against this detector, we also propose an alternative detector. In this case, we show that an alternative learning algorithm based on a robust variant of PCA is able to substantially mitigate the effect of the poisoning.

In the third part of the book, we consider attackers who passively exploit a learner's vulnerabilities without requiring data contamination, and we conduct a theoretical investigation of two tasks for secure learning: preserving the privacy of the learner's data and preventing evasion of the learner. In Chapter 7 we explore the task of releasing a support vector machine (SVM) classifier while preserving the privacy of its training data. We adopt the strong, semantic definition of privacy known as differential privacy Dwork et al. (2006), which guarantees the privacy of even a single training datum when the adversary has full knowledge of the remaining data and the release mechanism. We present mechanisms for privately releasing SVM-like classifiers, which we prove guarantee differential privacy while attaining a guaranteed level of utility. We also explore the limits of privately releasing classifiers that approximate SVMs through lower bounds. Last, we explore the near-optimal evasion problem for the family of convex-inducing classifiers and apply our framework to a theoretical model of classifier evasion in Chapter 8. To find a classifier's blind spots an adversary can systematically issue membership queries and use the classifier's responses to glean important structural information about its boundary. To study this problem, we generalize the near-optimal evasion framework of Lowd & Meek (2005a), which quantifies the evasion problem in terms of query complexity. Under this model, we study the evasion of a diverse family of classifiers called the convex-inducing classifiers , and we present algorithms for evading these classifiers based on the family of ℓ_p costs. We demonstrate both positive and negative results for the feasibility of classifier evasion within the family of convex-inducing classifiers and discuss future directions for studying the evasion problem.

In the final part of the book, we explore future directions for adversarial machine learning. In Chapter 9, we discuss important themes and open questions for the field of adversarial learning in security-sensitive domains.

This book provides machine learning practitioners with a framework for evaluating learning systems in the presence of an adversary. Under this framework we demonstrate the vulnerability of real-world learning systems, and we suggest alternative techniques that are resilient to the demonstrated exploits. Our approach and techniques provide a common foundation for secure learning, which is vital for the continued development and deployment of learning in security-sensitive or adversarial environments.

2   Background and Notation

In this chapter we establish the mathematical notation used throughout this book and introduce the basic foundation of machine learning that this text builds upon. Readers generally familiar with this field can cursorily read this chapter to become familiar with our notation. For a more thorough treatment of machine learning, the reader should refer to a text such as (Hastie, Tibshirani, & Friedman 2003) or (Vapnik 1995).

2.1   Basic Notation

Here we give a brief overview of the formal notation we use throughout this text. For more, along with foundations in basic logic, set theory, linear algebra, mathematical optimization, and probability we refer the reader to Appendix A.

We use $=$ to denote *equality* and $\triangleq$ to denote *defined as*. The typeface style of a character is used to differentiate between elements of a set, sets, and spaces as follows. Individual objects such as scalars are denoted with italic font (e.g., x) and multidimensional vectors are denoted with bold font (e.g., $\mathbf{x}$). A set is denoted using blackboard bold characters (e.g., $\mathbb{X}$). However, when referring to the *entire* set or universe that spans a particular kind of object (i.e., a space), we use calligraphic script such as in $\mathcal{X}$ to distinguish it from subsets $\mathbb{X}$ contained within this space.

2.2   Statistical Machine Learning

Machine learning encompasses a vast field of techniques that extract information from data as well as the theory and analysis relating to these algorithms. In describing the task of machine learning, Mitchell (1997) wrote,

A computer program is said to *learn* from experience E with respect to some class of tasks T and performance measure P, if its performance at tasks in T, as measured by P, improves with experience E.

This definition encompasses a broad class of methods. We present an overview of the terminology and mechanisms for a particular notion of learning that is often referred to as statistical machine learning. In particular, the notion of experience is cast as data, the task is to choose an action (or make a prediction/decision) from an action or

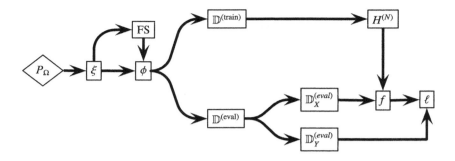

(a) The complete learning framework.

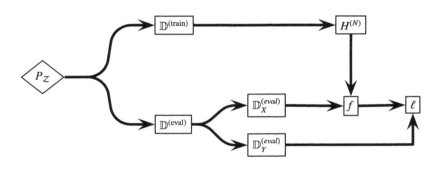

(b) The learning framework with implicit data collection.

Figure 2.1 Diagrams depicting the flow of information through different phases of learning.
(a) All major phases of the learning algorithm except for model selection. Here objects from the space Ω are drawn from the distribution P_Ω and parsed into measurements that then are used in the feature selector FS. It selects a feature mapping ϕ that is used to create training and evaluation datasets, $\mathbb{D}^{(\mathrm{train})}$ and $\mathbb{D}^{(\mathrm{eval})}$. The learning algorithm $H^{(N)}$ selects a hypothesis f based on the training data, and its predictions are assessed on $\mathbb{D}^{(\mathrm{eval})}$ according to the loss function ℓ.
(b) The training and prediction phases of learning with implicit data collection phases. Here the data are assumed to be drawn directly from P_Z instead of being drawn from P_Ω and subsequently mapped into the space Z by the measurement process.

decision space, and the performance metric is a loss function that measures the cost that the learner incurs for a particular prediction/action compared to the best or correct one. Figure 2.1 illustrates the data flow for learning in this setting. The data lies in a product space $Z = X \times Y$ composed of an input space X and an output space Y, which are discussed later. The training dataset $\mathbb{D}^{(\mathrm{train})}$ (consisting of N coupled training examples from the product space) is drawn from the distribution P_Z and is used by the learning procedure $H^{(N)}$ to produce a hypothesis (or classifier) f. This classifier is a function that makes predictions on a new set of data $\mathbb{D}^{(\mathrm{eval})}$ (assumed to be drawn from the same distribution) and is assessed according to the loss function ℓ. Figure 2.1(a) additionally depicts the data collection phase of learning discussed in Section 2.2.1. While measurement and initial feature extraction are important aspects for the security of a learning algorithm, our focus in this book is on the security of the learning algorithm.

Throughout this book, we only consider inductive learning methods for which learning takes the form of generalizing from prior experiences. The method of induction requires an inductive bias: a set of (implicit) assumptions used to create generalizations from a set of observations. An example of an inductive bias is Ockham's Razor—the preference for the simplest hypothesis that is consistent with the observations. Naive Bayes methods use *maximal conditional independence* as their inductive bias, while the inductive bias of a support vector machine is *maximal margin*. The inductive bias of most methods is an implicit bias built into the learning procedure.

In this book, we focus on techniques from statistical machine learning that can be described as empirical risk minimization procedures. Later, we summarize the components of these procedures and provide notation to describe them, but first, their overall goal is to minimize the expected loss (risk) incurred on predictions made for the unseen evaluation data, $\mathbb{D}^{(\text{eval})}$. Minimizing the average loss (or risk) on the training data is often used as a surrogate for minimizing the expected loss on unseen random evaluation data, and under the appropriate conditions, the error on the training data can be used to bound generalization error (cf. Vapnik 1995, Chapter 1). Underlying such results is the stationarity assumption that the training data and evaluation data are both drawn from the same distribution P_Z as depicted in Figure 2.1. Subsequently, we examine scenarios that violate this stationarity assumption and evaluate the impact these violations have on the performance of learning methods. However, while we study the impact on performance of empirical risk minimizers, these violations would have similar effects on any learner based on stationarity, which is often required to guarantee generalization. Further we demonstrate that these violations have less impact on alternative empirical risk minimizers that were designed to be robust against distributional deviations. Vulnerabilities are neither unique to empirical risk minimization procedures nor are they inherent to them, but rather guarding against these exploits requires learners designed to be resilient against violations of their assumptions. There is also a tradeoff between the robustness and the effectiveness of the procedure, which we emphasize in each chapter.

2.2.1   Data

Real-world objects such as emails or network packets are contained in a space Ω of all such objects. Usually, applying a learning algorithm directly to real-world objects is difficult because the learner cannot parse the objects' structures or the objects may have extraneous elements that are irrelevant to the learner's task. These objects are transformed into a more amenable representation by a mapping from real-world abstractions (e.g., objects or events) into a space of representative observations—the process of measurement. In this process, each real-world abstraction, $\omega \in \Omega$, is measured and represented to the learning algorithm as a composite object $x \in \mathcal{X}$. Often there are D simple measurements of ω; the ith measurement (or feature) x_i is from a space $\mathcal{X}_i$, and the composite representation (or data point) $\mathbf{x} \in \mathcal{X}$ is represented as a tuple $(x_1, x_2, \ldots, x_D)$. The space of all such data points is $\mathcal{X} \triangleq \mathcal{X}_1 \times \mathcal{X}_2 \times \ldots \times \mathcal{X}_D$. Each feature is usually real-valued $\mathcal{X}_i = \mathfrak{R}$, integer-valued $\mathcal{X}_i = \mathfrak{Z}$, boolean $\mathcal{X}_i = \{\text{true, false}\}$, or categorical $\mathcal{X}_i = \{A_1, A_2, \ldots, A_k\}$. Figure 2.1(a) formally represents the measurement process with the measurement map $\xi : \Omega \mapsto \mathcal{X}$, which represents the learner's perspective of the world.

Data collection is the application of a measurement map ξ to a sequence of N objects $\omega^{(1)}, \omega^{(2)}, \ldots, \omega^{(N)}$ resulting in an indexed set of N data points $\{x^{(i)}\}_{i=1}^{N} \subseteq \mathcal{X}^N$, which we refer to as a dataset and denote it by $\mathbb{D}$. The dataset represents a sequence of observations of the environment and serves as the basis for the learner's ability to generalize past experience to future events or observations. Various assumptions are made about the structure of the dataset, but most commonly, the learner assumes the data points are independent and identically distributed. All the learning algorithms we investigate assume that the data is independently sampled from an unknown but stationary distribution, although with various degrees of dependence on this assumption.

Labels

In many learning problems, the learner is tasked with learning to predict the unobserved state of the world based on its observed state. Observations are partitioned into two sets. Those that are observed are the explanatory variables (also referred to as the covariates, input, predictor, or controlled variables) and the unobserved quantities to be predicted comprise the response variables (also referred to as the output or outcome variables). In the context of this book and our focus on classification, we refer to the observed independent quantities as the data point (as discussed earlier) and to the dependent categorical quantity as its label. The learner is expected to be able to predict the label for a data point having seen past instances of data points coupled with their labels. In this form, each datum consists of two paired components: a data point x from an input space $\mathcal{X}$ and a label y from a response space $\mathcal{Y}$. The components of the datum are also referred to as the predictor (input) variable x and the response (output) variable y. These paired objects belong to the Cartesian product: $\mathcal{Z} \triangleq \mathcal{X} \times \mathcal{Y}$. We also assume these instances are randomly drawn from a joint distribution $P_{\mathcal{Z}}$ over this paired space that may also be denoted by $P_{\mathcal{X} \times \mathcal{Y}}$ when convenient.

In learning problems that include labels (e.g., supervised or semi-supervised learning), the learner trains on a set of paired data from $\mathcal{Z}$. In particular, a labeled dataset is an indexed set of N instances from $\mathcal{Z}$: $\mathbb{D} \triangleq \{z^{(1)}, z^{(2)}, \ldots, z^{(N)}\}$ where $z^{(i)} \in \mathcal{Z}$ is drawn from $P_{\mathcal{Z}}$. The indexed set of only the data points is $\mathbb{D}_X \triangleq \{x^{(1)}, x^{(2)}, \ldots, x^{(N)}\}$ and the indexed set of only the labels is $\mathbb{D}_Y \triangleq \{y^{(1)}, y^{(2)}, \ldots, y^{(N)}\}$. In the case that $\mathcal{X} = \mathcal{A}^D$ for some numeric set $\mathcal{A}$, the ith data point can be expressed as a D-dimensional vector $\mathbf{x}^{(i)}$ and the data can be expressed as an $N \times D$ matrix $\mathbf{X}$ defined by $\mathbf{X}_{i,\bullet} = \mathbf{x}^{(i)}$. Similarly, when $\mathcal{Y}$ is a scalar set (e.g., booleans, reals), $y^{(i)}$ is a scalar, and the labels can be expressed as a simple N-dimensional vector $\mathbf{y}$. In the remainder of this book, N will refer to the size of $\mathbb{D}$, and where applicable, D will refer to the dimension of its data points.

Feature Selection

Typically, measurement is only the first phase in the overall process of data extraction. After a dataset is collected, it is often altered through a process of feature selection. Feature selection is a mapping $\phi_\mathbb{D}$ of the original measurements into a space $\hat{\mathcal{X}}$ of features[1]: $\phi_\mathbb{D} : \mathcal{X} \to \hat{\mathcal{X}}$. Unlike the data-independent measurement mapping ξ, the feature selection map often is selected in a data-dependent fashion according to the entire dataset $\mathbb{D}$, to extract aspects of the data most relevant to the learning task. Further, measurement often is an irreversible physical process, whereas feature selection usually can be redone by reprocessing the original measurements. In many settings, one can retroactively alter the feature selection process by redefining the feature selection map and reapplying it to the measured data, whereas it is impossible to make retroactive measurements on the original objects unless the information required to reconstruct this raw data is still available. For the purposes of this book, we do not distinguish between the feature selection and measurement phases because the attacks we study target downstream aspects of learning. We merge them together into a single step and disregard $\hat{\mathcal{X}}$ except explicitly in reference to feature selection. We revisit potential roles for feature selection in security-sensitive settings in Section 9.1.1.2.

2.2.2   Hypothesis Space

A learning algorithm is tasked with selecting a hypothesis that best supports the data. Here we consider the hypothesis to be a function f mapping from the data space $\mathcal{X}$ to the response space $\mathcal{Y}$; i.e., $f : \mathcal{X} \to \mathcal{Y}$. Of course, there are many such hypotheses, which together form the family $\mathcal{F}$ of all possible hypotheses or the hypothesis space. This space is most generally the set of all functions that map $\mathcal{X}$ onto $\mathcal{Y}$ as we discussed in Appendix A.1: $\mathcal{F} \triangleq \{f \mid f : \mathcal{X} \to \mathcal{Y}\}$. The hypothesis space $\mathcal{F}$ may be constrained by assumptions made about the form of the hypotheses. For instance, when $\mathcal{X} = \Re^D$, the family may be restricted to generalized linear functions of the form $f_{\mathbf{a},b}^{\beta}(\mathbf{x}) \triangleq \beta(\mathbf{a}^\top \mathbf{x} + b)$ where $\beta : \Re \to \mathcal{Y}$ is some mapping from the reals to the response space. In the case that $\mathcal{Y} = \{0, 1\}$, the function $\beta(x) = \mathrm{I}[x > 0]$ yields the family of all halfspaces on $\Re^D$ parameterized by $(\mathbf{a}, b)$. In the case that $\mathcal{Y} = \Re$ the identity function $\beta(x) = x$ defines the family of linear functions on $\Re^D$ also parameterized by $(\mathbf{a}, b)$.

2.2.3   The Learning Model

We describe the learner as a model and a training procedure. The model captures assumptions made about the observed data—this model provides limitations on the space of hypotheses and also available prior knowledge or inductive bias on these hypotheses (e.g., a prior distribution in a Bayesian setting or a regularizer in a risk

---

[1] In the literature, feature selection chooses a subset of the measurements ($\hat{\mathcal{X}} \subseteq \mathcal{X}$), and feature extraction creates composite features from the original measurements. We do not differentiate between these two processes and will refer to both as feature selection.

minimization setting). That is, the model is a set of assumptions about the relationship between the observed data and the hypothesis space, but the model does not specify how hypotheses are selected—that is done by a training procedure as discussed later. For example, consider a simple location estimation procedure for normally distributed data. The data model specifies that the data points are independently drawn from a unit-variance Gaussian distribution centered at an unknown parameter θ; i.e., $X \sim N(\theta, 1)$. The mean and the median are procedures for estimating the location parameter θ. By distinguishing between the model and the training procedure, we can study two different aspects of a learner's vulnerabilities.

2.2.4   Supervised Learning

The primary focus of this work will be analyzing the task of prediction in a supervised learning setting. In the supervised learning framework, the observed data is a paired dataset $\mathbb{D} = \left\{ \left(x^{(i)}, y^{(i)} \right) \right\}$, which we assume to be drawn from an unknown distribution $P_{\mathcal{X} \times \mathcal{Y}}$. The objective of prediction is to select the best hypothesis or function $\hat{f}$ for predicting the response variable based on the observed predictor variable. More precisely, given a hypothesis space $\mathcal{F}$ of functions mapping from the input space $\mathcal{X}$ to the output space $\mathcal{Y}$, the prediction task is to select a classification hypothesis (classifier) $\hat{f} \in \mathcal{F}$ with the smallest expected prediction cost; i.e., the cost incurred in predicting the label y of a new random instance (x, y) when only the predictor variable x is revealed to the classifier. To accomplish this task, the learner is given a labeled training dataset $\mathbb{D}$ and a cost or loss function ℓ. This cost function assigns a numeric cost to each combination of data instance, true label, and classifier label (most commonly, however, the cost function used is identical for every data instance).

To accomplish the prediction task, a learning algorithm $H^{(N)}$ (also called a training algorithm) is used to select the best hypothesis from $\mathcal{F}$ based on the training data and the cost function. This learner is a mapping from a dataset $\mathbb{D} \in \mathcal{Z}^N$ to a hypothesis f in the hypothesis space: $H^{(N)} : \mathcal{Z}^N \to \mathcal{F}$; that is, a mapping from N training examples in $\mathcal{Z}$ to some hypothesis f in the hypothesis space $\mathcal{F}$. If the algorithm has a randomized element we use the notation $H^{(N)} : \mathcal{Z}^N \times \mathfrak{R} \to \mathcal{F}$ to capture that fact that the hypothesis depends on a random element $R \sim P_{\mathfrak{R}}$.

Training

The process we describe here is batch learning—the learner trains on a training set $\mathbb{D}^{(\text{train})}$ and is evaluated on an evaluation set $\mathbb{D}^{(\text{eval})}$. This setting can be generalized to a repeated process of online learning in which the learner continually retrains on evaluation data after obtaining evaluation labels (we return to this setting in Section 3.6). In a pure online setting, prediction and retraining occur every time a new data point is received. In the batch learning setting (or in a single epoch of online learning), the learner $H^{(N)}$ forms a hypothesis $\hat{f}$ based on the collected data $\mathbb{D}^{(\text{train})}$—the process known as training. A plethora of different training procedures have been used in the supervised learning setting for (regularized) empirical risk minimization under a wide variety of settings. We will not detail these methods further, but instead introduce the basic setting for classification.

In a classification problem the response space is a finite set of labels each of which corresponds to some subset of input space (although these subsets need not be disjoint). The learning task is to construct a classifier that can best assign these labels to new data points based on labeled training examples from each class. In a binary classification setting there are only two labels, "$-$" and "$+$"; i.e., the response space is $\mathcal{Y} = \{"-", "+"\}$. Where mathematically convenient, we will use 0 and 1 in place of the labels "$-$" and "$+$" respectively; i.e., we will implicitly redefine the label y to be I $[y = "+"]$. In binary classification, we refer to the two classes as the negative class ($y = "-"$) and the positive class ($y = "+"$). The training set $\mathbb{D}^{(\text{train})}$ consists of labeled instances from both classes. We primarily focus on binary classification for security applications in which a defender attempts to separate instances (i.e., data points), some or all of which come from a malicious attacker, into harmful and benign classes. This setting covers many important security applications, such as host and network intrusion detection, virus and worm detection, and spam filtering. In detecting malicious activity, the positive class (with label "$+$") indicates malicious intrusion instances while the negative class (with label "$-$") indicates benign or innocuous normal instances. In Chapter 6, we also consider the anomaly detection setting, in which the training set only contains normal instances from the negative class.

Risk Minimization

The goal of the learner is to find the *best* hypothesis $f^\star$ from the hypothesis space $\mathcal{F}$ that best predicts the target concept (according to some measure of correctness) on instances drawn according to the unknown distribution P_Z. Ideally the learner is able to distinguish $f^\star$ from any other hypothesis $f \in \mathcal{F}$, with high probability, based on the observed data $\mathbb{D}$ of data points drawn from P_Z, but this is seldom realistic or even possible. Instead, the learner should choose the *best* hypothesis in the space according to some criteria for preferring one hypothesis over another—this is the performance measure. The measure can be any assessment of a hypothesis; in statistical machine learning, the most common goal is *risk minimization*, which is based on a loss function $\ell : \mathcal{Y} \times \mathcal{Y} \mapsto \Re_{0+}$ the nonnegative reals. The learner selects a hypothesis $\hat{f} \in \mathcal{F}$ that minimizes the expected loss, or risk, over all hypotheses ($\hat{f} \in \operatorname{argmin}_{f \in \mathcal{F}} R(P_Z, f)$) where the risk is given by

$$R(P_Z, f) \triangleq \int_{(x,y) \in Z} \ell(y, f(x)) \, dP_Z(x, y)$$

and $P_Z(x, y)$ is a probability measure for the distribution P_Z. Unfortunately, this minimization is infeasible since this distribution is unknown. Instead, in the empirical risk minimization framework (cf. Vapnik 1995) the learner selects $\hat{f}$ to minimize the empirical risk on the dataset $\mathbb{D} \sim P_Z$ defined as

$$\tilde{R}_N(f) = \frac{1}{N} \sum_{(x,y) \in \mathbb{D}} \ell(y, f(x))$$

with $N = |\mathbb{D}|$.

Regularization

If the space of hypotheses $\mathcal{F}$ is too expressive, there will be a hypothesis that fits the empirical observations exactly, but it may not be able to make accurate predictions about unseen instances; e.g., consider constructing a lookup table mapping from observed data points to their responses: this classifier can perfectly predict observed instances, but does not generalize to unobserved instances. This phenomenon is known as overfitting the training data. One possibility to avoid overfitting is to only consider a small or restricted space of hypotheses; e.g., the space of linear functions. Alternatively, one could allow for a large space of hypotheses, but penalize the complexity of a hypothesis—a practice known as regularization. The learner selects a hypothesis $\hat{f}$ that minimizes the modified objective

$$\tilde{R}_N\left(f\right) + \lambda \cdot \rho\left(f\right) \tag{2.1}$$

where the function $\rho : \mathcal{F} \to \mathfrak{R}$ is a measure of the complexity of a hypothesis and $\lambda \in \mathfrak{R}_+$ the positive reals, is a regularization parameter that controls the tradeoff between risk minimization and hypothesis complexity.

Prediction and Evaluation

Once trained on a dataset, the learned hypothesis is subsequently used to predict the response variables for a set of unlabeled data. We call this the *evaluation phase* although it may also be referred to as the test or prediction phase. Initially, only a new data point x is presented to the predictor (or rather the predictor is queried with the data point). The learned hypothesis $\hat{f}$ predicts a value $\hat{y} = \hat{f}(x)$ in the space $\mathcal{Y}$ of all possible responses.[2] Finally, the actual label y is revealed, and the agent receives a loss $\ell(\hat{y}, y)$ as an assessment of its performance. In the binary classification setting, there are generally two types of classification mistakes: a false positive (FP) is a normal instance classified as positive, and a false negative (FN) is a malicious instance classified as negative. Selecting an appropriate tradeoff between false positives and false negatives is an application-specific task.

The performance of a learner is typically assessed on a labeled evaluation dataset, $\mathbb{D}^{(\text{eval})}$. Predictions are generated by $\hat{f}$ for each data point $x^{(i)} \in \mathbb{D}_X^{(\text{eval})}$ in the evaluation dataset, and the losses incurred are aggregated into various performance measures. In the binary classification setting, the typical performance measures are the false-positive rate (FPR), the fraction of negative instances classified as positive, and the false-negative rate (FNR), the fraction of positive instances classified as negatives. Often a classifier is tuned to have a particular (empirical) false-positive rate based on held-out training data (validation dataset), and its resulting false-negative rate is assessed at that FP level.

---

[2] The space of allowed predictions or actions $\mathcal{A}$ need not be the same as the space of allowed responses, $\mathcal{Y}$. This allows the learner to choose from a larger range of responses (hedging bets) or to restrict the learner to some desired subset. However, unless explicitly stated, we will assume $\mathcal{A} = \mathcal{Y}$.

2.2.5   Other Learning Paradigms

It is also important to consider cases where a classifier has more than two classes or a real-valued output. Indeed, the spam filter SpamBayes, which we study in Chapter 5, uses a third label, *unsure*, to allow the end-user to examine these potential spam more closely. However, generalizing the analysis of errors to more than two classes is not straightforward, and furthermore most systems in practice make a single fundamental distinction (for example, regardless of the label applied by the spam filter, the end-user will ultimately decide to treat each class as either junk messages or legitimate mail). For these reasons, and in keeping with common practice in the literature, we limit our analysis to binary classification and leave extensions to the multi-class or real-valued prediction as a future discussion.

In Chapter 6, we also study an anomaly detection setting. Like binary classification, anomaly detection consists of making one of two predictions: the data is normal ("−") or the data is anomalous ("+"). Unlike the classification setting, the training data usually only consist of examples from the negative class. Because of this, it is common practice to calibrate the detector to achieve a desired false-positive rate on held-out training data.

There are other interesting learning paradigms to consider such as semi-supervised, unsupervised, and reinforcement learning. However, as they do not directly affect our discussion in this text, we will not discuss these frameworks. For a thorough discussion of different learning settings refer to (Hastie et al. 2003) or (Mitchell 1997).

3   A Framework for Secure Learning

In this chapter we introduce a framework for qualitatively assessing the security of machine learning systems that captures a broad set of security characteristics common to a number of related adversarial learning settings. There has been a rich set of work that examines the security of machine learning systems; here we survey prior studies of learning in adversarial environments, attacks against learning systems, and proposals for making systems secure against attacks. We identify different classes of attacks on machine learning systems (Section 3.3), categorizing a threat in terms of three crucial properties.

We also present secure learning as a game between an *attacker* and a *defender*— the taxonomy determines the structure of the game and its cost model. Further, this taxonomy provides a basis for evaluating the resilience of the systems described by analyzing threats against them to construct defenses. The development of defensive learning techniques is more tentative, but we also discuss a variety of techniques that show promise for defending against different types of attacks.

The work we present not only provides a common language for thinking and writing about secure learning, but goes beyond that to show how the framework applies to both algorithm design and the evaluation of real-world systems. Not only does the framework elicit common themes in otherwise disparate domains but it has also motivated our study of practical machine learning systems as presented in Chapters 5, 6, and 8. These foundational principles for characterizing attacks against learning systems are an essential first step if secure machine learning is to reach its potential as a tool for use in real systems in security-sensitive domains.

This chapter builds on earlier research (Barreno, Nelson, Sears, Joseph, & Tygar 2006; Barreno, Nelson, Joseph, & Tygar 2010; Barreno 2008).

3.1   Analyzing the Phases of Learning

Attacks can occur at each of the phases of the learning process that were outlined in Section 2.2. Figure 2.1(a) depicts how data flows through each phase of learning. We briefly outline how attacks against these phases differ.

The Measuring Phase
With knowledge of the measurement process, an adversary can design malicious instances to mimic the measurements of innocuous data. After a successful attack

against the measurement mechanism, the system may require expensive re-instrumentation or redesign to accomplish its task.

The Feature Selection Phase

The feature selection process can be attacked in the same manner as the measuring phase, except countermeasures and recovery are less costly since feature selection is a dynamic process that can be more readily adapted. Potentially, retraining could even be automated. However, feature selection can also be attacked in the same manner as the training phase (below) if feature selection is based on training data that may be contaminated.

Learning Model Selection

Once the learning model is known, an adversary could exploit assumptions inherent in the model. Erroneous or unreasonable modeling assumptions about the training data may be exploited by an adversary; e.g., if a model erroneously assumes linear separability in the data, the adversary could use data that cannot be separated linearly to deceive the learner or make it perform poorly. It is essential to explicitly state and critique the modeling assumptions to identify potential vulnerabilities since changing the model may require that the system be redesigned.

The Training Phase

By understanding how the learner trains, an adversary can design data to fool the learner into choosing a poor hypothesis, or to aid a later privacy breach of the training data during prediction. Robust learning methods are promising techniques to counter the former attacks as discussed in Section 3.5.4.3. These methods are resilient to adversarial contamination although there are inherent tradeoffs between their robustness and performance. Differential privacy is a leading approach to providing strong guarantees on the level of privacy preserved by learners in the presence of powerful adversaries (Dwork et al. 2006). We explore mechanisms for differentially private approximation of support vector classification in Chapter 7.

The Prediction Phase

Once learned, an imperfect hypothesis can be exploited by an adversary who discovers prediction errors made by the learner. Assessing how difficult it is to discover such errors is an important question; e.g., the ACRE-learning framework of Lowd & Meek (2005a) as discussed in Section 3.4.4. In addition, an adversary can exploit an imperfect hypothesis to breach training data privacy during prediction. An interesting avenue of future research is detecting that an adversary is exploiting these errors and retraining to counter the attack.

To better understand these different abstract attacks, consider a spam filter that (*i*) has some simple set of measurements of email such as *hasAttachment, subjectLength, bodyLength, etc.*, (*ii*) selects the top-ten most frequently appearing features in spam, (*iii*) uses the naive Bayes model, (*iv*) trains class frequencies by empirical counts, and (*v*) classifies email by thresholding the model's predicted class probabilities. An attack against the measurement (or feature selection) phase would consist of first determining the features used (for classification) and then producing spams that are indistinguishable from normal email for those features. An attack against the learning model would entail discovering a set of spams and hams that could not be classified correctly due to the linearity of the naive Bayes boundary. Further, the training system (or feature selection) could be attacked by injecting spams with misleading spurious features, causing it to learn the wrong hypothesis or to learn a hypothesis that improves the odds of revealing privacy-sensitive training emails that were not tampered with. Finally, the prediction phase could be attacked by systematically probing the filter to find spams that are misclassified as ham (false negatives) or to infer information about the privacy-sensitive training dataset.

Many learning methods make a stationarity assumption: training data and evaluation data are drawn from the same distribution. Under this assumption minimizing the risk on the training set is a surrogate for risk on the evaluation data. However, real-world sources of data often are not stationary, and even worse, attackers can easily break the stationarity assumption with some control of either training or evaluation instances. Analyzing and strengthening learning methods to withstand or mitigate violations of the stationarity assumption are the crux of the *secure learning* problem.

Qualifying the vulnerable components of the learning system is only the first step to understanding the adversary. In the next section, we outline a framework designed to qualify the adversary's goals.

3.2   Security Analysis

Security is concerned with protecting assets from attackers. Properly analyzing the security of a system requires identifying the security goals and a threat model for the system. A security goal is a requirement that, if violated, results in the partial or total compromise of an asset. A threat model is a profile of attackers who wish to harm the system, describing their motivation and capabilities. Here we describe possible security goals and threat models for machine learning systems.

In a security-sensitive domain, classifiers can be used to make distinctions that advance the security goals of the system. For example, a virus detection system has the goal of reducing susceptibility to virus infection, either by detecting the virus in transit prior to infection or by detecting an extant infection to expunge. Another example is an intrusion detection system (IDS), which has the goal of preventing harm from malicious intrusion, either by identifying existing intrusions for removal or by detecting malicious traffic and preventing it from reaching its intended target.[1] In this section, we describe security goals and threat models that are specific to machine learning systems.

---

[1] In the case of preventing intrusion, the whole system is more properly called an intrusion prevention system (IPS). We have no need to distinguish between the two cases, so we use IDS to refer to both intrusion detection systems and intrusion prevention systems.

3.2.1   Security Goals

In a security context the classifier's purpose is to classify malicious events and prevent them from interfering with system operations. We split this general learning goal into three goals:

- **Integrity goal**: To prevent attackers from reaching system assets
- **Availability goal**: To prevent attackers from interfering with normal operation
- **Privacy goal**: To protect the confidentiality of potentially privacy-sensitive data used to train the classifier

There is a clear connection between false negatives and violation of the integrity goal: malicious instances that pass through the classifier can wreak havoc. Likewise, false positives tend to violate the availability goal because the learner itself denies benign instances. Finally while an attacker attempting to breach privacy may cause false positives or false negatives, these will typically not be the end goal.

3.2.2   Threat Model

Attacker Goal and Incentives

In general the attacker wants to access system assets (typically with false negatives or through inverting the learning process in the case of a training set privacy violation) or to deny normal operation (usually with false positives). For example, a virus author wants viruses to pass through the filter and take control of the protected system (a false negative). On the other hand, an unscrupulous merchant may want sales traffic to a competitor's web store to be blocked as intrusions (false positives). Finally an over-zealous health insurer might reverse engineer an automated cancer detector to breach the private medical records of the patients who make up the detector's training set.

We assume that the attacker and defender each have a cost function that assigns a cost either to each labeling for any given instance or to each training instance privacy violation. Cost can be positive or negative; a negative cost is a benefit. It is usually the case that low cost for the attacker parallels high cost for the defender and vice versa; the attacker and defender would not be adversaries if their goals aligned. Unless otherwise stated, for ease of exposition we assume that every cost for the defender corresponds to a similar benefit for the attacker and vice versa. However, this assumption is not essential to this framework, which extends easily to arbitrary cost functions. In this chapter, we take the defender's point of view and use *high cost* to mean high positive cost for the defender.

3.2.2.1   Attacker Capabilities

Making only weak assumptions on the adversary, we adopt a threat model in which the attacker has knowledge of the training algorithm and in many cases partial or complete information about the training set, such as its distribution. For example, the attacker may have the ability to eavesdrop on all network traffic over the period of time in which the learner gathers training data. We examine different degrees of the attacker's knowledge and assess how much it gains from different sources of potential information.

In general, we assume the attacker can generate arbitrary instances; however, many settings do impose significant restrictions on the instances generated by the attacker. For example, when the learner trains on data from the attacker, sometimes it is safe to assume that the attacker cannot choose the label for training, such as when training data is carefully hand labeled. As another example, an attacker may have complete control over data packets being sent from the attack source, but routers in transit may add to or alter the packets as well as affect their timing and arrival order.

We consider an attacker with the ability to modify or generate data used in training, and explore scenarios both when it has this capability and when it does not. When the attacker controls training data, an important limitation to consider is what fraction of the training data the attacker can control and to what extent. If the attacker has arbitrary control over 100% of the training data, it is difficult to see how the learner can learn anything useful; however, even in such cases there are learning strategies that can make the attacker's task more difficult (see Section 3.6). We examine intermediate cases and explore how much influence is required for the attacker to defeat the learning procedure.

3.2.3   Discussion of Machine Learning Applications in Security

Sommer & Paxson (2010) have raised a set of objections to some uses of machine learning in security applications. In Section III of that paper, the authors outline five challenges of using machine learning for network anomaly detection. Their first challenge is outlier detection, and the authors argue that network anomaly detection is best done using filtering, instead of the classification that machine learning provides. They also argue that machine learning excels at finding similar occurrences, but does not work for finding novel occurrences. Their second challenge is the high cost of errors, and the authors argue that network anomaly detection systems have a stringent limit on the number of false positive and true positive errors that they can tolerate, with false positives being particularly expensive due to the analyst time required to resolve them. Their third challenge is the semantic gap between anomaly detection systems and users/operators/analysts, and they argue that machine learning-based systems are opaque in decisions they make. Their fourth challenge is that the diversity of network traffic yields very bursty networks, making decision making challenging. They also argue that diversity reduction techniques like aggregation make networks noisy and also make decision making challenging. Their fifth challenge is around the difficulties with evaluation and has multiple components: a lack of usable public datasets, a semantic gap in explaining a machine learning-based system, decisions about novel attacks to users/operators/analysts, and the adversarial setting of network anomaly detection.

Sommer & Paxson (2010) raise interesting points, with a full discussion lying outside the scope of this book. Elsewhere (Miller, Kantchelian, Afroz, Bachwani, Dauber, Huang, Tschantz, Joseph, & Tygar 2014) we discuss frameworks based on adversarial active learning specifically designed to handle novel occurrences of attacks and to intelligently allocate human time required to respond to them, addressing the first two challenges presented by Sommer & Paxson (2010), and also the issue of evaluation in the adversarial setting of their fifth challenge. The field of *secure machine learning* is specifically designed to present robust machine learning, and in that paper we argue for a way to intelligently allocate human resources in dealing with malicious input. Note that the other challenges raised by Sommer & Paxson (2010) are challenges both for traditional filtering systems and for machine learning systems. For example, the question of the availability of datasets is an issue for both researchers of secure machine learning and traditional filtering systems. In a number of research projects including Intel's "Canary" algorithm (Chandrashekar, Orrin, Livadas, & Schooler 2009), Google's malicious advertising detection system (Sculley, Otey, Pohl, Spitznagel, Hainsworth, & Zhou 2011), and UC Berkeley's comment spam detection work (Kantchelian, Ma, Huang, Afroz, Joseph, & Tygar 2012), researchers have been able to gain access to real-world high-quality large datasets.

3.3 Framework

The framework we describe here has three primary components: a taxonomy based on the common characteristics of attacks against learning algorithms, a high-level description of the elements of the game played between the attacker and defender (learner), and set of common characteristics for an attacker's capabilities. Each of these elements helps organize and assess the threat posed by an attacker.

3.3.1 Taxonomy

A great deal of the work that has been done within secure learning is the analysis of attack and defense scenarios for particular learning applications. Together with Marco Barreno and Russell Sears, we developed a qualitative taxonomy of attacks against machine learning systems that we used to categorize others' research, to find commonalities between otherwise disparate domains, and ultimately to frame our own research. We present the taxonomy categorizing attacks against learning systems along three axes. Each of these dimensions operates independently, so we have at least 12 distinct classes of attacks on machine learning systems.

INFLUENCE
- *Causative* attacks influence learning with control over training data.
- *Exploratory* attacks exploit predictions, but do not affect training.

SECURITY VIOLATION
- *Integrity* attacks compromise assets via false negatives.
- *Availability* attacks cause denial of service, usually via false positives.
- *Privacy* attacks obtain information from the learner, compromising the privacy of the learner's training data.

SPECIFICITY
- *Targeted* attacks focus on a particular instance.
- *Indiscriminate* attacks encompass a wide class of instances.

The first axis describes the capability of the attacker: whether (a) the attacker has the ability to influence the training data that is used to construct the classifier (a *Causative* attack) or (b) the attacker does not influence the learned classifier, but can send new instances to the classifier and possibly observe its decisions on these carefully crafted instances (an *Exploratory* attack).

The second axis indicates the type of security violation the attacker causes: either (a) allowing harmful instances to slip through the filter as false negatives (an *Integrity* violation); (b) creating a denial-of-service event in which benign instances are incorrectly filtered as false positives (an *Availability* violation); or (c) using the filter's responses to infer confidential information used in the learning process (a *Privacy* violation).

The third axis refers to how specific the attacker's intention is: whether (a) the attack is highly *Targeted* to degrade the classifier's performance on one particular instance or to violate the privacy of one particular training instance or (b) the attack aims to cause the classifier to fail in an *Indiscriminate* fashion on a broad class of instances. Each axis, especially this one, can actually be a spectrum of choices, but for simplicity, we will categorize attacks and defenses into these groupings.

These axes define the space of attacks against learners and aid in identifying unconventional threats. By qualifying where an attack lies in this space, one can begin to quantify the adversary's capabilities and assess the risk posed by this threat. Laskov & Kloft (2009) have since extended these basic principles to propose a framework for quantitatively evaluating security threats.

In Table 3.1, we use our taxonomy to classify past work on adversarial learning with goals relating to misclassifications—*Integrity* and *Availability* attacks, but not *Privacy*

Table 3.1 Selected related work on misclassification attacks in the taxonomy

	Integrity	*Availability*
Causative: *Targeted*	Kearns & Li (1993); Newsome et al. (2006)	Kearns & Li (1993); Newsome et al. (2006); Chung & Mok (2007); Nelson, Barreno, Chi, Joseph, Rubinstein, Saini, Sutton, Tygar, & Xia (2008)
Indiscriminate	Kearns & Li (1993); Newsome et al. (2006)	Kearns & Li (1993); Newsome et al. (2006); Chung & Mok (2007); Nelson et al. (2008)
Exploratory: *Targeted*	Tan et al. (2002); Lowd & Meek (2005*a*, 2005*b*); Wittel & Wu (2004)	Moore, Shannon, Brown, Voelker, & Savage (2006)
Indiscriminate	Fogla & Lee (2006); Lowd & Meek (2005*b*); Wittel & Wu (2004)	Moore et al. (2006)

attacks. As we discuss in Section 3.7 while the taxonomy provides a useful classification of possible privacy attacks on machine learning systems, past work (with a few exceptions) tends to fall in most bins simultaneously.

3.3.2   The Adversarial Learning Game

We model the task of constructing a secure learning system as a game between an attacker and a defender—the attacker manipulates data to mistrain or evade or violate privacy of a learning algorithm chosen by the defender to thwart the attacker's objective. The characteristics specified by the taxonomy's axes also designate some aspects of this game. The INFLUENCE axis determines the structure of the game and the legal moves that each player can make. The SPECIFICITY and SECURITY VIOLATION axes of the taxonomy determine the general shape of the cost function: an *Integrity* attack benefits the attacker on false negatives, and therefore focuses high cost (to the defender) on false negatives; an *Availability* attack focuses high cost on false positives; and a *Privacy* attack focuses high cost on leaking information about training instances. Similarly a *Targeted* attack focuses high cost only on a small number of specific instances, while an *Indiscriminate* attack spreads high cost over a broad range of instances.

We formalize the game as a series of *moves*, or *steps*. Each move either is a strategic choice by one of the players or is a *neutral* move not controlled by either player. The choices and computations in a move depend on information produced by previous moves (when a game is repeated, this includes previous iterations) and on domain-dependent constraints that we highlight in discussing prior work. Generally, though, in an *Exploratory* attack, the attacker chooses a procedure $A^{(\mathrm{eval})}$ that affects the evaluation data $\mathbb{D}^{(\mathrm{eval})}$, and in a *Causative* attack, the attacker also chooses a procedure $A^{(\mathrm{train})}$ to manipulate the training data $\mathbb{D}^{(\mathrm{train})}$. In either setting, the defender chooses a learning algorithm $H^{(N)}$. This formulation gives us a theoretical basis for analyzing the interactions between attacker and defender.

3.3.3   Characteristics of Adversarial Capabilities

In this section we introduce three essential properties for constructing a model of an attack against a learning algorithm that refine the game played between the learner and the adversary as described by the taxonomy. These properties define a set of common domain-specific adversarial limitations that allow a security analyst to formally describe the capabilities of the adversary.

3.3.3.1   **Corruption Models**

The most important aspect of the adversary is how it can alter data to mislead or evade the classifier, or reveal information about the training data. As previously stated, learning against an unlimited adversary is futile. Instead, the security analysis we propose focuses on a limited adversary, but to do so, one must model the restrictions on the adversary and justify these restrictions for a particular domain. We outline two common models for adversarial corruption, and we describe how the adversary is limited within each.

Data Insertion Model

The first model assumes the adversary has unlimited control of a small fraction of the data; i.e., the adversary is restricted to only modifying a limited amount of data, but can alter those data points arbitrarily. We call this an *insertion model* because, in this scenario, the adversary crafts a small number of attack instances and *inserts* them into the dataset for training or evaluation (or perhaps replaces existing data points). For example, in the case of a spam filter, the adversary (spammer) can create any arbitrary message for their attack, but it is limited in the number of attack messages it can inject: the spammer does not have control over innocuous email messages sent by third parties. The spammer's attack on the spam filter can be analyzed in terms of how many messages are required for the attack to be effective. For this reason, we use this model of corruption in analyzing attacks on the SpamBayes spam filter in Chapter 5 and show that, even with a relatively small number of attack messages, the adversarial spammer can significantly mislead the filter.

Data Alteration Model

The second corruption model instead assumes that the adversary can alter any (or all) of the data points in the dataset, but is limited in the degree of alteration; i.e., an *alteration model*. For example, to attack a detector that is monitoring network traffic volumes over windows of time, the adversary can add or remove traffic within the network, but only can make a limited degree of alteration. Such an adversary cannot insert new data since each data point corresponds to a time slice and the adversary cannot arbitrarily control any single data point because other actors are also creating traffic in the network. Here the adversary is restricted by the total amount it can alter, and so the effectiveness of its attack can be analyzed in terms of the size of alteration required to achieve the attacker's objective. This is the model we use for analyzing attacks on a PCA-subspace detector for network anomaly detection in Chapter 6, and again we show that, with a relatively small degree of control, the adversary can dramatically degrade the effectiveness of this detector using data alterations.

3.3.3.2 Class Limitations

A second limitation on attackers involves which parts of the data the adversary is allowed to alter—the positive (malicious) class, the negative (benign) class, or both. Usually in settings where the adversary aims to affect misclassifications, attackers external to the system are only able to create malicious data and so they are limited to only manipulating positive instances. This is the model we use throughout this text. However, there is also an alternative threat that *insiders* could attack a learning system by altering negative instances. We do not analyze this threat in this book but return to the issue in the discussion in Chapter 9. In the setting of *Privacy* attacks, the learner may not necessarily be classifying instances as malicious or benign so there may not be any natural class limitation on the attacker's influence.

3.3.3.3   Feature Limitations

The final type of adversarial limitation we consider are limits on how an adversary can alter data points in terms of each *feature*. Features represent different aspects of the state of the world and have various degrees of vulnerability to attack. Some features can be arbitrarily changed by the adversary, but others may have stochastic aspects that the adversary cannot completely control, and some features may not be alterable at all. For instance, in sending an email, the adversary can completely control the content of the message, but cannot completely determine the routing of the message or its arrival time. Further, this adversary has no control over meta-information that is added to the message's header by mail relays while the message is en route. Providing an accurate description of the adversary's control over the features is essential.

3.3.4   Attacks

In the remainder of this chapter, we survey prior research, we discuss how attack and defense strategies were developed in different domains, we reveal their common themes, and we highlight important aspects of the secure learning game in the context of this taxonomy. The related work discussed later is also presented in the taxonomy in Table 3.1. For an *Exploratory* attack, we discuss realistic instances of the attacker's choice for $A^{(\mathrm{eval})}$ in Sections 3.4.2 and 3.4.3. Similarly, in Sections 3.5.2 and 3.5.3, we discuss practical examples of the attacker's choices in the *Causative* game.

We treat *Privacy* attacks separately from attacks aiming to produce misclassifications, with a dedicated discussion in Section 3.7.

3.3.5   Defenses

The game between attacker and defender and the taxonomy also provide a foundation on which to construct defense strategies against broad classes of attacks. We address *Exploratory* and *Causative* misclassification attacks separately. For *Exploratory* attacks, we discuss the defender's choice for an algorithm $H^{(N)}$ in Section 3.4.4 and we discuss the defender's strategies in a *Causative* setting in Section 3.5.4. Finally, in Section 3.6, we discuss the broader setting of an iterated game.

We treat defenses against *Exploratory* and *Causative Privacy* attacks together in Section 3.7.

In all cases, defenses present a tradeoff: changing the algorithms to make them more robust against (worst-case) attacks will generally make them *less* effective on non-adversarial data. Analyzing this tradeoff is an important part of developing defenses.

3.4   Exploratory Attacks

Based on the INFLUENCE axis of the taxonomy, the first category of attacks that we discuss are *Exploratory* attacks, which influence only the evaluation data as indicated in

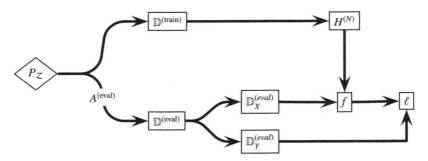

Figure 3.1 Diagram of an *Exploratory* attack against a learning system (see Figure 2.1).

Figure 3.1. The adversary's transformation $A^{(\mathrm{eval})}$ alters the evaluation data either by defining a procedure to change instances drawn from P_Z or by changing P_Z to an altogether different distribution $P_Z^{(\mathrm{eval})}$ chosen by the adversary. The adversary makes these changes based on (partial) information gleaned about the training data $\mathbb{D}^{(\mathrm{train})}$, the learning algorithm $H^{(N)}$, and the classifier f. Further, the adversary's transformation may evolve as the adversary learns more about the classifier with each additional prediction it makes.

3.4.1   The Exploratory Game

First we present the formal version of the game for *Exploratory* attacks and then explain it in greater detail.

1 **Defender**   Choose procedure $H^{(N)}$ for selecting an hypothesis
2 **Attacker**   Choose procedure $A^{(\mathrm{eval})}$ for selecting an evaluation distribution
3 Evaluation:
   - Reveal distribution $P_Z^{(\mathrm{train})}$
   - Sample dataset $\mathbb{D}^{(\mathrm{train})}$ from $P_Z^{(\mathrm{train})}$
   - Compute $f \leftarrow H^{(N)}\left(\mathbb{D}^{(\mathrm{train})}\right)$
   - Compute $P_Z^{(\mathrm{eval})} \leftarrow A^{(\mathrm{eval})}(\mathbb{D}^{(\mathrm{train})}, f)$
   - Sample dataset $\mathbb{D}^{(\mathrm{eval})}$ from $P_Z^{(\mathrm{eval})}$
   - Assess total cost: $\displaystyle\sum_{(x,y)\in\mathbb{D}^{(\mathrm{eval})}} \ell_x\left(f(x), y\right)$

The defender's move is to choose a learning algorithm (procedure) $H^{(N)}$ for creating hypotheses from datasets. Many procedures used in machine learning have the form of Equation (2.1). For example, the defender may choose a support vector machine (SVM) with a particular kernel, loss, regularization, and cross-validation plan. The attacker's move is then to choose a procedure $A^{(\mathrm{eval})}$ to produce a distribution on which to evaluate the hypothesis that $H^{(N)}$ generates. (The degree of control the attacker has in generating the dataset and the degree of information about $\mathbb{D}^{(\text{train})}$ and f that $A^{(\text{eval})}$ has access to are setting specific.)

After the defender and attacker have both made their choices, the game is evaluated. A training dataset $\mathbb{D}^{(\text{train})}$ is drawn from some fixed and possibly unknown distribution $P_{\mathcal{Z}}^{(\text{train})}$, and training produces $f = H^{(N)}\left(\mathbb{D}^{(\text{train})}\right)$. The attacker's procedure $A^{(\text{eval})}$ produces distribution $P_{\mathcal{Z}}^{(\text{eval})}$, which is based in general on $\mathbb{D}^{(\text{train})}$ and f, and an evaluation dataset $\mathbb{D}^{(\text{eval})}$ is drawn from $P_{\mathcal{Z}}^{(\text{eval})}$. Finally, the attacker and defender incur cost based on the performance of f evaluated on $\mathbb{D}^{(\text{eval})}$ according to the loss function $\ell_x(\cdot, \cdot)$. Note that, unlike in Section 2.2, here we allow the loss function to depend on the data point x. This generalization allows this game to account for an adversary (or learner) with instance-dependent costs (cf. Dalvi, Domingos, Mausam, Sanghai, & Verma 2004).

The procedure $A^{(\text{eval})}$ generally depends on $\mathbb{D}^{(\text{train})}$ and f, but the amount of information an attacker actually has is setting specific (in the least restrictive case the attacker knows $\mathbb{D}^{(\text{train})}$ and f completely). The attacker may know a subset of $\mathbb{D}^{(\text{train})}$ or the family $\mathcal{F}$ containing f. However, the procedure $A^{(\text{eval})}$ may also involve acquiring information dynamically. For instance, in some cases, the procedure $A^{(\text{eval})}$ can query the classifier, treating it as an oracle that provides labels for query instances; this is one particular degree of information that $A^{(\text{eval})}$ can have about f. An attack that uses this technique is called a probing attack. Probing can reveal information about the classifier. On the other hand, with sufficient prior knowledge about the training data and algorithm, the attacker may be able to find high-cost instances without probing.

3.4.2   Exploratory Integrity Attacks

A frequently studied attack is the *Exploratory Integrity* attack in which the adversary attempts to passively circumvent the learning mechanism to exploit blind spots in the learner that allow miscreant activities to go undetected. In an *Exploratory Integrity* attack, the attacker crafts intrusions so as to evade the classifier without direct influence over the classifier itself. Instead, attacks of this sort often attempt to systematically make the miscreant activity appear to be normal activity to the detector or obscure the miscreant activity's identifying characteristics. Some *Exploratory Integrity* attacks mimic statistical properties of normal traffic to camouflage intrusions; e.g., the attacker examines training data and the classifier, then crafts intrusion data. In the *Exploratory* game, the attacker's move produces malicious instances in $\mathbb{D}^{(\text{eval})}$ that statistically resemble normal traffic in the training data $\mathbb{D}^{(\text{train})}$.

EXAMPLE 3.1 (The Shifty Intruder)
An attacker modifies and obfuscates intrusions, such as by changing network headers and reordering or encrypting contents. If successful, these modifications prevent the IDS from recognizing the altered intrusions as malicious, so it allows them into the system. In the *Targeted* version of this attack, the attacker has a particular intrusion to get past the filter. In the *Indiscriminate* version, the attacker has no particular preference and can search for any intrusion that succeeds, such as by modifying a large number of different exploits to see which modifications evade the filter.

3.4.2.1   Polymorphic Blending Attack

Fogla & Lee (2006) introduce *polymorphic blending attacks* that evade intrusion detectors using encryption techniques to make attacks statistically indistinguishable from normal traffic according to the intrusion detection system. They present a formalism for reasoning about and generating polymorphic blending attack instances to evade intrusion detection systems. The technique is fairly general and is *Indiscriminate* in terms of the intrusion packets it modifies.

Feature deletion attacks instead specifically exclude high-value identifying features used by the detector (Globerson & Roweis 2006); this form of attack stresses the importance of proper feature selection as was also demonstrated empirically by Mahoney & Chan (2003) in their study of the behavior of intrusion detection systems on the DARPA/Lincoln Lab dataset.

3.4.2.2   Attacking a Sequence-Based IDS

Tan et al. (2002) describe a mimicry attack against the `stide` sequence-based intrusion detection system (IDS) proposed by Forrest et al. (1996) and Warrender et al. (1999). They modify exploits of the `passwd` and `traceroute` programs to accomplish the same ends using different sequences of system calls: the shortest subsequence in attack traffic that does not appear in normal traffic is longer than the IDS window size. By exploiting the finite window size of the detector, this technique makes attack traffic indistinguishable from normal traffic for the detector. This attack is more *Targeted* than polymorphic blending since it modifies particular intrusions to look like normal traffic. In subsequent work Tan, McHugh, & Killourhy (2003) characterize their attacks as part of a larger class of information hiding techniques that they demonstrate can make exploits mimic either normal call sequences or the call sequence of another less severe exploit.

Independently, Wagner & Soto (2002) have also developed mimicry attacks against a sequence-based IDS called pH proposed by Somayaji & Forrest (2000). Using the machinery of finite automata, they construct a framework for testing whether an IDS is susceptible to mimicry for a particular exploit. In doing so, they develop a tool for validating IDSs on a wide range of variants of a particular attack and suggest that similar tools should be more broadly employed to identify the vulnerabilities of an IDS.

Overall, these mimicry attacks against sequence-based anomaly detection systems underscore critical weaknesses in these systems that allow attackers to obfuscate the necessary elements of their exploits to avoid detection by mimicking normal behaviors. Further they highlight how an IDS may appear to perform well against a known exploit, but unless it captures necessary elements of the intrusion, the exploit can easily be adapted to circumvent the detector. See Section 3.4.4 for more discussion.

3.4.2.3   Good Word Attacks

Adding or changing words in a spam message can allow the message to bypass the filter. Like the attacks against an IDS described earlier, these attacks all use both training data and information about the classifier to generate instances intended to bypass the filter. They are somewhat independent of the *Targeted/Indiscriminate* distinction, but the *Exploratory* game captures the process used by all of these attacks.

Studying these techniques was first suggested by John Graham-Cumming. In his presentation *How to Beat an Adaptive Spam Filter* delivered at the 2004 MIT Spam Conference, he presented a *Bayes vs. Bayes* attack that uses a second statistical spam filter to find good words based on feedback from the filter under attack. Several authors have further explored evasion techniques used by spammers and demonstrated attacks against spam filters using similar principles as those against IDSs as discussed earlier. Lowd & Meek (2005*b*) and Wittel & Wu (2004) develop attacks against statistical spam filters that add *good words*, or words the filter considers indicative of non-spam, to spam emails. This good word attack makes spam emails appear innocuous to the filter, especially if the words are chosen to be ones that appear often in non-spam email and rarely in spam email. Finally, obfuscation of spam words (i.e., changing characters in the word or the spelling of the word so it is no longer recognized by the filter) is another popular technique for evading spam filters that has been formalized by several authors (cf. Liu & Stamm 2007 and Sculley, Wachman, & Brodley 2006).

3.4.2.4   Cost-Based Evasion

Another line of research focuses on the costs incurred due to the adversary's evasive actions; i.e., instances that evade detection may be less desirable to the adversary. By directly modeling adversarial cost, this work explicitly casts evasion as a problem in which the adversary wants to evade detection, but wants to do so using high-value instances (an assumption that was implicit in the other work discussed in this section).

Game-Theoretic Approaches

Dalvi et al. (2004) exploit these costs to develop a cost-sensitive game-theoretic classification defense that is able to successfully detect optimal evasion of the original classifier. Using this game-theoretic approach, this technique preemptively patches the naive classifier's blind spots by constructing a modified classifier designed to detect optimally modified instances.

Subsequent game-theoretic approaches to learning have extended this setting and solved for equilibria of the game (Brückner & Scheffer 2009; Kantarcioglu, Xi, & Clifton 2009). Further, Biggio, Fumera, & Roli (2010) extend this game-theoretic approach and propose hiding information or randomization as additional defensive mechanisms for this setting. Großhans, Sawade, Brückner, & Scheffer (2013) explore Bayesian games between Bayesian statistician defender and attacker, in the non-zero-sum case under incomplete information and with continuous action spaces. Here they model the defender's (partial) knowledge of the attacker as encoded in the prior, demonstrate sufficient conditions for unique equilbrium existence (under sufficiently strong regularization of costs), and present an algorithm for computing such an equilibrium.

Evasion by Membership Queries

Cost models of the adversary also led to a theory for query-based near-optimal evasion of classifiers first presented by Lowd & Meek (2005*a*), in which they cast the difficulty of evading a classifier into a abstract query complexity problem. They give algorithms for an attacker to reverse engineer a classifier. The attacker seeks the highest cost (lowest cost for the attacker) instance that the classifier labels *negative*. In *Near-Optimal Evasion of Convex-Inducing Classifiers*, we developed an extension to this work (Nelson, Rubinstein, Huang, Joseph, Lau, Lee, Rao, Tran, & Tygar 2010). We generalized the theory of near-optimal evasion to a broader class of classifiers and demonstrated that the problem is easier than reverse-engineering approaches. We go into greater detail on this work in Chapter 8. The ACRE framework (Lowd & Meek 2005*a*) is further extended by Stevens & Lowd (2013) to encompass concept classes that are convex polytopes representing unions or intersections of linear classifiers, in the difficult case of discrete features (contrasting with the continuous case explored for convex-inducing classifiers in Chapter 8). Query complexity upper bounds for this nonlinear discrete setting suggest that these classes are difficult to evade via membership queries, unlike their linear counterparts.

Attacks on Deployed Systems
Reverse-engineering attacks have been deployed by Tramèr, Zhang, Juels, Reiter, and Ristenpart (2016) against major cloud-based Machine-Learning-as-a-service systems. When target learning systems output prediction confidence values, the researchers probe the model randomly to obtain a set of instance-confidence pairs from which they solve a system of equations to determine decision boundaries in the case of logistic regression and neural networks. When the target model is a tree, they leverage the confidence values output at leaves to develop an efficient and exact path-finding algorithm to reconstruct the tree. Without access to the confidence values, the authors apply the idea of membership queries (see Chapter 8), specifically extending the technique of Lowd & Meek (2005*a*) when models are linear under an invertible feature mapping, such as used for certain support vector machine models. In an earlier work, the deployed system PDFrate—an online service for detecting PDF malware—is the subject of evasion attacks in Srndic & Laskov (2014). Given their work's focus on practical evasion attacks, the authors present a sub-taxonomy of attacks sharing the same goal, distinguishing between cases of attacker information around knowledge of the feature set, training data, and details of the classifier.

Attack Generation by Gradient Descent
Computing the best response in the game-theoretic formulation corresponds to finding (near) optimal attacks under adversary-agnostic learners. An apparent advantage of this approach, over computing equilibria over both attacker and defender actions, is that more nonlinear models and learners can be tackled efficiently. Building on their work formulating *Causative* attacks as optimization (see Section 3.5.2), Biggio, Corona, Maiorca, Nelson, Srndic, Laskov, Giacinto, & Roli (2013) formulate *Exploratory* attacks on the support vector machine as gradient descent. By the Representer Theorem, the prediction function for the SVM can be written as a sum of kernel terms; hence gradients exist and are easily computed provided the kernel function is differentiable in the test point.

3.4.2.5   Evasion of Deep Learning Methods

There has been a great deal of interest and success in the field of deep neural network learners (for example see LeCun, Bengio, & Hinton 2015), which focuses on training multilayer (deep) neural networks (DNNs). Unlike prior neural network architectures, DNNs use cascades of hidden layers to implicitly undertake complex tasks such as feature extraction and transformation as part of the learning process. However, because of the large model size, DNNs are prone to overfitting and may be susceptible to evasion attacks. In particular Goodfellow, Shlens, & Szegedy (2015) demonstrated a simple *fast gradient sign method* for generating adversarial examples. Their work showed that even models with multiple nonlinear layers can be easily misled by applying linear perturbations of the test data. The authors observed that these attacks are *transferable*; i.e., can be applied to other target DNN models with different architectures that are used for the same learning task. Based on the transferability of these attacks, Papernot, McDaniel, Goodfellow, Jha, Celik, and Swami (2017) demonstrated black-box attacks against deep neural network systems in which the adversary is able to train a surrogate DNN model based on the output of the targeted DNN and craft adversarial examples for the surrogate model that also can evade the targeted model. Liu, Chen, Liu, & Song (2017) explore these transferable attacks at scale: for larger datasets and larger architectures better reflecting the state-of-the-art models used in industrial systems. They find that while indiscriminate attacks transfer easily, an ensembling technique is required to generate an attack example when transferring in the targeted case.

The success of deep learning and the risk of DNN model overfitting have triggered broad interest in adversarial learning. The application of adversarial learning as a form of regularization has enjoyed particular interest; we return to the topic in Section 3.4.4.1.

3.4.3   Exploratory Availability Attacks

In an *Exploratory Availability* attack, the attacker interferes with the normal behavior of a learning system without influence over training. This type of attack against non-learning systems abounds in the literature: almost any denial-of-service (DoS) attack falls into this category, such as those described by Moore et al. (2006). However, *Exploratory Availability* attacks against the learning components of systems are not common and we are not aware of any studies of them. It seems the motivation for attacks of this variety is not as compelling as for other attacks against learners.

One possible attack is described in the following example: if a learning IDS has trained on intrusion traffic and has the policy of blocking hosts that originate intrusions, an attacker could send intrusions that appear to originate from a legitimate host, convincing the IDS to block that host. Another possibility is to take advantage of a computationally expensive learning component: for example, spam filters that use image processing to detect advertisements in graphical attachments can take significantly more time than text-based filtering (Dredze, Gevaryahu, & Elias-Bachrach 2007; Wang, Josephson, Lv, Charikar, & Li 2007). An attacker could exploit such overhead by sending many emails with images, causing the time-consuming processing to delay and perhaps even block messages.

EXAMPLE 3.2 (The Mistaken Identity)
An attacker sends intrusions that appear to come from the IP address of a legitimate machine. The IDS, which has learned to recognize intrusions, blocks that machine. In the *Targeted* version, the attacker has a particular machine to target. In the *Indiscriminate* version, the attacker may select any convenient machine or may switch IP addresses among many machines to induce greater disruption.

3.4.4 Defending against Exploratory Attacks

Exploratory attacks do not corrupt the training data, but attempt to find vulnerabilities in the learned hypothesis. Through control over the evaluation data, the attacker can violate the assumption of stationarity. When producing the evaluation distribution, the attacker attempts to construct an unfavorable evaluation distribution that concentrates probability mass on high-cost instances; in other words, the attacker's procedure $A^{(\text{eval})}$ constructs an evaluation distribution $P_Z^{(\text{eval})}$ on which the learner predicts poorly (violating stationarity); i.e., the attacker chooses $P_Z^{(\text{eval})}$ to maximize the cost computed in the last step of the *Exploratory* game. This section examines defender strategies that make it difficult for the attacker to construct such a distribution.

In the *Exploratory* game, the defender makes a move before observing contaminated data; that is, here we do not consider scenarios where the defender is permitted to react to the attack. The defender can impede the attacker's ability to reverse engineer the classifier by limiting access to information about the training procedure and data. With less information, $A^{(\text{eval})}$ has difficulty producing an unfavorable evaluation distribution. Nonetheless, even with incomplete information, the attacker may be able to construct an unfavorable evaluation distribution using a combination of prior knowledge and probing.

The defender's task is to design data collection and learning techniques that make it difficult for an attacker to reverse engineer the hypothesis. The primary task in analyzing *Exploratory* attacks is quantifying the attacker's ability to reverse engineer the learner.

3.4.4.1 Defenses against Attacks without Probing
Part of a security analysis involves identifying aspects of the system that should be kept secret. In securing a learner, the defender can limit information to make it difficult for an adversary to conduct its attack.

Training Data
Preventing the attacker from obtaining the training data limits the attacker's ability to reconstruct internal states of the classifier. There is a tension between collecting training data that fairly represents the real-world instances and keeping all aspects of that data secret. In most situations, it is difficult to use completely secret training data, though

the attacker may have only partial information about it. Securing training data relates to privacy-preserving learning (see Section 3.7).

Feature Selection

The defender can also harden classifiers against attacks through attention to features in the feature selection and learning steps (which are both internal steps of the defender's hypothesis selection procedure $H^{(N)}$). Feature selection is the process of choosing a feature map that transforms raw measurements into the feature space used by the learning algorithm. In the learning step, the learning algorithm builds its model or signature using particular features from the map's feature space; this choice of features for the model or signature is also sometimes referred to as feature selection, though we consider it to be part of the learning process, after the feature map has been established. For example, one feature map for email message bodies might transform each token to a Boolean feature indicating its presence; another map might specify a real-valued feature indicating the relative frequency of each word in the message compared to its frequency in natural language; yet another map might count sequences of n characters and specify an integer feature for each character n-gram indicating how many times it appears. In each of these cases, a learner will construct a model or signature that uses certain features (tokens present or absent; relative frequency of words present; character n-gram counts) to decide whether an instance is benign or malicious.

Obfuscation of spam-indicating words (an attack on the feature set) is a common *Targeted Exploratory Integrity* attack. Sculley et al. (2006) use inexact string matching in feature selection to defeat obfuscations of words in spam emails. They choose a feature map based on character subsequences that are robust to character addition, deletion, and substitution.

Globerson & Roweis (2006) present a feature-based learning defense for the feature deletion attack; an *Exploratory* attack on the evaluation data $\mathbb{D}^{(\mathrm{eval})}$. In feature deletion, features present in the training data, and perhaps highly predictive of an instance's class, are removed from the evaluation data by the attacker. For example, words present in training emails may not occur in evaluation messages, and network packets in training data may contain values for optional fields that are missing from future traffic. Globerson & Roweis formulate a modified support vector machine classifier that is robust in its choice of features against deletion of high-value features.

It has been observed that high dimensionality serves to increase the attack surface of *Exploratory* attacks (Sommer & Paxson 2010; Amsaleg, Bailey, Erfani, Furon, Houle, Radovanović, & Vinh 2016), suggesting that (possibly randomized) feature selection be used as a defensive strategy. In game-theoretic models of *Causative* attacks, high dimensions also have computational consequences on finding equilibrium solutions. Alpcan, Rubinstein, & Leckie (2016) approach such settings through random projections, exploring conditions where solutions lift from projected spaces to the original action spaces; as a case study they apply their ideas to *Causative* attacks on the linear support vector machine.

The work of Li & Vorobeychik (2014), however, should bring a note of caution: in exploring traditional approaches to feature reduction in applications to email spam, they observe vulnerabilities to attackers using feature substitution that is particularly well motivated in spam. Next they explore counter-measures including learning equivalence classes of features and then using these in feature reduction to mitigate feature substitution; and formulation of the Stackelberg game as a bilevel mixed linear integer program, with heuristics for making approximate solutions tractable that yield an interesting trade-off between sparse regularized learning and evasion, thereby producing an approach to adversarial feature selection. Zhang, Chan, Biggio, Yeung, & Roli (2016) also explore the interplay between feature selection and attacks. The authors propose a wrapper-based adversarial feature selector that optimizes both classifier generalization capability and classifier security with optimization via greedy approaches: forward feature selection or backward feature elimination.

One particularly important consideration when the learner builds its model or signature is to ensure that the learner uses features related to the intrusion itself. In their study of the DARPA/Lincoln Laboratory intrusion dataset, Mahoney & Chan (2003) demonstrate that spurious artifacts in training data can cause an IDS to learn to distinguish normal from intrusion traffic based on those artifacts rather than relevant features. Ensuring that the learner builds a model from features that describe the fundamental differences between malicious and benign instances should mitigate the effects of mimicry attacks (Section 3.4.2) and red herring attacks (Section 3.5.2).

Using spurious features in constructing a model or signature is especially problematic in cases where any given intrusion attempt may cause harm only probabilistically or depending on some internal state of the victim's system. If the features relevant to the intrusion are consistent for some set of instances but the actual cost of those instances varies widely, then a learner risks attributing the variation to other nonessential features.

Hypothesis Space/Learning Procedures
A complex hypothesis space may make it difficult for the attacker to infer precise information about the learned hypothesis. However, hypothesis complexity must be balanced against the capacity to generalize, through appropriate regularization.

Wang, Parekh, & Stolfo (2006) present *Anagram*, an anomaly detection system using *n-gram* models of bytes to detect intrusions. They incorporate two techniques to defeat *Exploratory* attacks that mimic normal traffic (mimicry attacks): *i*) they use high-order *n*-grams (with *n* typically between 3 and 7), which capture differences in intrusion traffic even when that traffic has been crafted to mimic normal traffic on the single-byte level; and *ii*) they randomize feature selection by randomly choosing several (possibly overlapping) subsequences of bytes in the packet and testing them separately, so the attack will fail unless the attacker makes not only the whole packet but also any subsequence mimic normal traffic.

Dalvi et al. (2004) develop a cost-sensitive game-theoretic classification defense to counter *Exploratory Integrity* attacks. In their model, the attacker can alter natural instance features in $A^{(\text{eval})}$ but incurs a known cost for each change. The defender can measure each feature at a different known cost. Each has a known cost function over classification/true label pairs. The classifier $H^{(N)}$ is a cost-sensitive naive Bayes learner that classifies instances to minimize expected cost, while the attacker modifies features to minimize its own expected cost. The defense constructs an adversary-aware classifier by altering the likelihood function of the learner to anticipate the attacker's changes. The defender adjusts the likelihood that an instance is malicious by considering that the observed instance may be the result of an attacker's optimal transformation of another instance. This defense relies on two assumptions: *i*) the defender's strategy is a step ahead of the attacker's strategy (i.e., their game differs from ours in that the attacker's procedure $A^{(\text{eval})}$ cannot take f into account), and *ii*) the attacker plays optimally against the original cost-sensitive classifier. It is worth noting that while the approach defends against optimal attacks, it does not account for nonoptimal attacks. For example, if the attacker does not modify any data, the adversary-aware classifier misclassifies some instances that the original classifier correctly classifies.

Some defensive methods for deep neural network learners in adversarial settings have been developed. Based on their *fast gradient sign method* for generating adversarial examples, Goodfellow et al. (2015) developed an alternative adversarial objective function for training DNN models. In this formulation, a regularizer is added to the original objective function. This regularizer is the objective function with an adversarial perturbation applied to each training instance; i.e., a gradient step in the opposing direction to the optimization. This regularizer transforms the objective into a minimax problem, which generally encourages flatter gradients in the neighborhood of the training data. An application of attacks on deep learners is represented by the framework of generative adversarial networks of Goodfellow, Pouget-Abadie, Mirza, Xu, Warde-Farley, Ozair, Courville, & Bengio (2014), whereby a pair of DNNs are trained: a generative (adversarial) model that captures the training data distribution and a discriminative model that is trained to discriminate between samples drawn from the training data and samples drawn from the generative network. The models together are trained via a minimax (zero-sum) game. Significant interest has followed from the approach's strong experimental results across several domains.

3.4.4.2   Defenses against Probing Attacks

In the game described in Section 3.4.1, the attacker chooses an evaluation distribution $P_{\mathcal{Z}}^{(\text{eval})}$ for selecting the evaluation data $\mathbb{D}^{(\text{eval})}$ based on knowledge obtained from the training data $\mathbb{D}^{(\text{train})}$ and/or the classifier f. However, the procedure $A^{(\text{eval})}$ need not select a stationary distribution $P_{\mathcal{Z}}^{(\text{eval})}$. In fact, the attacker may incrementally change the distribution based on the observed behavior of the classifier to each data point generated from $P_{\mathcal{Z}}^{(\text{eval})}$—a *probing* or query-based adaptive attack. The ability for $A^{(\text{eval})}$ to query a classifier gives an attacker powerful additional attack options, which several researchers have explored.

Analysis of Reverse Engineering

Lowd & Meek (2005*a*) observe that the attacker need not model the classifier explicitly, but only find lowest-attacker-cost instances as in the setting of Dalvi et al. (2004). They formalize a notion of reverse engineering as the adversarial classifier reverse-engineering (ACRE) problem. Given an attacker cost function, they analyze the complexity of finding a lowest-attacker-cost instance that the classifier labels as negative. They assume no general knowledge of training data, though the attacker does know the feature space and also must have one positive example and one negative example. A classifier is ACRE-learnable if there exists a polynomial-query algorithm that finds a lowest-attacker-cost negative instance. They show that linear classifiers are ACRE-learnable with linear attacker cost functions and some other minor technical restrictions.

The ACRE-learning problem provides a means of quantifying how difficult it is to use queries to reverse engineer a classifier from a particular hypothesis class using a particular feature space. We now suggest defense techniques that can increase the difficulty of reverse engineering a learner.

Randomization

A randomized hypothesis may decrease the value of feedback to an attacker. Instead of choosing a hypothesis $f : \mathcal{X} \rightarrow \{0, 1\}$, we generalize to hypotheses that predict a real value on $[0, 1]$. This generalized hypothesis returns a probability of classifying $x \in \mathcal{X}$ as 1; i.e., a *randomized* classifier. By randomizing, the expected performance of the hypothesis may decrease on regular data drawn from a nonadversarial distribution, but it also may decrease the value of the queries for the attacker.

Randomization in this fashion does not reduce the information available in principle to the attacker, but merely requires more work from the attacker. It is likely that this defense is appropriate in only a small number of scenarios.

Limiting/Misleading Feedback

Another potential defense is to limit the feedback given to an attacker. For example, common techniques in the spam domain include eliminating bounce emails, delivery notices, and remote image loading and imposing other limits on potential feedback channels. In most settings, it is impossible to remove all feedback channels; however, limiting feedback increases work for the attacker. Moreover in some settings, it may also be possible to mislead the attacker by sending fraudulent feedback. Actively misleading the attacker by fabricating feedback suggests an interesting battle of information between attacker and defender. In some scenarios the defender may be able to give the attacker no information via feedback, and in others the defender may even be able to return feedback that causes the attacker to come to incorrect conclusions. Of course, misinformation can also degrade the usefulness of the classifier when evaluated on benign data.

3.5   Causative Attacks

The second broad category of attacks according to the taxonomy's Influence axis are *Causative* attacks, which influence the training data (as well as potentially subsequently modifying the evaluation data) as indicated in Figure 3.2. Again, the adversary's transformation $A^{(\text{eval})}$ alters the evaluation data either by defining a procedure to change instances drawn from P_Z or by changing P_Z to an alternative distribution $P_Z^{(\text{eval})}$ chosen

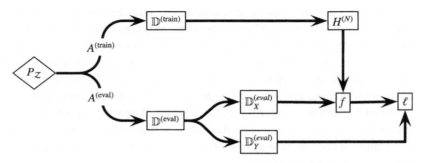

Figure 3.2 Diagram of a *Causative* attack against a learning system (see Figure 2.1).

by the adversary (see Section 3.4). However, in addition to changing evaluation data, *Causative* attacks also allow the adversary to alter the training data with a second transformation $A^{(\text{train})}$, which either transforms instances drawn from P_Z or changes P_Z to an alternative distribution $P_Z^{(\text{train})}$ during training. Of course, the adversary can synchronize $A^{(\text{train})}$ and $A^{(\text{eval})}$ to best achieve its desired objective, although in some *Causative* attacks, the adversary can only control the training data (e.g., the attacker we describe in Chapter 5 cannot control the non-spam messages sent during evaluation). Also note that, since the game described here corresponds to batch learning, an adaptive procedure $A^{(\text{train})}$ is unnecessary, although the distribution $P_Z^{(\text{train})}$ can be nonstationary.

3.5.1　The Causative Game

The game for *Causative* attacks is similar to the game for *Exploratory* attacks with an augmented move for the attacker.

1 **Defender**　Choose procedure $H^{(N)}$ for selecting hypothesis
2 **Attacker**　Choose procedures $A^{(\text{train})}$ and $A^{(\text{eval})}$ for selecting distributions
3 Evaluation:
- Compute $P_Z^{(\text{train})} \leftarrow A^{(\text{train})}\left(P_Z, H\right)$
- Sample dataset $\mathbb{D}^{(\text{train})}$ from $P_Z^{(\text{train})}$
- Compute $f \leftarrow H^{(N)}\left(\mathbb{D}^{(\text{train})}\right)$
- Compute $P_Z^{(\text{eval})} \leftarrow A^{(\text{eval})}\left(\mathbb{D}^{(\text{train})}, f\right)$
- Sample dataset $\mathbb{D}^{(\text{eval})}$ from $P_Z^{(\text{eval})}$
- Assess total cost: $\displaystyle\sum_{(x,y)\in\mathbb{D}^{(\text{eval})}} \ell_x\left(f(x), y\right)$

This game is very similar to the *Exploratory* game, but the attacker can choose $A^{(\text{train})}$ to affect the training data $\mathbb{D}^{(\text{train})}$. The attacker may have various types of influence over the data, ranging from arbitrary control over some fraction of instances to a small biasing influence on some aspect of data production; details depend on the setting. Again, the loss function $\ell_x(\,\cdot\,,\,\cdot\,)$ allows for instance-dependent costs.

Control over data used for training opens up new strategies to the attacker. Cost is based on the interaction of f and $\mathbb{D}^{(\text{eval})}$. In the *Exploratory* game the attacker chooses $\mathbb{D}^{(\text{eval})}$ while the defender controls f; in the *Causative* game the attacker also has influence on f. With this influence, the attacker can proactively cause the learner to produce bad classifiers.

Contamination in PAC Learning

Kearns & Li (1993) extend Valiant's *probably approximately correct* (PAC) learning framework (cf. Valiant 1984, 1985) to prove bounds for maliciously chosen errors in the training data. In PAC learning, an algorithm succeeds if it can, with probability at least $1 - \delta$, learn a hypothesis that has at most probability ϵ of making an incorrect prediction on an example drawn from the same distribution. Kearns & Li examine the case where an attacker has arbitrary control over some fraction β of the training examples (this specifies the form that $A^{(\text{train})}$ takes in our *Causative* game). They prove that in general the attacker can prevent the learner from succeeding if $\beta \geq \epsilon/(1 + \epsilon)$, and for some classes of learners they show this bound is tight.

This work provides important limits on the ability to succeed at PAC learning in a particular adversarial setting. The analysis broadly concerns both *Integrity* and *Availability* attacks as well as both *Targeted* and *Indiscriminate* variants. However, not all learning systems fall into the PAC learning model.

3.5.2   Causative Integrity Attacks

In these attacks, the adversary actively attempts to corrupt the learning mechanism so that miscreant activities can take place that would be otherwise disallowed. In a *Causative Integrity* attack, the attacker uses control over training to cause intrusions to slip past the classifier as false negatives.

EXAMPLE 3.3 (The Intrusion Foretold)
An attacker wants the defender's IDS not to flag a novel virus. The defender trains periodically on network traffic, so the attacker sends non-intrusion traffic that is carefully chosen to look like the virus and mis-train the learner to fail to block it. This example would be *Targeted* if the attacker already has a particular virus executable to send and needs to cause the learner to miss that particular instance. It would be *Indiscriminate*, on the other hand, if the attacker has a certain payload but could use any of a large number of existing exploit mechanisms to transmit the payload, in which case the attack need only fool the learner on any one of the malicious executables.

Red Herring Attack

Newsome et al. (2006) present *Causative Integrity* and *Causative Availability* attacks against Polygraph (Newsome et al. 2005), a polymorphic-virus detector that learns virus signatures using both a conjunction learner and a naive-Bayes-like learner. Their *red herring* attacks against conjunction learners exploit certain weaknesses not generally present in other learning algorithms. The attack introduces spurious features along with their payload; once the learner constructs a signature, the spurious features are removed from subsequent malicious instances to evade the conjunction rules, which require all identified features to be present to match the signature learned by Polygraph. This attack allows the attacker to maintain a high false-negative rate even when retraining occurs because the attacker can introduce many spurious features and remove them incrementally. Conceptually, this attack corresponds to a transformation of $P_{\mathcal{Z}}$ into $P_{\mathcal{Z}}^{(\text{train})}$ and $P_{\mathcal{Z}}^{(\text{eval})}$. This transformation introduces spurious features into all malicious instances that the defender uses for training. The malicious instances produced by $P_{\mathcal{Z}}^{(\text{eval})}$, however, lack some of the spurious features and therefore bypass the filter, which erroneously generalized that all the spurious features were necessary elements of the malicious behavior. Venkataraman, Blum, and Song (2008) also present lower bounds for learning worm signatures based on red herring attacks.

ANTIDOTE

We also collaborated with our colleagues at Berkeley and Intel Labs to explore the vulnerability of network-wide traffic anomaly detectors based on principal component analysis (PCA) as introduced by Lakhina et al. (2004b). Our work examines how an attacker can exploit the sensitivity of PCA to form *Causative Integrity* attacks (Rubinstein, Nelson, Huang, Joseph, Lau, Rao, Taft, & Tygar 2009a). In anticipation of a DoS attack, the attacker systematically injects traffic to increase variance along the links of their target flow and mislead the anomaly detection system. We also studied how the projection pursuit-based robust PCA algorithm of Croux, Filzmoser, & Oliveira (2007) significantly reduces the impact of poisoning. We detail this work in Chapter 6.

Optimization Formulations

Biggio, Nelson, & Laskov (2012) formulate *Causative* attacks on the support vector machine as optimization, leveraging work in incremental learning (Cauwenberghs & Poggio 2000) to determine contamination points to inject into the training set. The optimization is approximated via gradient descent. Attack as optimization has appeared many times in the literature since. The effect of feature selection on training robustness is examined by Xiao, Biggio, Brown, Fumera, Eckert, & Roli (2015), complementing the evaluation on *Exploratory* robustness by Li & Vorobeychik (2014), where it is demonstrated on malware samples for example that the performance of LASSO can be reduced to random choice with only 5% control over the training set. Li, Wang, Singh, & Vorobeychik (2016) explore *Causative* attacks on collaborative filtering methods also using gradient-descent based approaches, but for nonsmooth nuclear normed objectives, using alternating minimization and nuclear norm minimization.

Mei & Zhu (2015b) formulate early moves of the adversarial learning game for *Causative* attacks as a bilevel optimization where the defender learns in a lower-level optimization while the attacker contaminates training data at a top level. They show that under differentiability and convexity of the learner's objectives, the optimization can be reduced via KKT methods to a single-level optimization and use (projected) gradient descent to find attack training sets. Finally they draw connections to machine teaching and teaching dimension (Goldman & Kearns 1995), where training data is generated by a teacher guiding a learner to a predetermined hypothesis.

As an application of these ideas the authors explore the security of latent Dirichlet allocation (Mei & Zhu 2015a), demonstrating the promotion (demotion) of words to (from) topics. Alfeld, Zhu, & Barford (2016) also apply these attacks to autoregressive models for time series analysis, motivated by futures market manipulation in gas prices. The attacker possess a target forecast and optimizes poisoning data under the quadratic loss on forecasts achieved. The adversary is capable of perturbing past covariates at the time of attack optimization, modelling a scenario of "cooking the books" whereby past reporting may be manipulated. Hard and soft constraints on the attacker's perturbations are considered. While their examples are computed for weakly stationary models (where the first moment and covariance are stationary through time), their approach of convex optimization for finding contaminating data is general. Torkamani & Lowd (2013) consider adversarial learning for collective classification: a learning task where labels of instances may experience dependencies provided that related objects are more likely to have similar labels (associativity). They present a convex quadratic program formulation. Their experimental results show that in some cases techniques that increase robustness against attack also can lead to better non-attacked performance.

3.5.3 Causative Availability Attacks

This less common (but nonetheless well-motivated) attack attempts to corrupt the learning system to cause innocuous data to significantly be misclassified so as to disrupt normal system operation. In a *Causative Availability* attack, the attacker uses control over training instances to interfere with operation of the system, such as by blocking legitimate traffic.

EXAMPLE 3.4 (The Rogue IDS)
An attacker uses an intrusion detection system (IDS) to disrupt operations on the defender's network. The attacker wants traffic to be blocked so the destination does not receive it. The attacker generates attack traffic similar to benign traffic when the defender is collecting training data to train the IDS. When the learner retrains on the attack data, the IDS will start to filter away benign instances as if they were intrusions. This attack could be *Targeted* at a particular protocol or destination. On the other hand, it might be *Indiscriminate* and attempt to block a significant portion of all legitimate traffic.

Allergy Attack
Chung & Mok (2006, 2007) present *allergy* attacks against the Autograph worm signature generation system (Kim & Karp 2004). Autograph operates in two phases. First, it identifies infected nodes based on behavioral patterns, in particular scanning behavior. Second, it observes traffic from the suspect nodes and infers blocking rules based on observed patterns. Chung and Mok describe an attack that targets traffic to a particular

resource. In the first phase, an attack node convinces Autograph that it is infected by scanning the network. In the second phase, the attack node sends crafted packets mimicking targeted traffic, causing Autograph to learn rules that block legitimate access and create a denial-of-service event.

In the context of the *Causative* game, the attacker's choice of $P_Z^{(\text{train})}$ provides the traffic for both phases of Autograph's learning. When Autograph produces a hypothesis f that depends on the carefully crafted traffic from the attacker, it will block access to legitimate traffic from $P_Z^{(\text{eval})}$ that shares patterns with the malicious traffic.

Correlated Outlier Attack

Newsome et al. (2006) also suggest a *correlated outlier* attack against the Polygraph virus detector Newsome et al. (2005). This attack targets the naive-Bayes-like component of the detector by adding spurious features to positive training instances, causing the filter to block benign traffic with those features. As with the red herring attacks, these correlated outlier attacks fit neatly into the *Causative* game; this time $P_Z^{(\text{train})}$ includes spurious features in malicious instances, causing $H^{(N)}$ to produce an f that classifies many benign instances as malicious.

Attacking SpamBayes

In the spam filtering domain we also explored *Causative Availability* attacks against the SpamBayes statistical spam classifier (Nelson et al. 2008, Nelson, Barreno, Chi, Joseph, Rubinstein, Saini, Sutton, Tygar, & Xia 2009). In these attacks, we demonstrated that by sending emails containing entire dictionaries of tokens, the attacker can cause a significant fraction of normal email to be misclassified as spam with relatively little contamination (an *Indiscriminate* attack). Similarly, if an attacker can anticipate a particular target message, then the attacker can also poison the learner to misclassify the target as spam (a *Targeted* attack). We also investigated a principled defense to counter these *dictionary attacks*: the *reject on negative impact (RONI) defense*. We discuss this work in detail in Chapter 5.

Attacking Malheur

In the realm of unsupervised learners, the Malheur, an open-source behavioral malware clustering tool (Rieck, Trinius, Willems, & Holz 2011), has been found highly vulnerable to even very low levels of *Indiscriminate Causative Availability* attacks (Biggio, Rieck, Ariu, Wressnegger, Corona, Giacinto, & Roli 2014): DoS attacks against the malware clustering through poisoning of the data to which the clustering is fit. The authors avoid the feature inversion problem by essentially walking in the space of malware samples, performing only feature addition in a similar vein to dictionary attacks.

3.5.4   Defending against Causative Attacks

Most defenses presented in the literature of secure learning combat *Exploratory Integrity* attacks (as discussed earlier) while relatively few defenses have been presented to cope with *Causative* attacks. In *Causative* attacks, the attacker has a degree of control over not only the evaluation distribution but also the training distribution. Therefore the learning procedures we consider must be resilient against contaminated training data, as well as satisfy the evaluation considerations discussed in Section 3.4.4.

Two general strategies for defense are to remove malicious data from the training set and to harden the learning algorithm against malicious training data. We first present one method for the former and then describe two approaches to the latter that appear in the literature. The foundations of these approaches primarily lie in adapting game-theoretic techniques to analyze and design resilient learning algorithms.

3.5.4.1 The Reject on Negative Impact Defense

Insidious *Causative* attacks make learning inherently more difficult. In many circumstances, data sanitization may be the only realistic mechanism to achieve acceptable performance. For example, Nelson et al. (2009) introduce such a sanitization technique called *reject on negative impact*, a technique that measures the empirical effect of adding each training instance and discards instances that have a substantial negative impact on classification accuracy. To determine whether a candidate training instance is malicious or not, the defender trains a classifier on a base training set, then adds the candidate instance to the training set, and trains a second classifier. The defender applies both classifiers to a *quiz set* of instances with known labels and measures the difference in accuracy between the two classifiers. If adding the candidate instance to the training set causes the resulting classifier to produce substantially more classification errors, then the defender permanently removes the instance as detrimental in its effect. We refine and explore the reject on negative impact defense experimentally in Section 5.5.5.

3.5.4.2 Learning with Contaminated Data

Several approaches to learning under adversarial contamination have been studied in the literature. The effect of adversarial contamination on the learner's performance is incorporated into some existing learning frameworks. As outlined earlier, Kearns & Li (1993) extended the PAC learning model to allow for adversarial noise within the training data and bounded the amount of contamination a learner could tolerate. Separately, the field of robust statistics (Huber 1981; Hampel et al. 1986; Maronna, Martin, & Yohai 2006). has formalized adversarial contamination with a worst-case contamination model from which researchers derived criteria for designing and comparing the robustness of statistical procedures to adversarial noise. Research incorporated these robustness criteria with more traditional learning domains (Christmann & Steinwart 2004; Wagner 2004), but generally these techniques have not been widely incorporated within machine learning and even less so within security. We discuss this area further in the next section.

To derive secure kernel methods, Russu, Demontis, Biggio, Fumera, & Roli (2016) leverage results of Xu, Caramanis, & Mannor (2009) on the equivalence of support vector machine learning, with unregularized hinge-loss minimization under adversarial perturbations with size bounded by the dual norm of the original SVM problem. They upper-bound change to nonlinear SVM predicted values in terms of the change in a datum and the norm through which the change is measured. For sparse evasion attacks, the authors argue that Laplace kernels are more appropriate for defense, while for dense attacks the defender should employ the RBF kernel. The authors argue for choices of regularizer, kernel, and regularization parameters (potentially being class or example dependent), leveraging the connection between robustness and regularization parameters. Earlier, Torkamani & Lowd (2014) explored related questions for structured prediction models, specifically for the case of the structural SVM leveraging the connection between optimization robust to perturbation and appropriate regularization of a nonrobust learner. Here the space of structured outputs however is exponentially large.

Alfeld, Zhu, & Barford (2017) revisit their early work on *Causative* attacks on autoregressive models Alfeld et al. (2016) and consider defensive strategies based on bilevel optimization where the defender's action set includes linear projections that define an ellipse from which the attacker chooses a poisoning attack. By assuming a rational attacker in a zero-sum game, they frame the defense as a bilevel optimization that reduces to minimax. More generally the framework operates under discrete action sets. Under this framework they compute optimal defenses that significantly reduce defender loss in experiments on futures market datasets.

Another model of adversarial learning is based on the online expert learning setting (Cesa-Bianchi & Lugosi 2006). Rather than designing learners to be robust against adversarial contamination of well-behaved stationary, stochastic data, techniques here focus on regret minimization to construct aggregate learners that adapt to completely adversarial conditions. The objective of regret minimization techniques is to dynamically aggregate the decisions of many experts based on their past performance so that the composite learner does well with respect to the best single expert in hindsight. We discuss this set of techniques in Section 3.6.

3.5.4.3 Robustness

The field of robust statistics explores procedures that limit the impact of a small fraction of deviant (adversarial) training data. In the setting of robust statistics, it is assumed that the bulk of the data is generated from a known well-behaved stochastic model, but a fraction of the data comes from an unknown adversarial model—the goal is to bound the effect of this adversarial data on statistical estimates. There are a number of measures of a procedure's robustness: the breakdown point is the level of contamination required for the attacker to arbitrarily manipulate the procedure, and the influence function measures the impact of contamination on the procedure. Robustness measures can be used to assess the susceptibility of an existing system and to suggest alternatives that reduce or eliminate the vulnerability. Ideally one would like to use a procedure with a high breakdown point and a bounded influence function. These measures can be used to compare candidate procedures and to design procedures $H^{(N)}$ that are optimally robust against adversarial contamination of the training data. Here we summarize these concepts, but for a full treatment of these topics, refer to the books by Huber (1981), Hampel et al. (1986), and Maronna et al. (2006).

To motivate applications of robust statistics for adversarial learning, recall the traditional learning framework presented in Section 2.2. Particularly, in Section 2.2.4, we discuss selecting a hypothesis that minimizes the empirical risk. Unfortunately in adversarial settings, assumptions made by the learning model, such as stationarity leading to this empirical risk minimization, may be violated. Ideally one would hope that minor deviations from the modeling assumptions would not have a large impact on the optimal procedures that were derived under those assumptions. Unfortunately, this is not always the case—small adversarial deviations from the assumptions can have a profound impact on many real-world learning procedures. As stated by Tukey (1960),

A tacit hope in ignoring deviations from ideal models was that they would not matter; that statistical procedures which were optimal under the strict model would still be approximately optimal under the approximate model. Unfortunately, it turned out that this hope was often drastically wrong; even mild deviations often have much larger effects than were anticipated by most statisticians.

These flaws can also be exploited by an adversary to mistrain a learning algorithm even when limited to a small amount of contamination. To avoid such vulnerabilities, one must augment the notion of optimality to include some form of *robustness* to the assumptions of the model; as defined by Huber (1981), "robustness signifies insensitivity to small deviations from the assumptions." There is, however, a fundamental tradeoff between the efficiency of a procedure and its robustness—this issue is addressed in the field of robust statistics.

The model used to assess the distributional robustness of a statistical estimator H is known as the gross-error model, which is a mixture of the known distribution F_Z and some unknown distribution G_Z parameterized by some fraction of contamination ϵ,

$$\mathcal{P}_\epsilon (F_Z) \triangleq \{ (1 - \epsilon) F_Z + \epsilon G_Z \mid G_Z \in \mathcal{P}_Z \}$$

where $\mathcal{P}_Z$ is the collection of all probability distributions on $\mathcal{Z}$. This concept of a contamination neighborhood provides for the *minimax approach* to robustness by considering a worst-case distribution within the gross-error model. Historically, the minimax approach yielded a robust class of estimators known as *Huber estimators*. Further it introduced the concept of a breakdown point $\epsilon^\star$—intuitively, the smallest level of contamination where the minimax asymptotic bias of an estimator becomes infinite.

An alternative approach is to consider the (scaled) change in the estimator H due to an infinitesimal fraction of contamination. Again, consider the gross-error models and define a derivative in the direction of an infinitesimal contamination localized at a single point z. By analyzing the scaled change in the estimator due to the contamination, one can assess the *influence* that adding contamination at point z has on the estimator. This gives rise to a functional known as the influence function and is defined as

$$\text{IF} \, (z; H, F_Z) \triangleq \lim_{\epsilon \to 0} \frac{H \left((1 - \epsilon) F_Z + \epsilon \Delta_z \right) - H \left(F_Z \right)}{\epsilon}$$

where Δ_z is the distribution that has all its probability mass at the point z. This functional was derived for a wide variety of estimators and gives rise to several (infinitesimal) notions of robustness. The most prominent of these measures is the gross-error sensitivity defined as

$$\gamma^* (H, F_{\mathcal{Z}}) \triangleq \sup_z |\mathrm{IF} (z; H, F_{\mathcal{Z}})|.$$

Intuitively, a finite gross-error sensitivity gives a notion of robustness to infinitesimal point contamination.

Research has highlighted the importance of robust procedures in security and learning tasks. Wagner (2004) observes that common sensor net aggregation procedures, such as computing a mean, are not robust to adversarial point contamination, and he identifies robust alternatives as a defense against malignant or failed sensors. Christmann & Steinwart (2004) study robustness for a general family of learning methods. Their results suggest that certain commonly used loss functions, along with proper regularization, lead to robust procedures with a bounded influence function. These results suggest such procedures have desirable properties for secure learning, which we return to in Section 9.1.

3.6   Repeated Learning Games

In Sections 3.4.1 and 3.5.1, the considered learning games are one-shot games, in which the defender and attacker minimize their cost when each move happens only once. We generalize these games to an iterated game, in which the players make a series of K repetitions of the iterated *Causative* game with the ultimate aim of minimizing their total accumulated cost. We assume players have access to all information from previous iterations of the game, and grant the attacker unspecified (potentially arbitrary) control of the training data. At each iteration the defender produces a prediction after which it learns the true label and suffers some loss.

Evaluating the defender's absolute cumulative cost of playing—the analog of risk in the stochastic or PAC settings—is impossible due to the strongly adversarial nature of the data. Instead it is conventional to compare the accumulated cost incurred by the learner relative to the minimum cost achievable (in hindsight) by any one of M experts—i.e., a set of classifiers each designed to provide different security properties. This relative (additive) performance measure is known as regret, since it represents the regret that the learner feels for not heeding the advice of the best expert in hindsight. The analogous multiplicative ratio of the learner's total cost to the minimum total cost of an expert is the related competitive ratio.

Most commonly, online learners form a composite prediction based on the advice of the experts. As such, the experts can be seen as providing advice to the defender (hence their name), who weighs the advice to produce the composite prediction; e.g., the aggregate prediction could be a weighted majority of the experts' predictions (Littlestone & Warmuth 1994). Further, at the end of each iteration, the defender uses the newly revealed true label to reweigh each expert based on the expert's predictive performance. No assumption is made about how the experts form their advice or about their performance; in fact, their advice may be adversarial and may incur arbitrary loss.

By developing algorithms with provable small regret, the composite predictor performs comparably to the best expert without knowing which one will be best a priori. By designing strategies that minimize regret, online learning provides an elegant mechanism to combine several predictors, each designed to address the security problem in a different way, into a single predictor that adapts relative to the performance of its constituents—all while facing arbitrarily adversarial data. As a result, the attacker must design attacks that are uniformly successful on the set of predictors rather than just on a single predictor because the composite learner can perform almost as well as the best without knowing ahead of time which expert to follow.

We now delve more deeply into the online learning setting, but for a full description and several regret minimizing algorithms see Cesa-Bianchi & Lugosi (2006).

As discussed earlier, the learner forms a prediction from the M expert predictions and adapts its predictor $h^{(k)}$ based on their performance during K repetitions. At each step k of the game, the defender receives a prediction $\hat{y}^{(k,m)}$ from the mth expert[2] and makes a composite prediction $\hat{y}^{(k)}$ via $h^{(k)}$. After the defender's prediction is made, the true label $y^{(k)}$ is revealed, and the defender evaluates the instantaneous regret for each expert; i.e., the difference in the loss for the composite prediction and the loss for the mth expert's prediction. More formally, the kth round of the expert-based prediction game follows[3]:

1 **Defender**   Update function $h^{(k)} : \mathcal{Y}^M \to \mathcal{Y}$
2 **Attacker**   Choose distribution $P_{\mathcal{Z}}^{(k)}$
3 Evaluation:
   - Sample an instance $\left(x^{(k)}, y^{(k)}\right) \sim P_{\mathcal{Z}}^{(k)}$
   - Compute expert advice $\left\{\hat{y}^{(k,m)}\right\}_{m=1}^{M}$; e.g., $\hat{y}^{(k,m)} = f^{(m)}\left(x^{(k)}\right)$
   - Predict $\hat{y}^{(k)} = h^{(k)}\left(\hat{y}^{(k,1)}, \hat{y}^{(k,2)}, \ldots, \hat{y}^{(k,M)}\right)$
   - Compute instantaneous regret: $r^{(k,m)} = \ell\left(\hat{y}^{(k)}, y^{(k)}\right) - \ell\left(\hat{y}^{(k,m)}, y^{(k)}\right)$ for each expert $m = 1 \ldots M$

This game has a slightly different structure from the games we presented in Sections 3.4.1 and 3.5.1—here the defender chooses one strategy at the beginning of the game and then in each iteration updates the function $h^{(k)}$ according to that strategy. Based only on the past performance of each expert (i.e., the regrets observed over the previous $k - 1$ iterations of the game), the defender chooses an online strategy for updating $h^{(k)}$ at the kth step of the game to minimize regret (Cesa-Bianchi & Lugosi

---

[2] An expert's advice may be based on the data, but the defender makes no assumption about how experts form their advice.

[3] We again assume that costs are symmetric for the defender and adversary and are represented by the loss function. Further, as in Section 2.2.4 we simplify the game to use the surrogate loss function used in place of a 0-1 loss: Finally, this game is also easily generalized to the case where several instances/labels are generated in each round.

2006). The attacker, however, may select a new strategy at each iteration and can control the subsequent predictions made by each expert based on the defender's choice for $h^{(k)}$.

Finally, at the end of the game, the defender is assessed in terms of its worst-case regret R^*, which is defined in terms of the cumulative regret $R^{(m)}$ with respect to the mth expert as

$$R^{(m)} \triangleq \sum_{k=1}^{K} r^{(k,m)}$$

$$R^* \triangleq \max_m R^{(m)}. \tag{3.1}$$

If R^* is small (relative to K), then the defender's aggregation algorithm has performed almost as well as the best expert without knowing which expert would be best. Further, as follows from the Equation (3.1) and the definition of instantaneous regret, the average regret is simply the difference of the risk of $h^{(k)}$ and the risk of $f^{(m)}$. If the average worst-case regret is small (i.e., approaches 0 as K goes to infinity) and the best expert has small risk, the predictor $h^{(k)}$ also has a small risk. This motivates the study of regret minimization procedures. A substantial body of research has explored strategies for choosing $h^{(k)}$ to minimize regret in several settings.

Online expert-based prediction splits risk minimization into two subproblems: (i) minimizing the risk of each expert and (ii) minimizing the average regret; that is, as if we had known the best predictor $f^{(\star)}$ before the game started and had simply used its prediction at every step of the game. The defenses we have discussed approach the first problem. Regret minimization techniques address the second problem. For certain variants of the game, there exist composite predictors whose regret is $o(K)$—that is, the average regret approaches 0 as K increases. This effectively allows the defender to use several strategies simultaneously and forces the attacker to design attacks that do well against them all.

3.6.1   Repeated Learning Games in Security

Thus far the game-theoretic form of online learning outlined earlier has had relatively little application to security. While naturally aimed at managing a form of worst-case risk, these techniques have traditionally only been applied to mitigating risk in finance such as for universal portfolio management (Cover 1991; Helmbold, Singer, Schapire, & Warmuth 1998; Kalai & Vempala 2002).

There has been slowly growing interest in online learning within the security community, however. Our work with collaborators at Berkeley and Stanford applies online learning to develop a reactive risk management strategy for an abstract Chief Information Security Officer (CISO) (Barth, Rubinstein, Sundararajan, Mitchell, Song, & Bartlett 2012). In this game, the CISO must defend against a powerful adversary who can penetrate the CISO's organization passing from one state of intrusion to another (nodes in an attack graph) via various sets of actions (edges or hyperedges in general). The defender incurs certain costs when the attacker reaches certain nodes, but the defender can apply a limited defense budget to the graph's edges, forcing a cost on the attacker proportional to the applied budget. The defender faces a seemingly up-hill battle, since it is never made aware of the attacker's node payoffs and is only made aware of the graph's structure after it is first attacked. However we show that under the adaptive CISO, the attacker's return on investment/profit always approaches the attacker's ROI/profit under an optimal (minimax) fixed defensive strategy corresponding to proactive risk management. Further we show that in many realistic settings the adaptive defender performs significantly better. That is, in an abstract setting reactive security at worst approaches the performance of proactive security, or at best dominates it. Our algorithm and analysis draw heavily on existing results in online learning theory. Within the context of our present secure learning taxonomy, the adversary essentially aims to achieve *Causative Integrity* attacks on the defender, although the learner is not strictly performing binary classification.

Blocki, Christin, Datta, & Sinha (2011) have also applied online learning theory to security research. Their work proposes a learning-theoretic foundation for audit mechanisms, where the notion of regret in online learning theory is applied to define a desirable property of an adaptive audit mechanism: its cost (consisting of the numbers and types of transaction inspections performed and the cost of brand degradation due to missing violations that are detected by external agencies) should approach that of a hypothetical auditor employing an optimal fixed strategy. The authors develop an adaptive audit mechanism that provably asymptotically minimizes regret, with fast convergence.

Seeding online learning approaches with the results of computing equilibrium strategies—rather than starting with poor-performing uniformly random policies—is an idea proposed and explored in Klíma, Lisý, & Kiekintveld (2015). Potentially such hybrid approaches could enjoy the benefits of both communities.

Repeated learning games clearly possess the potential for suggesting useful adaptive algorithms for security-sensitive settings, where regret minimizing algorithms are suited to playing against powerful adversaries by design. Existing research is a step in the right direction, where defenses are designed to stand up against truly active adversaries. However, more work is needed to apply these ideas to other domains within security, and empirical research is needed to assess these methods in less idealized real-world settings.

3.7 Privacy-Preserving Learning

The aim of privacy-preserving learning is to release aggregate statistics, or the results of machine learning, on a dataset without disclosing local information about individual data elements. In the language of our taxonomy, privacy-preserving learning should be robust to *Exploratory* or *Causative* attacks which aim to violate *Privacy*. An attacker with access to a released statistic, model, or classifier may probe it in an attempt to reveal information about the training data (an *Exploratory Privacy* attack); moreover an attacker with influence over some proportion of the training examples may attempt to manipulate the mechanism into revealing information about unknown training examples (a *Causative Privacy* attack). In this way the *Privacy* goal represents an important extension of the security goals for machine learning systems considered by the taxonomy originally proposed by Barreno et al. (2006).

This section outlines the current state of the art in defending against *Privacy* attacks: most publicized privacy breaches are not strictly violations of a *Privacy* goal of an adaptive system, but are often linkage attacks or releases of sensitive data following the violation of a system's integrity (Narayanan & Shmatikov 2008; Sweeney 2002; Barbaro & Zeller 2006; Homer, Szelinger, Redman, Duggan, Tembe, Muehling, Pearson, Stephan, Nelson, & Craig 2008). As intimated earlier, we treat the *Privacy* goal separately here from the earlier discussion of misclassification attacks (*Integrity* or *Availability*) based around INFLUENCE and SPECIFICITY. While these axes apply equally well to categorizing *Privacy* attacks, the leading formalization for preserving privacy (i.e., defenses) provides for very strong theoretical guarantees spanning all levels of these axes.

Next we outline the leading measure of privacy preservation known as differential privacy, discuss how the definition provides for certain quantifiable protections against both *Exploratory* and *Causative* attacks, and describe existing research into the inherent tradeoffs between a learner's statistical utility and the level of training data privacy it provides.

3.7.1   Differential Privacy

Historically, formal measures for quantifying the level of privacy preserved by a data analysis or data release have been elusive. Numerous definitions have been proposed and put aside due to the propositions being of a syntactic rather than semantic nature, most notably k-anonymity and its variants (Sweeney 2002; Machanavajjhala, Kifer, Gehrke, & Venkitasubramaniam 2007). However, the concept of differential privacy due to Dwork et al. (2006) has emerged as a strong guarantee of privacy, with formal roots influenced by cryptography. This definition has enjoyed a significant amount of interest in the theory community (Dinur & Nissim 2003; Blum, Dwork, McSherry, & Nissim 2005; Dwork et al. 2006; Dwork 2006; Barak, Chaudhuri, Dwork, Kale, McSherry, & Talwar 2007; Blum, Ligett, & Roth 2008; Dwork, Naor, Reingold, Rothblum, & Vadhan 2009; Dwork, McSherry, & Talwar 2007; McSherry & Talwar 2007; Kasiviswanathan, Lee, Nissim, Raskhodnikova, & Smith 2008; Dwork & Yekhanin 2008; Dwork & Lei 2009; Beimel, Kasiviswanathan, & Nissim 2010; Hardt & Talwar 2010; Smith 2011; Hardt, Ligett, & Mcsherry 2012; Duchi, Jordan, & Wainwright 2013; Bassily, Smith, & Thakurta 2014) where the general consensus is that the formal definition is meaningful and appropriately strong, while allowing for statistical learning methods that preserve the notion of privacy to be of practical use (Rubinstein, Bartlett, Huang, & Taft 2009; McSherry & Mironov 2009; Barak et al. 2007; Kasiviswanathan et al. 2008; Dinur & Nissim 2003; Dwork & Yekhanin 2008, Machanavajjhala, Kifer, Abowd, Gehrke, & Vilhuber 2008; Beimel et al. 2010; Hardt & Talwar 2010; Chaudhuri, Monteleoni, & Sarwate 2011; Hardt et al. 2012; Cormode, Procopiuc, Srivastava, Shen, & Yu 2012; Zhang,

Zhang, Xiao, Yang, & Winslett 2012; Li, Hay, Miklau, & Wang 2014; He, Cormode, Machanavajjhala, Procopiuc, & Srivastava 2015; Wang, Fienberg, & Smola 2015) .We now recall the definition of differential privacy before discussing its prevailing features in the current context of adversarial machine learning. We follow the terminology that is most common in works on differential privacy and is influenced by roots in statistical databases research; the parallels to the existing notation and terminology introduced in Chapter 2 will be clear. A comprehensive treatment of differential privacy is provided by Dwork & Roth (2014).

A *database* $\mathbb{D}$ is a sequence of *rows* $\mathbf{x}^{(1)}, \ldots, \mathbf{x}^{(N)}$ that are typically binary or real vectors but could belong to any domain $\mathcal{X}$. Given access to $\mathbb{D}$, a *mechanism M* is tasked with releasing aggregate information about $\mathbb{D}$ while maintaining the privacy of individual rows. In particular we assume that the *response* $M(\mathbb{D}) \in \mathcal{T}_M$ is the only information released by the mechanism. This response could be a scalar statistic on $\mathbb{D}$, such as a mean, median, or variance, or a model such as the parameters to an estimated joint density or the weight vector to a learned classifier. We say that a pair of databases $\mathbb{D}^{(1)}, \mathbb{D}^{(2)}$ are *neighbors* if they differ on one row. With these definitions in hand we can describe the following formal measure of privacy due to Dwork et al. (2006).

DEFINITION 3.1 For any $\epsilon > 0$, a randomized mechanism M achieves ϵ-*differential privacy* if, for all pairs of neighboring databases $\mathbb{D}^{(1)}, \mathbb{D}^{(2)}$ and all measurable subsets of responses $T \subseteq \mathcal{T}_M$ the mechanism satisfies[4]

$$\Pr\left(M\left(\mathbb{D}^{(1)}\right) \in T\right) \le \exp(\epsilon)\Pr\left(M\left(\mathbb{D}^{(2)}\right) \in T\right).$$

To understand this definition, consider a differentially private mechanism M that preserves data privacy by adding noise to the response of some desired nonprivate deterministic statistic $S(\mathbb{D})$, say the average $N^{-1}\sum_{i=1}^{N}\mathbf{x}^{(i)}$ of a sequence of N scalars $\mathbf{x}^{(1)}, \ldots, \mathbf{x}^{(N)}$. The definition compares the distributions of M's noisy mean responses, when one scalar $\mathbf{x}^{(i)}$ (a database row) is changed. If the definition holds for privacy level $\epsilon \ll 1$, then the likelihood of M responding with noisy mean t on database $\mathbb{D}^{(1)}$ is exceedingly close to the likelihood of responding with the same t on database $\mathbb{D}^{(2)}$ with perturbed $\mathbf{x}^{(i)}$: the mechanism's response distributions on the two *neighboring* databases are pointwise close.

EXAMPLE 3.5 (Private Support Vector Machine Learning)
As a more practical example we have previously studied differentially private mechanisms for support vector machine (SVM) learning with collaborators from Berkeley and Intel (Rubinstein, Bartlett, Huang, & Taft 2009). There the setting is again a private database on which we wish to perform inference. However, the database is now composed of rows of feature vectors and binary labels, making up a training set of supervised binary classification. The desired inference is now the more sophisticated task of

---

[4] The probabilities in the definition are over the randomization of mechanism M, not over the databases, which are fixed.

SVM learning (Cristianini & Shawe-Taylor 2000): in the linear case we find a hyper-plane normal vector that maximizes margin on the training set, and in the nonlinear case we perform this margin maximization in a high-dimensional feature space induced by a user-defined kernel function. The mechanism here responds with the weight vector representing the learned classifier itself; the response is the parameterization of a function. Our mechanism for linear SVM simply adds Laplace noise to the weight vector, which we prove achieves differential privacy. For the nonlinear case we first solve linear SVM in a random feature space with an inner product approximating the desired kernel before adding noise to the corresponding solution; this first step allows us to achieve differential privacy even for kernels such as the radial basis function (RBF) that corresponds to learning in an infinite-dimensional feature space. Another approach to differentially private SVM learning is due to Chaudhuri et al. (2011), who instead of adding noise to the solution of SVM learning, randomly perturb the optimization used for SVM learning itself. We discuss privacy-preserving SVM learning in detail in Chapter 7.

Numerous other practical algorithms have been made differentially private, including regularized logistic regression (Chaudhuri & Monteleoni 2009), several collaborative filtering algorithms (McSherry & Mironov 2009), point estimation (Smith 2011), nearest neighbor, histograms, perceptron (Blum et al. 2005), range queries over databases with data structures such as KD trees (Li et al. 2014; He et al. 2015; Cormode et al. 2012), Bayesian probabilistic inference (Dimitrakakis, Nelson, Mitrokotsa, & Rubinstein 2014; Zhang, Rubinstein, & Dimitrakakis 2016; Wang et al. 2015), function release (Zhang et al. 2012; Aldà & Rubinstein 2017), and more.

3.7.2   Exploratory and Causative Privacy Attacks

An important observation on differential privacy is that the definition provides for very strong, semantic guarantees of privacy. Even with knowledge of M up to randomness and with knowledge of the first $N - 1$ rows of $\mathbb{D}$, an adversary cannot learn any additional information on the Nth row from a sublinear (in N) sample of $M(\mathbb{D})$. The adversary may even attempt a brute-force *Exploratory* attack with such auxiliary information and unbounded computational resources:

1 For each possible $\hat{\mathbf{x}}^{(N)}$ consider $\mathbb{D}' = \mathbf{x}^{(1)}, \ldots, \mathbf{x}^{(N-1)}, \hat{\mathbf{x}}^{(N)}$ neighboring database $\mathbb{D}$.
   - Offline: Calculate the response distribution $p_{\mathbb{D}'}$ of $M(\mathbb{D}')$ by simulation.
2 Estimate the distribution of $M(\mathbb{D})$ as $\hat{p}_{\mathbb{D}}$ by querying the mechanism repeatedly (a sublinear number of times).
3 Identify $\mathbf{x}^{(N)} = \hat{\mathbf{x}}^{(N)}$ by the $p_{\mathbb{D}'}$ most closely resembling $\hat{p}_{\mathbb{D}}$.

However, for high levels of privacy (sufficiently small ϵ), the sampling error in $\hat{p}_{\mathbb{D}}$ will be greater than the differences between alternate $p_{\mathbb{D}'}$, and so even this powerful brute-force exploratory attack will fail with high probability. The same robustness holds even in the setting of the analogous *Causative* attack, where the adversary can arbitrary manipulate the first $N - 1$ rows.

3.7.3   Utility despite Randomness

The more a target nonprivate estimator is randomized, the more privacy is preserved, but at a cost to utility. Several researchers have considered this inherent tradeoff between privacy and *utility*.

In our work on differentially private SVM learning (see Chapter 7), we define the utility of our private mechanism to be the pointwise difference between released privacy-preserving classifiers and nonprivate SVM classifiers. A private classifier (trained on D) that, with high probability yields very similar classifications to an SVM (trained on D), for all test points, is judged to be of high utility since it well approximates the desired nonprivate SVM classifier. Similar notions of utility are considered by Barak et al. (2007) when releasing contingency tables whose marginals are close to true marginals; Blum et al. (2008) whose mechanism releases anonymized data on which a class of analyses yield similar results to the original data; and Kasiviswanathan et al. (2008) and Beimel et al. (2010) who consider utility as corresponding to PAC learning where response and target concepts learned on sensitive data are averaged over the underlying measure. Others such as Chaudhuri & Monteleoni (2009) and Chaudhuri et al. (2011) measure the utility of a differential private mechanism not by its approximation of a target nonprivate algorithm, but rather by the absolute error it achieves. In all of these works, the differentially private mechanism is analyzed with the chosen utility in mind to produce an upper bound on the utility achieved by that particular mechanism.

Fundamental limits on the tradeoff between differential privacy and utility have also been of great interest in past work, through negative results (lower bounds) that essentially state that mechanisms cannot achieve both high levels of privacy preservation and utility simultaneously. In our work on differentially private SVM learning we establish lower bounds for approximating both linear and RBF SVM learning with any differentially private mechanism, quantifying levels of differential privacy and utility that cannot be achieved together. Dinur & Nissim (2003) show that if the noise of rate only $o\left(\sqrt{N}\right)$ is added to subset sum queries on a database $\mathbb{D}$ of bits, then an adversary can reconstruct a $1 - o(1)$ fraction of $\mathbb{D}$: if accuracy is too great, then privacy cannot be guaranteed at all. Hardt & Talwar (2010) and Beimel et al. (2010) conducted further studies establishing upper and lower bounds for the tradeoff between utility and privacy in respective settings where the mechanism responds with linear transformations of data and in the setting of private PAC learning. Generic approaches to establish lower bounds in differential privacy (for example, using volumetric packing arguments) are summarized by De (2012).

Moreover it is noteworthy that lower bounds, such as the above in theoretical differential privacy research, constitute powerful *Privacy* attacks that achieve guaranteed results on *any* privacy-preserving learner.

While significant progress has been made in achieving differential privacy and utility, understanding connections between differential privacy and learnability Beimel et al. (2010), algorithmic stability (Rubinstein, Bartlett, Huang, & Taft 2009; Wang, Lei, & Fienberg 2016), robust statistics (Dwork & Lei 2009), and even mechanism design (McSherry & Talwar 2007), many open problems remain in finding more complete understandings of these connections, making practical learning algorithms differentially private, and understanding the tradeoff between privacy and utility.

Part II

Causative Attacks on Machine Learning

4 Attacking a Hypersphere Learner

In the second part of this book, we elaborate on *Causative* attacks, in which an adversary actively mistrains a learner by influencing the training data. We begin in this chapter by considering a simple adversarial learning game that can be theoretically analyzed. In particular, we examine the effect of malicious data in the learning task of anomaly (or outlier) detection. Anomaly detectors are often employed for identifying novel malicious activities such as sending virus-laden email or misusing network-based resources. Because anomaly detectors often serve a role as a component of learning-based detection systems, they are a probable target for attacks. Here we analyze potential attacks specifically against hypersphere-based anomaly detectors, for which a learned hypersphere is used to define the region of normal data and all data that lies outside of this hypersphere's boundary are considered to be anomalous. Hypersphere detectors are used for anomaly detection because they provide an intuitive notion for capturing a subspace of normal points. These detectors are simple to train, and learning algorithms for hypersphere detectors can be kernelized, that is implicitly extended into higher dimensional spaces via a kernel function (Forrest et al. 1996; Rieck & Laskov 2006; Rieck & Laskov 2007; Wang & Stolfo 2004; Wang et al. 2006; Warrender et al. 1999). For our purposes in this chapter, hypersphere models provide a theoretical basis for understanding the types of attacks that can occur and their potential impact in a variety of different settings. The results we present in this chapter provide intriguing insights into the threat of causative attacks. Then, in Chapter 5 and 6, we proceed to describe practical studies of causative attacks motivated by real-world applications of machine learning algorithms.

The topic of hypersphere poisoning first arose in designing virus and intrusion detection systems for which anomaly detectors (including hypersphere detectors) have been used to identify abnormal emails or network packets, and therefor are targets for attacks. This line of work sought to investigate the vulnerability of proposed learning algorithms to adversarial contamination. The threat of an adversary systematically misleading an outlier detector led to the construction of a theoretical model for analyzing the impact of contamination. Nelson (2005) and Nelson & Joseph (2006) first analyzed a simple algorithm for anomaly detection based on bounding the normal data in a mean-centered hypersphere of fixed radius as depicted in Figure 4.1(a). We summarize the results of that work in Sections 4.3 and 4.4. This analysis was then substantially extended by Kloft & Laskov (2010, 2012), whose work we summarize in Sections 4.5 and 4.6.

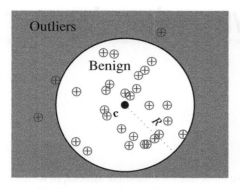 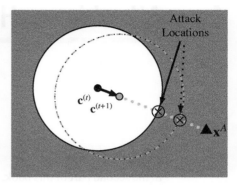

(a) Hypersphere Outlier Detection   (b) Attack on a Hypersphere

Figure 4.1 Depictions of the concept of hypersphere outlier detection and the vulnerability of naive approaches. **(a)** A bounding hypersphere centered at $\mathbf{c}$ of fixed radius R is used to encapsulate the empirical support of a distribution by excluding outliers beyond its boundary. Samples from the "normal" distribution are indicated by $\oplus$'s with three outliers on the exterior of the hypersphere. **(b)** An attack against a hypersphere outlier detector that shifts the detector's "normal" region toward the attacker's goal $\mathbf{x}^A$. It will take several iterations of attacks to sufficiently shift the hypersphere before it encompasses $\mathbf{x}^A$ and classifies it as benign.

The novelty detection learning algorithm considered throughout this chapter is a mean-centered hypersphere of fixed radius R. For this basic model for novelty detection, we analyze a contamination scenario whereby the attacker poisons the learning algorithm to subvert the learner's ability to adapt to a tool the adversary uses to accomplish its objective. The specific scenario we consider is that the adversary wants the novelty detector to misclassify a malicious target point, $\mathbf{x}^A$, as a normal instance. However, the initial detector would correctly classify $\mathbf{x}^A$ as malicious so the adversary must manipulate the learner to achieve its objective. Initially, the attacker's target point, $\mathbf{x}^A$, is located a distance D_R radii from the side of the hypersphere (or a total distance of $R(D_R + 1)$ from the initial center). Further, it is assumed that the initial hypersphere was already trained using N initial benign data points, and the adversary has M total attack points it can deploy during the attack, which takes place over the course of T retraining iterations of the hypersphere model. Analyzing this simple attack scenario yields a deeper understanding into the impact of data contamination on learning agents and quantifies the relationship between the attacker's effort (i.e., M, the number of attack points used by the attacker) and the attacker's impact (i.e., the number of radii, D_R, by which the hypersphere is shifted).

4.1   Causative Attacks on Hypersphere Detectors

Learning bounding hyperspheres is a basic technique for anomaly detection that can be accomplished by learning a hypersphere centered at the empirical mean of a training set or that encloses the (majority of the) training data (e.g., see Shawe-Taylor & Cristianini 2004, Chapter 5). These novelty detection models classify all data that lie within the bounding hypersphere as *normal* ("−") and all other data as *abnormal* ("+"). A simple version of this detector uses a mean-centered hypersphere of fixed radius R to bound the support of the underlying distribution as depicted in Figure 4.1(a). Such a detector is trained by averaging the training data, $\{\mathbf{x}^{(\ell)}\}$, to estimate the centroid as $\mathbf{c} = \sum_{\ell=1}^{N} \mathbf{x}^{(\ell)}$, and it classifies subsequent queries $\mathbf{x}$ as

$$f_{\mathbf{c},R}(\mathbf{x}) = \begin{cases} "+", & \text{if } \|\mathbf{x} - \mathbf{c}\| > R \\ "-", & \text{otherwise} \end{cases},$$

where we use $f_{\mathbf{c},R}$ to denote the classification function corresponding to the hypersphere centered at $\mathbf{c}$ with a radius R. Because we are considering a sequence of detectors with a fixed radius R but a changing centroid, we use the notation f_t to denote the tth such detector with centroid $\mathbf{c}^{(t)}$.

One can imagine several situations in which a malicious user wants to attack such an outlier detection algorithm. For example, an adversary may be searching for malicious points that erroneously lie within the hypersphere, or it could try to mislead the hypersphere by tampering with its training data. Here we consider a *Targeted Causative Integrity* attack on the simple mean-centered hypersphere outlier detector described earlier. This attack takes place over the course of T retraining iterations. In this attack, the goal of the attacker is to cause the hypersphere to have a final centroid, $\mathbf{c}^{(T)}$, that *incorrectly* classifies a specific attack point $\mathbf{x}^A$ as normal, making this a *Targeted Integrity* attack. We assume that, prior to the attack, the target $\mathbf{x}^A$ is correctly classified by the detector (i.e., $f_0(\mathbf{x}^A) = "+"$) and that the attacker does not want to modify $\mathbf{x}^A$, but rather wants to mistrain the learner so that, after the T retraining iterations, its objective is fulfilled (i.e., $f_T(\mathbf{x}^A) = "-"$). This is a *Repeated Causative* attack; see 3.6. To analyze this iterated game, we now specify the assumptions made about the learning process and attacker and then analyze optimal attacks on the detector in several different situations.

4.1.1 Learning Assumptions

This chapter focuses on iterated security games. As such, the learning algorithm discussed here is relatively simple: a novelty detector modeled as a mean-centered hypersphere of fixed radius R (possibly in a kernel space as discussed in Section 4.6.3) that contains most of the normal data. This outlier detector is trained from a corpus of data, which is initially assumed to be predominantly *benign* (perhaps the initial training set is vetted by human experts), and the initial (unattacked) centroid is $\mathbf{c}^{(0)}$. The radius R is typically selected to tightly bound the normal training data while having a low probability of false positives. Choosing the radius to meet these constraints is discussed in Shawe-Taylor & Cristianini (2004, Chapter 5), but for this work we assume the radius is specified a priori; i.e., it cannot be influenced by the adversary.

Importantly, as new data becomes available, it is used to periodically retrain the detector. We assume this new data remains unlabeled and is susceptible to adversarial contamination, but that the new data is filtered to limit this vulnerability by retraining *only on data points previously classified as normal*. In particular, we assume the novelty detector uses *bootstrapping retraining*, in which the latest detector is used to remove outliers from the newly received data, sanitizing the data before it is used for retraining. Under this policy, data points classified as *normal* are always used in subsequent retraining while any point classified as an *outlier* is immediately discarded. Finally, we initially assume there is no *replacement* of data; i.e., new points are added to the training set but no points are ever removed from it, regardless of how the model subsequently changes. We relax this last assumption in Section 4.5 where we examine the effect of different policies for data replacement. Regardless, as a result of retraining, the hypersphere detector is described by a sequence of centroids $\left(\mathbf{c}^{(t)}\right)_{t=0}^{T}$ produced by each retraining iteration.

4.1.2   Attacker Assumptions

We also make specific assumptions about the attacker's knowledge and capabilities. Throughout this chapter, we generally assume the attacker is *omnipotent*; that is, it knows the learner's feature representation, it knows the training data and current state (parameters) of the learning algorithm (although in most of the attack variants it only needs the state), it knows the learning algorithm and its retraining policy, and it can precisely predict the impact its attack has on the detector. We also assume that the attacker has strong capabilities. We assume the attacker can insert arbitrary points in feature space (i.e., it is not hindered by limitations of the measurement map ξ or feature map ϕ discussed in Section 2.2.1) and that it can control *all* data once the attack commences, but it cannot alter the representations of existing points (including the initial training data and its target data point $\mathbf{x}^A$). We modify the assumption that the attacker can control *all* data in Sections 4.5 and 4.6.

Finally, we assume the attacker has the *goal* of causing the retrained classifier to misclassify its target point $\mathbf{x}^A$ as normal. We quantify the attacker's task in terms of three quantities: the distance D_R that the attacker must displace the hypersphere to accomplish its goal, the total number of points M that the attacker can use in the attack, and the total number of retraining iterations T during which the attack is executed. The quantity $D_R > 0$ is expressed relative to the hypersphere radius R as

$$D_R = \frac{\|\mathbf{x}^A - \mathbf{c}^{(0)}\|}{R} - 1; \tag{4.1}$$

that is, the total number of radii by which the hypersphere must be shifted (in the direction of the attack) to achieve the attacker's goal.[1] The remaining quantities M and T are variables, and in this chapter, we explore bounds on them. First, in Section 4.3, we consider an attacker that only wants to use as few attack points as possible, and we investigate the minimum number of attack points M required to achieve its goal. Second, in Section 4.4, we consider an attacker that wants to affect its attack quickly, and we investigate both the minimum number of retraining iterations T required and the minimum number of attack points M required in a fixed execution time T.

---

[1] This displacement is nonpositive if the attack point $\mathbf{x}^A$ is initially classified as normal, in which case no attack is necessary.

Under these assumptions, an intuitive sketch of an attack strategy emerges. Because the outlier detector is only retraining on points falling within this hypersphere, this attacker must displace its centroid by inserting *attack points* within the hypersphere. Moreover, since the centroid is a linear combination of its training data, the attacker can achieve an optimal displacement by judiciously inserting its attack points at the intersection of the hypersphere's boundary and the line segment from the mean of the hypersphere to its goal $\mathbf{x}^A$. This attack strategy is depicted in Figure 4.1(b). As we show in Section 4.2, this observation reduces the task of attack optimization to a one-dimensional problem since it is assumed that the attacker has exact knowledge of the desired direction. The only complexity in optimizing the attack remains in choosing the number of points to place at each iteration of the attack; this task is addressed throughout the remainder of this chapter.

4.1.3   Analytic Methodology

Before delving into the details of the attacks, we sketch our analytic method. Namely, in the subsequent sections, we provide bounds on the number of attack points $M^\star$ or the number of retraining iterations $T^\star$ required by an adversary to achieve a desired displacement D_R. To do so, we find attacks that optimally displace the hypersphere toward $\mathbf{x}^A$ and upper bound the displacement such an attack can achieve under a given size M and duration T. We then invert this upper bounds to create lower bounds on M and T based on the following lemma.

LEMMA 4.1 *For any functions $f : \mathbb{X} \to \mathbb{Y}$ and $g : \mathbb{X} \to \mathbb{Y}$ mapping $\mathbb{X} \subseteq \mathfrak{R}$ to $\mathbb{Y} \subseteq \mathfrak{R}$ such that g is strictly monotonically increasing on $\mathbb{X}$ (and hence invertible) with g everywhere upper bounding f (i.e., $\forall\, x \in \mathbb{X},\quad f(x) \le g(x)$), if, for any $y \in \mathbb{Y}$, $z \in f^{-1}(y) = \{x \in \mathbb{X} \mid f(x) = y\}$, then we have*

$$z \ge g^{-1}(y).$$

It follows that, when f is invertible, $f^{-1}(y) \ge g^{-1}(y)$.

Proof [due to Matthias Bussas] By the contrapositive, suppose $z < g^{-1}(y)$. Then, it follows that $f(z) \le g(z) < g(g^{-1}(y)) = y$ where the strict inequality is due to the strict monotonicity of g. Thus, $z \notin f^{-1}(y)$. □

We use this result throughout this chapter to invert bounds on the maximum distance attainable by an optimal attack to bound $M^\star$ or $T^\star$. We now proceed with a formal description of attacks against these iteratively retrained hyperspheres.

4.2   Hypersphere Attack Description

As discussed earlier, the attacker's objective is to manipulate the retraining process and induce a sequence of hypersphere centroids $\left(\mathbf{c}^{(t)}\right)_{t=0}^{T}$ such that for some $T \in \mathfrak{N}_0$

it achieves its objective $f_T\left(\mathbf{x}^A\right) = \text{"}-\text{"}$, or rather

$$\left\|\mathbf{x}^A - \mathbf{c}^{(T)}\right\| \le R, \tag{4.2}$$

for which we assume T is the first such iteration satisfying this condition. Alternatively, we can frame this problem as minimizing the squared distance between $\mathbf{x}^A$ and $\mathbf{c}^{(T)}$ relative to the squared radius of the hypersphere, allowing us to formulate the attacker's objective as

$$\min_{\mathbf{c}^{(T)}} \frac{\left\|\mathbf{x}^A - \mathbf{c}^{(T)}\right\|^2}{R^2}. \tag{4.3}$$

Clearly, this objective is minimized by $\mathbf{c}^{(T)} = \mathbf{x}^A$, but the attacker cannot select $\mathbf{c}^{(T)}$ directly. Instead, it must choose a sequence of attack points that yield a sequence of centroids to ultimately achieve the desired effect as we detail below. However, first we further decompose the attacker's objective into a more convenient form.

To quantify the attack's progress, we introduce the *total relative displacement* achieved by an attack of t iterations. This vector is defined as the relative displacement of the centroid from its initial state to its position after t^{th} retraining iterations:

$$\mathbf{D}_t = \frac{\mathbf{c}^{(t)} - \mathbf{c}^{(0)}}{R}. \tag{4.4}$$

Using $\mathbf{D}_t$, we can rewrite the vector used in the adversary's optimization objective in Equation (4.3) as $\frac{\mathbf{x}^A - \mathbf{c}^{(t)}}{R} = \frac{\mathbf{x}^A - \mathbf{c}^{(0)}}{R} - \mathbf{D}_t$, which gives the following alternative optimization objective:

$$\frac{\left\|\mathbf{x}^A - \mathbf{c}^{(t)}\right\|^2}{R^2} = \frac{\left\|\mathbf{x}^A - \mathbf{c}^{(0)}\right\|^2}{R^2} + \|\mathbf{D}_t\|^2 - 2\frac{\left\|\mathbf{x}^A - \mathbf{c}^{(0)}\right\|}{R} \cdot \left(\mathbf{D}_t^\top \frac{\mathbf{x}^A - \mathbf{c}^{(0)}}{\left\|\mathbf{x}^A - \mathbf{c}^{(0)}\right\|}\right).$$

The first term $\frac{\left\|\mathbf{x}^A - \mathbf{c}^{(0)}\right\|^2}{R^2}$ is constant with respect to the attack and can be discarded. The remaining two terms express that the displacement $\mathbf{D}_t$ should align with the vector $\mathbf{x}^A - \mathbf{c}^{(0)}$ (i.e., the desired displacement vector) while not becoming too large. This latter constraint reflects the fact that if the displacement vector were too large, the shifted hypersphere would *overshoot* the target point $\mathbf{x}^A$ and subsequently still classify it as an outlier. However, overshooting the target is an implementation detail that can be easily avoided by halting the attack once the objective is achieved. It is not necessary to explicitly model this behavior as part of the optimization because it is not a practical concern. Further, in this chapter, we study attacks that use the minimal effort to achieve their effort and do not overshoot the target.

Moreover, as suggested by the above expression, the final term is expressed as two factors. The first, $2\frac{\left\|\mathbf{x}^A - \mathbf{c}^{(0)}\right\|}{R}$, is again constant with respect to $\mathbf{c}^{(t)}$. However, the second represents a particular geometric quantity. It is the length of the projection of $\mathbf{D}_t$ onto the desired attack direction $\mathbf{x}^A - \mathbf{c}^{(0)}$; i.e., $\text{proj}_{\mathbf{x}^A - \mathbf{c}^{(0)}}\left(\mathbf{D}_t\right) = \mathbf{D}_t^\top \frac{\mathbf{x}^A - \mathbf{c}^{(0)}}{\left\|\mathbf{x}^A - \mathbf{c}^{(0)}\right\|}$. By the

Cauchy-Schwarz inequality, we obtain the following pair of results:

$$\|\mathbf{D}_t\| \geq \left| \mathbf{D}_t^\top \frac{\mathbf{x}^A - \mathbf{c}^{(0)}}{\|\mathbf{x}^A - \mathbf{c}^{(0)}\|} \right|$$

$$\frac{\|\mathbf{x}^A - \mathbf{c}^{(t)}\|}{R} \geq \frac{\|\mathbf{x}^A - \mathbf{c}^{(0)}\|}{R} - \mathbf{D}_t^\top \frac{\mathbf{x}^A - \mathbf{c}^{(0)}}{\|\mathbf{x}^A - \mathbf{c}^{(0)}\|}.$$

This confirms that accomplishing $\text{proj}_{\mathbf{x}^A - \mathbf{c}^{(0)}}(\mathbf{D}_t) \geq D_R$ is necessary for the attack to achieve the original objective in Equation (4.2). Further, maximizing this projection for a fixed attack budget will generally find attacks that best align with the desired attack direction and have maximum magnitude. Hence, to simplify the results of this chapter, we consider the following alternative objective, which seeks the largest possible alignment to the desired displacement vector without regard to the possibility of overshooting. This notion of the attack's progress was originally introduced by Kloft & Laskov (2012), but there was called the *relative displacement*.

DEFINITION 4.2 *Optimal Displacement:* An attack achieves an *optimal displacement* at the tth retraining iteration if its relative displacement vector $\mathbf{D}_t$ has the highest alignment with the desired displacement vector $\frac{\mathbf{x}^A - \mathbf{c}^{(0)}}{R}$. The attack objective is given by the *displacement alignment*

$$\rho\left(\mathbf{D}_t\right) = \mathbf{D}_t^\top \frac{\mathbf{x}^A - \mathbf{c}^{(0)}}{\|\mathbf{x}^A - \mathbf{c}^{(0)}\|}. \tag{4.5}$$

The attacker seeks to find a $\mathbf{D}_t$ that maximizes $\rho\left(\mathbf{D}_t\right)$.

Optimizing this objective achieves the same optimal sequences as those from Equation 4.3 until the target is reached. In the remainder of this chapter, we study attacks that seek maximal displacement alignment.

Remark 4.3 When the tth displacement vector perfectly aligns with the attack direction (i.e., it has no residual), then the displacement vector is given by $\mathbf{D}_t = \kappa \frac{\mathbf{x}^A - \mathbf{c}^{(0)}}{\|\mathbf{x}^A - \mathbf{c}^{(0)}\|}$ for some $\kappa \in [0, D_R]$ and $\|\mathbf{D}_t\| = \kappa$. The progress of such an attack is given precisely in terms of κ as

$$\frac{\|\mathbf{x}^A - \mathbf{c}^{(t)}\|}{R} = \frac{\|\mathbf{x}^A - \mathbf{c}^{(0)}\|}{R} - \kappa.$$

This exact connection between the original goal and alignment objective is, in fact, attained in several of the attack scenarios discussed later.

4.2.1   Displacing the Centroid

Here we discuss the behavior of $\mathbf{c}^{(t)}$ and how the attacker can manipulate it to optimize Equation (4.3). By the bootstrap retraining policy, when an attacker adds a point, $\mathbf{a}^{(t)}$, to the tth training set, the tth centroid will be affected if the point is within a distance R of the current centroid; i.e., $\|\mathbf{a}^{(t)} - \mathbf{c}^{(t-1)}\| \leq R$. When that occurs, assuming that the attacker is the only source of new data during the attack, the attack point causes the hypersphere to shift in the next iteration to a new centroid given by

$$\mathbf{c}^{(t)} = \frac{\mu_{t-1}}{\mu_{t-1} + 1} \mathbf{c}^{(t-1)} + \frac{1}{\mu_{t-1} + 1} \mathbf{a}^{(t)}, \tag{4.6}$$

which is a convex combination of the prior centroid $\mathbf{c}^{(t-1)}$ and newly introduced attack point $\mathbf{a}^{(t)}$. This combination is defined by coefficients computed in terms of μ_{t-1}, the total number of training points used to train $\mathbf{c}^{(t-1)}$. This term μ_{t-1} is analogous to the *mass* that supports the prior hypersphere since it determines how difficult that hypersphere is to shift. Under the assumptions that data points are never removed and that, during the attack, the attacker is solely responsible for new data points, $\mu_t = \mu_{t-1} + 1$ with an initial mass $\mu_0 = N$ given by the number of benign data points that were present before the attack began.

More generally, during the tth retraining iteration, the attacker attacks the hypersphere with a set $\mathbb{A}^{(t)} = \left(\mathbf{a}^{(t,\ell)}\right)_{\ell=1}^{\alpha_t}$ consisting of α_t attack points all of which are within R of the current centroid. Again, we assume the attacker is the only source of new data during the attack. The number of data points in the tth retraining iteration is now given by $\mu_t = \mu_{t-1} + \alpha_t$ or more generally as the *cumulative sum of mass*:

$$\mu_t = N + \sum_{\ell=1}^{t} \alpha_\ell. \tag{4.7}$$

Further, the new centroid is now given by the convex combination

$$\begin{aligned}
\mathbf{c}^{(t)} &= \frac{\mu_{t-1}}{\mu_{t-1} + \alpha_t} \mathbf{c}^{(t-1)} + \frac{1}{\mu_{t-1} + \alpha_t} \sum_{\ell=1}^{\alpha_t} \mathbf{a}^{(t,\ell)} \\
&= \mathbf{c}^{(t-1)} + \frac{1}{\mu_t} \sum_{\ell=1}^{\alpha_t} \left(\mathbf{a}^{(t,\ell)} - \mathbf{c}^{(t-1)}\right),
\end{aligned} \tag{4.8}$$

which leads to a natural notion of the *relative displacement* at the tth iteration.

DEFINITION 4.4 The *relative displacement* at the tth retraining iteration is defined as the displacement vector of the hypersphere centroid from the $(t-1)^{\text{th}}$ to the tth iteration relative to the fixed radius R of the hypersphere. This vector is given by

$$\mathbf{r}_t \triangleq \frac{\mathbf{c}^{(t)} - \mathbf{c}^{(t-1)}}{R} = \frac{1}{R \cdot \mu_t} \sum_{\ell=1}^{\alpha_t} \left(\mathbf{a}^{(t,\ell)} - \mathbf{c}^{(t-1)}\right).$$

Further, the *total relative displacement* can be expressed as the sum of the attack's relative displacements: $\mathbf{D}_T = \sum_{t=1}^{T} \mathbf{r}_t$.

Remark 4.5 A deeper insight into the nature of this problem is revealed by Equation (4.8). In particular, it shows that the change in the mean after T iterations of the attack relative to the radius of hypersphere R is a sum of "cumulatively penalized gains." That is, the contribution of the tth iteration of the attack is weighed down by the sum of the *mass* used in all iterations up to and including the current iteration.

From the fact that $\left\| \mathbf{a}^{(t,\ell)} - \mathbf{c}^{(t)} \right\| \le R$ for all attack points, we can use the generalized triangle inequality to obtain our first bound:

$$\left\| \mathbf{r}_t \right\| = \frac{1}{R \cdot \mu_t} \left\| \sum_{\ell=1}^{\alpha_t} \left(\mathbf{a}^{(t,\ell)} - \mathbf{c}^{(t-1)} \right) \right\| \le \frac{\alpha_t}{\mu_t} \le 1,$$

since $\alpha_t \le \mu_t$. This leads to the following theorem and a general (albeit, weak) bound on the effort required by the adversary:

THEOREM 4.6 *The total relative displacement between $\mathbf{c}^{(T)}$ and $\mathbf{c}^{(0)}$ in T retraining iterations has a norm of at most T (i.e., $\left\| \mathbf{D}_T \right\| \le T$) and a displacement alignment of $\rho\left(\mathbf{D}_T \right) \le T$. Therefor, to achieve the desired total relative displacement of D_R, a successful attack must have at least $T \ge D_R$ attack iterations.*

Proof. The bound on the norm follows from the generalized triangle inequality and the fact that for all t, $\left\| \mathbf{r}_t \right\| \le 1$. Similarly, the bound on $\rho(\,\cdot\,)$ follows from the following application of the Cauchy-Schwarz inequality:

$$\rho\left(\mathbf{D}_T \right) = \mathbf{D}_T^\top \frac{\mathbf{x}^A - \mathbf{c}^{(0)}}{\left\| \mathbf{x}^A - \mathbf{c}^{(0)} \right\|} = \frac{1}{\left\| \mathbf{x}^A - \mathbf{c}^{(0)} \right\|} \sum_{t=1}^{T} \mathbf{r}_t^\top \left(\mathbf{x}^A - \mathbf{c}^{(0)} \right)$$

$$\le \frac{1}{\left\| \mathbf{x}^A - \mathbf{c}^{(0)} \right\|} \sum_{t=1}^{T} \left\| \mathbf{r}_t \right\| \left\| \mathbf{x}^A - \mathbf{c}^{(0)} \right\| \le T$$

$\square$

Ultimately, the attacker's goal is create a sequence of attack points (i.e., a set of attack points $\mathbb{A}^{(t)} = \left(\mathbf{a}^{(t,\ell)} \right)_{\ell=1}^{\alpha_t}$ at each attack iteration) such that the attacker's goal is satisfied. The following theorem states that the attacker can accomplish this in a greedy fashion by placing all its attack points at the point where the current hypersphere boundary intersects the line segment between the current centroid $\mathbf{c}^{(t-1)}$ and its goal point $\mathbf{x}^A$. Further, it shows that, when this greedy strategy is executed at every iteration, the resulting centroid at the tth iteration follows the line segment between the initial centroid $\mathbf{c}^{(t-1)}$ and the attacker's goal point $\mathbf{x}^A$, gradually shifting toward its goal.

THEOREM 4.7 *For every attack sequence $\boldsymbol{\alpha} = (\alpha_t \in \mathfrak{N}_0)$ and for all $t \in \mathfrak{N}$, at the tth iteration the set of attack vectors $\mathbb{A}^{(t)}$ that optimize $\rho(\,\cdot\,)$ according to Equation (4.5) consists of α_t copies of the vector $\mathbf{c}^{(t-1)} + R \cdot \frac{\mathbf{x}^A - \mathbf{c}^{(0)}}{\left\| \mathbf{x}^A - \mathbf{c}^{(0)} \right\|}$ and*

$$\mathbf{c}^{(t)} = \mathbf{c}^{(0)} + R \cdot \frac{\mathbf{x}^A - \mathbf{c}^{(0)}}{\left\| \mathbf{x}^A - \mathbf{c}^{(0)} \right\|} \cdot \sum_{\ell=1}^{t} \frac{\alpha_\ell}{\mu_\ell} \tag{4.9}$$

where μ_t is the cumulative sum of mass for the attack given by Equation (4.7).

Proof. The proof appears in Appendix B.1. $\square$

This theorem shows that the optimal centroid at the tth iteration can be computed in a greedy fashion only from the supplied parameters $\mathbf{c}^{(0)}$, R, $\mathbf{x}^A$, and $\boldsymbol{\alpha}$.

COROLLARY 4.8 *For every attack sequence* $\alpha = (\alpha_t \in \mathfrak{N}_0)$ *and for all* $T \in \mathfrak{N}$, *the total relative displacement achieved by an optimal attack following the attack sequence* α *after* T *iterations is* $\mathbf{D}_T = \frac{\mathbf{x}^A - \mathbf{c}^{(0)}}{\|\mathbf{x}^A - \mathbf{c}^{(0)}\|} \cdot \sum_{\ell=1}^{T} \frac{\alpha_\ell}{\mu_\ell}$, *which achieves a displacement alignment (Equation 4.5) of*

$$\rho(\mathbf{D}_T) = \sum_{\ell=1}^{T} \frac{\alpha_\ell}{\mu_\ell} \tag{4.10}$$

where μ_t *is the cumulative sum of mass for the attack given by Equation (4.7) and* D_R *is a parameter of the attack given by Equation (4.1).*

Proof. The result for $\mathbf{D}_T$ follows directly from substituting the optimal centroid given by Equation (4.9) into Equation (4.4). The resulting displacement alignment follows from $\left\|\mathbf{x}^A - \mathbf{c}^{(0)}\right\|^2 = \left(\mathbf{x}^A - \mathbf{c}^{(0)}\right)^\top \left(\mathbf{x}^A - \mathbf{c}^{(0)}\right)$ and Equation 4.1. □

Importantly, under our assumptions, this theorem shows that the attacker's objective depends solely on the sequence $\alpha = (\alpha_t)_{t=1}^{T}$; the actual attack vectors follow directly from its specification. The attacker can choose the elements of α; i.e., the number of attack points to employ at each iteration. Hence, we have reduced a multidimensional optimization problem to an optimization over a single sequence. In the next section, we formalize how the attacker can optimize this sequence based on the attack objective given in Equation (4.10).

However, before continuing, note that Equation (4.10) shows that the *success* of an attack at time t can be described solely as a function of this attack sequence. Moreover, since the optimal displacement vector $\mathbf{D}_T$ is a scalar multiple of the desired attack direction, $\mathbf{x}^A - \mathbf{c}^{(0)}$, its projection onto that direction has no residual component, and Remark 4.3 shows us that the progress of this attack is given by

$$\frac{\left\|\mathbf{x}^A - \mathbf{c}^{(t)}\right\|}{R} = \frac{\left\|\mathbf{x}^A - \mathbf{c}^{(0)}\right\|}{R} - \sum_{\ell=1}^{T} \frac{\alpha_\ell}{\mu_\ell}.$$

The success of this attack in minimizing $\frac{\|\mathbf{x}^A - \mathbf{c}^{(t)}\|}{R}$ is determined completely by the attacker's choice of α, which it chooses so as to maximize $\sum_{\ell=1}^{T} \frac{\alpha_\ell}{\mu_\ell}$. We now proceed to formalize this setting by describing these attack sequences.

Remark 4.9 (Nontrivial Initial Attack) The astute reader will have noticed that the above results, including all derivations from Equation (4.8) onward, rely on the assumption that $\forall t \in \{1, \dots, T\}$, $\mu_t > 0$. Equivalently, this requires that $\alpha_1 > 0$, which we assume throughout the remainder of this chapter—the *nontrivial initial attack assumption*. In fact, if the first nonzero attack occurs at the kth iteration (i.e., $\alpha_t = 0$ for $t < k$ and $\alpha_k > 0$), the first $k - 1$ iterations can be discarded from the attack, since there is no adversarial impact on the classifier during this period. Further, the attack sequence of all zeros, $\alpha = \mathbf{0}$, is the *trivial attack sequence* and need not be considered.

4.2.2 Formal Description of the Attack

Having described the problem and the assumptions made under it, a formal analysis can be conducted to reveal optimal attack strategies. This formal analysis begins with a formalization of the problem setting and of the objective. We refer to the number of *attack points* used at the tth retraining iteration as α_t and the optimal (under prescribed conditions) number of attack points to be used at the tth iteration as $\alpha_t^\star$. We use $\mathfrak{N}$ to denote the natural numbers $1, 2, 3, \ldots$, $\mathfrak{N}_0$ to denote the non-negative integers $0, 1, 2, 3, \ldots$, and $\mathfrak{N}_{0+}$ to denote the non-negative reals. Unless specifically mentioned otherwise, $\alpha_t, \alpha_t^\star \in \mathfrak{N}_0$ although later in the text we consider sequences in the non-negative reals, which we differentiate notationally by using $\beta_t, \beta_t^\star \in \mathfrak{N}_{0+}$, respectively.

Along with α_t and β_t, we also define the space of possible attack sequences. Formally, we define $\mathcal{A}$ to be the space of all legitimate sequence of attack points; that is, $\mathcal{A} = \left\{ (\alpha_t)_{t=1} \mid \forall t\ \alpha_t \in \mathfrak{N}_0 \right\}$ (in this space, any attack of a finite span is represented by concatenating an infinite trailing sequence of zeros). Similarly, we define the space of attacks of finite duration and limited size as $\mathcal{A}^{(M,T)} = \left\{ (\alpha_t)_{t=1}^T \mid \forall t\ \alpha_t \in \mathfrak{N}_0 \wedge \sum_{t=1}^T \alpha_t \leq M \right\}$; the space of attacks of a finite duration, T, but unlimited size as $\mathcal{A}^{(\infty,T)}$; and the space of attacks of a limited total size, M, but unlimited duration as $\mathcal{A}^{(M,\infty)}$. Finally, the analogous continuous versions of these spaces are denoted by $\mathcal{B}$, $\mathcal{B}^{(\infty,T)}$, $\mathcal{B}^{(M,\infty)}$, and $\mathcal{B}^{(M,T)}$ and defined by replacing α_t with $\beta_t \in \mathfrak{N}_{0+}$ in the corresponding definitions of $\mathcal{A}$.

With the notion of an attack sequence, we now formalize the notion of optimal strategies by reexamining the objective of the attacker. The attacker wishes to maximize the displacement alignment $\rho(\,\cdot\,)$ as described in Definition 4.2, which was shown in Corollary 4.8 to depend solely on the attack sequence. The objective function is defined with respect to a given attack sequence $\boldsymbol{\alpha} \in \mathcal{A}$ according to Equation (4.10) as

$$D(\boldsymbol{\alpha}) = \sum_{t=1} \frac{\alpha_t}{\mu_t} = \sum_{t=1} \delta_t(\boldsymbol{\alpha}) \tag{4.11}$$

$$\delta_t(\boldsymbol{\alpha}) = \frac{\alpha_t}{\mu_t}, \tag{4.12}$$

where $\mu_t = N + \sum_{\ell=1}^t \alpha_\ell$ from Equation (4.7) and the function $\delta_t(\,\cdot\,)$ assesses the *contribution* due to the tth iteration of the attack, which depends on only the first t elements of the attack sequence. The goal of the attacker is to maximize this objective function $D(\,\cdot\,)$ with respect to constraints on the size and duration of the attack.

DEFINITION 4.10 *Optimality:* An attack sequence $\boldsymbol{\alpha}^\star \in \mathcal{A}^{(M,\infty)}$ against a hypersphere with N initial non-attack points is an optimal strategy that uses a total of M attack points if $\forall \boldsymbol{\alpha} \in \mathcal{A}^{(M,\infty)}$, $D(\boldsymbol{\alpha}) \leq D(\boldsymbol{\alpha}^\star)$. The optimal distance achieved by such a sequence is denoted by $D_N^\star(M, \infty)$, where ∞ here represents the infinite attack duration. This optimality can be achieved for the attacker by solving the following program for $\boldsymbol{\alpha}^\star$:

$$\boldsymbol{\alpha}^\star \in \operatorname{argmax}_{\boldsymbol{\alpha}} D(\boldsymbol{\alpha}) \tag{4.13}$$

$$\text{s.t.} \qquad \boldsymbol{\alpha} \in \mathcal{A}^{(M,\infty)}$$

Thus, $D_N^{\star}(M, \infty)$, the optimal distance achievable for any sequence in the space $\mathcal{A}^{(M,\infty)}$, is expressed in terms of the problem's parameters M and N; i.e., if $\alpha^{\star}$ is an optimal strategy in $\mathcal{A}^{(M,\infty)}$, then $D(\alpha^{\star}) = D_N^{\star}(M, \infty)$. Similarly for attacks constrained to a finite duration T in the space of sequences $\mathcal{A}^{(M,T)}$, we define the optimal achievable distance to be $D_N^{\star}(M, T)$, which we return to in Section 4.4.

4.2.3   Characteristics of Attack Sequences

To better understand our problem, we characterize its properties and those of (optimal) attack sequences. These properties provide the foundation for the further analysis of the problem.

4.2.3.1   Invariance to Empty Attack Iterations

We discuss the behavior of the attack distance $D(\cdot)$ from Equation 4.11 with respect to zero elements in the attack sequence. First we show that the attack distance $D(\cdot)$ is invariant to the insertion of a zero at the kth position in the sequence (with $k > 1$ following Remark 4.9).

LEMMA 4.11 *For any $k > 1$, every sequence $\alpha \in \mathcal{A}^{(M,\infty)}$ achieves an identical distance as the sequence α' defined as*

$$\alpha_t' = \begin{cases} \alpha_t, & \text{if } t < k \\ 0, & \text{if } t = k \; ; \\ \alpha_{t-1}, & \text{if } t > k \end{cases}$$

i.e., $D(\alpha) = D(\alpha')$.

Proof. First, $\delta_t(\alpha') = \delta_t(\alpha)$ for $t < k$ since $\delta_t(\cdot)$ depends only on the first t elements of the sequence (see Equation 4.12). Second, $\delta_k(\alpha') = 0$ from Equation (4.12). Third, $\delta_t(\alpha') = \delta_{t-1}(\alpha)$ for $t > k$ since inserting a 0 at the kth position does not affect the denominator μ_t in the definition of $\delta_t(\cdot)$ (see Equations (4.7) and (4.12)) and the numerators are shifted, accordingly. The distance achieved by the sequence α' is

$$D(\alpha') = \sum_{t=1}^{k-1} \delta_t(\alpha') + \delta_k(\alpha') + \sum_{t=k+1} \delta_t(\alpha')$$

$$= \sum_{t=1}^{k-1} \delta_t(\alpha) + \sum_{t=k+1} \delta_{t-1}(\alpha) = D(\alpha).$$

$\square$

From this lemma, it follows that the insertion (or deletion) of zero elements ($\alpha_t = 0$) is irrelevant to the sequence's distance, and therefore all zeros can be removed in considering our notion of optimality. Intuitively, the distance achieved by an attack is not affected by the retraining iterations in which no adversarial data is used since, in this scenario, the adversarial data is the sole source of new data. This notion is captured by the following theorem:

THEOREM 4.12 *Every pair of sequences* $\alpha, \alpha' \in \mathcal{A}^{(M,\infty)}$ *with identical subsequences of nonzero elements—i.e.,* $(\alpha_t \mid \alpha_t > 0) = (\alpha'_t \mid \alpha'_t > 0)$*—achieve the same distance:* $D(\alpha) = D(\alpha')$*; that is, the distance achieved by a sequence is independent of the number of zeros in the sequence and their placement.* $D(\alpha)$ *only depends on the subsequence of nonzero elements of* α*. As a consequence, any finite sequence can be reordered as its positive subsequence followed by a subsequence of all zeros, and the two achieve identical distances.*

Proof. Since the sequences α and α' contain the same nonzero elements in the same order, one can transform α to α' by repeated applications of Lemma 4.11 to insert and delete zeros at the necessary positions in the sequence. Thus α, α', and all intermediate sequences used in this transformation have identical distances. □

It follows that zero elements can be arbitrarily inserted into or removed from any optimal attack sequence to form an equivalent optimal attack sequence with the same distance since zero elements neither add distance nor "weight" to the subsequent denominators. Theorem 4.12 allows us to disregard all zero elements in a sequence since they do not contribute to the effectiveness of the attack. Moreover, moving all zero elements to the end of the sequence corresponds to the notion that the attacker wants to minimize the time required for the attack since it does not benefit our attacker to prolong the attack. Finally, the fact that zero elements can be disregarded suggests the possibility of redefining $\alpha_t \in \mathfrak{N}$ rather than $\mathfrak{N}_0$.

4.2.3.2 Characteristics of Optimal Attack Sequences

Having shown that zero elements are irrelevant to our analysis, we now describe the properties of the nonzero elements in optimal attacks. To begin, in this attack formulation, there are no initial points supporting the hypersphere, so no matter how many points the attacker places in the first iteration, the same displacement is achieved. This is captured by the following lemma:

LEMMA 4.13 *For $N = 0$, the optimal initial attack iteration is given by $\alpha_1^\star = 1$.*

Proof. The contribution of the first attack iteration is given by $\delta_1(\alpha) = \frac{\alpha_1}{\mu_1} = \frac{\alpha_1}{\alpha_1} = 1$. Hence, for $\alpha_1 \in \mathfrak{N}$ (we exclude the possibility that $\alpha_1 = 0$ in accordance with Remark 4.9), we have $\delta_1(\alpha) = 1$, and since $\delta_t(\alpha) = \frac{\alpha_t}{\alpha_1 + \sum_{\ell=2}^t \alpha_\ell}$ is strictly decreasing in α_1 for $t > 1$, the optimal integer solution for this first iteration is given by $\alpha_1^\star = 1$. □

Additionally, if the total attack capacity is greater than one attack point and the attacker has the ability to distribute its attack over more than one retraining iteration, it is beneficial for it to do so; i.e., attacks that concentrate all their attack points in a single attack iteration are nonoptimal. This is captured by Lemma B.2 provided in Appendix B.3.

Further, the notion of cumulatively penalized gains from Remark 4.5 is crucial. There are two *forces* at work here. On the one hand, placing many points (large α_t) during iteration t improves the contribution of the term $\delta_t(\alpha)$ to the overall distance $D(\alpha)$. On the other hand, a large α_t will be detrimental to subsequent terms since it will increase the size of the denominator μ_τ in the contributions $\delta_\tau(\alpha)$ for $\tau > t$. This effect can be likened to having the mean of the points becoming heavier (harder to move) as more points are utilized. Intuitively, one does not want to place too much *weight* too quickly as it will cause the mean to become too *heavy* toward the end of the attack, making the latter efforts less effective. This suggests that any optimal attack sequence should be monotonically nondecreasing, which we prove in the following theorem:

THEOREM 4.14 *For any optimal sequence of attack points, $\boldsymbol{\alpha}^\star \in \mathcal{A}^{(M,\infty)}$, every subsequence of nonzero elements of $\boldsymbol{\alpha}^\star$ must be monotonically nondecreasing; that is, if $\mathbb{I}^{(nz)} = \{i_1, i_2, \ldots \mid \forall\, k \quad \alpha_{i_k}^\star > 0\}$ is a set of indexes corresponding to nonzero elements of $\boldsymbol{\alpha}^\star$, then $\forall\, i, j \in \mathbb{I}^{(nz)} \quad i \leq j \Leftrightarrow \alpha_i^\star \leq \alpha_j^\star$.*

Proof. The proof appears in Appendix B.2. $\square$

Note that Theorem 4.14 does not require strict monotonicity, which makes it consistent with Theorem 4.12.

While it has been shown that any optimal attack sequence should be monotonically nondecreasing in magnitude, the intuition that the mean becomes *heavier* as more points are utilized suggests more than just monotonicity. In fact, this notion will lead us to an optimal solution in Section 4.3.1.

4.2.3.3   Behavior of Optimal Attack Distances

While it can be difficult to describe optimal attacks, we can generally describe the behavior of the optimal displacement alignment (over all possible attacks) as functions of M and T. In particular, we would expect that as the number attack points available to the attacker, M, increases, the resulting optimal displacement alignment should increase. Similarly, as the attack duration T increases, we also expect the resulting optimal displacement alignment to increase. The following theorem shows that the function $D_N^\star(M, T)$ does, in fact, monotonically increase with respect to both M and T for any fixed $N \geq 0$.

THEOREM 4.15 *For all $N \in \mathfrak{N}_0$, the functions $D_N^\star(M, \infty)$ and $D_N^\star(M, T)$ (for any fixed $T > 0$) are strictly monotonically increasing with respect to $M \in \mathfrak{N}_0$ unless $N = 0$ and $T = 1$ in which case $D_0^\star(M, 1) = 1$ for all $M \in \mathfrak{N}_0$. Further, for any fixed $M > 0$, the function $D_N^\star(M, T)$ is strictly monotonically increasing with respect to $T \leq M$ and is constant for $T > M$; i.e., $D_N^\star(M, T) = D_N^\star(M, \infty)$ for any $T \geq M$.*

Proof. The proof appears in Appendix B.3. $\square$

Note that, with respect to T, the function $D_N^\star(M, T)$ is constant for $T \geq M$ because the attacker must use at least one attack point in every gainful retraining iteration (see Section 4.2.3.1). The attacker gains no additional benefit from attacks that exceed M in duration.

4.3   Optimal Unconstrained Attacks

We now present solutions to different variations of the hypersphere attack problem and find optimal attack strategies, as defined earlier. In this section, we explore attacks without any constraints on the attacker, and, in the following sections, we consider different constraints that make the attacks more realistic. For an unconstrained attacker, the strict monotonicity properties demonstrated in Theorem 4.15 suggest that an optimal sequence should use all M available attack points and space its points as uniformly as possible to maximally extend the attack duration, T, after discarding zero elements. Indeed, this is an optimal integer strategy for the optimization problem in Definition 4.10, which is proven in the following theorem:

THEOREM 4.16 *For $N \in \mathfrak{N}$, any optimal attack sequence, $\boldsymbol{\alpha}^\star \in \mathcal{A}^{(M,\infty)}$, must satisfy $\alpha_t^\star \in \{0, 1\}$ and $\sum_t \alpha_t^\star = M$; i.e., $\boldsymbol{\alpha}^\star$ must have exactly M ones. In particular, one such optimal sequence is $\mathbf{1}_M$, which is a sequence of M ones followed by zeros. Moreover, the optimal displacement achieved by any $\boldsymbol{\alpha}^\star \in \mathcal{A}^{(M,\infty)}$ is $D_N^\star(M, \infty) = h_{M+N} - h_N$ where $h_k = \sum_{\ell=1}^k \frac{1}{\ell}$ is the kth harmonic number.*

Proof. The proof appears in Appendix B.4.   □

As a result of this theorem, we have a tight upper bound on the effect of any attack that uses M attack points. While the harmonic numbers are computable, there is no closed-form formula to express them. However, using the fact that $h_{M+N} - h_N = \sum_{k=1}^M \frac{1}{k+N}$ is a series of a decreasing function in k, it is upper bounded by $\int_0^M \frac{dx}{x+N} = \ln\left(\frac{M+N}{N}\right)$ when $N > 0$ (Cormen, Leiserson, Rivest, & Stein 2001, Appendix A.2). Similarly, when $N = 0$, Cormen et al. (2001, Appendix A.2) show that $h_k \leq \ln(k) + 1$. Together, we have the following upper bound on the optimal displacement achieved by an attack with M points and no time limitations:

$$D_N^\star(M, \infty) \leq \begin{cases} \ln(M) + 1, & \text{if } N = 0 \\ \ln\left(\frac{M+N}{N}\right), & \text{if } N > 0 \end{cases}.$$

Since these upper bounds are strictly increasing functions in M, we apply Lemma 4.1 to invert the bounds and obtain the following lower bounds on the the number of attack points required to execute an attack that displaces the hypersphere by the desired relative displacement, D_R. These bounds are simply

$$M^\star \geq \begin{cases} \exp(D_R - 1), & \text{if } N = 0 \\ N(\exp(D_R) - 1), & \text{if } N > 0 \end{cases};$$

i.e., the effort required by the attacker to achieve its goal grows exponentially in D_R.

4.3.1   Optimal Unconstrained Attack: Stacking Blocks

The optimal strategy given by $\boldsymbol{\alpha}^\star = \mathbf{1}_M$ can alternatively be derived by transforming this problem into a center-of-mass problem. Recall that, in Remark 4.5, the distance achieved by the attack was likened to a sum of cumulatively penalized gains. We can think of this as a sequence of contributions attributable to each iteration of the attack; that is, the tth iteration of the attack contributes $\delta_t(\boldsymbol{\alpha}) = \frac{\alpha_t}{\sum_{\ell=1}^{t} \alpha_\ell}$ which is the "amount of weight" used at time t relative to the total weight used up to that time. This is analogous to a center-of-mass problem. In particular, if we model the attack points α_t as units of mass that are placed at a distance of R from the current center of mass $\mathbf{c}^{(t-1)}$, $\delta_t(\boldsymbol{\alpha})$ given by Equation (4.12) is the amount by which the center of mass $\mathbf{c}^{(t)}$ is shifted relative to R. Since viable attack points cannot be placed beyond distance R, this is analogous to placing a set of identical blocks below the current stack of blocks that was created at time $t - 1$ such that the stack does not topple (the structure being stable corresponds to the constraint that viable attack points cannot be beyond the radius R). Since the attack is constrained to only place points at the boundary, this analogy only holds when the stacking is done optimally or some of the blocks are vertically grouped (corresponding to placing several attack points in a single iteration, a notion that will be revisited in Section 4.4). Figure 4.2 depicts the correspondence between attacks on mean-centered hyperspheres and the stacking of blocks extending beyond the edge of a table.

Having likened the attack strategy to a classical physics problem, the optimal strategy reemerges from the latter's solution. As is discussed in (Johnson 1955), the blocks can be optimally stacked by extending the first by $\frac{1}{2}$, the second by $\frac{1}{4}$, and the tth by $\frac{1}{2t}$. The optimal integer strategy is given by placing a single point per iteration. Moreover, as is mentioned in Figure 4.2, since the blocks are of length $2R$, this optimal strategy achieves a displacement determined by the harmonic series $D_0^{\star}(M, \infty) = h_M = \sum_{t=1}^{M} \frac{1}{t}$. We arrive at a physical representation for the hypersphere attack and the corresponding optimal strategy that we derived in Theorem 4.16. (In fact, the single-block stacking strategy is not optimal if one allows more than one block per vertical layer, as per the multi-wide stacking problem (Hall 2005; Hohm, Egli, Gaehwiler, Bleuler, Feller, Frick, Huber, Karlsson, Lingenhag, Ruetimann, Sasse, Steiner, Stocker, & Zitzler 2007). However, due to the constraints of our problem, such stacking strategies do not correspond to realistic attacks as they would imply adding attack points outside of the hypersphere.

4.4   Imposing Time Constraints on the Attack

In the previous section, we showed that optimality was achieved by attacks that use at most one attack point at each retraining iteration. While this strategy achieves maximal possible displacement toward the attacker's target for any fixed attack budget M, it fails to capture the entire objective of the attacker. Namely, the goal of an attack is to achieve an objective (displace the mean a desired amount), but to do so within a minimal total attack duration T or with minimal effort (fewest possible points M). As the preceding analysis shows, the prescribed attack achieves maximal distance of $\approx \log M$ but does so in time $T = M$, and thus, such an attack only achieves a logarithmic effect in the time required to mount the attack, whereas Theorem 4.6 bounds the total displacement achieved linearly in T. This discrepancy between this upper bound and the actual effect achieved suggests that such an attack does not fully utilize the attacker's available resources; i.e., its attack budget, M. As such, we consider the case of an

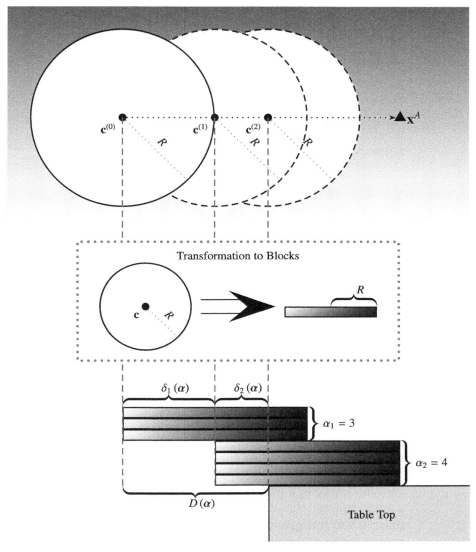

Figure 4.2 A figure depicting the physics analogy between the attack sequence $\alpha = (\alpha_1 = 3, \alpha_2 = 4)$ and the concept of optimally stacking blocks on the edge of a table to extend beyond the edge of the table. From top to bottom, the original effect of the attack α on the naive hypersphere outlier detector is transformed into the equivalent balancing problem. In this analogy, blocks of length $2R$ with a starting edge at $\mathbf{c}^{(t)}$ are equivalent to placing an attack point at the t retraining iteration of a hypersphere with mean $\mathbf{c}^{(t)}$ and radius R. This strange equivalence encapsulates the idea of a point of unit mass being placed at a distance R from the former mean. Vertical stacks can be interpreted as placing several points at time t, and time (oddly enough) flows down the blocks to the table. Also depicted are the contributions $\delta_1(\alpha)$ and $\delta_2(\alpha)$ along with their overall effect $D(\alpha_1, \alpha_2)$.

attacker, who must execute its attack within T retraining iterations for some $T \in \mathfrak{N}_0$, with the more realistic assumption that $T \ll M$; i.e., the attack must occur in a small time window relative to the total size of the attack. This leads to the following notion of constrained optimality:

DEFINITION 4.17 *Constrained Optimality* An attack sequence $\boldsymbol{\alpha}^\star \in \mathcal{A}^{(M,T)}$ is considered optimal with respect to M total available attack points and a given duration T if $\forall \boldsymbol{\alpha} \in \mathcal{A}^{(M,T)}$ $D(\boldsymbol{\alpha}) \leq D(\boldsymbol{\alpha}^\star)$ and the optimal distance achieved by such a sequence is denoted by $D_0^\star(M, T)$. This optimality can be achieved by the attacker by solving the following program to find an optimal attack sequence $\boldsymbol{\alpha}^\star$:

$$\boldsymbol{\alpha}^\star \in \text{argmax}_{\boldsymbol{\alpha}} \, D(\boldsymbol{\alpha}) \tag{4.14}$$
$$\text{s.t.} \qquad \boldsymbol{\alpha} \in \mathcal{A}^{(M,T)}$$

An equivalent formulation of constrained optimality would take a desired relative displacement D_R as an input and attempt to minimize the duration T required to achieve the desired distance with a total of M attack points. Similarly, another alternative would be to minimize M with respect to a fixed D_R and T. However, Equation (4.14) is a natural way to think about this optimization in terms of the attacker's goal. In the remainder of this section, we derive bounds that can be achieved for this constrained problem.

Before we continue, note that, when $M \geq T$, the constrained problem is equivalent to the original unconstrained problem. Further, by Theorem 4.15, the optimal displacement achieved strictly increases as the attack duration T increases, and using $T = M$ achieves the maximum extension distance for any fixed attack size $M \in \mathfrak{N}_0$. It is worth noting that all the results of Section 4.2 remain valid in this constrained domain; We need only rework the results obtained in the last section.

4.4.1   Stacking Blocks of Variable Mass

As was shown in Section 4.3.1, the original problem is equivalent to the problem of optimally extending a stack of identical blocks over the edge of a table—a reduction to a solved problem. Not surprisingly, the time-limited version of the attack on the hypersphere is also analogous to a constrained version of the stacking blocks problem. In this version, we have M points corresponding to M identical blocks. These points must be arranged into T vertical stacks such that all points in a given stack are bound together at the same (horizontal) location, which corresponds to placing points at a single time iteration. Thus, the tth vertical stack contains $\alpha_t \in \mathfrak{N}_0$ blocks of unit weight and has a combined *mass* of α_t. Additionally, to incorporate the initial supporting mass, there is an initial unmovable mass of $\alpha_0 = N$, which rests at the outer edge of the topmost block. The attacker must optimize the grouping of the M blocks such that the resulting T stacks achieve a maximal extension beyond the edge of the table; Figure 4.2 depicts this problem with three stacks. However, this constrained form of the stacking blocks problem is more difficult than the original one since it adds this vertical stacking constraint and, since the size of each stack is integral, this is an integer program.

To the best of our knowledge, there is no generally known (integer) solution for this problem. However, for our purpose of bounding the optimal progress an attacker can achieve, we are not required to find a provably optimal feasible strategy. Instead, if by relaxing the limitations on our adversary (i.e., giving it strictly more power than the problem allows), we can derive an optimal strategy, then the displacement achieved by this optimal relaxed strategy will bound the optimal strategy of the true (limited) adversary. One such intuitive relaxation is to remove the constraint that the vertical stacks contain an integer number of elements; instead, we allow them to be real-valued (but still non-negative). This leads to a new formulation: the attacker has T blocks of equal length but variable mass, and it wants to optimally allocate mass to those blocks so that their total mass is M and they achieve an optimal horizontal displacement beyond the table. This is the continuous variant of the problem: the *variable-mass block-stacking problem*.

By moving into the continuous realm, we consider continuous sequences $\boldsymbol{\beta} \in \mathcal{B}^{(M,T)}$ where $\beta_t \in \Re_{0+}$. For a given T and M, the (relaxed) attacker wants to find an $\boldsymbol{\beta}^\star$ such that for all $\boldsymbol{\beta} \in \mathcal{B}^{(M,T)}$ it achieves $D(\boldsymbol{\beta}^\star) \geq D(\boldsymbol{\beta})$. The optimization problems presented in Equations (4.13) and (4.14) naturally extend to the continuous context, and most of the observations of the original problem carry over to the continuous realm. In particular, it is clear that the location of zero-elements is still irrelevant as was shown in Theorem 4.12, and the zero-elements can again be discarded without affecting optimality. Moreover, the proof of Theorem 4.14 made no use of the fact that α_t were integers; only that $\alpha_t \geq 0$. The same line of reasoning can be applied to $\beta_t \in \Re_{0+}$ and any optimal continuous solution is monotonically increasing. In fact, the only result of Section 4.2 invalidated by this relaxation is Lemma 4.13—in the continuous domain, it is no longer generally optimal to have $\beta_1 = 1$ because any $\beta_1 = \epsilon > 0$ achieves the optimal initial contribution $\delta_1(\boldsymbol{\beta}) = 1$.

4.4.2   An Alternate Formulation

In the continuous mass setting, it is not straightforward to find an optimal strategy $\boldsymbol{\beta}_T^\star = (\beta_t \in \Re_{0+})$ for the program given in Equation (4.14). While the original stacking-blocks problem is a well-known example of a center-of-mass problem with a published solution, we are not aware of research addressing a block-stacking problem in which mass can be redistributed among the blocks. In the sections that follow, we provide a solution to this problem and bound the effort required by the attacker to achieve its goal in the analogous setting.

To solve this problem we return to the intuition given in Remark 4.5 that the attacker must balance current gains against past actions, and we rewrite the problem in terms of the mass accumulated in the tth retraining iteration. In particular, by considering that the relaxed cumulative sum of mass of Equation (4.7) is given by $\mu_t = \sum_{\ell=1}^{t} \beta_\ell$ with $\mu_0 = N$ and $\mu_T = M$, each element of the attack sequence can be rewritten as $\beta_t = \mu_t - \mu_{t-1}$. This allows us to rewrite the entire objective function in terms of the cumulative mass sequence, $\boldsymbol{\mu}$, which results in

$$D(\boldsymbol{\mu}) = T - \sum_{t=1}^{T} \frac{\mu_{t-1}}{\mu_t}, \qquad (4.15)$$

with $\mu_0 = N$. From the definition of μ_t as a *cumulative mass*, it follows that $\mu_0 \leq \mu_1 \leq \mu_2 \leq \ldots \leq \mu_T = M + N$. Finally, in the Tth iteration, the mass must total $M + N$ since, from Theorem 4.15, we have that attacks using less than M total points are nonoptimal, and hence, are excluded from consideration. Thus, optimality can be achieved for the attacker by solving the following program for $\boldsymbol{\mu}^{\star} = (\mu_t^{\star})$:

$$\boldsymbol{\mu}^{\star} \in \operatorname{argmax}_{\boldsymbol{\mu}} D(\boldsymbol{\mu}) = T - \sum_{t=1}^{T} \frac{\mu_{t-1}}{\mu_t} \qquad (4.16)$$

$$\text{s.t.} \qquad \begin{aligned} &\mu_0^{\star} \leq \mu_1^{\star} \leq \ldots \leq \mu_T^{\star} \\ &\mu_0^{\star} = N, \quad \mu_t^{\star} \in \Re_+, \quad \mu_T^{\star} = M + N \end{aligned}$$

In this reformulation, the total mass constraints still capture every aspect of the relaxed problem, and it is easier to optimize this reformulated version of the problem. This leads to our desired bounds on the optimal progress of an attacker in the time-constrained problem variant.

4.4.3   The Optimal Relaxed Solution

Using the alternative formulation of Program (4.16), we can calculate the optimal relaxed strategy for $T < M$ (for $T \geq M$, Theorem 4.16 applies). The results of this optimization are summarized by the following theorem:

THEOREM 4.18 *For any $N > 0$ and $T < M$, the sequence of masses described by the total mass sequence $\mu_t^{\star} = N \left(\frac{M+N}{N} \right)^{\left(\frac{t}{T} \right)}$ for $t \in 1 \ldots T$ is the unique solution of Program (4.16). Moreover, this total mass sequence provides the following bound on the optimal displacement alignment*

$$D_N^{\star}(M, T) \leq D(\boldsymbol{\mu}^{\star}) = T \left(1 - \left(\frac{N}{M+N} \right)^{1/T} \right). \qquad (4.17)$$

Finally, the actual optimal sequence of mass placements $\boldsymbol{\beta}^{\star}$ can be described by

$$\beta_t^{\star} = \begin{cases} N, & \text{if } t = 0 \\ N \left(\frac{M+N}{N} \right)^{\frac{t-1}{T}} \left(\left(\frac{M+N}{N} \right)^{\frac{1}{T}} - 1 \right), & \text{if } t \in 1 \ldots T \end{cases}. \qquad (4.18)$$

Also note that, as required this solution meets the conditions $\mu_0 = N$, $\sum_{t=1}^{T} \beta_t^{\star} = \mu_T = M + N$, and for all $t > 0$, $\mu_{t-1} \leq \mu_t$.

Proof. See Appendix B.5.   □

In general, the optimal relaxed strategy of Equation (4.18) does not produce integer strategies except in the case when $\left(\frac{M+N}{N} \right)^{\frac{1}{T}} \in \mathfrak{N}$. Thus, these strategies are not generally optimal according to the program given in Equation (4.14). Moreover, it is nontrivial to convert an optimal relaxed strategy to an optimal integer-valued one (rounding can produce good strategies but is not necessarily optimal). However, we need not explicitly compute the optimal integer-valued strategy to quantify its impact.

The utility of this result is that it allows us to bound the optimal displacement achieved by the optimal integer-valued attack sequence and subsequently invert these bounds using Lemma 4.1 since the function $T\left(1 - \left(\frac{N}{M+N}\right)^{1/T}\right)$ is monotonically increasing in both M and T. Also, in agreement with Theorem 4.6, this function is upper bounded by T and has an upper limit (as $T \to \infty$) of $\log\left(\frac{M+N}{N}\right)$. For any fixed T and M, the displacement achieved is at most $\min\left[T, \log\left(\frac{M+N}{N}\right)\right]$. The result is as follows:

$$M^\star \geq \begin{cases} N\left(\frac{T}{T-D_R}\right)^T - N \quad \geq \quad N\left(\exp\left(D_R\right) - 1\right), & \text{if } D_R < T \\ \infty, & \text{if } D_R \geq T \end{cases} \quad (4.19)$$

where the second case of this bound reflects the restriction that the total relative displacement cannot exceed the attack duration T, regardless of how many attack points are used (see Theorem 4.6). Similarly, the minimum number of retraining iterations required to achieve the displacement D_R for a given $N, M > 0$ can be determined as solutions to the following inequality

$$\left(\frac{D_R}{T} - 1\right)^T \geq \frac{N}{M+N},$$

which is computable using the Lambert-W function (i.e., the inverse of the function $f(w) = w \exp(w)$), but cannot be expressed in terms of elementary functions and does not contribute to our intuition about the problem except to say that the bound can be computed (see Figure 4.3).

We have now provided strong bounds on the effort required of the adversary to achieve its desired goal. However, before we conclude this section, note that the result

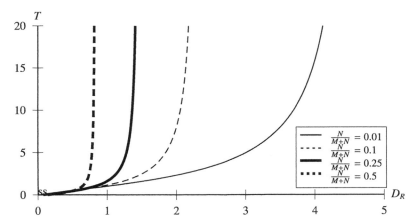

Figure 4.3 Plots depicting the lower bound on the number of retraining iterations T required to make the goal displacement D_R attainable. Each curve shows the lower bound for a particular fixed ratio $\frac{N}{M+N}$. As one expects, when $M \gg N$ the requirement is lessened, but in each case, there is a turning point in the curve where the bound sharply increases; e.g., it is practically impossible to achieve $D_R > 1$ when $\frac{N}{M+N} = 0.5$ because it would require an unreasonable attack duration to do so. The reader should note that, additionally, these lower bounds are loose unless $M \gg T$.

in Equation (4.19) is only applicable when $N \geq 1$. Briefly, we address this special case and then consider additional scenarios for attacks against hypersphere detectors.

4.4.3.1   Attacks against a Nonsupported Initial Hypersphere

As noted earlier, unlike Theorem 4.16, Theorem 4.18 and the subsequent bounds that result from it do not apply when $N = 0$. This is because, without an initial constraint on the sequence, increasingly large displacements can be obtained by starting with an ever-diminishing initial point, $\mu_1 > 0$. The problem is that for $N = 0$, the initial hypersphere centered at $\mathbf{c}^{(0)}$ is assumed to have no initial mass. Thus, the first mass placed by the attacker on the boundary displaces the mean to $\mathbf{c}^{(1)} = R$ regardless of its size. In the integer-valued case, this assumption has little effect on the outcome due to Lemma 4.13, but in the continuous case, this leads to an attack that places minuscule (but exponentially increasing) masses in the initial phase of the attack and then adds the overwhelming majority of the total mass in the final stages.

In the continuous domain, we can examine the sequence of optimal attacks given by Theorem 4.18 in the limit as $N \to 0$. In doing so, we derive that the optimal distance achieved by Equation (4.17) approaches T; i.e., $\lim_{N \to 0} D_N^\star (M, T) = T$. As shown in Theorem 4.6, this is, if fact, the maximal possible displacement alignment attainable by any sequence of T duration. However, such attack sequences do not correspond well to the feasible integer-valued attacks and do not improve our bounds.

To provide better bounds for the case of $N = 0$, we reintroduce the constraint $\mu_1 = \beta_1 = 1$ from the original integer-valued problem. That is, we now assume that the result of Lemma 4.13 hold; this constrains the continuous-valued sequences to more closely match the integer-valued ones. This is a reasonable assumption to make since the attack does not begin until the attacker uses at least one attack point as discussed in Remark 4.9.

This new constraint for the problem leads to a similar problem as was analyzed earlier in Equation (4.16) using $\mu_1 = 1$ instead of $\mu_0 = N$, and the subsequent results mirror those presented in Theorem 4.18 and its proof. In particular, we have that the total mass sequence given by $\mu_t^\star = M^{\frac{t-1}{T-1}}$ for $t \in 1 \ldots T$ is the unique solution and achieves an optimal displacement alignment of $D_0^\star (M, T) \leq T - (T - 1) \cdot M^{\frac{-1}{T-1}}$. Again, this bounding function is monotonically increasing in both M and T, which leads to the following bound on the adversary's effort when $N = 0$:

$$M^\star \geq \begin{cases} \left(\frac{T}{T - D_R} \right)^T & \geq \quad \exp\left(D_R - 1 \right), & \text{if } D_R < T \\ \infty, & & \text{if } D_R \geq T \end{cases},$$

where the second case again reflects the restriction that the total relative displacement cannot exceed the attack duration T. Also, a bound on the minimum number of retraining iterations, $T^\star$, required to achieve the displacement D_R for a given $M > 0$ can be computed from the above bound on $D_0^\star (M, T)$, but it cannot be expressed in terms of elementary functions and does not contribute further insight.

This concludes our results for attacks against the hypersphere model described in Section 4.1. In all cases we have thus far examined, the impact of the attacker on the model was extremely limited, and the number of attack points required to attain a desired displacement D_R was minimally exponential in D_R. These results provide a strong guarantee on the hypersphere's security, but, as discussed in the next section, the retraining model used is overly rigid. We now proceed by examining alternative retraining models.

4.5   Attacks against Retraining with Data Replacement

Now we consider an alternative learning scenario, in which new data replaces old data, allowing the hypersphere detector to adapt more agilely. This scenario was explored by Kloft & Laskov (2012), and here we summarize their results. We assume that each new point is introduced by the attacker and *replaces* exactly one existing point that was previously used to train the hypersphere in the last retraining iteration. This alters the centroid update formula given in Equation (4.6) to

$$\mathbf{c}^{(t)} = \mathbf{c}^{(t-1)} + \frac{1}{N}\left(\mathbf{a}^{(t)} - \mathbf{x}_{rep}^{(t)}\right),\tag{4.20}$$

where $\mathbf{x}_{rep}^{(t)}$ is the point to be replaced by $\mathbf{a}^{(t)}$. Notice that, unlike in Section 4.2, the mass supporting the new hypersphere's centroid does not change since we have both added and removed a point. As we show below, in this scenario, the attacker is no longer inhibited by past attack points, which makes its attack *considerably* more effective than in previous attack scenarios.

One can generalize this setting to again allow the attacker to use α_t attack points in each iteration (generally with $\alpha_t \in \{0, \dots, N\}$). However, doing so considerably complicates the subsequent analysis both in terms of choosing the set of optimal attack vectors $\mathbb{A}^{(t)}$ and optimally apportioning the attack points into an overall strategy $\boldsymbol{\alpha}$. Moreover, as we saw in Section 4.3, the strategy of placing a single attack point at each iteration ($\alpha_t = 1$) is the optimal strategy for placing M points without any time constraints and strictly dominates all time-constrained strategies. Hence, in this section, to simplify our presentation, we focus only on single-point attack strategies (assuming that $T = M$) and comment on the effects of this assumption.

Under this single-point replacement scenario, the *relative displacement* and *total relative displacement* are given, respectively, by

$$\mathbf{r}_t = \frac{1}{R \cdot N}\left(\mathbf{a}^{(t)} - \mathbf{x}_{rep}^{(t)}\right) \quad \text{and} \quad \mathbf{D}_T = \frac{1}{R \cdot N}\sum_{t=1}^{T}\left(\mathbf{a}^{(t)} - \mathbf{x}_{rep}^{(t)}\right).$$

Unlike the results derived in Section 4.2 and their subsequent consequences, we require more information about the specific replacement policy used by the hypersphere to optimize or analyze the impact of attacks in this scenario. Next we discuss various replacement policies for choosing $\mathbf{x}_{rep}^{(t)}$ and their effect on the attack's success. However, from the expression of $\mathbf{D}_T$ given above, it is obvious that the attacks will generally be more successful than those analyzed in previous sections. In fact, note that if for all t we have $\left(\mathbf{a}^{(t)} - \mathbf{x}_{rep}^{(t)}\right)^{\top}\left(\mathbf{x}^A - \mathbf{c}^{(0)}\right) \geq \kappa$ for some fixed constant $\kappa > 0$, then the attacker can achieve a displacement alignment of at least

$$\rho\left(\mathbf{D}_T\right) \geq \frac{\kappa}{RN \left\|\mathbf{x}^A - \mathbf{c}^{(0)}\right\|} T.$$

This suggests that, under replacement, attacks may potentially achieve a linear displacement alignment that *linearly increases* with the attack duration T using only a *single* attack point at each iteration (hence a total of $M = T$ attack points). This would be an astounding success for the attacker, especially compared to the exponential results that were demonstrated for retraining without replacement.

Below we discuss a number of potential replacement policies and how they affect the attacker's success. In this discussion, we will consider policies and effects that are random. To do so, we analyze attacks that are optimal for each step of the attack, but are not necessarily optimal with respect to the entire attack strategy. For this purpose, we consider the following notion of greedy optimal attacks.

DEFINITION 4.19 At the tth iteration of the attack, given the current centroid $\mathbf{c}^{(t-1)}$, an attack using attack point $\mathbf{a}^{(t)}$ is a *greedy optimal attack* if it optimizes

$$E\left[\rho\left(\mathbf{D}_t\right) \mid \mathbf{c}^{(t-1)}\right] \tag{4.21}$$

subject to the constraint that $\left\|\mathbf{a}^{(t)} - \mathbf{c}^{(t-1)}\right\| \leq R$.

4.5.1   Average-out and Random-out Replacement Policy

First, we examine two simple replacement policies: removing a copy of the previous centroid (*average-out replacement*) and removing a random point from the data (*random-out replacement*). These policies have a predictable impact on the displacement alignment, which allows the attacker to achieve its objective using relatively few attack points.

In *average-out replacement*, the point that is replaced by any new data point is always a copy of the current centroid; i.e., in the tth iteration, $\mathbf{x}_{rep}^{(t)} = \mathbf{c}^{(t-1)}$. Thus, from Equation (4.20), the tth centroid is given by $\mathbf{c}^{(t)} = \mathbf{c}^{(t-1)} + \frac{1}{N}\left(\mathbf{a}^{(t,\ell)} - \mathbf{c}^{(t-1)}\right)$, which yields a result similar to Theorem 4.7; namely, the optimal attack point at every iteration is $\mathbf{a}^{(t)} = \mathbf{c}^{(t-1)} + R \cdot \frac{\mathbf{x}^A - \mathbf{c}^{(0)}}{\left\|\mathbf{x}^A - \mathbf{c}^{(0)}\right\|}$ and the optimal T^{th} centroid is $\mathbf{c}^{(T)} = \mathbf{c}^{(0)} + \frac{RT}{N} \cdot \frac{\mathbf{x}^A - \mathbf{c}^{(0)}}{\left\|\mathbf{x}^A - \mathbf{c}^{(0)}\right\|}$. This yields the following optimal attack parameters:

$$\mathbf{r}_t = \frac{1}{N} \cdot \frac{\mathbf{x}^A - \mathbf{c}^{(0)}}{\left\|\mathbf{x}^A - \mathbf{c}^{(0)}\right\|} \quad \forall\, t \in \{1, \ldots, T\}$$

$$\mathbf{D}_T = \frac{T}{N} \cdot \frac{\mathbf{x}^A - \mathbf{c}^{(0)}}{\left\|\mathbf{x}^A - \mathbf{c}^{(0)}\right\|}.$$

Further, the resulting displacement alignment is thus $\rho\left(\mathbf{D}_T\right) = \frac{T}{N}$. In accordance with our discussion above, the relative displacement achieved under this policy at each iteration achieves a fixed inner product with the desired direction $\mathbf{x}^A - \mathbf{c}^{(0)}$ of $\kappa = \frac{\left\|\mathbf{x}^A - \mathbf{c}^{(0)}\right\|}{N}$. Each attack point contributes $\frac{1}{N}$ of a unit step in the desired direction, and the desired displacement can be achieved with $M^\star = T^\star = N \cdot D_R$; i.e., the goal only requires linearly many points in the desired relative displacement D_R.

Remark 4.20 Above, the attacker can optimally displace the hypersphere by using one attack point per iteration. However, note that the impact achieved on the centroid by each attack point is the same regardless of how many attack points are used in any iteration. The per-point impact is the same regardless of how many points are used in each iteration. In fact, if N attack points are used in each iteration, the displacement alignment is $\rho(\mathbf{D}_T) = T$, the maximum possible displacement alignment when replacement was not permitted (see Theorem 4.6). The attacker's goal can be achieved using only $T^\star = D_R$ iterations, although the number of points required remains as $M^\star = N \cdot D_R$. As such, it is more appropriate to write $\rho(\mathbf{D}_T) = M$, which holds for average-out replacement regardless of the allocation strategy.

For the *random-out replacement* policy, $\mathbf{x}_{rep}^{(t)}$ is a randomly selected element of the hypersphere's current training set. As such, it is no longer possible to compute the attack parameters precisely—namely, the terms $\left(\mathbf{a}^{(t)} - \mathbf{x}_{rep}^{(t)}\right)$ that are used to recursively compute the hypersphere's centroid depend on a random variable. However, we can consider greedy optimal attacks that locally optimize the *expected* displacement alignment at each iteration t with respect to the centroid $\mathbf{c}^{(t-1)}$ obtained from the previous iteration. In particular, the expected value of $\rho(\cdot)$ can be simplified by noting that $\mathrm{E}\left[\mathbf{D}_t \mid \mathbf{c}^{(t-1)}\right] = \frac{\mathrm{E}\left[\mathbf{c}^{(t)} \mid \mathbf{c}^{(t-1)}\right] - \mathbf{c}^{(0)}}{R}$. By the linearity of expectations and the definition of displacement alignment in Equation (4.5) we have

$$\mathrm{E}\left[\rho(\mathbf{D}_t) \mid \mathbf{c}^{(t-1)}\right] = \frac{\mathrm{E}\left[\mathbf{c}^{(t)} \mid \mathbf{c}^{(t-1)}\right]^\top \left(\mathbf{x}^A - \mathbf{c}^{(0)}\right)}{R \left\|\mathbf{x}^A - \mathbf{c}^{(0)}\right\|} - \frac{\left(\mathbf{c}^{(0)}\right)^\top \left(\mathbf{x}^A - \mathbf{c}^{(0)}\right)}{R \left\|\mathbf{x}^A - \mathbf{c}^{(0)}\right\|},$$

where the second term is a constant determined by the parameters of the problem. Thus, we seek to maximize the numerator of the first term, for which $\mathrm{E}\left[\mathbf{c}^{(t)} \mid \mathbf{c}^{(t-1)}\right] = \mathbf{c}^{(t-1)} + \frac{1}{N}\left(\mathbf{a}^{(t)} - \mathrm{E}\left[\mathbf{x}_{rep}^{(t)} \mid \mathbf{c}^{(t-1)}\right]\right)$ since $\mathbf{a}^{(t)}$ is not considered a random variable.

In general, the attacker does not know the distribution of the candidate replacement data points $\left\{\mathbf{x}^{(\ell)}\right\}$, which consist of a mixture of benign and adversarial points. However, it does know that they have an empirical mean of $\mathbf{c}^{(t-1)}$, since these data points are the sample used to center the hypersphere. Since the replacement point is selected randomly from this set (with equal probability), the required expectation is $\mathrm{E}\left[\mathbf{x}_{rep}^{(t)} \mid \mathbf{c}^{(t-1)}\right] = \mathbf{c}^{(t-1)}$. Thus, as with average-out replacement, the optimal greedy attack point is $\mathbf{a}^{(t)} = \mathbf{c}^{(t-1)} + R \cdot \frac{\mathbf{x}^A - \mathbf{c}^{(0)}}{\left\|\mathbf{x}^A - \mathbf{c}^{(0)}\right\|}$ and the expected displacement achieved is

$$\mathrm{E}\left[\mathbf{r}_t \mid \mathbf{c}^{(t-1)}\right] = \frac{1}{N} \cdot \frac{\mathbf{x}^A - \mathbf{c}^{(0)}}{\left\|\mathbf{x}^A - \mathbf{c}^{(0)}\right\|} \quad \forall\, t \in \{1, \ldots, T\}$$

$$\mathrm{E}\left[\mathbf{D}_T \mid \mathbf{c}^{(t-1)}\right] = \sum_{t=1}^{T} \mathrm{E}\left[\mathbf{r}_t \mid \mathbf{c}^{(t-1)}\right] = \frac{T}{N} \cdot \frac{\mathbf{x}^A - \mathbf{c}^{(0)}}{\left\|\mathbf{x}^A - \mathbf{c}^{(0)}\right\|}.$$

Naturally, the expected displacement alignment is again $\mathrm{E}\left[\rho\left(\mathbf{D}_T\right) \mid \mathbf{c}^{(t-1)}\right] = \frac{T}{N}$. Thus, randomly selecting the point to be replaced does not deter the attacker's expected progress compared to the average-out policy.

4.5.2   Nearest-out Replacement Policy

Here we consider a replacement rule that is intended to diminish the success of poisoning when old data is replaced by new data. In particular, we consider *nearest-out replacement*, in which each new datum replaces the old data point that lies closest to it. This policy is designed to reduce the effectiveness of attacks because it limits the total displacement caused by any attack point. However, under the assumption that the adversary knows all training data, Kloft & Laskov (2012) showed that an adversary can use a greedy optimization procedure to find the optimal point to insert conditioned on the current training data—in this case, such a strategy is *greedy* since it does not factor future gains when selecting the next best point to insert.

To counter nearest-out replacement, the strategy employed by the adversary is to find the best point to replace the jth point in the dataset; i.e., the point $\mathbf{a}^{(t,j)}$ that (i) lies within the tth hypersphere, (ii) will replace $\mathbf{x}^{(j)}$, and (iii) has the largest displacement alignment of any such point . To find this point, consider that the N data points divide $\mathcal{X}$ into N regions called *Voronoi cells*; the jth Voronoi cell is the set of points that are closer to $\mathbf{x}^{(j)}$ than any other data point in the dataset. As such, the sought-after point $\mathbf{a}^{(t,j)}$ must lie within the jth Voronoi region and thus can be found by solving the following optimization problem:

$$\mathbf{a}^{(t,j)} = \mathrm{argmax}_{\mathbf{x}} \; \frac{1}{RN} \left(\mathbf{x} - \mathbf{x}^{(j)}\right)^{\top} \frac{\left(\mathbf{x}^A - \mathbf{c}^{(t)}\right)}{\left\|\mathbf{x}^A - \mathbf{c}^{(t)}\right\|} \tag{4.22}$$

$$\text{s.t.} \qquad \begin{array}{cc} \forall\, k \in 1, \ldots, N & \left\|\mathbf{x} - \mathbf{x}^{(j)}\right\| \leq \left\|\mathbf{x} - \mathbf{x}^{(k)}\right\| \\ & \left\|\mathbf{x} - \mathbf{c}^{(t)}\right\| \leq R. \end{array}$$

The objective of this program maximizes the displacement alignment for replacing the jth point, the first constraint requires that the new point lie within the jth Voronoi cell, and the second constraint requires it to lie within the tth hypersphere. The attacker can thus solve for the best points relative to each of the N data points and select the one that achieves the largest displacement alignment as the tth attack point, $\mathbf{a}^{(t)}$, as depicted in Figure 4.4. This process is repeated at each attack iteration.

The program of Equation (4.22) is a quadratically constrained linear program, for which the quadratic constraints on $\mathbf{a}^{(t,j)}$ can be expressed in terms of a positive definite matrix. Thus, the programs are convex and have a unique optimum (Boyd & Vandenberghe 2004). They can generally be solved by convex optimizers, but current solvers do not scale well when N is large. However, an alternative approach is presented in Algorithm 4.1, which utilizes a quadratic program instead. This optimization problem minimizes the radius of the point within the neighborhood of the kth data point, but is constrained to obtain a minimum displacement alignment, $\hat{\rho}$. If such a point is feasible and lies within the radius R of $\mathbf{c}^{(t)}$, then $\hat{\rho}$ is a lower bound on the displacement

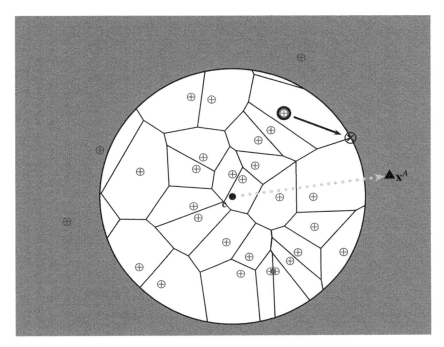

Figure 4.4 A depiction of an iteration of the optimal greedy attack against a hypersphere retrained using nearest-out replacement. The attacker wants to shift the current centroid **c** toward the target point $\mathbf{x}^A$, and the desired displacement direction is shown with a gray vector between them. Each training point is indicated with a $\oplus$. These points induce a Voronoi decomposition of the space depicted by the black grid within the hypersphere. Each such Voronoi cell is the set of points that would replace the enclosed training point. Finally, the optimal attack point is represented by a $\otimes$—it replaces the indicated training point and thereby yields the maximum possible displacement alignment according to Program (4.22).

alignment that can be achieved by replacing the kth point; otherwise, it is an upper bound. Thus, we can perform a binary search for the maximum attainable displacement alignment that can be achieved relative to each point. Further, since we are searching for the maximum possible displacement alignment, we can initialize the initial lower bound of the kth point to the maximum displacement alignment thus far achieved for the previous $(k-1)$ points. This overall procedure is captured in Algorithm 4.1.

However, there remains one aspect of this problem we have not yet addressed. Until now, we implicitly assumed that the Voronoi region of each point has a non-empty intersection with the hypersphere, but this assumption may be violated after many iterations of greedy optimal attacks. Such points are *abandoned* and act as a drag on the attack since they are no longer replaceable and lie far from the desired target $\mathbf{x}^A$. However, the attacker can prevent points from being abandoned by finding the optimal attack point, determining (through simulation) if the attack would cause any points to be abandoned, and, if so, finding the optimal attack point for the abandoned point. By ensuring that no points are abandoned, the attacker loses gain in that iteration, but prevents a long-term

---

ALGORITHM 4.1   NEAREST-OUT GREEDY ATTACK
_____

$Nout - Opt\left(\mathbf{x}^A, \mathbf{c}^{(0)}, R, \mathbf{c}^{(t)}, \left\{\mathbf{x}^{(j)}\right\}, \epsilon\right)$

Let $\rho^- \leftarrow -2 \cdot R$

for all $j \in 1, \ldots, N$ **do begin**

    Let $\rho^+ \leftarrow 2 \cdot R$

    while $\rho^+ - \rho^- > \epsilon$ **do begin**

        Solve for

$$\mathbf{a}^{(t,j)} = \text{argmin}_{\mathbf{x}} \left\| \mathbf{x} - \mathbf{c}^{(t)} \right\| \tag{4.23}$$

$$\text{s.t.} \quad \begin{array}{l} \forall\, k \in 1, \ldots, N \quad 2\left(\mathbf{x}^{(k)} - \mathbf{x}^{(j)}\right)^{\top} \mathbf{x} \leq \left\|\mathbf{x}^{(k)}\right\|^2 - \left\|\mathbf{x}^{(j)}\right\|^2 \\[2mm] \frac{1}{RN}\left(\mathbf{x} - \mathbf{x}^{(j)}\right)^{\top} \frac{\left(\mathbf{x}^A - \mathbf{c}^{(0)}\right)}{\left\|\mathbf{x}^A - \mathbf{c}^{(0)}\right\|} \geq \frac{\rho^+ - \rho^-}{2} \end{array}$$

        if Program 4.23 is feasible **and** $\left\| \mathbf{a}^{(t,j)} - \mathbf{c}^{(t)} \right\| \leq R$ **then** $\rho^- \leftarrow \frac{\rho^+ - \rho^-}{2}$ **and**
$\mathbf{a}^{(t)} \leftarrow \mathbf{a}^{(t,j)}$

        else $\rho^+ \leftarrow \frac{\rho^+ - \rho^-}{2}$

    end while

end for

return: $\mathbf{a}^{(t)}$

---

drag on its attack. This makes the attack more globally optimal, but more difficult to analyze precisely.

Because of this problem, there is no known exact result for this attack's total displacement alignment over T attack iterations. However, we can approximate it. Namely, in the worst case for the attacker, all training points would be co-linear along the direction $\mathbf{x}^A - \mathbf{c}^{(t)}$. As such, we can analyze the one-dimensional case. Here, assuming that no points will be abandoned, the displacement achieved by a single attack is at least $\frac{R}{2N}$ since, at worst, the N points are spread evenly between the centroid and the radius R. Thus, the total displacement is at least $\frac{1}{2N^2}$ times the number of iterations in which no points are abandoned. However, in practice, the gains are much greater in high-dimensional problems and are approximately linear in $\frac{T}{N}$. To see this, we followed the experimental procedure of Kloft & Laskov (2012) using $N = 100$ initial data points drawn from a standard normal distribution in $D \in \{2, 4, 8, 16, 32, 64, 100\}$ dimensions with a radius R selected to have a false-negative rate of 0.001. From this initial setting, we constructed over $T = 5 \cdot N = 500$ iterations of greedy attacks. The experiments were repeated 10 times, and the results are shown in Figure 4.5. As can be seen in these plots, the effects are approximately linear for $D > 4$ with a slope that approaches and even can perform slightly better than $D_R = \frac{T}{N}$.

4.6   Constrained Attackers

Reiterating our results thus far, in Sections 4.3 and 4.4, we showed that a hypersphere detector, which uses bootstrap retraining without any data replacement, is resilient to

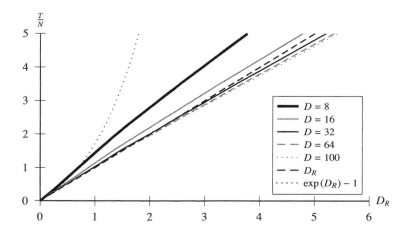

(a) Greedy Attack on Nearest-out Policy: High Dimensional

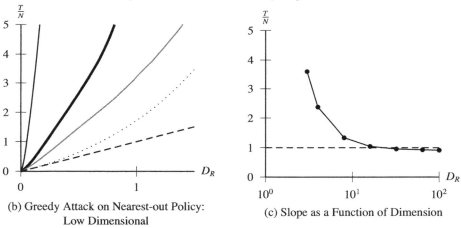

(b) Greedy Attack on Nearest-out Policy: Low Dimensional

(c) Slope as a Function of Dimension

Figure 4.5 These plots show the empirical effect of iterative greedy attacks against a hypersphere using nearest-out replacement. **(a)** In high dimensions, the required duration of the attack increases approximately linearly as a function of D_R, with a slope that decreases as dimension increases. **(b)** In small dimensions, the required duration can exceed the exponential bound due to the dense clustering of the data in the hypersphere. **(c)** When approximated as a linear function, the slope of the fit line decreases as the dimension of the hypersphere increases. For $D \approx N$, the slope can be slightly less than one.

attacks in the sense that an attacker must use exponentially many attack points in terms of its desired displacement, D_R. However, without any data replacement, the hypersphere becomes unadaptable as more data is received and retraining quickly becomes futile. However, as we saw in the last section, when data replacement is incorporated, an attacker can achieve its desired displacement, D_R, of the hypersphere detector using only linearly many attack points to do so under several possible replacement policies. These results suggest that having an adaptive hypersphere detector may be incompatible with having a model that is difficult for an attacker to coerce; i.e., iterative relearning and security are not simultaneously possible for hypersphere learning. However, to this point, we have been exceedingly pessimistic in assuming that the attacker can control all data points once the attack commences. In this section, we examine more realistic assumptions on the attacker's capabilities and show that in some settings, iteratively retrained hyperspheres are more resilient to poisoning attacks than indicated by the previous worst-case analysis. As with the last section, here we summarize results presented by Kloft & Laskov (2012).

To simplify the analysis, here we only consider *average-out replacement*, and we restrict ourselves to the scenario in which the hypersphere is retrained whenever it receives a new point; i.e., $\alpha_t = 1$ for all t. Through this restriction, we need only consider how the attacker designs a single optimal point $\mathbf{a}^{(t)}$ at the tth iteration, and we assume it does so greedily (i.e., only considering the current hypersphere).

In contrast to previous sections, we now assume that there are two sources of new data: attack data generated by the attacker and benign data generated by other users of the system. We assume that the benign data (i) comes from a natural distribution $P_\mathbf{x}$ that is neither advantageous nor detrimental to the adversary, (ii) is drawn independently and identically from that distribution, (iii) is randomly interleaved with the adversarial data, and most importantly, (iv) is always accepted for retraining regardless of the current state of the classifier (i.e., bootstrap retraining is relaxed for benign data).[2] In particular, we assume that each new data point given to the classifier is randomly selected to be either adversarial or benign according to a Bernoulli random variable with fixed parameter $\nu \in [0, 1]$; i.e., when the tth new data point is introduced, it is either the point $\mathbf{a}^{(t)}$ selected by the adversary with probability ν or it is a point $\mathbf{x}^{(t)} \sim P_\mathbf{x}$ with probability $1 - \nu$ and the attacker cannot alter the probability ν of its point being selected. Equivalently, we can model the new point $\mathbf{x}_{new}^{(t)}$ with a random variable $B^{(t)} \sim \text{Bern}(\nu)$ such that

$$\mathbf{x}_{new}^{(t)} = B^{(t)}\mathbf{a}^{(t)} + \left(1 - B^{(t)}\right)\mathbf{x}^{(t)} \tag{4.24}$$

where $\mathbf{x}^{(t)} \sim P_\mathbf{x}$ and $B^{(t)} \in \{0, 1\}$. Importantly, in selecting $\mathbf{a}^{(t)}$, we assume the adversary does not know $B^{(t)}$ or $\mathbf{x}^{(t)}$ but can still observe $\mathbf{c}^{(t)}$ that results and thus can compute $\mathbf{x}_{new}^{(t)}$ after retraining occurs. As before, the adversary must also choose $\mathbf{a}^{(t)}$ to be accepted for retraining, but here we assume that when $B^{(t)} = 0$, the benign $\mathbf{x}_{new}^{(t)}$ will always be accepted. Next, we discuss how the attacker can select $\mathbf{a}^{(t)}$ and analyze its impact under several constraints.

4.6.1   Greedy Optimal Attacks

In the scenario discussed above, new training data is a mixture of attack and benign data, but the attacker *cannot* alter the mixing ratio between them. Under this setting, we assume that the attacker produces an attack point at each iteration to optimize the expected displacement alignment according to Equation (4.21), and either this point

---

[2] This assumption is removed in alternative models studied by Kloft & Laskov (2012) that are not discussed here.

or a benign point $\mathbf{x}^{(t)} \sim P_{\mathbf{x}}$ will be used in retraining the hypersphere to obtain the tth centroid. Under average-out replacement (see Section 4.5.1), the outcome of this attack can be described by the resulting centroid and displacement vector, which are computed from $\mathbf{x}_{new}^{(t)}$ as

$$\mathbf{c}^{(t)} = \mathbf{c}^{(t-1)} + \frac{1}{N} \left(\mathbf{x}_{new}^{(t)} - \mathbf{c}^{(t-1)} \right)$$

$$= \mathbf{c}^{(t-1)} + \frac{1}{N} \left(B^{(t)} \left(\mathbf{a}^{(t)} - \mathbf{c}^{(t-1)} \right) + \left(1 - B^{(t)} \right) \left(\mathbf{x}^{(t)} - \mathbf{c}^{(t-1)} \right) \right)$$

$$\mathbf{D}_T = \frac{1}{R \cdot N} \sum_{t=1}^{T} \left(\mathbf{x}_{new}^{(t)} - \mathbf{c}^{(t-1)} \right)$$

$$= \frac{1}{R \cdot N} \sum_{t=1}^{T} \left(B^{(t)} \left(\mathbf{a}^{(t)} - \mathbf{c}^{(t-1)} \right) + \left(1 - B^{(t)} \right) \left(\mathbf{x}^{(t)} - \mathbf{c}^{(t-1)} \right) \right)$$

Due to the structure of these recursive expressions, it is difficult to optimize $\mathbf{D}_T$ over the entire attack sequence. However, given the centroid $\mathbf{c}^{(t-1)}$ from the last iteration, we can derive greedy optimal actions for the adversary under the assumption that all points $\{\mathbf{x}^{(t)}\}$ are drawn independently from the distribution $P_{\mathbf{x}}$. The result is given by the following lemma.

LEMMA 4.21 *Under average-out replacement, at the tth attack iteration, the greedy optimal attack point is given by*

$$\mathbf{a}^{(t)} = \mathbf{c}^{(t-1)} + R \cdot \frac{\mathbf{x}^A - \mathbf{c}^{(0)}}{\left\| \mathbf{x}^A - \mathbf{c}^{(0)} \right\|}.$$

Proof. From Equation (4.21), the greedy optimal strategy optimizes $\mathrm{E}\left[\rho\left(\mathbf{D}_t \right) \mid \mathbf{c}^{(t-1)} \right]$ but since $\mathrm{E}\left[\rho\left(\mathbf{D}_{t-1} \right) \mid \mathbf{c}^{(t-1)} \right] = \rho\left(\mathbf{D}_{t-1} \right)$—a fixed quantity relative to the attacker's actions in the tth step—the former is equivalent to optimizing $\mathrm{E}\left[\rho\left(\mathbf{D}_t \right) - \rho\left(\mathbf{D}_{t-1} \right) \mid \mathbf{c}^{(t-1)} \right]$; i.e., to optimizing the dot product of $\mathbf{r}_t$ with the desired direction $\mathbf{x}^A - \mathbf{c}^{(0)}$. This relative displacement is given by $\mathbf{r}_t = \frac{B^{(t)}}{R \cdot N} \cdot \left(\mathbf{a}^{(t)} - \mathbf{c}^{(t-1)} \right) + \frac{\left(1 - B^{(t)} \right)}{R \cdot N} \cdot \left(\mathbf{x}^{(t)} - \mathbf{c}^{(t-1)} \right)$. Computing the required expected value thus becomes

$$\mathrm{E}\left[\rho\left(\mathbf{D}_t \right) - \rho\left(\mathbf{D}_{t-1} \right) \mid \mathbf{c}^{(t-1)} \right] = \mathrm{E}\left[\mathbf{r}_t \mid \mathbf{c}^{(t-1)} \right]^{\top} \frac{\mathbf{x}^A - \mathbf{c}^{(0)}}{\left\| \mathbf{x}^A - \mathbf{c}^{(0)} \right\|}$$

$$= \frac{\nu}{R \cdot N} \left(\mathbf{a}^{(t)} - \mathbf{c}^{(t-1)} \right)^{\top} \frac{\mathbf{x}^A - \mathbf{c}^{(0)}}{\left\| \mathbf{x}^A - \mathbf{c}^{(0)} \right\|}$$

$$+ \frac{1 - \nu}{R \cdot N} \left(\mathrm{E}\left[\mathbf{x}^{(t)} \mid \mathbf{c}^{(t-1)} \right] - \mathbf{c}^{(t-1)} \right)^{\top} \frac{\mathbf{x}^A - \mathbf{c}^{(0)}}{\left\| \mathbf{x}^A - \mathbf{c}^{(0)} \right\|},$$

where $\mathrm{E}\left[\mathbf{x}^{(t)} \mid \mathbf{c}^{(t-1)} \right]$ is a fixed quantity since $\mathbf{x}^{(t)}$ is drawn independently from $P_{\mathbf{x}}$. By linearity, maximizing this quantity is equivalent to maximizing $\left(\mathbf{a}^{(t)} - \mathbf{c}^{(t-1)} \right)^{\top} \frac{\mathbf{x}^A - \mathbf{c}^{(0)}}{\left\| \mathbf{x}^A - \mathbf{c}^{(0)} \right\|}$ with respect to $\left\| \mathbf{a}^{(t)} - \mathbf{c}^{(t-1)} \right\| \leq R$. As we saw in Section 4.5.1, this yields the claimed form for optimal $\mathbf{a}^{(t)}$. $\qquad\square$

4.6.2   Attacks with Mixed Data

Here we analyze the expected net effect of applying the optimal greedy attack of Lemma 4.21 over T iterations and thus provide an analysis for the mixed data scenario described in Equation (4.24). To do so, we require an additional assumption about the benign data's distribution—namely we assume (i) that all benign data is drawn independently from $P_{\mathbf{x}}$, (ii) that the benign data has a stationary mean, $E_{\mathbf{x} \sim P_{\mathbf{x}}}[\mathbf{x}] = \mathbf{c}^{(0)}$, and (iii) that *benign data is never rejected*. These are strong assumptions about the benign data, but, in assuming that the benign data has a stationary mean and is always accepted, these are conservative assumptions on the attacker and yield the following theorem.[3]

THEOREM 4.22 (Paraphrased from Kloft & Laskov 2012) *Given a fixed mixture probability v, applying the greedy optimal attack strategy (given by Lemma 4.21) at each iteration yields an expected displacement alignment of*

$$E\left[\rho\left(\mathbf{D}_T\right)\right] = \frac{v}{1-v} \cdot \left(1 - \left(1 - \frac{(1-v)}{N}\right)^T\right) \leq \frac{v}{1-v}$$

after T iterations.

Proof. Under the optimal attack strategy of Lemma 4.21 the centroid becomes

$$\mathbf{c}^{(t)} = \mathbf{c}^{(t-1)} + \frac{1}{N}\left(B^{(t)}R \cdot \frac{\mathbf{x}^A - \mathbf{c}^{(0)}}{\left\|\mathbf{x}^A - \mathbf{c}^{(0)}\right\|} + \left(1 - B^{(t)}\right)\left(\mathbf{x}^{(t)} - \mathbf{c}^{(t-1)}\right)\right)$$

$$= \mathbf{c}^{(t-1)} + \frac{B^{(t)}R}{N}\frac{\mathbf{x}^A - \mathbf{c}^{(0)}}{\left\|\mathbf{x}^A - \mathbf{c}^{(0)}\right\|} + \frac{1}{N}\left(1 - B^{(t)}\right)\left(\mathbf{x}^{(t)} - \mathbf{c}^{(0)}\right)$$

$$- \frac{1}{N}\left(1 - B^{(t)}\right)\left(\mathbf{c}^{(t-1)} - \mathbf{c}^{(0)}\right),$$

where the summation has been conveniently reorganized for later. Now, using the definition of $\mathbf{D}_t = \frac{\mathbf{c}^{(t)} - \mathbf{c}^{(0)}}{R}$ from Equation (4.4), we substitute this form of $\mathbf{c}^{(t)}$ and use the linearity of $\rho(\cdot)$ to obtain

$$\mathbf{D}_t = \left(1 - \frac{1 - B^{(t)}}{N}\right)\mathbf{D}_{t-1} + \frac{\mathbf{x}^A - \mathbf{c}^{(0)}}{\left\|\mathbf{x}^A - \mathbf{c}^{(0)}\right\|}\frac{B^{(t)}}{N} + \frac{\left(1 - B^{(t)}\right)}{N}\frac{\left(\mathbf{x}^{(t)} - \mathbf{c}^{(0)}\right)}{R},$$

$$\rho\left(\mathbf{D}_t\right) = \left(1 - \frac{1 - B^{(t)}}{N}\right)\rho\left(\mathbf{D}_{t-1}\right) + \frac{B^{(t)}}{N} + \frac{\left(1 - B^{(t)}\right)}{N}\frac{\left(\mathbf{x}^{(t)} - \mathbf{c}^{(0)}\right)^{\top}\left(\mathbf{x}^A - \mathbf{c}^{(0)}\right)}{R\left\|\mathbf{x}^A - \mathbf{c}^{(0)}\right\|}.$$

Next we use the linearity of $E[\cdot]$ and the mutual independence of the random variables $B^{(t)}$ and $\mathbf{x}^{(t)}$ to compute the expectation of $\rho(\mathbf{D}_t)$. Importantly, $\mathbf{D}_{t-1}$ is also mutually independent of $B^{(t)}$ and $\mathbf{x}^{(t)}$ from the tth iteration. Finally, using the fact that $E\left[B^{(t)}\right] = v$ and $E\left[\mathbf{x}^{(t)}\right] = \mathbf{c}^{(0)}$, we arrive at the following recursive formula $E\left[\rho\left(\mathbf{D}_t\right)\right] = \left(1 - \frac{(1-v)}{N}\right)E\left[\rho\left(\mathbf{D}_{t-1}\right)\right] + \frac{1}{N}v$. Unwrapping this recursion and using the

---

[3] In a more realistic model, benign data would not always be accepted, particularly once the attack had significantly shifted the detector. This would motivate the attacker to concentrate its attack mass in the early iterations. Amenable models for this scenario are further explored in Kloft & Laskov (2012).

facts that $\mathbf{D}_0 = \mathbf{0}$ and thus $\rho(\mathbf{D}_0) = 0$ yield the following geometric series:

$$
\begin{aligned}
\mathrm{E}\left[\rho(\mathbf{D}_t)\right] &= \frac{\nu}{N} \cdot \sum_{t=1}^{T}\left(1 - \frac{(1-\nu)}{N}\right)^{T-t} \\
&= \frac{\nu}{N} \cdot \frac{1 - \left(1 - \frac{(1-\nu)}{N}\right)^T}{1 - \left(1 - \frac{(1-\nu)}{N}\right)} \\
&= \frac{\nu}{1-\nu}\left(1 - \left(1 - \frac{(1-\nu)}{N}\right)^T\right).
\end{aligned}
$$

The upper bound of $\frac{\nu}{1-\nu}$ on this quantity is derived from the fact that, for all T, the last factor in the above expression is less than or equal to one. □

In addition to the above result, Kloft & Laskov (2012) also bound the variance of $\rho(\mathbf{D}_t)$ and show that it vanishes as $T, N \to \infty$. Thus, for sufficiently large N, the above formula for $\mathrm{E}\left[\rho(\mathbf{D}_t)\right]$ should accurately predict $\rho(\mathbf{D}_t)$ as an attack progresses. According to this result, Figure 4.6 depicts the number of iterations T relative to N that are predicted for mixed-data attacks as a function of the desired relative displacement D_R for various values of ν. As suggested by the bound in Theorem 4.22, for $\nu < 1$, displacements that exceed $D_R > \frac{\nu}{1-\nu}$ are not achievable regardless of the attack's duration T or the initial number of points, N. Further, since this bound strictly increases in ν we can invert it using Lemma 4.1, which suggests the adversary must control a fraction $\nu \geq \frac{D_R}{1+D_R}$ of the new data to expect to be able to achieve its goal.

These results are analogous to those of Section 4.4 where $1 - \nu$ plays a similar role to $\frac{N}{N+M}$ (see Figure 4.3). The absolute upper bounds are obtained under replacement by

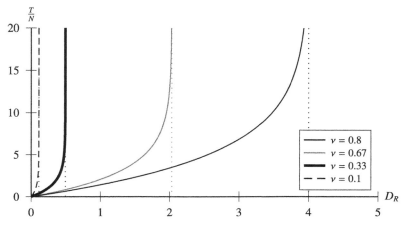

Figure 4.6 This plot show the theoretically predicted expected effect of the greedy optimal attacks of Theorem 4.22 for various values of the traffic mixture parameter: $\nu \in \{0.1, 0.33, 0.67, 0.8\}$. The plot shows the expected number of iterations T (relative to N) that are predicted for the mixed-data attacks as a function of the desired relative displacement D_R. The dotted lines depict the asymptotic maximum displacement that can be achieved for each ν.

limiting the fraction of data controlled by the adversary, rather than limiting the attack duration. However, the results here just give the expected behavior rather than a strict bound on attack performance. In fact, in the worst case, all adversarial points could be accepted, resulting in the linear behavior of Section 4.5.1. Nonetheless, these results show that such results are generally overly pessimistic about the adversary's power. However, they also relied on assumptions about the benign data's distribution. Alternatively, Kloft & Laskov (2012) also examined a scenario in which the hypersphere would be manually reset if its false-positive rate becomes too high. In this alternative scenario, we no longer need to assume that benign data is always accepted for retraining, and under it, Kloft & Laskov (2012) derive a result similar to Theorem 4.22; however, for the sake of brevity, we will not explore that scenario here.

4.6.3   Extensions

There are several straightforward extensions of this work. The first extends the results to a hyper-ellipsoid detector defined by the Mahalanobis norm $\|\mathbf{x}\|_{\Sigma} = \mathbf{x}^{\top}\Sigma^{-1}\mathbf{x}$ for a fixed positive-definite structure matrix Σ. Under this norm, the hyper-ellipsoid detector is defined as $f_{\mathbf{c},\Sigma,R}(\mathbf{x}) = $ "+" if $\|\mathbf{x} - \mathbf{c}\|_{\Sigma} > R$ and "−" otherwise. By transforming the problem into the space defined by $\mathbf{x}' \leftarrow \Sigma^{-\frac{1}{2}}\mathbf{x}$ (which is possible since Σ is positive definite), all of the results of this chapter can be directly applied. The only caveat is that Σ distorts the space—hence the hardness of the task (given by D_R) depends on where the target point $\mathbf{x}^A$ is relative to the principal axes of Σ.

A second extension involves hypersphere-based detection in an implicit feature space defined by a kernel function, which computes the inner product for data points implicitly projected into a Hilbert space $\mathcal{H}$. In particular, if $k : \mathcal{X} \times \mathcal{X} \to \Re$ is a kernel function and $\phi : \mathcal{X} \to \mathcal{H}$ is its corresponding projection function satisfying $k\left(\mathbf{x}^{(1)}, \mathbf{x}^{(2)}\right) = \phi\left(\mathbf{x}^{(1)}\right)^{\top}\phi\left(\mathbf{x}^{(1)}\right)$, then the centroid of the projected dataset is given by $\phi_C = \frac{1}{N}\sum_{i=1}^{N}\phi\left(\mathbf{x}^{(i)}\right)$ and the distance of the projected data point $\phi(\mathbf{x})$ from this centroid is

$$\|\phi(\mathbf{x}) - \phi_C\|_k = \left(k(\mathbf{x}, \mathbf{x}) - \frac{2}{N}\sum_{i=1}^{N} k\left(\mathbf{x}^{(i)}, \mathbf{x}\right) + \frac{1}{N^2}\sum_{i,j=1}^{N} k\left(\mathbf{x}^{(i)}, \mathbf{x}^{(j)}\right) \right)^{\frac{1}{2}},$$

which, as with all kernel algorithms, can be computed implicitly only using the kernel function. The corresponding classification function labels the point $\mathbf{x}$ as "+" if $\|\phi(\mathbf{x})\|_k > R$ and as "−" otherwise.

Attacks against these kernel-based hypersphere detectors are a straightforward extension of the work presented above *if* we assume the attacker can insert arbitrary attack points directly in the feature space $\mathcal{H}$. However, a true adversary is restricted to inserting data points in the space $\mathcal{X}$, for which there is not generally a one-to-one mapping to $\mathcal{H}$. It is generally nontrivial for the adversary to find a point $\mathbf{a}^{(t)} \in \mathcal{X}$ whose image in feature space maximizes the displacement alignment according to Definition (4.2)—this is the well-known pre-image problem (Fogla & Lee 2006), which we also revisit in this book in other contexts (for example, see Section 8.4.3). Nonetheless, Kloft & Laskov

(2010) examined attacks against kernel-based hypersphere detectors empirically under the stronger assumption that the attacker could create its attack points in feature space—a conservative security assumption.

4.7   Summary

In this chapter, we analyzed *Causative Integrity* attacks against a hypersphere learner, which iteratively retrains its centroid based on new data. This analysis provides, under a variety of different assumptions, a deep understanding of the impact an attack can have on a simple learning model. We showed how optimal attacks can be constructed when assuming different powers for the adversary using several models for retraining and the outcomes demonstrate that the adversary's success critically depends on the scenario's assumptions. First, in Sections 4.3 and 4.4 we proved that, without any data replacement or time constraints, the attacker requires at least $M^\star \geq \exp(D_R - 1)$ attack points when $N = 0$ or $M^\star \geq N(\exp(D_R) - 1)$ when $N > 0$ to achieve the desired relative displacement of D_R. Similarly, if the attack has a maximum duration of T, these bounds increase to $M^\star \geq \left(\frac{T}{T-D_R}\right)^T$ when $N = 0$ or $M^\star \geq N\left(\frac{T}{T-D_R}\right)^T - N$ when $N > 0$ (assuming, in both cases, that $T > D_R$ because otherwise the desired displacement is unachievable). In all of these cases, the attacker requires *exponentially many attack points* in the size of its objective; i.e., the relative displacement, D_R.

However, bootstrap retraining without any data replacement severely limits the model's ability to adapt to data drift over time—eventually the model will become rigidly fixed even without an attack. Thus, in Sections 4.5 and 4.6, we revisit the data replacement settings analyzed by Kloft & Laskov (2012), in which each new data point replaces an old data point. These results show that under average-out and random-out replacement, the attacker only requires *linearly many attack points* (relative to the number of initial points, N) to achieve the desired goal, D_R. Even the nearest-out replacement policy, which was selected to limit the adversary's influence, empirically also exhibited linear-like behavior (except in low-dimensional spaces). These results showed that when the attacker controls all the new data in this scenario, it can successfully execute its attack with relatively little effort. Be that as it may, in many circumstances it is too conservative to assume that the attacker controls all new training data. Thus, in the final part of this chapter, we explored the work of Kloft & Laskov (2012) in examining a mixed-data scenario, in which the new data is drawn both from benign and malicious sources. Under the assumption that each new data point is malicious with probability ν and otherwise benign (and that all benign data is always used for retraining), the attacker must control a fraction $\nu \geq \frac{D_R}{1+D_R}$ of the new data to expect to be able to achieve its goal. Further, the expected displacement of the attacker no longer increases linearly with the number of attack points; thus, under this more realistic setting, we see that the attacker cannot easily achieve its objective.

The analyses presented in this chapter demonstrate that the success of a poisoning attack against a iteratively retrained learner depends on several factors including how the learner restricts new training data and how much control the attacker has. However, the exact analysis provided in this chapter requires some assumptions that are not easily justified in practical settings and only apply to a relatively simple learning algorithm with bootstrap retraining. Nonetheless, these exact analyses provide interesting insights into the abstract problem of data poisoning and serve as a guide for less theoretical analysis of more complicated learning problems. This early work on contamination models heavily influenced our subsequent approach to the adversarial learning framework that we describe in the remainder of this book and was one of the first attempts to treat this problem as an adversarial game between a learner and an adversary.

5 Availability Attack Case Study: SpamBayes

Adversaries can also execute attacks designed to degrade the classifier's ability to distinguish between allowed and disallowed events. These *Causative Availability* attacks against learning algorithms cause the resulting classifiers to have unacceptably high false-positive rates; i.e., a successfully poisoned classifier will misclassify benign input as potential attacks, creating an unacceptable level of interruption in legitimate activity. This chapter provides a case study of one such attack on the SpamBayes spam detection system. We show that cleverly crafted attack messages—pernicious spam email that an uninformed human user would likely identify and label as spam—can exploit Spam-Bayes' learning algorithm, causing the learned classifier to have an unreasonably high false-positive rate. (Chapter 6 demonstrates *Causative* attacks that instead result in classifiers with an unreasonably high false-negative rate—these are *Integrity* attacks.) We also show effective defenses against these attacks and discuss the tradeoffs required to defend against them.

We examine several attacks against the SpamBayes spam filter, each of which embodies a particular insight into the vulnerability of the underlying learning technique. In doing so, we more broadly demonstrate attacks that could affect any system that uses a similar learning algorithm. The attacks we present target the learning algorithm used by the spam filter SpamBayes (spambayes.sourceforge.net), but several other filters also use the same underlying learning algorithm, including BogoFilter (bogofilter.sourceforge.net), the spam filter in Mozilla's Thunderbird email client (mozilla.org), and the machine learning component of SpamAssassin (spamassassin.apache.org). The primary difference between the learning elements of these three filters is in their tokenization methods; i.e., the learning algorithm is fundamentally identical, but each filter uses a different set of features. We demonstrate the vulnerability of the underlying algorithm for SpamBayes because it uses a pure machine learning method, it is familiar to the academic community (Meyer & Whateley 2004), and it is popular with over 700,000 downloads. Although here we only analyze SpamBayes, the fact that these other systems use the same learning algorithm suggests that other filters are also vulnerable to similar attacks. However, the overall effectiveness of the attacks would depend on how each of the other filters incorporates the learned classifier into the final filtering decision. For instance, filters such as Apache SpamAssassin (Apa n.d.), only use learning as one of several components of a broader filtering engine (the others are handcrafted non-adapting rules), so attacks against it would degrade the performance of the filter, but perhaps their overall impact would be lessened or muted entirely. In principle, though, it should be possible to replicate these results in these other filters. Finally, beyond spam filtering, we highlight the vulnerabilities in SpamBayes' learner because these same attacks could also be employed against similar learning algorithms in other domains. While the feasibility of these attacks, the attacker's motivation, or the contamination mechanism presented in this chapter may not be appropriate in other domains, it is nonetheless interesting to understand the vulnerability so that it can be similarly assessed for other applications.

We organize our approach to studying the vulnerability of SpamBayes' learning algorithm based on the framework discussed in Chapter 3. Primarily, we investigated *Causative Availability* attacks on the filter because this type of attack was an interesting new facet that could actually be deployed in real-world settings. Here the adversary has an additive contamination capability (i.e., the adversary has exclusive control of some subset of the user's training data), but is limited to only altering the positive (spam) class; we deemed this contamination model to be the most appropriate for a crafty spammer. Novel contributions of our research include a set of successful principled attacks against SpamBayes, an empirical study validating the effectiveness of the attacks in a realistic setting, and a principled defense that empirically succeeds against several of the attacks. We finally discuss the implications of the attack and defense strategies and the role that attacker information plays in the effectiveness of these attacks.

In this chapter, we discuss the background of the training model (see Section 5.1); we present three new attacks on SpamBayes (see Section 5.3); we give experimental results (see Section 5.5); and we present a defense against these attacks together with further experimental results (see Section 5.4). This chapter builds on the work of Nelson et al. (2008, 2009).

5.1   The SpamBayes Spam Filter

SpamBayes is a content-based statistical spam filter that classifies email using token counts in a model proposed by Robinson (2003) as inspired by Graham (2002). Meyer & Whateley (2004) describe the system in detail. SpamBayes computes a spam score for each token in the training corpus based on its occurrence in spam and non-spam emails; this score is motivated as a smoothed estimate of the posterior probability that an email containing that token is spam. The filter computes a message's overall spam score based on the assumption that the token scores are independent, and then it applies Fisher's method (cf. Fisher 1948) for combining significance tests to determine whether the email's tokens are sufficiently indicative of one class or the other. The message score is compared against two thresholds to select the label *spam*, *ham* (i.e., non-spam), or *unsure*. In the remainder of this section, we detail the statistical method SpamBayes uses to estimate and aggregate token scores.

5.1.1   SpamBayes' Training Algorithm

SpamBayes is a content-based spam filter that classifies messages based on the tokens (including header tokens) observed in an email. The spam classification model used by

SpamBayes was designed by Robinson (2003) and Meyer & Whateley (2004), based on ideas by Graham (2002), together with Fisher's method for combining independent significance tests (Fisher 1948). Intuitively, SpamBayes learns how strongly each token indicates *ham* or *spam* by counting the number of each type of email in which the token appears. When classifying a new email, SpamBayes considers all the message's tokens as evidence of whether the message is spam or ham and uses a statistical test to decide whether they indicate one label or the other with sufficient confidence; if not, SpamBayes returns *unsure*.

SpamBayes tokenizes each email X based on words, URL components, header elements, and other character sequences that appear in X. Each is treated as a unique token of the email independent of their order within the message, but for convenience, we place an ordering on the tokens so that each unique token has a fixed position i among the entire alphabet of tokens. Further, SpamBayes only records whether or not a token occurs in the message, not how many times it occurs. Email X is thus represented as a binary (potentially infinite length) vector $\mathbf{x}$ where

$$x_i = \begin{cases} 1, & \text{if the } i^{\text{th}} \text{ token occurs in } X \\ 0, & \text{otherwise} \end{cases}.$$

This message vector representation records which tokens occur in the message independent of their order or multiplicity.

The training data used by SpamBayes is a dataset of message vector (representing each training message) and label pairs: $\mathbb{D}^{(\text{train})} = \{ (\mathbf{x}^{(1)}, y^{(1)}), (\mathbf{x}^{(2)}, y^{(2)}), \dots, (\mathbf{x}^{(N)}, y^{(N)}) \}$ where $\mathbf{x}^{(i)} \in \{0, 1\}^D$ and $y^{(i)} \in \{ham, spam\}$. As in Section 2.2.1, this training data can be represented as a training matrix $\mathbf{X} = [\mathbf{x}^{(1)} \, \mathbf{x}^{(2)} \, \dots \, \mathbf{x}^{(N)}]^\top \in \{0, 1\}^{N \times D}$ along with its label vector $\mathbf{y} = [y^{(1)} \, y^{(2)} \, \dots \, y^{(N)}] \in \{0, 1\}^N$, using 1 to represent *spam* and 0 for *ham*. Using the training matrix, the token-counting statistics used by SpamBayes can be expressed as

$$\mathbf{n}^{(s)} \triangleq \mathbf{X}^\top \mathbf{y} \qquad \mathbf{n}^{(h)} \triangleq \mathbf{X}^\top (1 - \mathbf{y}) \qquad \mathbf{n} \triangleq \mathbf{n}^{(s)} + \mathbf{n}^{(h)}$$

which are vectors containing the cumulative token counts for each token in all, spam, and ham messages, respectively. We also define $N^{(s)} \triangleq \mathbf{y}^\top \mathbf{y}$ as the total number of training spam messages and $N^{(h)} \triangleq (1 - \mathbf{y})^\top (1 - \mathbf{y})$ as the total number of training ham messages (and, of course, $N = N^{(s)} + N^{(h)}$).

From these count statistics, SpamBayes computes a spam score for the ith token by estimating the posterior $\Pr(X \text{ is spam} | x_i = 1)$. First, the likelihoods $\Pr(x_i = 1 | X \text{ is spam})$ and $\Pr(x_i = 1 | X \text{ is ham})$ for observing the ith token in a spam/ham message are estimated using the maximum likelihood estimators yielding the likelihood vectors $L_i^{(s)} = \frac{1}{N^{(s)}} \cdot \mathbf{n}^{(s)}$ and $L_i^{(h)} = \frac{1}{N^{(h)}} \cdot \mathbf{n}^{(h)}$.

Second, using the likelihood estimates $\mathbf{L}^{(s)}$ and $\mathbf{L}^{(h)}$ and an estimate $\pi^{(s)}$ on the prior distribution $\Pr(X \text{ is spam})$, Bayes' Rule is used to estimate the posteriors as $\mathbf{P}^{(s)} \propto \frac{\pi^{(s)}}{N^{(s)}} \cdot \mathbf{n}^{(s)}$ and $\mathbf{P}^{(h)} \propto \frac{1 - \pi^{(s)}}{N^{(h)}} \cdot \mathbf{n}^{(h)}$ along with the constraints $\mathbf{P}^{(s)} + \mathbf{P}^{(h)} = 1$. However, instead of using the usual naive Bayes maximum likelihood prior estimator $\pi^{(s)} = \frac{N^{(s)}}{N^{(s)} + N^{(h)}}$, SpamBayes uses the agnostic prior distribution $\pi^{(s)} = \frac{1}{2}$, a choice that gives the learner unusual properties that we further discuss in Appendix C.2.1. Based on this choice of prior, SpamBayes then computes a *spam score vector* $\mathbf{P}^{(s)}$ specified for the ith token as

$$P_i^{(s)} = \frac{N^{(h)} n_i^{(s)}}{N^{(h)} n_i^{(s)} + N^{(s)} n_i^{(h)}}; \qquad (5.1)$$

i.e., this score is an estimator of the posterior $\Pr(X \text{ is spam}|x_i = 1)$. An analogous *token ham score* is given by $\mathbf{P}^{(h)} = 1 - \mathbf{P}^{(s)}$.

Robinson's method (Robinson 2003) smooths $P_i^{(s)}$ through a convex combination with a prior distribution belief x (default value of $x = 0.5$), weighting the quantities by n_i (the number of training emails with the ith token) and s (chosen for the strength of the prior with a default of $s = 1$), respectively:

$$q_i = \frac{s}{s + n_i} x + \frac{n_i}{s + n_i} P_i^{(s)}. \qquad (5.2)$$

Smoothing mitigates overfitting for rare tokens. For instance, if the token "floccinaucini-hilipilification" appears once in a spam and never in a ham in the training set, the posterior estimate would be $P_i^{(s)} = 1$, which would make any future occurrence of this word dominate the overall spam score. However, occurrence of this word only in spam may have only been an artifact of its overall rarity. In this case, smoothing is done by adding a prior distribution that the posterior for every token is $x = \frac{1}{2}$ (i.e., an agnostic score). For rare tokens, the posterior estimate is dominated by this prior. However, when a token is more frequently observed, its smoothed score approaches the empirical estimate of the posterior in Equation (5.1) according to the strength given to the prior by s. An analogous smoothed ham score is given by $1 - \mathbf{q}$.

5.1.2   SpamBayes' Predictions

After training, the filter computes the overall spam score $I(\hat{\mathbf{x}})$ of a new message $\hat{X}$ using Fisher's method (Fisher 1948) for combining the scores of the tokens observed in $\hat{X}$. SpamBayes uses at most 150 tokens from $\hat{X}$ with scores furthest from 0.5 and outside the interval $(0.4, 0.6)$ (see Appendix C.2.2 for more details). Let $\mathbb{T}_{\hat{\mathbf{x}}}$ be the set of tokens that SpamBayes incorporates into its spam score, and let $\boldsymbol{\delta}(\hat{\mathbf{x}})$ be the indicator function for this set. The token spam scores are combined into a *message spam score* for $\hat{X}$ by

$$S(\hat{\mathbf{x}}) = 1 - \chi_{2\tau_{\hat{\mathbf{x}}}}^2 \left(-2(\log \mathbf{q})^\top \boldsymbol{\delta}(\hat{\mathbf{x}}) \right), \qquad (5.3)$$

where $\tau_{\hat{\mathbf{x}}} \triangleq |\mathbb{T}_{\hat{\mathbf{x}}}|$ is the number of tokens from $\hat{X}$ used by SpamBayes and $\chi_{2\tau_{\hat{\mathbf{x}}}}^2(\cdot)$ denotes the cumulative distribution function of the chi-square distribution with $2\tau_{\hat{\mathbf{x}}}$ degrees of freedom. A ham score $H(\hat{\mathbf{x}})$ is similarly defined by replacing $\mathbf{q}$ with $1 - \mathbf{q}$ in Equation (5.3). Finally, SpamBayes constructs an overall spam score for $\hat{X}$ by averaging $S(\hat{\mathbf{x}})$ and $1 - H(\hat{\mathbf{x}})$ (both being indicators of whether $\hat{X}$ is spam), giving the final score

$$I(\hat{\mathbf{x}}) = \frac{1}{2}(S(\hat{\mathbf{x}}) + 1 - H(\hat{\mathbf{x}})) \qquad (5.4)$$

for a message: a quantity between 0 (strong evidence of ham) and 1 (strong evidence of spam). SpamBayes predicts by thresholding $I(\hat{\mathbf{x}})$ against two user-tunable thresholds $\theta^{(h)}$ and $\theta^{(s)}$, with defaults $\theta^{(h)} = 0.15$ and $\theta^{(s)} = 0.9$. SpamBayes predicts *ham*, *unsure*, or *spam* if $I(\hat{\mathbf{x}})$ falls into the interval $[0, \theta^{(h)}]$, $(\theta^{(h)}, \theta^{(s)}]$, or $(\theta^{(s)}, 1]$, respectively, and filters the message accordingly.

The inclusion of an *unsure* label in addition to *spam* and *ham* prevents us from purely using *ham-as-spam* and *spam-as-ham* misclassification rates (false positives and false negatives, respectively) for evaluation. We must also consider *spam-as-unsure* and *ham-as-unsure* misclassifications. Because of the practical effects on the user's time and effort discussed in Section 5.2.3, *ham-as-unsure* misclassifications are nearly as bad for the user as *ham-as-spam*.

5.1.3   SpamBayes' Model

Although the components of the SpamBayes algorithm (token spam scores, smoothing, and chi-squared test) were separately motivated, the resulting system can be described by a unified probability model for discriminating ham from spam messages. While Robinson motivates the SpamBayes classifier as a smoothed estimator of the posterior probability of spam, he never explicitly specifies the probabilistic model. We specify a discriminative model and show that the resulting estimation can be re-derived using empirical risk minimization. Doing so provides a better understanding of the modeling assumptions of the SpamBayes classifier and its vulnerabilities.

In this model, there are three random variables of interest: the spam label y_i of the ith message, the indicator variable $X_{i,j}$ of the jth token in the ith message, and the token score q_j of the jth token. We use the convention that a label is 1 to indicate *spam* or 0 to indicate *ham*. In the discriminative setting, given $\mathbf{X}_{i,\bullet}$ as a representation of the tokens in the ith message and the token scores $\mathbf{q}$, the message's label y_i is conditionally independent of all other random variables in the model. The conditional probability of the message label given the occurrence of a single token $X_{i,j}$ is specified by

$$\Pr\left(y_i | X_{i,j}, q_j\right) = \left((q_j)^{y_i} \cdot (1 - q_j)^{1-y_i}\right)^{X_{i,j}} \left(\tfrac{1}{2}\right)^{1-X_{i,j}}, \tag{5.5}$$

i.e., in the SpamBayes model, each token that occurs in the message is an indicator of its label, whereas tokens absent from the message have no impact on its label. Because SpamBayes' scores only incorporate tokens that occur in the message, traditional generative spam models (e.g., Figure 5.1(b)) are awkward to construct, but the above discriminative conditional probability captures this modeling nuance. Further, there is no prior distribution for the token indicators $X_{i,j}$ but there is a prior on the token scores. Treating these as binomial parameters, each has a beta prior with common parameters α and β, giving them a conditional probability of

$$\Pr\left(q_j | \alpha, \beta\right) = \tfrac{1}{\text{B}(\alpha,\beta)} \cdot (q_j)^{\alpha-1} \cdot (1 - q_j)^{\beta-1}, \tag{5.6}$$

where $\text{B}(\alpha, \beta)$ is the beta function (see the Glossary). As earlier mentioned, Robinson instead used an equivalent parameterization with a strength parameter s and prior parameter x for which $\alpha = s \cdot x + 1$ and $\beta = s(1-x) + 1$. Using this parameterization, x specifies the mode of the prior distribution distribution. In SpamBayes, these parameters are fixed a priori rather than treated as random hyper-parameters. Their default values are $\pi^{(s)} = \frac{1}{2}$, $x = \frac{1}{2}$, and $s = 1$.

Together, the label's probability conditioned on the jth token and the prior distribution on the jth token score are used to derive a spam score for the message (based only on the jth token). However, unlike a maximum likelihood derivation, SpamBayes' parameter estimation for q_j is not based on a joint probability model over all tokens. Instead, the score for each token is computed separately by maximizing the labels' likelihood within a per-token model as depicted in Figure 5.1(a); i.e., the model depicts a sequence of labels based solely on the presence of the jth token. Based on the independence assumption of Figure 5.1(a), the conditional distributions of Equation (5.5) combine together to make the following joint log probability based on the jth token (for

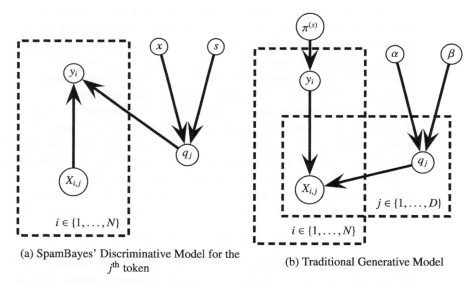

(a) SpamBayes' Discriminative Model for the jth token

(b) Traditional Generative Model

Figure 5.1 Probabilistic graphical models for spam detection. **(a)** A probabilistic model that depicts the dependency structure between random variables in SpamBayes for a *single* token (SpamBayes models each token as a separate indicator of ham/spam and then combines them together assuming each is an independent test). In this model, the label y_i for the ith email depends on the token score q_j for the jth token if it occurs in the message; i.e., $X_{i,j} = 1$. The parameters s and x parameterize a beta prior distribution on q_j. **(b)** A more traditional generative model for spam. The parameters $\pi^{(s)}$, α, and β parameterize the prior distributions for y_i and q_j. Each label y_i for the ith email is drawn independently from a Bernoulli distribution with $\pi^{(s)}$ as the probability of *spam*. Each token score for the jth token is drawn independently from a beta distribution with parameters α and β. Finally, given the label for a message and the token scores, $X_{i,j}$ is drawn independently from a Bernoulli. Based on the likelihood function for this model, the token scores q_j computed by SpamBayes can be viewed simply as the maximum likelihood estimators for the corresponding parameter in the model.

N messages):

$$\log \Pr\left(\mathbf{y}, \mathbf{X}_{\bullet,j} | \alpha, \beta\right) = \log \Pr\left(q_j | \alpha, \beta\right) + \sum_{i=1}^{N} \log \Pr\left(y_i | X_{i,j}, q_j\right)$$
$$= -\log\left(\mathrm{B}\left(\alpha, \beta\right)\right) + (\alpha - 1)\log\left(q_j\right) + (\beta - 1)\log\left(1 - q_j\right)$$
$$+ \sum_{i=1}^{N}\left[y_i X_{i,j}\log\left(q_j\right) + (1 - y_i)X_{i,j}\log\left(1 - q_j\right)\right]$$

Maximizing this joint distribution (nearly) achieves the token scores specified by Spam-Bayes. To solve for the maximum, differentiate the joint probability with respect to the jth token score, q_j, and set the derivative equal to 0. This yields

$$q_j = \frac{\sum_{i=1}^{N} y_i X_{i,j} + \alpha - 1}{\sum_{i=1}^{N} X_{i,j} + \alpha - 1 + \beta - 1}$$
$$= \frac{\alpha - 1}{n_j + \alpha - 1 + \beta - 1} + \frac{n_j^{(s)}}{n_j + \alpha - 1 + \beta - 1},$$

where the summations in the first equation are simplified to token counts based on the definitions of y_i and $X_{i,j}$. Using the equivalent beta parameterization with x and s and the usual posterior token score $P_i^{(s)} = \frac{n_i^{(s)}}{n_i^{(s)} + n_i^{(h)}}$ (which differs from the SpamBayes' token score used in Equation (5.1) unless $N^{(s)} = N^{(h)}$), this equation for the maximum-likelihood estimator of q_j is equivalent to the SpamBayes' estimator in Equation (5.2).

The above per-token optimizations can also be viewed as a joint maximization procedure by considering the overall spam and ham scores $S(\,\cdot\,)$ and $H(\,\cdot\,)$ for the messages in the training set (see Equation 5.3). These overall scores are based on Fisher's method for combining independent p-values and assume that each token score is independent. In fact, $S(\,\cdot\,)$ and $H(\,\cdot\,)$ are tests for the aggregated scores $s_{\mathbf{q}}(\,\cdot\,)$ and $h_{\mathbf{q}}(\,\cdot\,)$ defined by Equations (C.1) and (C.2)—tests that monotonically increase with $s_{\mathbf{q}}(\,\cdot\,)$ and $h_{\mathbf{q}}(\,\cdot\,)$, respectively. Thus, from the overall spam score $I(\,\cdot\,)$ defined by Equation (5.4), maximizing $s_{\mathbf{q}}(\,\cdot\,)$ for all spam and $h_{\mathbf{q}}(\,\cdot\,)$ for all ham is a surrogate for minimizing the prediction error of $I(\,\cdot\,)$; i.e., minimizing some loss for $I(\,\cdot\,)$. Hence, combining the individual tokens' conditional distributions (Equation 5.5) together to form

$$Q\left(y_i, \mathbf{X}_{i,\bullet}, \mathbf{q}\right) = -\log \prod_{j=1}^{D}\left((q_j)^{y_i} \cdot (1 - q_j)^{1 - y_i}\right)^{X_{i,j}},$$

can be viewed as the loss function for the score $I(\,\cdot\,)$, and the sum of the negative logarithm of the token score priors given by Equation 5.6 can be viewed as its regularizer.[1] Moreover, minimizing this *regularized empirical loss* again yields the

---

[1] This interpretation ignores the censoring function $\mathbb{T}$ in which SpamBayes only uses the scores of the most informative tokens when computing $I(\,\cdot\,)$ for a message. As discussed in Appendix C.1 this censoring action makes $I(\,\cdot\,)$ non-monotonic in the token scores q_j. Computing the token scores without considering $\mathbb{T}$ can be viewed as a tractable relaxation of the true objective.

SpamBayes' token scores from Equation (5.2). In this way, SpamBayes can be viewed as a regularized empirical risk minimization technique.

Unfortunately, the loss function Q is not a negative log-likelihood because the product of the scores is unnormalized. When the proper normalizer is added to Q, the resulting parameter estimates for q_j no longer are equivalent to SpamBayes' estimators. In fact, SpamBayes' parameter estimation procedure and its subsequent prediction rule do not appear to be compatible with a traditional joint probability distribution over all labels, tokens, and scores (or at least we were unable to derive a joint probability model that would yield these estimates). Nonetheless, through the loss function Q, SpamBayes can be viewed as a regularized empirical risk minimization procedure as discussed in Section 2.2.

By analyzing this model of SpamBayes, we now identify its potential vulnerabilities. First, by incorporating a prior distribution on the token scores for smoothing, Robinson prevented a simple attack. Without any smoothing on the token scores, all tokens that only appear in ham would have token scores of 0. Since the overall score $I(\,\cdot\,)$ is computed with products of the individual token scores, including any of these ham-only tokens would cause spam to be misclassified as *ham* (and vice versa for spam-only tokens), which the adversary could clearly exploit. Similarly, using the censor function $\mathbb{T}$ helps prevent attacks in which the adversary pads a spam with many *hammy* tokens to negate the effect of *spammy* tokens. However, despite these design considerations, SpamBayes is still vulnerable to attacks. The first vulnerability of SpamBayes comes from its assumption that the data and tokens are independent, for which each token score is estimated based solely on the presence of that token in ham and spam messages. The second vulnerability comes from its assumption that only tokens that occur in a message contribute to its label. While there is some intuition behind this assumption, in this model, it causes rare tokens to have little support so that their scores can be easily changed. Ultimately, these two vulnerabilities lead to a family of attacks that we call dictionary attacks that we present and evaluate in the rest of this chapter.

5.2   Threat Model for SpamBayes

In analyzing the vulnerabilities of SpamBayes, we were motivated by the taxonomy of attacks (see Section 3.3). Known real-world attacks that spammers use against deployed spam filters tend to be *Exploratory Integrity* attacks: either the spammer obfuscates the especially spam-like content of a spam email, or it includes content not indicative of spam. Both tactics aim to get the modified message into the victim's inbox. This category of attack has been studied in detail in the literature (e.g., see Lowd & Meek 2005*a*, 2005*b*, Wittel & Wu 2004; Dalvi et al. 2004). However, in this chapter we investigate the compelling threat of *Causative* attacks against spam filters, which are unique to machine learning systems and potentially more harmful since they alter the filter.

In particular, a *Causative Availability* attack can create a powerful denial of service. For example, if a spammer causes enough legitimate messages to be filtered by the user's spam filter, the user is likely to disable the filter and therefore see the spammer's unwanted messages. Alternatively, an unscrupulous business owner may wish to use spam filter denial of service to prevent a competitor from receiving email orders from potential customers. In this chapter, we present two novel *Causative Availability* attacks against SpamBayes: the dictionary attack is *Indiscriminate* and the focused attack is *Targeted*.

5.2.1 Attacker Goals

We consider an attacker with one of two goals: expose the victim to an advertisement or prevent the victim from seeing a legitimate message. The motivation for the first objective is obviously the potential revenue gain for the spammer if its marketing campaign is widely viewed. For the second objective, there are at least two motives for the attacker to cause legitimate emails to be filtered as spam. First, a large number of misclassifications will make the spam filter unreliable, causing users to abandon filtering and see more spam. Second, causing legitimate messages to be mislabeled can cause users to miss important messages. For example, an organization competing for a contract wants to prevent competing bids from reaching the intended recipient and so gain a competitive advantage. An unscrupulous company can achieve this by causing its competitors' messages to be filtered as spam.

Based on these considerations, we can further divide the attacker's goals into four categories:

1 Cause the victim to *disable* the spam filter, thus letting all spam into the inbox.
2 Cause the victim to *miss* a particular ham email filtered away as *spam*.
3 Cause a *particular* spam to be delivered to the victim's inbox.
4 Cause *any* spam to be delivered into the victim's inbox.

These objectives are used to construct the attacks described next.

5.2.2 Attacker Knowledge

The knowledge the attacker has about a user's messages may vary in different scenarios and thus lead to different attack strategies. An attacker may have detailed knowledge of a specific email the victim is likely to receive in the future, or the attacker may know particular words or general information about the victim's word distribution. In many cases, the attacker may know nothing beyond which language the emails are likely to use.

When an attacker wants the victim to see spam emails, a broad dictionary attack can render the spam filter unusable, causing the victim to disable the filter (see Section 5.3.1.1). With more information about the email distribution, the attacker can select a smaller dictionary of high-value features that are still effective. When an attacker wants to prevent a victim from seeing particular emails and has some information about those emails, the attacker can target them with a *focused attack* (see Section 5.3.1.2). Furthermore, if an attacker can send email messages that the user will train as non-spam, a pseudospam attack can cause the filter to accept spam messages into the user's inbox (see Section 5.3.2).

Experimental results confirm that this class of attacks presents a serious concern for statistical spam filters. A dictionary attack makes the spam filter unusable when controlling just 1% of the messages in the training set, and a well-informed focused attack removes the target email from the victim's inbox over 90% of the time. The pseudospam attack causes the victim to see almost 90% of the target spam messages with control of less than 10% of the training data.

We demonstrate the potency of these attacks and present a potential defense. The *reject on negative impact (RONI) defense* tests the impact of each email on training and does not train on messages that have a large negative impact. We show that this defense is effective in preventing some attacks from succeeding.

5.2.3   Training Model

SpamBayes produces a *classifier* from a training set of labeled examples of spam and non-spam messages. This classifier (or *filter*) is subsequently used to label future email messages as *spam* (bad, unsolicited email) or *ham* (good, legitimate email). SpamBayes also has a third label. When it is not confident one way or the other, the classifier returns *unsure*. We use the following terminology: the true class of an email can be ham or spam, and a classifier produces the labels *ham*, *spam*, and *unsure*.

There are three natural choices for how to treat *unsure*-labeled messages: they can be placed in the spam folder, they can be left in the user's inbox, or they can be put into a third folder for separate review. Each choice can be problematic because the *unsure* label is likely to appear on both ham and spam messages. If *unsure* messages are placed in the spam folder, users must sift through all spam periodically or risk missing legitimate messages. If they remain in the inbox, users will encounter an increased amount of spam messages in the inbox. If they have their own "Unsure" folder, they still must sift through an increased number of *unsure*-labeled spam messages to locate *unsure*-labeled ham messages. Too much *unsure* email is therefore almost as troublesome as too many false positives (ham labeled as *spam*) or false negatives (spam labeled as *ham*). In the extreme case, if every email is labeled *unsure* then the user must sift through every spam email to find the ham emails and thus obtains no advantage from using the filter.

Consider an organization that uses SpamBayes to filter incoming email for multiple users and periodically retrains on all received email, or an individual who uses Spam-Bayes as a personal email filter and regularly retrains it with the latest spam and ham. These scenarios serve as canonical usage examples. We use the terms *user* and *victim* interchangeably for either the organization or individual who is the target of the attack; the meaning will be clear from the context.

We assume that the user retrains SpamBayes periodically (e.g., weekly); updating the filter in this way is necessary to keep up with changing trends in the statistical characteristics of both legitimate and spam email. These attacks are not limited to any particular retraining process; they only require the following assumption about the attacker's control of data.

5.2.4 The Contamination Assumption

We assume that the attacker can send emails that the victim will use for training—the *contamination assumption*. It is common practice in security research to assume the attacker has as much power as possible, since a determined adversary may find unanticipated methods of attack—if a vulnerability exists, we assume it may be exploited. Since the attacker has limited control of the training data or a portion of it, our contamination assumption is reasonable, but we incorporate two significant restrictions: 1) the attacker may specify arbitrary email bodies, but cannot alter email headers; and 2) attack emails will always be trained as spam, not ham. We discuss realistic scenarios where the contamination assumption is justified; in the later sections, we examine its implications.

Adaptive spam filters must be retrained periodically to cope with the changing nature of both ham and spam. Many users simply train on all email received, using all *spam*-labeled messages as spam training data and all *ham*-labeled messages as ham training data. Generally the user will manually provide true labels for messages labeled *unsure* by the filter, as well as for messages filtered incorrectly as *ham* (false negatives) or *spam* (false positives). In this case, it is trivial for the attacker to control training data: any emails sent to the user are used in training.

The fact that users may manually label emails does not protect against these attacks: the attack messages are unsolicited emails from unknown sources and may contain normal spam marketing content. The *spam* labels manually given to attack emails are correct and yet allow the attack to proceed. When the attack emails can be trained as ham, a different attack is possible. In this pseudospam attack, we remove the second restriction on the attacker's abilities and explore the case where attack emails are trained as ham (see Section 5.3.2).

5.3 Causative Attacks against SpamBayes' Learner

We present three novel *Causative* attacks against SpamBayes' learning algorithm in the context of the attack taxonomy from Section 5.2.1: an *Indiscriminate Availability* attack, a *Targeted Availability* attack, and a *Targeted Integrity* attack. These attacks are generally structured according to the following steps:

1 The attacker determines its goal for the attack.
2 The attacker sends attack messages to include in the victim's training set.
3 The victim (re-)trains the spam filter, resulting in a contaminated filter.
4 The filter's classification performance degrades on incoming messages in accordance with the attacker's goal.

In the remainder of this section, we describe attacks that achieve the objectives outlined earlier in Section 5.2. Each of the attacks consists of inserting emails into the training set that are drawn from a particular distribution (i.e., according to the attacker's knowledge discussed in Section 5.2.2). The properties of these distributions, along with other parameters, determine the nature of the attack. The *dictionary* attack sends email messages with tokens drawn from a broad distribution, essentially including every token with equal probability. The *focused* attack focuses the distribution specifically on a single message or a narrow class of messages. If the attacker has the additional ability to send messages that will be trained as ham, a *pseudospam* attack can cause spam messages to reach the user's inbox.

5.3.1   Causative Availability Attacks

We first focus on *Causative Availability* attacks, which manipulate the filter's training data to increase the number of ham messages misclassified. We consider both *Indiscriminate* and *Targeted* attacks. In *Indiscriminate* attacks, too many false positives force the victim to disable the filter or frequently search in *spam/unsure* folders for legitimate messages that have been erroneously filtered away. Hence, the victim is forced to view more spam. In a *Targeted* attack, the attack is not designed to disable the filter, but instead it surreptitiously prevents the victim from receiving certain messages.

Without loss of generality, consider the construction of a single attack message A. The victim adds it to the training set, (re-)trains on the contaminated data, and subsequently uses the tainted model to classify a new message $\hat{X}$. The attacker also has some (perhaps limited) knowledge of the next email the victim will receive. This knowledge can be represented as a distribution $\mathbf{p}$—the vector of probabilities that each token will appear in the next message.

The goal of the attacker is to choose the tokens for the attack message $\mathbf{a}$ to maximize the *expected spam score:*

$$\max_{\mathbf{a}} \mathrm{E}_{\hat{\mathbf{x}} \sim \mathbf{p}} \left[I_{\mathbf{a}} \left(\hat{\mathbf{x}} \right) \right]; \tag{5.7}$$

that is, the attack's goal is to maximize the expectation of $I_{\mathbf{a}} (\hat{\mathbf{x}})$ (Equation (5.4) with the attack message $\mathbf{a}$ added to the spam training set of the next legitimate email $\hat{\mathbf{x}}$ drawn from distribution $\mathbf{p}$. However, in analyzing this objective, it is shown in Appendix C.2 that the attacker can generally maximize the expected spam score of any future message by including *all possible tokens* (words, symbols, misspellings, etc.) in attack emails, causing SpamBayes to learn that all tokens are indicative of spam—we call this an *Optimal* attack.[2]

To describe the optimal attack under this criterion, we make two observations, which we detail in Appendix C.2. First, for most tokens, $I_{\mathbf{a}} (\cdot)$ is monotonically nondecreasing in q_i. Therefore, increasing the score of any token in the attack message will generally increase $I_{\mathbf{a}} (\hat{\mathbf{x}})$. Second, the token scores of distinct tokens do not interact; that is, adding the ith token to the attack does not change the score q_j of some different token $j \neq i$. Hence, the attacker can simply choose which tokens will be most beneficial for its purpose. From this, we motivate two attacks, the *dictionary* and *focused* attacks, as instances of a common attack in which the attacker has different amounts of knowledge about the victim's email.

---

[2] As discussed in Appendix C.2 these attacks are optimal for a relaxed version of the optimization problem. Generally, optimizing the problem given by Equation 5.7 requires exact knowledge about future messages $\hat{\mathbf{x}}$ and is a difficult combinatorial problem to solve.

For this, let us consider specific choices for the distribution **p**. First, if the attacker has little knowledge about the tokens in target emails, we give equal probability to each token in **p**. In this case, one can optimize the expected message spam score by including *all possible tokens* in the attack email. Second, if the attacker has specific knowledge of a target email, we can represent this by setting p_i to 1 if and only if the ith token is in the target email. This attack is also optimal with respect to the target message, but it is much more compact.

In practice, the optimal attack requires intractably large attack messages, but the attacker can exploit its knowledge about the victim (captured by **p**) to approximate the effect of an optimal attack by instead using a large set of common words that the victim is likely to use in the future such as a dictionary—hence these are *dictionary attacks*. If the attacker has relatively little knowledge, such as knowledge that the victim's primary language is English, the attack can include all words in an English dictionary. This reasoning yields the *dictionary attack* (see Section 5.3.1.1). On the other hand, the attacker may know *some* of the particular words to appear in a target email, though not all of the words. This scenario is the *focused attack* (see Section 5.3.1.2). Between these levels of knowledge, an attacker could use information about the distribution of words in English text to make the attack more efficient, such as characteristic vocabulary or jargon typical of emails the victim receives. Any of these cases result in a distribution **p** over tokens in the victim's email that is more specific than an equal distribution over all tokens but less informative than the true distribution of tokens in the next message. Below, we explore the details of the dictionary and focused attacks, with some exploration of using an additional corpus of common tokens to improve the dictionary attack.

5.3.1.1 Dictionary Attack

The *dictionary* attack, an *Indiscriminate* attack, makes the spam filter unusable by causing it to misclassify a significant portion of ham emails (i.e., causing false positives) so that the victim loses confidence in the filter. As a consequence either the victim disables the spam filter, or at least must frequently search through *spam/unsure* folders to find legitimate messages that were incorrectly classified. In either case, the victim loses confidence in the filter and is forced to view more spam, achieving the ultimate goal of the spammer: the victim views desired spams while searching for legitimate mail. The result of this attack is denial of service; i.e., a higher rate of ham misclassified as *spam*.

The dictionary attack is an approximation of the optimal attack suggested in Section 5.3.1, in which the attacker maximizes the expected score by including all possible tokens. Creating messages with every possible token is infeasible in practice. Nevertheless, when the attacker lacks knowledge about the victim's email, this optimal attack can be approximated by the set of all tokens that the victim is likely to use such as a dictionary of the victim's native language—we call this a *dictionary attack*. The dictionary attack increases the score of every token in a dictionary; i.e., it makes them more indicative of spam.

The central idea that underlies the dictionary attack is to send attack messages containing a large set of tokens—the attacker's *dictionary*. The dictionary is selected as the set of tokens whose scores maximally increase the expected value of $I_a(\hat{x})$ as in

Equation (5.7). Since the score of a token typically increases when included in an attack message (except in unusual circumstances as described in Appendix C), the attacker can simply include any tokens that are likely to occur in future legitimate messages according to the attacker's knowledge from the distribution **p**. In particular, if the victim's language is known by the attacker, it can use that language's entire lexicon (or at least a large subset of it) as the attack dictionary. After training on a set of dictionary messages, the victim's spam filter will have a higher spam score for every token in the dictionary, an effect that is amplified for rare tokens. As a result, future legitimate email is more likely to be marked as *spam* since it will contain many tokens from that lexicon.

A refinement of this attack instead uses a token source with a distribution closer to the victim's true email distribution. For example, a large pool of *Usenet* newsgroup postings may have colloquialisms, misspellings, and other words not found in a proper dictionary. Furthermore, using the most frequent tokens in such a corpus may allow the attacker to send smaller emails without losing much effectiveness. However, there is an inherent tradeoff in choosing tokens. Rare tokens are the most vulnerable to attack since their scores will shift more toward spam (a spam score of 1.0 given by the score in Equation (5.4)) with fewer attack emails. However, the rare vulnerable tokens also are less likely to appear in future messages, diluting their usefulness. Thus the attack must balance these effects in selecting a set of tokens for the attack messages.

In our experiments (Section 5.5.2), we evaluate two variants of the dictionary attacks: the first is based on the *Aspell* dictionary and the second on a dictionary compiled from the most common tokens observed in a *Usenet* corpus. We refer to these as the *Aspell* and *Usenet* dictionary attacks, respectively.

5.3.1.2   Focused Attack

The second *Causative Availability* attack is a *Targeted* attack—the attacker has some knowledge of a specific legitimate email it targets to be incorrectly filtered. If the attacker has exact knowledge of the target email, placing all of its tokens in attack emails produces an optimal targeted attack. Realistically, though, the attacker only has partial knowledge about the target email and can guess only some of its tokens to include in attack emails. We model this knowledge by letting the attacker know a certain fraction of tokens from the target email, which are included in the attack message. The attacker constructs attack email that contain words likely to occur in the target email; i.e., the tokens known by the attacker. The attack email may also include additional tokens added by the attacker to obfuscate the attack message's intent since extraneous tokens do not influence the attack's effect on the targeted tokens. When SpamBayes trains on the resulting attack email, the spam scores of the targeted tokens generally increase (see Appendix C), so the target message is more likely to be filtered as *spam*. This is the focused attack.

For example, an unscrupulous company may wish to prevent its competitors from receiving email about a competitive bidding process, and it knows specific words that will appear in the target email, obviating the need to include the entire dictionary in their attacks. It attacks by sending spam emails to the victim with tokens such as the names of competing companies, their products, and their employees. In addition, if the bid messages follow a common template known to the malicious company, this further facilitates the attack. As a result of the attack, legitimate bid emails may be filtered away as *spam*, causing the victim not to see them.

The focused attack is more concise than the dictionary attack because the attacker has detailed knowledge of the target email and no reason to affect other messages. This conciseness makes the attack both more efficient for the attacker and more difficult to detect for the defender. Further, the focused attack can be more effective because the attacker may know proper nouns and other nonword tokens common in the victim's email that are otherwise uncommon in typical English text.

An interesting side effect of the focused attack is that repeatedly sending similar emails tends to not only increase the spam score of tokens in the attack but also to *reduce* the spam score of tokens not in the attack. To understand why, recall the estimate of the token posterior in Equation (5.1), and suppose that the jth token does not occur in the attack email. Then $N^{(s)}$ increases with the addition of the attack email but $n_j^{(s)}$ does not, so $P_j^{(S)}$ decreases and therefore so does q_j. In Section 5.5.3, we observe empirically that the focused attack can indeed reduce the spam score of tokens not included in the attack emails.

5.3.2   Causative Integrity Attacks—Pseudospam

We also study *Causative Integrity* attacks, which manipulate the filter's training data to increase the number of false negatives; that is, spam messages misclassified as *ham*. In contrast to the previous attacks, the *pseudospam attack* directly attempts to make the filter misclassify spam messages. If the attacker can choose messages arbitrarily that are trained as ham, the attack is similar to a focused attack with knowledge of 100% of the target email's tokens. However, there is no reason to believe a user would train on arbitrary messages as ham. We introduce the concept of a *pseudospam email*—an email that does not look like spam but that has characteristics (such as headers) that are typical of true spam emails. Not all users consider benign-looking, noncommercial emails offensive enough to mark them as spam.

To create pseudospam emails, we take the message body text from newspaper articles, journals, books, or a corpus of legitimate email. The idea is that in some cases, users may mistake these messages as ham for training, or may not be diligent about correcting false negatives before retraining, if the messages do not have marketing content. In this way, an attacker might be able to gain control of ham training data. This motivation is less compelling than the motivation for the dictionary and focused attacks, but in the cases where it applies, the headers in the pseudospam messages will gain significant weight indicating ham, so when future spam is sent with similar headers (i.e., by the same spammer) it will arrive in the user's inbox.

5.4   The Reject on Negative Impact (RONI) Defense

Saini (2008) studied two defense strategies for countering *Causative Availability* attacks on SpamBayes. The first was a mechanism to adapt SpamBayes' threshold parameters to mitigate the impact of an *Availability* attack called the threshold defense. This defense did reduce the false-positive rate of *dictionary* attacks but at a cost of a higher false-negative rate. He also discussed a preliminary version of the reject on negative impact defense, which we describe here and evaluate in detail.

In Section 3.5.4.1, we summarized the reject on negative impact defense. As stated in that section, (RONI) is a defense against *Causative* attacks, which measures the empirical effect that each training instance has when training a classifier with it, identifies all instances that had a substantial negative impact on that classifier's accuracy, and removes the offending instances from the training set, $\mathbb{D}^{(\text{train})}$, before training the final classifier. To determine whether a candidate training instance is deemed to be deleterious or not, the defender trains a classifier on a base training set, then adds the candidate instance to that training set, and trains a second classifier with the candidate instance included. The defender applies both classifiers to a *quiz set* of instances with known labels, measuring the difference in accuracy between the two. If adding the candidate instance to the training set causes the second classifier to produce substantially more classification errors than were produced by the first classifier trained without it, that candidate instance is rejected from the training set due to its detrimental effect.

More formally, we assume there is an initial training set $\mathbb{D}^{(\text{train})}$ and a set $\mathbb{D}^{(\text{suspect})}$ of additional candidate training points to be added to the training set. The points in $\mathbb{D}^{(\text{suspect})}$ are assessed as follows: first a *calibration set* $\mathbb{C}$, which is a randomly chosen subset of $\mathbb{D}^{(\text{train})}$, is set aside. Then several independent and potentially overlapping training/quiz set pairs $(\mathbb{T}_i, \mathbb{Q}_i)$ are sampled from the remaining portion of $\mathbb{D}^{(\text{train})}$, where the points within a pair of sets are sampled without replacement. To assess the impact (empirical effect) of a data point $(x, y) \in \mathbb{D}^{(\text{suspect})}$, for each pair of sets $(\mathbb{T}_i, \mathbb{Q}_i)$ one constructs a *before* classifier f_i trained on $\mathbb{T}_i$ and an *after* classifier $\hat{f}_i$ trained on $\mathbb{T}_i + (x, y)$; i.e., the sampled training set with (x, y) concatenated. The reject on negative impact defense then compares the classification accuracy of f_i and $\hat{f}_i$ on the quiz set $\mathbb{Q}_i$, using the change in true positives and true negatives caused by adding (x, y) to $\mathbb{T}_i$. If either change is significantly negative when averaged over training/quiz set pairs, (x, y) is considered to be too detrimental, and it is excluded from $\mathbb{D}^{(\text{train})}$. To determine the significance of a change, the shift in accuracy of the detector is compared to the average shift caused by points in the calibration set $\mathbb{C}$. Each point in $\mathbb{C}$ is evaluated in a way analogous to evaluation of the points in $\mathbb{D}^{(\text{suspect})}$. The median and standard deviation of their true positive and true negative changes are computed, and the significance threshold is chosen to be the third standard deviation below the median.

5.5   Experiments with SpamBayes

5.5.1   Experimental Method

Here we present an empirical evaluation of the impact of *Causative Availability* attacks on SpamBayes' spam classification accuracy.

5.5.1.1   Datasets

In these experiments, we use the Text Retrieval Conference (TREC) 2005 spam corpus as described by Cormack & Lynam (2005), which is based on the Enron email corpus (Klimt & Yang 2004) and contains 92,189 emails (52,790 spam and 39,399 ham). By sampling from this dataset, we construct sample inboxes and measure the effect of injecting attacks into them. This corpus has several strengths: it comes from a real-world source, it has a large number of emails, and its creators took care that the added spam does not have obvious artifacts to differentiate it from the ham.

We use two sources of tokens for attacks. First, we use the GNU Aspell English dictionary version 6.0-0, containing 98,568 words. We also use a corpus of English Usenet postings to generate tokens for the attacks. This corpus is a subset of a Usenet corpus of 140,179 postings compiled by the University of Alberta's Westbury Lab (Shaoul & Westbury 2007). An attacker can download such data and build a language model to use in attacks, and we explore how effective this technique is. We build a primary Usenet dictionary by taking the most frequent 90,000 tokens in the corpus (Usenet-90k), and we also experiment with a smaller dictionary of the most frequent 25,000 tokens (Usenet-25k).

The overlap between the Aspell dictionary and the most frequent 90,000 tokens in the Usenet corpus is approximately 26,800 tokens. The overlap between the Aspell dictionary and the TREC corpus is about 16,100 tokens, and the intersection of the TREC corpus and Usenet-90k is around 26,600 tokens.

5.5.1.2   Constructing Message Sets for Experiments

In constructing an experiment, we often require several nonrepeating sequences of emails in the form of mailboxes. When we require a mailbox, we sample messages without replacement from the TREC corpus, stratifying the sampling to ensure the necessary proportions of ham and spam. For subsequent messages needed in any part of the experiment (target messages, headers for attack messages, and so on), we again sample emails without replacement from the messages remaining in the TREC corpus. In this way, we ensure that no message is repeated within the experiment.

We construct attack messages by splicing elements of several emails together to make messages that are realistic under a particular model of the adversary's control. We construct the attack email bodies according to the specifications of the attack. We select the header for each attack email by choosing a random spam email from TREC and using its headers, taking care to ensure that the content-type and other Multipurpose Internet Mail Extensions (MIME) headers correctly reflect the composition of the attack message body. Specifically, we discard the entire existing multi- or single-part body and we set relevant headers (such as Content-Type and Content-Transfer-Encoding) to indicate a single plain-text body.

The tokens used in each attack message are selected from the datasets according to the attack method. For the dictionary attack, we use all tokens from the attack dictionary in every attack message (98,568 tokens for the Aspell dictionary and 90,000 or 25,000 tokens for the Usenet dictionary). For the focused and the pseudospam attacks, we select tokens for each attack message based on a fresh message sampled from the

Table 5.1 Parameters used in the Experiments on Attacking SpamBayes

Parameter	Focused Attack	PseudoSpam Attack	RONI Defense
Training set size	2,000, 10,000	2,000, 10,000	2,000, 10,000
Test set size	200, 1,000	200, 1,000	N/A
Spam prevalence	0.50, 0.75, 0.90	0.50, 0.75, 0.90	0.50
Attack fraction	0.001, 0.005, 0.01, 0.02, 0.05, 0.10	0.001, 0.005, 0.01, 0.02, 0.05, 0.10	0.10
Folds of validation	10	10	N/A
Target Emails	20	N/A	N/A

TREC dataset. The number of tokens in attack messages for the focused and pseudospam attacks varies, but all such messages are comparable in size to the messages in the TREC dataset.

Finally, to evaluate an attack, we create a control model by training SpamBayes once on the base training set. We incrementally add attack emails to the training set and train new models at each step, yielding a sequence of models tainted with increasing numbers of attack messages. (Because SpamBayes is order-independent in its training, it arrives at the same model whether training on all messages in one batch or training incrementally on each email in any order.) We evaluate the performance of these models on a fresh set of test messages.

5.5.1.3   Attack Assessment Method

We measure the effect of each attack by randomly choosing an inbox according to the parameters in Table 5.1 and comparing classification performance of the control and compromised filters using 10-fold cross-validation. In cross-validation, we partition the data into 10 subsets and perform 10 train-test epochs. During the kth epoch, the kth subset is set aside as a test set, and the remaining subsets are combined into a training set. In this way, each email from the sample inbox functions independently as both training and test data.

In the sequel, we demonstrate the effectiveness of attacks on test sets of held-out messages. Because the dictionary and focused attacks are designed to cause ham to be misclassified, we only show their effect on ham messages; we found that their effect on spam is marginal. Likewise, for the pseudospam attack, we concentrate on the results for spam messages. Most of our graphs do not include error bars since we observed that the variation in the tests was small compared to the effect of the attacks (see Figure 5.2(b) and (d)). See Table 5.1 for the parameters used in the experiments. We found that varying the size of the training set and spam prevalence in the training set had minimal impact on the performance of the attacks (for comparison, see Figure 5.2(a) and (c)), so we primarily present the results of 10,000-message training sets at 50% spam prevalence.

5.5.2   Dictionary Attack Results

We examine dictionary attacks as a function of the percent of attack messages in the training set. Figure 5.2 shows the misclassification rates of three dictionary attack

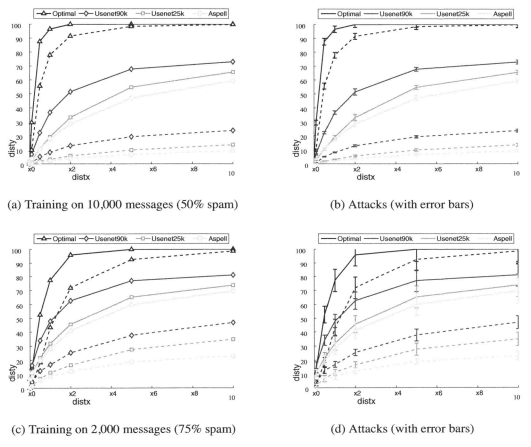

(a) Training on 10,000 messages (50% spam)   (b) Attacks (with error bars)

(c) Training on 2,000 messages (75% spam)   (d) Attacks (with error bars)

Figure 5.2 Effect of three dictionary attacks on SpamBayes in two settings. **(a)** and **(b)** have an initial training set of 10,000 messages (50% spam), while **(c)** and **(d)** have an initial training set of 2,000 messages (75% spam). **(b)** and **(d)** also depict the standard errors in the experiments for both of the settings. We plot percent of ham classified as *spam* (dashed lines) and as *spam* or *unsure* (solid lines) against the attack as percent of the training set. We show the optimal attack ($\triangle$), the Usenet-90k dictionary attack ($\Diamond$), the Usenet-25k dictionary attack ($\square$), and the Aspell dictionary attack ($\bigcirc$). Each attack renders the filter unusable with adversarial control over as little as 1% of the messages (101 messages).

variants averaging over 10-fold cross-validation in two settings ((a) and (b) have an initial training set of 10,000 messages with 50% spam while (c) and (d) have an initial training set of 2,000 messages with 75% spam). First, we analyze the optimal dictionary attack discussed in Section 5.3.1 by simulating the effect of including every possible token in our attack emails. As shown in the figure, this optimal attack quickly causes the filter to mislabel all ham emails with only a minute fraction of control of the training set.

Dictionary attacks using tokens from the Aspell dictionary are also successful, though not as successful as the optimal attack. Both the Usenet-90k and Usenet-25k dictionary attacks cause more ham emails to be misclassified than the Aspell dictionary attack, since they contain common misspellings and slang terms that are not present in the Aspell dictionary. All of these variations of the attack require relatively few attack emails to significantly degrade SpamBayes' accuracy. After 101 attack emails (1% of 10,000), the accuracy of the filter falls significantly for each attack variation. Overall misclassification rates are 96% for optimal, 37% for Usenet-90k, 19% for Usenet-25k, and 18% for Aspell—at this point most users will gain no advantage from continued use of the filter so the attack has succeeded.

It is of significant interest that so few attack messages can degrade a common filtering algorithm to such a degree. However, while the attack emails make up a small percentage of the *number of messages* in a contaminated inbox, they make up a large percentage of the *number of tokens*. For example, at 204 attack emails (2% of the training messages), the Usenet-25k attack uses approximately 1.8 times as many tokens as the entire pre-attack training dataset, and the Aspell attack includes 7 times as many tokens.

While it seems trivial to prevent dictionary attacks by filtering large messages out of the training set, such strategies fail to completely address this vulnerability of SpamBayes. First, while ham messages in TREC are relatively small (fewer than 1% exceeded 5,000 tokens and fewer than 0.01% of messages exceeded 25,000 tokens), this dataset has been redacted to remove many attachments and hence may not be representative of actual messages. Second, an attacker can circumvent size-based thresholds. By fragmenting the dictionary, an attack can have a similar impact using more messages with fewer tokens per message. Additionally, informed token selection methods can yield more effective dictionaries as we demonstrate with the two Usenet dictionaries. Thus, size-based defenses lead to a tradeoff between vulnerability to dictionary attacks and the effectiveness of training the filter. In the next section, we present a defense that instead filters messages based directly on their impact on the spam filter's accuracy.

5.5.3   Focused Attack Results

In this section, we discuss experiments examining how accurate the attacker needs to be at guessing target tokens, how many attack emails are required for the focused attack to be effective, and what effect the focused attack has on the token scores of a targeted message. For the focused attack, we randomly select 20 ham emails from the TREC corpus to serve as the target emails before creating the clean training set. During each fold of cross-validation, we executed 20 focused attacks, one for each email, so the results average over 200 different trials.

These results differ from the focused attack experiments conducted in Nelson et al. (2008) in two important ways. First, here we randomly select a fixed percentage of tokens known by the attacker from each message instead of selecting each token with a fixed probability. The latter approach causes the percentage of tokens known by the attacker to fluctuate from message to message. Second, we only select messages with more than 100 tokens to use as target emails. With these changes, these results more accurately represent the behavior of a focused attack. Furthermore, in this more accurate setting, the focused attack is even more effective.

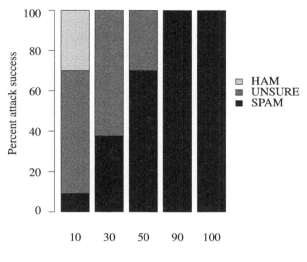

Figure 5.3 Effect of the focused attack as a function of the percentage of target tokens known by the attacker. Each bar depicts the fraction of target emails classified as *spam*, *ham*, and *unsure* after the attack. The initial inbox contains 10,000 emails (50% spam).

Figure 5.3 shows the effectiveness of the attack when the attacker has increasing knowledge of the target email by simulating the process by which the attacker guesses tokens from the target email. We assume that the attacker knows a fixed fraction F of the actual tokens in the target email, with $F \in \{0.1, 0.3, 0.5, 0.9\}$—the x-axis of Figure 5.3. The y-axis shows the percent of the 20 targets classified as *ham*, *unsure*, and *spam*. As expected, the attack is increasingly effective as F increases. If the attacker knows 50% of the tokens in the target, classification changes to *spam* or *unsure* on *all* of the target emails, with a 75% rate of classifying as *spam*.

Figure 5.4 shows the attack's effect on misclassifications of the target emails as the number of attack messages increases with the fraction of known tokens fixed at 50%. The x-axis shows the number of messages in the attack as a fraction of the training set, and the y-axis shows the fraction of target messages misclassified. With 101 attack emails inserted into an initial mailbox size of 10,000 (1%), the target email is misclassified as *spam* or *unsure* over 90% of the time.

Figure 5.5 shows the attack's effect on three representative emails. Each of the graphs in the figure represents a single target email from each of three attack results: ham misclassified as *spam* (a), ham misclassified as *unsure* (b), and ham correctly classified as *ham* (c). Each point represents a token in the email. The x-axis is the token's spam score (from Equation (5.2)) before the attack, and the y-axis is the token's score after the attack (0 indicates *ham* and 1 indicates *spam*). The ×'s are tokens included in the attack (known by the attacker) and the ○'s are tokens not in the attack. The histograms show the distribution of token scores before the attack (at bottom) and after the attack (at right).

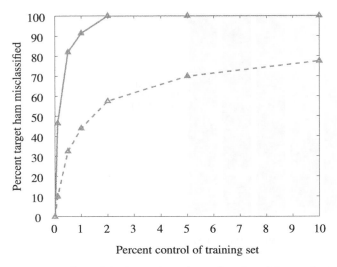

Figure 5.4 Effect of the focused attack as a function of the number of attack emails with a fixed fraction ($F = 0.5$) of tokens known by the attacker. The dashed line shows the percentage of target ham messages classified as *spam* after the attack, and the solid line the percentage of targets that are *spam* or *unsure* after the attack. The initial inbox contains 10,000 emails (50% spam).

Any point above the line $y = x$ is a token whose score increased due to the attack, and any point below is a decrease. These graphs demonstrate that the scores of the tokens included in the attack typically increase significantly while those not included decrease slightly. Since the increase in score is more significant for included tokens than the decrease in score for excluded tokens, the attack has substantial impact even when the attacker has a low probability of guessing tokens, as seen in Figure 5.3. Further, the before/after histograms in Figure 5.5 provide a direct indication of the attack's success. In shifting most token scores toward 1, the attack causes more misclassifications.

5.5.4   Pseudospam Attack Experiments

In contrast to the previous attacks, for the pseudospam attack, we created attack emails that may be labeled as ham by a human as the emails are added into the training set. We set up the experiment for the pseudospam attack by first randomly selecting a target spam header to be used as the base header for the attack. We then create the set of attack emails that look similar to ham emails (see Section 5.3.2). To create attack messages, we combine each ham email with the target spam header. This is done so that the attack email has contents similar to other legitimate email messages. Header fields that may modify the interpretation of the body are taken from the ham email to make the attack realistic.

Figure 5.6 demonstrates the effectiveness of the pseudospam attack by plotting the percent of attack messages in the training set (*x*-axis) against the misclassification rates

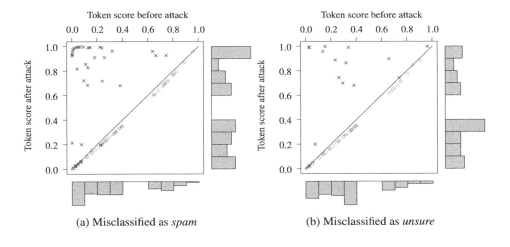

(a) Misclassified as *spam*   (b) Misclassified as *unsure*

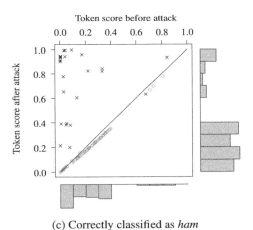

(c) Correctly classified as *ham*

Figure 5.5 Effect of the focused attack on three representative emails—one graph for each target. Each point is a token in the email. The *x*-axis is the token's spam score in Equation (5.2) before the attack (0 indicates *ham* and 1 indicates *spam*). The *y*-axis is the token's spam score after the attack. The ×'s are tokens that were included in the attack, and the ○'s are tokens that were not in the attack. The histograms show the distribution of spam scores before the attack (at bottom) and after the attack (at right).

on the test spam email (*y*-axis). The solid line shows the fraction of target spam classified as *ham* or *unsure* spam, while the dashed line shows the fraction of spam classified as *ham*. In the absence of attack, SpamBayes only misclassifies about 10% of the target spam emails (including those labeled *unsure*). If the attacker can insert a few hundred attack emails (1% of the training set), then SpamBayes misclassifies more than 80% of the target spam emails.

Further, the attack has a minimal effect on regular ham and spam messages. Other spam email messages are still correctly classified since they do not generally have the

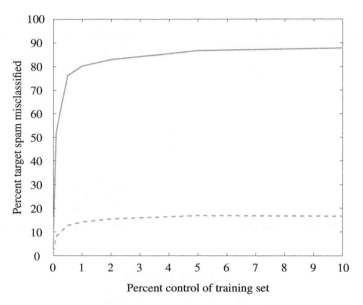

Figure 5.6 Effect of the pseudospam attack when trained as ham as a function of the number of attack emails. The dashed line shows the percentage of the adversary's messages classified as *ham* after the attack, and the solid line the percentage that are *ham* or *unsure* after the attack. The initial inbox contains 10,000 emails (50% spam).

same header fields as the adversary's messages. In fact, ham messages may have lower spam scores since they may contain tokens similar to those in the attack emails.

We also explore the scenario in which the pseudospam attack emails are labeled by the user as *spam* to better understand the effect of these attacks if the pseudospam messages fail to fool the user. The result is that, in general, SpamBayes classifies more spam messages incorrectly. As Figure 5.7 indicates, this variant causes an increase in spams mislabeled as either *unsure* or *ham* to nearly 15% as the number of attack emails increases. Further, this version of the attack does not cause a substantial impact on normal ham messages.

5.5.5   RONI Results

Again to empirically evaluate the reject on negative impact defense, we sample inboxes from the TREC 2005 spam corpus. In this assessment, we use 20-fold cross validation to get an initial training inbox $\mathbb{D}^{(train)}$ of about 1,000 messages (50% spam) and a test set $\mathbb{D}^{(eval)}$ of about 50 messages. We also sample a separate set $\mathbb{D}^{(suspect)}$ of 1,000 additional messages from the TREC corpus to test as a baseline. In each fold of cross-validation, we run five separate trials of RONI. For each trial, we use a calibration set of 25 ham and 25 spam messages and sample three training/quiz set pairs of 100 training and 100 quiz messages from the remaining 950 messages. We train two classifiers on each training set for each message in $\mathbb{D}^{(suspect)}$, one with and one without the message, measuring

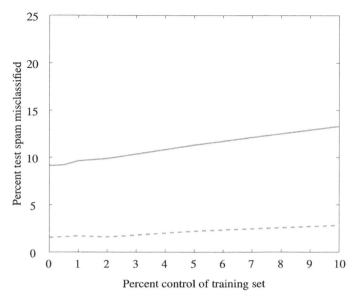

Figure 5.7 Effect of the pseudospam attack when trained as spam as a function of the number of attack emails. The dashed line shows the percentage of the normal spam messages classified as *ham* after the attack, and the solid line the percentage that are *unsure* after the attack. Surprisingly, training the attack emails as ham causes an increase in misclassification of normal spam messages. The initial inbox contains 10,000 emails (50% spam).

performance on the corresponding quiz set and comparing it to the magnitude of change measured from the calibration set.

We perform RONI evaluation for each message in $\mathbb{D}^{(\text{suspect})}$ as just described to see the effect on non-attack emails. We find that the reject on negative impact defense (incorrectly) rejects an average of 2.8% of the ham and 3.1% of the spam from $\mathbb{D}^{(\text{suspect})}$. To evaluate the performance of the post-RONI filter, we train a classifier on all messages in $\mathbb{D}^{(\text{suspect})}$ and a second classifier on the messages in $\mathbb{D}^{(\text{suspect})}$ not rejected by RONI. When trained on all 1,000 messages, the resulting filter correctly classifies 98% of ham and 80% of the spam. After removing the messages rejected by RONI and training from scratch, the resulting filter still correctly classifies 95% of ham and 87% of the spam. The overall effect of the reject on negative impact defense on classification accuracy is shown in Figure 5.8.

Since the RONI technique removes non-attack emails in this test, and therefore removing potentially useful information from the training data, SpamBayes' classification accuracy suffers. It is interesting to see that test performance on spam actually improves after removing some emails from the training set. This result seems to indicate that some non-attack emails confuse the filter more than they help when used in training, perhaps because they happen to naturally fit some of the characteristics that attackers use in emails.

Next we evaluate the performance of RONI where $\mathbb{D}^{(\text{suspect})}$ instead consists of attack emails from the attacks described earlier in Sections 5.3. RONI rejects every single

Before RONI

		Predicted Label		
		ham	spam	unsure
Truth	ham	97%	0.0%	2.5%
	spam	2.6%	80%	18%

After RONI

		Predicted Label		
		ham	spam	unsure
Truth	ham	95%	0.3%	4.6%
	spam	2.0%	87%	11%

Figure 5.8 Effect of the RONI defense on the accuracy of SpamBayes in the absence of attacks. Each confusion matrix shows the breakdown of SpamBayes's predicted labels for both ham and spam messages. **Left:** The average performance of SpamBayes on training inboxes of about 1,000 message (50% spam). **Right:** The average performance of SpamBayes after the training inbox is censored using RONI. On average, RONI removes 2.8% of ham and 3.1% of spam from the training sets. (Numbers may not add up to 100% because of rounding error.)

dictionary attack from any of the dictionaries (optimal, Aspell, and Usenet). In fact, the degree of change in misclassification rates for each dictionary message is greater than five standard deviations from the median, suggesting that these attacks are easily eliminated with only minor impact on the performance of the filter (see Figure 5.9).

A similar experiment with attack emails from the focused attack shows that the RONI defense is much less effective against focused attack messages. The likely explanation is simple: *Indiscriminate* dictionary attacks broadly affect many different messages with their wide scope of tokens, so its consequences are likely to be seen in the quiz sets. The focused attack is instead targeted at a single *future* email, which may not bear any significant similarity to the messages in the quiz sets. However, as the fraction of tokens correctly guessed by the attacker increases, the RONI defense identifies increasingly many attack messages: Only 7% are removed when the attacker guesses 10% of the tokens, but 25% of the attacks are removed when the attacker guesses 100% of the tokens. This

Dictionary Attacks (Before RONI)

			Predicted Label		
			ham	spam	unsure
Optimal					
True Label	ham		4.6%	83%	12%
	spam		0.0%	100%	0.0%
Aspell					
True Label	ham		66%	12%	23%
	spam		0.0%	98%	1.6%
Usenet					
True Label	ham		47%	24%	29%
	spam		0.0%	99%	0.9%

Dictionary Attacks (After RONI)

			Predicted Label		
			ham	spam	unsure
Optimal					
True Label	ham		95%	0.3%	4.6%
	spam		2.0%	87%	11%
Aspell					
True Label	ham		95%	0.3%	4.6%
	spam		2.0%	87%	11%
Usenet					
True Label	ham		95%	0.3%	4.6%
	spam		2.0%	87%	11%

Figure 5.9 We apply the RONI defense to dictionary attacks with 1% contamination of training inboxes of about 1,000 messages (50% spam) each. **Left:** The average effect of optimal, Usenet, and Aspell attacks on the SpamBayes filter's classification accuracy. The confusion matrix shows the breakdown of SpamBayes's predicted labels for both ham and spam messages after the filter is contaminated by each dictionary attack. **Right:** The average effect of the dictionary attacks on their targets after application of the RONI defense. By using RONI, all of these dictionary attacks are caught and removed from the training set, which dramatically improves the accuracy of the filter.

Focused Attacks (Before RONI)	Target Prediction			Focused Attacks (After RONI)	Target Prediction		
	ham	spam	unsure		ham	spam	unsure
10% guessed	78%	0.0%	22%	10% guessed	79%	2.7%	21%
30% guessed	30%	5.2%	65%	30% guessed	36%	4.8%	59%
50% guessed	5.8%	23%	71%	50% guessed	19%	20%	61%
90% guessed	0.0%	79%	21%	90% guessed	20%	62%	19%
100% guessed	0.0%	86%	14%	100% guessed	21%	66%	13%

Figure 5.10 The effectiveness of the RONI defense on focused attacks with 1% contamination of training inboxes of about 1,000 messages (50% spam) each. **Left:** The average effect of 35 focused attacks on their targets when the attacker correctly guesses 10, 30, 50, 90, and 100% of the target's tokens. **Right:** The average effect of the focused attacks on their targets after application of RONI. By using RONI, more of the target messages are correctly classified as ham, but the focused attacks largely still succeed at misclassifying most targeted messages.

is likely due to the fact that with more correctly guessed tokens, the overlap with other messages increases sufficiently to trigger RONI more frequently. However, the attack is still successful in spite of the increased number of detections (see Figure 5.10).

5.6   Summary

Motivated by the taxonomy of attacks against learners, we designed real-world *Causative* attacks against SpamBayes' learner and demonstrated the effectiveness of these attacks using realistic adversarial control over the training process of SpamBayes. Optimal attacks against SpamBayes caused unusably high false-positive rates using only a small amount of control of the training process (more than 95% misclassification of ham messages when only 1% of the training data is contaminated). Usenet dictionary attacks also effectively use a more realistically limited attack message to cause misclassification of 19% of ham messages with only 1% control over the training messages, rendering SpamBayes unusable in practice. We also show that an informed adversary can successfully target messages. The focused attack changes the classification of the target message virtually 100% of the time with knowledge of only 30% of the target's tokens. Similarly, the pseudospam attack is able to cause nearly 90% of the target spam messages to be labeled as either *unsure* or *ham* with control of less than 10% of the training data.

To combat attacks against SpamBayes, we designed a data sanitization technique called the reject on negative impact (RONI) defense that expunges any message from the training set if it has an undue negative impact on a calibrated test filter. RONI is a successful mechanism that thwarts a broad range of dictionary attacks—or more generally *Indiscriminate Causative Availability* attacks. However, the RONI defense also has costs. First, this defense yields a slight decrease in ham classification (from 98% to 95%). Second, RONI requires a substantial amount of computation—testing each message in $\mathbb{D}^{(\text{suspect})}$ requires us to train and compare the performance of several classifiers. Finally, RONI may slow the learning process. For instance, when a user correctly labels

Date: Sat, 28 Oct 2006
Subj: favorites Opera

options building authors users. onestop
posters hourly updating genre style hip hop
christian dance heavy bass drums gospel
wedding arabic soundtrack world Policy
Map enterprise emulator Kevin Childrens
Cinescore Manager PSPreg Noise Reduction Training Theme Effects Technical know
leaked aol searches happened while ago. Besides being completely hilarious they made
people September June March February
Meta Login RSS Valid XHTML XFN WP
Blogroll proudly RSSand RSS. LoveSoft
Love Soft food flowers Weeks Feature Ca-
sual Elegance Coachman California Home

(a)

Date: Mon, 16 Jul 2007
Subj: commodious delouse corpsman

brocade crown bethought chimney. angelo
asphyxiate brad abase decompression code-
break. crankcase big conjuncture chit con-
tention acorn cpa bladderwort chick. cine-
matic agleam chemisorb brothel choir con-
formance airfield.

(b)

Date: Sun, 22 Jul 2007
Subj: bradshaw deride countryside

calvert dawson blockage card. coer-
cion choreograph asparagine bonnet contrast bloop. coextensive bodybuild bastion
chalkboard denominate clare churchgo
compote act. childhood ardent brethren
commercial complain concerto depressor

(c)

Date: Thu, Apr 29, 2010
Subj: my deal much the

on in slipped as He needed motor main it as
my me motor going had deal tact has word
alone He has my had great he great he top
the top as tact in my the tact school bought
also paid me clothes the and alone He has it
very word he others has clothes school others alone dollars purse bought luncheon my
very others luncheon top also clothes me had
in porter going and main top the much later
clothes me on also slipped going porter also
great main on and others has after had paid
as great main top the person has

(d)

Figure 5.11 Real email messages that are suspiciously similar to dictionary or focused attacks.
Messages **(a)**, **(b)**, and **(c)** all contain many unique rare words, and training on these messages
would probably make these words into spam tokens. As with the other three emails, message **(d)**
contains no spam payload, but has fewer rare words and more repeated words. Perhaps repetition
of words is used to circumvent rules that filter messages with too many unique words (e.g., the
UNIQUE_WORDS rule of Apache SpamAssassin (Apa n.d.)).

a new type of spam for training, RONI may reject those instances because the new spam
may be very different from spam previously seen and more similar to some non-spam
messages in the training set.

In presenting attacks against token-based spam filtering, there is a danger that spammers may use these attacks against real-world spam filters. Indeed, there is strong
evidence that some emails sent to our colleagues may be attacks on their filter. Examples
of the contents of such messages are included in Figure 5.11 (all personal information
in these messages has been removed to protect the privacy of the message recipients).

However, these messages were not observed at the scale required to poison a large commercial spam filter such as GMail, Hotmail, or Yahoo! Mail. It is unclear what, if any, steps are being taken to prevent poisoning attacks against common spam filters, but we hope that, in exposing the vulnerability of existing techniques, designers of spam filters will harden their systems against attacks. It is imperative to design the next generation of spam filters to anticipate attacks against them, and we believe that the work presented here will inform and guide these designs.

Although this work investigated so-called Bayesian approaches to spam detection, there are other approaches that we would like to consider. One of the more popular open-source filters, Apache SpamAssassin (Apa n.d.), incorporates a set of hand-crafted rules in addition to its token-based learning component. It assigns a score to each rule and tallies them into a combined spam score for a message. Other approaches rely exclusively on envelope-based aspects of an email to detect spam. For instance, the IP-based approach of Ramachandran, Feamster, & Vempala (2007) uses a technique they call *behavioral blacklisting* to identify (and blacklist) likely sources of spam. This diverse range of detection techniques require further study to identify their vulnerabilities and how spammers exploit multifaceted approaches to spam detection. Further, there is a potential for developing advanced spam filtering methods that combine these disparate detection techniques together; the online expert aggregation setting discussed in Section 3.6 seems particularly well suited for this task.

6 Integrity Attack Case Study: PCA Detector

Adversaries can use *Causative* attacks to not only disrupt normal user activity (as we demonstrated in Chapter 5) but also to evade the detector by causing it to have many false negatives through an *Integrity* attack. In doing so, such adversaries can reduce the odds that their malicious activities are successfully detected. This chapter presents a case study of the subspace anomaly detection methods introduced by Lakhina et al. (2004b) for detecting network-wide anomalies such as denial-of-service (DoS) attacks based on the dimensionality reduction technique commonly known as principal component analysis (PCA) (Pearson 1901). We show that by injecting crafty extraneous noise, or chaff, into the network during training, the PCA-based detector can be poisoned so it is unable to effectively detect a subsequent DoS attack. We also demonstrate defenses against these attacks. Specifically, by replacing PCA with a more robust alternative subspace estimation procedure, we show that the resulting detector is resilient to poisoning and maintains a significantly lower false-positive rate when poisoned.

The PCA-based detector we analyze was first proposed by Lakhina et al. (2004b) as method for identifying volume anomalies in a backbone network. This basic technique led to a variety of extensions of the original method (e.g., Lakhina, Crovella & Diot 2004a, 2005a, 2005b) and to related techniques for addressing the problem of diagnosing large-volume network anomalies (e.g., Brauckhoff, Salamatian, & May 2009; Huang, Nguyen, Garofalakis, Jordan, Joseph, & Taft 2007; Li, Bian, Crovella, Diot, Govindan, Iannaccone, & Lakhina 2006; Ringberg, Soule, Rexford, & Diot 2007; Zhang, Ge, Greenberg, & Roughan 2005). While their subspace-based method is able to successfully detect DoS attacks in the network traffic, to do so it assumes the detector is trained on nonmalicious data (in an unsupervised fashion under the setting of anomaly detection). Instead, we consider an adversary that knows that an ISP is using a subspace-based anomaly detector and attempts to evade it by proactively poisoning the training data.

We consider an adversary whose goal is to circumvent detection by poisoning the training data; i.e., an *Integrity* goal to increase the detector's false-negative rate, which corresponds to the evasion success rate of the attacker's subsequent DoS attack. When trained on this poisoned data, the detector learns a distorted set of principal components that are unable to effectively discern the desired DoS attacks—a *Targeted* attack. Because PCA estimates the data's principal subspace solely on the covariance of the link traffic, we explore poisoning schemes that add chaff (additional traffic) into the network along the flow targeted by the attacker to systematically increase the targeted flow's variance; i.e., an additive contamination model. By increasing the targeted flow's variance, the attacker causes the estimated subspace to unduly shift toward the target flow, making large-volume events along that flow less detectable.

In this chapter, we explore attacks against and defenses for network anomaly detection. In Section 6.1, we introduce the PCA-based method for detecting network volume anomalies as first proposed by Lakhina et al. (2004*b*). Section 6.2 proposes attacks against the detector and Section 6.3 proposes a defense based on a robust estimator for the subspace. In Section 6.4, we evaluate the effect of attacks on both the original PCA-based approach and the proposed defense. We summarize the results of this study in Section 6.5. This chapter builds on (Rubinstein, Nelson, Huang, Joseph, Lau, Rao, Taft, & Tygar 2009*a*, 2009*b*).

Related Work

Several earlier studies examined attacks on specific learning systems for related applications. Ringberg, Soule, Rexford, & Diot (2007) performed a study of the sensitivities of the PCA method that illustrates how the PCA method can be sensitive to the number of principal components used to describe the normal subspace. This parameter can limit PCA's effectiveness if not properly configured. They also show that routing outages can pollute the normal subspace; this is a kind of perturbation to the subspace that is not adversarial but can still significantly degrade detection performance. Our work in this chapter differs in two key ways. First, we investigate malicious data poisoning; i.e., adversarial perturbations that are stealthy and subtle and are more challenging to circumvent than routing outages. Second, Ringberg et al. focus on showing the variability in PCA's performance to certain sensitivities, and not on defenses. In this work, we propose a robust defense against a malicious adversary and demonstrate its effectiveness. It is conceivable that this technique may limit PCA's sensitivity to routing outages, although such a study is beyond the scope of this work. A study by Brauckhoff, Salamatian, & May (2009) showed that the sensitivities observed by Ringberg et al. can be attributed to the inability of the PCA-based detector to capture temporal correlations. They propose to replace PCA by a Karhunen-Loeve expansion. This study indicates that it would be important to examine, in future work, the data poisoning robustness of the proposal of Brauckhoff et al. to understand how it fares under adversarial conditions.

Contributions

The first contribution of this chapter is a detailed analysis of how adversaries subvert the learning process in these *Causative Integrity* attacks using additive contamination. We explore a range of poisoning strategies in which the attacker's knowledge about the network traffic state and its time horizon (length of poisoning episode) vary. Through theoretical analysis of global poisoning strategies, we reveal simple and effective poisoning strategies for the adversary that can be used to successfully exploit various levels of knowledge that the attacker has about the system. To gain further insights as to why these attacks are successful, we demonstrate their impact on the normal model built by the PCA detector.

The second contribution is to design a robust defense against this type of poisoning. It is known that PCA can be strongly affected by outliers (Ringberg, Soule, Rexford, & Diot 2007). However, instead of finding the principal components along directions that maximize variance, alternative PCA-like techniques find more robust components by maximizing alternative dispersion measures with desirable robustness properties. Analogously in centroid estimation, the median is a more robust measure of location than the mean, in that it is far less sensitive to the influence of outliers—this is a form of distributional robustness (cf. Hampel et al. 1986). This concept was also extended to design and evaluate estimates of dispersion that are robust alternatives to variance (a nonrobust estimate of dispersion) such as the median absolute deviation (MAD), which is robust to outliers. PCA too can be thought of as an estimator of the underlying subspace of the data, which selects the subspace that minimizes the sum of the square of the data's residuals; i.e., the variance of the data in the residual subspace. This sum-of-squares estimator also is nonrobust and is thus sensitive to outliers (cf. Maronna et al. 2006). Over the past two decades a number of robust PCA algorithms have been developed that maximize alternative measures of dispersion such as the MAD instead of variance. The PCA-GRID algorithm was proposed by Croux et al. (2007) as an efficient method for estimating directions that maximize the MAD without underestimating variance (a flaw identified in previous solutions). We adapt PCA-GRID for anomaly detection by combining the method with a new robust cutoff threshold. Instead of modeling the squared prediction error as Gaussian (as in the original PCA method), we model the error using a Laplace distribution. The new threshold was motivated from observations of the residual that show longer tails than exhibited by Gaussian distributions. Together, we refer to the method that combines PCA-GRID with a Laplace cutoff threshold as ANTIDOTE. Because it builds on robust subspace estimates, this method substantially reduces the effect of outliers and is able to reject poisonous training data as we demonstrate empirically in Section 6.4.4.

The third contribution is an evaluation and comparison of both ANTIDOTE and the original PCA method when exposed to a variety of poisoning strategies and an assessment of their susceptibility to poisoning in terms of several performance metrics. To do this, we used traffic data from the Abilene Internet2 backbone network (Zhang, Ge, Greenberg, & Roughan 2005), a public network traffic dataset used in prior studies of PCA-based anomaly detection approaches. We show that the original PCA method can be easily compromised by the poisoning schemes we present using only small volumes of chaff (i.e., fake traffic used to poison the detector). In fact, for moderate amounts of chaff, the performance of the PCA detector approaches that of a random detector. However, ANTIDOTE is dramatically more robust to these attacks. It outperforms PCA in that it *i*) more effectively limits the adversary's ability to increase its evasion success; *ii*) can reject a larger portion of contaminated training data; and *iii*) provides robust protection for nearly all origin-destination flows through the network. The gains of ANTIDOTE for these performance measures are large, especially as the amount of poisoning increases. Most importantly, we demonstrate that when there is no poisoning ANTIDOTE incurs an insignificant decrease in its false-negative and false-positive performance, compared to PCA. However, when poisoning does occur, ANTIDOTE incurs significantly less degradation than PCA with respect to both of these performance measures. Fundamentally, the original PCA-based approach was not designed to be robust, but these results show that it is possible to adapt the original technique to bolster its performance under an adversarial setting by using robust alternatives.

Finally, we also summarize episodic poisoning and its effect on both the original PCA-based detector and ANTIDOTE as further discussed in Rubinstein (2010). Because the network behaviors are nonstationary, the baseline models must be periodically retrained to capture evolving trends in the underlying data, but a *patient* adversary can exploit the periodic retraining to slowly poison the filter over many retraining periods. In previous usage scenarios (Lakhina, Crovella, & Diot 2004*b*; Soule, Salamatian, & Taft 2005), the PCA detector is retrained regularly (e.g., weekly), meaning that attackers could poison PCA slowly over long periods of time, thus poisoning PCA in a more stealthy fashion. By perturbing the principal components gradually over several retraining epochs, the attacker decreases the chance that the poisoning activity itself is detected—an episodic poisoning scheme. As we show in Section 6.4.5, these poisoning schemes can boost the false-negative rate as high as the nonstealthy strategies, with almost unnoticeable increases in weekly traffic volumes, albeit over a longer period of time.

6.1   PCA Method for Detecting Trafffic Anomalies

To uncover anomalies, many network anomography detection techniques analyze the network-wide flow traffic matrix (TM), which describes the traffic volume between all pairs of points-of-presence (PoP) in a backbone network and contains the observed traffic volume time series for each origin-destination (OD) flow. PCA-based techniques instead uncover anomalies using the more readily available link traffic matrix. In this section, we define traffic matrices and summarize the PCA-based anomaly detection method of Lakhina et al. (2004*b*) using the notation introduced in Section 2.1.

6.1.1   Traffic Matrices and Volume Anomalies

We begin with a brief overview of the volume anomaly detection problem, in which a network administrator wants to identify unusual traffic in *origin-destination* (OD) flows between *points-of-presence* (PoP) nodes in a backbone network (see Figure 6.1). The flow traffic is routed along a network represented as an undirected graph $(\mathbb{V}, \mathbb{E})$ on $V \triangleq |\mathbb{V}|$ *nodes* and $D \triangleq |\mathbb{E}|$ unidirectional *links*. There are $Q \triangleq V^2$ OD flows in this network (between every pair of PoP nodes), and the amount of traffic transmitted along the qth flow during the tth time slice is $Q_{t,q}$. All OD flow traffic observed in T time intervals is summarized by the matrix $\mathbf{Q} \in \mathfrak{N}^{T \times Q}$. Ideally, one would like to identify a pair (t, q) as anomalous if the traffic along flow q is unusually large at time t, but $\mathbf{Q}$ is not directly observable within the backbone network. Instead what is observable is the network link traffic during the tth time slice.

More specifically, network link traffic is the superposition of all OD flows; i.e., the data transmitted along the qth flow contributes to the overall observed link traffic along the links traversed by the qth flow's route from its origin to its destination. Consider

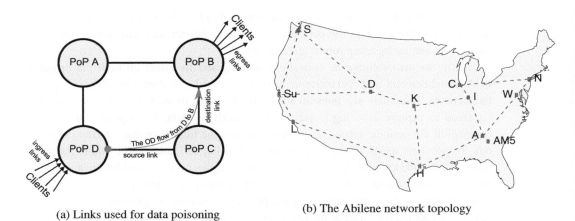

(a) Links used for data poisoning   (b) The Abilene network topology

Figure 6.1 Depictions of network topologies, in which subspace-based detection methods can be used as traffic anomaly monitors. **(a)** A simple four-node network with four edges. Each node represents a PoP, and each edge represents a bidirectional link between two PoPs. Ingress links are shown at node D although all nodes have ingress links that carry traffic from clients to the PoP. Similarly, egress links are shown at node B carrying traffic from the PoP to its destination client. Finally, a flow from D to B is depicted flowing through C; this is the route taken by traffic sent from PoP D to PoP B. **(b)** The Abilene backbone network overlaid on a map of the United States representing the 12 PoP nodes in the network and the 15 links between them. PoPs AM5 and A are actually co-located together in Atlanta, but the former is displayed to the southeast to highlight its connectivity.

a network with Q OD flows and D links and measure traffic on this network over T time intervals. The relationship between link traffic and OD flow traffic is concisely captured by the *routing matrix* $\mathbf{R}$. This matrix is a $D \times Q$ matrix such that $R_{i,j} = 1$ if the jth OD flow passes over the ith link, and otherwise is zero. Thus, if $\mathbf{Q}$ is the $T \times Q$ traffic matrix containing the time-series of all OD flows and $\mathbf{X}$ is the $T \times D$ link TM containing the time-series of all links, then $\mathbf{X} = \mathbf{Q}\mathbf{R}^{\top}$. We denote the tth row of $\mathbf{X}$ as $\mathbf{x}^{(t)} = \mathbf{X}_{t,\bullet}$ (the vector of D link traffic measurements at time t) and the traffic observed along a particular *source link*, s, by $x_s^{(t)}$. We denote column q of routing matrix $\mathbf{R}$ by $\mathbf{R}_q$; i.e., the indicator vector of the links used by the qth flow.

We consider the problem of detecting OD flow volume anomalies across a top-tier network by observing link traffic volumes. Anomalous flow volumes are unusual traffic load levels in a network caused by anomalies such as DoS attacks, distributed DoS (DDoS) attacks, flash crowds, device failures, misconfigured devices, and other abnormal network events. DoS attacks serve as the canonical example of an attack throughout this chapter.

6.1.2   Subspace Method for Anomaly Detection

Here we briefly summarize the PCA-based anomaly detector introduced by Lakhina, Crovella, & Diot (2004*b*). They observed that the high degree of traffic aggregation on ISP backbone links often causes OD flow volume anomalies to become indistinct within normal traffic patterns. They also observe that although the measured data has high dimensionality, D, the normal traffic patterns lie in a subspace of low-dimension $K \ll D$; i.e., the majority of normal traffic can be described using a smaller representation because of temporally static correlations caused by the aggregation. Fundamentally, they found that the link data is dominated by a small number of flows. Inferring this normal traffic subspace using PCA (which finds the principal components within the traffic) facilitates the identification of volume anomalies in the residual (abnormal) subspace. For the Abilene (Internet2 backbone) network, most variance can be captured by the first $K = 4$ principal components; i.e., the link traffic of this network effectively resides in a (low) K-dimensional subspace of $\Re^D$.

PCA is a dimensionality reduction technique that finds K orthogonal *principal components* to define a K-dimensional subspace that captures the maximal amount of variance from the data. First, PCA centers the data by replacing each data point $\mathbf{x}^{(t)}$ with $\mathbf{x}^{(t)} - \hat{\mathbf{c}}$ where $\hat{\mathbf{c}}$ is the central location estimate, which in this case is the mean vector $\hat{\mathbf{c}} = \frac{1}{T}\mathbf{X}^\top \mathbf{1}$. Let $\hat{\mathbf{X}}$ be the centered link traffic matrix; i.e., with each column of $\mathbf{X}$ translated to have zero mean. Next, PCA estimates the principal subspace on which the mean-centered data lies by computing its principal components. The kth principal component satisfies

$$\mathbf{v}^{(k)} \in \underset{\mathbf{w}:\|\mathbf{w}\|_2=1}{\text{argmax}} \left[\left\| \hat{\mathbf{X}} \left(\mathbf{I} - \sum_{i=1}^{k-1} \mathbf{v}^{(i)}(\mathbf{v}^{(i)})^\top \right) \mathbf{w} \right\|_2 \right]. \tag{6.1}$$

The resulting K-dimensional subspace spanned by the first K principal components is represented by a $D \times K$ dimensional matrix $\mathbf{V}^{(K)} = [\mathbf{v}^{(1)}, \mathbf{v}^{(2)}, \ldots, \mathbf{v}^{(K)}]$ that maps to the *normal* traffic subspace $\dot{\mathbb{S}}$ and has a projection matrix $\dot{\mathbf{P}} = \mathbf{V}^{(K)} \left(\mathbf{V}^{(K)}\right)^\top$ into $\Re^D$. The residual $(D - K)$-dimensional subspace is spanned by the remaining principal components $\mathbf{W}^{(K)} = \left[\mathbf{v}^{(K+1)}, \mathbf{v}^{(K+2)}, \ldots, \mathbf{v}^{(D)}\right]$. This matrix maps to the abnormal traffic subspace $\ddot{\mathbb{S}}$ with a corresponding projection matrix $\ddot{\mathbf{P}} = \mathbf{W}^{(K)} \left(\mathbf{W}^{(K)}\right)^\top = \mathbf{I} - \dot{\mathbf{P}}$ onto $\Re^D$.

Volume anomalies can be detected by decomposing the link traffic into normal and abnormal components such that $\mathbf{x}^{(t)} = \dot{\mathbf{x}}^{(t)} + \ddot{\mathbf{x}}^{(t)} + \hat{\mathbf{c}}$ where $\dot{\mathbf{x}}^{(t)} \triangleq \dot{\mathbf{P}}\left(\mathbf{x}^{(t)} - \hat{\mathbf{c}}\right)$ is the modeled normal traffic and $\ddot{\mathbf{x}}^{(t)} \triangleq \ddot{\mathbf{P}}\left(\mathbf{x}^{(t)} - \hat{\mathbf{c}}\right)$ is the residual traffic, corresponding to projecting $\mathbf{x}^{(t)}$ onto $\dot{\mathbb{S}}$ and $\ddot{\mathbb{S}}$, respectively. A volume anomaly at time t typically results in a large change to $\ddot{\mathbf{x}}^{(t)}$, which can be detected by thresholding the squared prediction error $\left\| \ddot{\mathbf{x}}^{(t)} \right\|_2^2$ against the threshold Q_β, which is chosen to be the Q-statistic at the $1 - \beta$ confidence level (Jackson & Mudholkar 1979). This PCA-based detector defines the following classifier:

$$f\left(\mathbf{x}^{(t)}\right) = \begin{cases} \text{"+"}, & \left\|\ddot{\mathbf{P}}\left(\mathbf{x}^{(t)} - \hat{\mathbf{c}}\right)\right\|_2^2 > Q_\beta \\ \text{"−"}, & \text{otherwise} \end{cases} \tag{6.2}$$

for a link measurement vector, where "+" indicates that the tth time slice is *anomalous* and "−" indicates it is *innocuous*. Due to the nonstationarity of normal network traffic (gradual drift), periodic retraining is necessary. We assume the detector is retrained weekly.

6.2   Corrupting the PCA Subspace

In this section, we survey a number of data poisoning schemes and discuss how each is designed to affect the training phase of a PCA-based detector. Three general categories of attacks are considered based on the attacker's capabilities: uninformed attacks, locally informed attacks, and globally informed attacks. Each of these reflects different levels of knowledge and resources available to the attacker.

6.2.1   The Threat Model

The adversary's goal is to launch a DoS attack on some victim and to have the attack traffic successfully transit an ISP's network without being detected en route. The DoS traffic traverses the ISP from an ingress point-of-presence (PoP) node to an egress PoP of the ISP. To avoid detection prior to the desired DoS attack, the attacker poisons the detector during its periodic retraining phase by injecting additional traffic (chaff) along the OD flow (i.e., from an ingress PoP to an egress PoP) that it eventually intends to attack. Based on the anticipated threat against the PCA-based anomaly detector, the contamination model we consider is a *data alteration* model where the adversary is limited to only altering the traffic from a single source node. This poisoning is possible if the adversary gains control over clients of an ingress PoP or if the adversary compromises a router (or set of routers) within the ingress PoP. For a poisoning strategy, the attacker must decide how much chaff to add and when to do so. These choices are guided by the degree of covertness required by the attacker and the amount of information available to it.

We consider poisoning strategies in which the attacker has various potential levels of information at its disposal. The weakest attacker is one that knows nothing about the traffic at the ingress PoP and adds chaff randomly (called an *uninformed* attack). Alternatively, a partially informed attacker knows the current volume of traffic on the ingress link(s) that it intends to inject chaff on. Because many networks export SNMP records, an adversary might intercept this information or possibly monitor it itself (i.e., in the case of a compromised router). We call this type of poisoning a *locally informed* attack because this adversary only observes the local state of traffic at the ingress PoP of the attack. In a third scenario, the attacker is *globally informed* because its global view over the network enables it to know the traffic levels on all network links and this attacker has knowledge of all future traffic link levels. (Recall that in the locally informed scheme, the attacker only knows the *current* traffic volume of a link.) Although these attacker capabilities are impossible to achieve, we study this scenario to better understand the limits of variance injection poisoning schemes.

We assume the adversary does not have control over existing traffic (i.e., it cannot delay or discard traffic). Similarly, the adversary cannot falsify SNMP reports to PCA.

Such approaches are more conspicuous because the inconsistencies in SNMP reporting from neighboring PoPs could expose the compromised router. Stealth is a major goal of this attacker—it does not want its DoS attack or its poisoning to be detected until the DoS attack has successfully been executed.

So far we have focused primarily on nondistributed poisoning of DoS detectors and on nondistributed DoS attacks. *Distributed* poisoning that aims to evade a DoS detector is also possible; the globally informed poisoning strategy presented later is an example since this adversary potentially can poison any network link. We leave the study of distributed forms of poisoning to future work. Nonetheless, by demonstrating that poisoning can effectively achieve evasion in the nondistributed setting, this work shows that distributing the poisoning is unnecessary, although it certainly should result in even more powerful attacks.

For each of these scenarios of different poisoning strategies and the associated level of knowledge available to the adversary, we now detail specific poisoning schemes. In each, the adversary decides on the quantity of $a^{(t)}$ chaff to add to the target flow time series at a time t, and during the training period it sends a total volume of chaff $A \triangleq \sum_{t=1}^{T} a^{(t)}$. Each strategy has an attack parameter θ, which controls the intensity of the attack. Ultimately, in each strategy, the attacker's goal is to maximally increase traffic variance along the target flow to mislead the PCA detector to give that flow undue representation in its subspace, but each strategy differs in the degree of information the attacker has to achieve its objective. For each scenario, we present only one representative poisoning scheme, although others were studied in prior work (Rubinstein, Nelson, Huang, Joseph, Lau, Taft, & Tygar 2008).

6.2.2 Uninformed Chaff Selection

In this setting, the adversary has no knowledge about the network and randomly injects chaff traffic. At each time t, the adversary decides whether or not to inject chaff according to a Bernoulli random variable. If it decides to inject chaff, the amount of chaff added is of size θ, i.e., $a^{(t)} = \theta$. This method is independent of the network traffic since this attacker is uninformed—we call it the *Random* poisoning scheme.

6.2.3 Locally Informed Chaff Selection

In the locally informed scenario, the attacker observes the volume of traffic in the ingress link it controls at each point in time, $x_s^{(t)}$. Hence this attacker only adds chaff when the current traffic volume is already reasonably large. In particular, it adds chaff when the traffic volume on the link exceeds a threshold parameter α (typically the mean of the overall flow's traffic). The amount of chaff added is then $a^{(t)} = \left(\max \left\{ 0, x_s^{(t)} - \alpha \right\} \right)^{\theta}$. In other words, if the difference between the observed link traffic and a parameter α is non-negative, the chaff volume is that difference to the power θ; otherwise, no chaff is added during the interval. In this scheme (called *add-more-if-bigger*), the farther the traffic is from the mean link traffic, the larger the deviation of chaff inserted.

6.2.4   Globally Informed Chaff Selection

The *globally informed* scheme captures an omnipotent adversary with full knowledge of $\mathbf{X}$, $\mathbf{R}$, and the future measurements $\tilde{\mathbf{x}}$, and that is capable of injecting chaff into *any* network flow during training. This latter point is important. In previous poisoning schemes the adversary can only inject chaff along the compromised link, whereas in this scenario, the adversary can inject chaff into any link. For each link n and each time t, the adversary must select the amount of chaff $A_{t,n}$. We cast this process into an optimization problem that the adversary solves to maximally increase its chance of a DoS evasion along the target flow q. Although these capabilities are unrealistic, we study the globally informed poisoning strategy to understand the limits of variance injection methods.

The PCA evasion problem considers an adversary wishing to launch an undetected DoS attack of volume δ along the qth target flow at the tth time window. If the vector of link volumes at future time t is $\tilde{\mathbf{x}}$, where the tilde distinguishes this future measurement from past training data $\hat{\mathbf{X}}$, then the vectors of anomalous DoS volumes are given by $\tilde{\mathbf{x}}(\delta, q) = \tilde{\mathbf{x}} + \delta \cdot \mathbf{R}_q$. Denote by $\mathbf{A}$ the matrix of link traffic injected into the network by the adversary during training. Then the PCA-based anomaly detector is trained on an altered link traffic matrix $\hat{\mathbf{X}} + \mathbf{A}$ to produce the mean traffic vector μ, the top K eigenvectors $\mathbf{V}^{(K)}$, and the squared prediction error threshold Q_β. The adversary's objective is to enable as large a DoS attack as possible (maximizing δ) by optimizing $\mathbf{A}$ accordingly. The PCA evasion problem corresponds to solving the following:

$$\max_{\delta \in \Re, \ \mathbf{A} \in \Re^{T \times Q}} \delta$$

$$\text{s.t.} \ \ (\mu, \mathbf{V}, Q_\beta) = \text{PCA}(\mathbf{X} + \mathbf{A}, K)$$

$$\left\| \ddot{\mathbf{P}}(\tilde{\mathbf{x}}(\delta, q) - \mu) \right\|_2 \le Q_\beta$$

$$\|\mathbf{A}\|_1 \le \theta \qquad \forall t, q \ A_{t,q} \ge 0,$$

where θ is a constant constraining total chaff and the matrix 1-norm is here defined as $\|\mathbf{A}\|_1 \triangleq \sum_{t,q} |A_{t,q}|$. The second constraint guarantees evasion by requiring that the contaminated link volumes at time t are classified as innocuous according to Equation 6.2. The remaining constraints upper-bound the total chaff volume by θ and constrain the chaff to be non-negative.

Unfortunately, this optimization is difficult to solve analytically. Thus we construct a relaxed approximation to obtain a tractable analytic solution. We make a few assumptions and derivations,[1] and show that the above objective seeks to maximize the attack direction $\mathbf{R}_q$'s projected length in the normal subspace $\max_{\mathbf{A} \in \Re^{T \times Q}} \left\| \left(\mathbf{V}^{(K)} \right)^\top \mathbf{R}_q \right\|_2$. Next, we restrict our focus to traffic processes that generate spherical k-rank link traffic covariance matrices.[2] This property implies that the eigen-spectrum consists of K ones followed by all zeroes. Such an eigen-spectrum allows us to approximate the top

---

[1] The full proof is omitted due to space constraints.
[2] While the spherical assumption does not hold in practice, the assumption of low-rank traffic matrices is met by published datasets (Lakhina et al. 2004b).

eigenvectors $\mathbf{V}^{(K)}$ in the objective, with the matrix of all eigenvectors weighted by their corresponding eigenvalues $\Sigma \mathbf{V}$. This transforms the PCA evasion problem into the following relaxed optimization:

$$\max_{\mathbf{A} \in \mathfrak{R}^{T \times Q}} \left\| (\hat{\mathbf{X}} + \mathbf{A}) \mathbf{R}_q \right\|_2 \qquad (6.3)$$
$$\text{s.t.} \quad \|\mathbf{A}\|_1 \leq \theta$$
$$\forall t, q \ A_{t,q} \geq 0.$$

Solutions to this optimization are obtained by a standard projection pursuit method from optimization: iteratively take a step in the direction of the objective's gradient and then project onto the feasible set.

These solutions yield an interesting insight. Recall that the globally informed adversary is capable of injecting chaff along *any* flow. One could imagine that it might be useful to inject chaff along an OD flow whose traffic dominates the choice of principal components (i.e., an elephant flow), and then send the DoS traffic along a different flow (that possibly shares a subset of links with the poisoned OD flow). However the solutions of Equation (6.3) indicates that the best strategy to evade detection is to inject chaff only along the links $\mathbf{R}_q$ associated with the target flow q. This follows from the form of the initializer $\mathbf{A}^{(0)} \propto \hat{\mathbf{X}} \mathbf{R}_q \mathbf{R}_q^\top$ (obtained from an L_2 relaxation) as well as the form of the projection and gradient steps. In particular, all these objects preserve the property that the solution only injects chaff along the target flow. In fact, the only difference between this globally informed solution and the locally informed scheme is that the former uses information about the entire traffic matrix $\mathbf{X}$ to determine chaff allocation along the flow whereas the latter uses only local information.

6.2.5   Boiling Frog Attacks

In the above attacks, chaff was designed to affect a single training period (one week) in the training cycle of the detector, but here we consider the possibility of episodic poisoning that is carried out over multiple weeks of retraining the subspace detector to adapt to changing traffic trends. As with previous studies, we assume that the PCA-subspace method is retrained on a weekly basis using the traffic observed in the previous week to retrain the detector at the beginning of the new week; i.e., the detector for the mth week is learned from the traffic of week $m - 1$. Further, as with the outlier model discussed in Chapter 4, we sanitize the data from the prior week before retraining so that all detected anomalies are removed from it. This sort of poisoning could be used by a realistic adversary that plans to execute a DoS attack in advance; e.g., to lead up to a special event like the Super Bowl or an election.

Multiweek poisoning strategies vary the attack according to the time horizon over which they are carried out. As with single-week attacks, during each week the adversary inserts chaff along the target OD flow throughout the training period according to its poisoning strategy. However, in the multiweek attack the adversary increases the total amount of chaff used during each subsequent week according to a poisoning schedule. This poisons the model over several weeks by initially adding small amounts of chaff and increasing the chaff quantities each week so that the detector is gradually acclimated to chaff and fails to adequately identify the eventually large amount of poisoning—this is analogous to the attacks against the hypersphere detector in Chapter 4. We call this type of episodic poisoning the *boiling frog poisoning attack* after the folk tale that one can boil a frog by slowly increasing the water temperature over time.[3]

The boiling frog poisoning attack can use any of the preceding chaff schemes to select $a^{(t)}$ during each week of poisoning; the only week-to-week change is in the total volume of chaff used, which increases as follows. During the first week, the subspace-based detector is trained on unpoisoned data. In the second week, an initial total volume of chaff is $A^{(1)}$ is selected, and the target flow is injected with chaff generated using a parameter θ_1 to achieve the desired total chaff volume. After classifying the traffic from the new week, PCA is retrained on that week's sanitized data with any detected anomalies removed. During each subsequent week, the poisoning is increased according to its schedule; the schedules we considered increase the total chaff volumes geometrically as $A^{(t)} = \kappa A^{(t-1)}$ where κ is the rate of weekly increase. The goal of boiling frog poisoning is to slowly rotate the normal subspace, injecting low levels of chaff relative to the previous week's traffic levels so that PCA's rejection rates stay low and a large portion of the present week's poisoned traffic matrix is trained on. Although PCA is retrained each week, the training data will include some events not caught by the previous week's detector. Thus, more malicious training data will accumulate each successive week as the PCA subspace is gradually shifted. This process continues until the week of the DoS attack, when the adversary stops injecting chaff and executes its desired DoS; again we measure the success rate of that final attack. Episodic poisoning is considered more fully in Rubinstein (2010), but we summarize the results of this poisoning scheme on subspace detectors in Section 6.4.5.

6.3   Corruption-Resilient Detectors

We propose using techniques from robust statistics to defend against *Causative Integrity* attacks on subspace-based anomaly detection and demonstrate their efficacy in that role. Robust methods are designed to be less sensitive to outliers and are consequently ideal defenses against variance injection schemes that perturb data to increase variance along the target flow. There have been two general approaches to make PCA robust: the first computes the principal components as the eigen-spectrum of a robust esti-mate of the covariance matrix (Devlin, Gnanadesikan, & Kettenring 1981), while the second approach searches for directions that maximize a robust scale estimate of the data projection. In this section, we propose using a method from the second approach as a defense against poisoning. After describing the method, we also propose a new

---

[3] Note that there is nothing inherent in the choice of a one-week poisoning period. For a general learning algorithm, our strategies would correspond to poisoning over one training period (whatever its length) or multiple training periods.

threshold statistic that can be used for any subspace-based method including robust PCA and better fits their residuals. Robust PCA and the new robust Laplace threshold together form a new network-wide traffic anomaly detection method, ANTIDOTE, that is less sensitive to poisoning attacks.

6.3.1 Intuition

Fundamentally, to mitigate the effect of poisoning attacks, the learning algorithm must be stable despite data contamination; i.e., a small amount of data contamination should not dramatically change the model produced by our algorithm. This concept of stability has been studied in the field of robust statistics in which *robust* is the formal term used to qualify a related notion of stability often referred to as distributional robustness (see Section 3.5.4.3). There have been several approaches to developing robust PCA algorithms that construct a low-dimensional subspace that captures most of the data's dispersion[4] and are stable under data contamination (Croux et al. 2007; Croux & Ruiz-Gazen 2005; Devlin et al. 1981; Li & Chen 1985; Maronna 2005). As stated earlier, the approach we selected finds a subspace that maximizes an alternative dispersion measure instead of the usual variance.

The robust PCA algorithms search for a unit direction $\mathbf{v}$ whose projections maximize some univariate dispersion measure $S\{\,\cdot\,\}$ after centering the data according to the location estimator $\hat{\mathbf{c}}\{\,\cdot\,\}$; that is,[5]

$$\mathbf{v} \in \underset{\|\mathbf{w}=1\|_2}{\operatorname{argmax}}\left[\, S\left\{\mathbf{w}^\top\left(\mathbf{x}^{(t)} - \hat{\mathbf{c}}\left\{\mathbf{x}^{(t)}\right\}\right)\right\}\right]. \qquad (6.4)$$

The standard deviation is the dispersion measure used by PCA; i.e., $S^{\mathrm{SD}}\left\{r^{(1)}, \ldots, r^{(T)}\right\} = \left(\frac{1}{T-1}\sum_{t=1}^{T}\left(r^{(t)} - \bar{r}\right)^2\right)^{\frac{1}{2}}$ where $\bar{r}$ is the mean of the values $\left\{r^{(t)}\right\}$. However, it is well known that the standard deviation is sensitive to outliers (cf. Hampel et al. 1986, Chapter 2), making PCA nonrobust to contamination. Robust PCA algorithms instead use measures of dispersion based on the concept of *robust projection pursuit (RPP)* estimators (Li & Chen 1985). As is shown by Li & Chen, RPP estimators achieve the same breakdown points as their dispersion measure (recall that the breakdown point is the [asymptotic] fraction of the data an adversary must control to arbitrarily change an estimator and is a common measure of statistical robustness) as well as being qualitatively robust; i.e., the estimators are stable.

However, unlike the eigenvector solutions that arise in PCA, there is generally no efficiently computable solution for robust dispersion measures, and so these estimators must be approximated. In the next section, we describe the PCA-GRID algorithm, a successful method for approximating robust PCA subspaces developed by Croux et al.

---

[4] Dispersion is an alternative term for variation since the latter is often associated with statistical variation. A dispersion measure is a statistic that measures the variability or spread of a variable according to a particular notion of dispersion.

[5] Here we use the notation $g\{r^{(1)}, \ldots, r^{(T)}\}$ to indicate that the function g acts on an enumerated set of objects. This notation simplifies the notation $g(\{r^{(1)}, \ldots, r^{(T)}\})$ to a more legible form.

(2007). Of several other projection pursuit techniques (Croux & Ruiz-Gazen 2005; Maronna 2005), PCA-GRID proved to be most resilient to our poisoning attacks. It is worth emphasizing that the procedure described in the next section is simply a technique for approximating a projection pursuit estimator and does not itself contribute to the algorithm's robustness—that robustness comes from the definition of the projection pursuit estimator in Equation (6.4).

First, to better understand the efficacy of a robust PCA algorithm, we demonstrate the effect our poisoning techniques have on the PCA algorithm and contrast them with the effect on the PCA-GRID algorithm. Figure 6.2 shows an example of the impact that a globally informed poisoning attack has on both algorithms. As demonstrated in Figure 6.2(a), initially the data was approximately clustered in an ellipse, and both algorithms construct reasonable estimates for the center and first principal component for this data. However, Figure 6.2(b) shows that a large amount of poisoning dramatically perturbs some of the data in the direction of the target flow, and as a result, the PCA subspace is dramatically shifted toward the target flow's direction (y-axis). Due to this shift, DoS attacks along the target flow will be less detectable. Meanwhile, the subspace of PCA-GRID is considerably less affected by the poisoning and only rotates slightly toward the direction of the target flow.

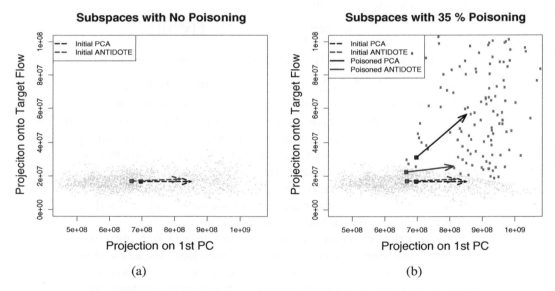

(a)   (b)

Figure 6.2 In these figures, the Abilene data was projected into the 2D space spanned by the first principal component and the direction of the attack flow #118. **(a)** The first principal component learned by PCA and PCA-GRID on clean data (represented by small gray dots). **(b)** The effect on the first principal components of PCA and PCA-GRID is shown under a globally informed attack (represented by o's). Note that some contaminated points were too far from the main cloud of data to include in the plot.

6.3.2   PCA-GRID

The PCA-GRID algorithm introduced by Croux et al. (2007) is a projection pursuit technique as described in Equation 6.4. It finds a K-dimensional subspace that approximately maximizes $S\{\,\cdot\,\}$, a *robust* measure of dispersion, for the data $\mathbf{X}$ as in Equation (6.4). The robust measure of dispersion used by Croux et al. and also incorporated into ANTIDOTE is the well-known MAD estimator because of its high degree of distributional robustness—it attains the highest achievable breakdown point of $\epsilon^\star = 50\%$ and is the most robust M-estimator of dispersion (cf. Hampel et al. 1986, Chapter 2). For scalars $r^{(1)}, \ldots, r^{(T)}$ the MAD is defined as

$$\mathrm{MAD}\left\{r^{(1)}, \ldots, r^{(T)}\right\} = \mathrm{median}\left\{\left|r^{(i)} - \mathrm{median}\left\{r^{(1)}, \ldots, r^{(T)}\right\}\right|\right\} \quad (6.5)$$
$$S^{\mathrm{MAD}}\left\{r^{(1)}, \ldots, r^{(T)}\right\} = \omega \cdot \mathrm{MAD}\left\{r^{(1)}, \ldots, r^{(T)}\right\},$$

where the coefficient $\omega = \frac{1}{\Phi^{-1}(3/4)} \approx 1.4826$ rescales the MAD so that $S^{\mathrm{MAD}}\{\,\cdot\,\}$ is an estimator of the standard deviation that is asymptotically consistent for normal distributions.

The next step requires choosing an estimate of the data's central location. In PCA, this estimate is simply the mean of the data. However, the mean is also not a robust estimator, so we center the data using the spatial median instead:

$$\hat{\mathbf{c}}\left\{\mathbf{x}^{(t)}\right\} \in \operatorname*{argmin}_{\boldsymbol{\mu} \in \mathfrak{R}^D} \sum_{t=1}^{T} \left\|\mathbf{x}^{(t)} - \boldsymbol{\mu}\right\|_2,$$

which is a convex optimization that can be efficiently solved using techniques developed by Hössjer & Croux (1995).

After centering the data based on the location estimate $\hat{\mathbf{c}}\left\{\mathbf{x}^{(t)}\right\}$ obtained above, PCA-GRID finds a unitary direction $\mathbf{v}$ that is an approximate solution to Equation (6.4) for the scaled MAD dispersion measure. The PCA-GRID algorithm uses a grid search for this task. To motivate this search procedure, suppose one wants to find the best candidate between some pair of unit vectors $\mathbf{w}^{(1)}$ and $\mathbf{w}^{(2)}$ (a 2D search space). The search space is the unit circle parameterized by ϕ as $\mathbf{w}(\phi) = \cos(\phi)\,\mathbf{w}^{(1)} + \sin(\phi)\,\mathbf{w}^{(2)}$ with $\phi \in \left[-\frac{\pi}{2}, \frac{\pi}{2}\right]$. The grid search splits the domain of ϕ into a mesh of $G + 1$ candidates $\phi^{(k)} = \frac{\pi}{2}\left(\frac{2k}{G} - 1\right)$, $k = 0, \ldots, G$. Each candidate vector $\mathbf{w}\left(\phi^{(k)}\right)$ is assessed, and the one that maximizes $S\left\{\left(\mathbf{x}^{(t)}\right)^\top \mathbf{w}\left(\phi^{(k)}\right)\right\}$ is selected as the approximate maximizer $\hat{\mathbf{w}}$.

To search a more general D-dimensional space, the search iteratively refines its current best candidate $\hat{\mathbf{w}}$ by performing a grid search between $\hat{\mathbf{w}}$ and each of the unit directions $\mathbf{e}^{(j)}$ with $j \in 1 \ldots D$. With each iteration, the range of angles considered progressively narrows around $\hat{\mathbf{w}}$ to better explore its neighborhood. This procedure (outlined in Algorithm 6.1) approximates the direction of maximal dispersion analogous to an eigenvector in PCA.

To find the K-dimensional subspace $\left\{\mathbf{v}^{(k)} \mid \forall j = 1, \ldots, K\, (\mathbf{v}^{(k)})^\top \mathbf{v}^{(j)} = \delta_{k,j}\right\}$ that maximizes the dispersion measure, the GRID-SEARCH is repeated K-times. After each

---

ALGORITHM 6.1   GRID-SEARCH $(\mathbf{X})$

Require: $\mathbf{X}$ is a $T \times D$ matrix

$\hat{\mathbf{v}} \leftarrow \mathbf{e}^{(1)}$

for $i = 1$ to C **do begin**

    for $j = 1$ to D **do begin**

        for $k = 0$ to G **do begin**

            $\phi^{(k)} \leftarrow \frac{\pi}{2^i} \left(\frac{2k}{G} - 1 \right)$

            $\mathbf{w} \left(\phi^{(k)} \right) \leftarrow \cos \left(\phi^{(k)} \right) \hat{\mathbf{w}} + \sin \left(\phi^{(k)} \right) \mathbf{e}^{(j)}$

            if $S \left\{ \left(\mathbf{x}^{(t)} \right)^{\top} \mathbf{w} \left(\phi^{(k)} \right) \right\} > S \left\{ \left(\mathbf{x}^{(t)} \right)^{\top} \hat{\mathbf{v}} \right\}$ **then** $\hat{\mathbf{v}} \leftarrow \mathbf{w} \left(\phi^{(k)} \right)$

        end for

    end for

end for

return: $\hat{\mathbf{v}}$

ALGORITHM 6.2   PCA-GRID $(\mathbf{X}, K)$

Center $\mathbf{X}$: $\mathbf{X} \leftarrow \mathbf{X} - \hat{\mathbf{c}} \left\{ \mathbf{x}^{(t)} \right\}$

for $i = 1$ to K **do begin**

    $\mathbf{v}^{(k)} \leftarrow$ GRID-SEARCH $(\mathbf{X})$

    $\mathbf{X} \leftarrow$ projection of $\mathbf{X}$ onto the complement of $\mathbf{v}^{(k)}$

end for

Return subspace centered at $\hat{\mathbf{c}} \left\{ \mathbf{x}^{(t)} \right\}$ with principal directions $\left\{ \mathbf{v}^{(k)} \right\}_{k=1}^{K}$

---

repetition, the data is deflated to remove the dispersion captured by the last direction from the data. This process is detailed in Algorithm 6.2.

6.3.3   Robust Laplace Threshold

In addition to the robust PCA-GRID algorithm, we also design a robust estimate for its residual threshold that replaces the Q-statistic described in Section 6.1.2. The use of the Q-statistic as a threshold by Lakhina et al. was implicitly motivated by an assumption of normally distributed residuals (Jackson & Mudholkar 1979). However, we found that the residuals for both the PCA and PCA-GRID subspaces were empirically non-normal, leading us to conclude that the Q-statistic is a poor choice for a detection threshold. The non-normality of the residuals was also observed by Brauckhoff et al. (2009). Instead, to account for the outliers and heavy-tailed behavior we observed from our method's residuals, we choose the threshold as the $1 - \beta$ quantile of a Laplace distribution fit with robust location and scale parameters. The alternative subspace-based anomaly detector, ANTIDOTE, is the combination of the PCA-GRID algorithm for normal-subspace estimation and the Laplace threshold to estimate the threshold for flagging anomalies.

As with the Q-statistic described in Section 6.1.2, we construct the Laplace threshold $Q_{L,\beta}$ as the $1 - \beta$ quantile of a parametric distribution fit to the residuals in the training data. However, instead of the normal distribution assumed by the Q-statistic, we use the quantiles of a Laplace distribution specified by a location parameter c and a scale parameter b. Critically, though, instead of using the mean and standard deviation, we robustly fit the distribution's parameters. We estimate c and b from the squared residuals $\left\{ \left\| \ddot{\mathbf{x}}^{(t)} \right\|_2^2 \right\}$ using robust consistent estimates $\hat{c}$ and $\hat{b}$ of location (median) and scale (MAD), respectively,

$$\hat{c} = \text{median} \left\{ \left\| \ddot{\mathbf{x}}^{(t)} \right\|_2^2 \right\}$$

$$\hat{b} = \frac{1}{\sqrt{2}P^{-1}(0.75)} \, \text{MAD} \left\{ \left\| \ddot{\mathbf{x}}^{(t)} \right\|_2^2 \right\}$$

where $P^{-1}(q)$ is the qth quantile of the standard Laplace distribution. The Laplace quantile function has the form $P_{c,b}^{-1}(q) = c + b \cdot k_L(q)$ for the function $k_{Laplace}$ that is independent of the location and shape parameters of the distribution.[6] Thus, the Laplace threshold only depends linearly on the (robust) estimates $\hat{c}$ and $\hat{b}$ making the threshold itself robust. This form is also shared by the normal quantiles (differing only in its standard quantile function k_{Normal}), but because nonrobust estimates for c and b are implicitly used by the Q-statistic, it is not robust. Further, by choosing the heavy-tailed Laplace distribution, the quantiles are more appropriate for the observed heavy-tailed behavior, but the robustness of this threshold is due to robust parameter estimation.

Empirically, the Laplace threshold also proved to be better suited for thresholding the residuals for ANTIDOTE than the Q-statistic. Figure 6.3(a) shows that both the Q-statistic and the Laplace threshold produce a reasonable threshold on the residuals of the PCA algorithm; however, as seen in Figure 6.3(b), the Laplace threshold produces a reasonable threshold for the residuals of the PCA-GRID algorithm, whereas the Q-statistic vastly underestimates the spread of the residuals. In the experiments described in the next section, the Laplace threshold is consistently more reliable than the Q-statistic.

6.4   Empirical Evaluation

We evaluate how the performance of PCA-based methods is affected by the poisoning strategies described in Section 6.2. We compare the original PCA-based detector and the alternative ANTIDOTE detector under these adversarial conditions using a variety of performance metrics.

6.4.1   Setup

To assess the effect of poisoning, we test their performance under a variety of poisoning conditions. Here we describe the data used for that evaluation, the method used to test the detectors, and the different types of poisoning scenarios used in their evaluation.

---

[6] For the Laplace distribution, this function is given by $k_L(q) \triangleq \text{sign}\left(q - \frac{1}{2}\right) \cdot \ln\left(1 - 2\left|q - \frac{1}{2}\right|\right)$.

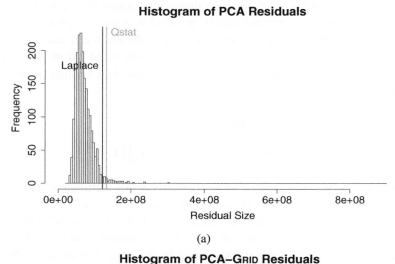

(a)

(b)

Figure 6.3 A comparison of the Q-statistic and the Laplace threshold for choosing an anomalous cutoff threshold for the residuals from an estimated subspace. **(a)** Histograms of the residuals for the original PCA algorithm and **(b)** of the PCA-GRID algorithm (the largest residual is excluded as an outlier). Pale and dark vertical lines demarcate the threshold selected using the Q-statistic and the Laplace threshold (see the labels adjacent to the vertical lines). For the original PCA method, both methods choose nearly the same reasonable threshold to the right of the majority of the residuals. However, for the residuals of the PCA-GRID subspace, the Laplace threshold is reasonable, whereas the Q-statistic is not; it would misclassify too much of the normal data to be an acceptable choice.

6.4.1.1 Traffic Data

The dataset we use for evaluation is OD flow data collected from the Abilene (Internet2 backbone) network to simulate attacks on PCA-based anomaly detection. This data was collected over an almost continuous 6-month period from March 1, 2004, through

September 10, 2004 (Zhang, Ge, Greenberg, & Roughan 2005). Each week of data consists of 2016 measurements across all 144 network OD flows binned into five-minute intervals. At the time of collection the network consisted of 12 PoPs and 15 inter-PoP links; 54 virtual links are present in the data corresponding to two directions for each inter-PoP link and an ingress and egress link for each PoP.

6.4.1.2   Validation

Although there are a total of 24 weeks of data in the dataset, these experiments are primarily based on the 20th and 21st weeks that span the period from August 7–20, 2004. These weeks were selected because PCA achieved the lowest false-negative rate on these during testing, and thus this data was most ideal for the detector. To evaluate a detector, it is trained on the 20th week's traffic and tested on the data from the 21st week during which DoS attacks are injected to measure how often the attacker can evade detection. To simulate the single training period attacks, the training traffic from week 21 is first poisoned by the attacker.

To evaluate the impact of poisoning on the ability of the original PCA-subspace method and ANTIDOTE to detect DoS attacks, two consecutive weeks of data are used (again, the subsequent results use the 20th and 21st weeks)—the first for training and the second for testing. The poisoning occurs throughout the training phase, while the DoS attack occurs during the test week. An alternate evaluation method (described in detail later) is needed for the boiling frog poisoning attack scheme where training and poisoning occur over multiple weeks. The success of the poisoning strategies is measured by their impact on the subspace-based detector's false-negative rate (FNR). The FNR is the ratio of the number of successful evasions to the total number of attacks (i.e., the attacker's success rate is PCA's FNR rate). We also use receiver operating characteristic (ROC) curves to visualize a detection method's tradeoff between the true-positive rate (TPR) and the false-positive rate (FPR).

To compute the FNRs and FPRs, synthetic anomalies are generated according to the method of Lakhina et al. (2004b) and are injected into the Abilene data. While there are disadvantages to this method, such as the conservative assumption that a single volume size is anomalous for all flows, it is convenient for the purposes of relative comparison between PCA and robust PCA, to measure relative effects of poisoning, and for consistency with prior studies. The training sets used in these experiments consist of week-long traffic traces; a week is a sufficiently long time scale to capture weekday and weekend cyclic trends (Ringberg et al. 2007), and it is also the same time scale used in previous studies (Lakhina et al. 2004b). Because the data is binned into five-minute windows (corresponding to the reporting interval of SNMP), a decision about whether or not an anomaly occurred can be made at the end of each window; thus attacks can be detected within five minutes of their occurrence.

Unfortunately, computing the false-positive rate of a detector is difficult since there may be actual anomalous events in the Abilene data. To estimate the FPR, negative examples (benign OD flows) are generated as follows. The data is fit to an EWMA model that is intended to capture the main trends of the data with little noise. This model is used to select points in the Abilene flow's time series to use as negative examples. The actual data is then compared to the EWMA model; if the difference is small (not in the flow's top one percentile) for a particular flow at a particular time, $Q_{t,q}$, then the element $Q_{t,q}$ is labeled as *benign*. This process is repeated across all flows. The FPR of a detector is finally estimated based on the (false) alarms raised on the time slots that were deemed to be benign.

DoS attacks are simulated by selecting a target flow, q, and time window, t, and injecting a traffic spike along this target flow during the time window. Starting with the flow traffic matrix **Q** for the test week, a positive example (i.e., an anomalous flow event) is generated by setting the qth flow's volume at the tth time window, $Q_{t,q}$, to be a large value known to correspond to an anomalous flow (replacing the original traffic volume in this time slot). This value was defined by Lakhina et al. (2004*b*) to be 1.5 times a cutoff of 8×10^7. After multiplying by the routing matrix **R**, the link volume measurement at time t is anomalous. This process is repeated for each time t (i.e., each five-minute window) in the test week to generate 2016 anomalous samples for the qth target flow.

A DoS attack is simulated along every flow at every time, and the detector's alarms are recorded for each such attack. The FNR is estimated by averaging over all 144 flows and all 2016 time slots. When reporting the effect of an attack on traffic volumes, we first average over links within each flow and then over flows. Furthermore, we generally report average volumes relative to the preattack average volumes. Thus, a single poisoning experiment was based on one week of poisoning with FNRs computed during the test week that includes $144 \times 2,016$ samples coming from the different flows and time slots. Because the poisoning is deterministic in add-more-if-bigger, this experiment was run once for that scheme. In contrast, for the *Random* poisoning scheme, we ran 20 independent repetitions of poisoning experiments data because the poisoning is random.

The squared prediction errors produced by the detection methods (based on the anomalous and normal examples from the test set) are used to produce ROC curves. By varying the method's threshold from $-\infty$ to ∞ a curve of possible (FPR, TPR) pairs is produced from the set of squared prediction errors; the Q-statistic and Laplace threshold each correspond to one such point in ROC space. We adopt the area under curve (AUC) statistic to directly compare ROC curves. The ideal detector has an AUC of 1, while the random predictor achieves an AUC of $\frac{1}{2}$.

6.4.2   Identifying Vulnerable Flows

There are two ways that a flow can be vulnerable. A flow is considered *vulnerable to DoS attack* (unpoisoned scenario) if a DoS attack along it is likely to be undetected when the resulting traffic data is projected onto the abnormal subspace. *Vulnerability to poisoning* means that if the flow is first poisoned, then the subsequent DoS attack is likely to be undetected because the resulting projection in abnormal space is no longer significant. To examine the vulnerability of flows, we define the residual rate statistic, which measures the change in the size of the residual (i.e., $\Delta \|\tilde{\mathbf{x}}\|_2$) caused by adding a single unit of traffic volume along a particular target flow. This statistic assesses how vulnerable a detector is to a DoS attack because it measures how rapidly the residual grows as the size of the DoS increases and thus is an indicator of whether a large DoS attack will be undetected along a target flow. Injecting a unit volume along the qth target flow causes an additive increase to the link measurement vector $\mathbf{R}_q$ and also increases the residual by

$$\nu\left(q; \ddot{\mathbf{P}}\right) \triangleq \left\|\ddot{\mathbf{P}}\mathbf{R}_q\right\|_2.$$

The residual rate measures how well a flow aligns with the normal subspace. If the flow aligns perfectly with the normal subspace, its residual rate will be 0 since changes along the directions of the subspace do not change the residual component of the traffic at all. More generally, a low residual rate indicates that (per unit of traffic sent) a DoS attack will not significantly affect the squared prediction error. Thus, for a detector to be effective, the residual rate must be high for most flows; otherwise the attacker will be able to execute large undetected DoS attacks.

By running PCA on each week of the Abilene data, we computed the residual rate of each flow for each week's model and estimated the spread in their residual rates. Figure 6.4 displays box plots of the residual rates for each flow over the 24 weeks of data. These plots show that when trained on uncontaminated data 99% of the flows have a median residual rate above 1.0; i.e., for every unit of traffic added to any of these flows in a DoS attack, the residual component of the traffic increases by at least 1.0 unit and for many flows the increase is higher.[7] This result indicates that PCA trained on clean data is not vulnerable to DoS attacks on the majority of flows since each unit of traffic used in the attack increases the residual by at least one unit. However, PCA is very vulnerable to DoS attacks along flows 32 and 87 because their residual rates are small even without poisoning.

All of this is good news from the point of view of the attacker. Without poisoning, an attacker might only succeed if it were lucky enough to be attacking along the two highly vulnerable flows. However, after poisoning, it is clear that whatever the attack's target might be, the flow it chooses to attack, on average, is likely to be vulnerable.

6.4.3   Evaluation of Attacks

In this section, we present experimental validation that adversarial poisoning can have a significant detrimental impact on the PCA-based anomaly detector. We evaluate the effectiveness of the three data poisoning schemes from Section 6.2 for single training period attacks. During the testing week, the attacker launches a DoS attack in each five-minute time window. The results of these attacks are displayed in Figure 6.5(a). Although the objective of these poisoning schemes is to add variance along the target flow, the mean of the target OD flow being poisoned increases as well, increasing the

---

[7] Many flows have residual rates well above 1 because these flows traverse many links, and thus adding a single unit of traffic along the flow adds many units in link space. On average, flows in the Abilene dataset have 4.5 links per flow.

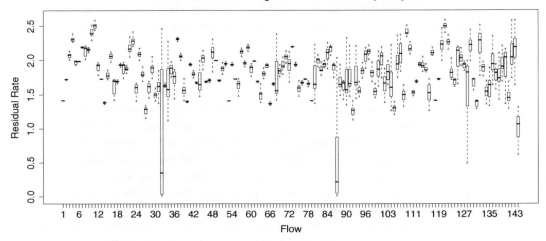

(a) Residual Rates for PCA

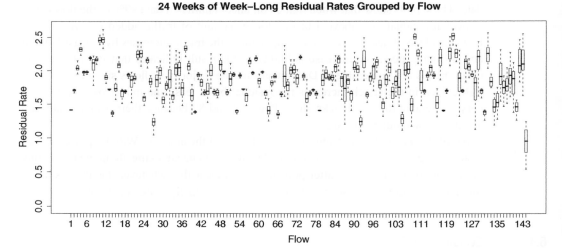

(b) Residual Rates for PCA-GRID

Figure 6.4 Comparison of the original PCA subspace and PCA-GRID subspace in terms of their residual rates. Shown here are box plots of the 24 weekly residual rates for each flow to demonstrate the variation in residual rate for the two methods. **(a)** Distribution of the per-flow residual rates for the original PCA method and **(b)** for PCA-GRID. For PCA, flows 32 and 87 (the flows connecting Chicago and Los Angeles in Figure 6.1(b)), have consistently low residual rates, making PCA susceptible to evasion along these flows. Both methods also have a moderate susceptibility along flow 144 (the ingress/egress link for Washington). Otherwise, PCA-GRID has overall high residual rates along all flows, indicating little vulnerability to evasion.

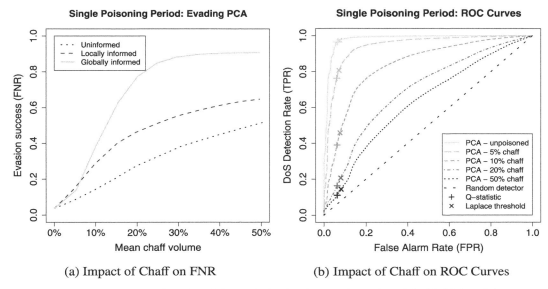

(a) Impact of Chaff on FNR   (b) Impact of Chaff on ROC Curves

Figure 6.5 Effect of single training period poisoning attacks on the original PCA-based detector. **(a)** Evasion success of PCA versus relative chaff volume under single training period poisoning attacks using three chaff methods: uninformed (dotted line), locally informed (dashed line), and globally informed (solid line). **(b).** Comparison of the ROC curves of PCA for different volumes of chaff (using add-more-if-bigger chaff). Also depicted are the points on the ROC curves selected by the Q-statistic and Laplace threshold, respectively.

means of all links over which the OD flow traverses. The x-axis in Figure 6.5 is the relative increase in the mean rate. The y-axis is the average FNR for that level of poisoning (i.e., averaged over all OD flows).

As expected the increase in evasion success is smallest for the uninformed strategy, intermediate for the locally informed scheme, and largest for the globally informed poisoning scheme. A locally informed attacker can use the add-more-if-bigger scheme to raise its evasion success to 28% from the baseline FNR of 3.67% via a 10% average increase in the mean link rates due to chaff; i.e., the attacker's rate of successful evasion increases nearly eightfold from the rate of the unpoisoned PCA detector. With a globally informed strategy, a 10% average increase in the mean link rates causes the unpoisoned FNR to increase by a factor of 10 to 38% success and eventually to over 90% FNR as the size of the attack increases. The primary difference between the performance of the locally informed and globally informed attacker is intuitive to understand. Recall that the globally informed attacker is privy to the traffic on all links for the entire training period while the locally informed attacker only knows the traffic status of a single ingress link. Considering this information disparity, the locally informed adversary is quite successful with only a small view of the network. An adversary is unlikely to be able to acquire, in practice, the capabilities used in the globally informed poisoning attack. Moreover, adding 30% chaff to obtain a 90% evasion success is dangerous in that the poisoning activity itself is likely to be detected. Therefore add-more-if-bigger offers a nice tradeoff, from the adversary's point of view, in terms of poisoning effectiveness, and the attacker's capabilities and risks.

We also evaluate the PCA detection algorithm on both anomalous and normal data, as described in Section 6.4.1.2, to produce the ROC curves in Figure 6.5(b). We produce a series of ROC curves (as shown) by first training a PCA model on the unpoisoned data from the 20th week and then training on data poisoned by progressively larger add-more-if-bigger attacks.

To validate PCA-based detection on poisoned training data, each flow is poisoned separately in different trials of the experiment as dictated by the threat model. Thus, for relative chaff volumes ranging from 5% to 50%, add-more-if-bigger chaff is added to each flow separately to construct 144 separate training sets and 144 corresponding ROC curves for the given level of poisoning. The poisoned curves in Figure 6.5(b) display the averages of these ROC curves; i.e., the average TPR over the 144 flows for each FPR.

The sequence of ROC curves show that the add-more-if-bigger poisoning scheme creates an unacceptable tradeoff between false positives and false negatives of the PCA detector: the detection and false alarm rates drop together rapidly as the level of chaff is increased. At 10% relative chaff volume performance degrades significantly from the ideal ROC curve (lines from $(0, 0)$ to $(0, 1)$ to $(1, 1)$) and at 20% the PCA's mean ROC curve is already close to that of a random detector (the $y = x$ line with an AUC of $1/2$).

6.4.4   Evaluation of ANTIDOTE

We assess the effect of poisoning attacks on ANTIDOTE performance during a single training period. As with the PCA-based detector, we evaluate the success of this detector with each of the different poisoning schemes and compute ROC curves using the add-more-if-bigger poisoning scheme to compare to the original PCA-subspace method.

Figure 6.6(a) depicts ANTIDOTE's FNR for various levels of average poisoning that occur in a single training period attack compared to the results depicted in Figure 6.5(a) using the same metric for the original PCA detector. Comparing these results, the evasion success of the attack is dramatically reduced for ANTIDOTE. For any particular level of chaff, the evasion success rate of ANTIDOTE is approximately half that of the original PCA approach. Interestingly, the most effective poisoning scheme on PCA (globally informed poisoning) is the least effective poisoning scheme against ANTIDOTE. The globally informed scheme was designed in an approximately optimal fashion to circumvent PCA, but for the alternative detector, globally informed chaff is not optimized and empirically has little effect on PCA-GRID. For this detector, *Random* remains equally effective because constant shifts in a large subset of the data create a bimodality that is difficult for any subspace method to reconcile—since roughly half the data shifts by a constant amount, it is difficult to distinguish between the original and shifted subspaces. However, this effect is still small compared to the dramatic success of locally informed and globally informed chaff strategies against the original detector.

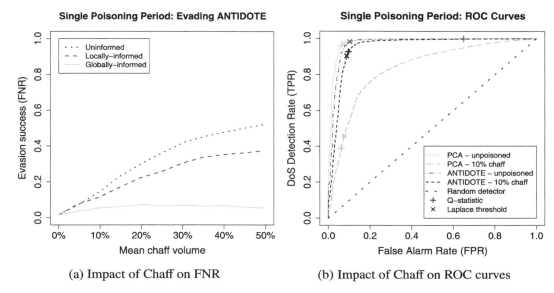

(a) Impact of Chaff on FNR   (b) Impact of Chaff on ROC curves

Figure 6.6 Effect of single training period poisoning attacks on the ANTIDOTE detector.
(a) Evasion success of ANTIDOTE versus relative chaff volume under single training period
poisoning attacks using three chaff methods: uninformed (dotted black line), locally informed
(dashed line), and globally informed (solid line). **(b)** Comparison of the ROC curves of
ANTIDOTE and the original PCA detector when unpoisoned and under 10% chaff (using
add-more-if-bigger chaff). The PCA detector and ANTIDOTE detector have similar performance
when unpoisoned but PCA's ROC curve is significantly degraded with chaff, whereas
ANTIDOTE's is only slightly affected.

Since poisoning distorts the detector, it affects both the false-negative and false-positive rates. Figure 6.6(b) provides a comparison of the ROC curves for both ANTIDOTE and PCA when the training data is both unpoisoned and poisoned. For the poisoned training scenario, each point on the curve is the average over 144 poisoning scenarios in which the training data is poisoned along one of the 144 possible flows using the add-more-if-bigger strategy. While ANTIDOTE performs very similarly to PCA on unpoisoned training data, PCA's performance is significantly degraded by poisoning while ANTIDOTE remains relatively unaffected. With a moderate mean chaff volume of 10%, ANTIDOTE's average ROC curve remains close to optimal, while PCA's curve considerably shifts toward the $y = x$ curve of the random detector. This means that under a moderate level of poisoning, PCA cannot achieve a reasonable tradeoff between false positives and false negatives while ANTIDOTE retains a good operating point for these two common performance measures. *In summary, in terms of false positives and false negatives, ANTIDOTE incurs insignificant performance shifts when no poisoning occurs, but is resilient against poisoning and provides enormous performance gains compared to PCA when poisoning attacks do occur.*

Given Figures 6.6(a) and 6.6(b) alone, it is conceivable that ANTIDOTE outperforms PCA only on average, and not on all flows targeted for poisoning. In place of plotting

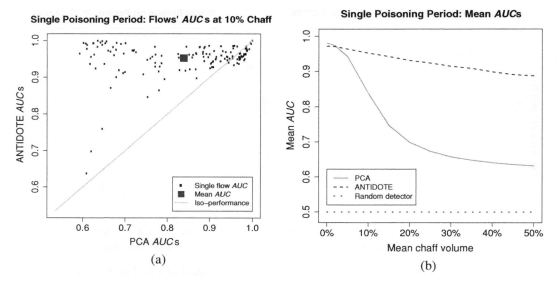

Figure 6.7 Comparison of the original PCA detector in terms of the area under their (ROC) curves (*AUC*s). **(a)** The *AUC* for the PCA detector and the ANTIDOTE detector under 10% add-more-if-bigger chaff for each of the 144 target flows. Each point in this scatter plot is a single target flow; its *x*-coordinate is the *AUC* of PCA and its *y*-coordinate is the *AUC* of ANTIDOTE. Points above the line $y = x$ represent flows where ANTIDOTE has a better *AUC* than the PCA detector, and those below $y = x$ represent flows for which PCA outperforms ANTIDOTE. The mean *AUC* for both methods is indicated by the square symbol. **(b)** The mean *AUC* of each detector versus the mean chaff level of an add-more-if-bigger poisoning attack for increasing levels of relative chaff. The methods compared are a random detector (dotted black line), the PCA detector (solid line), and ANTIDOTE (dashed line).

all 144 poisoned ROC curves, Figure 6.7(a) compares the *AUC*s for the two detection methods under 10% chaff. Not only is average performance much better for robust PCA, but it in fact outperforms PCA on most flows and by a decidedly large amount. Although PCA indeed performs slightly better for some flows, in these cases both methods have excellent detection performance (because their *AUC*s are close to 1), and hence the distinction between the two is insignificant for those specific flows.

Figure 6.7(b) plots the mean AUC (averaged from the 144 ROC curves' *AUC*s where flows are poisoned separately) achieved by the detectors for an increasing level of poisoning. ANTIDOTE behaves comparably to (albeit slightly worse than) PCA under no-chaff conditions, yet its performance remains relatively stable as the amount of contamination increases while PCA's performance rapidly degrades. In fact, with as little as 5% poisoning, ANTIDOTE already exceeds the performance of PCA, and the gap only widens with increasing contamination. As PCA's performance drops, it approaches a random detector (equivalently, $AUC = 1/2$), for amounts of poisoning exceeding 20%. As these experiments demonstrate, ANTIDOTE is an effective defense and dramatically outperforms a solution that was not designed to be robust. This is strong evidence that the robust techniques are a promising instrument for designing machine learning algorithms used in security-sensitive domains.

6.4.5   Empirical Evaluation of the Boiling Frog Poisoning Attack

6.4.5.1   Experimental Methodology for Episodic Poisoning

To test the boiling frog poisoning attack, several weeks of traffic data are simulated using a generative model inspired by Lakhina, Crovella, & Diot (2004b). These simulations produce multiple weeks of data generated from a stationary distribution. While such data is unrealistic in practice, stationary data is the ideal dataset for PCA to produce a reliable detector. Anomaly detection under nonstationary conditions is more difficult due to the learner's inability to distinguish between benign data drift and anomalous conditions. By showing that PCA is susceptibility to episodic poisoning even in this stationary case, these experiments suggest that the method can also be compromised in more realistic settings. Further, the six-month Abilene dataset of Zhang et al. (2005) proved to be too nonstationary for PCA to consistently operate well from one week to the next—PCA often performed poorly even without poisoning. It is unclear whether the nonstationarity observed in this data is prevalent in general or whether it is an artifact of the dataset, but nonetheless, these experiments show PCA is susceptible to poisoning even when the underlying data is well behaved.

To synthesize a stationary multiweek dataset of OD flow traffic matrices, a three-step generative procedure is used to model each OD flow separately. First the underlying daily cycle of the qth OD flow's time series is modeled by a sinusoidal approximation. Then the times at which the flow is experiencing an anomaly are modeled by a binomial arrival process with interarrival times distributed according to the geometric distribution. Finally Gaussian white noise is added to the base sinusoidal model during times of benign OD flow traffic, and exponential traffic is added to the base model during times of anomalous traffic.

In the first step, the underlying cyclic trends are captured by fitting the coefficients for Fourier basis functions. Following the model proposed by Lakhina et al. (2004b), the basis functions are sinusoids of periods of 7, 5, and 3 days, and 24, 12, 6, 3, and 1.5 hours, as well as a constant function. For each OD flow, the Fourier coefficients are estimated by projecting the flow onto this basis. The portion of the traffic modeled by this Fourier forecaster is removed, and the remaining residual traffic is modeled with two processes—a zero-mean Gaussian noise process captures short-term benign traffic variance, and an exponential distribution is used to model nonmalicious volume anomalies.

In the second step, one of the two noise processes is selected for each time interval. After computing the Fourier model's residuals (the difference between the observed and predicted traffic), the smallest negative residual value $-m$ is recorded. We assume that residuals in the interval $[-m, m]$ correspond to benign traffic and that residuals exceeding m correspond to traffic anomalies (this is an approximation, but it works reasonably well for most OD flows). Periods of benign variation and anomalies are then modeled separately since these effects behave quite differently. After classifying residual traffic as benign or anomalous, anomaly arrival times are modeled as a Bernoulli arrival process, and the inter-anomaly arrival times are geometrically distributed. Further, since we consider only spatial PCA methods, the temporal placement of anomalies is unimportant.

In the third and final step, the parameters for the two residual traffic volume and the inter-anomaly arrival processes are inferred from the residual traffic using the maximum likelihood estimates of the Gaussian's variance and exponential and geometric rates, respectively. Positive goodness-of-fit results (Q-Q plots not shown) have been obtained for small, medium, and large flows.

In the synthesis, all link volumes are constrained to respect the link capacities in the Abilene network: 10 gbps for all but one link that operates at one fourth of this rate. We also cap chaff that would cause traffic to exceed the link capacities.

6.4.5.2   Effect of Episodic Poisoning on the PCA Detector

We now evaluate the effectiveness of the boiling frog poisoning attack strategy, that contaminates the training data over multiple training periods. Figure 6.8(a) plots the FNRs against the poisoning duration for the PCA detector for four different *poisoning*

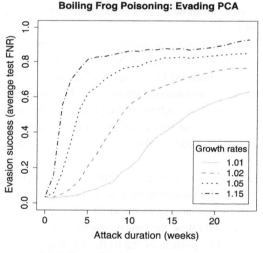

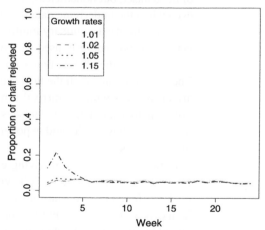

(a) Effect of boiling frog on PCA   (b) Rejection of chaff by PCA

Figure 6.8 Effect of boiling frog poisoning attack on the original PCA-subspace detector (see Figure 6.9 for comparison with the PCA-based detector). **(a)** Evasion success of PCA under boiling frog poisoning attack in terms of the average FNR after each successive week of poisoning for four different poisoning schedules (i.e., a weekly geometric increase in the size of the poisoning by factors 1.01, 1.02, 1.05, and 1.15 respectively). More aggressive schedules (e.g., growth rates of 1.05 and 1.15) significantly increase the FNR within a few weeks while less aggressive schedules take many weeks to achieve the same result, but are more stealthy in doing so. **(b)** Weekly chaff rejection rates by the PCA-based detector for the boiling frog poisoning attacks from (a). The detector only detects a significant amount of the chaff during the first weeks of the most aggressive schedule (growth rate of 1.15); subsequently, the detector is too contaminated to accurately detect the chaff.

schedules with growth rates of 1.01, 1.02, 1.05, and 1.15 respectively. The schedule's growth rate corresponds to the rate of increase in the attacked links' average traffic from week to week. The attack strength parameter θ (see Section 6.2) is selected to achieve this goal. We see that the FNR dramatically increases for all four schedules as the poison duration increases. With a 15% growth rate the FNR is increased from 3.67% to more than 70% over three weeks of poisoning; even with a 5% growth rate the FNR is increased to 50% over 3 weeks. Thus boiling frog attacks are effective even when the amount of poisoned data increases rather slowly. Further, in comparing Figure 6.5(a) for a single training period to Figure 6.8(a), the success of boiling frog attacks becomes clear. For the single training period attack, to raise the FNR to 50%, an immediate increase in mean traffic of roughly 18% is required, whereas in the boiling frog attack the same result can be achieved with only a 5% average traffic increase spread across three weeks.

Recall that the two methods are retrained every week using the data collected from the previous week. However, the data from the previous week is also filtered by the detector itself, and for any time window flagged as anomalous, the training data is thrown out. Figure 6.8(b) shows the proportion of chaff rejected each week by PCA (*chaff rejection rate*) for the boiling frog poisoning attack strategy. The three slower schedules enjoy a relatively small constant rejection rate close to 5%. The 15% schedule begins with a relatively high rejection rate, but after a month sufficient amounts of poisoned traffic mistrain PCA, after whichpoint the rates drop to the level of the slower schedules. Thus, the boiling frog strategy with a moderate growth rate of 2–5% can significantly poison PCA, dramatically increasing its FNR while still going unnoticed by the detector.

6.4.5.3   Effect of Episodic Poisoning on ANTIDOTE

We now evaluate the effectiveness of ANTIDOTE against the boiling frog strategy that occurs over multiple successive training periods. Figure 6.9(a) shows the FNRs for ANTIDOTE with the four poisoning schedules (recall from Section 6.4.5.2 that each is the weekly growth factor for the increase in size of a add-more-if-bigger poisoning strategy). First, for the two most stealthy poisoning strategies (1.01 and 1.02), ANTIDOTE shows remarkable resistance in that the evasion success increases very slowly, e.g., after ten training periods it is still below 20% evasion success. This is in stark contrast to PCA (see Figure 6.8(a)); for example, after ten weeks the evasion success against PCA exceeds 50% for the 1.02 poisoning growth rate scenario.

Second, under PCA the evasion success consistently increases with each additional week. However, with ANTIDOTE, the evasion success of these more aggressive schedules actually decreases after several weeks. The reason is that as the chaff levels rise, ANTIDOTE increasingly is able to identify the chaff as abnormal and then reject enough of it from the subsequent training data that the poisoning strategy loses its effectiveness.

Figure 6.9(b) shows the proportion of chaff rejected by ANTIDOTE under episodic poisoning. The two slower schedules almost have a constant rejection rate close to 9% (which is higher than PCA's rejection rate of around 5%). For the more aggressive growth schedules (5% and 15%), however, ANTIDOTE rejects an increasing amount of the poison data. This reflects a good target behavior for any robust detector—to

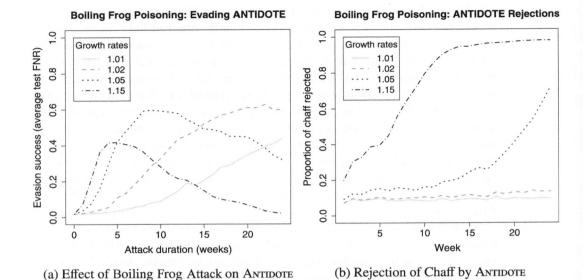

(a) Effect of Boiling Frog Attack on ANTIDOTE   (b) Rejection of Chaff by ANTIDOTE

Figure 6.9 Effect of boiling frog poisoning attack on the ANTIDOTE detector (see Figure 6.8 for comparison with the PCA-based detector). **(a)** Evasion success of ANTIDOTE under boiling frog poisoning attacks in terms of the average FNR after each successive week of poisoning for four different poisoning schedules (i.e., a weekly geometric increase in the size of the poisoning by factors 1.01, 1.02, 1.05, and 1.15 respectively). Unlike the weekly FNRs for the boiling frog poisoning in Figure 6.8(a), the more aggressive schedules (e.g., growth rates of 1.05 and 1.15) reach their peak FNR after only a few weeks of poisoning after which their effect declines (as the detector successfully rejects increasing amounts of chaff). The less aggressive schedules (with growth rates of 1.01 and 1.02) still have gradually increasing FNRs, but also seem to eventually plateau. **(b)** Weekly chaff rejection rates by the ANTIDOTE detector for the boiling frog poisoning attacks from (a). Unlike PCA (see Figure 6.8(b)), ANTIDOTE rejects increasingly more chaff from the boiling frog attack. For all poisoning schedules, ANTIDOTE has a higher baseline rejection rate (around 10%) than the PCA detector (around 5%), and it rejects most of the chaff from aggressive schedules within a few weeks. This suggests that, unlike PCA, ANTIDOTE is not progressively poisoned by increasing week-to-week chaff volumes.

reject more training data as the contamination grows. *Overall, these experiments pro-vide empirical evidence that the combination of techniques used by* ANTIDOTE, *namely a subspace-based detector designed with a robust subspace estimator combined with a Laplace-based cutoff threshold, maintains a good balance between false-negative and false-positive rates throughout a variety of poisoning scenarios (different amounts of poisoning, on different OD flows, and on different time horizons) and thus provides a resilient alternative to the original PCA-based detector.*

6.5   Summary

To subvert the PCA-based detector proposed by Lakhina et al. (2004*b*), we stud-ied *Causative Integrity* attacks that poison the training data by adding malicious chaff; i.e., spurious traffic sent across the network by compromised nodes that reside within it. This chaff is designed to interfere with PCA's subspace estimation procedure. Based on a relaxed objection function, we demonstrated how an adversary can approximate optimal noise using a global view of the traffic patterns in the network. Empirically, we found that by increasing the mean link rate by 10% with globally informed chaff traffic, the FNR increased from 3.67% to 38%—a 10-fold increase in misclassification of DoS attacks. Similarly, by only using local link information the attacker is able to mount a more realistic add-more-if-bigger attack. For this attack, increasing the mean link rate by 10% with add-more-if-bigger chaff traffic, the FNR increased from 3.67% to 28%—an eightfold increase in misclassification of DoS attacks. These attacks demonstrate that with sufficient information about network patterns, adversaries can mount attacks against the PCA detector that severely compromise its ability to detect future DoS attacks traversing the networking it is monitoring.

We also demonstrated that an alternative robust method for subspace estimation could be used instead to make the resulting DoS detector less susceptible to poisoning attacks. The alternative detector was constructed using a subspace method for robust PCA developed by Croux et al. and a more robust method for estimating the residual cutoff threshold. The resulting ANTIDOTE detector is affected by poisoning, but its performance degrades more gracefully. Under nonpoisoned traffic, ANTIDOTE performs nearly as well as PCA, but for all levels of contamination using add-more-if-bigger chaff traffic, the misclassification rate of ANTIDOTE is approximately half the FNR of the PCA-based solution. Moreover, the average performance of ANTIDOTE is much better than the original detector; it outperforms ordinary PCA for more flows and by a large amount. For the multiweek boiling frog poisoning attack ANTIDOTE also outperformed PCA and would catch progressively more attack traffic in each subsequent week.

Several important questions about subspace detection methods remain unanswered. While we have demonstrated that ANTIDOTE is resilient to poisoning attacks, it is not yet known if there are alternative poisoning schemes that significantly reduce ANTIDOTE's detection performance. Because ANTIDOTE is founded on robust estimators, it is unlikely that there is a poisoning strategy that completely degrades its performance. However, to better understand the limits of attacks and defenses, it is imperative to continue investigating worst-case attacks against the next generation of defenders; in this case, ANTIDOTE.

QUESTION 6.1 What are the worst-case poisoning attacks against the ANTIDOTE-subspace detector for large-volume network anomalies? What are game-theoretic equilibrium strategies for the attacker and defender in this setting? How does ANTIDOTE's performance compare to these strategies?

There are also several other approaches for developing effective anomaly detectors for large volume anomalies (e.g., Brauckhoff et al. 2009). To compare these alternatives to ANTIDOTE, one must first identify their vulnerabilities and assess their performance when under attack. More importantly though, we think detectors could be substantially improved by combining them together.

QUESTION 6.2 Can subspace-based detection approaches be adapted to incorporate the alternative approaches? Can they find both temporal and spatial correlations and use both to detect anomalies? Can subspace-based approaches be adapted to incorporate domain-specific information such as the topology of the network?

Developing the next generation of network anomaly detectors is a critical task that perhaps can incorporate several of the themes we promote in this dissertation to create secure learners.

Part III

Exploratory Attacks on Machine Learning

7 Privacy-Preserving Mechanisms for SVM Learning

High-profile privacy breaches have trained the spotlight of public attention on data privacy. Until recently privacy, a relative laggard within computer security, could be enhanced only weakly by available technologies, when releasing aggregate statistics on sensitive data: until the mid-2000s definitions of privacy were merely syntactic. Contrast this with the state of affairs within cryptography that has long offered provably strong guarantees on maintaining the secrecy of encrypted information, based on computational limitations of attackers. Proposed as an answer to the challenge of bringing privacy on equal footing with cryptography, differential privacy (Dwork et al. 2006; Dwork & Roth 2014) has quickly grown in stature due to its formal nature and guarantees against powerful attackers. This chapter continues the discussion begun in Section 3.7, including a case study on the release of trained support vector machine (SVM) classifiers while preserving training data privacy. This chapter builds on (Rubinstein, Bartlett, Huang, & Taft 2012).

7.1 Privacy Breach Case Studies

We first review several high-profile privacy breaches achieved by privacy researchers. Together these have helped shape the discourse on privacy and in particular have led to important advancements in privacy-enhancing technologies. This section concludes with a discussion of lessons learned.

7.1.1 Massachusetts State Employees Health Records

An early privacy breach demonstrated the difficulty in defining the concept of *personally identifiable information* (PII) and led to the highly influential development of *k*-anonymity (Sweeney 2002).

In the mid-1990s the Massachusetts Group Insurance Commission released private health records of state employees, showing individual hospital visits, for the purpose of fostering health research. To mitigate privacy risks to state employees, the Commission scrubbed all suspected PII: names, addresses, and Social Security numbers. What was released was pure medical information together with (what seemed to be innocuous) demographics: birthdate, gender, and zipcode.

Security researcher Sweeney realized that the demographic information not scrubbed was in fact partial PII. To demonstrate her idea, Sweeney obtained readily available public voter information for the city of Cambridge, Massachusetts, which included birthdates, zipcodes, and names. She then linked this public data to the "anonymized" released hospital records, thereby re-identifying many of the employees including her target, then Governor William Weld who originally oversaw the release of the health data.

Sweeney (2002) measured the success rate of her technique more broadly, estimating that 87% of the U.S. population was uniquely identified by birthdate, gender, and zipcode. Focusing on preventing such unique identification, she proposed k-anonymity: the information on each individual in a release must be indistinguishable to at least $k - 1$ other individuals in the release. Typically attributes/values identified as PII are either suppressed completely, or aggregated in a higher level of quantization.

Since the initial work on k-anonymity, vulnerabilities in the definition have been identified and in some cases repaired by follow-up derivative proposals such as ℓ-diversity (Machanavajjhala et al. 2007) and t-closeness (Li, Li, & Venkatasubramanian 2007).

7.1.2   AOL Search Query Logs

In 2006 AOL publicly released three months of search logs for over 650,000 AOL users, for the purpose of fostering Web search research (Barbaro & Zeller 2006). While queries were not labeled by user name, queries were linked to common user IDs, and search terms included PII and sensitive information regarding users' online activity.

Shortly after the data release, *New York Times* journalists identified AOL users in the query log. The misstep of releasing the data cost AOL's CTO her job and resulted in a class-action lawsuit brought against AOL by the affected users. The AOL search data episode put a dampener on data sharing for research, and highlights the difficulty in defining PII only in terms of structured data fields like name and address.

7.1.3   The Netflix Prize

In 2006—the same year as the AOL data release—Netflix launched a three-year-long movie recommendation competition with a $1,000,000 first prize (Bennett, Lanning et al. 2007). The released competition data consisted of about 100 million ratings of about 17 thousand movies by 480k users. The Netflix dataset was highly sparse with over 200 ratings on average per user and over 5k ratings on average per movie, but high variance on both counts.

While Netflix did not release information directly identifying users—indeed the ratings of some users were apparently perturbed in an attempt to preserve privacy (Bennett et al. 2007)—the identities of movies were released. Competitors were permitted to leverage movie identities to make use of external data that could assist in making more accurate recommendations. Researchers Narayanan & Shmatikov (2008) used publicly available IMDb data with movie ratings from non-anonymized users, to link PII in public IMDb profiles with anonymized users in the Netflix data, thereby re-identifying users in the competition dataset. The sexual orientation of one Netflix user became public. Netflix lost a class-action lawsuit launched as a result of the de-anonymization, with one stipulation being the cancellation of the sequel Netflix Prize II competition.

7.1.4   Deanonymizing Twitter Pseudonyms

A year after Narayanan & Shmatikov re-identified Netflix users, the same researchers demonstrated the inherent difficulty of anonymizing social network data (Narayanan & Shmatikov 2009).

Privacy is a serious concern in social networks. For example, Twitter played a crucial role in the Arab Spring uprising, with political dissidents taking to the online site to coordinate peaceful protest and document government abuses. Pseudonyms in online profiles promote anonymity, but are not foolproof. And while companies like Twitter may attempt to keep user privacy protected, they have competing drives for profit (sharing data with advertisers) and complying with legal warrants for information. Narayanan & Shmatikov showed that even in the absence of any profile information, network connections alone can identify many users. Linking nodes in the Twitter social graph with nodes in the Flickr photo-sharing website's social graph, they were able to re-identify a third of the users verified to have accounts on both Twitter and Flickr with 88% accuracy.

We have extended the approach, with Narayanan and Shi, to recover test labels in a social network link prediction challenge (Narayanan, Shi, & Rubinstein 2011): effectively a privacy attack applied to cheating at a machine learning competition. Where Narayanan & Smatikov linked different graphs from two sites crawled at the same time, our result demonstrates that even over a six-month period graph evolution is insufficient to mitigate linkage attacks.

7.1.5   Genome-Wide Association Studies

Genome-wide Association Studies (GWAS) are an important statistical tool for analyzing medical assay data, in which the nucleotide frequencies at specific locii on the genome are compared between a control group of healthy subjects and a case group of individuals with a particular disease. Significant differences in occurrence frequencies imply an association between the disease and genetic markers. Homer et al. (2008) demonstrated the possibility of detecting whether a target individual participated in a GWAS case group—characterized as a mixture of participant genetic data—from the target DNA sequence information. This opened the possibility that participants of previously published GWAS data could be identified and led the National Institutes of Health to control the publication of study statistics.

Several other avenues exist for breaching "genetic privacy" (Erlich & Narayanan 2014) such as triangulating genealogical data to determine a study participant's surname (Gymrek, McGuire, Golan, Halperin, & Erlich 2013).

7.1.6   Ad Microtargeting

Sharing personal data such as demographics and browsing history with online advertisers has long led to objections from privacy advocates. But what if no directly identifying information is shared with advertisers? What if no information is directly shared at all? Even in this seemingly innocuous setting, user privacy may be breached. Korolova (2011) showed that ad microtargeting on Facebook can be exploited to infer private information on users. The basic attack aims to infer some unknown private attribute (such as sexual orientation) of a selected target, for whom some identifying information is known already, such as age, location, workplace, or education. The attacker launches two ad campaigns on the social network, both targeting the fine details of the target user: one targeting users having the private attribute and the other targeting users without the attribute. Even though Facebook does not *directly* share the details of users viewing the ad, the attacker can determine this information depending on which ad campaign's dollar balance changes. By examining the PII that is provided by Facebook, both campaigns can target the specific user, and an ad from exactly one of the two campaigns will be presented and be charged back to the attacker. This reveals which attribute value is possessed by the target user.

7.1.7   Lessons Learned

A number of patterns recur within the above case studies:

- It is dangerous to dismiss privacy breaches as trivially unlikely or requiring too much work on the part of the attacker. Time and time again, highly sophisticated attacks have been demonstrated. They were publicized to highlight misuses of sensitive data (due to initial data releases) and advance privacy research. In reality, much more valuable incentives exist to breach privacy without disclosure.
- Many breaches are accomplished via linkage attack: Records of an "anonymized" dataset are linked with an external data source that is easily obtained or even public. The combined data ties sensitive information (from the released private data) to re-identified individuals (from public records).
- It is exceedingly difficult to identify attributes that constitute PII, a necessary condition of employing *syntactic* measures such as k-anonymity and its derivatives. Many attributes can act like fingerprints: a *curse of dimensionality* exists in private data analysis in which high-dimensional data associated with individuals is likely to be unique.

7.2   Problem Setting: Privacy-Preserving Learning

Our goal in this chapter is to release aggregate information about a dataset while maintaining the privacy of each individual datum. These two goals of *utility* and *privacy* are inherently discordant. However, we will see that an effective balance can be achieved with practical release mechanisms.

For a release mechanism to be useful, its responses must closely resemble some target statistic of the data. In particular since we will be releasing classifiers learned on training data, our formal measure of utility will compare the released classifiers with a desired nonprivate classifier trained on the same data. In this case, our target classifier is the support vector machine (SVM), one of the most widely used supervised learners in practice.

Within the context of the previous section, any claim of data confidentiality *must* be backed up by a semantic guarantee of privacy: Time and time again weakly anonymized data has been re-identified. To this end, it is necessary for the mechanism's response to be "smoothed out": the mechanism must be randomized to reduce any individual datum's influence on this distribution. This is exactly the approach when establishing a property due to Dwork et al. (2006) known as differential privacy. We adopt this strong guarantee on privacy.

Those in the area of statistical databases, studied by the databases and theory communities, hope to understand when the goals of utility and privacy can be efficiently achieved simultaneously (Dinur & Nissim 2003; Barak et al. 2007; Blum et al. 2008; Chaudhuri & Monteleoni 2009; Kasiviswanathan et al. 2008; Duchi et al. 2013; Dwork & Roth 2014; Aldà & Rubinstein 2017). We will thus adopt their terminology while examining their approaches. While this chapter's discussion involves theoretical analyses, the mechanisms presented here—developed in our past work (Rubinstein, Bartlett, Huang, & Taft 2009; Rubinstein et al. 2012)—are easily implemented and efficient, and release classifiers that are close to the corresponding nonprivate SVM under the ℓ_∞-norm, with high probability. In our setting this notion of utility is stronger than closeness of risk.

7.2.1   Differential Privacy

We now cover background on differential privacy. Given access to database $\mathbb{D}$, a *mechanism M* must release aggregate information about $\mathbb{D}$ while maintaining the privacy of individual entries. We assume that the *response M* $(\mathbb{D})$, belonging to range space $\mathcal{T}_M$, is the only information released by the mechanism. The statistical databases terminology we adopt should be understood to have analogs in machine learning, where for example database corresponds to dataset, record or item corresponds to datum, mechanism to learning algorithm, and the released quantity as the learned classifier.

We say that a pair of databases $\mathbb{D}^{(1)}, \mathbb{D}^{(2)}$ are neighbors if they differ on exactly one entry; in other words the two datasets are separated by hamming (or ℓ_1) distance 1. We adopt the following strong notion of privacy due to Dwork et al. (2006).

DEFINITION 7.1 For any $\beta > 0$, a randomized mechanism M provides *β-differential privacy*, if, for all neighboring databases $\mathbb{D}^{(1)}, \mathbb{D}^{(2)}$ and all responses $t \in \mathcal{T}_M$, the mechanism satisfies

$$\log\left(\frac{\Pr\left(M\left(\mathbb{D}^{(1)}\right) = t\right)}{\Pr\left(M\left(\mathbb{D}^{(2)}\right) = t\right)}\right) \leq \beta.$$

The probability in the definition is over the randomization in M, not the databases. For continuous $\mathcal{T}_M$ we mean by this ratio a Radon-Nikodym derivative of the distribution of $M\left(\mathbb{D}^{(1)}\right)$ with respect to the distribution of $M\left(\mathbb{D}^{(2)}\right)$.[1] In the sequel we assume without loss of generality that each pair of neighboring databases differs on their last entry.

To understand the definition, consider a mechanism M preserving a high level of differential privacy (low β) and a powerful attacker with the following capabilities:

- Knowledge of the mapping M up to randomness;
- Unbounded computational resources that could be used to simulate M's responses on any number of databases;
- Knowledge of the first $N-1$ entries of $\mathbb{D}$; and
- The ability to sample linearly many responses from $M(\mathbb{D})$.

Then the attacker's optimal approach to re-identify the Nth entry of $\mathbb{D}$ is to

1 Construct an empirical distribution approximating the unknown response distribution $M(\mathbb{D})$ by querying the mechanism the maximum order of N times and forming a histogram of responses;
2 Construct all candidate databases $\mathbb{D}'$ from the known $N-1$ first entries of $\mathbb{D}$;
3 For each $\mathbb{D}'$:
   1. Simulate the response distribution of $M(\mathbb{D}')$ using knowledge of $M(\cdot)$;
   2. Compare the exact candidate response distribution with the approximate empirical distribution; and
4 Return the $\mathbb{D}'$ that most closely matches the empirical distribution.

Even with this optimal procedure the adversary cannot infer additional information on the true identity of the Nth entry of $\mathbb{D}$, under suitably small β. Differential privacy guarantees that each response distribution $M(\mathbb{D}')$ is pointwise close to the true distribution $M(\mathbb{D})$. In other words the response distributions are indistinguishable because the unknown datum is varied over all possibilities. When attempting to match candidate response distribution to the queried actual empirical distribution, it will not be possible to distinguish true $\mathbb{D}$ from incorrect neighboring $\mathbb{D}'$. Indistinguishability is effective, provided β is close to the estimation error between the sampled empirical distribution and the actual response distribution $M(\mathbb{D})$—this estimation error is guaranteed not to be too small since the number of queries is limited.

We have argued in this section that differential privacy provides a strong, semantic guarantee of privacy for each individual datum, while allowing the release of some aggregate information. Indeed in certain situations one may argue the definition is unnecessarily strong. Some possible relaxations are natural; for example a "grouped privacy" variation models an adversary with knowledge of the data up to some fixed $k \geq 1$ rows of $\mathbb{D}$ (Dwork et al. 2006). In other words knowledge of the data is relaxed to a hamming-k ball centered on $\mathbb{D}$.

---

[1] More generally, for each measurable $T \subseteq \mathcal{T}_M$, $\Pr\left(M\left(\mathbb{D}^{(1)}\right) \in T\right) \leq \exp(\beta)\Pr\left(M\left(\mathbb{D}^{(2)}\right) \in T\right)$.

7.2.1.1   The Laplace Mechanism

The earliest pattern of establishing differential privacy is to add (possibly multivariate) zero-mean Laplace noise to a nonprivate mechanism. Typically the nonprivate mechanism being privatized is a deterministic function of data—in our case it will be the support vector machine. The scale of the zero-mean Laplace noise depends on the level β of differential privacy desired and the so-called global sensitivity of the nonprivate mechanism.

DEFINITION 7.2 Deterministic mechanism M with real-vector-valued responses, has ℓ_1-global sensitivity $\Delta > 0$ if for every pair $\mathbb{D}^{(1)}, \mathbb{D}^{(2)}$ of neighboring databases, $\left\| M\left(\mathbb{D}^{(1)}\right) - M\left(\mathbb{D}^{(2)}\right) \right\|_1 \le \Delta$.

This is essentially a Lipschitz condition on the nonprivate mechanism with metric in the co-domain induced by the ℓ_1-norm, and similarly on databases in the domain. Intuitively global sensitivity measures the continuity of the nonprivate map: how much does the response to be released vary with small perturbations to the input dataset.

With global sensitivity of a nonprivate mechanism in hand, it is a simple matter to prove differential privacy of suitable Laplace noise added to the nonprivate mechanism.

LEMMA 7.3 (Dwork et al. 2006) *Let M be a deterministic mechanism with ℓ_1-global sensitivity $\Delta > 0$, let $\beta > 0$, and $\lambda \overset{iid}{\sim} Laplace(\mathbf{0}, \beta/\Delta)$. Then mechanism $M\left(\mathbb{D}\right) + \lambda$ preserves β-differential privacy.*

Proof Consider neighboring databases $\mathbb{D}^{(1)}, \mathbb{D}^{(2)}$, any $t \in \mathcal{T}_M$, and two multivariate random variables $\lambda_1, \lambda_2 \overset{iid}{\sim} Laplace(\mathbf{0}, \Delta/\beta)$

$$
\frac{\Pr\left(M\left(\mathbb{D}^{(1)}\right) + \lambda_1 = t\right)}{\Pr\left(M\left(\mathbb{D}^{(2)}\right) + \lambda_2 = t\right)} = \frac{\exp\left(\left\| t - M\left(\mathbb{D}^{(1)}\right) \right\|_1 / (\Delta/\beta)\right)}{\exp\left(\left\| t - M\left(\mathbb{D}^{(2)}\right) \right\|_1 / (\Delta/\beta)\right)}
$$
$$
\le \exp\left(\left\| M\left(\mathbb{D}^{(1)}\right) - M\left(\mathbb{D}^{(2)}\right) \right\|_1 / (\Delta/\beta)\right)
$$
$$
\le \exp(\beta).
$$

The equality follows from the definition of the Laplace probability density function, the first inequality follows from the triangle inequality, and the final inequality follows from the bound on global sensitivity. Taking logs of both sides yields β-differential privacy.   □

7.2.2   Utility

Intuitively the more an "interesting" mechanism M is perturbed to guarantee differential privacy, the less like M the resulting mechanism $\hat{M}$ will become. The next definition formalizes the notion of "likeness."

DEFINITION 7.4 Consider two mechanisms $\hat{M}$ and M with the same domains and with response spaces $\mathcal{T}_{\hat{M}}$ and $\mathcal{T}_M$. Let $\mathcal{X}$ be some set and let $\mathcal{F} \subseteq \mathfrak{R}^{\mathcal{X}}$ be parametrized by the response spaces: For every $t \in \mathcal{T}_{\hat{M}} \cup \mathcal{T}_M$ define some corresponding function $f_t \in \mathcal{F}$. Finally assume $\mathcal{F}$ is endowed with norm $\| \cdot \|_{\mathcal{F}}$. Then for $\epsilon > 0$ and $0 < \delta < 1$ we say that[2] $\hat{M}$ is (ϵ, δ)-*useful* with respect to M if, for all databases $\mathbb{D}$,

$$\Pr\left(\left\|f_{\hat{M}(\mathbb{D})} - f_{M(\mathbb{D})}\right\|_{\mathcal{F}} \le \epsilon\right) \ge 1 - \delta.$$

Typically $\hat{M}$ will be a privacy-preserving (perturbed) version of M, such as the Laplace mechanism of M. In the sequel we take $\|\cdot\|_{\mathcal{F}}$ to be $\|f\|_{\infty;\mathcal{M}} = \sup_{\mathbf{x}\in\mathcal{M}} |f(\mathbf{x})|$ for some $\mathcal{M} \subseteq \mathfrak{R}^D$ containing the data. It will also be convenient to define $\|k\|_{\infty;\mathcal{M}} = \sup_{\mathbf{x},\mathbf{z}\in\mathcal{M}} |k(\mathbf{x}, \mathbf{z})|$ for bivariate $k(\cdot, \cdot)$.

7.2.3   Historical Research Directions in Differential Privacy

A rich literature of prior work on differential privacy exists. We provide an overview some of this work in the context of privacy-preserving learning of support vector machines.

Range Spaces Parametrizing Vector-Valued Statistics or Simple Functions

Early work on private interactive mechanisms focused on approximating real- and vector-valued statistics (e.g., Dinur & Nissim 2003; Blum et al. 2005; Dwork et al. 2006; Dwork 2006; Barak et al. 2007) McSherry & Talwar (2007) first considered private mechanisms with range spaces parametrizing sets more general than real-valued vectors and used such differentially private mappings for mechanism design. The first work to develop private mechanisms for releasing classifiers, which specifically regularized logistic regression, was due to Chaudhuri & Monteleoni (2009). There the mechanism's range space parametrizes the VC-dimension $D + 1$ class of linear hyperplanes in $\mathfrak{R}^D$. One of their mechanisms injects a random term into the primal objective to achieve differential privacy. Their simpler mechanism adds noise to the learned weight vector. Both of these approaches have analogs in SVM learning as explored in this chapter. The calculation of SVM sensitivity (see Section 7.4) presented here is a generalization of the derivation of the sensitivity of regularized logistic regression (Chaudhuri & Monteleoni 2009), to the setting of nondifferentiable loss functions, with the condition on the gradient replaced by the Lipschitz condition and the condition on the Hessian replaced by strong convexity. Kasiviswanathan et al. (2008) show that discretized concept classes can be PAC or agnostically learned privately, albeit via an inefficient mechanism. Blum et al. (2008) show that noninteractive mechanisms can privately release anonymized data such that utility is guaranteed over classes of predicate queries with polynomial VC-dimension, when the domain is discretized. Dwork et al. (2009) has since characterized when utility and privacy can be achieved by efficient noninteractive mechanisms. In this chapter we consider efficient mechanisms for private SVM learning, whose range spaces parametrize real-valued functions. One case considered here is learning with a RBF (or Gaussian) kernel, which corresponds to learning over a rich class of infinite dimension. Differential privacy has been explored under Bayesian probabilistic inference in the exact (Dimitrakakis, Nelson, Mitrokotsa,

---

[2] Our definition of (ϵ, δ)-usefulness for releasing a single function is analogous to the notion of the same name introduced by Blum et al. (2008) for anonymization mechanisms.

& Rubinstein 2014; Zhang, Rubinstein, & Dimitrakakis 2016) and sampled settings (Wang et al. 2015). Other work develops generic mechanisms for function release under differential privacy: Hall, Rinaldo, & Wasserman (2013) add Gaussian process noise, yielding a weaker form of differential privacy, without general results on utility rates; Wang, Fan, Zhang, & Wang (2013) release privatized projections, in a trigonometric basis, of functions that are separable in the training data, similar to Zhang et al. (2012); Aldà & Rubinstein (2017) propose the Bernstein mechanism as a functional form of the Laplace mechanism for vector release, which achieves differential privacy and strong utility guarantees under general conditions of smoothness of the nonprivate function, by using iterated Bernstein polynomial approximation.

Practical Privacy-Preserving Learning (Mostly) via Subset Sums
Most work in differential privacy has focused on the deep analysis of mechanisms for relatively simple statistics (with histograms and contingency tables as explored by Blum et al. 2005 and Barak et al. 2007, respectively, as examples) and learning algorithms (e.g., interval queries and halfspaces as explored by Blum et al. 2008), or on constructing learning algorithms that can be decomposed into subset-sum operations (e.g., perceptron, k-NN, ID3 as described by Blum et al. 2005, and various recommender systems as shown by McSherry & Mironov 2009). Some early work in function release focuses on functions separable (expressable as sums) over training data (Zhang et al. 2012; Wang et al. 2013). By contrast, this chapter explores the more practical goal of SVM learning, which does not generally decompose into a subset sum (Rubinstein et al. 2012; Appendix A). It is also notable that the mechanisms here run in polynomial time.

The Privacy-Utilty Tradeoff
Like several early studies, we explore here the tradeoff between privacy and utility. Barak et al. (2007) present a mechanism for releasing contingency tables that guarantees differential privacy and also guarantees a notion of accuracy: with high probability all marginals from the released table are close in ℓ_1-norm to the true marginals. As mentioned earlier, Blum et al. (2008) develop a private noninteractive mechanism that releases anonymized data such that all predicate queries in a VC class take on similar values regardless of whether they are taken over the anonymized data and original data. Kasiviswanathan et al. (2008) consider utility as corresponding to PAC learning: with high probability the response and target concepts are close, averaged over the underlying measure.

Early negative results show that any mechanism providing overly accurate responses cannot be private (Dinur & Nissim 2003; Dwork & Yekhanin 2008; Beimel et al. 2010; Hardt & Talwar 2010). Dinur & Nissim (2003) show that if a noise of rate only $o\left(\sqrt{N}\right)$ is added to subset-sum queries on a database of bits, then an adversary can reconstruct a $1 - o(1)$ fraction of the bits. This threshold phenomenon says that if accuracy is too great, privacy cannot be guaranteed at all. A similar negative result can be shown for the case of private SVM learning: i.e., requiring very high accuracy with respect to the SVM prevents high levels of privacy. De (2012) summarizes approaches to lower-bounding utility under differential privacy such as the volumetric packing approach used here.

The results presented here are qualitatively closer to those of Hardt & Talwar (2010) and Beimel et al. (2010). The former work finds almost matching upper and lower bounds for the tradeoff between differential privacy and accuracy through the lens of convex geometry, in the following setting that encompasses releasing histograms and recommender systems. Queries submitted to the interactive mechanism are linear mappings on a private database of reals. Nonprivate responses are the vector image of the query applied to the database, the mechanism's responses are a randomized version of this target image, and the mechanism's accuracy is the expected Euclidean distance between nonprivate also private and private responses. Beimel et al. (2010) focus on the notion of private learning (Kasiviswanathan et al. 2008) in which a private learner not only PAC learns but the release of its hypothesis is differentially private with respect to the training data. Beimel et al. (2010) delve into the sample complexity of private learning and demonstrate separation results between proper and improper private learning[3]—which do not exist for nonprivate PAC learning—and between efficient and inefficient proper private learners. Both papers consider negative results on the tradeoff between notions of utility and differential privacy. In SVM learning, concept classes are not necessarily linear or have finite VC-dimension.

The ϵ-packing proof technique used in the lower bound for SVM learning with the RBF kernel, although discovered independently, is similar to the technique used by Hardt & Talwar (2010) to establish lower bounds for their setting of privately responding to linear map queries. See also (De 2012) for a general account.

Connections between Stability and Differential Privacy
To prove differential privacy in this chapter, a proof technique is borrowed from algorithmic stability. In passing, Kasiviswanathan et al. (2008) predict a possible relationship between algorithmic stability and differential privacy; however, they do not describe in detail how to exploit this. Since then, Wang et al. (2016) have drawn connections between stability, learnability, and privacy.

7.3   Support Vector Machines: A Brief Primer

Empirical risk minimization (ERM) can lead to overfitting or poor generalization (risk of the minimizer), so in theory and practice it is more desirable to perform regularized empirical risk minimization, which minimizes the sum of the empirical risk and uses a regularization term that imposes a soft smoothness constraint on the classifier. A well-known example is the soft-margin support vector machine that has the following primal program, for convex loss $\ell\,(\cdot, \cdot)$,

$$\min_{\mathbf{w} \in \mathfrak{R}^F} \frac{1}{2} \|\mathbf{w}\|_2^2 + \frac{C}{N} \sum_{i=1}^{N} \ell\left(y^{(i)}, f_{\mathbf{w}}\left(\mathbf{x}^{(i)}\right)\right),$$

---

[3] A proper learner outputs a hypothesis from the target concept class.

where for chosen *feature mapping* $\phi : \Re^D \to \Re^F$ taking points in input space $\Re^D$ to some (possibly infinite) F-dimensional *feature space*, and hyperplane normal $\mathbf{w} \in \Re^F$, we define

$$f_{\mathbf{w}}(\mathbf{x}) = \langle \phi(\mathbf{x}), \mathbf{w} \rangle.$$

Parameter $C > 0$ is the soft-margin parameter that controls the degree of regularization. Let $\mathbf{w}^\star$ denote an optimizing weight vector. Then predictions are taken as the sign of $f^\star(\mathbf{x}) = f_{\mathbf{w}^\star}(\mathbf{x})$. We will refer to both $f_{\mathbf{w}}(\,\cdot\,)$ and sign $(f_{\mathbf{w}}(\,\cdot\,))$ as *classifiers*, with the exact meaning apparent from the context.

An overview of the relevant details on learning follows (for full details, see, for example Burges 1998; Cristianini & Shawe-Taylor 2000; Schölkopf & Smola 2001; Bishop 2006) In order for the primal to be convex and the process of SVM learning to be tractable, $\ell(y, \hat{y})$ is chosen to be a loss function that is convex in $\hat{y}$. A common convex surrogate for the 0-1 loss and the loss most commonly associated with the SVM, is the hinge loss $\ell(y, \hat{y}) = \max[1 - y\hat{y}, 0]$ that upper bounds the 0-1 loss and is non-differentiable at $y\hat{y} = 1$. Other example losses include the square loss $(1 - y\hat{y})^2$ and the logistic loss $\log(1 + \exp(-y\hat{y}))$. We consider general convex losses in this chapter, and a detailed case study of private SVM learning under the hinge loss in Section 7.7.1.

Remark 7.5 We say that a learning algorithm is *universally consistent* if for all distributions μ it is *consistent*: its expected risk converges to the minimum achievable (Bayes) risk with increasing sample size (Devroye, Györfi, & Lugosi 1996). For universal consistency, the SVM's parameter C should increase like $\sqrt{N}$.

When F is large the solution may be more easily obtained via the dual. For example, the following is the dual formulation on the N dual variables for learning with hinge loss:

$$\max_{\boldsymbol{\alpha} \in \Re^N} \sum_{i=1}^{N} \alpha_i - \frac{1}{2} \sum_{i=1}^{N} \sum_{j=1}^{N} \alpha_i \alpha_j y^{(i)} y^{(j)} k\left(\mathbf{x}^{(i)}, \mathbf{x}^{(j)}\right) \qquad (7.1)$$

$$\text{s.t. } 0 \le \alpha_i \le \frac{C}{N} \ \forall i \in [n],$$

where $k(\mathbf{x}, \mathbf{z}) = \langle \phi(\mathbf{x}), \phi(\mathbf{z}) \rangle$ is the kernel function.

The vector of maximizing duals $\boldsymbol{\alpha}^\star$ parametrizes the function $f^\star = f_{\boldsymbol{\alpha}^\star}$ as

$$f_{\boldsymbol{\alpha}}(\cdot) = \sum_{i=1}^{N} \alpha_i y^{(i)} k\left(\,\cdot\,, \mathbf{x}^{(i)}\right).$$

The space of SVM classifiers endowed with the kernel function forms a reproducing kernel Hilbert space $\mathcal{H}$.

Algorithm 7.1 SVM

Inputs: database $\mathbb{D} = \left\{(\mathbf{x}^{(i)}, y^{(i)})\right\}_{i=1}^{N}$ with $\mathbf{x}^{(i)} \in \mathfrak{R}^D$, $y^{(i)} \in \{-1, 1\}$; kernel $k : \mathfrak{R}^D \times \mathfrak{R}^D \to \mathfrak{R}$; convex loss ℓ; parameter $C > 0$.

1 $\boldsymbol{\alpha}^\star \leftarrow$ Solve the SVM's dual in Equation (7.1).
2 Return vector $\boldsymbol{\alpha}^\star$.

DEFINITION 7.6 A *reproducing kernel Hilbert space (RKHS)* is a Hilbert space[4] of real-valued functions on the space $\mathcal{X}$, which includes, for each point $\mathbf{x} \in \mathcal{X}$, a point-evaluation function $k(\cdot, \mathbf{x})$ having the reproducing kernel property $\langle f, k(\cdot, \mathbf{x})\rangle_{\mathcal{H}} = f(\mathbf{x})$ for all $f \in \mathcal{H}$.

In particular $\langle k(\cdot, \mathbf{x}), k(\cdot, \mathbf{z})\rangle_{\mathcal{H}} = k(\mathbf{x}, \mathbf{z})$. The Representer Theorem (Kimeldorf & Wahba 1971) implies that the minimizer $f^\star = \operatorname{argmin}_{f \in \mathcal{H}} \left[\frac{1}{2}\|f\|_{\mathcal{H}}^2 + \frac{C}{N}\sum_{i=1}^{n} \ell\left(y^{(i)}, f(\mathbf{x}^{(i)})\right)\right]$ lies in the span of the functions $k(\cdot, \mathbf{x}^{(i)}) \in \mathcal{H}$. Indeed the above dual expansion shows that the coordinates in this subspace are given by the $\alpha_i^\star y^{(i)}$. We define the SVM *mechanism* to be the dual optimization that responds with the vector $\boldsymbol{\alpha}^\star$, as described by Algorithm 7.1.

7.3.1   Translation-Invariant Kernels

A number of kernels/feature mappings have been proposed in the literature (Burges 1998; Cristianini & Shawe-Taylor 2000; Schölkopf & Smola 2001; Bishop 2006). The *translation-invariant kernels* are an important class of kernel that we study in the sequel (see Table 7.1 for examples).

DEFINITION 7.7 A kernel function of the form $k(\mathbf{x}, \mathbf{z}) = g(\mathbf{x} - \mathbf{z})$, for some function g, is called *translation invariant*.

Table 7.1 Example of translation-invariant kernels and their g functions as defined on the vector $\boldsymbol{\Delta} = \mathbf{x} - \mathbf{z}$

Kernel	$g(\boldsymbol{\Delta})$
RBF	$\exp\left(-\frac{\|\boldsymbol{\Delta}\|_2^2}{2\sigma^2}\right)$
Laplacian	$\exp(-\|\boldsymbol{\Delta}\|_1)$
Cauchy	$\prod_{i=1}^{D} \frac{2}{1+\Delta_i^2}$

---

[4] A Hilbert space is an inner-product space that is complete with respect to its norm-induced metric.

7.3.2 Algorithmic Stability

In proving bounds on the differential privacy of our mechanisms for private SVM learning, we will exploit the uniform stability of regularized ERM as established by Bousquet & Elisseeff (2002).

Recall that we say that a pair of databases $\mathbb{D}^{(1)}$, $\mathbb{D}^{(2)}$ are *neighbors* if they differ on one entry, and we define the learning stability with respect to neighboring databases as follows.

DEFINITION 7.8 A *learning map* $\mathcal{A}$, that takes databases $\mathbb{D}$ to classifiers is said to have γ-*uniform stability* with respect to loss $\ell\,(\,\cdot\,,\,\cdot\,)$ if for all neighboring databases $\mathbb{D}, \mathbb{D}'$, the losses of the classifiers trained on $\mathbb{D}$ and $\mathbb{D}'$ are close on all test examples $\left\| \ell\,(\,\cdot\,, \mathcal{A}\,(\mathbb{D})) - \ell\,(\,\cdot\,, \mathcal{A}\,(\mathbb{D}')) \right\|_\infty \leq \gamma$.

Stability corresponds to smoothness of the learning map, and the concept is typically used in statistical learning theory to yield tight risk bounds, sometimes when class capacity-based approaches (such as VC-dimension-based approaches) do not apply (Devroye & Wagner 1979; Kearns & Ron 1999; Bousquet & Elisseeff 2002; Kutin & Niyogi 2002). Intuitively if a learning map is stable, then it is not overly influenced by noise and is less likely to suffer from overfitting.

7.4 Differential Privacy by Output Perturbation

We now focus on an output perturbation approach we developed with collaborators Bartlett, Huang, and Taft, based on the Laplace mechanism (Rubinstein, Bartlett, Huang, & Taft 2009; Rubinstein et al. 2012). We consider differentially private SVM learning with finite F-dimensional feature maps. We begin by describing the mechanism, then prove the range of noise parameters required to guarantee privacy (Theorem 7.10), and derive the conditions under which the mechanism yields close approximations to the nonprivate SVM (Theorem 7.11).

Algorithm 7.2 describes the PRIVATESVM-FINITE mechanism, which is an application of the Laplace mechanism (cf. Section 7.2.1.1): After forming the primal solution to the SVM—weight vector $\mathbf{w} \in \Re^F$—the mechanism adds i.i.d. zero-mean, scale λ, and Laplace noise to $\mathbf{w}$. Differential privacy follows from the ℓ_1-sensitivity Δ of $\mathbf{w}$ to data perturbations taking the Laplace-noise scale to be $\lambda = \Delta / \beta$.

To calculate sensitivity—the change in $\mathbf{w}$ with respect to the ℓ_1-norm when a training example is perturbed—we exploit the uniform stability of regularized ERM (cf. Definition 7.8).

LEMMA 7.9 *Consider a loss function* $\ell\,(y, \hat{y})$ *that is convex and L-Lipschitz in* $\hat{y}$, *and RKHS* $\mathcal{H}$ *induced by finite F-dimensional feature mapping* ϕ *with bounded kernel* $k\,(\mathbf{x}, \mathbf{x}) \leq \kappa^2$ *for all* $\mathbf{x} \in \Re^D$. *For each database* $\mathbb{S} = \left\{ \left(\mathbf{x}^{(i)}, y^{(i)} \right) \right\}_{i=1}^N$, *define*

$$\mathbf{w}^{(\mathbb{S})} \in \operatorname*{argmin}_{\mathbf{w} \in \Re^F} \left[\frac{C}{N} \sum_{i=1}^N \ell\left(y^{(i)}, f_\mathbf{w}\left(\mathbf{x}^{(i)} \right) \right) + \frac{1}{2} \left\| \mathbf{w} \right\|_2^2 \right].$$

Algorithm 7.2 PRIVATESVM-FINITE

Inputs: database $\mathbb{D} = \left\{(\mathbf{x}^{(i)}, y^{(i)})\right\}_{i=1}^{N}$ with $\mathbf{x}^{(i)} \in \Re^D$, $y^{(i)} \in \{-1, 1\}$; finite feature map $\phi : \Re^D \to \Re^F$ and induced kernel k; convex loss function ℓ; and parameters $\lambda, C > 0$.

1   $\boldsymbol{\alpha}^\star \leftarrow$ Run Algorithm 7.1 on $\mathbb{D}$ with parameter C, kernel k, and loss ℓ;
2   $\tilde{\mathbf{w}} \leftarrow \sum_{i=1}^{N} \alpha_i^\star y^{(i)} \phi\left(\mathbf{x}^{(i)}\right)$;
3   $\boldsymbol{\mu} \leftarrow$ Draw i.i.d. sample of F scalars from Laplace $(0, \lambda)$; and
4   Return $\hat{\mathbf{w}} = \tilde{\mathbf{w}} + \boldsymbol{\mu}$.

Then for every pair of neighboring databases $\mathbb{D}, \mathbb{D}'$ *of* N *entries, we have* $\left\|\mathbf{w}^{(\mathbb{D})} - \mathbf{w}^{(\mathbb{D}')}\right\|_2 \le 4LC\kappa/N$, *and* $\left\|\mathbf{w}^{(\mathbb{D})} - \mathbf{w}^{(\mathbb{D}')}\right\|_1 \le 4LC\kappa\sqrt{F}/N$.

Proof The argument closely follows the proof of the SVM's uniform stability (Schölkopf & Smola 2001, Theorem 12.4). For convenience we define for any training set $\mathbb{S}$

$$R_{\text{reg}}(\mathbf{w}, \mathbb{S}) = \frac{C}{N} \sum_{i=1}^{N} \ell\left(y^{(i)}, f_{\mathbf{w}}\left(\mathbf{x}^{(i)}\right)\right) + \frac{1}{2}\|\mathbf{w}\|_2^2$$

$$R_{\text{emp}}(\mathbf{w}, \mathbb{S}) = \frac{1}{N} \sum_{i=1}^{N} \ell\left(y^{(i)}, f_{\mathbf{w}}\left(\mathbf{x}^{(i)}\right)\right).$$

Then the first-order necessary KKT conditions imply

$$\mathbf{0} \in \partial_{\mathbf{w}} R_{\text{reg}}(\mathbf{w}^{(\mathbb{D})}, \mathbb{D}) = C\partial_{\mathbf{w}} R_{\text{emp}}(\mathbf{w}^{(\mathbb{D})}, \mathbb{D}) + \mathbf{w}^{(\mathbb{D})}, \tag{7.2}$$

$$\mathbf{0} \in \partial_{\mathbf{w}} R_{\text{reg}}(\mathbf{w}^{(\mathbb{D}')}, \mathbb{D}') = C\partial_{\mathbf{w}} R_{\text{emp}}(\mathbf{w}^{(\mathbb{D}')}, \mathbb{D}') + \mathbf{w}^{(\mathbb{D}')}. \tag{7.3}$$

where $\partial_{\mathbf{w}}$ is the subdifferential operator wrt $\mathbf{w}$. Define the auxiliary risk function

$$\tilde{R}(\mathbf{w}) = C\left\langle \partial_{\mathbf{w}} R_{\text{emp}}(\mathbf{w}^{(\mathbb{D})}, \mathbb{D}) - \partial_{\mathbf{w}} R_{\text{emp}}(\mathbf{w}^{(\mathbb{D}')}, \mathbb{D}'), \mathbf{w} - \mathbf{w}^{(\mathbb{D}')} \right\rangle + \frac{1}{2}\left\|\mathbf{w} - \mathbf{w}^{(\mathbb{D}')}\right\|_2^2.$$

Note that $\tilde{R}(\cdot)$ maps to sets of reals. It is easy to see that $\tilde{R}(\mathbf{w})$ is strictly convex in $\mathbf{w}$. Substituting $\mathbf{w}^{(\mathbb{D}')}$ into $\tilde{R}(\mathbf{w})$ yields

$$\tilde{R}(\mathbf{w}^{(\mathbb{D}')}) = C\left\langle \partial_{\mathbf{w}} R_{\text{emp}}\left(\mathbf{w}^{(\mathbb{D})}, \mathbb{D}\right) - \partial_{\mathbf{w}} R_{\text{emp}}\left(\mathbf{w}^{(\mathbb{D}')}, \mathbb{D}'\right), \mathbf{0} \right\rangle + \frac{1}{2}\|0\|_2^2$$
$$= \{0\},$$

and by Equation (7.3)

$$C\partial_{\mathbf{w}} R_{\text{emp}}(\mathbf{w}^{(\mathbb{D})}, \mathbb{D}) + \mathbf{w} \in C\partial_{\mathbf{w}} R_{\text{emp}}(\mathbf{w}^{(\mathbb{D})}, \mathbb{D}) - C\partial_{\mathbf{w}} R_{\text{emp}}(\mathbf{w}^{(\mathbb{D}')}, \mathbb{D}') + \mathbf{w} - \mathbf{w}^{(\mathbb{D}')}$$
$$= \partial_{\mathbf{w}} \tilde{R}(\mathbf{w}),$$

which combined with Equation (7.2) implies $\mathbf{0} \in \partial_{\mathbf{w}} \tilde{R}(\mathbf{w}^{(\mathbb{D})})$, so that $\tilde{R}(\mathbf{w})$ is minimized at $\mathbf{w}^{(\mathbb{D})}$. Thus there exists some nonpositive $r \in \tilde{R}(\mathbf{w}^{(\mathbb{D})})$. Next simplify the first term of $\tilde{R}(\mathbf{w}^{(\mathbb{D})})$, scaled by N/C for notational convenience. In what follows we denote by

$\ell'\left(y,\hat{y}\right)$ the subdifferential $\partial_{\hat{y}}\ell\left(y,\hat{y}\right)$.

$$N\left\langle\partial_{\mathbf{w}}R_{\text{emp}}(\mathbf{w}^{(\mathbb{D})},\mathbb{D})-\partial_{\mathbf{w}}R_{\text{emp}}(\mathbf{w}^{(\mathbb{D}')},\mathbb{D}'),\ \mathbf{w}^{(\mathbb{D})}-\mathbf{w}^{(\mathbb{D}')}\right\rangle$$

$$=\sum_{i=1}^{N}\left\langle\partial_{\mathbf{w}}\ell\left(y^{(i)},f_{\mathbf{w}^{(\mathbb{D})}}\left(\mathbf{x}^{(i)}\right)\right)-\partial_{\mathbf{w}}\ell\left(\hat{y}^{(i)},f_{\mathbf{w}^{(\mathbb{D}')}}\left(\hat{\mathbf{x}}^{(i)}\right)\right),\ \mathbf{w}^{(\mathbb{D})}-\mathbf{w}^{(\mathbb{D}')}\right\rangle$$

$$=\sum_{i=1}^{N-1}\left(\ell'\left(y^{(i)},f_{\mathbf{w}^{(\mathbb{D})}}\left(\mathbf{x}^{(i)}\right)\right)-\ell'\left(y^{(i)},f_{\mathbf{w}^{(\mathbb{D}')}}\left(\mathbf{x}^{(i)}\right)\right)\right)\left(f_{\mathbf{w}^{(\mathbb{D})}}\left(\mathbf{x}^{(i)}\right)-f_{\mathbf{w}^{(\mathbb{D}')}}\left(\mathbf{x}^{(i)}\right)\right)$$

$$+\ell'\left(y^{(N)},f_{\mathbf{w}^{(\mathbb{D})}}\left(\mathbf{x}^{(N)}\right)\right)\left(f_{\mathbf{w}^{(\mathbb{D})}}\left(\mathbf{x}^{(N)}\right)-f_{\mathbf{w}^{(\mathbb{D}')}}\left(\mathbf{x}^{(N)}\right)\right)$$

$$-\ell'\left(\hat{y}^{(N)},f_{\mathbf{w}^{(\mathbb{D}')}}\left(\hat{\mathbf{x}}^{(N)}\right)\right)\left(f_{\mathbf{w}^{(\mathbb{D})}}\left(\hat{\mathbf{x}}^{(N)}\right)-f_{\mathbf{w}^{(\mathbb{D}')}}\left(\hat{\mathbf{x}}^{(N)}\right)\right)$$

$$\geq\ell'\left(y^{(N)},f_{\mathbf{w}^{(\mathbb{D})}}\left(\mathbf{x}^{(N)}\right)\right)\left(f_{\mathbf{w}^{(\mathbb{D})}}\left(\mathbf{x}^{(N)}\right)-f_{\mathbf{w}^{(\mathbb{D}')}}\left(\mathbf{x}^{(N)}\right)\right)$$

$$-\ell'\left(\hat{y}^{(N)},f_{\mathbf{w}^{(\mathbb{D}')}}\left(\hat{\mathbf{x}}^{(N)}\right)\right)\left(f_{\mathbf{w}^{(\mathbb{D})}}\left(\hat{\mathbf{x}}^{(N)}\right)-f_{\mathbf{w}^{(\mathbb{D}')}}\left(\hat{\mathbf{x}}^{(N)}\right)\right).$$

Here the second equality follows from $\partial_{\mathbf{w}}\ell\left(y,f_{\mathbf{w}}\left(\mathbf{x}\right)\right)=\ell'\left(y,f_{\mathbf{w}}\left(\mathbf{x}\right)\right)\phi\left(\mathbf{x}\right)$, and $\hat{\mathbf{x}}^{(i)}=\mathbf{x}^{(i)}$ and $\hat{y}^{(i)}=y^{(i)}$ for each $i\in[N-1]$. The inequality follows from the convexity of ℓ in its second argument.[5] Combined with the existence of nonpositive $r\in\tilde{R}(\mathbf{w}^{(\mathbb{D})})$ this yields that there exists

$$g\in\ell'\left(\hat{y}^{(N)},f_{\mathbf{w}^{(\mathbb{D}')}}\left(\hat{\mathbf{x}}^{(N)}\right)\right)\left(f_{\mathbf{w}^{(\mathbb{D})}}\left(\hat{\mathbf{x}}^{(N)}\right)-f_{\mathbf{w}^{(\mathbb{D}')}}\left(\hat{\mathbf{x}}^{(N)}\right)\right)$$

$$-\ell'\left(y^{(N)},f_{\mathbf{w}^{(\mathbb{D})}}\left(\mathbf{x}^{(N)}\right)\right)\left(f_{\mathbf{w}^{(\mathbb{D})}}\left(\mathbf{x}^{(N)}\right)-f_{\mathbf{w}^{(\mathbb{D}')}}\left(\mathbf{x}^{(N)}\right)\right)$$

such that

$$0\geq\frac{N}{C}r$$

$$\geq g+\frac{N}{2C}\left\|\mathbf{w}^{(\mathbb{D})}-\mathbf{w}^{(\mathbb{D}')}\right\|_{2}^{2}.$$

And since $|g|\leq2L\left\|f_{\mathbf{w}^{(\mathbb{D})}}-f_{\mathbf{w}^{(\mathbb{D}')}}\right\|_{\infty}$ by the Lipschitz continuity of ℓ, this in turn implies

$$\frac{N}{2C}\left\|\mathbf{w}^{(\mathbb{D})}-\mathbf{w}^{(\mathbb{D}')}\right\|_{2}^{2}\leq2L\left\|f_{\mathbf{w}^{(\mathbb{D})}}-f_{\mathbf{w}^{(\mathbb{D}')}}\right\|_{\infty}.\qquad(7.4)$$

Now by the reproducing property and Cauchy-Schwarz inequality we can upper bound the classifier difference's infinity norm by the Euclidean norm on the weight vectors: For each $\mathbf{x}$

$$\left|f_{\mathbf{w}^{(\mathbb{D})}}\left(\mathbf{x}\right)-f_{\mathbf{w}^{(\mathbb{D}')}}\left(\mathbf{x}\right)\right|=\left|\left\langle\phi\left(\mathbf{x}\right),\mathbf{w}^{(\mathbb{D})}-\mathbf{w}^{(\mathbb{D}')}\right\rangle\right|$$

$$\leq\left\|\phi\left(\mathbf{x}\right)\right\|_{2}\left\|\mathbf{w}^{(\mathbb{D})}-\mathbf{w}^{(\mathbb{D}')}\right\|_{2}$$

$$=\sqrt{k\left(\mathbf{x},\mathbf{x}\right)}\left\|\mathbf{w}^{(\mathbb{D})}-\mathbf{w}^{(\mathbb{D}')}\right\|_{2}$$

$$\leq\kappa\left\|\mathbf{w}^{(\mathbb{D})}-\mathbf{w}^{(\mathbb{D}')}\right\|_{2}.$$

---

[5] Namely for convex f and any $a,b\in\Re$, $(g_a-g_b)(a-b)\geq0$ for all $g_a\in\partial f(a)$ and all $g_b\in\partial f(b)$.

Combining this with Inequality (7.4) yields $\left\| \mathbf{w}^{(\mathbb{D})} - \mathbf{w}^{(\mathbb{D}')} \right\|_2 \leq 4LC\kappa/N$ as claimed. The ℓ_1-based sensitivity then follows from $\|\mathbf{w}\|_1 \leq \sqrt{F} \|\mathbf{w}\|_2$ for all $\mathbf{w} \in \Re^F$. $\qquad\square$

For a SVM with a Gaussian kernel, we have $L = 1$ and $\kappa = 1$. Then the bounds can be simplified as $\left\| \mathbf{w}^{(\mathbb{D})} - \mathbf{w}^{(\mathbb{D}')} \right\|_2 \leq 4C/N$ and $\left\| \mathbf{w}^{(\mathbb{D})} - \mathbf{w}^{(\mathbb{D}')} \right\|_1 \leq 4C\sqrt{F}/N$. With the weight vector's sensitivity in hand, differential privacy follows immediately (cf. Lemma 7.3)

THEOREM 7.10 (Privacy of PRIVATESVM-FINITE) *For any $\beta > 0$, database $\mathbb{D}$ of size N, $C > 0$, loss function $\ell\,(y, \hat{y})$ that is convex and L-Lipschitz in $\hat{y}$, and finite F-dimensional feature map with kernel $k\,(\mathbf{x}, \mathbf{x}) \leq \kappa^2$ for all $\mathbf{x} \in \Re^D$, PRIVATESVM-FINITE run on $\mathbb{D}$ with loss ℓ, kernel k, noise parameter $\lambda \geq 4LC\kappa\sqrt{F}/(\beta N)$, and regularization parameter C guarantees β-differential privacy.*

This result states that higher levels of privacy require more noise, while more training examples reduce the level of required noise. We next establish the (ϵ, δ)-usefulness of PRIVATESVM-FINITE, using the exponential tails of the noise vector $\boldsymbol{\mu}$. By contrast to privacy, utility demands that the noise not be too large.

THEOREM 7.11 (Utility of PRIVATESVM-FINITE) *Consider any $C > 0$, $N > 1$, database $\mathbb{D}$ of N entries, arbitrary convex loss ℓ, and finite F-dimensional feature mapping ϕ with kernel k and $|\phi\,(\mathbf{x})_i| \leq \Phi$ for all $\mathbf{x} \in \mathcal{M}$ and $i \in [F]$ for some $\Phi > 0$ and $\mathcal{M} \subseteq \Re^D$. For any $\epsilon > 0$ and $\delta \in (0, 1)$, PRIVATESVM-FINITE run on $\mathbb{D}$ with loss ℓ, kernel k, noise parameter $0 < \lambda \leq \frac{\epsilon}{2\Phi\left(F + \log_e \frac{1}{\delta}\right)}$, and regularization parameter C is (ϵ, δ)-useful with respect to the SVM under the $\|\cdot\|_{\infty;\mathcal{M}}$-norm.*

In other words, run with arbitrary noise parameter $\lambda > 0$, PRIVATESVM-FINITE is (ϵ, δ)-useful for $\epsilon = \Omega\left(\lambda\Phi\left(F + \log_e \frac{1}{\delta}\right)\right)$.

Proof Consider the SVM and PRIVATESVM-FINITE classifications on an arbitrary point $\mathbf{x} \in \mathcal{M}$:

$$\left| f_{\hat{M}(\mathbb{D})}\,(\mathbf{x}) - f_{M(\mathbb{D})}\,(\mathbf{x}) \right| = \left| \langle \hat{\mathbf{w}}, \phi\,(\mathbf{x}) \rangle - \langle \tilde{\mathbf{w}}, \phi\,(\mathbf{x}) \rangle \right|$$
$$= \left| \langle \boldsymbol{\mu}, \phi\,(\mathbf{x}) \rangle \right|$$
$$\leq \|\boldsymbol{\mu}\|_1 \|\phi\,(\mathbf{x})\|_\infty$$
$$\leq \Phi \|\boldsymbol{\mu}\|_1 \,.$$

The absolute value of a zero-mean Laplace random variable with scale λ is exponentially distributed with scale λ^{-1}. Moreover, the sum of q i.i.d. exponential random variables has an Erlang q-distribution with the same scale parameter. Thus we have, for Erlang F-distributed random variable X and any $t > 0$,

$$\forall \mathbf{x} \in \mathcal{M}, \ \left| f_{\hat{M}(\mathbb{D})}\,(\mathbf{x}) - f_{M(\mathbb{D})}\,(\mathbf{x}) \right| \leq \Phi X$$
$$\Rightarrow \ \forall \epsilon > 0, \ \Pr\left(\left\| f_{\hat{M}(\mathbb{D})} - f_{M(\mathbb{D})} \right\|_{\infty;\mathcal{M}} > \epsilon \right) \leq \Pr\left(X > \epsilon/\Phi \right)$$
$$\leq \frac{\mathrm{E}\left[e^{tX} \right]}{e^{\epsilon t/\Phi}} \,. \qquad (7.5)$$

Algorithm 7.3 PRIVATEERM-OBJECTIVE

Inputs: database $\mathbb{D} = \left\{ (\mathbf{x}^{(i)}, y^{(i)}) \right\}_{i=1}^{N}$ with $\mathbf{x}^{(i)} \in \mathfrak{R}^D$, $y^{(i)} \in \{-1, 1\}$; regularizer $\rho\,(\cdot)$; loss function $\ell(\cdot)$; $c > 0$ a bound on the 2nd derivative of ℓ; regularization parameter $\lambda > 0$; and privacy parameter $\beta > 0$.

1 Let $\beta' = \beta - \log\left(1 + \frac{2c}{N\lambda} + \frac{c^2}{N^2\lambda^2}\right)$;
2 If $\beta' > 0$, then let $\Delta = 0$; otherwise let $\Delta = \frac{c}{N(e^{\beta/4}-1)} - \lambda$ and let $\beta' = \beta/2$;
3 Sample $\mathbf{b} \sim \exp(-\beta'\|\mathbf{b}\|_2/2)$; and
4 Return $\mathbf{f}_{priv} = \arg\min_{\mathbf{f}} J_{priv}(\mathbf{f}, \mathbb{D}) + \frac{1}{2}\Delta\|\mathbf{f}\|_2^2$.

Here we have employed the Chernoff tail bound technique using Markov's inequality. The numerator of (7.5), the moment-generating function of the Erlang F-distribution with parameter λ, is $(1 - \lambda t)^{-F}$ for $t < \lambda^{-1}$. With the choice of $t = (2\lambda)^{-1}$, this gives

$$
\Pr\left(\left\| f_{\hat{M}(\mathbb{D})} - f_{M(\mathbb{D})} \right\|_{\infty;\mathcal{M}} > \epsilon\right) \leq (1 - \lambda t)^{-F} e^{-\epsilon t/\Phi}
$$
$$
= 2^F e^{-\epsilon/(2\lambda\Phi)}
$$
$$
= \exp\left(F\log_e 2 - \frac{\epsilon}{2\lambda\Phi}\right)
$$
$$
< \exp\left(F - \frac{\epsilon}{2\lambda\Phi}\right).
$$

And provided that $\epsilon \geq \left(2\lambda\Phi\left(F + \log_e \frac{1}{\delta}\right)\right)$ this probability is bounded by δ. $\qquad\square$

7.5 Differential Privacy by Objective Perturbation

We briefly review another early independent approach to differentially private SVM learning due to Chaudhuri, Monteleoni, & Sarwate (2011). Their mechanism for linear SVM guarantees differential privacy by adding a random term to the objective, as performed previously by the same group for regularized logistic regression (Chaudhuri & Monteleoni 2009) and as is suitable for a general class of regularized empirical risk minimizers (Chaudhuri et al. 2011). While we limit our discussion to the linear SVM for clarity of exposition, all results go through essentially unchanged for SVM under finite-dimensional feature mappings. It is also notable that further general connections and treatments of (regularized) empirical risk minimization and differential privacy have been made; for example, with Bassily et al. (2014) providing matching rates under bounded Lipschitz influence of each training datum on loss and bounded parameter domains; and Duchi et al. (2013) demonstrating minimax rates for efficient convex risk minimization under a definition of local privacy (when data is unavailable to the statistician) with lower/upper bounds matching up to constant factors.

We repeat here the objective of regularized empirical risk minimization, found in Equation (2.1):

$$
J(f, \mathbb{D}) = \frac{1}{N} \sum_{(x,y) \in \mathbb{D}} \ell\,(y, f(x)) + \lambda \cdot \rho\,(f),
$$

where $\rho\,(\cdot)$ is a regularization functional that for the SVM is one-half the ℓ_2-norm, and where $\lambda > 0$ is the regularization parameter equivalent to $1/C$ for the SVM as introduced earlier. The mechanism PRIVATEERM-OBJECTIVE, as described by Algorithm 7.3, aims to minimize

$$J_{priv}(\mathbf{f}, \mathbb{D}) = J(\mathbf{f}, \mathbb{D}) + \frac{1}{N}\langle \mathbf{b}, \mathbf{f}\rangle,$$

where $\mathbf{b}$ is zero-mean random noise. Intuitively, the perturbed objective minimizes regularized empirical risk while favoring models that align with a random direction. The strength of alignment preferred—the degree of objective perturbation—depends on the level of privacy required. To provide a flavor of the results known for PRIVATEERM-OBJECTIVE, we state privacy and utility guarantees due to Chaudhuri et al. (2011), directing the interested reader to the original paper for detailed discussion and proofs.

THEOREM 7.12 (Privacy of PRIVATEERM-OBJECTIVE; Chaudhuri et al. 2011, Theorem 6) *If regularization functional $\rho\,(\cdot)$ is 1-strongly convex and doubly differentiable, and loss function $\ell(\cdot)$ is convex and doubly differentiable with first and second derivatives bounded by 1 and $c > 0$, respectively, then PRIVATEERM-OBJECTIVE is β-differentially private.*

It is noteworthy that preserving privacy via the randomized objective can only apply to convex differentiable loss functions, ruling out the most common case for the SVM: the nondifferentiable hinge loss. The output perturbation approach of the previous section preserves privacy for any convex loss—a very weak condition since convexity is required for the formulation of SVM learning to be convex. Chaudhuri et al. (2011) explore two instantiations of PRIVATEERM-OBJECTIVE for the SVM with this limitation in mind. The more complex approach is to use the Huber loss, which is not globally doubly differentiable, but nonetheless can be shown to achieve differential privacy. The simpler alternative is to use the following loss function that satisfies the conditions of Theorem 7.12 with $c = \frac{3}{4h}$.

$$\ell_s(z) = \begin{cases} 0, & \text{if } z > 1 + h \\ -\frac{(1-z)^4}{16h^3} + \frac{3(1-z)^2}{8h} + \frac{1-z}{2} + \frac{3h}{16}, & \text{if } |1 - z| \le h. \\ 1 - z, & \text{if } z < 1 - h \end{cases}$$

As the bandwidth $h \to 0$, this loss approaches the hinge loss. And using this loss with resulting $c = \frac{3}{4h}$, and regularization functional $\rho\,(\cdot) = \frac{1}{2}\|\mathbf{f}\|_2^2$, PRIVATEERM-OBJECTIVE yields a β-differentially private approximation of the SVM (Chaudhuri et al. 2011, Corollary 12).

While the definition of utility of Section 7.2.2 measures the pointwise similarity of the private SVM classifier to the nonprivate SVM classifier, Chaudhuri et al. (2011) measure utility in terms of bounds on excess risk.

THEOREM 7.13 (Excess Risk of PRIVATEERM-OBJECTIVE; (Chaudhuri et al. 2011), Theorem 18) *Consider regularization functional $\rho\,(\mathbf{f}) = \frac{1}{2}\|\mathbf{f}\|_2^2$, D-dimensional data $\mathbb{D}$ drawn i.i.d. according to distribution P_Z, and $\mathbf{f}_0$ a reference classifier with some risk $R\,(P_Z, \mathbf{f}) = R^\star$. Under the same conditions as in Theorem 7.12, there exists a constant*

$A > 0$ *such that for* $\delta > 0$, *if the training set size satisfies*

$$N > A \cdot \max \left\{ \frac{\|\mathbf{f}_0\|_2^2 \log(1/\delta)}{\epsilon^2}, \frac{c\|\mathbf{f}_0\|_2^2}{\epsilon\beta}, \frac{D\log\left(\frac{D}{\delta}\right)\|\mathbf{f}_0\|_2^2}{\epsilon\beta} \right\}.$$

then the excess risk of PRIVATEERM-OBJECTIVE *is bounded with high probability*

$$\Pr\left(R\left(P_Z, \mathbf{f}_{priv}\right) \leq R^\star + \epsilon\right) \geq 1 - 2\delta.$$

For the purpose of comparison, nonprivate SVM requires data size of at least a constant times $\|\mathbf{f}_0\|_2^2 \log(1/\delta)/\epsilon^2$ to achieve the same guarantee on excess risk (Shalev-Shwartz & Srebro 2008). This corresponds to the first term of the max in the sample complexity of PRIVATEERM-OBJECTIVE.

It is noteworthy that for SVM learning with the hinge loss, guarantees on pointwise similarity utility are strictly stronger than risk bounds.

Remark 7.14 Since the hinge loss is Lipschitz in the classifier output by the SVM, any mechanism $\hat{M}$ having utility with respect to the SVM also has expected hinge loss that is within ϵ of the SVM's hinge loss with high probability; i.e., (ϵ, δ)-usefulness with respect to the sup-norm is stronger than guaranteed closeness of risk.

The stronger definition of utility offers a natural advantage: An arbitrary differentially private mechanism that enjoys low risk is not necessarily an approximation of a given learning algorithm of interest; it is natural to expect that a private SVM approximates the classifications of a nonprivate SVM. Guarantees with respect to this utility imply such approximation and (for the SVM) low risk.

While analytical results for PRIVATESVM-FINITE and PRIVATEERM-OBJECTIVE are not directly comparable, the excess risk bounds for PRIVATEERM-OBJECTIVE enjoy better growth rates than those proved by Chaudhuri et al. (2011) for output perturbation, and early experiments on benchmark datasets suggest that objective perturbation can outperform output perturbation.

Finally, Chaudhuri et al. (2011) also develop a method for tuning the regularization parameter while preserving privacy, using a comparison procedure due to McSherry & Talwar (2007).

For the remainder of this chapter, we focus on the mechanism of output perturbation.

7.6 Infinite-Dimensional Feature Spaces

We now consider the problem of privately learning in an RKHS $\mathcal{H}$ induced by an infinite-dimensional feature mapping ϕ. We begin the section by deriving the mechanism, then establish the range of noise parameters required to guarantee privacy (Corollary 7.15), and derive the conditions under which the mechanism yields close approximations to the nonprivate SVM (Theorem 7.16).

It is natural to look to the dual SVM as a starting point: an optimizing $f^\star \in \mathcal{H}$ must lie in the span of the data by the Representer Theorem (Kimeldorf & Wahba 1971). While the coordinates with respect to this data basis—the $\alpha_i^\star$ dual variables—could be perturbed to guarantee differential privacy, the basis is also needed to parametrize $f^\star$. The

---

Algorithm 7.4 PRIVATESVM

Inputs: database $\mathbb{D} = \left\{(\mathbf{x}^{(i)}, y^{(i)})\right\}_{i=1}^{N}$ with $\mathbf{x}^{(i)} \in \Re^D$, $y^{(i)} \in \{-1, 1\}$; translation-invariant kernel $k(\mathbf{x}, \mathbf{z}) = g(\mathbf{x} - \mathbf{z})$ with Fourier transform $p(\boldsymbol{\omega}) = 2^{-1} \int e^{-j\langle \boldsymbol{\omega}, \mathbf{x} \rangle} g(\mathbf{x}) \, d\mathbf{x}$; convex loss function ℓ; parameters $\lambda, C > 0$, and $\hat{D} \in \mathfrak{N}$.

1 $\boldsymbol{\rho}_1, \ldots, \boldsymbol{\rho}_{\hat{D}} \leftarrow$ Draw i.i.d. sample of $\hat{D}$ vectors in $\Re^D$ from p;
2 $\hat{\boldsymbol{\alpha}} \leftarrow$ Run Algorithm 7.1 on $\mathbb{D}$ with parameter C, kernel $\hat{k}$ induced by map (7.6), and loss ℓ;
3 $\tilde{\mathbf{w}} \leftarrow \sum_{i=1}^{N} y^{(i)} \hat{\alpha}_i \hat{\phi}\left(\mathbf{x}^{(i)}\right)$ where $\hat{\phi}$ is defined in Equation (7.6);
4 $\boldsymbol{\mu} \leftarrow$ Draw i.i.d. sample of $2\hat{D}$ scalars from Laplace $(\mathbf{0}, \lambda)$; and
5 Return $\hat{\mathbf{w}} = \tilde{\mathbf{w}} + \boldsymbol{\mu}$ and $\boldsymbol{\rho}_1, \ldots, \boldsymbol{\rho}_{\hat{D}}$.

---

basis is the original data itself, so such an approach appears to be a dead end. Instead we approach the problem by approximating $\mathcal{H}$ with a random RKHS $\hat{\mathcal{H}}$ induced by a random finite-dimensional map $\hat{\phi}$, which admits a response based on a primal parametrization. This idea was applied independently by both Chaudhuri et al. (2011) and Rubinstein et al. (2012) to the output- and objective-perturbation mechanisms. Algorithm 7.4 summarizes this mechanism from Rubinstein (2010).

As noted by Rahimi & Recht (2008), the Fourier transform p of the kernel function g, a continuous positive-definite translation-invariant function, is a non-negative measure (Rudin 1994). If the kernel g is properly scaled, Bochner's theorem guarantees that p is a proper probability distribution. Rahimi & Recht (2008) exploit this fact to construct a random RKHS $\hat{\mathcal{H}}$ by drawing $\hat{D}$ vectors $\boldsymbol{\rho}_1, \ldots, \boldsymbol{\rho}_{\hat{D}}$ from p, and defining the random $2\hat{D}$-dimensional feature map

$$\hat{\phi}(\,\cdot\,) = \hat{D}^{-1/2} \left[\cos\left(\langle \boldsymbol{\rho}_1, \,\cdot\, \rangle\right), \sin\left(\langle \boldsymbol{\rho}_1, \,\cdot\, \rangle\right), \ldots, \cos\left(\langle \boldsymbol{\rho}_{\hat{D}}, \,\cdot\, \rangle\right), \sin\left(\langle \boldsymbol{\rho}_{\hat{D}}, \,\cdot\, \rangle\right)\right]^T. \tag{7.6}$$

Table 7.2 presents three translation-invariant kernels and their transformations. Inner products in the random feature space $\hat{k}(\,\cdot\,, \,\cdot\,)$ approximate $k(\,\cdot\,, \,\cdot\,)$ uniformly and arbitrary precision depending on parameter $\hat{D}$, as restated in Lemma 7.21. Rahimi & Recht (2008) apply this approximation to large-scale learning, finding good approximations for $\hat{D} \ll N$. We perform regularized ERM in $\hat{\mathcal{H}}$, not to avoid complexity in N, but to provide a direct finite representation $\tilde{\mathbf{w}}$ of the primal solution in the case of infinite-dimensional feature spaces. Subsequently, Laplace noise is added to the primal solution $\tilde{\mathbf{w}}$ to guarantee differential privacy as before.

Unlike PRIVATESVM-FINITE, PRIVATESVM must release a parametrization of feature map $\hat{\phi}$—the sample $\left\{\boldsymbol{\rho}_i\right\}_{i=1}^{\hat{D}}$—to classify as $\hat{f}^{\star} = \langle \hat{\mathbf{w}}, \hat{\phi}(\,\cdot\,) \rangle$. Of PRIVATESVM's response, only $\hat{\mathbf{w}}$ depends on $\mathbb{D}$; the $\boldsymbol{\rho}_i$ are data-independent draws from the kernel's transform p, which we assume to be known by the adversary (to wit the adversary knows the mechanism, including k). Thus to establish differential privacy we need only consider the weight vector, as we did for PRIVATESVM-FINITE.

Table 7.2 Translation-invariant kernels of Table 7.1, their g functions, and the corresponding Fourier transforms p

Kernel	$g(\boldsymbol{\Delta})$	$p(\boldsymbol{\omega})$
RBF	$\exp\left(-\frac{\|\boldsymbol{\Delta}\|_2^2}{2\sigma^2}\right)$	$\frac{1}{(2\pi)^{D/2}}\exp\left(\frac{-\|\boldsymbol{\omega}\|_2^2}{2}\right)$
Laplacian	$\exp\left(-\|\boldsymbol{\Delta}\|_1\right)$	$\prod_{i=1}^{D}\frac{1}{\pi\left(1+\omega_i^2\right)}$
Cauchy	$\prod_{i=1}^{D}\frac{2}{1+\Delta_i^2}$	$\exp\left(-\|\boldsymbol{\omega}\|_1\right)$

COROLLARY 7.15 (Privacy of PRIVATESVM) *For any $\beta > 0$, database $\mathbb{D}$ of size N, $C > 0$, $\hat{D} \in \mathfrak{N}$, loss function $\ell\,(y, \hat{y})$ that is convex and L-Lipschitz in $\hat{y}$, and translation-invariant kernel k, PRIVATESVM run on $\mathbb{D}$ with loss ℓ, kernel k, noise parameter $\lambda \geq 2^{2.5}LC\sqrt{\hat{D}}/(\beta N)$, approximation parameter $\hat{D}$, and regularization parameter C guarantees β-differential privacy.*

Proof The result follows from Theorem 7.10 since $\tilde{\mathbf{w}}$ is the primal solution of SVM with kernel $\hat{k}$, the response vector $\hat{\mathbf{w}} = \tilde{\mathbf{w}} + \boldsymbol{\mu}$, and $\hat{k}\,(\mathbf{x}, \mathbf{x}) = 1$ for all $\mathbf{x} \in \mathfrak{R}^D$. The extra factor of $\sqrt{2}$ comes from the fact that $\hat{\phi}\,(\,\cdot\,)$ is a $2\hat{d}$-dimensional feature map. $\square$

This result is surprising, in that PRIVATESVM is able to guarantee privacy for regularized ERM over a function class of infinite dimension, where the obvious way to return the learned classifier (responding with the dual variables and feature mapping) reveals all the entries corresponding to the support vectors completely.

The remainder of this section considers the following result, which states that PRIVATESVM is useful with respect to the SVM.

THEOREM 7.16 (Utility of PRIVATESVM) *Consider any database $\mathbb{D}$, compact set $\mathcal{M} \subseteq \mathfrak{R}^D$ containing $\mathbb{D}$, convex loss ℓ, translation-invariant kernel k, and scalars $C, \epsilon > 0$ and $\delta \in (0, 1)$. Suppose the SVM with loss ℓ, kernel k, and parameter C has dual variables with ℓ_1-norm bounded by Λ. Then Algorithm 7.4 run on $\mathbb{D}$ with loss ℓ, kernel k, parameters $\hat{D} \geq \frac{4(D+2)}{\theta(\epsilon)}\log_e\left(\frac{2^9\left(\sigma_p \mathrm{diam}(\mathcal{M})\right)^2}{\delta\theta(\epsilon)}\right)$ where $\theta(\epsilon) =$*

$$\min\left\{1, \frac{\epsilon^4}{2^4\left(\Lambda+2\sqrt{(CL+\Lambda/2)\Lambda}\right)^4}\right\},\ \lambda \leq \min\left\{\frac{\epsilon}{2^4\log_e 2\sqrt{\hat{D}}}, \frac{\epsilon\sqrt{\hat{D}}}{8\log_e\frac{2}{\delta}}\right\},\ \textit{and } C \textit{ is } (\epsilon, \delta)\textit{-useful}$$

with respect to Algorithm 7.1 run on $\mathbb{D}$ with loss ℓ, kernel k and parameter C, with respect to the $\|\cdot\|_{\infty;\mathcal{M}}$-norm.

Remark 7.17 Theorem 7.16 introduces the assumption that the SVM has a dual solution vector with bounded ℓ_1-norm. The motivation for this condition is the most common case for SVM classification: learning with the hinge loss. Under this loss the dual program (7.1) has box constraints that ensure that this condition is satisfied.

The result of Theorem 7.16 bounds the pointwise distance between classifiers $f^\star$ output by SVM and $\hat{f}^\star$ output by PRIVATESVM with high probability. Let $\tilde{f}$ be the function parametrized by intermediate-weight vector $\tilde{\mathbf{w}}$. Then we establish the main result by proving that both f^* and $\hat{f}^*$ are close to $\tilde{f}$ with high probability and applying the triangle inequality. We begin by relating $\tilde{f}$ and f^*. As f^* is the result of adding Laplace noise to $\tilde{w}$, the task of relating these two classifiers is almost the same as proving the utility of PRIVATESVM-FINITE (see Theorem 7.11).

COROLLARY 7.18 *Consider a run of Algorithms 7.1 and 7.4 with $\hat{D} \in \mathfrak{N}$, $C > 0$, convex loss, and translation-invariant kernel. Denote by $\hat{f}^*$ and $\tilde{f}$ the classifiers parametrized by weight vectors $\hat{w}$ and $\tilde{w}$, respectively, where these vectors are related by $\hat{w} = \tilde{w} + \mu$ with $\mu \overset{iid}{\sim} \text{Laplace}(0, \lambda)$ in Algorithm 7.4. For any $\epsilon > 0$ and $\delta \in (0, 1)$, if $0 < \lambda \leq \min\left\{ \frac{\epsilon}{2^4 \log_e 2\sqrt{\hat{D}}}, \frac{\epsilon\sqrt{\hat{D}}}{8 \log_e \frac{2}{\delta}} \right\}$ then $\Pr\left(\left\| \hat{f}^* - \tilde{f} \right\|_\infty \leq \frac{\epsilon}{2} \right) \geq 1 - \frac{\delta}{2}$.*

Proof As in the proof of Theorem 7.11 we can use the Chernoff trick to show that, for an Erlang $2\hat{D}$-distributed random variable X, the choice of $t = (2\lambda)^{-1}$, and for any $\epsilon > 0$

$$\Pr\left(\left\| \hat{f}^* - \tilde{f} \right\|_\infty > \epsilon/2 \right) \leq \frac{\mathrm{E}\left[e^{tX} \right]}{e^{\epsilon t \sqrt{\hat{D}}/2}}$$
$$\leq (1 - \lambda t)^{-2\hat{D}} e^{-\epsilon t \sqrt{\hat{D}}/2}$$
$$= 2^{2\hat{D}} e^{-\epsilon\sqrt{\hat{D}}/(4\lambda)}$$
$$= \exp\left(\hat{D} \log_e 4 - \epsilon\sqrt{\hat{D}}/(4\lambda) \right).$$

Provided that $\lambda \leq \epsilon/\left(2^4 \log_e 2\sqrt{\hat{D}} \right)$ this is bounded by $\exp\left(-\epsilon\sqrt{\hat{D}}/(8\lambda) \right)$. Moreover, if $\lambda \leq \epsilon\sqrt{\hat{D}}/\left(8 \log_e \frac{2}{\delta} \right)$, then the claim follows. $\square$

To relate f^* and $\tilde{f}$, we exploit smoothness of regularized ERM with respect to small changes in the RKHS itself. We begin with a technical lemma that we will use to exploit the convexity of the regularized empirical risk functional; it shows a kind of converse to Remark 7.14 relating that functions with risks that are close in value will also be close in proximity.

LEMMA 7.19 *Let R be a functional on Hilbert space $\mathcal{H}$ satisfying $R[f] \geq R[f^*] + \frac{a}{2} \left\| f - f^* \right\|_\mathcal{H}^2$ for some $a > 0$, $f^* \in \mathcal{H}$, and all $f \in \mathcal{H}$. Then $R[f] \leq R[f^*] + \epsilon$ implies $\left\| f - f^* \right\|_{\hat{\mathcal{H}}} \leq \sqrt{\frac{2\epsilon}{a}}$, for all $\epsilon > 0$, $f \in \mathcal{H}$.*

Proof By assumption and the antecedent

$$\left\| f - f^* \right\|_{\hat{\mathcal{H}}}^2 \leq \frac{2}{a} \left(R[f] - R[f^*] \right)$$
$$\leq \frac{2}{a} \left(R[f^*] + \epsilon - R[f*] \right)$$
$$= \frac{2\epsilon}{a}.$$

Taking square roots of both sides yields the result. $\square$

Provided that the kernels $k, \hat{k}$ are uniformly close, we now show that $f^\star$ and $\tilde{f}$ are pointwise close, using the insensitivity of regularized ERM to feature mapping perturbation.

LEMMA 7.20 *Let $\mathcal{H}$ be an RKHS with translation-invariant kernel k, and let $\hat{\mathcal{H}}$ be the random RKHS corresponding to feature map (7.6) induced by k. Let C be a positive scalar and loss $\ell(y, \hat{y})$ be convex and L-Lipschitz continuous in $\hat{y}$. Consider the regularized empirical risk minimizers in each RKHS, where $R_{\mathrm{emp}}[f] = n^{-1} \sum_{i=1}^{N} \ell\left(y^{(i)}, f\left(\mathbf{x}^{(i)}\right)\right)$,*

$$f^\star \in \operatorname*{argmin}_{f \in \mathcal{H}} \left[C R_{\mathrm{emp}}[f] + \frac{1}{2} \|f\|_{\mathcal{H}}^2, \right]$$

$$g^\star \in \operatorname*{argmin}_{g \in \hat{\mathcal{H}}} \left[C R_{\mathrm{emp}}[g] + \frac{1}{2} \|g\|_{\hat{\mathcal{H}}}^2 \right].$$

Let $\mathcal{M} \subseteq \Re^D$ be any set containing $\mathbf{x}^{(1)}, \ldots, \mathbf{x}^{(N)}$. For any $\epsilon > 0$, if the dual variables from both optimizations have ℓ_1-norms bounded by some $\Lambda > 0$ and $\left\| k - \hat{k} \right\|_{\infty; \mathcal{M}} \leq$

$$\min \left\{ 1, \frac{\epsilon^2}{2^2 \left(\Lambda + 2\sqrt{(CL + \Lambda/2)\Lambda} \right)^2} \right\} \text{ then } \|f^\star - g^\star\|_{\infty; \mathcal{M}} \leq \epsilon/2.$$

Proof Define regularized empirical risk functional $R_{\mathrm{reg}}[f] = C R_{\mathrm{emp}}[f] + \|f\|^2/2$, for the appropriate RKHS norm. Let minimizer $f^\star \in \mathcal{H}$ be given by parameter vector $\boldsymbol{\alpha}^\star$, and let minimizer $g^\star \in \hat{\mathcal{H}}$ be given by parameter vector $\boldsymbol{\beta}^\star$. Let $g_{\boldsymbol{\alpha}^\star} = \sum_{i=1}^{N} \alpha_i^\star y^{(i)} \hat{\phi}\left(\mathbf{x}^{(i)}\right)$ and $f_{\boldsymbol{\beta}}^\star = \sum_{i=1}^{N} \beta_i^\star y^{(i)} \phi\left(\mathbf{x}^{(i)}\right)$ denote the images of $f^\star$ and $g^\star$ under the natural mapping between the spans of the data in RKHS's $\hat{\mathcal{H}}$ and $\mathcal{H}$, respectively. We will first show that these four functions have arbitrarily close regularized empirical risk in their respective RKHS, and then that this implies uniform proximity of the functions themselves. Observe that for any $g \in \hat{\mathcal{H}}$,

$$R_{\mathrm{reg}}^{\hat{\mathcal{H}}}[g] = C R_{\mathrm{emp}}[g] + \frac{1}{2} \|g\|_{\hat{\mathcal{H}}}^2$$

$$\geq C \langle \partial_g R_{\mathrm{emp}}[g^\star], g - g^\star \rangle_{\hat{\mathcal{H}}} + C R_{\mathrm{emp}}[g^\star] + \frac{1}{2} \|g\|_{\hat{\mathcal{H}}}^2$$

$$= \langle \partial_g R_{\mathrm{reg}}^{\hat{\mathcal{H}}}[g^\star], g - g^\star \rangle_{\hat{\mathcal{H}}} - \langle g^\star, g - g^\star \rangle_{\hat{\mathcal{H}}} + C R_{\mathrm{emp}}[g^\star] + \frac{1}{2} \|g\|_{\hat{\mathcal{H}}}^2.$$

The inequality follows from the convexity of $R_{\mathrm{emp}}[\cdot]$ and holds for all elements of the subdifferential $\partial_g R_{\mathrm{emp}}[g^\star]$. The subsequent equality holds by $\partial_g R_{\mathrm{reg}}^{\hat{\mathcal{H}}}[g] = C \partial_g R_{\mathrm{emp}}[g] + g$. Now since $\mathbf{0} \in \partial_g R_{\mathrm{reg}}^{\hat{\mathcal{H}}}[g^\star]$, it follows that

$$R_{\mathrm{reg}}^{\hat{\mathcal{H}}}[g] \geq C R_{\mathrm{emp}}[g^\star] + \frac{1}{2} \|g\|_{\hat{\mathcal{H}}}^2 - \langle g^\star, g - g^\star \rangle_{\hat{\mathcal{H}}}$$

$$= R_{\mathrm{reg}}^{\hat{\mathcal{H}}}[g^\star] + \frac{1}{2} \|g\|_{\hat{\mathcal{H}}}^2 - \langle g^\star, g \rangle_{\hat{\mathcal{H}}} + \frac{1}{2} \|g^\star\|_{\hat{\mathcal{H}}}^2$$

$$= R_{\mathrm{reg}}^{\hat{\mathcal{H}}}[g^\star] + \frac{1}{2} \|g - g^\star\|_{\hat{\mathcal{H}}}^2.$$

With this, Lemma 7.19 states that for any $g \in \hat{\mathcal{H}}$ and $\epsilon' > 0$,

$$R_{\text{reg}}^{\hat{\mathcal{H}}}[g] \leq R_{\text{reg}}^{\hat{\mathcal{H}}}[g^\star] + \epsilon' \implies \|g - g^\star\|_{\hat{\mathcal{H}}} \leq \sqrt{2\epsilon'}. \tag{7.7}$$

Next we show that the antecedent is true for $g = g_{\alpha^\star}$. Conditioned on $\left\{ \|k - \hat{k}\|_{\infty; \mathcal{M}} \leq \epsilon' \right\}$, for all $\mathbf{x} \in \mathcal{M}$

$$
\begin{aligned}
|f_\Gamma^\star](\mathbf{x}) - g_{\alpha^\star}(\mathbf{x})| &= \left| \sum_{i=1}^{N} \alpha_i^\star y^{(i)} \left(k\left(\mathbf{x}^{(i)}, \mathbf{x}\right) - \hat{k}\left(\mathbf{x}^{(i)}, \mathbf{x}\right) \right) \right| \\
&\leq \sum_{i=1}^{N} |\alpha_i^\star| \left| k\left(\mathbf{x}^{(i)}, \mathbf{x}\right) - \hat{k}\left(\mathbf{x}^{(i)}, \mathbf{x}\right) \right| \\
&\leq \epsilon' \|\alpha^\star\|_1 \\
&\leq \epsilon' \Lambda, \tag{7.8}
\end{aligned}
$$

by the bound on $\|\alpha^\star\|_1$. This and the Lipschitz continuity of the loss lead to

$$
\begin{aligned}
\left| R_{\text{reg}}^{\mathcal{H}}[f^\star] - R_{\text{reg}}^{\hat{\mathcal{H}}}[g_{\alpha^\star}] \right| &= \left| C R_{\text{emp}}[f^\star] - C R_{\text{emp}}[g_{\alpha^\star}] + \frac{1}{2}\|f^\star\|_{\mathcal{H}}^2 - \frac{1}{2}\|g_{\alpha^\star}\|_{\hat{\mathcal{H}}}^2 \right| \\
&\leq \frac{C}{N} \sum_{i=1}^{N} \left| \ell\left(y^{(i)}, f_\Gamma^\star](\mathbf{x}^{(i)})\right) - \ell\left(y^{(i)}, g_{\alpha^\star}(\mathbf{x}^{(i)})\right) \right| \\
&\quad + \frac{1}{2}\left| (\alpha^\star)^\top (\mathbf{K} - \hat{\mathbf{K}}) \alpha^\star \right| \\
&\leq C L \|f^\star - g_{\alpha^\star}\|_{\infty; \mathcal{M}} + \frac{1}{2}\|\alpha^\star\|_1 \|(\mathbf{K} - \hat{\mathbf{K}})\alpha^\star\|_\infty \\
&\leq C L \epsilon' \Lambda + \Lambda^2 \epsilon'/2 \\
&= \left(C L + \frac{\Lambda}{2} \right) \Lambda \epsilon',
\end{aligned}
$$

where $\mathbf{K}$ and $\hat{\mathbf{K}}$ are the kernel matrices of the kernels k and $\hat{k}$, respectively. Similarly,

$$\left| R_{\text{reg}}^{\hat{\mathcal{H}}}[g^\star] - R_{\text{reg}}^{\mathcal{H}}[f_{\beta^\star}] \right| \leq (C L + \Lambda/2)\Lambda\epsilon'$$

by the same argument. And since $R_{\text{reg}}^{\mathcal{H}}[f_{\beta^\star}] \geq R_{\text{reg}}^{\mathcal{H}}[f^\star]$ and $R_{\text{reg}}^{\hat{\mathcal{H}}}[g_{\alpha^\star}] \geq R_{\text{reg}}^{\hat{\mathcal{H}}}[g^\star]$, we have proved that

$$
\begin{aligned}
R_{\text{reg}}^{\hat{\mathcal{H}}}[g_{\alpha^\star}] &\leq R_{\text{reg}}^{\mathcal{H}}[f^\star] + (C L + \Lambda/2)\Lambda\epsilon' \\
&\leq R_{\text{reg}}^{\mathcal{H}}[f_{\beta^\star}] + (C L + \Lambda/2)\Lambda\epsilon' \\
&\leq R_{\text{reg}}^{\hat{\mathcal{H}}}[g^\star] + 2(C L + \Lambda/2)\Lambda\epsilon'.
\end{aligned}
$$

And by implication (7.7),

$$\left\| g_{\alpha^\star} - g^\star \right\|_{\hat{\mathcal{H}}} \leq 2\sqrt{\left(CL + \frac{\Lambda}{2} \right) \Lambda \epsilon'}. \tag{7.9}$$

Now $\hat{k}(\mathbf{x}, \mathbf{x}) = 1$ for each $\mathbf{x} \in \mathfrak{R}^D$ implies

$$
\begin{aligned}
\left| g_{\alpha^\star}(\mathbf{x}) - g^\star(\mathbf{x}) \right| &= \left\langle g_{\alpha^\star} - g^\star, \hat{k}(\mathbf{x}, \cdot) \right\rangle_{\hat{\mathcal{H}}} \\
&\leq \left\| g_{\alpha^\star} - g^\star \right\|_{\hat{\mathcal{H}}} \sqrt{\hat{k}(\mathbf{x}, \mathbf{x})} \\
&= \left\| g_{\alpha^\star} - g^\star \right\|_{\hat{\mathcal{H}}}.
\end{aligned}
$$

This combines with Inequality (7.9) to yield $\left\| g_{\alpha^\star} - g^\star \right\|_{\infty;\mathcal{M}} \leq 2\sqrt{\left(CL + \frac{\Lambda}{2} \right) \Lambda \epsilon'}$. Together with Inequality (7.8) this implies $\left\| f^\star - g^\star \right\|_{\infty;\mathcal{M}} \leq \epsilon' \Lambda + 2\sqrt{\left(CL + \Lambda/2 \right) \Lambda \epsilon'}$, conditioned on event $P_{\epsilon'} = \left\{ \left\| k - \hat{k} \right\|_\infty \leq \epsilon' \right\}$. For desired $\epsilon > 0$, conditioning on event $P_{\epsilon'}$ with $\epsilon' = \min \left\{ \epsilon / \left[2 \left(\Lambda + 2\sqrt{\left(CL + \Lambda/2 \right) \Lambda} \right) \right], \ \epsilon^2 / \left[2 \left(\Lambda + 2\sqrt{\left(CL + \Lambda/2 \right) \Lambda} \right) \right]^2 \right\}$ yields bound $\left\| f^\star - g^\star \right\|_{\infty;\mathcal{M}} \leq \epsilon/2$: if $\epsilon' \leq 1$, then $\epsilon/2 \geq \sqrt{\epsilon'} \left(\Lambda + 2\sqrt{\left(CL + \Lambda/2 \right) \Lambda} \right) \geq \epsilon' \Lambda + 2\sqrt{\left(CL + \Lambda/2 \right) \Lambda \epsilon'}$ provided that $\epsilon' \leq \epsilon^2 / \left[2 \left(\Lambda + 2\sqrt{\left(CL + \Lambda/2 \right) \Lambda} \right) \right]^2$. Otherwise if $\epsilon' > 1$, then we have $\epsilon/2 \geq \epsilon' \left(\Lambda + 2\sqrt{\left(CL + \Lambda/2 \right) \Lambda} \right) \geq \epsilon' \Lambda + 2\sqrt{\left(CL + \Lambda/2 \right) \Lambda \epsilon'}$ provided $\epsilon' \leq \epsilon / \left[2 \left(\Lambda + 2\sqrt{\left(CL + \Lambda/2 \right) \Lambda} \right) \right]$. Since for any $H > 0$, $\min \left\{ H, H^2 \right\} \geq \min \left\{ 1, H^2 \right\}$, the result follows. $\qquad\square$

We now recall the result due to Rahimi & Recht (2008) that establishes the non-asymptotic uniform convergence of the kernel functions required by the previous lemma (i.e., an upper bound on the probability of event $P_{\epsilon'}$).

LEMMA 7.21 (Rahimi & Recht, 2008, Claim 1) *For any $\epsilon > 0$, $\delta \in (0, 1)$, translation-invariant kernel k, and compact set $\mathcal{M} \subseteq \mathfrak{R}^D$, if $\hat{D} \geq \frac{4(D+2)}{\epsilon^2} \log_e \left(\frac{2^8 \left(\sigma_p \mathrm{diam}(\mathcal{M}) \right)^2}{\delta \epsilon^2} \right)$, then Algorithm 7.4's random mapping $\hat{\phi}$ from Equation (7.6) satisfies $\mathrm{Pr}\left(\left\| k - \hat{k} \right\|_\infty < \epsilon \right) \geq 1 - \delta$, where $\sigma_p^2 = \mathrm{E}\left[\langle \boldsymbol{\omega}, \boldsymbol{\omega} \rangle \right]$ is the second moment of the Fourier transform p of k's g function.*

Combining these ingredients establishes utility for PRIVATESVM.

Proof Lemma 7.20 and Corollary 7.18 combined via the triangle inequality with Lemma 7.21, together establish the result as follows. Define $\mathbb{P}$ to be the conditioning event regarding the approximation of k by $\hat{k}$, denote the events in Lemmas 7.20 and

7.11 by Q and R, and the target event in the theorem by $\mathbb{S}$.

$$\mathbb{P} = \left\{ \left\| k - \hat{k} \right\|_{\infty;\mathcal{M}} < \min \left\{ 1, \frac{\epsilon^2}{2^2 \left(\Lambda + 2\sqrt{\left(CL + \frac{\Lambda}{2} \right) \Lambda} \right)^2} \right\} \right\}$$

$$\mathbb{Q} = \left\{ \left\| f^\star - \tilde{f} \right\|_{\infty;\mathcal{M}} \leq \frac{\epsilon}{2} \right\}$$

$$\mathbb{R} = \left\{ \left\| \hat{f}^\star - \tilde{f} \right\|_{\infty} \leq \frac{\epsilon}{2} \right\}$$

$$\mathbb{S} = \left\{ \left\| f^\star - \hat{f}^\star \right\|_{\infty;\mathcal{M}} \leq \epsilon \right\}.$$

The claim is a bound on $\Pr(\mathbb{S})$. By the triangle inequality, events $\mathbb{Q}$ and $\mathbb{R}$ together imply $\mathbb{S}$. Second note that event $\mathbb{R}$ is independent of $\mathbb{P}$ and $\mathbb{Q}$. Thus $\Pr(\mathbb{S} \mid \mathbb{P}) \geq \Pr(\mathbb{Q} \cap \mathbb{R} \mid \mathbb{P}) = \Pr(\mathbb{Q} \mid \mathbb{P})\Pr(\mathbb{R}) \geq 1 \cdot (1 - \delta/2)$, for sufficiently small λ. Finally Lemma 7.21 bounds $\Pr(\mathbb{P})$: Provided that $\hat{D} \geq 4(D+2)\log_e \left(2^9 \left(\sigma_p \mathrm{diam}(\mathcal{M}) \right)^2 / (\delta\theta(\epsilon)) \right) / \theta(\epsilon)$ where $\theta(\epsilon) = \min \left\{ 1, \epsilon^4 / \left[2 \left(\Lambda + 2\sqrt{(CL + \Lambda/2)\Lambda} \right) \right]^4 \right\}$ we have $\Pr(\mathbb{P}) \geq 1 - \delta/2$. Together this yields $\Pr(\mathbb{S}) = \Pr(\mathbb{S} \mid \mathbb{P})\Pr(\mathbb{P}) \geq (1 - \delta/2)^2 \geq 1 - \delta$. $\qquad\square$

7.7   Bounds on Optimal Differential Privacy

In this section we delve deeper into the special case of the hinge loss. We begin by plugging hinge loss $\ell(y, \hat{y}) = (1 - y\hat{y})_+$ into the main results on privacy and utility of the previous sections. Similar computations can be done for other convex losses; we select hinge loss because it is the most common among SVM classification losses. We then proceed to combine the obtained privacy and utility bounds into an upper bound on the optimal differential privacy for SVM learning with the hinge loss. This notion, while presented here specifically for the SVM, in general quantifies the highest level of privacy achievable over all (ϵ, δ)-useful mechanisms with respect to a target mechanism M.

DEFINITION 7.22 For $\epsilon, C > 0$, $\delta \in (0, 1)$, $N > 1$, loss function $\ell(y, \hat{y})$ convex in $\hat{y}$, and kernel k, the *optimal differential privacy for the SVM* is the function

$$\beta^\star(\epsilon, \delta, C, N, \ell, k) = \inf_{\hat{M} \in \mathcal{I}} \sup_{(\mathbb{D}^{(1)}, \mathbb{D}^{(2)}) \in \mathcal{D}} \sup_{t \in \mathcal{T}_{\hat{M}}} \log \left(\frac{\Pr\left(\hat{M}\left(\mathbb{D}^{(1)} \right) = t \right)}{\Pr\left(\hat{M}\left(\mathbb{D}^{(2)} \right) = t \right)} \right),$$

where $\mathcal{I}$ is the set of all (ϵ, δ)-useful mechanisms with respect to the SVM with parameter C, loss ℓ, and kernel k; and $\mathcal{D}$ is the set of all pairs of neighboring databases with N entries.

7.7.1   Upper Bounds

Combining Theorems 7.10 and 7.11 immediately establishes the upper bound on the optimal differential privacy $\beta^\star$ for mechanisms achieving a given desired level (ϵ, δ) of usefulness.

COROLLARY 7.23 *The optimal differential privacy $\beta^\star$ among all mechanisms that are (ϵ, δ)-useful with respect to the* SVM *with finite F-dimensional feature mapping inducing bounded norms $k(\mathbf{x}, \mathbf{x}) \le \kappa^2$ and $\|\phi(\mathbf{x})\|_\infty \le \Phi$ for all $\mathbf{x} \in \mathfrak{R}^D$, hinge loss, parameter $C > 0$, on N training, is at most*

$$\beta^\star \le \frac{8\kappa \Phi C \left(F \log_e 2 + \log_e \frac{1}{\delta} \right)}{N\epsilon}$$
$$= \mathcal{O}\left(\frac{C}{\epsilon N} \log \frac{1}{\delta} \right).$$

Proof The proof is a straightforward calculation for general L-Lipschitz loss. In the general case the bound has the numerator leading coefficient $8\kappa \Phi CL$. The result then follows from the fact that hinge loss is 1-Lipschitz on $\mathfrak{R}$: i.e., $\partial_{\hat{y}} \ell = \mathbf{1}[1 \ge y\hat{y}] \le 1$. $\square$

Observe that $\Phi \ge \kappa/\sqrt{F}$, so κ could be used in place of Φ to simply the result's statement; however, doing so would yield a slightly looser bound. Also note that by this result, if we set $C = \sqrt{N}$ (needed for universal consistency, see Remark 7.5) and fix β and δ, then the error due to preserving privacy is on the same order as the error in estimating the "true" parameter $\mathbf{w}$.

Recall the dual program for learning under hinge loss from Section 7.3 repeated here for convenience:

$$\max_{\boldsymbol{\alpha} \in \mathfrak{R}^N} \sum_{i=1}^N \alpha_i - \frac{1}{2} \sum_{i=1}^N \sum_{j=1}^N \alpha_i \alpha_j y^{(i)} y^{(j)} k\left(\mathbf{x}^{(i)}, \mathbf{x}^{(j)} \right) \qquad (7.10)$$
$$\text{s.t. } 0 \le \alpha_i \le \frac{C}{N} \ \forall i \in [n].$$

We split the calculation of the upper bound for the translation-invariant kernel case into the following two steps because they are slightly more involved than the finite-dimensional feature mapping case.

COROLLARY 7.24 *Consider any database $\mathbb{D}$ of size N, scalar $C > 0$, and translation-invariant kernel k. For any $\beta > 0$ and $\hat{D} \in \mathfrak{N}$,* PRIVATESVM *run on $\mathbb{D}$ with hinge loss, noise parameter $\lambda \ge \frac{2^{2.5} C \sqrt{\hat{D}}}{\beta N}$, approximation parameter $\hat{D}$, and regularization parameter C guarantees β-differential privacy. Moreover, for any compact set $\mathcal{M} \subseteq \mathfrak{R}^D$ containing $\mathbb{D}$, and scalars $\epsilon > 0$ and $\delta \in (0, 1)$,* PRIVATESVM *run on $\mathbb{D}$ with hinge loss, kernel k, noise parameter $\lambda \le \min\left\{ \frac{\epsilon}{2^4 \log_e 2\sqrt{\hat{D}}}, \frac{\epsilon\sqrt{\hat{D}}}{8 \log_e \frac{2}{\delta}} \right\}$, approximation parameter $\hat{D} \ge \frac{4(D+2)}{\theta(\epsilon)} \log_e \left(\frac{2^9 \left(\sigma_p \operatorname{diam}(\mathcal{M}) \right)^2}{\delta\theta(\epsilon)} \right)$ with $\theta(\epsilon) = \min\left\{ 1, \frac{\epsilon^4}{2^{12} C^4} \right\}$, and parameter C is (ϵ, δ)-useful with respect to hinge-loss SVM run on $\mathbb{D}$ with kernel k and parameter C.*

Proof The first result follows from Theorem 7.10 and the fact that hinge loss is convex and 1-Lipschitz on $\mathfrak{R}$ (as justified in the proof of Corollary 7.23). The second result follows almost immediately from Theorem 7.16. For hinge loss we have that feasible α_i's are bounded by C/N (and so $\Lambda = C$) by the dual's box constraints and that $L = 1$, implying we take $\theta(\epsilon) = \min\left\{1, \frac{\epsilon^4}{2^4 C^4 (1+\sqrt{6})^4}\right\}$. This is bounded by the stated $\theta(\epsilon)$. $\square$

Combining the competing requirements on λ upper-bounds optimal differential privacy of hinge-loss SVM.

THEOREM 7.25 *The optimal differential privacy for hinge-loss* SVM *on translation-invariant kernel k is bounded by $\beta^\star(\epsilon, \delta, C, N, \ell, k) = \mathcal{O}\left(\frac{C}{\epsilon^3 N} \log^{1.5} \frac{C}{\delta \epsilon}\right)$.*

Proof Consider hinge loss in Corollary 7.24. Privacy places a lower bound of $\beta \geq 2^{2.5} C \sqrt{\hat{D}}/(\lambda N)$ for any chosen λ, which we can convert to a lower bound on β in terms of ϵ and δ as follows. For small ϵ, we have $\theta(\epsilon) = \mathcal{O}\left(\epsilon^4/C^4\right)$ and so to achieve (ϵ, δ)-usefulness we must take $\hat{D} = \Omega\left(\frac{1}{\epsilon^4} \log_e\left(\frac{C^4}{\delta \epsilon^4}\right)\right)$. There are two cases for utility. The first case is with $\lambda = \epsilon/\left(2^4 \log_e\left(2\sqrt{\hat{D}}\right)\right)$, yielding

$$\beta = \mathcal{O}\left(\frac{C\sqrt{\hat{D}} \log \sqrt{\hat{D}}}{\epsilon N}\right)$$

$$= \mathcal{O}\left(\frac{C}{\epsilon^3 N} \sqrt{\log \frac{C}{\delta \epsilon}} \left(\log \frac{1}{\epsilon} + \log \log \frac{C}{\delta \epsilon}\right)\right)$$

$$= \mathcal{O}\left(\frac{C}{\epsilon^3 N} \log^{1.5} \frac{C}{\delta \epsilon}\right).$$

In the second case, $\lambda = \frac{\epsilon \sqrt{\hat{D}}}{8 \log_e \frac{2}{\delta}}$ yields $\beta = \mathcal{O}\left(\frac{C}{\epsilon N} \log \frac{1}{\delta}\right)$ which is dominated by the first case as $\epsilon \downarrow 0$. $\square$

A natural question arises from this discussion: given any mechanism that is (ϵ, δ)-useful with respect to hinge SVM, for how small a β can we possibly hope to guarantee β-differential privacy? In other words, what lower bounds exist for the optimal differential privacy for the SVM?

7.7.2   Lower Bounds

Lower bounds peg the level of differential privacy achievable for *any* mechanism approximating SVMs with high accuracy. The following lemma establishes a negative sensitivity result for the SVM mechanism run with the hinge loss and linear kernel.

LEMMA 7.26 *For any $C > 0$ and $N > 1$, there exists a pair of neighboring databases $\mathbb{D}^{(1)}, \mathbb{D}^{(2)}$ on N entries, such that the functions $f_1^\star, f_2^\star$ parametrized by SVM run with parameter C, linear kernel, and hinge loss on $\mathbb{D}^{(1)}, \mathbb{D}^{(2)}$, respectively, satisfy $\left\|f_1^\star - f_2^\star\right\|_\infty > \frac{\sqrt{C}}{N}.$*

Proof We construct the two databases on the line as follows. Let $0 < m < M$ be scalars to be chosen later. Both databases share negative examples $x_1 = \ldots = x_{\lfloor n/2 \rfloor} = -M$ and positive examples $x_{\lfloor n/2 \rfloor + 1} = \ldots = x_{N-1} = M$. Each database has $x_N = M - m$, with $y^{(N)} = -1$ for $\mathbb{D}^{(1)}$ and $y^{(N)} = 1$ for $\mathbb{D}^{(2)}$. In what follows we use subscripts to denote an example's parent database, so $(x_{i,j}, y^{(i,j)})$ is the jth example from $\mathbb{D}^{(i)}$. Consider the result of running primal SVM on each database:

$$
w_1^\star = \underset{w \in \Re}{\mathrm{argmin}} \left[\frac{1}{2} w^2 + \frac{C}{N} \sum_{i=1}^{N} \left(1 - y^{(1,i)} w x_{1,i} \right)_+ \right]
$$

$$
w_2^\star = \underset{w \in \Re}{\mathrm{argmin}} \left[\frac{1}{2} w^2 + \frac{C}{N} \sum_{i=1}^{N} \left(1 - y^{(2,i)} w x_{2,i} \right)_+ \right].
$$

Each optimization is strictly convex and unconstrained, so the optimizing $w_1^\star, w_2^\star$ are characterized by the first-order KKT conditions $0 \in \partial_w f_i(w)$ for f_i being the objective function for learning on $\mathbb{D}^{(i)}$, and ∂_w denoting the subdifferential operator. Now for each $i \in [2]$

$$
\partial_w f_i(w) = w - \frac{C}{N} \sum_{j=1}^{N} y^{(i,j)} x_{i,j} \tilde{\mathbf{1}} \left[1 - y^{(i,j)} w x_{i,j} \right],
$$

where

$$
\tilde{\mathbf{1}}[x] = \begin{cases} \{0\}, & \text{if } x < 0 \\ [0, 1], & \text{if } x = 0 \\ \{1\}, & \text{if } x > 0 \end{cases}
$$

is the subdifferential of $(x)_+$.

Thus for each $i \in [2]$, we have that $w_i^\star \in \frac{C}{N} \sum_{j=1}^{N} y^{(i,j)} x_{i,j} \tilde{\mathbf{1}} \left[1 - y^{(i,j)} w_i^\star x_{i,j} \right]$ that is equivalent to

$$
w_1^\star \in \frac{CM(N-1)}{N} \tilde{\mathbf{1}} \left[\frac{1}{M} - w_1^\star \right] + \frac{C(m-M)}{N} \tilde{\mathbf{1}} \left[w_1^\star - \frac{1}{m-M} \right]
$$

$$
w_2^\star \in \frac{CM(N-1)}{N} \tilde{\mathbf{1}} \left[\frac{1}{M} - w_2^\star \right] + \frac{C(M-m)}{N} \tilde{\mathbf{1}} \left[\frac{1}{M-m} - w_2^\star \right].
$$

The RHSs of these conditions correspond to decreasing piecewise-constant functions, and the conditions are met when the corresponding functions intersect with the diagonal $y = x$ line, as shown in Figure 7.1. If $\frac{C(M(N-2)+m)}{N} < \frac{1}{M}$ then $w_1^\star = \frac{C(M(N-2)+m)}{N}$. And if $\frac{C(MN-m)}{N} < \frac{1}{M}$ then $w_2^\star = \frac{C(MN-m)}{N}$. So provided that

$$
\frac{1}{M} > \frac{C(MN-m)}{N} = \max \left\{ \frac{C(M(N-2)+m)}{N}, \frac{C(MN-m)}{N} \right\},
$$

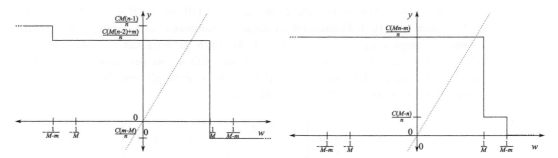

Figure 7.1 For each $i \in [2]$, the SVM's primal solution $w_i^\star$ on database $\mathbb{D}^{(i)}$ constructed in the proof of Lemma 7.26, corresponds to the crossing point of line $y = w$ with $y = w - \partial_w f_i(w)$. Database $\mathbb{D}^{(1)}$ is shown on the left; database $\mathbb{D}^{(2)}$ is shown on the right.

we have $\left| w_1^\star - w_2^\star \right| = \frac{2C}{N} |M - m|$. So taking $M = \frac{2n\epsilon}{C}$ and $m = \frac{N\epsilon}{C}$, this implies

$$\left\| f_1^\star - f_2^\star \right\|_\infty \geq \left| f_{[1}^\star 1](1) - f_{[2}^\star](1) \right|$$
$$= \left| w_1^\star - w_2^\star \right|$$
$$= 2\epsilon,$$

provided $\epsilon < \frac{\sqrt{C}}{2N}$. In particular taking $\epsilon = \frac{\sqrt{C}}{2N}$ yields the result. $\qquad\square$

With this negative sensitivity result in hand, we can lower bound the optimal differential privacy for any mechanism approximating the SVM with hinge loss.

THEOREM 7.27 (Lower bound on optimal differential privacy for linear SVM) *For any $C > 0$, $N > 1$, $\delta \in (0, 1)$, and $\epsilon \in \left(0, \frac{\sqrt{C}}{2N}\right)$, the optimal differential privacy for the hinge-loss SVM with linear kernel is lower bounded by $\log_e \frac{1-\delta}{\delta} = \Omega\left(\log \frac{1}{\delta}\right)$.*

Proof Consider (ϵ, δ)-useful mechanism $\hat{M}$ with respect to SVM learning mechanism M with parameter $C > 0$, hinge loss, and linear kernel on N training examples, where $\delta > 0$ and $\frac{\sqrt{C}}{2N} > \epsilon > 0$. By Lemma 7.26 there exists a pair of neighboring databases $\mathbb{D}^{(1)}, \mathbb{D}^{(2)}$ on N entries, such that $\left\| f_1^\star - f_2^\star \right\|_\infty > 2\epsilon$ where $f_i^\star = f_{M(\mathbb{D}^{(i)})}$ for each $i \in [2]$. Let $\hat{f}_i = f_{\hat{M}(\mathbb{D}^{(i)})}$ for each $i \in [2]$. Then by the utility of $\hat{M}$,

$$\Pr\left(\hat{f}_1 \in \mathcal{B}_\epsilon^\infty \left(f_1^\star \right) \right) \geq 1 - \delta, \tag{7.11}$$

$$\Pr\left(\hat{f}_2 \in \mathcal{B}_\epsilon^\infty \left(f_1^\star \right) \right) \leq \Pr\left(\hat{f}_2 \notin \mathcal{B}_\epsilon^\infty \left(f_2^\star \right) \right) < \delta. \tag{7.12}$$

Let $\hat{\mathcal{P}}_1$ and $\hat{\mathcal{P}}_2$ be the distributions of $\hat{M}\left(\mathbb{D}^{(1)}\right)$ and $\hat{M}\left(\mathbb{D}^{(2)}\right)$, respectively, so that $\hat{\mathcal{P}}_i(t) = \Pr\left(\hat{M}\left(\mathbb{D}^{(i)}\right) = t\right)$. Then by Inequalities (7.11) and (7.12)

$$\mathbb{E}_{T \sim \mathcal{P}_1}\left[\frac{d\mathcal{P}_2(T)}{d\mathcal{P}_1(T)} \;\middle|\; T \in \mathcal{B}_\epsilon^\infty\left(f_1^\star\right) \right] = \frac{\int_{\mathcal{B}_\epsilon^\infty(f_1^\star)} \frac{d\mathcal{P}_2(t)}{d\mathcal{P}_1(t)} d\mathcal{P}_1(t)}{\int_{\mathcal{B}_\epsilon^\infty(f_1^\star)} d\mathcal{P}_1(t)} \leq \frac{\delta}{1 - \delta}.$$

Thus there exists a t such that $\log \frac{\Pr(\hat{M}(\mathbb{D}^{(1)})=t)}{\Pr(\hat{M}(\mathbb{D}^{(2)})=t)} \geq \log \frac{1-\delta}{\delta} = \Omega\left(\log \frac{1}{\delta}\right)$. $\qquad\square$

Remark 7.28 Equivalently this result can be written as follows. For any $C > 0$, $\beta > 0$, and $N > 1$, if a mechanism $\hat{M}$ is (ϵ, δ)-useful and β-differentially private, then either $\epsilon \geq \frac{\sqrt{C}}{2N}$ or $\delta \geq \exp(-\beta)$.

We have now presented both upper bounds (Corollary 7.23 with $L = 1$) and lower bounds on the optimal differential privacy for the case of the linear SVM with hinge loss. Ignoring constants and using the scaling of C (see Remark 7.5) we have that

$$\Omega\left(\log\frac{1}{\delta}\right) = \beta^\star = \mathcal{O}\left(\frac{1}{\epsilon\sqrt{N}}\log\frac{1}{\delta}\right).$$

It is noteworthy that the bounds agree in their scaling on utility confidence δ, but that they disagree on linear and square-root terms in their dependence on ϵ and N, respectively. Moreover under the appropriate scaling of C, the lower bound holds only for $\epsilon = \mathcal{O}\left(N^{-0.75}\right)$; under which the upper asymptotic bound becomes $\mathcal{O}\left(N^{0.25}\log(1/\delta)\right)$. Finding better-matching bounds remains an interesting open problem.

We refer the reader to Rubinstein et al. (2012) for a similar lower bound under the RBF kernel. There a negative sensitivity result is achieved not through a pair of neighboring databases that induce very different SVM results, but through a sequence of K pairwise-neighboring databases whose images under SVM learning form an ϵ-packing.

7.8 Summary

In this chapter we presented mechanisms for private SVM learning due to Chaudhuri et al. (2011) and Rubinstein et al. (2012), which release a classifier based on a privacy-sensitive database of training data. The former approach is one of objective perturbation while the latter performs output perturbation, calibrated by the algorithmic stability of regularized ERM—a property that is typically used in learning theory to prove risk bounds of learning algorithms.

In addition to measuring the training data differential privacy preserved by the output perturbation mechanisms, we also focused on their utility: the similarity of the classifiers released by private and nonprivate SVM. This form of utility implies good generalization error of the private SVM. To achieve utility under infinite-dimensional feature mappings, both families of approach perform regularized empirical risk minimization (ERM) in a random reproducing kernel Hilbert space whose kernel approximates the target kernel. This trick, borrowed from large-scale learning, permits the mechanisms to privately respond with a finite representation of a maximum-margin hyperplane classifier. We explored the high-probability, pointwise similarity between the resulting function and the nonprivate SVM classifier through a smoothness result of regularized ERM with respect to perturbations of the RKHS.

Interesting directions involve extending the ideas of this chapter to other learning algorithms:

QUESTION 7.1 Can the mechanisms and proof techniques used for differentially private SVM by output perturbation be extended to other kernel methods?

QUESTION 7.2 Is there a general connection between algorithmic stability and global sensitivity?

Such a connection would immediately suggest a number of practical privacy-preserving learning mechanisms for which calculations on stability are available: stability would dictate the level of (possibly Laplace) noise required for differential privacy, and for finite-dimensional feature spaces utility would likely follow a similar pattern as presented here for the SVM. The application of the random RKHS with kernel approximating a target kernel would also be a useful tool in making kernelized learners differentially private for translation-invariant kernels.

Bounds on differential privacy and utility combine to upper bound the optimal level of differential privacy possible among all mechanisms that are (ϵ, δ)-useful with respect to the hinge-loss SVM. Lower bounds on this quantity establish that any mechanism that is too accurate with respect to the hinge SVM, with any nontrivial probability, cannot be β-differentially private for small β.

QUESTION 7.3 An important open problem is to reduce the gap between upper and lower bounds on the optimal differential privacy of the SVM.

8 Near-Optimal Evasion of Classifiers

In this chapter, we explore a theoretical model for quantifying the difficulty of *Exploratory* attacks against a trained classifier. Unlike the previous work, since the classifier has already been trained, the adversary can no longer exploit vulnerabilities in the learning algorithm to mistrain the classifier as we demonstrated in the first part of this book. Instead, the adversary must exploit vulnerabilities that the classifier accidentally acquired from training on benign data (or at least data not controlled by the adversary in question). Most nontrivial classification tasks will lead to some form of vulnerability in the classifier. All known detection techniques are susceptible to blind spots (i.e., classes of miscreant activity that fail to be detected), but simply knowing that they exist is insufficient. The principal question is how difficult it is for an adversary to discover a blind spot that is most advantageous for the adversary. In this chapter, we explore a framework for quantifying how difficult it is for the adversary to search for this type of vulnerability in a classifier.

At first, it may appear that the ultimate goal of these *Exploratory* attacks is to reverse engineer the learned parameters, internal state, or the entire boundary of a classifier to discover its blind spots. However, in this work, we adopt a more refined strategy; we demonstrate successful *Exploratory* attacks that only *partially* reverse engineer the classifier. Our techniques find blind spots using only a *small* number of queries and yield near-optimal strategies for the adversary. They discover data points that the classifier will classify as benign and that are close to the adversary's desired attack instance.

While learning algorithms allow the detection algorithm to adapt over time, real-world constraints on the learning algorithm typically allow an adversary to programmatically find blind spots in the classifier. We consider how an adversary can systematically discover blind spots by querying the filter to find a low-cost (for some cost function) instance that evades the filter. Consider, for example, a spammer who wishes to minimally modify a spam message so it is not classified as spam (here cost is a measure of how much the spam must be modified). By observing the responses of the spam detector,[1] the spammer can search for a modification while using few queries. The design of an exploit that must avoid intrusion detection systems can also be cast into this setting (here cost may be a measure of the exploit's severity).

---

[1] There are a variety of domain-specific mechanisms an adversary can use to observe the classifier's response to a query; e.g., the spam filter of a public email system can be observed by creating a *test* account on that system and sending the queries to that account. In this chapter, we assume the filter is able to be queried.

The problem of near-optimal evasion (i.e., finding a low-cost negative instance with few queries) was introduced by Lowd & Meek (2005a). We continue studying this problem by generalizing it to the family of convex-inducing classifiers—classifiers that partition their feature space into two sets, one of which is convex. The family of convex-inducing classifiers is a particularly important and natural set of classifiers to examine that includes the family of linear classifiers studied by Lowd & Meek, as well as anomaly detection classifiers using bounded PCA (Lakhina et al. 2004b), anomaly detection algorithms that use hypersphere boundaries (Bishop 2006), one-class classifiers that predict anomalies by thresholding the log-likelihood of a log-concave (or unimodal) density function, and quadratic classifiers with a decision function of the form $\mathbf{x}^\top \mathbf{A} \mathbf{x} + \mathbf{b}^\top \mathbf{x} + c \geq 0$ if $\mathbf{A}$ is semidefinite (cf. Boyd & Vandenberghe 2004, Chapter 3), to name a few. The family of convex-inducing classifiers also includes more complicated bodies such as the countable intersection of halfspaces, cones, or balls.

We further show that near-optimal evasion does not require complete reverse engineering of the classifier's internal state or decision boundary, but instead only partial knowledge about its general structure. The algorithm of Lowd & Meek (2005a) for evading linear classifiers in a continuous domain reverse engineers the decision boundary by estimating the parameters of their separating hyperplane. The algorithms we present for evading convex-inducing classifiers do not require fully estimating the classifier's boundary (which is hard in the case of general convex bodies; see Rademacher & Goyal 2009) or its parameters (internal state). Instead, these algorithms directly search for a minimal cost-evading instance. These search algorithms require only polynomially many queries, with one algorithm solving the linear case with better query complexity than the previously published reverse-engineering technique. Finally, we also extend near-optimal evasion to general ℓ_p costs. We show that the algorithms for ℓ_1 costs can also be extended to near-optimal evasion on ℓ_p costs, but are generally not efficient. However, in the cases when these algorithms are not efficient, we show that there is no efficient query-based algorithm.

The rest of this chapter is organized as follows. We first present an overview of the prior work most closely related to the near-optimal evasion problem in the remainder of this section (see Chapter 3 for additional related work). In Section 8.1, we formalize the near-optimal evasion problem and review Lowd & Meek (2005a) definitions and results. We present algorithms for evasion that are near-optimal under weighted ℓ_1 costs in Section 8.2, and we provide results for minimizing general ℓ_p costs in Section 8.3.

This chapter builds on (Nelson, Rubinstein, Huang, Joseph, Lau, Lee, Rao, Tran, & Tygar 2010; Nelson, Rubinstein, Huang, Joseph, & Tygar 2010; and Nelson, Rubinstein, Huang, Joseph, Lee, Rao, & Tygar 2012).

Related Work

Lowd & Meek (2005a) first explored near-optimal evasion and developed a method that reverse engineered linear classifiers in a continuous domain, as is discussed in Sections 3.4.2.4 and 3.4.4. The theory we present here generalizes that result and provides three significant improvements:

- This analysis considers a more general family of classifiers: the family of convex-inducing classifiers that partition the space of instances into two sets, one of which is convex. This family subsumes the family of linear classifiers considered by Lowd & Meek.

- The approach we present does not fully estimate the classifier's decision boundary, which is generally hard for arbitrary convex bodies (Rademacher & Goyal 2009) or reverse engineer the classifier's state. Instead, the algorithms search directly for an instance that the classifier labels as negative and is close to the desired attack instance; i.e., an evading instance of near-minimal cost. Lowd & Meek previously demonstrated a direct search technique for linear classifiers in Boolean spaces, but it is not applicable to the classifiers we consider.

- Despite being able to evade a more general family of classifiers, these algorithms still only use a limited number of queries: they require only polynomially many queries in the dimension of the feature space and the desired accuracy of the approximation. Moreover, the K-step MULTILINESEARCH (Algorithm 8.3) solves the linear case with asymptotically fewer queries than the previously published reverse-engineering technique for this case.

Further, as summarized in Section 3.4.2.4, Dalvi et al., Brückner & Scheffer, and Kantarcioglu et al. studied cost-sensitive game-theoretic approaches to preemptively patch a classifier's blind spots and developed techniques for computing an equilibrium for their games. This prior work is complementary to query-based evasion problems; the near-optimal evasion problem studies how an adversary can use queries to find blind spots of a classifier that is unknown but is able to be queried, whereas their game-theoretic approaches assume the adversary knows the classifier and can optimize their evasion accordingly at each step of an iterated game. Thus, the near-optimal evasion setting studies how difficult it is for an adversary to optimize its evasion strategy only by querying, and cost-sensitive game-theoretic learning studies how the adversary and learner can optimally play and adapt in the evasion game given knowledge of each other: These are two separate aspects of evasion.

A number of authors also have studied evading sequence-based IDSs as discussed in Section 3.4.2.2 (cf. Tan et al. 2002, 2003; Wagner & Soto 2002). In exploring mimicry attacks, these authors used offline analysis of the (IDS) to construct their modifications; by contrast, the adversary in near-optimal evasion constructs optimized modifications designed by querying the classifier.

The field of active learning also studies a form of query-based optimization (e.g., see Schohn & Cohn 2000). As summarized by Settles (2009), the three primary approaches to active learning are membership query synthesis, stream-based selective sampling, and pool-based sampling. Our work is most closely related to the membership query synthesis subfield introduced by Angluin (1988), in which the learner can request the label for any instance in feature space, rather than for unlabeled instances drawn from a distribution. However, while active learning and near-optimal evasion are similar in their exploration of query strategies, the objectives for these two settings are quite different—evasion approaches search for low-cost negative instances within a factor

$1 + \epsilon$ of the optimal cost, whereas active learning algorithms seek to obtain hypotheses with low-generalization error, often in a PAC setting (see Section 8.1.2 for a discussion on reverse-engineering approaches to evasion and active learning). It is interesting to note, nonetheless, that results in active learning settings (e.g., Dasgupta, Kalai, & Monteleoni 2009; Feldman 2009) have also achieved polynomial query complexities in specific settings. However, the focus of this chapter is solely on the evasion objective, and we leave the exploration of relationships between our results and those in active learning to future work.

Another class of related techniques that use query-based optimization are nongradient global optimization methods often referred to as direct search. Simple examples of these techniques include bisection and golden-section search methods for finding roots and extrema of univariate functions, as well as derivative approximation approaches such as the secant method and interpolation methods (e.g., Burden & Faires 2000). Combinations of these approaches include Brent's (1973) algorithms, which exhibit superlinear convergence under certain conditions on the query function; i.e., the number of queries is inversely quadratic in the desired error tolerance. However, while these approaches can be adapted to multiple dimensions, their query complexity grows exponentially with the dimension. Other approaches include the simplex method of Nelder & Mead (1965) and the DIRECT search algorithm introduced by Jones, Perttunen, & Stuckman (1993) (refer to Jones 2001, and Kolda, Lewis & Torczon 2003, for surveys of direct search methods); however, we are unaware of query bounds for these methods. While any direct search methods can be adapted for near-optimal evasion, these methods were designed to optimize an irregular function in a regular domain with few dimensions, whereas the near-optimal evasion problem involves optimizing regular known functions (the cost function) over an unknown, possibly irregular, and high-dimensional domain (the points labeled as negative by the classifier). The methods we present specifically exploit the regular structure of ℓ_p costs and of the convex-inducing classifiers to achieve near-optimality with only polynomially many queries.

8.1   Characterizing Near-Optimal Evasion

We begin by introducing the assumptions made for this problem. First, we assume that feature space $\mathcal{X}$ for the learner is a real-valued D-dimensional Euclidean space; i.e., $\mathcal{X} = \Re^D$ such as for some intrusion detection systems (e.g., Wang & Stolfo 2004). (Lowd & Meek also consider integer- and Boolean-valued feature spaces and provide interesting results for several classes of Boolean-valued learners, but these spaces are not compatible with the family of convex-inducing classifiers we study in this chapter.) We assume the feature space representation is known to the adversary and there are no restrictions on the adversary's queries; i.e., any point $\mathbf{x}$ in feature space $\mathcal{X}$ can be queried by the adversary to learn the classifier's prediction $f(\mathbf{x})$ at that point. These assumptions may not be true in every real-world setting (for instance, spam detectors are often defined with discrete features, and designers often attempt to hide or randomize their feature set; e.g., see Wang et al. 2006), but allow us to consider a worst-case adversary.

As in Section 2.2.4, we assume the target classifier f is a member of a family of classifiers $\mathcal{F}$—the adversary does not know f but knows the family $\mathcal{F}$. (This knowledge is congruous with the security assumption that the adversary knows the learning algorithm, but not the training set or parameters used to tune the learner.) We also restrict our attention to binary classifiers and use $\mathcal{Y} = \{"-", "+"\}$. We assume the adversary's attack will be against a fixed f so the learning method and the training data used to select f are irrelevant for this problem. Further, we assume $f \in \mathcal{F}$ is deterministic, and so it partitions $\mathcal{X}$ into two sets—the positive class $\mathcal{X}_f^+ = \{\mathbf{x} \in \mathcal{X} \mid f(\mathbf{x}) = "+"\}$ and the negative class $\mathcal{X}_f^- = \{\mathbf{x} \in \mathcal{X} \mid f(\mathbf{x}) = "-"\}$. As before, we take the negative set to be *normal* instances where the sought-after blind spots reside. We assume that the adversary is aware of at least one instance in each class, $\mathbf{x}^- \in \mathcal{X}_f^-$ and $\mathbf{x}^A \in \mathcal{X}_f^+$, and can observe the class for any $\mathbf{x}$ by issuing a membership query: $f(\mathbf{x})$.

8.1.1   Adversarial Cost

We assume the adversary has a notion of utility over the feature space, which we quantify with a cost function $A : \mathcal{X} \mapsto \Re_{0+}$. The adversary wishes to optimize A over the negative class, $\mathcal{X}_f^-$; e.g., a spammer wants to send spam that will be classified as normal email ("−") rather than as spam ("+"). We assume this cost function is a distance to some target instance $\mathbf{x}^A \in \mathcal{X}_f^+$ that is most desirable to the adversary; e.g., for a spammer, this could be a string edit distance required to change $\mathbf{x}^A$ to a different message. We focus on the general class of weighted ℓ_p ($0 < p \leq \infty$) cost functions relative to $\mathbf{x}^A$ defined in terms of the ℓ_p norm $\| \cdot \|_p$ as

$$A_p^{(\mathbf{c})} \left(\mathbf{x} - \mathbf{x}^A \right) = \left\| \mathbf{c} \odot \left(\mathbf{x} - \mathbf{x}^A \right) \right\|_p = \left(\sum_{d=1}^{D} c_d^p \left| x_d - x_d^A \right|^p \right)^{1/p}, \qquad (8.1)$$

where $0 < c_d < \infty$ is the relative cost the adversary associates with altering the dth feature. When the relative costs are uniform, $c_d = 1$ for all d, we use the simplified notation A_p to refer to the cost function. Similarly, when referring to a generic weighted cost function with weights $\mathbf{c}$, we use the notation $A^{(\mathbf{c})}$. In Section 8.2.1.3, we also consider the special cases when some features have $c_d = 0$ (the adversary does not care about the dth feature) or $c_d = \infty$ (the adversary requires the dth feature to match x_d^A), but otherwise, the weights are on the interval $(0, \infty)$. We use $\mathbb{B}^C (A; \mathbf{y})$ to denote the C-cost ball (or sublevel set) centered at $\mathbf{y}$ with cost no more than the threshold, C; i.e., $\mathbb{B}^C (A; \mathbf{y}) = \{\mathbf{x} \in \mathcal{X} \mid A (\mathbf{x} - \mathbf{y}) \leq C\}$. For instance, $\mathbb{B}^C (A_1; \mathbf{x}^A)$ is the set of instances that do not exceed an ℓ_1 cost of C from the target $\mathbf{x}^A$. For convenience, we also use $\mathbb{B}^C (A) \triangleq \mathbb{B}^C (A; \mathbf{x}^A)$ to denote the C-cost-ball of A recentered at the adversary's target, $\mathbf{x}^A$, since we focus on costs relative to this instance.

Unfortunately, ℓ_p costs do not include many interesting costs such as string edit distances for spam, and in other real-world settings, such as the intrusion detection example given earlier, there may be no natural notion of distance between points. Nevertheless, the objective of this chapter is not to provide practical evasion algorithms, but rather to understand the theoretic capabilities of an adversary on the analytically tractable, albeit practically restrictive, family of ℓ_p costs. Weighted ℓ_1 costs are, however, particularly appropriate for adversarial problems in which the adversary is interested in some features more than others and its cost is assessed based on the degree to which a feature is altered. The ℓ_1-norm is a natural measure of edit distance for email spam, while larger weights can model tokens that are more costly to remove (e.g., a payload URL). We focus first on the weighted ℓ_1 costs studied by Lowd & Meek in Section 8.2 and then explore general ℓ_p costs in Section 8.3. In the latter case, our discussion will focus on uniform weights for ease of exposition, but the results easily extend to the cost-sensitive case as presented for weighted ℓ_1 costs.

Lowd & Meek (2005a) define minimal adversarial cost (*MAC*) of a classifier f to be the value

$$MAC\,(f, A) \triangleq \inf_{\mathbf{x} \in \mathcal{X}_f^-} \left[A\left(\mathbf{x} - \mathbf{x}^A\right) \right];$$ (8.2)

i.e., the greatest lower bound on the cost obtained by any negative instance. They further define a data point to be an ϵ-approximate *instance of minimal adversarial cost (ϵ-IMAC)* if it is a negative instance with a cost no more than a factor $(1 + \epsilon)$ of the *MAC*; i.e., every ϵ-*IMAC* is a member of the set[2]

$$\epsilon\text{-}IMAC\,(f, A) \triangleq \left\{ \mathbf{x} \in \mathcal{X}_f^- \;\middle|\; A\left(\mathbf{x} - \mathbf{x}^A\right) \leq (1 + \epsilon) \cdot \mathrm{MAC}\,(f, A) \right\}.$$ (8.3)

Alternatively, this set can be characterized as the intersection of the negative class and the ball of A of costs within a factor $(1 + \epsilon)$ of $MAC\,(f, A)$ (i.e., ϵ-$IMAC\,(f, A) = \mathcal{X}_f^- \cap \mathbb{B}^{(1+\epsilon)\cdot MAC}\,(A)$); a fact we exploit in Section 8.2.2. The adversary's goal is to find an ϵ-*IMAC* efficiently while issuing as few queries as possible. In the next section, we introduce formal notions to quantify how effectively an adversary can achieve this objective.

8.1.2   Near-Optimal Evasion

Lowd & Meek (2005a) introduce the concept of *adversarial classifier reverse engineering (ACRE) learnability* to quantify the difficulty of finding an ϵ-*IMAC* instance for a particular family of classifiers, $\mathcal{F}$, and a family of adversarial costs, $\mathcal{A}$.

Using our notation, their definition of *ACRE* ϵ-learnable is as follows: A set of classifiers $\mathcal{F}$ is *ACRE* ϵ-learnable under a set of cost functions $\mathcal{A}$ if an algorithm exists such that for all $f \in \mathcal{F}$ and $A \in \mathcal{A}$, it can find an $\mathbf{x} \in \epsilon$-*IMAC* (f, A) using only polynomially many membership queries in terms of the dimensionality D, the encoded size of f, and the encoded size of $\mathbf{x}^+$ and $\mathbf{x}^-$.

In this definition, Lowd & Meek use encoded size to refer to the length of the string of digits used to encode f, $\mathbf{x}^+$, and $\mathbf{x}^-$. In generalizing their result, we use a slightly altered definition of query complexity. First, to quantify query complexity, we only use

---

[2] We use the term ϵ-*IMAC* to refer both to this set and members of it. The usage will be clear from the context.

the dimension, D, and the number of steps, L_ϵ, required by a unidirectional binary search to narrow the gap to within a factor $1 + \epsilon$, the desired accuracy. By including $L_\epsilon^{(*)}$ in our definition of query complexity, we do not require the encoded size of x^+ and x^- since L_ϵ implicitly captures the size of the distance between these points as discussed earlier.

Using the encoded sizes of f, x^+, and x^- in defining ϵ-*IMAC* searchable is problematic. For our purposes, it is clear that the encoded size of both x^+ and x^- is D so it is unnecessary to include additional terms for their size. Further we allow for families of nonparametric classifiers for which the notion of *encoding size* is ill defined, but is also unnecessary for the algorithms we present. In extending beyond linear and parametric family of classifiers, it is not straightforward to define the encoding size of a classifier f. One could use notions such as the VC-dimension of $\mathcal{F}$ or its covering number, but it is unclear why size of the classifier is important in quantifying the complexity of ϵ-*IMAC* search. Moreover, as we demonstrate in this chapter, there are families of classifiers for which ϵ-*IMAC* search is polynomial in D and L_ϵ alone.

Second, we assume the adversary only has two initial points $x^- \in \mathcal{X}_f^-$ and $x^A \in \mathcal{X}_f^+$ (the original setting used a third $x^+ \in \mathcal{X}_f^+$); this yields simpler search procedures. As is apparent in the algorithms we demonstrate, using $x^+ = x^A$ makes the attacker less covert since it is significantly easier to infer the attacker's intentions based on its queries. Covertness is not an explicit goal in ϵ-*IMAC* search, but it would be a requirement of many real-world attackers. However, since the goal of the near-optimal evasion problem is not to design real attacks but rather to analyze the best possible attack so as to understand a classifier's vulnerabilities, we exclude any covertness requirement but return to the issue in Section 8.4.2.1.

Finally, our algorithms do not reverse engineer so ACRE would be a misnomer. Instead, we call the overall problem near-optimal evasion and replace *ACRE* ϵ-learnable with the following definition of ϵ-*IMAC* searchable: a family of classifiers $\mathcal{F}$ is ϵ-*IMAC* *searchable* under a family of cost functions $\mathcal{A}$ if for all $f \in \mathcal{F}$ and $A \in \mathcal{A}$, there is an algorithm that finds some $x \in \epsilon$-*IMAC* (f, A) using polynomially many membership queries in D and L_ϵ. We will refer to such an algorithm as *efficient*.

Our definition does not include the encoded size of the classifier, f, because our approach to near-optimal evasion does not reverse engineer the classifier's parameters as we now discuss in detail.

Near-optimal evasion is only a *partial* reverse-engineering strategy. Unlike Lowd & Meek's approach for continuous spaces, we introduce algorithms that construct queries to provably find an ϵ-*IMAC* without *fully* reverse engineering the classifier; i.e., estimating the decision surface of f or estimating the parameters that specify it. Efficient query-based reverse engineering for $f \in \mathcal{F}$ is sufficient for minimizing A over the estimated negative space. However, generally reverse engineering is an expensive approach for near-optimal evasion, requiring query complexity that is exponential in the feature space dimension D for general convex classes (Rademacher & Goyal 2009), while finding an ϵ-*IMAC* need not be as we demonstrate in this chapter.[3] In fact, the requirements

---

[3] Lowd & Meek (2005a) also previously showed that the reverse-engineering technique of finding a feature's sign witness is NP-complete for linear classifiers with Boolean features, but also that this family was nonetheless 2-*IMAC* searchable.

for finding an ϵ-*IMAC* differ significantly from the objectives of reverse-engineering approaches such as active learning. Both approaches use queries to reduce the size of version space $\hat{\mathcal{F}} \subseteq \mathcal{F}$; i.e., the set of classifiers consistent with the adversary's membership queries. Reverse-engineering approaches minimize the expected number of disagreements between members of $\hat{\mathcal{F}}$. In contrast, to find an ϵ-*IMAC*, the adversary only needs to provide a single instance, $\mathbf{x}^\dagger \in \epsilon$-*IMAC* (f, A), for all $f \in \hat{\mathcal{F}}$, while leaving the classifier largely unspecified; i.e., we need to show that

$$\bigcap_{f \in \hat{\mathcal{F}}} \epsilon\text{-}IMAC\,(f, A) \neq \emptyset.$$

This objective allows the classifier to be unspecified over much of $\mathcal{X}$. We present algorithms for ϵ-*IMAC* search on a family of classifiers that generally cannot be efficiently reverse engineered—the queries necessarily only elicit an ϵ-*IMAC*; the classifier itself will be underspecified in large regions of $\mathcal{X}$ so these techniques do not reverse engineer the classifier's parameters or decision boundary except in a shrinking region near an ϵ-*IMAC*. Similarly, for linear classifiers in Boolean spaces, Lowd & Meek demonstrated an efficient algorithm for near-optimal evasion that does not reverse engineer the classifier—it too searches directly for an ϵ-*IMAC*, and it shows that this family is 2-*IMAC* searchable for ℓ_1 costs with uniform feature weights, $\mathbf{c}$.

8.1.3   Search Terminology

The notion of near-optimality introduced in Equation (8.3) and of the overall near-optimal evasion problem in the previous section is that of multiplicative optimality; i.e., an ϵ-*IMAC* must have a cost within a factor of $(1 + \epsilon)$ of the *MAC*. However, the results of this chapter can also be immediately adopted for additive optimality in which the adversary seeks instances with cost no more than $\eta > 0$ *greater* than the *MAC*. To differentiate between these notions of optimality, we use the notation ϵ-*IMAC*$^{(*)}$ to refer to the set in Equation (8.3) and define an analogous set η-*IMAC*$^{(+)}$ for additive optimality as

$$\eta\text{-}IMAC^{(+)}\,(f, A) \triangleq \left\{ \mathbf{x} \in \mathcal{X}_f^- \;\middle|\; A\left(\mathbf{x} - \mathbf{x}^A\right) \leq \eta + \text{MAC}\,(f, A) \right\}. \qquad (8.4)$$

We use the terms ϵ-*IMAC*$^{(*)}$ and η-*IMAC*$^{(+)}$ to refer both to the sets defined in Equation (8.3) and (8.4) as well as the members of them—the usage will be clear from the context.

We consider algorithms that achieve either additive or multiplicative optimality of the family of convex-inducing classifiers. For either notion of optimality one can efficiently use bounds on the *MAC* to find an ϵ-*IMAC*$^{(*)}$ or an η-*IMAC*$^{(+)}$. Suppose there is a negative instance, $\mathbf{x}^-$, with cost C^-, and there is a $C^+ > 0$ such that all instances with cost no more than C^+ are positive; i.e., C^- is an upper bound and C^+ is a lower bound on the *MAC*; i.e., $C^+ \leq MAC\,(f, A) \leq C^-$. Under that supposition, then the negative instance $\mathbf{x}^-$ is ϵ-multiplicatively optimal if $C^-/C^+ \leq (1 + \epsilon)$, whereas it is η-additively optimal if $C^- - C^+ \leq \eta$. We consider algorithms that can achieve either additive or multiplicative optimality via binary search. Namely, if the adversary can determine whether an intermediate cost establishes a new upper or lower bound on the MAC, then binary search strategies can iteratively reduce the tth gap between any bounds C_t^- and C_t^+ with the fewest steps. We now provide common terminology for the binary search, and in Section 8.2 we use convexity to establish a new bound at the tth iteration.

Remark 8.1 If an algorithm can provide bounds $0 < C^+ \leq MAC(f, A) \leq C^-$, then this algorithm has achieved $(C^- - C^+)$-additive optimality and $(\frac{C^-}{C^+} - 1)$-multiplicative optimality.

In the tth iteration of an additive binary search, the additive gap between the tth bounds, C_t^- and C_t^+, is given by $G_t^{(+)} = C_t^- - C_t^+$ with $G_0^{(+)}$ defined accordingly by the initial bounds $C_0^- = C^-$ and $C_0^+ = C^+$. The search uses a proposal step of $C_t = \frac{C_t^- + C_t^+}{2}$, a stopping criterion of $G_t^{(+)} \leq \eta$, and achieves η-additive optimality in

$$L_\eta^{(+)} = \left\lceil \log_2 \left(\frac{G_0^{(+)}}{\eta} \right) \right\rceil \tag{8.5}$$

steps. In fact, binary search has the least worst-case query complexity for achieving the η-additive stopping criterion for a unidirectional search (e.g., search along a ray).

Binary search can also be used for multiplicative optimality by searching in exponential space. Assuming that $C^- \geq C^+ > 0$, we can rewrite the upper and lower bounds as $C^- = 2^a$ and $C^+ = 2^b$, and thus the multiplicative optimality condition becomes $a - b \leq \log_2 (1 + \epsilon)$; i.e., an additive optimality condition. Thus, binary search on the exponent achieves ϵ-multiplicative optimality and does so with the best worst-case query complexity (again in a unidirectional search). The multiplicative gap of the tth iteration is $G_t^{(*)} = C_t^- / C_t^+$ with $G_0^{(*)}$ defined accordingly by the initial bounds C_0^- and C_0^+. The tth query is $C_t = \sqrt{C_t^- \cdot C_t^+}$, the stopping criterion is $G_t^{(*)} \leq 1 + \epsilon$, and it achieves ϵ-multiplicative optimality in

$$L_\epsilon^{(*)} = \left\lceil \log_2 \left(\frac{\log_2 \left(G_0^{(*)} \right)}{\log_2 (1 + \epsilon)} \right) \right\rceil \tag{8.6}$$

steps. Notice that multiplicative optimality only makes sense when both C_0^- and C_0^+ are strictly positive.

It is also worth noting that both $L_\epsilon^{(+)}$ and $L_\epsilon^{(*)}$ can be instead replaced by $\log \left(\frac{1}{\epsilon} \right)$ for asymptotic analysis. As pointed out by Rubinstein (2010), the near-optimal evasion problem is concerned with the difficulty of making accurate estimates of the MAC, and this difficulty increases as $\epsilon \downarrow 0$. In this sense, clearly $L_\epsilon^{(+)}$ and $\log \left(\frac{1}{\epsilon} \right)$ are asymptotically equivalent. Similarly, comparing $L_\epsilon^{(*)}$ and $\log \left(\frac{1}{\epsilon} \right)$ as $\epsilon \downarrow 0$, the limit of their ratio (by application of L'Hôpital's rule) is

$$\lim_{\epsilon \downarrow 0} \frac{L_\epsilon^{(*)}}{\log \left(\frac{1}{\epsilon} \right)} = 1;$$

i.e., they are also asymptotically equivalent. Thus, in the following asymptotic results, $L_\epsilon^{(*)}$ can be replaced by $\log\left(\frac{1}{\epsilon}\right)$.

Binary searches for additive and multiplicative optimality differ in their proposal step and their stopping criterion. For additive optimality, the proposal is the arithmetic mean $C_t = \frac{C_t^- + C_t^+}{2}$ and search stops when $G_t^{(+)} \leq \eta$, whereas for multiplicative optimality, the proposal is the geometric mean $C_t = \sqrt{C_t^- \cdot C_t^+}$ and search stops when $G_t^{(*)} \leq 1 + \epsilon$. In the remainder of this chapter, we will use the fact that binary search is optimal for unidirectional search to search the cost space. At each step in the search, we use several probes in the feature space $\mathcal{X}$ to determine if the proposed cost is a new upper or lower bound and then continue the binary search accordingly.

8.1.4   Multiplicative vs. Additive Optimality

Additive and multiplicative optimality are intrinsically related by the fact that the optimality condition for multiplicative optimality $C_t^-/C_t^+ \leq 1 + \epsilon$ can be rewritten as additive optimality condition $\log_2\left(C_t^-\right) - \log_2\left(C_t^+\right) \leq \log_2\left(1 + \epsilon\right)$. From this equivalence one can take $\eta = \log_2\left(1 + \epsilon\right)$ and utilize the additive optimality criterion on the logarithm of the cost. However, this equivalence also highlights two differences between these notions of optimality.

First, multiplicative optimality only makes sense when C_0^+ is strictly positive, whereas additive optimality can still be achieved if $C_0^+ = 0$. Taking $C_0^+ > 0$ is equivalent to assuming that $\mathbf{x}^A$ is in the interior of $\mathcal{X}_f^+$ (a requirement for our algorithms to achieve multiplicative optimality). Otherwise, when $\mathbf{x}^A$ is on the boundary of $\mathcal{X}_f^+$, there is no ϵ-$IMAC^{(*)}$ for any $\epsilon > 0$ unless there is some point $\mathbf{x}^\star \in \mathcal{X}_f^-$ that has 0 cost. Practically though, the need for a lower bound is a minor hindrance—as we demonstrate in Section 8.2.1.3, there is an algorithm that can efficiently establish a lower bound C_0^+ for any ℓ_p cost if such a lower bound exists.

Second, the additive optimality criterion is not scale invariant (i.e., any instance $\mathbf{x}^\dagger$ that satisfies the optimality criterion for cost A also satisfies it for $A'\left(\mathbf{x}\right) = s \cdot A\left(\mathbf{x}\right)$ for any $s > 0$), whereas multiplicative optimality is scale invariant. Additive optimality is, however, shift invariant (i.e., any instance $\mathbf{x}^\dagger$ that satisfies the optimality criterion for cost A also satisfies it for $A'\left(\mathbf{x}\right) = s + A\left(\mathbf{x}\right)$ for any $s \geq 0$), whereas multiplicative optimality is not. Scale invariance is more salient in near-optimal evasion because if the cost function is also scale invariant (all proper norms are), then the optimality condition is invariant to a rescaling of the underlying feature space; e.g., a change in units for all features. Thus, multiplicative optimality is a unit-less notion of optimality whereas additive optimality is not. The following result is a consequence of additive optimality's lack of scale invariance.

PROPOSITION 8.2 *Consider any hypothesis space $\mathcal{F}$, target instance $\mathbf{x}^A$, and cost function A. If there exists some $\bar{\epsilon} > 0$ such that no efficient query-based algorithm can find an ϵ-$IMAC^{(*)}$ for any $0 < \epsilon \leq \bar{\epsilon}$, then there is no efficient query-based algorithm that can find an η-$IMAC^{(+)}$ for any $0 < \eta \leq \bar{\epsilon} \cdot MAC\left(f, A\right)$. In particular consider a sequence of classifiers f_n admitting unbounded MACs, and a sequence $\epsilon_n > 0$ such that*

$1/\epsilon_n = o(MAC\,(f_n, A))$. *Then if no general algorithm can efficiently find an ϵ_n-IMAC$^{(*)}$ on each f_n, no general algorithm can efficiently find an η_n-IMAC$^{(+)}$ for $\eta_n \to \infty$.*

Proof Consider any classifier $f \in \mathcal{F}$ such that $MAC\,(f, A) > 0$. Suppose there exists some $\mathbf{x} \in \eta$-IMAC$^{(+)}$ for some $\eta > 0$. Let $\epsilon = \eta/MAC\,(f, A)$; then by definition

$$A\left(\mathbf{x} - \mathbf{x}^A\right) \le \eta + MAC\,(f, A) = (1 + \epsilon)\,MAC\,(f, A), \qquad (8.7)$$

implying that $\mathbf{x} \in \epsilon$-IMAC$^{(*)}$. Then by the contrapositive, if no ϵ-IMAC$^{(*)}$ can be efficiently found for any $0 < \epsilon \le \bar{\epsilon}$, no η-IMAC$^{(+)}$ can be efficiently found for any $0 < \eta \le \bar{\epsilon} \cdot MAC\,(f, A)$. The last result is an immediate corollary. $\square$

The last statement is, in fact, applicable to many common settings. For instance, for any of the weighted ℓ_p costs (with $0 < p \le \infty$ and $0 < c_d < \infty$ for all d) the family of linear classifiers and the family of hypersphere classifiers are both sufficiently diverse to yield such a sequence of classifiers that admit unbounded MACs as required by the last statement. Thus, the family of convex-inducing classifiers can also yield such a sequence. Moreover, as we show in Section 8.3, there are indeed ℓ_p costs for which there exists $\bar{\epsilon} > 0$ such that no efficient query-based algorithm can find an ϵ-IMAC$^{(*)}$ for any $0 < \epsilon \le \bar{\epsilon}$. The consequence of this is that there is no general algorithm capable of achieving additive optimality for any fixed η with respect to the convex-inducing classifiers for these ℓ_p costs, as is shown by the following theorem:

THEOREM 8.3 *If for some hypothesis space $\mathcal{F}$, cost function A, and any initial bounds $0 < C_0^+ < C_0^-$ on the $MAC\,(f, A)$ for some $f \in \mathcal{F}$, there exists some $\bar{\epsilon} > 0$ such that no efficient query-based algorithm can find an ϵ-IMAC$^{(*)}$ for any $0 < \epsilon \le \bar{\epsilon}$, then there is no efficient query-based algorithm that can find an η-IMAC$^{(+)}$ for any $0 < \eta \le \bar{\epsilon} \cdot C_0^-$. As a consequence, if there is $\bar{\epsilon} > 0$ as stated above, then there is generally no efficient query-based algorithm that can find an η-IMAC$^{(+)}$ for any $\eta \ge 0$ since C_0^- could be arbitrarily large.*

Proof By contraposition. If there is an efficient query-based algorithm that can find an $\mathbf{x} \in \eta$-IMAC$^{(+)}$ for some $0 < \eta \le \bar{\epsilon} \cdot C_0^-$, then, by definition of η-IMAC$^{(+)}$, $A\left(\mathbf{x} - \mathbf{x}^A\right) \le \eta + MAC\,(f, A)$. Equivalently, by taking $\eta = \epsilon \cdot MAC\,(f, A)$ for some $\epsilon > 0$, this algorithm achieved $A\left(\mathbf{x} - \mathbf{x}^A\right) \le (1 + \epsilon)MAC\,(f, A)$; i.e., $\mathbf{x} \in \epsilon$-IMAC$^{(*)}$. Moreover, since $MAC\,(f, A) \le C_0^-$, this efficient algorithm is able to find an ϵ-IMAC$^{(*)}$ for some $\epsilon \le \bar{\epsilon}$. The last remark follows directly from the fact that there is no efficient query-based algorithm for any $0 < \eta \le \bar{\epsilon} \cdot C_0^-$ and C_0^- could generally be arbitrarily large. $\square$

This result further suggests that additive optimality in near-optimal evasion is an awkward notion. If there is a cost function A for which some family of classifiers $\mathcal{F}$ cannot be efficiently evaded within any accuracy $0 < \epsilon \le \bar{\epsilon}$, then the question of whether efficient additive optimality can be achieved for some $\eta > 0$ depends on the scale of the cost function. That is, if η-additive optimality can be efficiently achieved for A, the feature space could be rescaled to make η-additive optimality no longer generally efficiently since the rescaling could be chosen to make C_0^- large. This highlights the limitation of the lack of scale invariance in additive optimality: *the units of the cost determine whether a particular level of additive accuracy can be achieved, whereas multiplicative optimality is unit-less.* For (weighted) ℓ_1 costs, this is not an issue since, as Section 8.2 shows, there is an efficient algorithm for ϵ-multiplicative optimality for any $\epsilon > 0$. However, as we demonstrate in Section 8.3, there are ℓ_p costs where this becomes problematic.

For the remainder of this chapter, we primarily only address ϵ-multiplicative optimality for an ϵ-*IMAC* (except where explicitly noted) and define $G_t = G_t^{(*)}$, $C_t = \sqrt{C_t^- \cdot C_t^+}$, and $L_\epsilon = L_\epsilon^{(*)}$. Nonetheless, the algorithms we present can be immediately adapted to additive optimality by simply changing the proposal step, stopping condition, and the definitions of $L_\epsilon^{(*)}$ and G_t, although they may not be generally efficient as discussed earlier.

8.1.5   The Family of Convex-Inducing Classifiers

We introduce the family of convex-inducing classifiers, $\mathcal{F}^{\text{convex}}$; i.e., the set of classifiers that partition the feature space $\mathcal{X}$ into a positive and negative class, one of which is convex. The convex-inducing classifiers include the linear classifiers studied by Lowd & Meek, as well as anomaly detection classifiers using boundeds PCA (Lakhina et al. 2004b), anomaly detection algorithms that use hypersphere boundaries (Bishop 2006), one-class classifiers that predict anomalies by thresholding the log-likelihood of a log-concave (or unimodal) density function, and quadratic classifiers of the form $\mathbf{x}^\top \mathbf{A} \mathbf{x} + \mathbf{b}^\top \mathbf{x} + c \geq 0$ if $\mathbf{A}$ is semidefinite (cf. Boyd & Vandenberghe 2004, Chapter 3). The convex-inducing classifiers also include complicated bodies such as any intersections of a countable number of halfspaces, cones, or balls.

There is a correspondence between the family of convex-inducing classifiers and the set of all convex sets; i.e., $\mathbb{C} = \{\mathbb{X} \mid convex(\mathbb{X})\}$. By definition of the convex-inducing classifiers, every classifier $f \in \mathcal{F}^{\text{convex}}$ corresponds to some convex set in $\mathbb{C}$. Further, for any convex set $\mathbb{X} \in \mathbb{C}$, there are at least two trivial classifier that create that set; namely the classifiers $f_{\mathbb{X}}^{"+"}(\mathbf{x}) = I[\mathbf{x} \in \mathbb{X}]$ and $f_{\mathbb{X}}^{"-"}(\mathbf{x}) = I[\mathbf{x} \notin \mathbb{X}]$. Thus, in the remainder of this chapter, we use the existence of particular convex sets to prove results about the convex-inducing classifiers since there is always a corresponding classifier.

It is also worth mentioning the following alternative characterization of the near-optimal evasion problem on the convex-inducing classifiers. For any convex set $\mathbb{C}$ with a non-empty interior, let $\mathbf{x}^{(c)}$ be a point in its interior and define the Minkowski metric (recentered at $\mathbf{x}^{(c)}$) as $m_{\mathbb{C}}(\mathbf{x}) = \inf\{\lambda \mid (\mathbf{x} - \mathbf{x}^{(c)}) \in \lambda(\mathbb{C} - \mathbf{x}^{(c)})\}$. This function is convex and non-negative, and it satisfies $m_{\mathbb{C}}(\mathbf{x}) \leq 1$ if and only if $\mathbf{x} \in \mathbb{C}$. Thus, we can rewrite the definition of the *MAC* of a classifier in terms of the Minkowski metric—if $\mathcal{X}_f^+$ is convex we require $m_{\mathcal{X}_f^+}(\mathbf{x}) > 1$, and if $\mathcal{X}_f^-$ is convex we require $m_{\mathcal{X}_f^-}(\mathbf{x}) \leq 1$. In this way, the near-optimal evasion problem (for $\mathcal{X}_f^-$ convex) can be rewritten as

$$\operatorname{argmin}_{\mathbf{x} \in \mathcal{X}} \left[A\left(\mathbf{x} - \mathbf{x}^A\right) \right] \tag{8.8}$$

$$\text{s.t.} \qquad m_{\mathcal{X}_f^-}(\mathbf{x}) \leq 1$$

If A is convex, the fact that $m_C(\cdot)$ is convex makes this a convex program that can be solved by optimizing its Lagrangian

$$\operatorname*{argmin}_{\mathbf{x}\in\mathcal{X}, \gamma\in\Re_{0+}}\left[A\left(\mathbf{x}-\mathbf{x}^A\right)+\gamma\left(1-m_{\mathcal{X}_f^-}(\mathbf{x})\right)\right].$$

In cases where $m_{\mathcal{X}_f^-}(\cdot)$ has a closed form, this optimization may have a closed-form solution, but generally this approach seems difficult. Instead, we use the special structure of the ℓ_1 cost function to construct efficient search over the family of convex-inducing classifiers.

8.2 Evasion of Convex Classes for ℓ_1 Costs

We generalize ϵ-*IMAC* searchability to the family of convex-inducing classifiers. Restricting $\mathcal{F}$ to be the family of convex-inducing classifiers simplifies ϵ-*IMAC* search. In our approach to this problem, we divide $\mathcal{F}^{\text{convex}}$, the family of convex-inducing classifiers, into $\mathcal{F}^{\text{convex},"-"}$ and $\mathcal{F}^{\text{convex},"+"}$ corresponding to the classifiers that induce a convex set $\mathcal{X}_f^-$ or $\mathcal{X}_f^+$, respectively (of course, linear classifiers belong to both). When the negative class $\mathcal{X}_f^-$ is convex (i.e., $f \in \mathcal{F}^{\text{convex},"-"}$), the problem reduces to minimizing a (convex) function A constrained to a convex set—if $\mathcal{X}_f^-$ were known to the adversary, this problem reduces simply to solving a convex optimization program (cf. Boyd & Vandenberghe 2004, Chapter 4). When the positive class $\mathcal{X}_f^+$ is convex (i.e., $f \in \mathcal{F}^{\text{convex},"+"}$), however, the problem becomes minimizing a (convex) function A outside of a convex set; this is generally a difficult problem (see Section 8.3.1.4 where we show that minimizing an ℓ_2 cost can require exponential query complexity). Nonetheless for certain cost functions A, it is easy to determine whether a particular cost ball $\mathbb{B}^C(A)$ is completely contained within a convex set. This leads to efficient approximation algorithms that we present in this section.

We construct efficient algorithms for query-based optimization of the (weighted) ℓ_1 cost $A_1^{(\mathbf{c})}$ of Equation (8.1) for the family of convex-inducing classifiers. There is, however, an asymmetry in this problem depending on whether the positive or negative class is convex as illustrated in Figure 8.1. When the positive set is convex, determining whether the ℓ_1 ball $\mathbb{B}^C\left(A_1^{(\mathbf{c})}\right)$ is a subset of $\mathcal{X}_f^+$ only requires querying the vertexes of the ball as depicted in Figure 8.1(a). When the negative set is convex, determining whether or not $\mathbb{B}^C\left(A_1^{(\mathbf{c})}\right)\cap\mathcal{X}_f^- = \emptyset$ is nontrivial since the intersection need not occur at a vertex as depicted in Figure 8.1(b). We present an efficient algorithm for optimizing (weighted) ℓ_1 costs when $\mathcal{X}_f^+$ is convex and a polynomial random algorithm for optimizing any convex cost when $\mathcal{X}_f^-$ is convex, although in both cases, we only consider convex sets with non-empty interiors. The algorithms we present achieve multiplicative optimality via the binary search strategies discussed in the previous section. In the sequel, we use Equation (8.6) to define L_ϵ as the number of phases required by binary

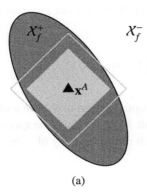
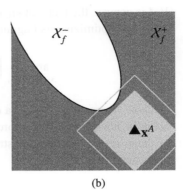

(a)   (b)

Figure 8.1 Geometry of convex sets and ℓ_1 balls. **(a)** If the positive set $\mathcal{X}_f^+$ is convex, finding an ℓ_1 ball contained within $\mathcal{X}_f^+$ establishes a lower bound on the cost; otherwise at least one of the ℓ_1 ball's corners witnesses an upper bound. **(b)** If the negative set $\mathcal{X}_f^-$ is convex, the adversary can establish upper and lower bounds on the cost by determining whether or not an ℓ_1 ball intersects with $\mathcal{X}_f^-$, but this intersection need not include any corner of the ball.

search[4] and $C_0^- = A_1^{(\mathbf{c})}\left(\mathbf{x}^- - \mathbf{x}^A\right)$ as an initial upper bound on the *MAC*. We also assume there is some $C_0^+ > 0$ that lower bounds the *MAC* (i.e., $\mathbf{x}^A \in int\left(\mathcal{X}_f^+\right)$).

8.2.1 ϵ-*IMAC* Search for a Convex $\mathcal{X}_f^+$

Solving the ϵ-*IMAC* search problem when $f \in \mathcal{F}^{\mathrm{convex},\text{"+"}}$ is difficult for the general case of optimizing a convex cost A. We demonstrate algorithms for the (weighted) ℓ_1 cost of Equation (8.1) that solve the problem as a binary search. Namely, given initial costs C_0^+ and C_0^- that bound the *MAC*, we introduce an algorithm that efficiently determines whether $\mathbb{B}^{C_t}(A_1) \subseteq \mathcal{X}_f^+$ for any intermediate cost $C_t^+ < C_t < C_t^-$. If the ℓ_1 ball is contained in $\mathcal{X}_f^+$, then C_t becomes the new lower bound C_{t+1}^+. Otherwise C_t becomes the new upper bound C_{t+1}^-. Since the objective given in Equation (8.3) is to obtain multiplicative optimality, the steps will be $C_t = \sqrt{C_t^+ \cdot C_t^-}$ (for additive optimality, see Section 8.1.3).

The existence of an efficient query-based algorithm relies on three facts: (1) $\mathbf{x}^A \in \mathcal{X}_f^+$; (2) every weighted ℓ_1 cost C-ball centered at $\mathbf{x}^A$ intersects with $\mathcal{X}_f^-$ only if at least one of its vertexes is in $\mathcal{X}_f^-$; and (3) C-balls of weighted ℓ_1 costs only have $2 \cdot D$ vertexes. The vertexes of the weighted ℓ_1 ball $\mathbb{B}^C(A_1)$ are axis-aligned instances differing from $\mathbf{x}^A$ in exactly one feature (e.g., the dth feature) and can be expressed in the form

$$\mathbf{x}^A \pm \frac{C}{c_d} \cdot \mathbf{e}^{(d)} \tag{8.9}$$

---

[4] As noted in Section 8.1.3, the results of this section can be replicated for additive optimality by using Equation (8.5) for L_ϵ and by using the regular binary search proposal and stopping criterion.

which belongs to the C-ball of the weighted ℓ_1 cost (the coefficient $\frac{C}{c_d}$ normalizes for the weight c_d on the dth feature). The second fact is formalized as the following lemma:

LEMMA 8.4 *For all $C > 0$, if there exists some $\mathbf{x} \in \mathcal{X}_f^-$ that achieves a cost of $C = A_1^{(\mathbf{c})}\left(\mathbf{x} - \mathbf{x}^A\right)$, then there is some feature d such that a vertex of the form of Equation (8.9) is in $\mathcal{X}_f^-$ (and also achieves cost C by Equation 8.1).*

Proof Suppose not; then there is some $\mathbf{x} \in \mathcal{X}_f^-$ such that $A_1^{(\mathbf{c})}\left(\mathbf{x} - \mathbf{x}^A\right) = C$ and $\mathbf{x}$ has $M \geq 2$ features that differ from $\mathbf{x}^A$ (if $\mathbf{x}$ differs in one or no features it would be of the form of Equation 8.9). Let $\{d_1, \ldots, d_M\}$ be the differing features, and let $b_{d_i} = \text{sign}\left(x_{d_i} - x_{d_i}^A\right)$ be the sign of the difference between $\mathbf{x}$ and $\mathbf{x}^A$ along the d_i^{th} feature. For each d_i, let $\mathbf{w}_{d_i} = \mathbf{x}^A + \frac{C}{c_{d_i}} \cdot b_{d_i} \cdot \mathbf{e}^{(d_i)}$ be a vertex of the form of Equation (8.9) that has a cost C (from Equation 8.1). The M vertices $\mathbf{w}_{d_i}$ form an M-dimensional equi-cost simplex of cost C on which $\mathbf{x}$ lies; i.e., $\mathbf{x} = \sum_{i=1}^{M} \alpha_i \cdot \mathbf{w}_{d_i}$ for some $0 \leq \alpha_i \leq 1$. If all $\mathbf{w}_{d_i} \in \mathcal{X}_f^+$, then the convexity of $\mathcal{X}_f^+$ implies that all points in their simplex are in $\mathcal{X}_f^+$ and so $\mathbf{x} \in \mathcal{X}_f^+$, which violates the premise. Thus, if any instance in $\mathcal{X}_f^-$ achieves cost C, there is always at least one vertex of the form Equation (8.9) in $\mathcal{X}_f^-$ that also achieves cost C. $\square$

As a consequence, if all such vertexes of any C ball $\mathbb{B}^C\left(A_1\right)$ are positive, then all $\mathbf{x}$ with $A_1^{(\mathbf{c})}\left(\mathbf{x}\right) \leq C$ are positive, thus establishing C as a lower bound on the *MAC*. Conversely, if any of the vertexes of $\mathbb{B}^C\left(A_1\right)$ are negative, then C is an upper bound on *MAC*. Thus, by simultaneously querying all $2 \cdot D$ equi-cost vertexes of $\mathbb{B}^C\left(A_1\right)$, the adversary either establishes C as a new lower or upper bound on the *MAC*. By performing a binary search on C the adversary iteratively halves the multiplicative gap until it is within a factor of $1 + \epsilon$. This yields an ϵ-*IMAC* of the form of Equation (8.9).

A general form of this multi-line search procedure is presented as Algorithm 8.1 and depicted in Figure 8.3. MULTILINESEARCH simultaneously searches along all

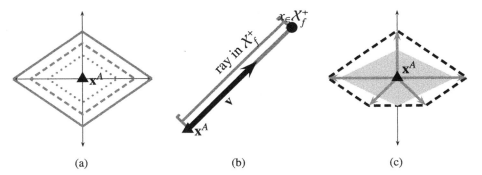

(a)   (b)   (c)

Figure 8.2 The geometry of multi-line search. **(a)** Weighted ℓ_1 balls are centered around the target $\mathbf{x}^A$ and have $2 \cdot D$ vertexes. **(b)** Search directions in multi-line search radiate from $\mathbf{x}^A$ to probe specific costs. **(c)** In general, the adversary leverages convexity of the cost function when searching to evade. By probing all search directions at a specific cost, the convex hull of the positive queries bounds the ℓ_1 cost ball contained within it.

unit-cost search directions in the set $\mathbb{W}$, which contains search directions that radiate from their origin at $\mathbf{x}^A$ and are unit vectors for their cost; i.e., $A(\mathbf{w}) = 1$ for every $\mathbf{w} \in \mathbb{W}$. Of course, any set of non-normalized search vectors $\{\mathbf{v}\}$ can be transformed into unit search vectors simply by applying a normalization constant of $A(\mathbf{v})^{-1}$ to each. At each step, MULTILINESEARCH (Algorithm 8.1) issues at most $|\mathbb{W}|$ queries to construct a bounding shell (i.e., the convex hull of these queries will either form an upper or lower bound on the MAC) to determine whether $\mathbb{B}^C(A_1) \subseteq \mathcal{X}_f^+$. Once a negative instance is found at cost C, the adversary ceases further queries at cost C since a single negative instance is sufficient to establish a lower bound. We call this policy *lazy querying*[5]—a practice that will lead to better bounds for a malicious classifier. Further, when an upper bound is established for a cost C (i.e., a negative vertex is found), the algorithm prunes all directions that were positive at cost C. This pruning is sound; by the convexity assumption, these pruned directions are positive for all costs less than the new upper bound C on the MAC so no further queries will be required along such a direction. Finally, by performing a binary search on the cost, MULTILINESEARCH finds an ϵ-$IMAC$ with no more than $|\mathbb{W}| \cdot L_\epsilon$ queries but at least $|\mathbb{W}| + L_\epsilon$ queries. Thus, this algorithm has a best-case query complexity of $\mathcal{O}(|\mathbb{W}| \cdot L_\epsilon)$ and a worst-case query complexity of $\mathcal{O}(|\mathbb{W}| \cdot L_\epsilon)$.

It is worth noting that, in its present form, MULTILINESEARCH has two implicit assumptions. First, we assume all search directions radiate from a common origin, $\mathbf{x}^A$, and $A(\mathbf{0}) = 0$. Without this assumption, the ray-constrained cost function $A(s \cdot \mathbf{w})$ is still convex in $s \geq 0$, but not necessarily monotonic as required for binary search. Second, we assume the cost function A is a positive homogeneous function along any ray from $\mathbf{x}^A$; i.e., $A(s \cdot \mathbf{w}) = |s| \cdot A(\mathbf{w})$. This assumption allows MULTILINESEARCH to scale its unit search vectors to achieve the same scaling of their cost. Although the algorithm could be adapted to eliminate these assumptions, the cost functions in Equation (8.1) satisfy both assumptions since they are norms recentered at $\mathbf{x}^A$.

Algorithm 8.2 uses MULTILINESEARCH for (weighted) ℓ_1 costs by making $\mathbb{W}$ be the vertexes of the unit-cost ℓ_1 ball centered at $\mathbf{x}^A$. In this case, the search issues at most $2 \cdot D$ queries to determine whether $\mathbb{B}^C(A_1)$ is a subset of $\mathcal{X}_f^+$ and thus is $\mathcal{O}(L_\epsilon \cdot D)$. However, MULTILINESEARCH does not rely on its directions being vertexes of the ℓ_1 ball, although those vertexes are sufficient to span the ℓ_1 ball. Generally, MULTILINESEARCH is agnostic to the configuration of its search directions and can be adapted for any set of directions that can provide a sufficiently tight bound on the cost using the convexity of $\mathcal{X}_f^+$ (see Section 8.3.1.1 for the bounding requirements that the search directions must satisfy). However, as we show in Section 8.3.1, the number of search directions required to adequately bound an ℓ_p-cost ball for $p > 1$ can be exponential in D.

---

[5] The search algorithm could continue to query at any distance B^- where there is a known negative instance as it may expedite the pruning of additional search directions early in the search. However, in analyzing the malicious classifier, these additional queries will not lead to further pruning, but instead will prevent improvements on the worst-case query complexity, as demonstrated in Section 8.2.1.1. Thus, the algorithms we present only use lazy querying and only queries at costs below the upper bound C_t^- on the MAC.

ALGORITHM 8.1   MULTILINESEARCH

$MLS\left(\mathbb{W}, \mathbf{x}^A, \mathbf{x}^-, C_0^+, C_0^-, \epsilon\right)$

$\mathbf{x}^\star \leftarrow \mathbf{x}^-$

$t \leftarrow 0$

while $C_t^- / C_t^+ > 1 + \epsilon$ **do begin**

    $C_t \leftarrow \sqrt{C_t^+ \cdot C_t^-}$

    for all $\mathbf{w} \in \mathbb{W}$ **do begin**

        Query: $f_\mathbf{w}^t \leftarrow f\left(\mathbf{x}^A + C_t \cdot \mathbf{w}\right)$

        if $f_\mathbf{w}^t = "-"$ **then begin**

            $\mathbf{x}^\star \leftarrow \mathbf{x}^A + C_t \cdot \mathbf{w}$

            Prune $\mathbf{i}$ from $\mathbb{W}$ if $f_\mathbf{i}^t = "+"$

            break for-loop

        end if

    end for

    $C_{t+1}^+ \leftarrow C_t^+$ and $C_{t+1}^- \leftarrow C_t^-$

    if $\forall \mathbf{w} \in \mathbb{W}\ f_\mathbf{w}^t = "+"$ **then** $C_{t+1}^+ \leftarrow C_t$

    else $C_{t+1}^- \leftarrow C_t$

    $t \leftarrow t + 1$

end while

return: $\mathbf{x}^\star$

ALGORITHM 8.2   CONVEX $\mathcal{X}_f^+$ SEARCH

$ConvexSearch\left(\mathbf{x}^A, \mathbf{x}^-, \mathbf{c}, \epsilon, C^+\right)$

$D \leftarrow dim\left(\mathbf{x}^A\right)$

$C^- \leftarrow A^{(\mathbf{c})}\left(\mathbf{x}^- - \mathbf{x}^A\right)$

$\mathbb{W} \leftarrow \emptyset$

for $i = 1$ **to** D **do begin**

    $\mathbf{w}^i \leftarrow \frac{1}{c_i} \cdot \mathbf{e}^{(i)}$

    $\mathbb{W} \leftarrow \mathbb{W} \cup \left\{\pm \mathbf{w}^i\right\}$

end for

return: $MLS\left(\mathbb{W}, \mathbf{x}^A, \mathbf{x}^-, C^+, C^-, \epsilon\right)$

Figure 8.3 Algorithms for multi-line search. Algorithm 8.1 is a generic procedure for performing simultaneous binary searches along multiple search directions emanating from $\mathbf{x}^A$; each direction, $\mathbf{w} \in \mathbb{W}$, must be a unit-cost direction. Algorithm 8.2 uses this MULTILINESEARCH procedure to minimize weighted ℓ_1 costs when the positive class of a classifier is convex. For this procedure, every weight, c_i, must be on the range $(0, \infty)$, although extensions are discussed in Section 8.2.1.3.

8.2.1.1   *K*-step Multi-line Search

Here we present a variant of the multi-line search algorithm that better exploits pruning to reduce the query complexity of Algorithm 8.1. The original MULTILINESEARCH algorithm is $2 \cdot |\mathbb{W}|$ simultaneous binary searches (i.e., a breadth-first search simultaneously along all search directions). This strategy prunes directions most effectively when the convex body is asymmetrically elongated relative to $\mathbf{x}^A$, but fails to prune for symmetrically round bodies. The algorithm could instead search sequentially (i.e., a depth-first search of L_ϵ steps along each direction sequentially). This alternative search strategy also obtains a best case of $\mathcal{O}\left(L_\epsilon + |\mathbb{W}|\right)$ queries (for a body that is symmetrically round about $\mathbf{x}^A$, it uses L_ϵ queries along the first direction to establish an upper and lower bound within a factor of $1 + \epsilon$, and then D queries to verify the lower bound) and a worst case of $\mathcal{O}\left(L_\epsilon \cdot |\mathbb{W}|\right)$ queries (for asymmetrically elongated bodies, in the worst case, the strategy would require L_ϵ queries along each of the D search directions). Surprisingly, these two alternatives have opposite best-case and worst-case convex bodies, which inspired a hybrid approach called *K*-STEP MULTILINESEARCH. This algorithm mixes simultaneous and sequential strategies to achieve a better worst-case query complexity than either pure search strategy.[6]

At each phase, the K-STEP MULTILINESEARCH (Algorithm 8.3) chooses a single direction $\mathbf{w}$ and queries it for K steps to generate candidate bounds B^- and B^+ on the *MAC*. The algorithm makes substantial progress toward reducing G_t without querying other directions (a depth-first strategy). It then iteratively queries all remaining directions at the candidate lower bound B^+ (a breadth-first strategy). Again, we use lazy querying and stop as soon as a negative instance is found since B^+ is then no longer a viable lower bound. In this case, although the candidate bound is invalidated, the algorithm can still prune all directions that were positive at B^+ (there will always be at least one such direction). Thus, in every iteration, either the gap is substantially decreased or at least one search direction is pruned. We show that for $K = \lceil \sqrt{L_\epsilon} \rceil$, the algorithm achieves a delicate balance between the usual breadth-first and depth-first approaches to attain a better worst-case complexity than either.

THEOREM 8.5 *Algorithm 8.3 will find an ϵ-IMAC with at most $\mathcal{O}\left(L_\epsilon + \sqrt{L_\epsilon}\,|\mathbb{W}|\right)$ queries when $K = \lceil \sqrt{L_\epsilon} \rceil$.*

The proof of this theorem appears in Appendix D. As a consequence of Theorem 8.5, finding an ϵ-IMAC with Algorithm 8.3 for a (weighted) ℓ_1 cost requires $\mathcal{O}\left(L_\epsilon + \sqrt{L_\epsilon}D\right)$ queries. Further, Algorithm 8.2 can incorporate K-step MULTILINESEARCH directly by replacing its function call to MULTILINESEARCH with K-STEP MULTILINESEARCH and using $K = \lceil \sqrt{L_\epsilon} \rceil$.

8.2.1.2   Lower Bound

Here we find a lower bound on the number of queries required by any algorithm to find an ϵ-IMAC when $\mathcal{X}_f^+$ is convex for any convex cost function; e.g., Equation (8.1) for $p \geq 1$. Below, we present theorems for additive and multiplicative optimality. Notably, since an ϵ-IMAC uses multiplicative optimality, we incorporate a bound $C_0^+ > 0$ on the *MAC* into the theorem statement.

THEOREM 8.6 *For any $D > 0$, any positive convex function $A : \mathfrak{R}^D \mapsto \mathfrak{R}_+$, any initial bounds $0 \leq C_0^+ < C_0^-$ on the MAC, and $0 < \eta < C_0^- - C_0^+$, all algorithms must submit at least $\max\{D, L_\eta^{(+)}\}$ membership queries in the worst case to be η-additive optimal on $\mathcal{F}^{\text{convex},\text{"+"}}$.*

THEOREM 8.7 *For any $D > 0$, any positive convex function $A : \mathfrak{R}^D \mapsto \mathfrak{R}_+$, any initial bounds $0 < C_0^+ < C_0^-$ on the MAC, and $0 < \epsilon < \frac{C_0^-}{C_0^+} - 1$, all algorithms must submit at least $\max\{D, L_\epsilon^{(*)}\}$ membership queries in the worst case to be ϵ-multiplicatively optimal on $\mathcal{F}^{\text{convex},\text{"+"}}$.*

The proof of both of these theorems is in Appendix D. Note that these theorems only apply to $\eta \in \left(0, C_0^- - C_0^+\right)$ and $\epsilon \in \left(0, \frac{C_0^-}{C_0^+} - 1\right)$, respectively. In fact, outside of these intervals the query strategies are trivial. For either $\eta = 0$ or $\epsilon = 0$, no approximation

---

[6] K-STEP MULTILINESEARCH also has a best case of $\mathcal{O}\left(L_\epsilon + |\mathbb{W}|\right)$.

ALGORITHM 8.3   *K*-STEP MULTILINESEARCH

$KMLS\left(\mathbb{W}, \mathbf{x}^A, \mathbf{x}^-, C_0^+, C_0^-, \epsilon, K\right)$

$\mathbf{x}^\star \leftarrow \mathbf{x}^-$

$t \leftarrow 0$

while $C_t^-/C_t^+ > 1 + \epsilon$ **do begin**

    Choose a direction $\mathbf{w} \in \mathbb{W}$

    $B^+ \leftarrow C_t^+$

    $B^- \leftarrow C_t^-$

    for K steps **do begin**

        $B \leftarrow \sqrt{B^+ \cdot B^-}$

        Query: $f_\mathbf{w} \leftarrow f\left(\mathbf{x}^A + B \cdot \mathbf{w}\right)$

        if $f_\mathbf{w} =$ "+" **then** $B^+ \leftarrow B$

        else $B^- \leftarrow B$ **and** $\mathbf{x}^\star \leftarrow \mathbf{x}^A + B \cdot \mathbf{w}$

    end for

    for all $\mathbf{i} \in \mathbb{W} \setminus \{\mathbf{w}\}$ **do begin**

        Query: $f_\mathbf{i}^t \leftarrow f\left(\mathbf{x}^A + (B^+) \cdot \mathbf{i}\right)$

        if $f_\mathbf{i}^t =$ "$-$" **then begin**

            $\mathbf{x}^\star \leftarrow \mathbf{x}^A + (B^+) \cdot \mathbf{i}$

            Prune $\mathbf{k}$ from $\mathbb{W}$ if $f_\mathbf{k}^t =$ "+"

            break for-loop

        end if

    end for

    $C_{t+1}^- \leftarrow B^-$

    if $\forall \mathbf{i} \in \mathbb{W} \ f_\mathbf{i}^t =$ "+" **then** $C_{t+1}^+ \leftarrow B^+$

    else $C_{t+1}^- \leftarrow B^+$

    $t \leftarrow t + 1$

end while

return: $\mathbf{x}^\star$

---

algorithm terminates. Similarly, for $\eta \geq C_0^- - C_0^+$ or $\epsilon \geq \frac{C_0^-}{C_0^+} - 1$, $\mathbf{x}^-$ is an *IMAC* since it has a cost $A\left(\mathbf{x}^- - \mathbf{x}^A\right) = C_0^-$, so no queries are required.

Theorems 8.6 and 8.7 show that η-additive optimality and ϵ-multiplicative optimality require $\Omega\left(L_\eta^{(+)} + D\right)$ and $\Omega\left(L_\epsilon^{(*)} + D\right)$ queries, respectively. Thus, the *K*-STEP MULTILINESEARCH algorithm (Algorithm 8.3) has close to the optimal query complexity for weighted ℓ_1-costs with its $\mathcal{O}\left(L_\epsilon + \sqrt{L_\epsilon}D\right)$ queries. This lower bound also applies to any ℓ_p cost with $p > 1$, but in Section 8.3 we present tighter lower bounds for $p > 1$ that substantially exceed this result for some ranges of ϵ and any range of η.

8.2.1.3   Special Cases

Here we present a number of special cases that require minor modifications to Algorithms 8.1 and 8.3 by adding preprocessing steps.

Revisiting Linear Classifiers

Lowd & Meek originally developed a method for reverse engineering linear classifiers for a (weighted) ℓ_1 cost. First their method isolates a sequence of points from $\mathbf{x}^-$ to $\mathbf{x}^A$ that cross the classifier's boundary, and then it estimates the hyperplane's parameters using D binary line searches. However, as a consequence of the ability to efficiently minimize our objective when $\mathcal{X}_f^+$ is convex, we immediately have an alternative method for linear classifiers (i.e., halfspaces). Because linear classifiers are a special case of convex-inducing classifiers, Algorithm 8.2 can be applied, and our K-STEP MULTILINESEARCH algorithm improves on complexity of their reverse-engineering technique's $\mathcal{O}\left(L_\epsilon \cdot D\right)$ queries and applies to a broader family of classifiers.

While Algorithm 8.2 has better complexity, it uses $2 \cdot D$ search directions rather than the D directions used in the approach of Lowd & Meek, which may require our technique to issue more queries in some practical settings. However, for some restrictive classifier families, it is also possible to eliminate search directions if they can be proven to be infeasible based on the current set of queries. For instance, given a set $\mathbb{W}$ of search directions, t queries $\left\{\mathbf{x}^{(i)}\right\}_{i=1}^t$ and their corresponding responses $\left\{y^{(i)}\right\}_{i=1}^t$, a search direction $\mathbf{e}$ can be eliminated from $\mathbb{W}$ if for all $C_t^+ \leq \alpha < C_t^-$ there does not exist any classifier $f \in \mathcal{F}$ consistent with all previous queries (i.e., $f\left(\mathbf{x}^-\right) = "-"$, $f\left(\mathbf{x}^A\right) = "+"$ and for all $i \in \{1, \ldots, t\}$, $f\left(\mathbf{x}^{(i)}\right) = y^{(i)}$) that also has $f(\alpha \cdot \mathbf{e}) = "-"$ and $f(\alpha \cdot \mathbf{i}) = "+"$ for every $\mathbf{i} \in \mathbb{W} \setminus \{\mathbf{e}\}$). That is, $\mathbf{e}$ is feasible if and only if it is the only search direction among the set of remaining search directions, $\mathbb{W}$, that would be classified as a negative for a cost α by some consistent classifier. Further, since subsequent queries only restrict the feasible space of α and the set of consistent classifiers $\hat{\mathcal{F}}$, pruning these infeasible directions is sound for the remainder of the search.

For restrictive families of convex-inducing classifiers, these feasibility conditions can be efficiently verified and may be used to prune search directions without issuing further queries. In fact, for the family of linear classifiers written as $f(\mathbf{x}) = \mathrm{sign}\left(\mathbf{w}^\top \mathbf{x} + b\right)$ for a normal vector $\mathbf{w}$ and displacement b, the above conditions become a set of linear inequalities along with quadratic inequalities corresponding to the constraint involving search directions. This can be cast as the following optimization program with respect to α, $\mathbf{w}$, and b:

$$\min_{\alpha, \mathbf{w}, b} \quad \alpha \cdot \mathbf{w}^\top \mathbf{e} + b$$

$$
\text{s.t.} \quad
\begin{aligned}
\alpha &\in [C_t^+, C_t^-) \\
\mathbf{w}^\top \mathbf{x}^- + b &\leq 0 \\
\mathbf{w}^\top \mathbf{x}^A + b &\geq 0 \\
y^i(\mathbf{w}^\top \mathbf{x}^{(i)} + b) &\geq 0 \quad \forall\, i \in \{1, \ldots, t\} \\
\alpha \cdot \mathbf{w}^\top \mathbf{i} + b &\geq 0 \quad \forall\, \mathbf{i} \neq \mathbf{e} \in \mathbb{W}
\end{aligned}
$$

If the resulting minimum is less than zero, direction $\mathbf{e}$ is feasible; otherwise, it can be pruned. Such programs can be efficiently solved and may allow the adversary to rapidly eliminate infeasible search directions without issuing additional queries. However, refining these pruning procedures further is beyond the scope of this chapter.

Extending MULTILINESEARCH *Algorithms to* $c_d = \infty$ *or* $c_d = 0$ *Weights*
In Algorithm 8.2, we reweighted the dth axis-aligned directions by a factor $\frac{1}{c_d}$ to make unit cost vectors by implicitly assuming $c_d \in (0, \infty)$. The case where $c_d = \infty$ (e.g., immutable features) is dealt with by simply removing those features from the set of search directions $\mathbb{W}$ used in the MULTILINESEARCH. In the case when $c_d = 0$ (e.g., useless features), MULTILINESEARCH-like algorithms no longer ensure near-optimality because they implicitly assume that cost balls are bounded sets. If $c_d = 0$, $\mathbb{B}^0(A)$ is no longer a bounded set, and 0 cost can be achieved if $\mathcal{X}_f^-$ anywhere intersects the subspace spanned by the 0-cost features—this makes near-optimality unachievable unless a negative 0-cost instance can be found. In the worst case, such an instance could be arbitrarily far in any direction within the 0-cost subspace, making search for such an instance intractable. Nonetheless, one possible search strategy is to assign all 0-cost features a nonzero weight that decays quickly toward 0 (e.g., $c_d = 2^{-t}$ in the tth iteration) as we repeatedly rerun MULTILINESEARCH on the altered objective for T iterations. The algorithm will either find a negative instance that only alters 0-cost features (and hence is a 0-*IMAC*), or it terminates with a nonzero cost instance, which is an ϵ-*IMAC* if no 0-cost negative instances exist. This algorithm does not ensure near-optimality, but may be suitable for practical settings using some fixed T runs.

Lack of an Initial Lower Bound
Thus far, to find an ϵ-*IMAC* the algorithms we presented searched between initial bounds C_0^+ and C_0^-, but in general, C_0^+ may not be known to a real-world adversary. We now present an algorithm called SPIRALSEARCH that efficiently establishes a lower bound on the *MAC* if one exists. This algorithm performs a halving search on the exponent along a single direction to find a positive example and then queries the remaining directions at this candidate bound. Either the lower bound is verified or directions that were positive can be pruned for the remainder of the search.

ALGORITHM 8.4   SPIRALSEARCH

$spiral\left(\mathbb{W}, \mathbf{x}^A, C_0^-\right)$
$t \leftarrow 0$ and $\mathbb{V} \leftarrow \emptyset$
repeat
  Choose a direction $\mathbf{w} \in \mathbb{W}$
  Remove $\mathbf{w}$ from $\mathbb{W}$ and $\mathbb{V} \leftarrow \mathbb{V} \cup \{\mathbf{w}\}$
  Query: $f_{\mathbf{w}} \leftarrow f\left(\mathbf{x}^A + C_0^- \cdot 2^{-2^t} \cdot \mathbf{w}\right)$
  if $f_{\mathbf{w}} = $ "$-$" **then begin**
    $\mathbb{W} \leftarrow \mathbb{W} \cup \{\mathbf{w}\}$ and $\mathbb{V} \leftarrow \emptyset$
    $t \leftarrow t + 1$
  end if
until $\mathbb{W} = \emptyset$
$C_0^+ \leftarrow C_0^- \cdot 2^{-2^t}$
if $t > 0$ **then** $C_0^- \leftarrow C_0^- \cdot 2^{-2^{t-1}}$
return: $(\mathbb{V}, C_0^+, C_0^-)$

At the tth iteration of SPIRALSEARCH, a direction is selected and queried at the candidate lower bound of $(C_0^-)2^{-2^t}$. If the query is positive, that direction is added to the set $\mathbb{V}$ of directions consistent with the lower bound. Otherwise, all positive directions in $\mathbb{V}$ are pruned, a new upper bound is established, and the candidate lower bound is lowered with an exponentially decreasing exponent. By definition of the MAC, this algorithm will terminate after $t = \left\lceil \log_2 \log_2 \frac{C_0^-}{MAC(f,A)} \right\rceil$ iterations. Further, in this algorithm, multiple directions are probed only during iterations with positive queries, and it makes at most one positive query for each direction. Thus, given that some lower bound $C_0^+ > 0$ does exist, SPIRALSEARCH will establish a lower bound with $\mathcal{O}\left(L'_\epsilon + D\right)$ queries, where L'_ϵ is given by Equation (8.6) defined using $C_0^+ = MAC(f, A)$: the largest possible lower bound.

This algorithm can be used as a precursor to any of the previous searches[7] and can be adapted to additive optimality by halving the lower bound instead of the exponent (see Section 8.1.3). Upon completion, the upper and lower bounds it establishes have a multiplicative gap of $2^{2^{t-1}}$ for $t > 0$ or 2 for $t = 0$. From the definition of t provided above in terms of the MAC, MULTILINESEARCH can hence proceed using $L_\epsilon = L'_\epsilon$. Further, the search directions pruned by SPIRALSEARCH are also invalid for the subsequent MULTILINESEARCH so the set $\mathbb{V}$ returned by SPIRALSEARCH will be used as the initial set $\mathbb{W}$ for the subsequent search. Thus, the query complexity of the subsequent search is the same as if it had started with the best possible lower bound.

Lack of a Negative Example

The MULTILINESEARCH algorithms can also naturally be adapted to the case when the adversary has no negative example $\mathbf{x}^-$. This is accomplished by querying ℓ_1 balls of doubly exponentially increasing cost until a negative instance is found. During the tth iteration, the adversary probes along every search direction at a cost $(C_0^+)2^{2^t}$; either all probes are positive (a new lower bound), or at least one is negative (a new upper bound) and search can terminate. Once a negative example is located (having probed for T iterations), we must have $(C_0^+)2^{2^{T-1}} < MAC(f, A) \leq (C_0^+)2^{2^T}$; thus, $T = \left\lceil \log_2 \log_2 \left(\frac{MAC(f,A)}{C_0^+} \right) \right\rceil$. After this preprocessing, the adversary can subsequently perform MULTILINESEARCH with $C_0^+ = 2^{2^{T-1}}$ and $C_0^- = 2^{2^T}$; i.e., $\log_2(G_0) = 2^{T-1}$. This precursor step requires at most $|\mathbb{W}| \cdot T$ queries to initialize the MULTILINESEARCH algorithm with a gap such that $L_\epsilon = \left\lceil (T-1) + \log_2 \left(\frac{1}{\log_2(1+\epsilon)} \right) \right\rceil$ according to Equation (8.6).

If there is neither an initial upper bound or lower bound, the adversary can proceed by probing each search direction at unit cost using additional $|\mathbb{W}|$ queries. This will either establish an upper or lower bound, and the adversary can then proceed accordingly.

---

[7] If no lower bound on the cost exists, no algorithm can find an ϵ-$IMAC$. As presented, this algorithm would not terminate, but in practice, the search would be terminated after sufficiently many iterations.

8.2.2 ϵ-$IMAC$ Learning for a Convex $\mathcal{X}_f^-$

In this section, we minimize convex cost function A with bounded cost balls (we focus on weighted ℓ_1 costs in Equation 8.1) when the feasible set $\mathcal{X}_f^-$ is convex. Any convex function can be efficiently minimized within a known convex set (e.g., using an ellipsoid method or interior point methods; see Boyd & Vandenberghe 2004). However, in the near-optimal evasion problem, the convex set is only accessible via membership queries. We use a randomized polynomial algorithm of Bertsimas & Vempala (2004) to minimize the cost function A given an initial point $\mathbf{x}^- \in \mathcal{X}_f^-$. For any fixed cost, C^t, we use their algorithm to determine (with high probability) whether $\mathcal{X}_f^-$ intersects with $\mathbb{B}^{C^t}(A)$; i.e., whether C^t is a new lower or upper bound on the MAC. With high probability, this approach can find an ϵ-$IMAC$ in no more than L_ϵ repetitions using binary search. The following theorem is the main result of this section.

THEOREM 8.8 *Let cost function A be convex and have bounded balls; i.e., bounded sublevel sets. Let the feasible set $\mathcal{X}_f^-$ be convex and assume there is some $r > 0$ and $\mathbf{y} \in \mathcal{X}_f^-$ such that $\mathcal{X}_f^-$ contains the cost ball $\mathbb{B}^r(A; \mathbf{y})$. Then given access to an oracle returning separating hyperplanes for the A cost balls, Algorithm 8.7 will find an ϵ-$IMAC$ using $\mathcal{O}^*\left(D^5\right)$ queries with high probability.*[8]

The proof of this result is outlined in the remainder of this section and is based on Bertsimas & Vempala (2004, theorem 14). We first introduce their randomized ellipsoid algorithm, then we elaborate on their procedure for efficient sampling from a convex body, and finally we present our application to optimization. In this section, we focus only on weighted ℓ_1 costs (Equation 8.1) and return to more general cases in Section 8.3.2.

8.2.2.1   **Intersection of Convex Sets**

Bertsimas & Vempala present a query-based procedure for determining whether two convex sets (e.g., $\mathcal{X}_f^-$ and $\mathbb{B}^{C^t}(A_1)$) intersect. Their INTERSECTSEARCH procedure, which we present as Algorithm 8.5 (see Figure 8.4) is a randomized ellipsoid method for determining whether there is an intersection between two bounded convex sets: $\mathbb{P}$ is only accessible through membership queries, and $\mathbb{B}$ provides a separating hyperplane for any point not in $\mathbb{B}$. They use efficient query-based approaches to uniformly sample from $\mathbb{P}$ to obtain sufficiently many samples such that cutting $\mathbb{P}$ through the centroid of these samples with a separating hyperplane from $\mathbb{B}$ significantly reduces the volume of $\mathbb{P}$ with high probability. Their technique thus constructs a sequence of progressively smaller feasible sets $\mathbb{P}^{(s)} \subseteq \mathbb{P}^{(s-1)}$ until either the algorithm finds a point in $\mathbb{P} \cap \mathbb{B}$ or it is highly likely that the intersection is empty.

As noted earlier, the cost optimization problem reduces to finding the intersection between $\mathcal{X}_f^-$ and $\mathbb{B}^{C^t}(A_1)$. Though $\mathcal{X}_f^-$ may be unbounded, we are minimizing a cost with bounded cost balls, so we can instead use the set $\mathbb{P}^{(0)} = \mathcal{X}_f^- \cap \mathbb{B}^{2R}\left(A_1; \mathbf{x}^-; \mathbf{x}^-\right)$ (where $R = A\left(\mathbf{x}^- - \mathbf{x}^A\right) > C^t$), which is a (convex) subset of $\mathcal{X}_f^-$. Since, by the triangle

---

[8] $\mathcal{O}^*(\cdot)$ denotes the standard complexity notation $\mathcal{O}(\cdot)$ without logarithmic terms. The dependence on $\epsilon*$ is in these logarithmic terms; see Bertsimas & Vempala (2004) for details.

ALGORITHM 8.5   INTERSECT SEARCH

$IntersectSearch\left(\mathbb{P}^{(0)}, \mathbb{Q} = \left\{\mathbf{x}^{(j)} \in \mathbb{P}^{(0)}\right\}, \mathbf{x}^{A}, C\right)$

for $s = 1$ to T **do begin**

(1) Generate $2N$ samples $\left\{\mathbf{x}^{(j)}\right\}_{j=1}^{2N}$
    Choose $\mathbf{x}$ from $\mathbb{Q}$
    $\mathbf{x}^{(j)} \leftarrow HitRun\left(\mathbb{P}^{(s-1)}, \mathbb{Q}, \mathbf{x}^{(j)}\right)$

(2) If any $\mathbf{x}^{(j)}$, $A\left(\mathbf{x}^{(j)} - \mathbf{x}^{A}\right) \leq C$ terminate the
    for-loop

(3) Put samples into 2 sets of size N
    $\mathbb{R} \leftarrow \left\{\mathbf{x}^{(j)}\right\}_{j=1}^{N}$ and $\mathbb{S} \leftarrow \left\{\mathbf{x}^{(j)}\right\}_{j=N+1}^{2N}$

(4) $\mathbf{z}^{(s)} \leftarrow \frac{1}{N} \sum_{\mathbf{x}^{(j)} \in \mathbb{R}} \mathbf{x}^{(j)}$

(5) Compute $\mathbb{H}^{\left(\mathbf{h}(\mathbf{z}^{(s)}), \mathbf{z}^{(s)}\right)}$ using Equation (8.11)

(6) $\mathbb{P}^{(s)} \leftarrow \mathbb{P}^{(s-1)} \cap \mathbb{H}^{\left(\mathbf{h}(\mathbf{z}), \mathbf{z}^{(s)}\right)}$

(7) Keep samples in $\mathbb{P}^{(s)}$
    $\mathbb{Q} \leftarrow \mathbb{S} \cap \mathbb{P}^{(s)}$

end for

Return: the found $[\mathbf{x}^{(j)}, \mathbb{P}^{(s)}, \mathbb{Q}]$; or No Intersect

ALGORITHM 8.6   HIT-AND-RUN SAMPLING

$HitRun\left(\mathbb{P}, \left\{\mathbf{y}^{(j)}\right\}, \mathbf{x}^{(0)}\right)$

for $i = 1$ to K **do begin**

(1) Choose a random direction:
    $\nu_j \sim N(0, 1)$
    $\mathbf{v} \leftarrow \sum_j \nu_j \cdot \mathbf{y}^{(j)}$

(2) Sample uniformly along $\mathbf{v}$ using
    rejection sampling:
    Choose $\hat{\omega}$ s.t. $\mathbf{x}^{(i-1)} + \hat{\omega} \cdot \mathbf{v} \notin \mathbb{P}$

repeat
    $\omega \sim Unif(0, \hat{\omega})$
    $\mathbf{x}^{(i)} \leftarrow \mathbf{x}^{(i-1)} + \omega \cdot \mathbf{v}$
    $\hat{\omega} \leftarrow \omega$
until $\mathbf{x}^{(i)} \in \mathbb{P}$

end for

Return: $\mathbf{x}^{(K)}$

Figure 8.4 Algorithms INTERSECTSEARCH and HIT-AND-RUN are used for the randomized ellipsoid algorithm of Bertsimas & Vempala (2004). INTERSECTSEARCH is used to find the intersection between a pair of convex sets: $\mathbb{P}^{(0)}$ is queryable and $\mathbb{B}$ provides a separating hyperplane from Equation (8.11). Note that the ROUNDING algorithm discussed in Section 8.2.2.2 can be used as a preprocessing step so that $\mathbb{P}^{(0)}$ is near-isotropic and to obtain the samples for $\mathbb{Q}$. The HIT-AND-RUN algorithm is used to efficiently obtain uniform samples from a bounded near-isotropic convex set, $\mathbb{P}$, based on a set of uniform samples from it, $\left\{\mathbf{y}^{(j)}\right\}$, and a starting point $\mathbf{x}^{(0)}$.

inequality, the ball $\mathbb{B}^{2R}\left(A_1; \mathbf{x}^{-}\right)$ centered at $\mathbf{x}^{-}$ envelops all of $\mathbb{B}^{C^{t}}\left(A_1; \mathbf{x}^{A}\right)$ centered at $\mathbf{x}^{A}$, the set $\mathbb{P}^{(0)}$ contains the entirety of the desired intersection, $\mathcal{X}_{f}^{-} \cap \mathbb{B}^{C^{t}}(A_1)$, if it exists. We also assume that there is some $r > 0$ such that there is an r-ball contained in the convex set $\mathcal{X}_{f}^{-}$; i.e., there exists $\mathbf{y} \in \mathcal{X}_{f}^{-}$ such that the r-ball centered at $\mathbf{y}$, $\mathbb{B}^{r}(A_1; \mathbf{y})$, is a subset of $\mathcal{X}_{f}^{-}$. This assumption both ensures that $\mathcal{X}_{f}^{-}$ has a non-empty interior (a requirement for the HIT-AND-RUN algorithm discussed later) and provides a stopping condition for the overall intersection search algorithm.

The foundation of Bertsimas & Vempala's search algorithm is the ability to sample uniformly from an unknown but bounded convex body by means of the HIT-AND-RUN random walk technique introduced by Smith (1996) (Algorithm 8.6). Given an instance $\mathbf{x}^{(j)} \in \mathbb{P}^{(s-1)}$, HIT-AND-RUN selects a random direction $\mathbf{v}$ through $\mathbf{x}^{(j)}$ (we revisit the selection of $\mathbf{v}$ in Section 8.2.2.2). Since $\mathbb{P}^{(s-1)}$ is a bounded convex set, the set $\mathbb{W} = \left\{\omega \geq 0 \mid \mathbf{x}^{(j)} + \omega\mathbf{v} \in \mathbb{P}^{(s-1)}\right\}$ is a bounded interval (i.e., there is some $\hat{\omega} \geq 0$ such that $\mathbb{W} \subseteq [0, \hat{\omega}]$) that indexes all feasible points along direction $\mathbf{v}$ through $\mathbf{x}^{(j)}$. Sampling ω uniformly from $\mathbb{W}$ yields the next step of the random walk: $\mathbf{x}^{(j)} + \omega\mathbf{v}$. Even though $\hat{\omega}$ is generally unknown, it can be upper bounded, and ω can be sampled using rejection sampling along the interval as demonstrated in Algorithm 8.6. As noted earlier, this random walk will not make progress if the interior of $\mathbb{P}^{(s-1)}$ is empty (which we preclude by assuming that $\mathcal{X}_f^-$ contains an r-ball), and efficient sampling also requires that $\mathbb{P}^{(s-1)}$ is sufficiently round. However, under the conditions discussed in Section 8.2.2.2, the HIT-AND-RUN random walk generates a sample uniformly from the convex body after $\mathcal{O}^*\left(D^3\right)$ steps (Lovász & Vempala 2004). We now detail the overall INTERSECTSEARCH procedure (Algorithm 8.5) and then discuss the mechanism used to maintain efficient sampling after each successive cut. It is worth noting that Algorithm 8.5 requires $\mathbb{P}^{(0)}$ to be in near-isotropic position and that $\mathbb{Q}$ is a set of samples from it; these requirements are met by using the ROUNDING algorithm of Lovász & Vempala discussed at the end of Section 8.2.2.2.

Randomized Ellipsoid Method

We use HIT-AND-RUN to obtain $2N$ samples $\left\{\mathbf{x}^{(j)}\right\}$ from $\mathbb{P}^{(s-1)} \subseteq \mathcal{X}_f^-$ for a single phase of the randomized ellipsoid method. If any satisfy the condition $A\left(\mathbf{x}^{(j)} - \mathbf{x}^A\right) \leq C^t$, then $\mathbf{x}^{(j)}$ is in the intersection of $\mathcal{X}_f^-$ and $\mathbb{B}^{C^t}(A_1)$, and the procedure is complete. Otherwise, the search algorithm must significantly reduce the size of $\mathbb{P}^{(s-1)}$ without excluding any of $\mathbb{B}^{C^t}(A_1)$ so that sampling concentrates toward the desired intersection (if it exists)— for this we need a separating hyperplane for $\mathbb{B}^{C^t}(A_1)$. For any point $\mathbf{y} \notin \mathbb{B}^{C^t}(A_1)$, the (sub)gradient denoted as $\mathbf{h}(\mathbf{y})$ of the weighted ℓ_1 cost is given by

$$[\mathbf{h}(\mathbf{y})]_f = c_f \cdot \text{sign}\left(y_f - x_f^A\right). \tag{8.10}$$

and thus the hyperplane specified by $\left\{\mathbf{x} \mid (\mathbf{x} - \mathbf{y})^\top \mathbf{h}(\mathbf{y})\right\}$ is a separating hyperplane for $\mathbf{y}$ and $\mathbb{B}^{C^t}(A_1)$.

To achieve sufficient progress, the algorithm chooses a point $\mathbf{z} \in \mathbb{P}^{(s-1)}$ so that cutting $\mathbb{P}^{(s-1)}$ through $\mathbf{z}$ with the hyperplane $\mathbf{h}(\mathbf{z})$ eliminates a significant fraction of $\mathbb{P}^{(s-1)}$. To do so, $\mathbf{z}$ must be centrally located within $\mathbb{P}^{(s-1)}$. We use the empirical centroid of half of the samples in $\mathbb{R}$: $\mathbf{z} = \frac{1}{N}\sum_{\mathbf{x} \in \mathbb{R}} \mathbf{x}$ (the other half will be used in Section 8.2.2.2). We cut $\mathbb{P}^{(s-1)}$ with the hyperplane $\mathbf{h}(\mathbf{z})$ through $\mathbf{z}$; i.e., $\mathbb{P}^{(s)} = \mathbb{P}^{(s-1)} \cap \mathbb{H}^{(\mathbf{h}(\mathbf{z}),\mathbf{z})}$ where $\mathbb{H}^{(\mathbf{h}(\mathbf{z}),\mathbf{z})}$ is the halfspace

$$\mathbb{H}^{(\mathbf{h}(\mathbf{z}),\mathbf{z})} = \left\{\mathbf{x} \mid \mathbf{x}^\top \mathbf{h}(\mathbf{z}) < \mathbf{z}^\top \mathbf{h}(\mathbf{z})\right\}. \tag{8.11}$$

As shown by Bertsimas & Vempala, this cut achieves $vol\left(\mathbb{P}^{(s)}\right) \leq \frac{2}{3}vol\left(\mathbb{P}^{(s-1)}\right)$ with high probability if $N = \mathcal{O}^*(D)$ and $\mathbb{P}^{(s-1)}$ is near-isotropic (see Section 8.2.2.2). Since the ratio of volumes between the initial circumscribing and inscribed balls of the feasible set is $\left(\frac{R}{r}\right)^D$, the algorithm can terminate after $T = \mathcal{O}\left(D\log\left(\frac{R}{r}\right)\right)$ unsuccessful iterations with a high probability that the intersection is empty.

Because every iteration in Algorithm 8.5 requires $N = \mathcal{O}^*(D)$ samples, each of which needs $K = \mathcal{O}^*\left(D^3\right)$ random walk steps, and there are $T = \mathcal{O}^*(D)$ iterations, the total number of membership queries required by Algorithm 8.5 is $\mathcal{O}^*\left(D^5\right)$.

8.2.2.2 Sampling from a Queryable Convex Body

In the randomized ellipsoid method, random samples are used for two purposes: estimating the convex body's centroid and maintaining the conditions required for the HIT-AND-RUN sampler to efficiently generate points uniformly from a sequence of shrinking convex bodies. Until now, we assumed the HIT-AND-RUN random walk efficiently produces uniformly random samples from any bounded convex body $\mathbb{P}$ using $K = \mathcal{O}^* \left(D^3 \right)$ membership queries. However, if the body is asymmetrically elongated, randomly selected directions will rarely align with the long axis of the body, and the random walk will take small steps (relative to the long axis) and mix slowly in $\mathbb{P}$. For the sampler to mix effectively, the convex body $\mathbb{P}$ has to be sufficiently round, or more formally near-isotropic; i.e., for any unit vector $\mathbf{v}$,

$$\frac{1}{2} vol\left(\mathbb{P} \right) \;\leq\; E_{\mathbf{x} \sim \mathbb{P}} \left[\left(\mathbf{v}^\top \left(\mathbf{x} - E_{\mathbf{x} \sim \mathbb{P}} \left[\mathbf{x} \right] \right) \right)^2 \right] \;\leq\; \frac{3}{2} vol\left(\mathbb{P} \right). \tag{8.12}$$

If the body is not near-isotropic, $\mathcal{X}$ can be rescaled with an appropriate affine transformation $\mathbf{T}$ so the resulting transformed body $\mathbb{P}' = \{ \mathbf{T}\mathbf{x} \mid \mathbf{x} \in \mathbb{P} \}$ is near-isotropic. With sufficiently many samples from $\mathbb{P}$ we can estimate $\mathbf{T}$ as their empirical covariance matrix. Instead, we rescale $\mathcal{X}$ implicitly using a technique described by Bertsimas & Vempala (2004). We maintain a set $\mathbb{Q}$ of sufficiently many uniform samples from the body $\mathbb{P}^{(s)}$, and in the HIT-AND-RUN algorithm (Algorithm 8.6), we sample the direction $\mathbf{v}$ based on this set. Intuitively, because the samples in $\mathbb{Q}$ are distributed uniformly in $\mathbb{P}^{(s)}$, the directions we sample based on the points in $\mathbb{Q}$ implicitly reflect the covariance structure of $\mathbb{P}^{(s)}$. This is equivalent to sampling the direction $\mathbf{v}$ from a normal distribution with zero mean and covariance of $\mathbb{P}$.

Further, the set $\mathbb{Q}$ must retain sufficiently many samples from $\mathbb{P}^{(s)}$ after each cut: $\mathbb{P}^{(s)} \leftarrow \mathbb{P}^{(s-1)} \cap \mathbb{H}^{\left(\mathbf{h}\left(\mathbf{z}^{(s)} \right), \mathbf{z}^{(s)} \right)}$. To do so, we initially resample $2N$ points from $\mathbb{P}^{(s-1)}$ using HIT-AND-RUN—half of these, $\mathbb{R}$, are used to estimate the centroid $\mathbf{z}^{(s)}$ for the cut, and the other half, $\mathbb{S}$, are used to repopulate $\mathbb{Q}$ after the cut. Because $\mathbb{S}$ contains independent uniform samples from $\mathbb{P}^{(s-1)}$, those in $\mathbb{P}^{(s)}$ after the cut constitute independent uniform samples from $\mathbb{P}^{(s)}$ (i.e., rejection sampling). By choosing N sufficiently large, the cut will be sufficiently deep, and there will be sufficiently many points to resample $\mathbb{P}^{(s)}$ after the cut.

Finally, for this sampling approach to succeed, we need the initial set $\mathbb{P}^{(0)}$ to be transformed into near-isotropic position, and we also need an initial set $\mathbb{Q}$ of uniform samples from the transformed $\mathbb{P}^{(0)}$ as input to Algorithm 8.5. However, in the near-optimal evasion problem, we only have a single point $\mathbf{x}^- \in \mathcal{X}_f^-$ and our set, $\mathbb{P}^{(0)}$, need not be near-isotropic. Fortunately, there is an iterative procedure that uses the HIT-AND-RUN algorithm to simultaneously transform the initial convex set, $\mathbb{P}^{(0)}$, into a near-isotropic position and construct our initial set of samples, $\mathbb{Q}$. This algorithm, the ROUNDING algorithm as described by Lovász & Vempala (2003), uses $\mathcal{O}^* \left(D^4 \right)$ membership queries to find a transformation that places $\mathbb{P}^0$ into a near-isotropic position and produces an initial set of samples from it. We use this as a preprocessing step for Algorithms 8.5 and 8.7; that is, given $\mathcal{X}_f^-$ and $\mathbf{x}^- \in \mathcal{X}_f^-$, we construct $\mathbb{P}^{(0)} = \mathcal{X}_f^- \cap \mathbb{B}^{2R} \left(A_1; \mathbf{x}^- \right)$ and then can use the ROUNDING algorithm to transform $\mathbb{P}^{(0)}$ and produce an initial uniform sample from it; i.e., $\mathbb{Q} = \left\{ \mathbf{x}^{(j)} \in \mathbb{P}^{(0)} \right\}$. These sets are then the inputs to our search algorithms.

8.2.2.3 Optimization over ℓ_1 Balls

We now revisit the outermost optimization loop (for searching the minimum feasible cost) of the algorithm to optimize the naive approach, which repeats the intersection search at each step of the binary search over cost balls. These improvements are reflected in our final procedure SETSEARCH in Algorithm 8.7 (as with previous binary search procedures, this algorithm can be trivially adapted for η-additive optimality simply by changing its stopping criterion and proposal step as explained in Section 8.1.3)—the total number of queries required is also $\mathcal{O}^*\left(D^5\right)$ since the algorithm only takes L_ϵ binary search steps (see Figure 8.5). Again, Algorithm 8.7 requires $\mathbb{P}$ to be near-isotropic and that $\mathbb{Q}$ is a set of samples from it, which is accomplished by the ROUNDING algorithm discussed at the end of Section 8.2.2.2. First, notice that $\mathbf{x}^A$ and $\mathbf{x}^-$ are the same for every iteration of the optimization procedure. Further, in each iteration of Algorithm 8.7, the new set, $\mathbb{P}$, remains near-isotropic, and the new $\mathbb{Q}$ is a set of samples from it since the sets returned by Algorithm 8.5 retain these properties. Thus, the set, $\mathbb{P}$, and the set of samples, $\mathbb{Q} = \left\{\mathbf{x}^{(j)} \in \mathbb{P}\right\}$, maintained by Algorithm 8.7 are sufficient to initialize INTERSECTSEARCH at each stage of its overall binary search over C^t, and we only need to execute the ROUNDING procedure once as a preprocessing step rather than re-invoking it before every invocation of INTERSECTSEARCH. Second, the separating hyperplane $\mathbf{h}\left(\mathbf{y}\right)$ given by Equation (8.10) does not depend on the target cost C^t but only on $\mathbf{x}^A$, the common center of all the ℓ_1 balls used in this search. In fact, the separating hyperplane at point $\mathbf{y}$ is valid for all ℓ_1-balls of cost $C < A\left(\mathbf{y} - \mathbf{x}^A\right)$. Further, if $C < C^t$, then $\mathbb{B}^C\left(A_1\right) \subseteq \mathbb{B}^{C^t}\left(A_1\right)$. Thus, the final state from a successful call to INTERSECTSEARCH for the C^t-ball can be used as the starting state for any subsequent call to INTERSECTSEARCH for all $C < C^t$. Hence, in Algorithm 8.7, we update $\mathbb{P}$ and $\mathbb{Q}$ only when Algorithm 8.5 succeeds.

8.3 Evasion for General ℓ_p Costs

Here we further extend ϵ-*IMAC* searchability over the family of convex-inducing classifiers to the full family of ℓ_p costs for any $0 < p \leq \infty$. As we demonstrate in this section, many ℓ_p costs are not generally ϵ-*IMAC* searchable for all $\epsilon > 0$ over the family of convex-inducing classifiers (i.e., we show that finding an ϵ-*IMAC* for this family can require exponentially many queries in D and L_ϵ). In fact, only the weighted ℓ_1 costs have known (randomized) polynomial query strategies when either the positive or negative set is convex.

8.3.1 Convex Positive Set

We explore the ability of the MULTILINESEARCH and K-STEP MULTILINESEARCH algorithms presented in Section 8.2.1 to find solutions to the near-optimal evasion problem for ℓ_p cost functions with $p \neq 1$. Particularly for $p > 1$, we explore the consequences of using the MULTILINESEARCH algorithms using more search directions than just the $2 \cdot D$

ALGORITHM 8.7   CONVEX $\mathcal{X}_f^-$ SET SEARCH

$SetSearch\left(\mathbb{P}, \mathbb{Q} = \left\{\mathbf{x}^{(j)} \in \mathbb{P}\right\}, \mathbf{x}^A, \mathbf{x}^-, C_0^+, C_0^-, \epsilon\right)$
$\mathbf{x}^\star \leftarrow \mathbf{x}^-$ and $t \leftarrow 0$
while $C_t^- / C_t^+ > 1 + \epsilon$ **do begin**
 $C_t \leftarrow \sqrt{C_t^- \cdot C_t^+}$
 $[\mathbf{x}^\star, \mathbb{P}', \mathbb{Q}'] \leftarrow IntersectSearch\left(\mathbb{P}, \mathbb{Q}, \mathbf{x}^A, C_t\right)$
 if intersection found **then begin**
  $C_{t+1}^- \leftarrow A\left(\mathbf{x}^\star - \mathbf{x}^A\right)$ and $C_{t+1}^+ \leftarrow C_t^+$
  $\mathbb{P} \leftarrow \mathbb{P}'$ and $\mathbb{Q} \leftarrow \mathbb{Q}'$
 else
  $C_{t+1}^- \leftarrow C_t^-$ and $C_{t+1}^+ \leftarrow C_t$
 end if
 $t \leftarrow t + 1$
end while
Return: $\mathbf{x}^\star$

Figure 8.5 Algorithm SETSEARCH that efficiently implements the randomized ellipsoid algorithm of Bertsimas & Vempala (2004). SETSEARCH performs a binary search for an ϵ-*IMAC* using the randomized INTERSECTSEARCH procedure to determine, with high probability, whether or not $\mathcal{X}_f^-$ contains any points less than a specified cost, C_t. Note that the ROUNDING algorithm discussed in Section 8.2.2.2 can be used as a preprocessing step so that $\mathbb{P}$ is near-isotropic and to obtain the samples for $\mathbb{Q}$.

axis-aligned directions. Figure 8.6 demonstrates how queries can be used to construct upper and lower bounds on general ℓ_p costs. The following lemma also summarizes well-known bounds on general ℓ_p costs using an ℓ_1 cost.

LEMMA 8.9 *The largest ℓ_p $(p > 1)$ ball enclosed within a C-cost ℓ_1 ball has a cost of $C \cdot D^{\frac{1-p}{p}}$ and for $p = \infty$ the cost is $C \cdot D^{-1}$.*

Proof By symmetry, the point $\mathbf{x}^\star$ on the simplex $\left\{\mathbf{x} \in \Re^D \mid \sum_{i=1}^D x_i = 1, x_i \geq 0 \forall i\right\}$ that minimizes the ℓ_p norm for any $p > 1$ is

$$\mathbf{x}^\star = \frac{1}{D}(1, 1, \ldots, 1).$$

The ℓ_p norm (cost) of the minimizer is

$$\|\mathbf{x}^\star\|_p = \frac{1}{D}\left(\sum_{i=1}^D 1^p\right)^{1/p}$$

$$= \frac{1}{D}D^{1/p}$$

$$= D^{\frac{1-p}{p}}$$

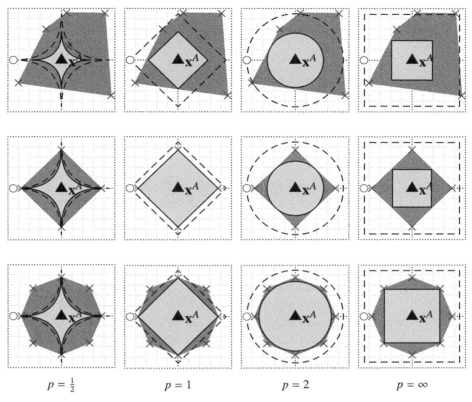

$$p = \tfrac{1}{2} \qquad\qquad p = 1 \qquad\qquad p = 2 \qquad\qquad p = \infty$$

Figure 8.6 The convex hull for a set of queries and the resulting bounding balls for several ℓ_p costs. Each row represents a unique set of positive ("×" points) and negative (black "○" points) queries, and each column shows the implied upper bound (the black dashed line) and lower bound (the black solid line) for a different ℓ_p cost. In the first row, the body is defined by a random set of seven queries, in the second, the queries are along the coordinate axes, and in the third, the queries are around a circle.

for $p \in (1, \infty)$ and is otherwise

$$\|\mathbf{x}^\star\|_\infty = \max\left[\frac{1}{D}, \frac{1}{D}, \dots, \frac{1}{D}\right]$$
$$= D^{-1}.$$

$\square$

8.3.1.1 Bounding ℓ_p Balls

In general, suppose one probes along some set of M unit directions, and eventually there is at least one negative point supporting an upper bound of C_0^- and M positive points supporting a lower bound of C_0^+. However, the lower bound provided by those M positive points is the cost of the largest ℓ_p cost ball that fits entirely within their convex hull; let's say this cost is $C^\dagger \leq C_0^+$. To achieve ϵ-multiplicative optimality, we need $\frac{C_0^-}{C^\dagger} \leq 1 + \epsilon$, which can be rewritten as

$$\left(\frac{C_0^-}{C_0^+}\right)\left(\frac{C_0^+}{C^\dagger}\right) \leq 1 + \epsilon.$$

This divides the problem into two parts. The first ratio C_0^-/C_0^+ is controlled solely by the accuracy ϵ achieved by running the MULTILINESEARCH algorithm for L_ϵ steps, whereas the second ratio $C_0^+/C^\dagger$ depends only on how well the ℓ_p ball is approximated by the convex hull of the M search directions. These two ratios separate the search task into choosing M and L_ϵ sufficiently so that their product is less than $1 + \epsilon$. First we select parameters $\alpha \geq 0$ and $\beta \geq 0$ such that $(1 + \alpha)(1 + \beta) \leq 1 + \epsilon$. Then we choose M so that $\frac{C_0^+}{C^\dagger} = 1 + \beta$ and use L_α steps so that MULTILINESEARCH with M directions will achieve $\frac{C_0^-}{C_0^+} = 1 + \alpha$. This process describes a generalized MULTILINESEARCH that achieves ϵ-multiplicative optimality for costs whose cost balls are not spanned by the convex hull of equi-cost probes along the M search directions.

In the case of $p = 1$, we demonstrated in Section 8.2.1 that choosing the $M = 2 \cdot D$ axis-aligned directions $\{\pm\mathbf{e}^{(d)}\}$ spans the ℓ_1 ball so that $C_0^+/C^\dagger = 1$ (i.e., $\beta = 0$). Thus, choosing $\alpha = \epsilon$ recovers the original multi-line search result.

We now address costs where $\beta > 0$. For a MULTILINESEARCH algorithm to be efficient, it is necessary that $\frac{C_0^+}{C^\dagger} = 1 + \beta$ can be achieved with polynomially many search directions (in D and L_ϵ) for some $\beta \leq \epsilon$; otherwise, $(1 + \alpha)(1 + \beta) > 1 + \epsilon$, and the MULTILINESEARCH approach cannot succeed for any $\alpha > 0$. Thus, we quantify how many search directions (or queries) are required to achieve $\frac{C_0^+}{C^\dagger} \leq 1 + \epsilon$. Note that this ratio is independent of the relative size of these costs, so without loss of generality we only consider bounds for unit-cost balls. Thus, we compute the largest value of $C^\dagger$ that can be achieved for the unit-cost ℓ_p ball (i.e., let $C_0^+ = 1$) within the convex hull of M queries. In particular, we quantify how many queries are required to achieve

$$C^\dagger \geq \frac{1}{1 + \epsilon}. \tag{8.13}$$

If this can be achieved with only polynomially many queries, then the generalized MULTILINESEARCH approach is efficient. More generally,

LEMMA 8.10 *If there exists a configuration of M unit search directions with a convex hull that yields a bound $C^\dagger$ for the cost function A, then MULTILINESEARCH algorithms can use those search directions to achieve ϵ-multiplicative optimality with a query complexity that is polynomial in M and $L_\epsilon^{(*)}$ for any*

$$\epsilon > \frac{1}{C^\dagger} - 1.$$

Moreover, if the M search directions yield $C^\dagger = 1$ for the cost function A, then MULTILINESEARCH algorithms can achieve ϵ-multiplicative optimality with a query complexity that is polynomial in M and $L_\epsilon^{(*)}$ for any $\epsilon > 0$.

Notice that this lemma also reaffirms that, for $p = 1$, using the $M = 2 \cdot D$ axis-aligned directions allows MULTILINESEARCH algorithms to achieve ϵ-multiplicative optimality for any $\epsilon > 0$ with a query complexity that is polynomial in M and $L_\epsilon^{(*)}$ since in this case $C^\dagger = 1$. Also recall that as a consequence of Theorem 8.3, if a particular multiplicative accuracy ϵ cannot be efficiently achieved, then additive optimality cannot be generally achieved for any additive accuracy $\eta > 0$.

8.3.1.2 Multi-Line Search for $0 < p < 1$

A simple result holds here. Namely, since the unit ℓ_1 ball bounds any unit ℓ_p balls with $0 < p < 1$, one can achieve $C_0^+/C^\dagger = 1$ using only the $2 \cdot D$ axis-aligned search directions. Thus, for any $0 < p < 1$, evasion is efficient for any value of $\epsilon > 0$. Whether or not any ℓ_p $(0 < p < 1)$ cost function can be efficiently searched with fewer search directions is an open question.

8.3.1.3 Multi-Line Search for $p > 1$

For this case, one can trivially use the ℓ_1 bound on ℓ_p balls as summarized by the following corollary.

COROLLARY 8.11 *For* $1 < p < \infty$ *and* $\epsilon \in \left(D^{\frac{p-1}{p}} - 1, \infty \right)$ *any multi-line search algorithm can achieve ϵ-multiplicative optimality on A_p using $M = 2 \cdot D$ search directions. Similarly for $\epsilon \in (D - 1, \infty)$ any multi-line search algorithm can achieve ϵ-multiplicative optimality on A_∞ also using $M = 2 \cdot D$ directions.*

Proof From Lemma 8.9, the largest co-centered ℓ_p ball contained within the unit ℓ_1 ball has radius $D^{\frac{1-p}{p}}$ cost (or D for $p = \infty$). The bounds on ϵ then follow from Lemma 8.10. $\qquad\square$

Unfortunately, this result only applies for a range of ϵ that grows with D, which is insufficient for ϵ-*IMAC* searchability. In fact, for some fixed values of ϵ, there is no query strategy that can bound ℓ_p costs using polynomially many queries in D as the following result shows.

THEOREM 8.12 *For* $p > 1$, $D > 0$, *any initial bounds* $0 < C_0^+ < C_0^-$ *on the MAC, and* $\epsilon \in \left(0, 2^{\frac{p-1}{p}} - 1 \right)$ *(or* $\epsilon \in (0, 1)$ *for* $p = \infty$)*, all algorithms must submit at least* $\alpha_{p,\epsilon}^D$ *membership queries (for some constant* $\alpha_{p,\epsilon} > 1$*) in the worst case to be ϵ-multiplicatively optimal on* $\mathcal{F}^{\text{convex},\,\text{"+"}}$ *for* ℓ_p *costs.*

The proof of this theorem is provided in Appendix D, and the definitions of $\alpha_{p,\epsilon}$ and $\alpha_{\infty,\epsilon}$ are provided by Equations (D.7) and (D.8), respectively. A consequence of this result is that there is no query-based algorithm that can efficiently find an ϵ-*IMAC* of any ℓ_p cost $(p > 1)$ for any *fixed* ϵ within the range $0 < \epsilon < 2^{\frac{p-1}{p}} - 1$ (or $0 < \epsilon < 1$ for $p = \infty$) on the family $\mathcal{F}^{\text{convex},\,\text{"+"}}$. However, from Theorem 8.11 and Lemma 8.10, multi-line search type algorithms efficiently find the ϵ-*IMAC* of any ℓ_p cost $(p > 1)$ for any $\epsilon \in \left(D^{\frac{p-1}{p}} - 1, \infty \right)$ (or $D - 1 < \epsilon < \infty$ for $p = \infty$). It is generally unclear if efficient algorithms exist for any values of ϵ between these intervals, but in the following section, we derive a stronger bound for the case $p = 2$.

8.3.1.4   Multi-Line Search for $p = 2$

THEOREM 8.13 *For any $D > 1$, any initial bounds $0 < C_0^+ < C_0^-$ on the MAC, and $0 < \epsilon < \frac{C_0^-}{C_0^+} - 1$, all algorithms must submit at least $\alpha_\epsilon^{\frac{D-2}{2}}$ membership queries (where $\alpha_\epsilon = \frac{(1+\epsilon)^2}{(1+\epsilon)^2-1} > 1$) in the worst case to be ϵ-multiplicatively optimal on $\mathcal{F}^{convex,"+"}$ for ℓ_2 costs.*

The proof of this result is in Appendix D.2.

This result says that there is no algorithm that can generally achieve ϵ-multiplicative optimality for ℓ_2 costs for any *fixed* $\epsilon > 0$ using only polynomially many queries in D since the ratio $\frac{C_0^-}{C_0^+}$ could be arbitrarily large. It may appear that Theorem 8.13 contradicts Corollary 8.11. However, Corollary 8.11 only applies for an interval of ϵ that depends on D; i.e., $\epsilon > \sqrt{D} - 1$. Interestingly, by substituting this lower bound on ϵ into the bound given by Theorem 8.13, the number of required queries for $\epsilon > \sqrt{D} - 1$ need only be

$$M \;\geq\; \left(\frac{(1+\epsilon)^2}{(1+\epsilon)^2 - 1} \right)^{\frac{D-2}{2}} \;=\; \left(\frac{D}{D-1} \right)^{\frac{D-2}{2}},$$

which is a monotonically increasing function in D that asymptotes at $\sqrt{e} \approx 1.64$. Thus, Theorem 8.13 and Corollary 8.11 are in agreement since for $\epsilon > \sqrt{D} - 1$, Theorem 8.13 only requires at least two queries, which is a trivial bound for all D. Indeed, this occurs because the ϵ considered here is bounded below by a function that increases with D.

A Tighter Bound

The bound derived for Lemma A.1 was sufficient to demonstrate that there is no algorithm that can generally achieve ϵ-multiplicative optimality for ℓ_2 costs for any fixed $\epsilon > 0$. It is, however, possible to construct a tighter lower bound on the number of queries required for ℓ_2 costs, although it is not easy to express this result as an exponential in D. A straightforward way to construct a better lower bound is to make a tighter upper bound on the integral $\int_0^\phi \sin^D (t) \, dt$ as is suggested in Appendix A.2. Namely, the result given in Equation (A.4) upper bounds this integral by

$$\frac{\sin^{D+1} (\phi)}{(D+1) \cos (\phi)},$$

which is tighter for large D and $\phi < \frac{\pi}{2}$. Applying this bound to the covering number result of Theorem 8.13 achieves the following bound on the number of queries required to achieve multiplicative optimality:

$$M \geq \frac{\sqrt{\pi}}{1+\epsilon} \cdot \frac{D \cdot \Gamma \left(\frac{D+1}{2} \right)}{\Gamma \left(1 + \frac{D}{2} \right)} \left(\frac{(1+\epsilon)^2}{(1+\epsilon)^2 - 1} \right)^{\frac{D-1}{2}}. \tag{8.14}$$

While not as obvious as the result presented in Appendix D.2, this bound is also exponential in D for any ϵ. Also, as with the previous result, this bound does not contradict the polynomial result for $\epsilon \geq \sqrt{D} - 1$. For $D = 1$ Equation 8.14 requires exactly two queries (in exact agreement with the number of queries required to bound an ℓ_2 ball in 1-dimension); for $D = 2$ it requires more than π queries (whereas at least four queries are actually required); and for $D > 2$ the bound asymptotes at $\sqrt{2e\pi} \approx 4.13$ queries. Again, this tighter bound does not contradict the efficient result achieved by bounding ℓ_2 balls with ℓ_1 balls.

8.3.2 Convex Negative Set

Algorithm 8.7 generalizes immediately to all weighted ℓ_p costs ($p \geq 1$) centered at $\mathbf{x}^A$ since these costs are convex. For these costs, an equivalent separating hyperplane for $\mathbf{y}$ can be used in place of Equation (8.10). They are given by the equivalent (sub)-gradients for ℓ_p cost balls:

$$h_{p,d}^{(\mathbf{y})} = c_d \cdot \text{sign}\left(y_d - x_d^A\right) \cdot \left(\frac{|y_d - x_d^A|}{A_p^{(\mathbf{c})}\left(\mathbf{y} - \mathbf{x}^A\right)}\right)^{p-1},$$

$$h_{\infty,d}^{(\mathbf{y})} = c_d \cdot \text{sign}\left(y_d - x_d^A\right) \cdot \mathrm{I}\left[|y_d - x_d^A| = A_\infty^{(\mathbf{c})}\left(\mathbf{y} - \mathbf{x}^A\right)\right].$$

By only changing the cost function A and the separating hyperplane $\mathbf{h}\left(\mathbf{y}\right)$ used for the halfspace cut in Algorithms 8.5 and 8.7, the randomized ellipsoid method can also be applied for any weighted ℓ_p cost $A_p^{(\mathbf{c})}$ with $p > 1$.

For more general convex costs A, every C-cost ball is a convex set (i.e., the sublevel set of a convex function is a convex set; see Boyd & Vandenberghe 2004, Chapter 3) and thus has a separating hyperplane. Further, since for any $D > C$, $\mathbb{B}^C(A) \subseteq \mathbb{B}^D(A)$, the separating hyperplane of the D-cost ball is also a separating hyperplane of the C-cost ball and can be reused in Algorithm 8.7. Thus, this procedure is applicable for any convex cost function, A, so long as one can compute the separating hyperplanes of any cost ball of A for any point $\mathbf{y}$ not in the cost ball.

For nonconvex costs A such as weighted ℓ_p costs with $0 < p < 1$, minimization over a convex set $\mathcal{X}_f^-$ is generally hard. However, there may be special cases when minimizing such a cost can be accomplished efficiently.

8.4 Summary

In this chapter we primarily studied membership query algorithms that efficiently accomplish ϵ-$IMAC$ search for convex-inducing classifiers with weighted ℓ_1 costs. When the positive class is convex, we demonstrated efficient techniques that outperform the previous reverse-engineering approaches for linear classifiers in a continuous space. When the negative class is convex, we appied the randomized ellipsoid method introduced by Bertsimas & Vempala to achieve efficient ϵ-$IMAC$ search. If the adversary is unaware of which set is convex, it can trivially run both searches to discover an ϵ-$IMAC$ with a combined polynomial query complexity; thus, for ℓ_1 costs, the family of convex-inducing classifiers can be efficiently evaded by an adversary; i.e., this family is ϵ-$IMAC$ searchable.

Further, we also extended the study of convex-inducing classifiers to the full family of ℓ_p costs. We showed that $\mathcal{F}^{convex}$ is only generally $\epsilon\text{-}IMAC$ searchable for both positive and negative convexity for any $\epsilon > 0$ when $p = 1$. For $0 < p < 1$, the MULTI-LINESEARCH algorithms of Section 8.2.1 achieve identical results when the positive set is convex, but the nonconvexity of these ℓ_p costs precludes the use of the randomized ellipsoid method when the negative class is convex. The ellipsoid method does provide an efficient solution for convex negative sets when $p > 1$ (since these costs are convex). However, for convex positive sets, we show that for $p > 1$ there is no algorithm that can efficiently find an $\epsilon\text{-}IMAC$ for all $\epsilon > 0$. Moreover, for $p = 2$, we prove that there is no efficient algorithm for finding an $\epsilon\text{-}IMAC$ for any fixed value of ϵ.

8.4.1   Open Problems in Near-Optimal Evasion

By investigating near-optimal evasion for the convex-inducing classifiers and ℓ_1 costs, we have significantly expanded the extent of the framework established by Lowd & Meek , but there are still a number of interesting unanswered questions about the near-optimal evasion problem. We summarize the problems we believe are most important and suggest potential directions for pursuing them.

As we showed in this chapter, the current upper bound on the query complexity to achieve near-optimal evasion for the convex positive class is $\mathcal{O}\left(L_\epsilon + \sqrt{L_\epsilon}D\right)$ queries, but the tightest known lower bound is $\mathcal{O}\left(L_\epsilon + D\right)$. Similarly, for the case of convex negative class, the upper bound is given by the randomized ellipsoid method of Bertsimas & Vempala that finds a near-optimal instance with high probability using $\mathcal{O}^*\left(D^5\right)$ queries (ignoring logarithmic terms). In both cases, there is a gap between the upper and lower bound.

QUESTION 8.1 Can we find matching upper and lower bounds for evasion algorithms? Is there a deterministic strategy with polynomial query complexity for all convex-inducing classifiers?

The algorithms we present in this chapter built on the machinery of convex optimization over convex sets, which relies on family of classifiers inducing a convex set. However, many interesting classifiers are not convex-inducing classifiers. Currently, the only known result for non-convex-inducing classifiers is due to Lowd & Meek; they found that linear classifiers on Boolean feature space are $2\text{-}IMAC$ searchable for unweighted ℓ_1 costs. In this case, the classifiers are linear, but the integer-valued domains do not have a usual notion of convexity. This raises questions about the extent to which near-optimal evasion is efficient.

QUESTION 8.2 Are there families larger than the convex-inducing classifiers that are $\epsilon\text{-}IMAC$ searchable? Are there families outside of the convex-inducing classifiers for which near-optimal evasion is efficient?

A particularly interesting family of classifiers to investigate is the family of support vector machines (SVMs) defined by a particular nonlinear kernel. This popular learning technique can induce nonconvex positive and negative sets (depending on its kernel), but it also has a great deal of structure. An SVM classifier can be nonconvex in its input space $\mathcal{X}$, but it is always linear in its kernel's reproducing kernel Hilbert space (RKHS; see Definition 7.6). However, optimization within the RKHS is complicated because mapping the cost balls into the RKHS destroys their structure and querying in the RKHS is nontrivial. However, SVMs also have additional structure that may facilitate near-optimal evasion. For instance, the usual SVM formulation encourages a sparse representation that could be exploited; i.e., in classifiers with few support vectors, the adversary would only need to find these instances to reconstruct the classifier.

QUESTION 8.3 Is some family of SVMs (e.g., with a known kernel) ϵ-*IMAC* searchable for some ϵ? Can an adversary incorporate the structure of a nonconvex classifier into the ϵ-*IMAC* search?

In addition to studying particular families of classifiers, it is also of interest to further characterize general properties of a family that lead to efficient search algorithms or preclude their existence. As we showed in this chapter, convexity of the induced sets allows for efficient search for some ℓ_p-costs but not others. Aside from convexity, other properties that describe the shape of the induced sets $\mathcal{X}_f^+$ and $\mathcal{X}_f^-$ could be explored. For instance, one could investigate the family of contiguous-inducing classifiers (i.e., classifiers for which either $\mathcal{X}_f^+$ or $\mathcal{X}_f^-$ is a contiguous, or connected, set). However, it appears that this family is not generally ϵ-*IMAC* searchable since it includes induced sets with many locally minimal cost regions, which rule out global optimization procedures like the MULTILINESEARCH or the randomized ellipsoid method. More generally, for families of classifiers that can induce noncontiguous bodies, ϵ-*IMAC* searchability seems impossible to achieve (disconnected components could be arbitrarily close to $\mathbf{x}^A$) unless the classifiers' structure can be exploited. However, even if near-optimal evasion is generally not possible in these cases, perhaps there are subsets of these families that are ϵ-*IMAC* searchable; e.g., as we discussed for SVMs earlier. Hence, it is important to identify what characteristics make near-optimal evasion inefficient.

QUESTION 8.4 Are there characteristics of nonconvex, contiguous bodies that are indicative of the hardness of the body for near-optimal evasion? Similarly, are there characteristics of noncontiguous bodies that describe their query complexity?

Finally, as discussed in Section 8.1.2, reverse engineering a classifier (i.e., using membership queries to estimate its decision boundary) is a strictly more difficult problem than the near-optimal evasion problem. Reverse engineering is sufficient for solving the evasion problem, but we show that it is not necessary. Lowd & Meek showed that reverse engineering linear classifiers is efficient, but here we show that reverse engineering is strictly more difficult than evasion for convex-inducing classifiers. It is unknown whether there exists a class in between linear and convex-inducing classifiers on which the two tasks are efficient.

QUESTION 8.5 For what families of classifiers is reverse engineering as easy as evasion?

8.4.2   Alternative Evasion Criteria

We suggest variants of near-optimal evasion that generalize or reformulate the problem investigated in this chapter to capture additional aspects of the overall challenge.

8.4.2.1   Incorporating a Covertness Criterion

As mentioned in Section 8.1.2, the near-optimal evasion problem does not require the attacker to be covert in its actions. The primary concern for the adversary is that a defender may detect the probing attack and make it ineffectual. For instance, the MUL-TILINESEARCH algorithms we present in Section 8.2 are very overt about the attacker's true intention; i.e., because the queries are issued in ℓ_p shells about $\mathbf{x}^A$, it is trivial to infer $\mathbf{x}^A$. The queries issued by the randomized ellipsoid method in Section 8.2.2 are less overt due to the random walks, but still the queries occur in shrinking cost balls centered around $\mathbf{x}^A$. The reverse-engineering approach of Lowd & Meek (2005a), however, is quite covert. In their approach, all queries are based only on the features of $\mathbf{x}^-$ and a third $\mathbf{x}^+ \in \mathcal{X}_f^+$—$\mathbf{x}^A$ is not used until an ϵ-*IMAC* is discovered.

QUESTION 8.6 What covertness criteria are appropriate for a near-optimal evasion problem? Can a defender detect nondiscrete probing attacks against a classifier? Can the defender effectively mislead a probing attack by falsely answering suspected queries?

Misleading an adversary is an especially promising direction for future exploration. If probing attacks can be detected, a defender could frustrate the attacker by falsely responding to suspected queries. However, if too many benign points are incorrectly identified as queries, such a defense could degrade the classifier's performance. Thus, strategies to mislead could backfire if an adversary fooled the defender into misclassifying legitimate data—yet another security game between the adversary and defender.

8.4.2.2   Additional Information about Training Data Distribution

Consider an adversary that knows the training algorithm and obtains samples drawn from a natural distribution. A few interesting settings include scenarios where the adversary's samples are *i)* a subset of the training data, *ii)* from the same distribution P_Z as the training data, or *iii)* from a perturbation of the training distribution. With these forms of additional information, the adversary could estimate its own classifier $\tilde{f}$ and analyze it offline. Open questions about this variant include.

QUESTION 8.7 What can be learned from $\tilde{f}$ about f? How can $\tilde{f}$ best be used to guide search? Can the sample data be directly incorporated into ϵ-*IMAC*-search without $\tilde{f}$?

Relationships between f and $\tilde{f}$ can build on existing results in learning theory. One possibility is to establish bounds on the difference between $MAC(f, A)$ and $MAC(\tilde{f}, A)$ in one of the above settings. If, with high probability, the difference is sufficiently small, then a search for an ϵ-*IMAC* could use $MAC(\tilde{f}, A)$ to initially lower bound $MAC(f, A)$. This should reduce search complexity since lower bounds on the MAC are typically harder to obtain than upper bounds.

8.4.2.3   Beyond the Membership Oracle

In this scenario, the adversary receives more from the classifier than just a "+"/"−" label. For instance, suppose the classifier is defined as $f(x) = I[g(x) > 0]$ for some real-valued function g (as is the case for SVMs) and the adversary receives $g(x)$ for every query instead of $f(x)$. If g is linear, the adversary can use $D + 1$ queries and solve a linear regression problem to reverse engineer g. This additional information may also be useful for approximating the support of an SVM.

QUESTION 8.8 What types of additional feedback may be available to the adversary, and how do they affect the query complexity of ϵ-$IMAC$-search?

8.4.2.4   Evading Randomized Classifiers

In this variant of near-optimal evasion, we consider randomized classifiers that generate random responses from a distribution conditioned on the query x. To analyze the query complexity of such a classifier, we first generalize the concept of the MAC to randomized classifiers. We propose the following generalization:

$$RMAC(f, A) = \inf_{x \in \mathcal{X}} \left\{ A\left(x - \mathbf{x}^A\right) + \lambda P\left(f(x) = \text{"}-\text{"}\right) \right\}.$$

Instead of the unknown set $\mathcal{X}_f^-$ in the near-optimal evasion setting, the objective function here contains the term $P\left(f(x) = \text{"}-\text{"}\right)$ that the adversary does not know and must approximate. If f is deterministic , $P\left(f(x) = \text{"}-\text{"}\right) = I\left[f(x) = \text{"}-\text{"}\right]$, this definition is equivalent to Equation (8.2) only if $\lambda \geq MAC(f, A)$ (e.g., $\lambda = A\left(\mathbf{x}^- - \mathbf{x}^A\right) + 1$ is sufficient); otherwise, a trivial minimizer is $\mathbf{x}^A$. For a randomized classifier, λ balances the cost of an instance with its probability of successful evasion.

QUESTION 8.9 Given access to the membership oracle only, how difficult is near-optimal evasion of randomized classifiers? Are there families of randomized classifiers that are ϵ-$IMAC$ searchable?

Potential randomized families include classifiers (*i*) with a fuzzy boundary of width δ around a deterministic boundary, and (*ii*) based on the class-conditional densities for a pair of Gaussians, a logistic regression model, or other members of the exponential family. Generally, evasion of randomized classifiers seems to be more difficult than for deterministic classifiers as each query provides limited information about the query probabilities. Based on this argument, Biggio et al. (2010) promote randomized classifiers as a defense against evasion. However, it is not known if randomized classifiers have provably worse query complexities.

8.4.2.5   Evading an Adaptive Classifier

Finally, we consider a classifier that periodically retrains on queries. This variant is a multi-fold game between the attacker and learner, with the adversary now able to issue queries that degrade the learner's performance. Techniques from game-theoretic online learning should be well suited to this setting (Cesa-Bianchi & Lugosi 2006).

QUESTION 8.10 Given a set of adversarial queries (and possibly additional innocuous data) will the learning algorithm converge to the true boundary, or can the adversary deceive the learner and evade it simultaneously? If the algorithm does converge, then at what rate?

To properly analyze retraining, it is important to have an oracle that labels the points sent by the adversary. If all points sent by the adversary are labeled "+", the classifier may prevent effective evasion, but with large numbers of false positives due to the adversary queries in $\mathcal{X}_f^-$, this itself constitutes an attack against the learner (Barreno et al. 2010).

8.4.3   Real-World Evasion

While the cost-centric evasion framework presented by Lowd & Meek formalizes the near-optimal evasion problem, it fails to capture some aspects of reality. From the theory of near-optimal evasion, certain classes of learners have been shown to be easy to evade, whereas others require a practically infeasible number of queries for evasion to be successful. However, real-world adversaries often do not require near-optimal cost evasive instances to be successful; it would suffice if they could find any low-cost instance able to evade the detector. Real-world evasion differs from the near-optimal evasion problem in several ways. Understanding query strategies and the query complexity for a real-world adversary requires incorporating real-world constraints that were relaxed or ignored in the theoretical version of this problem. We summarize the challenges for real-world evasion.

To adapt to these challenges, we propose a *realistic evasion problem* that weakens several of the assumptions of the theoretical near-optimal evasion problem for studying real-world evasion techniques. We still assume the adversary does not know f and may not even know the family $\mathcal{F}$; we only assume that the classifier is a deterministic classifier that uniquely maps each instance in $\mathcal{X}$ to {"+", *negLbl*}. For a real-world adversary, we require that the adversary send queries that are representable as actual objects in Ω; e.g., emails cannot have 1.7 occurrences of the word "viagra" in a message and IP addresses must have four integers between $0 - -255$. However, we no longer assume that the adversary knows the feature space of the classifier or its feature mapping.

Real-world near-optimal evasion is also more difficult (i.e., requires more queries) than is suggested by the theory because the theory simplifies the problem faced by the adversary. Even assuming that a real-world adversary can obtain query responses from the classifier, it cannot directly query it in the feature space $\mathcal{X}$. Real-world adversaries must make their queries in the form of real-world objects like email that are subsequently mapped into $\mathcal{X}$ via a feature map. Even if this mapping is known by the adversary, designing an object that maps to a desired query in $\mathcal{X}$ is itself a difficult problem—there may be many objects that map to a single query (e.g., permuting the order of words in a message yields the same unigram representation), and certain portions of $\mathcal{X}$ may not correspond to any real-world object (e.g., for the mapping $x \mapsto (x, x^2)$ no point x can map to $(1, 7)$).

QUESTION 8.11 How can the feature mapping be inverted to design real-world instances to map to desired queries? How can query-based algorithms be adapted for approximate querying?

Real-world evasion also differs dramatically from the near-optimal evasion setting in defining an *efficient* classifier. For a real-world adversary, even polynomially many queries in the dimensionality of the feature space may not reasonable. For instance, if the dimensionality of the feature space is large (e.g., hundreds of thousands of words in unigram models) the adversary may require the number of queries to be sub-linear, $o(D)$, but in the near-optimal evasion problem this is not even possible for linear classifiers. However, real-world adversaries do not need to be provably near-optimal. Near-optimality is a surrogate for the adversary's true evasion objective: to use a small number of queries to find a negative instance with acceptably low cost; i.e., below some maximum cost threshold. This corresponds to an alternative cost function $A'(x) = \max[A(x), \delta]$ where δ is the maximum allowable cost. Clearly, if an ϵ-*IMAC* is obtained, either it satisfies this condition or the adversary can cease searching. Thus, ϵ-*IMAC* searchability is sufficient to achieve the adversary's goal, but the near-optimal evasion problem ignores the maximum cost threshold even though it may allow for the adversary to terminate its search using far fewer queries. To accurately capture real-world evasion with sub-linearly many queries, query-based algorithms must efficiently use every query to glean essential information about the classifier. Instead of quantifying the query complexity required for a family of classifiers, perhaps it is more important to quantify the query performance of an evasion algorithm for a fixed number of queries based on a target cost.

QUESTION 8.12 In the real-world evasion setting, what is the worst-case or expected reduction in cost for a query algorithm after making M queries to a classifier $f \in \mathcal{F}$? What is the expected value of each query to the adversary, and what is the best query strategy for a fixed number of queries?

The final challenge for real-world evasion is to design algorithms that can thwart attempts to evade the classifier. Promising potential defensive techniques include randomizing the classifier, identifying queries, and sending misleading responses to the adversary. We discuss these and other defensive techniques in Section 9.1.2.

Part IV

Future Directions in Adversarial Machine Learning

9   Adversarial Machine Learning Challenges

Machine learning algorithms provide the ability to quickly adapt and find patterns in large diverse data sources and therefore are a potential asset to application developers in enterprise systems, networks, and security domains. They make analyzing the security implications of these tools a critical task for machine learning researchers and practitioners alike, spawning a new subfield of research into adversarial learning for security-sensitive domains. The work presented in this book advanced the state of the art in this field of study with five primary contributions: a taxonomy for qualifying the security vulnerabilities of a learner, two novel practical attack/defense scenarios for learning in real-world settings, learning algorithms with theoretical guarantees on training-data privacy preservation, and a generalization of a theoretical paradigm for evading detection of a classifier. However, research in adversarial machine learning has only begun to address the field's complex obstacles—many challenges remain. These challenges suggest several new directions for research within both fields of machine learning and computer security. In this chapter we review our contributions and list a number of open problems in the area.

Above all, we investigated both the practical and theoretical aspects of applying machine learning in security domains. To understand potential threats, we analyzed the vulnerability of learning systems to adversarial malfeasance. We studied both attacks designed to optimally affect the learning system and attacks constrained by real-world limitations on the adversary's capabilities and information. We further designed defense strategies, which we showed significantly diminish the effect of these attacks. Our research focused on learning tasks in virus, spam, and network anomaly detection, but also is broadly applicable across many systems and security domains and has far-reaching implications to any system that incorporates learning. Here is a summary of the contributions of each component of this book followed by a discussion of open problems and future directions for research.

Framework for Secure Learning
The first contribution discussed in this book was a framework for assessing risks to a learner within a particular security context (see Table 3.1). The basis for this work is a taxonomy of the characteristics of potential attacks. From this taxonomy (summarized in Table 9.1), we developed security games between an attacker and defender tailored to the particular type of threat posed by the attacker. The structure of these games was primarily determined by whether or not the attacker could influence the training data; either

Table 9.1 Our Taxonomy of Attacks against Machine Learning Systems

Axis	Attack Properties		
Influence	**Causative** – influences training and test data		**Exploratory** – influences test data
Security violation	**Confidentiality** – goal is to uncover training data	**Integrity** – goal is false negatives (FNs)	**Availability** – goal is false positives (FPs)
Specificity	**Targeted** – influence prediction of particular test instance		**Indiscriminate** – influence prediction of all test instances

a *Causative* or *Exploratory* attack. The goal of the attacker contributed to the game in two ways. First, it generically specifies the attack function (i.e., whether the attack had an *Integrity*, *Availability*, or *Privacy* goal specifying which class of data points is desirable for the adversary). Second, it specifies whether that goal is focused on a small number of points (a *Targeted* attack) or is agnostic to which errors occur (an *Indiscriminate* attack).

Beyond security games, we augmented the taxonomy by further exploring the contamination mechanism used by the attacker. We proposed a variety of different possible contamination models for an attacker. Each of these models is appropriate in different scenarios, and it is important for an analyst to identify the most appropriate contamination model in the threat assessment. We further demonstrated the use of different contamination models in our subsequent investigation of practical systems.

Causative Attacks against Real-World Learners

The second major contribution we presented was a practical and theoretical evaluation of two risk minimization procedures in two separate security domains (spam filtering and network anomalous flow detection) under different contamination models. Within these settings we not only analyzed attacks against real-world systems but we also suggested defense strategies that substantially mitigate the impact of these attacks.

The first system, which we analyzed in Chapter 5, was the spam filter SpamBayes' learning algorithm. This algorithm is based on a simple probabilistic model for spam and has also been used by other spam filtering systems (BogoFilter, Thunderbird's spam filter, and the learning component of Apache SpamAssassin filter (Apa n.d.)), suggesting that the attacks we developed would also be effective against other spam filters. Similarly, they may also be effective against analogous learning algorithms used in different domains. We demonstrated that the vulnerability of SpamBayes originates from its modeling assumptions that a message's label depends only on the tokens present in the message and that those tokens are conditionally independent. While these modeling assumptions are not an inherent vulnerability, in this setting, conditional independence coupled with the rarity of most tokens and the ability of the adversary to poison large numbers of vulnerable tokens with every attack message makes SpamBayes' learner highly vulnerable to malicious contamination.

Motivated by the taxonomy of attacks against learners, we designed real-world *Causative* attacks against SpamBayes' learner and demonstrated the effectiveness of these attacks using realistic adversarial control over the training process of SpamBayes. Optimal attacks against SpamBayes caused unreasonably high false-positive rates using only a small amount of control of the training process (causing more than 95% misclassification of ham messages when only 1% of the training data is contaminated). The Usenet dictionary attack also effectively used a more realistically limited attack message to cause misclassification of 19% of ham messages with only 1% control over the training messages, rendering SpamBayes unusable in practice. We also showed that an informed adversary can successfully target messages. The focused attack changed the classification of the target message virtually 100% of the time with knowledge of only 30% of the target's tokens. Similarly, a pseudospam attack was able to cause nearly 90% of the target spam messages to be labeled as either *unsure* or *ham* with control of less than 10% of the training data.

To combat attacks against SpamBayes, we designed a data sanitization technique; reject on negative impact. RONI expunges any message from the training set if it has an undue negative impact on a calibrated test filter. This technique proved to be a successful defense against dictionary attacks as it detected and removed all of the malicious messages we injected. However, RONI also has costs: it causes a slight decrease in ham classification, it requires a substantial amount of computation, and it may slow the learning process. Nonetheless, this defense demonstrates that attacks against learners can be detected and prevented.

The second system, which we presented in Chapter 6, was a PCA-based classifier for detecting anomalous traffic in a backbone network using only volume measurements. This anomaly detection system inherited the vulnerabilities of the underlying PCA algorithm; namely, we demonstrated that PCA's sensitivity to outliers can be exploited by contaminating the training data, allowing the adversary to dramatically decrease the detection rate for DoS attacks along a particular target flow.

To counter the PCA-based detector, we studied *Causative Integrity* attacks that poison the training data by adding malicious noise; i.e., spurious traffic sent across the network by compromised nodes that reside within it. This malicious noise was designed to interfere with PCA's subspace estimation procedure. Based on a relaxed objective function, we demonstrated how an adversary can approximate optimal noise using a global view of the traffic patterns in the network. Empirically, we found that by increasing the mean link rate by 10% with globally informed chaff traffic, the FNR increased from 3.67% to 38%—a 10-fold increase in misclassification of DoS attacks. Similarly, by only using local link information the attacker was able to mount a more realistic add-more-if-bigger attack. For this attack, when the mean link rate was increased by 10% with add-more-if-bigger chaff traffic, the FNR increased from 3.67% to 28%—an eight-fold increase in misclassification of DoS attacks. These attacks demonstrate that with sufficient information about network patterns, attackers can mount attacks against the PCA detector that severely compromise its ability to detect future DoS attacks traversing the network it is monitoring.

We also demonstrated that an alternative robust method for subspace estimation can be used to make the resulting DoS detector less susceptible to poisoning attacks. The alternative detector was constructed using a subspace method for robust PCA developed by Croux et al. and a more robust method for estimating the residual cutoff threshold. Our resulting ANTIDOTE detector was affected by poisoning, but its performance degraded more gracefully than PCA. Under nonpoisoned traffic, ANTIDOTE performed nearly as well as PCA, but for all levels of contamination using add-more-if-bigger chaff traffic, the misclassification rate of ANTIDOTE was approximately half the FNR of the PCA-based solution. Moreover, the average performance of ANTIDOTE was much better than the original detector; it outperforms ordinary PCA for more flows and by a large amount. For multiweek boiling frog attacks, ANTIDOTE also outperformed PCA and caught progressively more attack traffic in each subsequent week.

Privacy-Preserving Learning

In Chapter 7, we explored learning under attacks on *Privacy*. After contributing a brief survey of pivotal breaches that influenced thinking on data privacy, we laid the foundation for differential privacy—a formal semantic property that guarantees that information released does not significantly depend on any individual datum. We reviewed the simplest generic mechanism for establishing differential privacy: the Laplace mechanism that introduces additive noise to nonprivate releases, with a scale that depends on sensitivity of releases to data perturbation. After briefly introducing the support vector machine (SVM), we provided an overview of the objective perturbation approach of Chaudhuri et al. (2011). Instead of optimizing the SVM's convex program, we minimized the same program with a random linear term added to the objective.

We discussed our own output perturbation approach (Rubinstein et al. 2012) in Section 7.4. We applied existing results on SVM algorithmic stability to determine the level of classifier perturbation; i.e., the scale of our Laplace noise. We next formulated the utility of privacy-preserving approximations, as the high-probability pointwise similarity of the approximate response predictions compared to nonprivate classifications. We demonstrated results on the utility of both approaches to differentially private SVMs. We generalized our results from the linear SVM (or SVMs with finite-dimensional feature mappings) to SVMs trained with translation-invariant kernels. These results work even for the RBF kernel that corresponds to an infinite-dimensional feature mapping. To do so, we used a technique from large-scale SVM learning that constructs a low-dimensional random kernel that uniformly approximates the desired translation-invariant kernel. Finally we explored lower bounds, which frame fundamental limits on what can possibly be learned privately while achieving high utility. The mechanisms explored, while endowed with theoretical guarantees on privacy and utility, are easily implemented and practical.

Evasion Attacks

In Chapter 8, we generalized Lowd & Meek's near-optimal evasion framework for quantifying query complexity of classifier evasion to the family of convex-inducing classifiers; i.e., classifiers that partition space into two regions, one of which is convex. For the ℓ_p costs, we demonstrated algorithms that efficiently use polynomially many queries to find a near-optimal evading instance for any classifier in the convex-inducing classifiers, and we showed that for some ℓ_p costs efficient near-optimal evasion cannot be achieved generally for this family of classifiers. Further, the algorithms we presented achieve near-optimal evasion without reverse engineering the classifier boundary and, in some cases, achieve better asymptotic query complexity than reverse-engineering approaches. Further, we showed that the near-optimal evasion problem is generally easier than reverse engineering the classifier's boundary.

A contribution from this work was an extensive study of membership query algorithms that efficiently accomplish ϵ-$IMAC$ search for convex-inducing classifiers with weighted ℓ_1 costs (see Section 8.2). When the positive class is convex, we demonstrated efficient techniques that outperform the previous reverse-engineering approaches for linear classifiers. When the negative class is convex, we applied the randomized ellipsoid method introduced by Bertsimas & Vempala to achieve efficient ϵ-$IMAC$ search. If the adversary is unaware of which set is convex, it can trivially run both searches to discover an ϵ-$IMAC$ with a combined polynomial query complexity; thus, for ℓ_1 costs, the family of convex-inducing classifiers can be efficiently evaded by an adversary; i.e., this family is ϵ-$IMAC$ searchable.

Further, we also extended the study of convex-inducing classifiers to general ℓ_p costs (see Section 8.3). We showed that $\mathcal{F}^{convex}$ is only ϵ-$IMAC$ searchable for both positive and negative convexity for any $\epsilon > 0$ if $p = 1$. For $0 < p < 1$, the MULTILINESEARCH algorithms of Section 8.2.1 achieve identical results when the positive set is convex, but the nonconvexity of these ℓ_p costs precludes the use of the randomized ellipsoid method. The ellipsoid method does provide an efficient solution for convex negative sets when $p > 1$ (since these costs are convex). However, for convex positive sets, we showed that for $p > 1$ there is no algorithm that can efficiently find an ϵ-$IMAC$ for all $\epsilon > 0$. Moreover, for $p = 2$, we proved that there is no efficient algorithm for finding an ϵ-$IMAC$ for any fixed value of ϵ.

9.1   Discussion and Open Problems

In the course of our research, we have encountered many challenges and learned important lessons that have given us some insight into the future of the field of adversarial learning in security-sensitive domains. Here we suggest several intriguing research directions for pursuing secure learning. We organize these directions into two topics: *i*) unexplored components of the adversarial game and *ii*) directions for defensive technologies . Finally, we conclude by enumerating the open problems we suggested throughout this book.

9.1.1   Unexplored Components of the Adversarial Game

As suggested in Chapter 3, adversarial learning and attacks against learning algorithms have received a great deal of attention. While many types of attacks have been explored, there are still many elements of this security problem that are relatively unexplored. We summarize some promising ones for future research.

9.1.1.1   Research Direction: The Role of Measurement and Feature Selection

As discussed in Section 2.2.1, the measurement process and feature selection play an important role in machine learning algorithms that we have not addressed in this book. As suggested in Section 3.1, these components of a learning algorithm are also susceptible to attacks. Some prior work has suggested vulnerabilities based on the features used by a learner (e.g., Mahoney & Chan 2003; Venkataraman et al. 2008; Wagner & Soto 2002), and others have suggested defenses to particular attacks on the feature set (e.g., Globerson & Roweis 2006; Sculley et al. 2006) It has been observed that high dimensionality serves to increase the attack surface of *Exploratory* attacks (Sommer & Paxson 2010; Amsaleg et al. 2016), suggesting that (randomized) feature selection be used as a defensive strategy. In game-theoretic models of *Causative* attacks, high dimensions also have computational consequences on finding equilibrium solutions (Alpcan et al. 2016). However, it has also been observed that traditional approaches to feature reduction can be vulnerable to feature substitution (Li & Vorobeychik 2014). The full role of feature selection remains unknown.

Selecting a set of measurements is a critical decision in any security-sensitive domain. As has been repeatedly demonstrated (e.g., Wagner & Soto 2002) irrelevant features can be leveraged by the adversary to cripple the learner's ability to detect malicious instances with little cost to the attacker. For example, in Chapter 5, we showed that tokens unrelated to the spam concept can be used to poison a spam filter. These vulnerabilities require a concerted effort to construct tamper-resistant features, to identify and eliminate features that have been corrupted, and to establish guidelines for practitioners to meet these needs.

Further, feature selection may play a pivotal role in the future of secure learning. As discussed in Direction 9.1.1.2, these methods can provide some secrecy for the learning algorithm and can eliminate irrelevant features. In doing so, feature selection methods may provide a means to gain an advantage against adversaries, but they may also be attacked. Exploring these possibilities remains a significant research challenge.

9.1.1.2   Research Direction: The Effect of Attacker Capabilities

In Section 1.2, we acknowledge that adversarial learning should adhere to Kerckhoffs' Principle: resilient learning systems should not assume secrecy to provide security. However, to understand under what threat models learnability is possible, it is important to characterize the impact of the adversary's capabilities on attack effectiveness.

QUESTION 9.1   Consider underlying stochastic data. How is learning on such data affected by the attacker's information about the data and learner, as well as the attacker's control over the data? What are appropriate parameterizations of attacker capabilities for characterizing learnability?

As learning algorithms generally find patterns in their training data, it is not necessary to exactly reproduce the training data to discover information about the learned hypothesis. In many cases, to approximate the learned hypothesis, the adversary need only have access to a similar dataset.

As observed by Papernot, McDaniel, Goodfellow, Jha, Celik, & Swami (2016) for a special case, reverse-engineered models can be used as surrogates in successful evasion attacks. To the extent that this approach works in general, reverse engineering can amplify an adversary's ability to launch subsequent misclassification attacks.

QUESTION 9.2 How accurate must a surrogate model be for effective misclassification attacks against a target?

As in the near-optimal evasion framework in Chapter 8, the adversary can procure a great deal of information about the learned hypothesis with little information about the training algorithm and hypothesis space.

One motivation for studying reverse-engineering attacks—outside their use in enabling low-information misclassification attacks—is situations in which the defender wishes to protect commercial-in-confidence information about the learner. Tramèr et al. (2016) develop practical reverse-engineering attacks against cloud-based ML-as-a-service systems, both for cases where the model returns only class labels and where the model returns precise confidence values permitting an approach based on solving systems of (nonlinear) equations.

QUESTION 9.3 In general, how effective is reverse engineering at building surrogate models? What guarantees, in terms of query complexity, are possible?

Perhaps the most obvious ingredient to be protected is the training data used to create the learned hypothesis. Settings discussed throughout this book consider adversaries that (partially) control inputs; even in such settings, differential privacy guarantees (as explored in Chapter 7) hold for arbitrary manipulation of all but a single private training datum.

Feature selection (as presented in Section 2.2.1) could potentially play a role in defending against an adversary by allowing the defender to use dynamic feature selection. In many cases, the goal of the adversary is to construct malicious data instances that are inseparable from innocuous data from the perspective of the learner. However, as the attack occurs, dynamic feature selection could be employed to estimate a new feature mapping $\phi'_{\mathbb{D}}$ that would allow the classifier to continue to separate the classes in spite of the adversary's alterations.

9.1.2 Development of Defensive Technologies

The most important challenge remaining for learning in security-sensitive domains is to develop general-purpose secure learning technologies. In Section 3.3.5, we suggested several promising approaches to defend against learning attacks, and several secure learners have been proposed (e.g., Dalvi et al. 2004; Globerson & Roweis 2006; Wang et al. 2006) However, the development of defenses will inevitably create an arms race, so successful defenses must anticipate potential counterattacks and demonstrate that they are resilient against reasonable threats. With this in mind, the next step is to explore general defenses against larger classes of attack to exemplify trustworthy secure learning.

9.1.2.1 Research Direction: Game-Theoretic Approaches to Secure Learning

Since suggested by Dalvi et al. (2004), the game-theoretic approach to designing defensive classifiers has rapidly expanded (e.g., Brückner & Scheffer 2009; Kantarcioglu et al. 2009; Biggio et al. 2010; Großhans et al. 2013) In this approach, adversarial learning is treated as a game between a learner (which chooses a model) and an adversary (which chooses data or a data transform). Both players are constrained and seek to optimize an objective function (typically at odds with the other player's objective). These approaches find an optimal model against the adversary and one that is thus robust against attacks. This game-theoretic approach is particularly appealing for secure learning because it incorporates the adversary's objective and limitations directly into the classifier's design through an adversarial cost function. However, this cost function is difficult to specify for a real-world adversary, and using an inaccurate cost function may again lead to inadvertent blind spots in the classifier. This raises interesting questions:

QUESTION 9.4 How can a machine learning practitioner design an accurate cost function for a game-theoretic cost-sensitive learning algorithm? How sensitive are these learners to the adversarial cost? Can the cost itself be learned?

Game-theoretic learning approaches are especially interesting because they directly incorporate the adversary as part of the learning process. In doing so, they make a number of assumptions about the adversary and its capabilities, but the most dangerous assumption made is that the adversary behaves *rationally* according to its interests. While this assumption seems reasonable, it can cause the learning algorithm to be overly reliant on its model of the adversary. For instance, the original adversary-aware classifier proposed by Dalvi et al. attempts to preemptively detect evasive data, but will classify data points as benign if a rational adversary would have altered them; i.e., in this case, the adversary can evade this classifier by simply not changing its behavior. Such strange properties are an undesirable side effect of the assumption that the adversary is rational, which raises another question:

QUESTION 9.5 How reliant are adversary-aware classifiers on the assumption that the adversary will behave rationally? Are there game-theoretic approaches that are less dependent on this assumption?

9.1.2.2 Research Direction: Broader Incorporation of Research Methods

Currently, choosing a learning method for a particular task is usually based on the structure of application data, the speed of the algorithm in training and prediction, and expected accuracy (often assessed on a static dataset). However, as our research has demonstrated, understanding how an algorithm's performance can change in security-sensitive domains is critical for its success and for widespread adoption in these domains. Designing algorithms to be resilient in these settings is a critical challenge.

Generally, competing against an adversary is a difficult problem and can be computationally intractable. However, the framework of robust statistics as outlined in Section 3.5.4.3 partially addresses the problem of adversarial contamination in training data. This framework provides a number of tools and techniques to construct learners robust against security threats from adversarial contamination. Many classical statistical methods often make strong assumptions that their data is generated by a stationary distribution, but adversaries can defy that assumption. For instance, in Chapter 6, we demonstrated that a robust subspace estimation technique significantly outperformed the original PCA method under adversarial contamination.

Robust statistics augment classical techniques by instead assuming that the data comes from two sources: a known distribution and an unknown adversarial distribution. Under this setting, robust variants exist for parameter estimation, testing, linear models, and other classic statistical techniques. Further, the breakdown point and influence function provide quantitative measurements of robustness, which designers of learning systems can use to evaluate the vulnerability of learners in security-sensitive tasks and select an appropriate algorithm accordingly. However, relatively few learning systems are currently designed explicitly with statistical robustness in mind. We believe, though, that as the field of adversarial learning grows, robustness considerations and techniques will become an increasingly prevalent part of practical learning design. The challenge remains to broadly integrate robust procedures into learning for security-sensitive domains and use them to design learning systems resilient to attacks.

9.1.2.3   Research Direction: Online Learning

An alternative complementary direction for developing defenses in security-sensitive settings is addressed by the game-theoretic expert aggregation setting described in Section 3.6. Recall that in this setting, the learner receives advice from a set of experts and makes a prediction by weighing the experts' advice based on their past performance. Techniques for learning within this framework have been developed to perform well with respect to the best expert in hindsight. A challenge that remains is designing sets of experts that together can better meet a security objective. Namely,

QUESTION 9.6 How can one design a set of experts (learners) so that their aggregate is resilient to attacks in the online learning framework?

Ideally, even if the experts may be individually vulnerable, they are difficult to attack as a group. We informally refer to such a set of experts as being *orthogonal*. Orthogonal learners have several advantages in a security-sensitive environment. They allow us to combine learners designed to capture different aspects of the task. These learners may use different feature sets and different learning algorithms to reduce common vulnerabilities; e.g., making them more difficult to reverse engineer. Finally, online expert aggregation techniques are flexible: existing experts can be altered or new ones can be added to the system whenever new vulnerabilities in the system are identified.

To properly design a system of orthogonal experts for secure learning, the designer must first assess the vulnerability of several candidate learners. With that analysis, the designer should then choose a base set of learners and sets of features for them to learn on. Finally, as the aggregate predictor matures, the designer should identify new security threats and patch the learners appropriately. This patching could be done by adjusting the algorithms, changing their feature sets, or even adding new learners to the aggregate. Perhaps this process could itself be automated or learned.

9.2   Review of Open Problems

Many exciting challenges remain in the field of adversarial learning in security-sensitive domains. Here we recount the open questions we suggested throughout this manuscript.

PROBLEMS FROM CHAPTER 9

9.3   Concluding Remarks

The field of adversarial learning in security-sensitive domains is a new and rapidly expanding subdiscipline that holds a number of interesting research topics for researchers in both machine learning and computer security. The research presented in this book has both significantly affected this community and highlighted several important lessons. First, to design effective learning systems, practitioners must follow the principle of proactive design as discussed in Section 1.2. To avoid security pitfalls, designers must develop reasonable threat models for potential adversaries and develop learning systems to meet their desired security requirements. At the same time, machine learning designers should promote the security properties of their algorithms in addition to other traditional metrics of performance.

A second lesson that has reemerged throughout this book is that there are inherent tradeoffs between a learner's performance on regular data and its resilience to attacks. Understanding these tradeoffs is important not only for security applications but also for understanding how learners behave in any non-ideal setting.

Finally, throughout this book, we suggested a number of promising approaches toward secure learning, but a clear picture of what is required for secure learning has yet to emerge. Each of the approaches we discussed are founded in game theory, but have different benefits: the adversary-aware classifiers directly incorporate the threat model into their learning procedure, the robust statistics framework provides procedures that are generally resilient against any form of contamination, and the expert aggregation setting constructs classifiers that can do nearly as well as the best expert in hindsight. However, by themselves, none of these form a complete solution for secure learning. Integrating these different approaches or developing a new approach remains the most important challenge for this field.

Part V

Appendixes

Appendix A   Background for Learning and Hyper-Geometry

This appendix contains background material we use throughout this book. In Section A.1, we introduce basic foundations and notation in mathematics and probability necessary for the machine learning concepts built upon in this book. Section A.2 summarizes technical properties of hyperspheres and spherical caps used in the proofs for near-optimal evasion.

A.1   Overview of General Background Topics

We use standard terms and symbols from several fields, as detailed below to avoid ambiguities. We expect that the reader is familiar with the topics in logic, set theory, linear algebra, mathematical optimization, and probability as reviewed in this section. We use $=$ to denote *equality* and $\triangleq$ to denote *defined as*.

Typesetting of Elements, Sets, and Spaces
The typeface Style of a character is used to differentiate between elements of a set, sets, and spaces as follows. Individual objects such as scalars are denoted with italic roman font (e.g., x), and multidimensional vectors are denoted with bold roman font (e.g., $\mathbf{x}$). As discussed below, sets are denoted using blackboard bold characters (e.g., $\mathbb{X}$). However, when referring to the *entire* set or universe that spans a particular kind of object (i.e., a space), we use calligraphic script such as in $\mathcal{X}$ to distinguish it from subsets $\mathbb{X}$ contained within this space.

Sequences and Indexes
In this book, we differentiate between two types of indexing of objects. The first type is used to refer to an element in a sequence of similar objects. This type of index occurs in the superscript following the referenced object and is enclosed within parentheses. For instance, $x^{(1)}, x^{(2)}, \ldots, x^{(N)}$ are a sequence of objects with $x^{(t)}$ denoting the tth object in the sequence. The second type of index refers to a component of a composite object (e.g., within a multidimensional object) and is indexed by the subscript following the object. For instance $x_1, x_2, \ldots, x_D$ are the components of the vector $\mathbf{x}$. Thus, $\mathbf{x}^{(t)}$ refers to the tth vector in a sequence of vectors, $x_i^{(t)}$ refers to its ith coordinate, and x_i^k is the kth power of x_i.

First-Order Logic

We next describe a formal syntax for expressing logical statements. The notation $a \wedge b$ denotes the logical *conjunction*, a and b; $a \vee b$ denotes the logical *disjunction*, a or b; $\neg a$ is the logical *negation*, not a; $a \Rightarrow b$ is the logical implication defined as $(\neg a) \vee b$; and $a \Leftrightarrow b$ is logical equivalence (i.e., *if and only if*) defined as $(a \Rightarrow b) \wedge (b \Rightarrow a)$. We use the symbols $\forall$ and $\exists$ for universal and existential quantification, respectively. When necessary, predicates can be formalized as functions such as $p(\cdot)$, which evaluates to true if and only if its argument exhibits the property represented by the predicate. The special *identity predicate* is defined as $I[a] \Leftrightarrow a$. For convenience, we overload this notation for the indicator function, which instead evaluates to 1 if its argument is true and to 0 otherwise.

Sets

A set, or a collection of objects, is denoted using blackboard bold characters such as $\mathbb{X}$ as noted above and the empty set is given by $\emptyset$. To group a collection of objects as a set we use curly braces such as $\mathbb{X} = \{a, b, c\}$. To specify set membership we use $x \in \mathbb{X}$, and to explicitly enumerate the elements of a set we use the notation $\mathbb{X} = \{x_1, x_2, \ldots, x_N\}$ for a finite set and $\mathbb{X} = \{x_1, x_2, \ldots\}$ for a countably infinite sequence. To qualify the elements within a set, we use the notation $\mathbb{X} = \{x \mid A(x)\}$ to denote a set of objects that satisfy a logical condition represented here by the predicate $A(\cdot)$. We use $\mathbb{Y} \subseteq \mathbb{X}$ to denote that $\mathbb{Y}$ is a *subset* of $\mathbb{X}$; i.e., $\forall y\, (y \in \mathbb{Y} \Rightarrow y \in \mathbb{X})$. For finite sets, we use the notation $|\mathbb{X}|$ to denote the size of $\mathbb{X}$. We denote the *union* of two sets as $\mathbb{X} \cup \mathbb{Y} \triangleq \{a \mid (a \in \mathbb{X}) \vee (a \in \mathbb{Y})\}$, the *intersection* of two sets as $\mathbb{X} \cap \mathbb{Y} \triangleq \{a \mid (a \in \mathbb{X}) \wedge (a \in \mathbb{Y})\}$, and the *set difference* of two sets as $\mathbb{X} \setminus \mathbb{Y} \triangleq \{a \mid (a \in \mathbb{X}) \wedge (a \notin \mathbb{Y})\}$; i.e., the elements in $\mathbb{X}$ but not in $\mathbb{Y}$. We also use the predicate $I_{\mathbb{X}}[\cdot]$ to denote the set indicator function for $\mathbb{X}$; i.e., $I_{\mathbb{X}}[x] \triangleq I[x \in \mathbb{X}]$ (again we overload this function to map onto $\{0, 1\}$ for convenience).

Integers and Reals

Common sets include the set of all integers $\mathfrak{Z}$ and the set of all real numbers $\mathfrak{R}$. Special subsets of the integers are the natural numbers $\mathfrak{N} \triangleq \{z \in \mathfrak{Z} \mid z > 0\} = \{1, 2, \ldots\}$ and the whole numbers $\mathfrak{N}_0 \triangleq \{z \in \mathfrak{Z} \mid z \geq 0\} = \{0, 1, \ldots\}$. Similarly, special subsets of the reals are the positive reals $\mathfrak{R}_+ \triangleq \{r \in \mathfrak{R} \mid r > 0\}$ and the non-negative reals $\mathfrak{R}_{0+} \triangleq \{r \in \mathfrak{R} \mid r \geq 0\}$. *Intervals* are subsets of the reals spanning between two bounds; these are denoted by $(a, b) \triangleq \{r \in \mathfrak{R} \mid a < r < b\}$, $[a, b) \triangleq \{r \in \mathfrak{R} \mid a \leq r < b\}$, $(a, b] \triangleq \{r \in \mathfrak{R} \mid a < r \leq b\}$, and $[a, b] \triangleq \{r \in \mathfrak{R} \mid a \leq r \leq b\}$. For instance, $\mathfrak{R}_+ = (0, \infty)$ and $\mathfrak{R}_{0+} = [0, \infty)$.

Indexed Sets

To order the elements of a set, we use an index set as a mapping to each element. For a finite indexable set, we use the notation $\left\{x^{(i)}\right\}_{i=1}^{N}$ to denote the sequence of N objects, $x^{(i)}$, indexed by $\{1, \ldots, N\}$. More generally, a set indexed by some $\mathbb{I}$ is denoted $\left\{x^{(i)}\right\}_{i \in \mathbb{I}}$. An infinite sequence can be indexed by using infinite index sets such as $\mathfrak{N}$ or $\mathfrak{R}$ depending on the cardinality of the sequence.

Multidimensional Sets

Sets can also be coupled to describe multidimensional objects or *ordered tuples*. In refering to an object that is a tuple, we use a (lowercase) bold character such as **x** and use parenthetical brackets (·) to specify the contents of the tuple. The simplest tuple is an *ordered pair* $(x, y) \in \mathbb{X} \times \mathbb{Y}$, which is a pair of objects from two sets: $x \in \mathbb{X}$ and $y \in \mathbb{Y}$. The set of all such ordered pairs is called the *Cartesian product* of the sets $\mathbb{X}$ and $\mathbb{Y}$ denoted by $\mathbb{X} \times \mathbb{Y} \triangleq \{(x, y) \mid x \in \mathbb{X} \wedge y \in \mathbb{Y}\}$. This concept extends beyond ordered pairs to objects of any dimension. A *D-tuple* is an ordered list of D objects belonging to D sets: $(x_1, x_2, \ldots, x_D) \in \bigtimes_{i=1}^{D} \mathbb{X}_i$ where the generalized Cartesian product $\bigtimes_{i=1}^{D} \mathbb{X}_i \triangleq \mathbb{X}_1 \times \mathbb{X}_2 \times \ldots \times \mathbb{X}_D = \{(x_1, x_2, \ldots, x_D) \mid x_1 \in \mathbb{X}_1 \wedge x_2 \in \mathbb{X}_2 \wedge \ldots \wedge x_D \in \mathbb{X}_D\}$; i.e., the set of all such *D*-tuples. The *dimension* of this Cartesian product space and any member tuple is D, and the function *dim* (·) returns the dimension of a tuple. When each element of a D-tuple belongs to a common set $\mathbb{X}$, the generalized Cartesian product is denoted with exponential notation as $\mathbb{X}^D \triangleq \bigtimes_{i=1}^{D} \mathbb{X}$; e.g., the Euclidean space $\mathfrak{R}^D$ is the D-dimensional real-valued space.

Vectors

For our purposes, a vector is a special case of ordered D-tuples that we represent with a (usually lowercase) bold character such as **v**; unlike general tuples, vector spaces are endowed with an addition operator and a scalar multiplication operator, which obey properties discussed here. Consider a D-dimensional vector $\mathbf{v} \in \mathbb{X}^D$ with elements in the set $\mathbb{X}$. The ith element or *coordinate* of **v** is a scalar denoted by $v_i \in \mathbb{X}$ where $i \in \{1, 2, \ldots, D\}$. Special real-valued vectors include the all ones vector $\mathbf{1} = (1, 1, \cdots, 1)$, the all zeros vector $\mathbf{0} = (0, 0, \cdots, 0)$, and the coordinate or *basis* vector $\mathbf{e}^{(d)} \triangleq (0, \ldots, 1, \ldots, 0)$, which has a one only in its dth coordinate and is zero elsewhere.

A vector space, $\mathcal{X}$, is a set of vectors that can be added to one another or multiplied by a scalar to yield a new element within the space; i.e., the space is closed under vector addition and scalar multiplication operations that obey associativity, commutativity, and distributivity and have an identity (vector and scalar, respectively) as well as additive inverses. For example, the Euclidean space $\mathfrak{R}^n$ is a vector space for any $n \in \mathfrak{N}$ under the usual vector addition and real multiplication. A convex set $\mathbb{C} \subseteq \mathcal{X}$ is a subset of a vector space with real scalars, with the property that $\forall \alpha \in [0, 1]$, $x, y \in \mathbb{C} \Rightarrow (1 - \alpha)x + \alpha y \in \mathbb{C}$; i.e., $\mathbb{C}$ is closed under convex combinations. A vector space $\mathcal{X}$ is a *normed vector space* if it is endowed with a norm function $\|\cdot\| : \mathcal{X} \to \mathfrak{R}$ such that for all vectors $x, y \in \mathcal{X}$, *i*) there is a zero element 0 that satisfies $\|x\| = 0 \Leftrightarrow x = 0$, *ii*) for any scalar α, $\|\alpha x\| = |\alpha| \|x\|$, and *iii*) the triangle inequality holds: $\|x + y\| \leq \|x\| + \|y\|$. A common family of norms are the ℓ_p norms defined as

$$\|\mathbf{x}\|_p \triangleq \sqrt[p]{\sum_{i=1}^{D} |x_i|^p} \tag{A.1}$$

for $p \in \mathfrak{R}_+$. An extension of this family includes the ℓ_∞ norm, which is defined as $\|\mathbf{x}\|_\infty \triangleq \max [|x_i|]$.

Matrices

Usually denoted with an uppercase bold character such as $\mathbf{A}$, a *matrix* is a multi-dimensional object with two indices, which represent a row and column. The $(i, j)^{\text{th}}$ element of $\mathbf{A}$ is denoted by $A_{i,j} \in \mathbb{X}$ where $i \in \{1, 2, \ldots, M\}$ and $j \in \{1, 2, \ldots, N\}$. The full matrix can then be expressed element-wise using the bracket notation:

$$\mathbf{A} = \begin{bmatrix} A_{1,1} & A_{1,2} & \cdots & A_{1,N} \\ A_{2,1} & A_{2,2} & \cdots & A_{2,N} \\ \vdots & \vdots & \ddots & \vdots \\ A_{M,1} & A_{M,2} & \cdots & A_{M,N} \end{bmatrix}.$$

As suggested by this notation, a matrix's first index specifies its *row* and the second specifies its *column*. Each row and column are themselves vectors and are denoted by $\mathbf{A}_{i,\bullet}$ and $\mathbf{A}_{\bullet,j}$ respectively. We also use the bracket notation $[\,\cdot\,]_{i,j}$ to refer to the $(i, j)^{\text{th}}$ element of a matrix-valued expression; e.g., $[\mathbf{A} + \mathbf{B}]_{i,j}$ is the $(i, j)^{\text{th}}$ element of the matrix $\mathbf{A} + \mathbf{B}$. Special matrices include the identity matrix $\mathbf{I}$, with 1's along its diagonal and 0's elsewhere, and the zero matrix $\mathbf{0}$ with zero in every element. The transpose of an $M \times N$-dimensional matrix is an $N \times M$-dimensional matrix denoted as $\mathbf{A}^{\top}$ and defined as $\left[\mathbf{A}^{\top}\right]_{i,j} = A_{j,i}$.

Matrix Multiplication

Here we consider vectors and matrices whose elements belong to a scalar field $\mathcal{X}$ endowed with multiplication and addition (e.g., $\mathfrak{Z}$, $\mathfrak{R}$). For the purpose of matrix multiplication, we represent an N-dimensional vector as the equivalent $N \times 1$ matrix for notational convenience. The *inner product* between two vectors $\mathbf{v}$ and $\mathbf{w}$, with $dim\,(\mathbf{v}) = dim\,(\mathbf{w}) = N$, is the scalar denoted by $\mathbf{v}^{\top}\mathbf{w} = \sum_{i=1}^{N} v_i \cdot w_i$. The *outer product* between M-dimensional vector $\mathbf{v}$ and N-dimensional vector $\mathbf{w}$ is an $M \times N$-dimensional matrix denoted by $\mathbf{v}\mathbf{w}^{\top}$ with elements $\left[\mathbf{v}\mathbf{w}^{\top}\right]_{i,j} = v_i \cdot w_j$. The product between an $M \times N$-dimensional matrix $\mathbf{A}$ and an N-dimensional vector $\mathbf{w}$ is denoted $\mathbf{A}\mathbf{w}$ and defined as the M-dimensional vector of inner products between the ith row $\mathbf{A}_{i,\bullet}$ and the vector $\mathbf{w}$; i.e., $[\mathbf{A}\mathbf{w}]_i = \mathbf{A}_{i,\bullet}^{\top}\mathbf{w}$. It follows that $\mathbf{v}^{\top}\mathbf{A}\mathbf{w}$ is a scalar defined as $\mathbf{v}^{\top}\mathbf{A}\mathbf{w} = \sum_{i,j} v_i \cdot A_{i,j} \cdot w_j$. The *matrix product* between an $M \times N$-dimensional matrix $\mathbf{A}$ and an $N \times K$-dimensional matrix $\mathbf{B}$ is an $M \times K$-dimensional matrix denoted by $\mathbf{A}\mathbf{B}$ whose $(i, j)^{\text{th}}$ element is the inner product between the ith row of $\mathbf{A}$ and the jth column of $\mathbf{B}$; i.e., $[\mathbf{A}\mathbf{B}]_{i,j} = \mathbf{A}_{i,\bullet}^{\top}\mathbf{B}_{\bullet,j}$.

We also use the *Hadamard (element-wise) product* of vectors and matrices that we denote with the $\odot$ operator. The Hadamard product of vectors $\mathbf{v}$ and $\mathbf{w}$, with $dim\,(\mathbf{v}) = dim\,(\mathbf{w})$, is a vector defined as $[\mathbf{v} \odot \mathbf{w}]_i \triangleq v_i \cdot w_i$. Similarly, the Hadamard product of matrices $\mathbf{A}$ and $\mathbf{B}$, with $dim\,(\mathbf{A}) = dim\,(\mathbf{B})$, is the matrix $[\mathbf{A} \odot \mathbf{B}]_{i,j} \triangleq A_{i,j} \cdot B_{i,j}$.

Functions

We denote a function using regular italic font; e.g., the function *g*. However, for common named functions (such as logarithm and sine) we use the non-italicized Roman typeface (e.g., log and sin). A function is a mapping from its *domain* $\mathbb{X}$ to its *co-domain* or *range*

$\mathbb{Y}$; $g : \mathbb{X} \to \mathbb{Y}$. To apply g to x, we use the usual notation $g(x)$; $x \in \mathbb{X}$ is the argument and $g(x) \in \mathbb{Y}$ is the value of g at x. We also use this notation to refer to parameterized objects, but in this case, we will name the object according to its type. For instance, $\mathbb{B}^C(g) \triangleq \{x \mid g(x) < C\}$ is a set parameterized by the function g called the C-ball of g, and so we call attention to the fact that this object is a set by using the set notation $\mathbb{B}$ in naming it.

A convex function is any real-valued function $g : \mathbb{X} \to \mathfrak{R}$ whose domain $\mathbb{X}$ is a convex set in a vector space such that, for any $x^{(1)}, x^{(2)} \in \mathbb{X}$ and any $\alpha \in [0, 1]$, the function satisfies the inequality

$$f\left(\alpha x^{(1)} + (1 - \alpha)x^{(2)}\right) \leq \alpha f\left(x^{(1)}\right) + (1 - \alpha) f\left(x^{(2)}\right).$$

Families of Functions
A family of functions is a set of functions, for which we extend the previous concept of multidimensional sets. Functions can be defined as tuples of (possibly) infinite length—instead of indexing the tuple with natural numbers, it is indexed by the domain of the function; e.g., the reals. To represent the set of all such functions, we use the generalized Cartesian product over an index set $\mathbb{I}$ as $\times_{i \in \mathbb{I}} \mathbb{X}$ where $\mathbb{X}$ is the co-domain of the family of functions. For instance, the set of all real-valued functions is $\mathcal{G} = \times_{x \in \mathfrak{R}} \mathfrak{R}$; i.e., every function $g \in \mathcal{G}$ is a mapping from the reals to the reals: $g : \mathfrak{R} \to \mathfrak{R}$. We also consider special subsets such as the set of all continuous real-valued functions $\mathcal{G}^{(\text{continuous})} = \{g \in \mathcal{G} \mid continuous(g)\}$ or the set of all convex functions $\mathcal{G}^{(\text{convex})} = \{g \in \mathcal{G} \mid \forall t \in [0, 1] \ \ g(tx + (1 - t)y) \leq tg(x) + (1 - t)g(y)\}$. Particularly, we use the family of all classifiers (as defined in Section 2.2.2) in a D-dimensional space in Chapter 8. This family is the set of functions mapping $\mathfrak{R}^D$ to the set $\{"-", "+"\}$ and is denoted by $\mathcal{F} \triangleq \times_{x \in \mathfrak{R}^D} \{"-", "+"\}$.

Optimization
Learning theory makes heavy use of mathematical optimization. Optimization typically is cast as finding a *best* object x from a space $\mathcal{X}$ in terms of finding a minimizer of an objective function $f : \mathcal{X} \to \mathfrak{R}$:

$$x^\star \in \underset{x \in \mathcal{X}}{\operatorname{argmin}} [f(x)]$$

where argmin $[\ \cdot\ ]$ is a mapping from the space of all objects $\mathcal{X}$ to a subset $\mathbb{X}' \subseteq \mathcal{X}$, which is the set of all objects in $\mathcal{X}$ that minimize f (or equivalently maximize $-f$). Optimizations can additionally be restricted to obey a set of *constraints*. When specifying an optimization with constraints, we use the following notation:

$$\operatorname{argmin}_{x \in \mathcal{X}} [f(x)]$$
$$\text{s.t.} \qquad C(x)$$

where f is the function being optimized and C represents the constraints that need to be satisfied. Often there will be several constraints C_i that must be satisfied in the optimization.

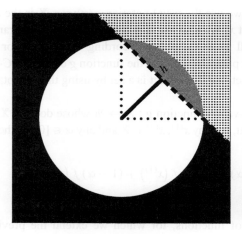 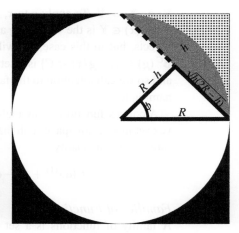

(a) A Spherical Cap on a Circle   (b) An Angular Cap on a Circle

Figure A.1 This figure shows various depictions of spherical caps. **(a)** A depiction of a spherical cap of height h, which is created by a halfspace that passes through the sphere. The gray region represents the area of the cap. **(b)** The geometry of the spherical cap: The intersecting halfspace forms a right triangle with the centroid of the hypersphere. The length of the side of this triangle adjacent to the centroid is $R - h$, its hypotenuse has length R, and the side opposite the centroid has length $\sqrt{h(2R - h)}$. The half-angle ϕ, given by $\sin(\phi) = \frac{\sqrt{h(2R-h)}}{R}$, of the right circular cone is used to parameterize the cap.

Probability and Statistics

We denote a probability distribution over the space $\mathcal{X}$ by $P_{\mathcal{X}}$. It is a function that is defined on the subsets in a σ-field of $\mathcal{X}$ (i.e., a set of subsets $\mathbb{A}^{(i)} \subseteq \mathcal{X}$ that is closed under complements and countable unions) and satisfies *(i)* $P_{\mathcal{X}}\left(\mathbb{A}^{(i)}\right) \geq 0$ for all subsets $\mathbb{A}^{(i)}$, *(ii)* $P_{\mathcal{X}}(\mathcal{X}) = 1$, and *(iii)* for pairwise disjoint subsets $\mathbb{A}^{(1)}$, $\mathbb{A}^{(2)}$, ..., it yields $P_{\mathcal{X}}\left(\bigcup_i \mathbb{A}^{(i)}\right) = \sum_i P_{\mathcal{X}}\left(\mathbb{A}^{(i)}\right)$. For a more thorough treatment, we refer the interested reader to Billingsley (1995). A random variable drawn from distribution $P_{\mathcal{X}}$ is denoted by $X \sim P_{\mathcal{X}}$—notice that we do not use a special notation for the random variable, but we make it clear in the text that they are random. The expected value of a random variable is denoted by $\mathrm{E}_{X \sim P_{\mathcal{X}}}[X] = \int x\, dP_{\mathcal{X}}(x)$ or simply by $\mathrm{E}[X]$ when the distribution of the random variables is known from the context. The family of all probability distributions on $\mathcal{X}$ is denoted by $\mathcal{P}_{\mathcal{X}}$; as above, this is the family of all functions that assign probability to elements of the σ-field of $\mathcal{X}$.

A.2   Covering Hyperspheres

Here we summarize the properties of hyperspheres and spherical caps and a covering number result provided by Wyner (1965) and Shannon (1959). This covering result will be used to bound the number of queries required by any evasion algorithm for ℓ_2 costs in Appendix D.2.

A D-dimensional *hypersphere* is simply the set of all points with ℓ_2 distance less than or equal to its radius R from its centroid (in Chapter 8, x^A); i.e.,; the ball $\mathbb{B}^R$ (A_2). Any D-dimensional hypersphere of radius, R, $\mathbb{S}^R$, has volume

$$vol\left(\mathbb{S}^R\right) = \frac{\pi^{\frac{D}{2}}}{\Gamma\left(1+\frac{D}{2}\right)} \cdot R^D \tag{A.2}$$

and surface area

$$surf\left(\mathbb{S}^R\right) = \frac{D \cdot \pi^{\frac{D}{2}}}{\Gamma\left(1+\frac{D}{2}\right)} \cdot R^{D-1}.$$

A D-dimensional *spherical cap* is the outward region formed by the intersection of a halfspace and a hypersphere as depicted in Figure A.1(a). The cap has a height of h, which represents the maximum length between the plane and the spherical arc. A cap of height h on a D-dimensional hypersphere of radius R will be denoted by $\mathbb{C}_h^R$ and has a volume

$$vol\left(\mathbb{C}_h^R\right) = \frac{\pi^{\frac{D-1}{2}} R^D}{\Gamma\left(\frac{D+1}{2}\right)} \int_0^{\arccos\left(\frac{R-h}{R}\right)} \sin^D(t)\ dt$$

and surface area

$$surf\left(\mathbb{C}_h^R\right) = \frac{(D-1) \cdot \pi^{\frac{D-1}{2}} R^{D-1}}{\Gamma\left(\frac{D+1}{2}\right)} \int_0^{\arccos\left(\frac{R-h}{R}\right)} \sin^{D-2}(t)\ dt.$$

Alternatively, the cap can be parameterized in terms of the hypersphere's radius R and the half-angle ϕ about a central radius (through the peak of the cap) as in Figure A.1(b). A cap of half-angle ϕ forms the right triangle depicted in the figure, for which $R - h = R\cos(\phi)$ so that h can be expressed in terms of R and ϕ as $h = R * (1 - \cos\phi)$. Substituting this expression for h into the above formulas yields the volume of the cap as

$$vol\left(\mathbb{C}_\phi^R\right) = \frac{\pi^{\frac{D-1}{2}} R^D}{\Gamma\left(\frac{D+1}{2}\right)} \int_0^\phi \sin^D(t)\ dt \tag{A.3}$$

and its surface area as

$$surf\left(\mathbb{C}_\phi^R\right) = \frac{(D-1) \cdot \pi^{\frac{D-1}{2}} R^{D-1}}{\Gamma\left(\frac{D+1}{2}\right)} \int_0^\phi \sin^{D-2}(t)\ dt.$$

Based on these formulas, we now bound the number of spherical caps of half-angle ϕ required to cover the sphere mirroring the result of Wyner (1965).

LEMMA A.1 *(Result based on Wyner (1965) Covering the surface of D-dimensional hypersphere of radius R, $\mathbb{S}^R$, requires at least*

$$\left(\frac{1}{\sin(\phi)}\right)^{D-2}$$

spherical caps of half-angle $\phi \in \left(0, \frac{\pi}{2}\right)$.

Proof Suppose there are M caps that cover the hypersphere. The total surface area of the M caps must be at least the surface area of the hypersphere. Thus,

$$M \geq \frac{surf\left(\mathbb{S}^R\right)}{surf\left(\mathbb{C}_\phi^R\right)}$$

$$\geq \frac{\frac{D \cdot \pi^{\frac{D}{2}}}{\Gamma\left(1+\frac{D}{2}\right)} \cdot R^{D-1}}{\frac{(D-1) \cdot \pi^{\frac{D-1}{2}} R^{D-1}}{\Gamma\left(\frac{D+1}{2}\right)} \int_0^\phi \sin^{D-2}(t) \, dt}$$

$$\geq \frac{D\sqrt{\pi}\,\Gamma\left(\frac{D+1}{2}\right)}{(D-1)\Gamma\left(1+\frac{D}{2}\right)} \left[\int_0^\phi \sin^{D-2}(t) \, dt\right]^{-1},$$

which is the result derived by Wyner (although applied as a bound on the packing number rather than the covering number). We continue by lower bounding the above integral. As demonstrated above, integrals of the form $\int_0^\phi \sin^D(t) \, dt$ arise in computing the volume or surface area of a spherical cap. To upper bound the volume of such a cap, note that *i*) the spherical cap is defined by a hypersphere and a hyperplane, *ii*) their intersection forms a $(D-1)$-dimensional hypersphere as the base of the cap, *iii*) the projection of the center of the first hypersphere onto the hyperplane is the center of the $(D-1)$-dimensional hyperspherical intersection, *iv*) the distance between these centers is $R - h$, and *v*) this projected point achieves the maximum height of the cap; i.e., continuing along the radial line achieves the remaining distance h—the height of the cap. We use these facts to upper bound the volume of the cap by enclosing the cap within a D-dimensional hypersphere. As seen in Figure A.1(b), the center of the $(D-1)$-dimensional hyperspherical intersection forms a right triangle with the original hypersphere's center and the edge of the intersecting spherical region (by symmetry, all such edge points are equivalent). That right triangle has one side of length $R - h$ and a hypotenuse of R. Hence, the other side has length $s = \sqrt{h(2R-h)} = R\sin(\phi)$. Moreover, $R \geq h$ implies $s \geq h$. Thus, a D-dimensional hypersphere of radius s encloses the cap, and its volume from Equation (A.2) bounds the volume of the cap as

$$vol\left(\mathbb{C}_\phi^R\right) \leq vol\left(\mathbb{S}^s\right) = \frac{\pi^{\frac{D}{2}}}{\Gamma\left(1+\frac{D}{2}\right)} \cdot (R\sin(\phi))^D.$$

Applying this bound to the formula for the volume of the cap in Equation A.3 then yields the following bound on the integral:

$$\frac{\pi^{\frac{D-1}{2}} R^D}{\Gamma\left(\frac{D+1}{2}\right)} \int_0^\phi \sin^D(t) \, dt \leq \frac{\pi^{\frac{D}{2}}}{\Gamma\left(1+\frac{D}{2}\right)} \cdot (R\sin(\phi))^D$$

$$\int_0^\phi \sin^D(t) \, dt \leq \frac{\sqrt{\pi}\,\Gamma\left(\frac{D+1}{2}\right)}{\Gamma\left(1+\frac{D}{2}\right)} \cdot \sin^D(\phi).$$

Using this bound on the integral, the bound on the size of the covering from Wyner reduces to the following (weaker) bound:

$$M \geq \frac{D\sqrt{\pi}\,\Gamma\left(\frac{D+1}{2}\right)}{(D-1)\Gamma\left(1+\frac{D}{2}\right)} \left[\frac{\sqrt{\pi}\,\Gamma\left(\frac{D-1}{2}\right)}{\Gamma\left(\frac{D}{2}\right)} \cdot \sin^{D-2}\left(\phi\right)\right]^{-1}.$$

Finally, using properties of the gamma function, it can be shown that $\frac{\Gamma\left(\frac{D+1}{2}\right)\Gamma\left(\frac{D}{2}\right)}{\Gamma\left(1+\frac{D}{2}\right)\Gamma\left(\frac{D-1}{2}\right)} = \frac{D-1}{D}$ which simplifies the above expression to

$$M \geq \left(\frac{1}{\sin\left(\phi\right)}\right)^{D-2}.$$

$\square$

It is worth noting that by further bounding the integral $\int_0^\phi \sin^D\left(t\right)\,dt$, the bound in Lemma A.1 is weaker than the original bound on the covering derived in Wyner (1965). However, the bound provided by the lemma is more useful for later results because it is expressed in a closed form (see the proof for Theorem 8.13 in Appendix D.2).

Of course, there are other tighter bounds on this power-of-sine integral. In Lemma A.1, this quantity is controlled using a bound on the volume of a spherical cap, but here we instead bound the integral directly. A naive bound can be accomplished by observing that all the terms in the integral are less than the final term, which yields

$$\int_0^\phi \sin^D\left(t\right)\,dt \leq \phi \cdot \sin^D\left(\phi\right),$$

but this bound is looser than the bound achieved in the lemma. However, by first performing a variable substitution, a tighter bound on the integral can be obtained. The variable substitution is given by letting $p = \sin^2\left(t\right)$, $t = \arcsin\left(\sqrt{p}\right)$, and $dt = \frac{dp}{2\sqrt{1-p}\sqrt{p}}$. This yields

$$\int_0^\phi \sin^D\left(t\right)\,dt = \frac{1}{2}\int_0^{\sin^2\left(\phi\right)} \frac{p^{\frac{D-1}{2}}}{\sqrt{1-p}}\,dp.$$

Within the integral, the denominator is monotonically decreasing in p since, for the interval of integration, $p \leq 1$. Thus it achieves its minimum value at the upper limit $p = \sin^2\left(\phi\right)$. Fixing the denominator at this value therefore results in the following upper bound on the integral:

$$\int_0^\phi \sin^D\left(t\right)\,dt \leq \frac{1}{2\cos\left(\phi\right)}\int_0^{\sin^2\left(\phi\right)} p^{\frac{D-1}{2}}\,dp = \frac{\sin^{D+1}\left(\phi\right)}{(D+1)\cos\left(\phi\right)}. \qquad (A.4)$$

This bound is not strictly tighter than the bound applied in Lemma A.1, but for large D and $\phi < \frac{\pi}{2}$, this result does achieve a tighter bound. We apply this bound for additional analysis in Section 8.3.1.4.

A.3   Covering Hypercubes

Here we introduce results for covering D-dimensional *hypercube graphs*—a collection of 2^D nodes of the form $(\pm 1, \pm 1, \ldots, \pm 1)$ where each node has an edge to every other node that is Hamming distance 1 from it. The following lemma summarizes coverings of a hypersphere and is utilized in Appendix D for a general query complexity result for ℓ_p distances:

LEMMA A.2 *For any $0 < \delta \leq \frac{1}{2}$ and $D \geq 1$, to cover a D-dimensional hypercube graph so that every vertex has a Hamming distance of at most $h = \lfloor \delta D \rfloor$ to some vertex in the covering, the minimum number of vertexes in the covering is bounded by*

$$Q(D, h) \geq 2^{D(1 - H(\delta))},$$

where $H(\delta) = -\delta \log_2 (\delta) - (1 - \delta) \log_2 (1 - \delta)$ is the entropy of δ.

Proof There are 2^D vertices in the D-dimensional hypercube graph. Each vertex in the covering is within a Hamming distance of at most h for exactly $\sum_{k=0}^{h} \binom{D}{k}$ vertexes. Thus, one needs at least $2^D / \left(\sum_{k=0}^{h} \binom{D}{k} \right)$ vertexes to cover the hypercube graph. Now we apply the following bound (cf. Flum & Grohe 2006, page 427)

$$\sum_{k=0}^{\lfloor \delta D \rfloor} \binom{D}{k} \leq 2^{H(\delta)D}$$

to the denominator,[1] which is valid for any $0 < \delta \leq \frac{1}{2}$.   □

LEMMA A.3 *The minimum of the ℓ_p cost function A_p from the target $\mathbf{x}^A$ to the halfspace $\mathbb{H}^{(\mathbf{w}, \mathbf{b})} = \left\{ \mathbf{x} \mid \mathbf{x}^\top \mathbf{w} \geq \mathbf{b}^\top \mathbf{w} \right\}$ can be expressed in terms of the equivalent hyperplane $\mathbf{x}^\top \mathbf{w} \geq d$ parameterized by a normal vector $\mathbf{w}$ and displacement $d = \left(\mathbf{b} - \mathbf{x}^A \right)^\top \mathbf{w}$ as*

$$\min_{\mathbf{x} \in \mathbb{H}^{(\mathbf{w}, d)}} A_p \left(\mathbf{x} - \mathbf{x}^A \right) = \begin{cases} d \cdot \| \mathbf{w} \|_{\frac{p}{p-1}}^{-1}, & \text{if } d > 0 \\ 0, & \text{otherwise} \end{cases} \tag{A.5}$$

for all $1 < p < \infty$ and for $p = \infty$ it is

$$\min_{\mathbf{x} \in \mathbb{H}^{(\mathbf{w}, d)}} A_\infty \left(\mathbf{x} - \mathbf{x}^A \right) = \begin{cases} d \cdot \| \mathbf{w} \|_1^{-1}, & \text{if } d > 0 \\ 0, & \text{otherwise} \end{cases} . \tag{A.6}$$

Proof For $1 < p < \infty$, minimizing A_p on the halfspace $\mathbb{H}^{(\mathbf{w}, \mathbf{b})}$ is equivalent to finding a minimizer for

$$\min_{\mathbf{x}} \frac{1}{p} \sum_{i=1}^{D} |x_i|^p \quad \text{s.t.} \quad \mathbf{x}^\top \mathbf{w} \leq d.$$

Clearly, if $d \leq 0$ then the vector $\mathbf{0}$ (corresponding to $\mathbf{x}^A$ in the transformed space) trivially satisfies the constraint and minimizes the cost function with cost 0, which yields

---

[1] Gottlieb, Kontorovich, & Mossel (2011) present a tighter entropy bound on this sum of binomial coefficients, but it is unnecessary for our result.

the second case of Equation (A.5). For the case $d > 0$, we construct the Lagrangian

$$\mathcal{L}(\mathbf{x}, \lambda) \triangleq \frac{1}{p} \sum_{i=1}^{D} |x_i|^p - \lambda \left(\mathbf{x}^\top \mathbf{w} - d \right).$$

Differentiating this with respect to $\mathbf{x}$ and setting that partial derivative equal to zero yield

$$x_i^\star = \text{sign}(w_i) (\lambda |w_i|)^{\frac{1}{p-1}}.$$

Plugging this back into the Lagrangian yields

$$\mathcal{L}(\mathbf{x}^\star, \lambda) = \frac{1-p}{p} \lambda^{\frac{p}{p-1}} \sum_{i=1}^{D} |w_i|^{\frac{p}{p-1}} + \lambda d,$$

which we differentiate with respect to λ and set the derivative equal to zero to yield

$$\lambda^\star = \left(\frac{d}{\sum_{i=1}^{D} |w_i|^{\frac{p}{p-1}}} \right)^{p-1}.$$

Plugging this solution into the formula for $\mathbf{x}^\star$ yields the solution

$$x_i^\star = \text{sign}(w_i) \left(\frac{d}{\sum_{i=1}^{D} |w_i|^{\frac{p}{p-1}}} \right) |w_i|^{\frac{1}{p-1}}.$$

The ℓ_p cost of this optimal solution is given by

$$A_p \left(\mathbf{x}^\star - \mathbf{x}^A \right) = d \cdot \|\mathbf{w}\|_{\frac{p}{p-1}}^{-1},$$

which is the first case of Equation (A.5).

For $p = \infty$, once again if $d \le 0$ then the vector $\mathbf{0}$ trivially satisfies the constraint and minimizes the cost function with cost 0, which yields the second case of Equation (A.6). For the case $d > 0$, we use the geometry of hypercubes (the equi-cost balls of a ℓ_∞ cost function) to derive the second case of Equation (A.6). Any optimal solution must occur at a point where the hyperplane given by $\mathbf{x}^\top \mathbf{w} = \mathbf{b}^\top \mathbf{w}$ is tangent to a hypercube about $\mathbf{x}^A$—this can either occur along a side (face) of the hypercube or at a corner. However, if the plane is tangent along a side (face), it is also tangent at a corner of the hypercube. Hence, there is always an optimal solution at some corner of the optimal cost hypercube.

The corner of the hypercube has the following property:

$$|x_1^\star| = |x_2^\star| = \ldots = |x_D^\star|;$$

that is, the magnitude of all coordinates of this optimal solution is the same value. Further, the sign of the optimal solution's i^{th} coordinate must agree with the sign of the hyperplane's i^{th} coordinate, w_i. These constraints, along with the hyperplane constraint, lead to the following formula for an optimal solution:

$$x_i = d \cdot \text{sign}(w_i) \|\mathbf{w}\|_1^{-1}$$

for all i. The ℓ_∞ cost of this solution is simply $d \cdot \|\mathbf{w}\|_1^{-1}$. $\qquad\square$

Appendix B Full Proofs for Hypersphere Attacks

In this appendix, we give proofs for the theorems from Chapter 4. For this purpose, we introduce the concept of (τ, k)-*differing sequences*, which are a pair of sequences $\mathbf{a}, \mathbf{b} \in \mathcal{A}^{(M,\infty)}$ that are everywhere identical except in the τth, $\tau + 1^{\text{th}}$, ..., $\tau + k^{\text{th}}$ consecutive elements and have the following mass-balance property:

$$\sum_{t=\tau}^{\tau+k} a_t = \sum_{t=\tau}^{\tau+k} b_t. \tag{B.1}$$

The following lemma for $(\tau, 1)$-differing sequences simplifies several of the subsequent proofs.

LEMMA B.1 *For any $(\tau, 1)$-differing sequences $\mathbf{a}, \mathbf{b} \in \mathcal{A}^{(M,\infty)}$ that are identical except in their τ^{th} and $(\tau + 1)^{th}$ elements (with $a_\tau + a_{\tau+1} = b_\tau + b_{\tau+1}$ from Equation (B.1)), the difference between the distances of these sequences, $\Delta_{\mathbf{a},\mathbf{b}} \triangleq D(\mathbf{a}) - D(\mathbf{b})$, can be expressed as*

$$\Delta_{\mathbf{a},\mathbf{b}} = \frac{\left(\mu_{\tau-1}^{(\mathbf{a})} + b_\tau\right) \cdot a_\tau \cdot a_{\tau+1} - \left(\mu_{\tau-1}^{(\mathbf{a})} + a_\tau\right) \cdot b_\tau \cdot b_{\tau+1}}{\left(\mu_{\tau-1}^{(\mathbf{a})} + a_\tau\right)\left(\mu_{\tau-1}^{(\mathbf{a})} + b_\tau\right)\left(\mu_{\tau-1}^{(\mathbf{a})} + a_\tau + a_{\tau+1}\right)} \tag{B.2}$$

where $\mu_t^{(\mathbf{a})} = N + \sum_{\ell=1}^t a_\ell$ is the cumulative sum of the first t elements of the sequence $\mathbf{a}$ as in Equation (4.7). This holds so long as either $\mu_{\tau-1}^{(\mathbf{a})} > 0$ or both $a_\tau > 0$ and $b_\tau > 0$.

Proof First, for $t < \tau$, $\mu_t^{(\mathbf{a})} = \mu_t^{(\mathbf{b})}$ since the two sequences are identical until the τth element. Similarly, for $t > \tau + 1$ we again have $\mu_t^{(\mathbf{a})} = \mu_t^{(\mathbf{b})}$ since the sequences only differ in their τ^{th} and $(\tau + 1)^{\text{th}}$ elements and they are mass-balanced according to Equation (B.1) for which we define $\gamma \triangleq a_\tau + a_{\tau+1} = b_\tau + b_{\tau+1}$ as the balance constant for these sequences. Using these two facts and that, from Equation (4.12), $\delta_t(\mathbf{a}) = \frac{a_t}{\mu_t^{(\mathbf{a})}}$, we have that $\delta_t(\mathbf{a}) = \delta_t(\mathbf{b})$ if $t < \tau$ or $t > \tau + 1$. Thus difference in the distances achieved by these two sequences is given from Equations (4.11) can be expressed as

$$\Delta_{\mathbf{a},\mathbf{b}} = \sum_{t=1} [\delta_t(\mathbf{a}) - \delta_t(\mathbf{b})]$$

$$= \underbrace{\sum_{t=1}^{\tau-1} [\delta_t(\mathbf{a}) - \delta_t(\mathbf{b})]}_{=0} + \delta_\tau(\mathbf{a}) - \delta_\tau(\mathbf{b}) + \delta_{\tau+1}(\mathbf{a}) - \delta_{\tau+1}(\mathbf{b})$$

$$+ \underbrace{\sum_{t=\tau+2} [\delta_t(\mathbf{a}) - \delta_t(\mathbf{b})]}_{=0}$$

$$= \frac{a_\tau}{\mu_\tau^{(\mathbf{a})}} - \frac{b_\tau}{\mu_\tau^{(\mathbf{b})}} + \frac{a_{\tau+1}}{\mu_{\tau+1}^{(\mathbf{a})}} - \frac{b_{\tau+1}}{\mu_{\tau+1}^{(\mathbf{b})}}$$

$$= \frac{a_\tau}{\mu_{\tau-1}^{(\mathbf{a})} + a_\tau} - \frac{b_\tau}{\mu_{\tau-1}^{(\mathbf{a})} + b_\tau} + \frac{a_{\tau+1}}{\mu_{\tau-1}^{(\mathbf{a})} + \gamma} - \frac{b_{\tau+1}}{\mu_{\tau-1}^{(\mathbf{a})} + \gamma}.$$

To combine these four terms, we can obtain a common denominator of $\Gamma = \left(\mu_{\tau-1}^{(\mathbf{a})} + a_\tau\right)\left(\mu_{\tau-1}^{(\mathbf{a})} + b_\tau\right)\left(\mu_{\tau-1}^{(\mathbf{a})} + \gamma\right)$ for which the combined numerator is given by

$$\left[a_\tau \left(\mu_{\tau-1}^{(\mathbf{a})} + b_\tau\right) - b_\tau \left(\mu_{\tau-1}^{(\mathbf{a})} + a_\tau\right) \right] \left(\mu_{\tau-1}^{(\mathbf{a})} + \gamma\right)$$

$$+ (a_{\tau+1} - b_{\tau+1})\left(\mu_{\tau-1}^{(\mathbf{a})} + a_\tau\right)\left(\mu_{\tau-1}^{(\mathbf{a})} + b_\tau\right)$$

$$= \mu_{\tau-1}^{(\mathbf{a})} a_\tau a_{\tau+1} - \mu_{\tau-1}^{(\mathbf{a})} b_\tau b_{\tau+1} + b_\tau a_\tau a_{\tau+1} - a_\tau b_\tau b_{\tau+1}$$

$$= \left(\mu_{\tau-1}^{(\mathbf{a})} + b_\tau\right) \cdot a_\tau \cdot a_{\tau+1} - \left(\mu_{\tau-1}^{(\mathbf{a})} + a_\tau\right) \cdot b_\tau \cdot b_{\tau+1},$$

in which we used the definition of γ to cancel terms. Combining this numerator with the denominator Γ yields Equation (B.2). Finally the condition that either $\mu_{\tau-1}^{(\mathbf{a})} > 0$ or both $a_\tau > 0$ and $b_\tau > 0$ is necessary to prevent the denominator from becoming zero. ☐

B.1   Proof of Theorem 4.7

Here we show that the optimal attack according to Equation (4.5) can be optimized in a greedy fashion. Further, we show that the optimal attack points are all placed at the intersection of the hypersphere's boundary and the desired attack direction.

Proof Consider the tth iteration of the attack for any $t \in \mathfrak{N}$. The attacker's goal in the tth iteration is to maximize the displacement alignment given in Equation (4.5). The attacker accomplishes this by crafting a set of $\alpha_t \in \mathfrak{N}$ attack points: $\mathbb{A}^{(t)} = \{\mathbf{a}^{(t,\ell)}\}_{\ell=1}^{\alpha_t}$. These points are designed to maximize $\mathbf{D}_t^\top \frac{\mathbf{x}^A - \mathbf{c}^{(0)}}{\|\mathbf{x}^A - \mathbf{c}^{(0)}\|}$ where $\mathbf{D}_t = \frac{\mathbf{c}^{(t)} - \mathbf{c}^{(0)}}{R}$ by Equation (4.4), $\mathbf{c}^{(t)}$ is defined recursively by Equation (4.8), and each attack vector is constrained to lie within the $(t-1)^{\text{th}}$ hypersphere; i.e., $\|\mathbf{a}^{(t,\ell)} - \mathbf{c}^{(t-1)}\| \le R$ for all $\ell = 1, \ldots, \alpha_t$. The attacker's objective can be modified without loss of generality by first transforming the space so that $\mathbf{c}^{(t-1)} = \mathbf{0}$ (via the transform $\hat{\mathbf{x}} \mapsto \mathbf{x} - \mathbf{c}^{(t-1)}$). This yields the following equivalent program that the attack optimizes:

$$\max_{\mathbb{A}^{(t)}} \rho\left(\hat{\mathbf{D}}_t\right) = \hat{\mathbf{D}}_t^\top \frac{\hat{\mathbf{x}}^A - \hat{\mathbf{c}}^{(0)}}{\left\|\hat{\mathbf{x}}^A - \hat{\mathbf{c}}^{(0)}\right\|}$$

$$\text{s.t.} \qquad \forall\, \ell \in 1, \ldots, \alpha_t \quad \left\|\hat{\mathbf{a}}^{(t,\ell)}\right\|^2 \le R^2,$$

where $\hat{\mathbf{D}}_t = \frac{\hat{\mathbf{c}}^{(t)} - \hat{\mathbf{c}}^{(0)}}{R}$ and $\hat{\mathbf{c}}^{(t)}$ takes the simplified form $\hat{\mathbf{c}}^{(t)} = \frac{1}{\mu_t}\sum_{\ell=1}^{\alpha_t} \hat{\mathbf{a}}^{(t,\ell)}$. The Lagrangian for this program at the tth attack iteration is

$$\mathcal{L}_t\left(\left\{\hat{\mathbf{a}}^{(t,\ell)}\right\}, \lambda\right) = \hat{\mathbf{D}}_t^\top \frac{\hat{\mathbf{x}}^A - \hat{\mathbf{c}}^{(0)}}{\left\|\hat{\mathbf{x}}^A - \hat{\mathbf{c}}^{(0)}\right\|} - \sum_{\ell=1}^{\alpha_t} \lambda_\ell\left(\left\|\hat{\mathbf{a}}^{(t,\ell)}\right\|^2 - R^2\right)$$

$$= \frac{1}{R\mu_t\left\|\hat{\mathbf{x}}^A - \hat{\mathbf{c}}^{(0)}\right\|}\sum_{\ell=1}^{\alpha_t}\left(\hat{\mathbf{a}}^{(t,\ell)}\right)^\top\left(\hat{\mathbf{x}}^A - \hat{\mathbf{c}}^{(0)}\right) - \sum_{\ell=1}^{\alpha_t}\lambda_\ell(\hat{\mathbf{a}}^{(t,\ell)})^\top\hat{\mathbf{a}}^{(t,\ell)}$$

$$- \frac{\left(\hat{\mathbf{c}}^{(0)}\right)^\top\left(\hat{\mathbf{x}}^A - \hat{\mathbf{c}}^{(0)}\right)}{R\left\|\hat{\mathbf{x}}^A - \hat{\mathbf{c}}^{(0)}\right\|} + R^2\sum_{\ell=1}^{\alpha_t}\lambda_\ell$$

where the variables $\lambda_\ell \ge 0$ are the Lagrangian multipliers and the second equality follows from expanding the above form of $\hat{\mathbf{D}}_t$.

We compute the partial derivatives of $\mathcal{L}_t\left(\left\{\hat{\mathbf{a}}^{(t,\ell)}\right\}, \lambda\right)$ with respect to the Lagrangian multipliers λ and set them to zero to reveal that, at a solution, $\left\|\hat{\mathbf{a}}^{(t,\ell)}\right\| = R$. Further, by the complementary slackness conditions that arise from the dual of the above program, it follows that the Lagrangian multipliers are non-zero; i.e., $\forall\, i \; \lambda_i \ge 0$. Then computing the partial derivatives of $\mathcal{L}_t\left(\left\{\hat{\mathbf{a}}^{(t,\ell)}\right\}, \lambda\right)$ with respect to each $\hat{\mathbf{a}}^{(t,\ell)}$ and setting them to zero reveals that, at a solution, we must have for all ℓ,

$$\hat{\mathbf{a}}^{(t,\ell)} = \frac{1}{2\lambda_\ell R\mu_t}\frac{\hat{\mathbf{x}}^A - \hat{\mathbf{c}}^{(0)}}{\left\|\hat{\mathbf{x}}^A - \hat{\mathbf{c}}^{(0)}\right\|},$$

which demonstrates that all optimal attack vectors must be a scaled version of the vector $\hat{\mathbf{x}}^A - \hat{\mathbf{c}}^{(0)}$. Thus, by the fact that $\left\|\hat{\mathbf{a}}^{(t,\ell)}\right\| = R$, we must have

$$\hat{\mathbf{a}}^{(t,\ell)} = R \cdot \frac{\hat{\mathbf{x}}^A - \hat{\mathbf{c}}^{(0)}}{\left\|\hat{\mathbf{x}}^A - \hat{\mathbf{c}}^{(0)}\right\|} \qquad \text{and} \qquad \hat{\mathbf{c}}^{(t)} = R \cdot \frac{\alpha_t}{\mu_t} \cdot \frac{\hat{\mathbf{x}}^A - \hat{\mathbf{c}}^{(0)}}{\left\|\hat{\mathbf{x}}^A - \hat{\mathbf{c}}^{(0)}\right\|}.$$

By reversing the transform making $\mathbf{c}^{(t-1)} = \mathbf{0}$, the attack vectors can be expressed as

$$\mathbf{a}^{(t,\ell)} = \mathbf{c}^{(t-1)} + R \cdot \frac{\mathbf{x}^A - \mathbf{c}^{(0)}}{\left\|\mathbf{x}^A - \mathbf{c}^{(0)}\right\|},$$

which gives the first part of the theorem. Similarly by reversing this transform for the centroids and solving the resulting simple recursion we arrive at

$$\mathbf{c}^{(t)} = \mathbf{c}^{(t-1)} + R \cdot \frac{\alpha_t}{\mu_t} \cdot \frac{\mathbf{x}^A - \mathbf{c}^{(0)}}{\left\|\mathbf{x}^A - \mathbf{c}^{(0)}\right\|} \qquad = \mathbf{c}^{(0)} + R \cdot \frac{\mathbf{x}^A - \mathbf{c}^{(0)}}{\left\|\mathbf{x}^A - \mathbf{c}^{(0)}\right\|} \cdot \sum_{\ell=1}^{t}\frac{\alpha_\ell}{\mu_\ell},$$

as was to be shown. $\qquad\qquad\qquad\qquad\qquad\qquad\qquad\qquad\qquad\qquad\qquad\qquad\qquad\square$

B.2   Proof of Theorem 4.14

Proof We show that any optimal sequence with $M \in \mathfrak{N}_0$ attack points (in the sense of Definition 4.10) must have a monotonically increasing sequence of non-zero elements. For $M = 0$, the trivial sequence $\boldsymbol{\alpha}^\star = \mathbf{0}$ is the only sequence in $\mathcal{A}^{(M,\infty)}$ and thus is optimal (and trivially satisfies the theorem).

For $M > 0$, the proof proceeds *by contradiction* by assuming that there exists an such that there is an optimal sequence, $\boldsymbol{\alpha}^\star \in \mathcal{A}^{(M,\infty)}$ with a sub-sequence of non-zero elements that is not monotonically non-decreasing. To simplify the proof, we instead consider an equivalent sequence (with respect to the distance function) with all interleaving zero elements removed from $\boldsymbol{\alpha}^\star$. As shown in Theorem 4.12, the placement of zero elements in the sequence *does not affect* the distance function $D(\cdot)$. Thus, the sequence $\boldsymbol{\alpha}^\star$ achieves the same distance as the sequence $\boldsymbol{\alpha}^{opt}$ created by removing the zero elements of $\boldsymbol{\alpha}^\star$. Moreover, for $\boldsymbol{\alpha}^\star$ to not be non-decreasing in some non-zero sub-sequence, the sequence $\boldsymbol{\alpha}^{opt}$ *must* have at least one pair of adjacent decreasing elements. That is, there exists an index τ such that the τth and $(\tau + 1)^{\text{th}}$ elements decrease: $\alpha_\tau^{opt} > \alpha_{\tau+1}^{opt}$.

We show that, by switching these elements, the distance achieved by the resulting sequence exceeds that of $\boldsymbol{\alpha}^{opt}$; i.e., $\boldsymbol{\alpha}^{opt}$ is not optimal. Formally, we assume that

$$\exists \boldsymbol{\alpha}^{opt} \in \mathcal{A}^{(M,\infty)} \quad \text{s.t.} \quad \forall \boldsymbol{\alpha} \in \mathcal{A}^{(M,\infty)} \quad D\left(\boldsymbol{\alpha}^{opt}\right) \geq D(\boldsymbol{\alpha}) \tag{B.3}$$

$$\text{and} \quad \exists \tau \in \mathfrak{N} \quad \text{s.t.} \quad \alpha_\tau^{opt} > \alpha_{\tau+1}^{opt} > 0. \tag{B.4}$$

Now we consider an alternative sequence $\boldsymbol{\alpha}' \in \mathcal{A}^{(M,\infty)}$ that switches the τth and $(\tau + 1)^{\text{th}}$ element of $\boldsymbol{\alpha}^{opt}$:

$$\alpha_t' = \begin{cases} \alpha_t^{opt}, & \text{if } t < \tau \\ \alpha_{t+1}^{opt}, & \text{if } t = \tau \\ \alpha_{t-1}^{opt}, & \text{if } t = \tau + 1 \\ \alpha_t^{opt}, & \text{if } t > \tau + 1 \end{cases}.$$

By design, $\boldsymbol{\alpha}^{opt}$ and $\boldsymbol{\alpha}'$ are $(\tau, 1)$-differing sequences and thus we can compute the difference in their distances by applying Lemma B.1 to yield[1]

$$\Delta_{\boldsymbol{\alpha}^{opt}, \boldsymbol{\alpha}'} = \frac{\left(\mu_{\tau-1}^{(\boldsymbol{\alpha}^{opt})} + \alpha_\tau'\right) \cdot \alpha_\tau^{opt} \cdot \alpha_{\tau+1}^{opt} - \left(\mu_{\tau-1}^{(\boldsymbol{\alpha}^{opt})} + \alpha_\tau^{opt}\right) \cdot \alpha_\tau' \cdot \alpha_{\tau+1}'}{\left(\mu_{\tau-1}^{(\boldsymbol{\alpha}^{opt})} + \alpha_\tau^{opt}\right)\left(\mu_{\tau-1}^{(\boldsymbol{\alpha}^{opt})} + \alpha_\tau'\right)\left(\mu_{\tau-1}^{(\boldsymbol{\alpha}^{opt})} + \alpha_\tau^{opt} + \alpha_{\tau+1}^{opt}\right)}$$

$$= \frac{\left(\alpha_{\tau+1}^{opt} - \alpha_\tau^{opt}\right) \cdot \alpha_\tau^{opt} \cdot \alpha_{\tau+1}^{opt}}{\left(\mu_{\tau-1}^{(\boldsymbol{\alpha}^{opt})} + \alpha_\tau^{opt}\right)\left(\mu_{\tau-1}^{(\boldsymbol{\alpha}^{opt})} + \alpha_{\tau+1}^{opt}\right)\left(\mu_{\tau-1}^{(\boldsymbol{\alpha}^{opt})} + \alpha_\tau^{opt} + \alpha_{\tau+1}^{opt}\right)},$$

in which $\mu_t^{(\boldsymbol{\alpha}^{opt})} = N + \sum_{\ell=1}^t \alpha_\ell^{opt}$ from Lemma B.1.

---

[1] Although $\mu_{\tau-1}^{(\boldsymbol{\alpha}^{opt})}$ may be zero (e.g., if $\tau = 0$), the lemma is applicable since we assumed $\alpha_\tau^{opt} > \alpha_{\tau+1}^{opt} > 0$.

The denominator in the above expression is strictly positive since $\alpha_\tau^{opt} > 0$, $\alpha_{\tau+1}^{opt} >$ 0 and $\mu_{\tau-1}^{(\alpha^{opt})} \geq 0$. Further, from assumption (B.4), we have that $\alpha_\tau^{opt} > \alpha_{\tau+1}^{opt} > 0$, and hence, the above numerator is strictly less than zero.[2] Thus, we have $\Delta_{\alpha^{opt},\alpha'} = D(\alpha^{opt}) - D(\alpha') < 0$, from which we conclude that $D(\alpha^\star) = D(\alpha^{opt}) < D(\alpha')$. This contradicts assumption (B.3) that $\alpha^\star$ is optimal, thus showing that any sequence with a sub-sequence of its non-zero elements that is not monotonically non-decreasing is non-optimal. Hence, every sub-sequence of the non-zero elements of any optimal attack sequence must be monotonically non-decreasing. $\square$

B.3   Proof of Theorem 4.15

We show that the optimal distances achieved by attack sequences are strictly monotonically increasing in the attack capacity available to the attacker and the attack duration during which the attack is executed. To do so, we first demonstrate that it is non-optimal to use all attack points during a single retraining iteration unless there is only a single attack point or retraining iteration.

LEMMA B.2 *For $M > 1$ and $T > 1$, any attack α with only a single non-zero element τ (i.e., such that $\alpha_\tau > 0$ and $\alpha_t = 0$ for all $t \neq \tau$) is a non-optimal sequence.*

Proof Any such sequence α described above achieves distance 1 by Equations (4.11) and (4.12). For $\alpha_\tau = 1$, we construct the alternative sequence $\alpha'_1 = 1$ and $\alpha'_2 = 1$, which is in $\mathcal{A}^{(M,T)}$ for $M > 1$ and $T > 1$ and achieves a distance of $\frac{3}{2} > 1$. Thus, this alternative sequence achieves a higher distance than any sequence with a single element that is one and so these are not optimal sequences.

Similarly, for $\alpha_\tau > 1$, we again construct an alternative sequence α' with $\alpha'_1 = \alpha_\tau - 1$ and $\alpha'_2 = 1$, which has the same attack size as α and also has a duration of 2, which places it in $\mathcal{A}^{(M,T)}$ for $M > 1$ and $T > 1$. Further, the alternative sequence achieves a distance of $1 + \frac{1}{\alpha_\tau} > 1$. Thus, we have demonstrated an alternative sequence in this space that achieves a higher distance and so any such sequence with a single non-zero element is not optimal. $\square$

This lemma is one of several results needed for the proof of Theorem 4.15 below. Additionally, it assumes that there is a greatest non-zero element within any sequence of finite attack size, M. This is true for all integral sequences, but does not hold for continuously valued sequences as discussed below. We now present the main proof of this section.

Proof of Theorem 4.15 First we show that, for any fixed $N > 0$, $D_N^\star(M, \infty)$ and $D_N^\star(M, T)$ are strictly monotonically increasing with respect to $M \in \mathfrak{N}_0$; i.e., $\forall M^{(1)} < M^{(2)} \in \mathfrak{N}_0$, we claim $D_N^\star(M^{(1)}, \infty) < D_N^\star(M^{(2)}, \infty)$ and that, for any fixed $T \in \mathfrak{N}$, $D_N^\star(M^{(1)}, T) < D_N^\star(M^{(2)}, T)$. By Definition 4.10 of $D_N^\star(\cdot, \infty)$, there exists a

---

[2] Notice that, if either $\alpha_\tau^{opt} = 0$ or $\alpha_{\tau+1}^{opt} = 0$, the numerator would be zero, thus giving the two sequences equal distances and making this result consistent with Theorem 4.12.

sequence $\alpha^\star \in \mathcal{A}^{(M^{(1)},\infty)}$ such that $D(\alpha^\star) = D_N^\star(M^{(1)}, \infty)$. However, we also have $\alpha^\star \in \mathcal{A}^{(M^{(2)},\infty)}$; that is, any optimal sequence from $\mathcal{A}^{(M^{(1)},\infty)}$ is also in the space $\mathcal{A}^{(M^{(2)},\infty)}$ but uses at most $M^{(1)} < M^{(2)}$ of its total attack capacity. Moreover, since $\sum_t \alpha_t^\star \leq M^{(1)}$ and all sequences consist of elements $\alpha_t^\star \in \mathfrak{N}_0$, there must exist a last non-zero index $\tau \in \mathfrak{N}$ of $\alpha_t^\star$; i.e., for all $t > \tau, \alpha_t^\star = 0$. From this, we construct an alternate sequence α', which is identical to $\alpha^\star$ except that we add the excess attack capacity to its last non-zero element: $\alpha_\tau' = \alpha_\tau^\star + m$ where $m = M^{(2)} - M^{(1)} > 0$. The difference in the distances of these two sequences is simply the difference in their final non-zero contributions:

$$
\begin{aligned}
D(\alpha^\star) - D(\alpha') &= \delta_\tau(\alpha^\star) - \delta_\tau(\alpha') \\
&= \frac{\alpha_\tau^\star}{M^{(1)} + N} - \frac{\alpha_\tau^\star + m}{M^{(2)} + N} \\
&= \frac{\alpha_\tau^\star M^{(2)} + \alpha_\tau^\star N - \alpha_\tau^\star M^{(1)} - \alpha_\tau^\star N - mM^{(1)} - mN}{(M^{(1)} + N)(M^{(2)} + N)} \\
&= \frac{(\alpha_\tau^\star - M^{(1)} - N) m}{(M^{(1)} + N)(M^{(2)} + N)},
\end{aligned}
$$

where $m > 0$ and $M^{(2)} > M^{(1)} \geq 0$. All terms in this ratio are *positive* except the term $(\alpha_\tau^\star - M^{(1)} - N)$, which is *negative* since $\alpha_\tau^\star \leq M^{(1)}$ and $N \geq 1$. Thus, the above difference is negative and $D_N^\star(M^{(2)}, \infty) \geq D(\alpha') > D(\alpha^\star) = D_N^\star(M^{(1)}, \infty)$. This proof also holds for any fixed $T \geq 1$, thus also showing that $D_N^\star(M^{(2)}, T) > D_N^\star(M^{(1)}, T)$.

Second, for $N = 0$, we demonstrate strict monotonicity of $D_0^\star(\cdot, \infty)$ and $D_0^\star(\cdot, T)$ for any $T > 1$. Since $D_0^\star(M, \infty) \geq 0$ for any $M \in \mathfrak{N}_0$, and $D_0^\star(M, \infty) = 0$ if and only if $M = 0$, we have that $D_0^\star(M, \infty) > D_0^\star(0, \infty)$ for any $M > 0$, as required. In the case $M^{(2)} > M^{(1)} = 1$, every sequence in $\mathcal{A}^{(1,\infty)}$ (or $\mathcal{A}^{(1,T)}$) achieves $D_0^\star(1, \infty) = D_0^\star(1, T) = 1$. Further the sequence $(1, 1)$ is in $\mathcal{A}^{(M^{(2)},\infty)}$ for all $M^{(2)} > 1$ (and also in $\mathcal{A}^{(M^{(2)},T)}$ for any $T > 1$), and it achieves a distance of $1 + \frac{1}{2}$, thus exceeding $D_0^\star(1, \infty)$. Thus, it again follows that $D_0^\star(M^{(2)}, \infty) > D_0^\star(1, \infty)$ and for any fixed $T > 1$, $D_0^\star(M^{(2)}, T) > D_0^\star(1, T)$. Finally, for $M^{(2)} > M^{(1)} > 1$, we use a similar proof as was used above for $N > 0$. Again, there is a sequence $\alpha^\star \in \mathcal{A}^{(M^{(1)},\infty)}$ such that $D(\alpha^\star) = D_0^\star(M^{(1)}, \infty)$ and we take τ to be index of the last non-zero element of $\alpha^\star$. We again contruct an alternate sequence α' that is identical to $\alpha^\star$ except the excess attack capacity is added to its last non-zero element: $\alpha_\tau' = \alpha_\tau^\star + m$ where $m = M^{(2)} - M^{(1)} > 0$. Then, as above, in examining the difference in the distances of these two sequences, it can be shown that

$$
D(\alpha^\star) - D(\alpha') = \frac{(\alpha_\tau^\star - M^{(1)}) m}{M^{(1)} \cdot M^{(2)}},
$$

where $m > 0$ and $M^{(2)} > M^{(1)} > 1$. Again, all terms in the fraction are *positive* except the term $(\alpha_\tau^\star - M^{(1)})$. But, by Lemma B.2, $\alpha^\star \in \mathcal{A}^{(M^{(1)},\infty)}$ for $M^{(1)} > 1$ cannot be optimal unless $\alpha_\tau^\star < M^{(1)}$. Thus the above difference is negative and $D_0^\star(M^{(2)}, \infty) \geq D(\alpha') > D(\alpha^\star) = D_0^\star(M^{(1)}, \infty)$. This proof construction also holds for any fixed duration $T > 1$, thus also showing that $D_0^\star(M^{(2)}, T) > D_0^\star(M^{(1)}, T)$.

Thirdly, we show that $D_N^\star (M, T)$ is strictly monotonically increasing with respect to $T \in \{1, \ldots, M\}$; that is, for any fixed $N \in \mathfrak{N}_0$ and $M \in \mathfrak{N}$ and $\forall\, T_1 < T_2 \in \{1, \ldots, M\}$, we claim $D_N^\star (M, T_1) < D_N^\star (M, T_2)$.

For $T_1, T_2 \leq M$, by Definition 4.10 of $D_N^\star (M, T)$, there exists a sequence $\boldsymbol{\alpha}^\star \in \mathcal{A}^{(M,T_1)}$ such that $D(\boldsymbol{\alpha}^\star) = D_N^\star (M, T_1)$. However, since $T_2 > T_1$, we also have $\boldsymbol{\alpha}^\star \in \mathcal{A}^{(M,T_2)}$; that is, any optimal sequence from $\mathcal{A}^{(M,T_1)}$ is also in the space $\mathcal{A}^{(M,T_2)}$ but has a trailing sequence of zeros: $\alpha_{T_1+1}^\star = \ldots = \alpha_{T_2}^\star = 0$. Alternatively, there is some last index $\tau < T_2$ such that $\alpha_\tau^\star > 0$ and $\alpha_t^\star = 0$ for all $t > \tau$.

In fact, this τ^{th} element must be greater than 1 since, by Theorem 4.14, the non-zero elements of $\boldsymbol{\alpha}^\star$ must be non-decreasing. Thus, either $\alpha_\tau^\star > 1$ or all previous elements must be in $\{0, 1\}$. However, since $\tau < T_2 \leq M$, such a sequence can have at most $M - 1$ elements, but the first part of this theorem already showed that such a sequence is not optimal. Hence, $\alpha_\tau^\star > 1$.

Using this fact, we can construct an alternative sequence $\boldsymbol{\alpha}' \in \mathcal{A}^{(M,T_2)}$ that moves one attack point from the τth element of $\boldsymbol{\alpha}^\star$ to its $(\tau + 1)^{\text{th}}$ element:

$$
\alpha_t' = \begin{cases}
\alpha_t^\star, & \text{if } t < \tau \\
\alpha_t^\star - 1, & \text{if } t = \tau \\
1, & \text{if } t = \tau + 1 \\
\alpha_{t-1}^\star, & \text{if } t > \tau + 1
\end{cases}.
$$

By design, $\boldsymbol{\alpha}^\star$ and $\boldsymbol{\alpha}'$ are $(\tau, 1)$-differing sequences and Lemma B.1 yields

$$
\Delta_{\boldsymbol{\alpha}^\star, \boldsymbol{\alpha}'} = \frac{\left(\mu_{\tau-1}^{(\boldsymbol{\alpha}^\star)} + \alpha_\tau' \right) \cdot \alpha_\tau^\star \cdot \alpha_{\tau+1}^\star - \left(\mu_{\tau-1}^{(\boldsymbol{\alpha}^\star)} + \alpha_\tau^\star \right) \cdot \alpha_\tau' \cdot \alpha_{\tau+1}'}{\left(\mu_{\tau-1}^{(\boldsymbol{\alpha}^\star)} + \alpha_\tau^\star \right) \left(\mu_{\tau-1}^{(\boldsymbol{\alpha}^\star)} + \alpha_\tau' \right) \left(\mu_{\tau-1}^{(\boldsymbol{\alpha}^\star)} + \alpha_\tau^\star + \alpha_{\tau+1}^\star \right)}
$$

$$
= \frac{-1 \cdot \left(\mu_{\tau-1}^{(\boldsymbol{\alpha}^\star)} + \alpha_\tau^\star \right) \cdot \left(\alpha_\tau^\star - 1 \right)}{\left(\mu_{\tau-1}^{(\boldsymbol{\alpha}^\star)} + \alpha_\tau^\star \right) \left(\mu_{\tau-1}^{(\boldsymbol{\alpha}^\star)} + \alpha_\tau' \right) \left(\mu_{\tau-1}^{(\boldsymbol{\alpha}^\star)} + \alpha_\tau^\star + \alpha_{\tau+1}^\star \right)}
$$

in which $\mu_t^{(\boldsymbol{\alpha}^{opt})} = N + \sum_{\ell=1}^t \alpha_\ell^{opt}$. This difference is negative, from which we conclude that $D(\boldsymbol{\alpha}^\star) < D(\boldsymbol{\alpha}')$. This contradicts assumption (B.3) that $\boldsymbol{\alpha}^\star$ is optimal in $\mathcal{A}^{(M,T_2)}$; i.e., we have shown there is a sequence in $\mathcal{A}^{(M,T_2)}$ whose distance exceeds $D_N^\star (M, T_1)$. Thus, $D_N^\star (M, T)$ is strictly monotonically increasing for $T \leq M$.

Finally, to see that $D_N^\star (M, T) = D_N^\star (M, \infty)$ for $T \geq M$, any sequence in $\mathcal{A}^{(M,T)}$ must have at least $M - T$ zero elements. As we showed in Theorem 4.12, the distance of a sequence is invariant to the placement of these zero elements so, without loss of generality, we can place them at the end. Thus, any sequence in $\mathcal{A}^{(M,T)}$ achieves the same distance as a sequence in $\mathcal{A}^{(M,M)}$, and the optimal distances achieved within these two spaces is equal. $\qquad\square$

Notice that the above argument does not hold for the space $\mathcal{B}^{(M,\infty)}$ of all positive-real-valued sequences with total mass of M since there need not be a greatest non-zero element in such a sequence. However, optimality is not well-defined on such a space. This proof does, however, extend directly to sequences in $\mathcal{B}^{(M,T)}$ since the finite attack duration T implies the existence of a greatest non-zero element.

B.4   Proof of Theorem 4.16

The proof of this theorem is again similar to the proofs in the previous sections.

Proof We show that any optimal sequence $\boldsymbol{\alpha}^\star \in \mathcal{A}^{(M,\infty)}$ only has elements in the set $\{0, 1\}$. This is trivially satisfied for $\mathbf{0}$, the only sequence in $\mathcal{A}^{(0,\infty)}$, and thus is optimal.

For $M > 0$, the proof proceeds *by contradiction* by assuming that there is an optimal sequence, $\boldsymbol{\alpha}^\star \in \mathcal{A}^{(M,\infty)}$, for which there exists a τ such that $\alpha_\tau^\star > 1$. We will arrive at a contradiction to the claim that this $\boldsymbol{\alpha}^\star$ achieves an optimal displacement within $\mathcal{A}^{(M,\infty)}$ by instead considering the equivalent (with respect to the distance function) sequence $\boldsymbol{\alpha}^{opt}$, which is identical to $\boldsymbol{\alpha}^\star$ except that a zero is inserted after the τth element and all subsequent elements are shifted to the next index; i.e., $\alpha_\tau^{opt} > 1$ and $\alpha_{\tau+1}^{opt} = 0$. As shown in Lemma 4.11, removing (or inserting) a zero elements in the sequence *does not affect* the distance function $D(\,\cdot\,)$. Thus, the sequence $\boldsymbol{\alpha}^\star$ achieves the same distance as the sequence $\boldsymbol{\alpha}^{opt}$.

We show that there is an alternative sequence, whose distance exceeds that of $\boldsymbol{\alpha}^{opt}$; i.e., $\boldsymbol{\alpha}^{opt}$ is not optimal. Formally, we first assume that

$$\exists \boldsymbol{\alpha}^{opt} \in \mathcal{A}^{(M,\infty)} \text{ s.t.} \quad \forall \boldsymbol{\alpha} \in \mathcal{A}^{(M,\infty)} \quad D\left(\boldsymbol{\alpha}^{opt}\right) \geq D\left(\boldsymbol{\alpha}\right) \tag{B.5}$$

$$\text{and} \quad \exists \tau \in \mathfrak{N} \text{ s.t.} \quad \alpha_\tau^{opt} > 1 \wedge \alpha_{\tau+1}^{opt} = 0. \tag{B.6}$$

Now we consider an alternative sequence $\boldsymbol{\alpha}' \in \mathcal{A}^{(M,\infty)}$ that shifts 1 unit from α_τ^{opt} to $\alpha_{\tau+1}^{opt}$

$$\alpha_t' = \begin{cases} \alpha_t^{opt}, & \text{if } t < \tau \\ \alpha_t^{opt} - 1, & \text{if } t = \tau \\ 1, & \text{if } t = \tau + 1 \\ \alpha_t^{opt}, & \text{if } t > \tau + 1 \end{cases}.$$

By design, $\boldsymbol{\alpha}^{opt}$ and $\boldsymbol{\alpha}'$ are $(\tau, 1)$-differing sequences and thus we can compute the difference in their distances by applying Lemma B.1 to yield[3]

$$\Delta_{\boldsymbol{\alpha}^{opt},\boldsymbol{\alpha}'} = \frac{\left(\mu_{\tau-1}^{(\boldsymbol{\alpha}^{opt})} + \alpha_\tau'\right) \cdot \alpha_\tau^{opt} \cdot \alpha_{\tau+1}^{opt} - \left(\mu_{\tau-1}^{(\boldsymbol{\alpha}^{opt})} + \alpha_\tau^{opt}\right) \cdot \alpha_\tau' \cdot \alpha_{\tau+1}'}{\left(\mu_{\tau-1}^{(\boldsymbol{\alpha}^{opt})} + \alpha_\tau^{opt}\right)\left(\mu_{\tau-1}^{(\boldsymbol{\alpha}^{opt})} + \alpha_\tau'\right)\left(\mu_{\tau-1}^{(\boldsymbol{\alpha}^{opt})} + \alpha_\tau^{opt} + \alpha_{\tau+1}^{opt}\right)}$$

$$= \frac{\left(\mu_{\tau-1}^{(\boldsymbol{\alpha}^{opt})} + \alpha_\tau^{opt}\right) \cdot \left(1 - \alpha_\tau^{opt}\right)}{\left(\mu_{\tau-1}^{(\boldsymbol{\alpha}^{opt})} + \alpha_\tau^{opt}\right)^2 \left(\mu_{\tau-1}^{(\boldsymbol{\alpha}^{opt})} + \alpha_\tau^{opt} - 1\right)},$$

in which $\mu_t^{(\boldsymbol{\alpha}^{opt})} = N + \sum_{\ell=1}^t \alpha_\ell^{opt}$ from Lemma B.1.

The denominator in the above expression is strictly positive since $\alpha_\tau^{opt} > 1$ and $\mu_{\tau-1}^{(\boldsymbol{\alpha}^{opt})} \geq 0$. Further, from assumption (B.6), we have that $\alpha_\tau^{opt} > 1$, and hence, the

---

[3] Although $\mu_{\tau-1}^{(\boldsymbol{\alpha}^{opt})}$ may be zero (e.g., if $\tau = 0$), the lemma is applicable since we assumed $\alpha_\tau^{opt} > 1$.

above numerator is negative.[4] Thus, we have $\Delta_{\alpha^{opt},\alpha'} = D(\alpha^{opt}) - D(\alpha') < 0$, from which we conclude that $D(\alpha^\star) = D(\alpha^{opt}) < D(\alpha')$. This contradicts assumption (B.5) that $\alpha^\star$ is optimal, thus showing that any sequence with an element not in $\{0, 1\}$ is non-optimal. Hence, any optimal sequence must have $\alpha_t^\star \in \{0, 1\}$ for all t. Further, an optimal sequence $\alpha^\star \in \mathcal{A}^{(M,\infty)}$ must have exactly M ones since, by Theorem 4.15, $D_0^\star(M, \infty)$ strictly increases in M.

Finally, the optimal displacement can be derived by supposing first that the adversary can control all $M + N$ points, including the initial N points. As we showed above, one optimal sequence is $\mathbf{1}_{M+N}$. It then follows from substituting $\alpha_t = 1$ and $\mu_t = t$ into Equation (4.11) that $D(\mathbf{1}_{M+N}) = \sum_t^{M+N} \frac{1}{t} = h_{M+N}$. Now we subtract the contribution from the first N points, which is h_N. This yields the result for $D_N^\star(M, \infty)$.   □

B.5   Proof of Theorem 4.18

The final proof we present here is for optimal attacks of a limited duration T using the relaxation to continuous attack sequences introduced in Section 4.4.1. In this continuous domain, we optimize Program (4.16) using optimization techniques.

Proof To optimize the objection function of Equation (4.15) in terms of the continuous sequences μ, we first verify that this function is well-behaved for feasible sequences. For all t, $\mu_t > 0$ since μ_t is monotonically non-decreasing in t and $\mu_0 = N > 0$. Any such sequence thus can be characterized as a positive-valued vector; i.e., $\mu \in (0, \infty)^T$. On this domain, the objective function given in Equation (4.15) is continuous as are its first derivatives. Thus, by Theorem 1.2.3 of Peressini, Sullivan & Jerry J. Uhl (1988), the extrema of this function are either its stationary points or lie on the boundary.

First, we eliminate the possibility that an optimum exists at the boundary. Any sequence on the boundary of this domain must have two or more consecutive elements in the total mass sequence that are equal, or rather, in the original formulation, there must be an element $\beta_j = 0$. By Theorem 4.12, such a boundary sequence is equivalent to a sequence of length $T - 1$. However, by Theorem 4.15, the function $D_0^\star(M, T)$ is increasing in T, unless $T \geq M$. Thus, no boundary point of the total mass formulation is an optimal sequence and so every optimal sequence must be a critical point of the objective.

Second, to find the stationary points of this objective function, we solve for sequences that make its partial derivatives equal zero. For each $\tau \in 1 \dots T - 1$, the partial

---

[4] An astute reader may wonder what this analysis implies when $\alpha_\tau^{opt} \in \{0, 1\}$. For $\alpha_\tau^{opt} = 0$, the sequence α' would have have a negative τth element and thus is not in $\mathcal{A}^{(M,\infty)}$. For $\alpha_\tau^{opt} = 1$, the above numerator is zero, but the denominator also may be zero so Lemma B.1 does not always apply. Instead, the alternate sequence α' can be viewed as simply swapping the position of a 1 with a 0 in the sequence. Thus, Theorem 4.12 can be applied to show that α^{opt} and α' have equal distances and no contradiction arises.

derivative with respect to the τth element, μ_τ, yields the following condition:

$$\frac{\partial}{\partial \mu_\tau} \left[T - \sum_{t=1}^T \frac{\mu_{t-1}}{\mu_t} \right] = 0 \quad \Rightarrow \quad \frac{\mu_{\tau-1}}{\mu_\tau^2} = \frac{1}{\mu_{\tau+1}}.$$

These conditions do not hold for $\tau = 0$ or $\tau = T$, but we already have $\mu_0 = N$ and $\mu_T = M + N$. Further, since $\mu_t^\star \in \Re_+$, we can instead consider the logarithm of these variables: $\ell\mu_t \triangleq \log(\mu_t)$), for which any stationary point must satisfy the following system of equations:

$$\ell\mu_0 = \log(N)$$
$$2 \cdot \ell\mu_t = \ell\mu_{t-1} + \ell\mu_{t+1} \quad \forall\, t \in \{1 \ldots T-1\} \tag{B.7}$$
$$\ell\mu_T = \log(M + N),$$

The second condition is equivalently defined by the recurrence relation $\ell\mu_t = 2\ell\mu_{t-1} - \ell\mu_{t-2}$, for $t \geq 2$. This recurrence has a characteristic polynomial given by $\chi(r) = r^2 - 2r + 1$. Solving $\chi(r) = 0$ yields the single root $r = 1$, for which there must exist ϕ and ψ such that $\ell\mu_t = \phi \cdot r^t + \psi \cdot t \cdot r^t = \phi + \psi \cdot t$. Using the boundary conditions $\ell\mu_0 = \log(N)$ and $\ell\mu_T = \log(M + N)$, we find that $\phi = \log(N)$ and $\psi = \frac{1}{T} \log\left(\frac{M+N}{N}\right)$. Thus, the *unique* solution to this linear recurrence relation is given by

$$\ell\mu_t = \log(N) + \tfrac{t}{T} \log\left(\tfrac{M+N}{N}\right).$$

Naturally, this corresponds to the sequence $\mu_t^\star = N \left(\frac{M+N}{N}\right)^{\left(\frac{t}{T}\right)}$, which satisfies $\mu_0^\star = N$ and $\mu_T^\star = N + M$ and is a non-decreasing sequence. Moreover, the logarithmic conditions given in Equation (B.7) must hold for any optimal positive sequence, but specify a system of $T + 1$ equalities in terms of $T + 1$ variables and thus have a unique solution. Thus, $\boldsymbol{\mu}^\star$ is the unique positive sequence that maximizes the program given in Equation (4.16).

Having established optimality, the optimal distance achieved is

$$D_N^\star(M, T) = T - \sum_{t=1}^T \frac{N}{N} \left(\frac{M+N}{N}\right)^{\left(\frac{t-1}{T}\right)} \left(\frac{M+N}{N}\right)^{\left(\frac{-t}{T}\right)} = T\left(1 - \left(\frac{N}{M+N}\right)^{\frac{1}{T}}\right)$$

as was to be shown. Finally, using the definition of total mass in Equation (4.7), for $t \geq 1$, $\beta_t^\star = \mu_t^\star - \mu_{t-1}^\star = N \left(\frac{M+N}{N}\right)^{\frac{t-1}{T}} \left(\left(\frac{M+N}{N}\right)^{\frac{1}{T}} - 1\right)$. This completes the proof. $\square$

Appendix C Analysis of SpamBayes for Chapter 5

In this appendix, we analyze the effect of attack messages on SpamBayes. This analysis serves as the motivation for the attacks presented in Section 5.3.

C.1   SpamBayes' $I(\cdot)$ message score

As mentioned in Section 5.1.1, the SpamBayes $I(\cdot)$ function used to estimate spaminess of a message, is the average between its score $S(\cdot)$ and one minus its score $H(\cdot)$. Both of these scores are expressed in terms of the *chi-squared* cumulative distribution function (CDF): $\chi^2_{2n}(\cdot)$. In both these score functions, the argument to the CDF is an inner product between the logarithm of a scores vector and the indicator vector $\delta(\hat{\mathbf{x}})$ as in Equation (5.3). These terms can be re-arranged to rewrite these functions as $S(\hat{\mathbf{x}}) = 1 - \chi^2_{2n}\left(-2\log s_{\mathbf{q}}(\hat{\mathbf{x}})\right)$ and $H(\hat{\mathbf{x}}) = 1 - \chi^2_{2n}\left(-2\log h_{\mathbf{q}}(\hat{\mathbf{x}})\right)$ where $s_{\mathbf{q}}(\cdot)$ and $h_{\mathbf{q}}(\cdot)$ are scalar functions that map $\hat{\mathbf{x}}$ onto $[0, 1]$ defined as

$$s_{\mathbf{q}}(\hat{\mathbf{x}}) \triangleq \prod_i q_i^{\delta(\hat{\mathbf{x}})_i} \tag{C.1}$$

$$h_{\mathbf{q}}(\hat{\mathbf{x}}) \triangleq \prod_i (1 - q_i)^{\delta(\hat{\mathbf{x}})_i}. \tag{C.2}$$

We further explore these functions in the next section, but first we expound on the properties of $\chi^2_k(\cdot)$.

The $\chi^2_k(\cdot)$ CDF can be written out exactly using gamma functions. For $k \in \mathfrak{N}$ and $x \in \mathfrak{R}_{0+}$ it is simply

$$\chi^2_k(x) = \frac{\gamma(k/2, x/2)}{\Gamma(k/2)}$$

where the *lower-incomplete gamma function* is $\gamma(k, y) = \int_0^y t^{k-1}e^{-t}dt$, the *upper-incomplete gamma function* is $\Gamma(k, y) = \int_y^\infty t^{k-1}e^{-t}dt$, and the *gamma function* is $\Gamma(k) = \int_0^\infty t^{k-1}e^{-t}dt$. By these definitions, it follows that for any k and y, the gamma functions are related by $\Gamma(k) = \gamma(k, x) + \Gamma(k, x)$. Also note that for $k \in \mathfrak{N}$

$$\Gamma(k, y) = (k-1)!\, e^{-y} \sum_{j=0}^{k-1} \frac{y^j}{j!} \qquad \Gamma(k) = (k-1)!.$$

Based on these properties, the $S(\cdot)$ score can be rewritten as

$$S(\hat{\mathbf{x}}) = \frac{\Gamma\left(n, -\log s_{\mathbf{q}}(\hat{\mathbf{x}})\right)}{\Gamma(n)} = s_{\mathbf{q}}(\hat{\mathbf{x}}) \sum_{j=0}^{n-1} \frac{\left(-\log s_{\mathbf{q}}(\hat{\mathbf{x}})\right)^j}{j!}$$

$$H(\hat{\mathbf{x}}) = \frac{\Gamma\left(n, -\log h_{\mathbf{q}}(\hat{\mathbf{x}})\right)}{\Gamma(n)} = h_{\mathbf{q}}(\hat{\mathbf{x}}) \sum_{j=0}^{n-1} \frac{\left(-\log h_{\mathbf{q}}(\hat{\mathbf{x}})\right)^j}{j!}.$$

It is easy shown that both these functions are monotonically non-decreasing in $s_{\mathbf{q}}(\hat{\mathbf{x}})$ and $h_{\mathbf{q}}(\hat{\mathbf{x}})$ respectively. For either of these functions, the following derivative can be taken (with respect to $s_{\mathbf{q}}(\hat{\mathbf{x}})$ or $h_{\mathbf{q}}(\hat{\mathbf{x}})$):

$$\frac{d}{dz}\left[z \sum_{j=0}^{n-1} \frac{(-\log z)^j}{j!}\right] = \frac{1}{(n-1)!}(-\log z)^{n-1},$$

which is non-negative for $0 \le z \le 1$.

C.2 Constructing Optimal Attacks on SpamBayes

As indicated by Equation (5.7) in Section 5.3.1, an attacker with objectives described in Section 5.2.1 would like to have the maximal (deleterious) impact on the performance of SpamBayes. In this section, we analyze SpamBayes' decision function $I(\cdot)$ to optimize the attacks' impact. Here we show that the attacks proposed in Section 5.3.1 are (nearly) optimal strategies for designing a single attack message that maximally increases $I(\cdot)$.

In the attack scenario described in Section 5.3.1.1, the attacker will send a series of attack messages which will increase $N^{(s)}$ and $n_j^{(s)}$ for the tokens that are included in the attacks. We will show how $I(\cdot)$ changes as the token counts $n_j^{(s)}$ are increased to understand which tokens the attacker should choose to maximize the impact per message. This analysis separates into two parts based on the following observation.

Remark C.1 Given a fixed number of attack spam messages, q_j is independent of the number of those messages containing the kth token for all $k \ne j$.

This remark follows from the fact that the inclusion of the jth token in attack spams affects $n_j^{(s)}$ and n_j but not $n_k^{(h)}$, $N^{(s)}$, $N^{(h)}$, $n_k^{(s)}$, $n_k^{(h)}$, or n_k for all $k \ne j$ (see Equations (5.1) and (5.2) in Section 5.1.1).

After an attack consisting of a fixed number of attack spam messages, the score $I(\hat{\mathbf{x}})$ of an incoming test message $\hat{\mathbf{x}}$ can be maximized by maximizing each q_j separately. This motivates dictionary attacks and focused attacks—intuitively, the attacker would like to maximally increase the q_j of tokens appearing (or most likely to appear) in $\hat{\mathbf{x}}$ depending on the information the attacker has about future messages.

Thus, we first analyze the effect of increasing $n_j^{(s)}$ on its score q_i in Section C.2.1. Based on this, we subsequently analyze the change in $I(\hat{\mathbf{x}})$ that is caused altering the token score q_i in Section C.2.2. As one might expect, since increasing the number of occurrences of the jth token in spam should increase the posterior probability that a message with the jth token is spam, we show that including the jth token in an attack message generally increases the corresponding score q_j more than not including that token (except in unusual situations which we identify below). Similarly, we show that increasing q_j generally increases the overall spam score $I(\cdot)$ of a message containing the jth token. Based on these results, we motivate the attack strategies presented in Section 5.3.1.

C.2.1   Effect of poisoning on token scores

In this section, we establish how token spam scores change as the result of attack messages in the training set. Intuitively, one might expect that the jth score q_j should increase when the jth token is added to the attack email. This would be the case, in fact, if the token score in Equation (5.1) were computed according to Bayes' Rule. However, as noted Section 5.1, the score in Equation (5.1) is derived by applying Bayes' Rule with an additional assumption that the prior distribution of spam and ham is equal. As a result, there are circumstances in which the spam score q_j can decrease when the jth token is included in the attack email—specifically when the assumption is violated. We show that this occurs when there is an extraordinary imbalance between the number of ham and spam in the training set.

As in Section 5.3, we consider an attacker whose attack messages are composed a single set of attack tokens; i.e., each token is either included in *all* attack messages or *none*. In this fashion, the attacker creates a set of k attack messages used in the retraining of the filter, after which the counts become

$$N^{(s)} \mapsto N^{(s)} + k$$
$$N^{(h)} \mapsto N^{(h)}$$
$$n_j^{(s)} \mapsto \begin{cases} n_j^{(s)} + k, & \text{if } a_j = 1 \\ n_j^{(s)}, & \text{otherwise} \end{cases}$$
$$n_j^{(h)} \mapsto n_j^{(h)}.$$

Using these count transformations, we compute the difference in the smoothed Spam-Bayes score q_j between training on an attack spam message **a** that contains the jth token and an attack spam that does not contain it. If the jth token is included in the attack (i.e., $a_j = 1$), then the new score for the jth token (from Equation 5.1) is

$$P_j^{(s,k)} \triangleq \frac{N^{(h)} \left(n_j^{(s)} + k \right)}{N^{(h)} \left(n_j^{(s)} + k \right) + \left(N^{(s)} + k \right) n_j^{(h)}}.$$

If the token is not included in the attack (i.e., $a_j = 0$), then the new token score is

$$P_j^{(s,0)} \triangleq \frac{N^{(h)} n_j^{(s)}}{N^{(h)} n_j^{(s)} + \left(N^{(s)} + k \right) n_j^{(h)}}.$$

Similarly, we use $q_j^{(k)}$ and $q_j^{(0)}$ to denote the smoothed spam score after the attack depending on whether or not the jth token was used in the attack message. We will analyze the quantity

$$\Delta^{(k)} q_j \triangleq q_j^{(k)} - q_j^{(0)}.$$

One might reasonably expect this difference to always be non-negative, but here we show that there are some scenarios in which $\Delta^{(k)} q_j < 0$. This unusual behavior is a direct result of the assumption made by SpamBayes that $N^{(h)} = N^{(s)}$ rather than using a proper prior distribution. In fact, it can be shown that the usual spam model depicted in Figure 5.1(b) does not exhibit these irregularities. Below, we will show how SpamBayes' assumption can lead to situations where $\Delta^{(k)} q_j < 0$ but also that these irregularities only occur when there is *many* more spam messages than ham messages in the training dataset. By expanding $\Delta^{(k)} q_j$ and rearranging terms, the difference can be expressed as:

$$\Delta^{(k)} q_j = \frac{s \cdot k}{(s + n_j + k)(s + n_j)} \left(P_j^{(s,k)} - x \right)$$

$$+ \frac{k \cdot N^{(h)} \cdot n_j}{(s + n_j)\left(N^{(h)} \cdot n_j^{(s)} + \left(N^{(s)} + k \right) n_j^{(h)} \right)} P_j^{(h,k)},$$

where $P_j^{(h,k)} = 1 - P_j^{(s,k)}$ is the altered ham score of the jth token. The difference can be rewritten as

$$\Delta^{(k)} q_j = \frac{k}{(s + n_j + k)(s + n_j)} \cdot \alpha_j$$

$$\alpha_j \triangleq s(1-x)$$

$$+ P_j^{(h,k)} \cdot \frac{N^{(h)} \cdot n_j (n_j + k) + s \cdot N^{(h)} \cdot n_j^{(h)} - s\left(N^{(s)} + k \right) n_j^{(h)}}{N^{(h)} \cdot n_j^{(s)} + \left(N^{(s)} + k \right) n_j^{(h)}}.$$

The first factor $\frac{k}{(s+n_j+k)(s+n_j)}$ in the above expression is non-negative so only α_j can make $\Delta^{(k)} q_j$ negative. From this, it is easy to show that $N^{(s)} + k$ must be greater that $N^{(h)}$ for $\Delta^{(k)} q_j$ to be negative, but we demonstrate stronger conditions. Generally, we demonstrate that for $\Delta^{(k)} q_j$ to be negative there must be a large disparity between the number of spams after the attack, $N^{(s)} + k$, and the number of ham messages, $N^{(h)}$. This reflects the effect of violating the implicit assumption made by SpamBayes that $N^{(h)} = N^{(s)}$.

Expanding the expression for α_j, the following condition is necessary for $\Delta^{(k)} q_j$ to be negative:

$$\frac{s\left(N^{(s)} + k \right) n_j^{(h)} x}{N^{(h)}} > \frac{s(1-x)\left(n_j^{(s)} + k \right)}{n_j^{(h)}\left(N^{(s)} + k \right)} \left[\left(N^{(s)} + k \right) n_j^{(h)} + N^{(h)} \cdot n_j^{(s)} \right]$$

$$+ n_j (n_j + k) + s n_j^{(s)} (1-x) + s \cdot n_j^{(h)}.$$

Because $1 - x \geq 0$ (since $x \leq 1$) and $n_j = n_j^{(s)} + n_j^{(h)}$, the right-hand side of the above expression is strictly increasing in $n_j^{(s)}$ while the left-hand side is constant in $n_j^{(s)}$. Thus, the weakest condition to make $\Delta^{(k)} q_j$ negative occurs when $n_j^{(s)} = 0$; i.e., tokens that were not observed in any spam prior to the attack are most susceptible to having $\Delta^{(k)} q_j < 0$ while tokens that were observed more frequently in spam prior distribution to the attack require an increasingly larger disparity between $N^{(h)}$ and $N^{(s)}$ for $\Delta^{(k)} q_j < 0$ to occur. Here we analyze the case when $n_j^{(s)} = 0$ and, using the previous constraints that $s > 0$ and $n_j^{(h)} > 0$, we arrive at the weakest condition for which $\Delta^{(k)} q_j$ can be negative. This condition can be expressed succinctly as the following condition on x for the attack to cause a token's score to decrease:[1]

$$x > \frac{N^{(h)} \left(n_j^{(h)} + s\right) \left(n_j^{(h)} + k\right)}{s \left(n_j^{(h)} \left(N^{(s)} + k\right) + kN^{(h)}\right)}.$$

First, notice that the right-hand side is always positive; i.e., there will always be some non-trivial threshold on the value of x to allow for $\Delta^{(k)} q_j$ to be negative. Further, when the right-hand side of this bound is at least one, there are no tokens that have a negative $\Delta^{(k)} q_j$ since the parameter $x \in [0, 1]$. For instance, this occurs when $n_j^{(h)} = 0$ or when $N^{(h)} \geq N^{(s)} + k$ (as previously noted).

Reorganizing the terms, the bound on the number of spams can be expressed as,

$$N^{(s)} + k > N^{(h)} \cdot \frac{\left(n_j^{(h)}\right)^2 + (s + k) n_j^{(h)} + s(1 - x)k}{s n_j^{(h)} x}.$$

This bound shows that the number of spam after the attack, $N^{(s)} + k$, must be larger than a multiple of total number of ham, $N^{(h)}$, to have any token with $\Delta^{(k)} q_j < 0$. The factor in this multiple is always greater than one, but depends on the $n_j^{(h)}$ of the jth token. In fact, the factor is strictly increasing in $n_j^{(h)}$; thus, the weakest bound occurs when $n_j^{(h)} = 1$ (recall that when $n_j^{(h)} = 0$, $\Delta^{(k)} q_j$ is always non-negative). When we examine SpamBayes' default values of $s = 1$ and $x = \frac{1}{2}$, the weakest bound (for tokens with $n_j^{(h)} = 1$ and $n_j^{(s)} = 0$) is

$$N^{(s)} + k > N^{(h)} \cdot (4 + 3k).$$

Thus, when the number of spam after the attack, $N^{(s)} + k$, is sufficiently larger than the number of ham, $N^{(h)}$, it is possible that the score of a token will be lower if it is *included* in the attack message than if it were excluded. This is a direct result of the assumption made by SpamBayes that $N^{(s)} = N^{(h)}$. We have shown that such aberrations will occur most readily in tokens with low initial values of $n_j^{(h)}$ and $n_j^{(s)}$; i.e., those seen infrequently in the dataset. However, for any significant number of attacks, k, the disparity between $N^{(s)} + k$ and $N^{(s)}$ must be tremendous for such aberrations to occur. Under the default SpamBayes settings, there would have to be at least 7 times as many spam as ham with

---

[1] In the case that $n_j^{(s)} > 0$, the condition is stronger but the expression is more complicated.

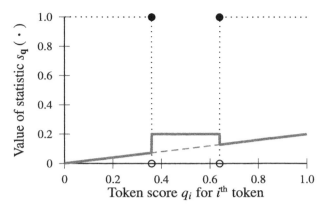

Figure C.1 Plot of the aggregation statistic $s_{\mathbf{q}}(\,\cdot\,)$ relative to a single token score q_i; on the x-axis is q_i and on the y-axis is $s_{\mathbf{q}}(\,\cdot\,)$. Here we consider a scenario where $\tau_{\hat{\mathbf{x}}} = 0.14$ and without the ith token $s_{\mathbf{q}}(\hat{\mathbf{x}} \setminus \{i\}) = 0.2$. The black dotted line is the value of $\delta(\hat{\mathbf{x}})_i$, the gray dotted line is the value of $q_i \prod_{j \neq i} q_j$ (i.e., $s_{\mathbf{q}}(\hat{\mathbf{x}})$ without including $\delta(\hat{\mathbf{x}})$), and the gray solid line is the value of $s_{\mathbf{q}}(\hat{\mathbf{x}})$ as q_i varies.

only a single attack message. For more attack messages ($k > 1$), this bound is even greater. Thus, in designing attacks against SpamBayes, we ignore the extreme cases outlined here and we assume that $\Delta^{(k)} q_j$ always increases if the jth token is included in the attack. Further, none of the experiments presented in Section 5.5 meet the criteria required to have $\Delta^{(k)} q_j < 0$.

C.2.2 Effect of poisoning on $I(\,\cdot\,)$

The key to understanding effect of attacks and constructing optimal attacks against SpamBayes is characterizing conditions under which SpamBayes' score $I(\hat{\mathbf{x}})$ increases when the training corpus is injected with attack spam messages. To do this, we dissect the method used by SpamBayes to aggregate token scores.

The statistics $s_{\mathbf{q}}(\hat{\mathbf{x}})$ and $h_{\mathbf{q}}(\hat{\mathbf{x}})$ from Equation (C.1) and (C.2) are measures of the *spaminess* and *haminess* of the message represented by $\hat{\mathbf{x}}$, respectively. Both assume that each token in the message presents an assessment of the *spaminess* of the message—the score q_i is the evidence for spam given by observing the ith token. Further, by assuming independence, $s_{\mathbf{q}}(\hat{\mathbf{x}})$ and $h_{\mathbf{q}}(\hat{\mathbf{x}})$ aggregate this evidence into a measure of the overall message's *spaminess*. For instance, if all tokens have $q_i = 1$, $s_{\mathbf{q}}(\hat{\mathbf{x}}) = 1$ indicates that the message is very *spammy* and $1 - h_{\mathbf{q}}(\hat{\mathbf{x}}) = 1$ concurs. Similarly, when all tokens have $q_i = 0$, both scores indicate that the message is ham.

These statistics also are (almost) nicely behaved. If we instead consider the ordinary product of the scores of all tokens in the message $\hat{\mathbf{x}}$, $\tilde{s}_{\mathbf{q}}(\hat{\mathbf{x}}) \triangleq \prod_{i:\hat{x}_i=1} q_i$, it is a linear function with respect to each q_i, and is monotonically non-decreasing. Similarly, the product $\tilde{h}_{\mathbf{q}}(\hat{\mathbf{x}}) \triangleq \prod_{i:\hat{x}_i=1}(1 - q_i)$ is linear with respect to each q_i and is monotonically non-increasing. Thus, if we increase any score q_i, the first product will not decrease and the second will not increase, as expected.[2] In fact, by redefining the scores $I(\cdot)$, $S(\cdot)$, and $H(\cdot)$ in terms of the simple products $\tilde{s}_{\mathbf{q}}(\hat{\mathbf{x}})$ and $\tilde{h}_{\mathbf{q}}(\hat{\mathbf{x}})$ (which we refer to as $\tilde{I}(\cdot)$, $\tilde{S}(\cdot)$, and $\tilde{H}(\cdot)$, respectively), the following lemma shows that $\tilde{I}(\cdot)$ is non decreasing in q_i.

LEMMA C.2 *The modified $\tilde{I}(\hat{\mathbf{x}})$ score is non-decreasing in q_i for all tokens (indexed by i).*

Proof We show that the derivative of $\tilde{I}(\hat{\mathbf{x}})$ with respect to q_k is non-negative for all k. By rewriting, Equation (5.3) in terms of $\tilde{s}_{\mathbf{q}}(\hat{\mathbf{x}})$ as $\tilde{S}(\hat{\mathbf{x}}) = 1 - \chi^2_{2n}\left(-2\log\left(\tilde{s}_{\mathbf{q}}(\hat{\mathbf{x}})\right)\right)$, the chain rule can be applied as follows:

$$\frac{\partial}{\partial q_k}\tilde{S}(\hat{\mathbf{x}}) = \frac{d}{d\tilde{s}_{\mathbf{q}}(\hat{\mathbf{x}})}\left[1 - \chi^2_{2n}\left(-2\log\left(\tilde{s}_{\mathbf{q}}(\hat{\mathbf{x}})\right)\right)\right] \cdot \frac{\partial}{\partial q_k}\tilde{s}_{\mathbf{q}}(\hat{\mathbf{x}})$$

$$\frac{d}{d\tilde{s}_{\mathbf{q}}(\hat{\mathbf{x}})}\left[1 - \chi^2_{2n}\left(-2\log\left(\tilde{s}_{\mathbf{q}}(\hat{\mathbf{x}})\right)\right)\right] = \frac{1}{(n-1)!}\left(-\log\left(\tilde{s}_{\mathbf{q}}(\hat{\mathbf{x}})\right)\right)^{n-1}.$$

The second derivative is non-negative since $0 \le \tilde{s}_{\mathbf{q}}(\hat{\mathbf{x}}) \le 1$. Further, the partial derivative of $\tilde{s}_{\mathbf{q}}(\hat{\mathbf{x}})$ with respect to q_k is simply $\frac{\partial}{\partial q_k}\tilde{s}_{\mathbf{q}}(\hat{\mathbf{x}}) = \prod_{i \ne k: \hat{x}_i = 1} q_i \ge 0$. Thus, for all k,

$$\frac{\partial}{\partial q_k}\tilde{S}(\hat{\mathbf{x}}) \ge 0.$$

By an analogous derivation, replacing q_i by $1 - q_i$,

$$\frac{\partial}{\partial q_k}\tilde{H}(\hat{\mathbf{x}}) \le 0.$$

The final result is then give by

$$\frac{\partial}{\partial q_k}\tilde{I}(\hat{\mathbf{x}}) = \frac{1}{2}\frac{\partial}{\partial q_k}\tilde{S}(\hat{\mathbf{x}}) - \frac{1}{2}\frac{\partial}{\partial q_k}\tilde{H}(\hat{\mathbf{x}}) \ge 0.$$

$\square$

However, unlike the simple products, the statistics $s_{\mathbf{q}}(\cdot)$ and $h_{\mathbf{q}}(\cdot)$ have unusual behavior because the function $\delta(\cdot)$ sanitizes the token scores. Namely, $\delta(\cdot)$ is the indicator function of the set $\mathbb{T}_{\hat{\mathbf{x}}}$. Membership in this set is determined by absolute distance of a token's score from the agnostic score of $\frac{1}{2}$; i.e., by the value $g_i \triangleq \left|q_i - \frac{1}{2}\right|$. The ith token belongs to $\mathbb{T}_{\hat{\mathbf{x}}}$ if *i*) $\hat{x}_i = 1$ *ii*) $g_i \ge Q$ (by default $Q = 0.1$ so all tokens in $(0.4, 0.6)$ are excluded) and *iii*) of the remaining tokens, the token has among the largest T values of g_i (by default $T = 150$).

For our purposes, for every message $\hat{\mathbf{x}}$, there is some value $\tau_{\hat{\mathbf{x}}} < \frac{1}{2}$ that defines an interval $\left(\frac{1}{2} - \tau_{\hat{\mathbf{x}}}, \frac{1}{2} + \tau_{\hat{\mathbf{x}}}\right)$ to exclude tokens. That is

$$\delta(\hat{\mathbf{x}})_i = \hat{x}_i \cdot \begin{cases} 0 & \text{if } q_i \in \left(\frac{1}{2} - \tau_{\hat{\mathbf{x}}}, \frac{1}{2} + \tau_{\hat{\mathbf{x}}}\right) \\ 1 & \text{otherwise} \end{cases}.$$

---

[2] These statistics also behave oddly in another sense. Namely, adding an additional token will always decrease both products and removing a token will always increase both products. Applying the chi-squared distribution rectifies this effect.

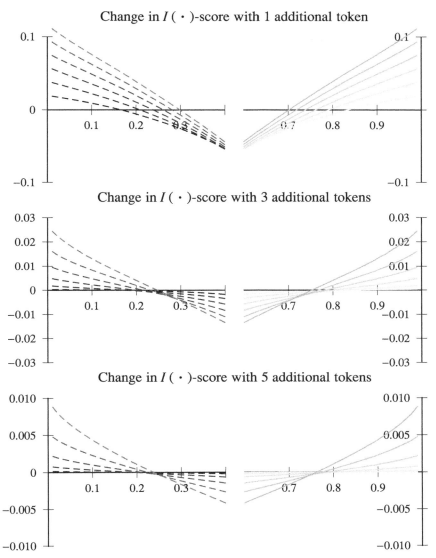

Figure C.2 The effect of the $\delta(\cdot)$ function on $I(\cdot)$ as the score of the ith token, q_i, increases causing q_i to move into or out of the region $(0.4, 0.6)$ where all tokens are ignored. In each plot, the x-axis is the value of q_i before it's removal and the y-axis is the change in $I(\cdot)$ due to the removal; note that the scale on the y-axis decreases from top to bottom. For the top-most row of plots there is 1 unchanged token scores in addition to the changing one, for the middle row there are 3 additional unchanged token scores, and for the bottom row there are 5 additional unchanged token scores. The plots in the left-most column demonstrate the effect of removing the ith token when initially $q_i \in (0, 0.4)$; the scores of the additional unchanging tokens are all fixed to the same value of 0.02 (dark dashed black), 0.04, 0.06, 0.08, 0.10, or 0.12 (light dashed black). The plots in the right-most column demonstrate the effect of adding the ith token when initially $q_i \in (0.4, 0.6)$; the scores of the additional unchanging tokens are all fixed to the same value of 0.88 (dark gray), 0.90, 0.92, 0.94, 0.96, or 0.98 (light gray).

Clearly, for tokens in $\hat{\mathbf{x}}$, $\delta(\hat{\mathbf{x}})_i$ steps from 1 to 0 and back to 1 as q_i increases. This causes $s_{\mathbf{q}}(\hat{\mathbf{x}})$ to have two discontinuities with respect to q_i: it increases linearly on the intervals $\left[0, \frac{1}{2} - \tau_{\hat{\mathbf{x}}}\right]$ and $\left[\frac{1}{2} + \tau_{\hat{\mathbf{x}}}, 1\right]$, but on the middle interval $\left(\frac{1}{2} - \tau_{\hat{\mathbf{x}}}, \frac{1}{2} + \tau_{\hat{\mathbf{x}}}\right)$ it jumps discontinuously to its maximum value. This behavior of is depicted in Figure C.1. Similarly, $h_{\mathbf{q}}(\hat{\mathbf{x}})$ decreases linearly except on the middle interval $\left(\frac{1}{2} - \tau_{\hat{\mathbf{x}}}, \frac{1}{2} + \tau_{\hat{\mathbf{x}}}\right)$ where it also jumps to its maximum value. Thus, neither $s_{\mathbf{q}}(\hat{\mathbf{x}})$ or $h_{\mathbf{q}}(\hat{\mathbf{x}})$ have monotonic behavior on the interval $[0, 1]$.

To better understand how $I(\hat{\mathbf{x}})$ behaves when q_i increases given that neither $s_{\mathbf{q}}(\hat{\mathbf{x}})$ or $h_{\mathbf{q}}(\hat{\mathbf{x}})$ are monotonic, we analyze its behavior on a case by case basis. For this purpose, we refer to the three intervals $\left[0, \frac{1}{2} - \tau_{\hat{\mathbf{x}}}\right]$, $\left(\frac{1}{2} - \tau_{\hat{\mathbf{x}}}, \frac{1}{2} + \tau_{\hat{\mathbf{x}}}\right)$, and $\left[\frac{1}{2} + \tau_{\hat{\mathbf{x}}}, 1\right]$ as $\mathbb{A}$, $\mathbb{B}$, and $\mathbb{C}$, respectively. Clearly, if q_i increases but stays within the same interval, $I(\hat{\mathbf{x}})$ also increases. This follows from Lemma C.2 and the fact that $I(\hat{\mathbf{x}})$ will not change if q_i remains within interval $\mathbb{B}$. Similarly, $I(\hat{\mathbf{x}})$ also increases if q_i increases from interval $\mathbb{A}$ to interval $\mathbb{C}$; this too follows from Lemma C.2. The only cases when $I(\hat{\mathbf{x}})$ may decrease when q_i increases occur when either q_i transitions from interval $\mathbb{A}$ to $\mathbb{B}$ or q_i transitions from interval $\mathbb{B}$ to $\mathbb{C}$, but in these cases, the behavior of $I(\hat{\mathbf{x}})$ depends heavily on the scores for the other tokens in $\hat{\mathbf{x}}$ and the value of q_i before it increases as depicted by Figure C.2. It is also worth noting that $I(\hat{\mathbf{x}})$ in fact will *never* decrease if $\hat{\mathbf{x}}$ has more than 150 tokens outside the interval $(0.4, 0.6)$, since in this case increasing q_i either into or out of $\mathbb{B}$ also corresponds to either adding or removing a second token score q_j. The effect in this case is that $I(\hat{\mathbf{x}})$ always increases.

The attacks against SpamBayes that we introduced in Section 5.3 ignore the fact that $I(\hat{\mathbf{x}})$ may decrease when increasing some token scores. In this sense, these attacks are not truly optimal. However, determining which set of tokens will optimally increase the overall $I(\cdot)$ of a set of future messages $\{\hat{\mathbf{x}}\}$ is a combinatorial problem that seems infeasible for a real-world adversary. Instead, we consider attacks that are optimal for the relaxed version of the problem that incorporates *all* tokens from $\hat{\mathbf{x}}$ in computing $I(\hat{\mathbf{x}})$. Further, in Section 5.5, we show that these approximate techniques are extraordinarily effective against SpamBayes in spite of the fact some non-optimal tokens are included in the attack messages.

Appendix D   Full Proofs for Near-Optimal Evasion

In this appendix, we give proofs for the theorems from Chapter 8. First, we show that the query complexity of K-STEP MULTILINESEARCH is $\mathcal{O}\left(L_\epsilon + \sqrt{L_\epsilon}|\mathbb{W}|\right)$ when $K = \lceil \sqrt{L_\epsilon} \rceil$. Second, we show three lower bounds for different cost functions. Each of the lower bound proofs follows a similar argument: We use classifiers based on the cost-ball and classifiers based on the convex hull of the queries to construct two alternative classifiers with different ϵ-*IMAC*s. This allows us to show results on the minimal number of queries required.

Proof of K-step MultiLineSearch Theorem

To analyze the worst case of K-STEP MULTILINESEARCH (Algorithm 8.3), we analyze the malicious classifier that seeks to maximize the number of queries. It is completely aware of the state of the adversary; i.e., the dimension of the space D, the adversary's goal L_ϵ, the cost function A, the bounds on the cost function C_t^+ and C_t^-, and so forth. In this proof, we refer to the querier as the *adversary*.

Proof of Theorem 8.5 At each iteration of Algorithm 8.3, the adversary chooses some direction, $\mathbf{e}$ not yet eliminated from $\mathbb{W}$. Every direction in $\mathbb{W}$ is feasible (i.e., could yield an ϵ-*IMAC*), and the malicious classifier, by definition, will make this choice as costly as possible. During the K steps of binary search along this direction, regardless of which direction $\mathbf{e}$ is selected or how the malicious classifier responds, the candidate multiplicative gap (see Section 8.1.3) along $\mathbf{e}$ will shrink by an exponent of 2^{-K}; i.e.,

$$\frac{B^-}{B^+} = \left(\frac{C^-}{C^+}\right)^{2^{-K}} \tag{D.1}$$

$$\log\left(G'_{t+1}\right) = \log\left(G_t\right) \cdot 2^{-K} \tag{D.2}$$

The primary decision for the malicious classifier occurs when the adversary begins querying other directions besides $\mathbf{e}$. At iteration t, the malicious classifier has two options:

    Case 1 ($t \in \mathbb{C}_1$): Respond with "+" for all remaining directions. Here the bound candidates B^+ and B^- are verified, and thus the new gap is reduced by an exponent of 2^{-K}; however, no directions are eliminated from the search.

Case 2 ($t \in \mathbb{C}_2$): Choose at least one direction to respond with "$-$". Here since only the value of C^- changes, the malicious classifier can choose to respond to the first K queries so that the gap decreases by a negligible amount (by always responding with "$+$" during the first K queries along $\mathbf{e}$, the gap only decreases by an exponent of $\left(1 - 2^{-K}\right)$). However, the malicious classifier must choose some number $E_t \geq 1$ of directions that will be eliminated.

By conservatively assuming the gap only decreases in case 1, the total number of queries is bounded for both cases independent of the order in which the malicious classifier applies them.

At the tth iteration, the malicious classifier can either decide to be in case 1 ($t \in \mathbb{C}_1$) or case 2 ($t \in \mathbb{C}_2$). We assume that the gap only decreases in case 1. That is, we define $G_0 = C_0^- / C_0^+$ so that if $t \in \mathbb{C}_1$, then $G_t = G_{t-1}^{2^{-K}}$ whereas if $t \in \mathbb{C}_2$, then $G_t = G_{t-1}$. This assumption yields an upper bound on the algorithm's performance and decouples the analysis of the queries for $\mathbb{C}_1$ and $\mathbb{C}_2$. From it, we derive the following upper bound on the number of case 1 iterations that must occur before our algorithm terminates; simply stated, there must be a total of at least L_ϵ binary search steps made during the case 1 iterations and every case 1 iteration makes exactly K steps. More formally, each case 1 iteration reduces the gap by an exponent of 2^{-K} and our termination condition is $G_T \leq 1 + \epsilon$. Since our algorithm will terminate as soon as the gap $G_T \leq 1 + \epsilon$, iteration T must be a case 1 iteration and $G_{T-1} > 1 + \epsilon$ (otherwise the algorithm would have terminated earlier). From this the total number of iterations must satisfy

$$\log_2 (G_{T-1}) > \log_2 (1 + \epsilon)$$

$$\underbrace{\log_2 (G_0) \prod_{i \in \mathbb{C}_1 \wedge i < T} 2^{-K}}_{\text{by Equation (D.2)}} > \log_2 (1 + \epsilon)$$

$$2^{-\sum_{i \in \mathbb{C}_1 \wedge i < T} K} > \frac{\log_2 (1 + \epsilon)}{\log_2 (G_0)}$$

$$\sum_{i \in \mathbb{C}_1 \wedge i < T} K > \log_2 \underbrace{\frac{\log_2 (G_0)}{\log_2 (1 + \epsilon)}}_{=L_\epsilon \text{ by Equation (8.6)}}$$

$$(|\mathbb{C}_1| - 1)K < L_\epsilon$$

where the factor $(|\mathbb{C}_1| - 1)$ comes as a result of excluding the last case 1 iteration, T. A similar derivation for $G_T \leq 1 + \epsilon$ yields $|\mathbb{C}_1| \cdot K \geq L_\epsilon$, and the only integer that satisfies both these conditions is

$$|\mathbb{C}_1| = \left\lceil \frac{L_\epsilon}{K} \right\rceil. \tag{D.3}$$

Now, at every case 1 iteration, the adversary makes exactly $K + |\mathbb{W}_t| - 1$ queries where $\mathbb{W}_t$ is the set of feasible directions remaining at the tth iteration. While $\mathbb{W}_t$ is controlled by the malicious classifier, it is bounded by $|\mathbb{W}_t| \leq |\mathbb{W}|$. Using this and the relation from Equation (D.3), we bound the number of queries, Q_1, used in case 1 by

$$Q_1 = \sum_{t \in C_1} (K + |\mathbb{W}_t| - 1)$$

$$\leq \sum_{t \in C_1} (K + |\mathbb{W}| - 1)$$

$$= \left\lceil \frac{L_\epsilon}{K} \right\rceil \cdot (K + |\mathbb{W}| - 1)$$

$$\leq \left(\frac{L_\epsilon}{K} + 1 \right) \cdot K + \left\lceil \frac{L_\epsilon}{K} \right\rceil \cdot (|\mathbb{W}| - 1)$$

$$= L_\epsilon + K + \left\lceil \frac{L_\epsilon}{K} \right\rceil \cdot (|\mathbb{W}| - 1).$$

For each case 2 iteration, the adversary makes exactly $K + E_t$ queries, and each eliminates $E_t \geq 1$ directions; hence, $|\mathbb{W}_{t+1}| = |\mathbb{W}_t| - E_t$. The malicious classifier will always make $E_t = 1$ in every case 2 instance since that maximally limits how much the adversary gains. Nevertheless, since case 2 requires the elimination of at least one direction, the following bound applies: $|\mathbb{C}_2| \leq |\mathbb{W}| - 1$. Moreover, regardless of the choice of E_t, $\sum_{t \in \mathbb{C}_2} E_t \leq |\mathbb{W}| - 1$ since each direction can be eliminated no more than once and at least one direction must remain. Thus,

$$Q_2 = \sum_{i \in \mathbb{C}_2} (K + E_t)$$

$$\leq |\mathbb{C}_2| \cdot K + |\mathbb{W}| - 1$$

$$\leq (|\mathbb{W}| - 1)(K + 1).$$

The total number of queries used by Algorithm 8.3 is

$$Q = Q_1 + Q_2 \leq L_\epsilon + K + \left\lceil \frac{L_\epsilon}{K} \right\rceil \cdot (|\mathbb{W}| - 1) + (|\mathbb{W}| - 1)(K + 1)$$

$$= L_\epsilon + K + \left\lceil \frac{L_\epsilon}{K} \right\rceil \cdot |\mathbb{W}| - \left\lceil \frac{L_\epsilon}{K} \right\rceil + K \cdot |\mathbb{W}| - K + |\mathbb{W}| - 1$$

$$= L_\epsilon + \left\lceil \frac{L_\epsilon}{K} \right\rceil \cdot |\mathbb{W}| + K \cdot |\mathbb{W}| + |\mathbb{W}| - \left\lceil \frac{L_\epsilon}{K} \right\rceil - 1$$

$$\leq L_\epsilon + \left\lceil \frac{L_\epsilon}{K} \right\rceil \cdot |\mathbb{W}| + K \cdot |\mathbb{W}| + |\mathbb{W}|$$

$$= L_\epsilon + \left(\left\lceil \frac{L_\epsilon}{K} \right\rceil + K + 1 \right) |\mathbb{W}|$$

Finally, choosing $K = \lceil \sqrt{L_\epsilon} \rceil$ minimizes this expression. Substituting this K into Q's bound and using the bound $L_\epsilon / \lceil \sqrt{L_\epsilon} \rceil \leq \sqrt{L_\epsilon}$, yield

$$Q \leq L_\epsilon + \left(2\lceil \sqrt{L_\epsilon} \rceil + 1 \right) |\mathbb{W}|$$

so $Q = \mathcal{O} \left(L_\epsilon + \sqrt{L_\epsilon} |\mathbb{W}| \right)$. $\qquad\square$

Proof of Lower Bounds

Here we give proofs for the lower bound theorems from Section 8.2.1.2 using the same arguments for the multiplicative and additive cases. Recall that, for these lower bounds, D is the dimension of the space, $A : \mathfrak{R}^D \mapsto \mathfrak{R}_+$ is any positive convex function, and $0 < C_0^+ < C_0^-$ are initial upper and lower bounds on the *MAC*. We also have that $\hat{\mathcal{F}}^{\text{convex,"+"}} \subseteq \mathcal{F}^{\text{convex,"+"}}$ is the set of classifiers consistent with the constraints on the *MAC*; i.e., for $f \in \hat{\mathcal{F}}^{\text{convex,"+"}}$ the set $\mathcal{X}_f^+$ is convex, $\mathbb{B}^{C_0^+}(A) \subseteq \mathcal{X}_f^+$ and $\mathbb{B}^{C_0^-}(A) \not\subseteq \mathcal{X}_f^+$. As in K-step MultiLineSearch, we again consider a malicious classifier.

Proof of Theorem 8.7 and 8.6 Suppose a query-based algorithm submits $N < D+1$ membership queries $\mathbf{x}^{(1)}, \ldots, \mathbf{x}^{(N)} \in \mathfrak{R}^D$ to the classifier. For the algorithm to be ϵ-optimal, these queries must constrain the family of all consistent classifiers, $\hat{\mathcal{F}}^{\text{convex,"+"}}$, to have a common point among their ϵ-*IMAC* sets. Suppose that the responses to the queries are consistent with the classifier f defined as

$$f(\mathbf{x}) = \begin{cases} +1, & \text{if } A\left(\mathbf{x} - \mathbf{x}^A\right) < C_0^- \\ -1, & \text{otherwise} \end{cases}.$$
(D.4)

For this classifier, $\mathcal{X}_f^+$ is convex since A is a convex function, $\mathbb{B}^{C_0^+}(A) \subseteq \mathcal{X}_f^+$ since $C_0^+ < C_0^-$, and $\mathbb{B}^{C_0^-}(A) \not\subseteq \mathcal{X}_f^+$ since $\mathcal{X}_f^+$ is the open C_0^--ball, whereas $\mathbb{B}^{C_0^-}(A)$ is the closed C_0^--ball. Moreover, since $\mathcal{X}_f^+$ is the open C_0^--ball, $\not\exists\, \mathbf{x} \in \mathcal{X}_f^+$ such that $A\left(\mathbf{x} - \mathbf{x}^A\right) < C_0^-$. Therefore, $MAC(f, A) = C_0^-$, and any ϵ-optimal points $\mathbf{x}' \in \epsilon\text{-}IMAC^{(*)}(f, A)$ must satisfy $C_0^- \le A\left(\mathbf{x}' - \mathbf{x}^A\right) \le (1 + \epsilon)C_0^-$. Similarly, any η-optimal points $\mathbf{x}' \in \eta\text{-}IMAC^{(+)}(f, A)$ must satisfy $C_0^- \le A\left(\mathbf{x}' - \mathbf{x}^A\right) \le C_0^- + \eta$.

Consider an alternative classifier g that responds identically to f for $\mathbf{x}^{(1)}, \ldots, \mathbf{x}^{(N)}$ but has a different convex positive set $\mathcal{X}_g^+$. Without loss of generality, suppose the first $M \le N$ queries are positive and the remaining are negative. Let $\mathbb{G} = conv\left(\mathbf{x}^{(1)}, \ldots, \mathbf{x}^{(M)}\right)$; that is, the convex hull of these M positive queries. Now let $\mathcal{X}_g^+$ be the convex hull of $\mathbb{G}$ and the C_0^+-ball of A: $\mathcal{X}_g^+ = conv\left(\mathbb{G} \cup \mathbb{B}^{C_0^+}(A)\right)$. Since $\mathbb{G}$ contains all positive queries and $C_0^+ < C_0^-$, the convex set $\mathcal{X}_g^+$ is consistent with the observed responses, $\mathbb{B}^{C_0^+}(A) \subseteq \mathcal{X}_g^+$ by definition, and $\mathbb{B}^{C_0^-}(A) \not\subseteq \mathcal{X}_g^+$ since the positive queries are all inside the open C_0^--sublevel set. Further, since $M \le N < D+1$, $\mathbb{G}$ is contained in a proper linear subspace of $\mathfrak{R}^D$ and hence the interior of $\mathbb{G}$ is empty; i.e., $int(\mathbb{G}) = \emptyset$. Thus, there is always some point from $\mathbb{B}^{C_0^+}(A)$ that is on the boundary of $\mathcal{X}_g^+$; i.e., $\mathbb{B}^{C_0^+}(A) \not\subseteq int(\mathbb{G})$ because $int(\mathbb{G}) = \emptyset$, hence, there must be at least one point from $\mathbb{B}^{C_0^+}(A)$ on the boundary of the convex hull of $\mathbb{B}^{C_0^+}(A)$ and $\mathbb{G}$. Hence, $MAC(g, A) = \inf_{\mathbf{x} \in \mathcal{X}_g^-}\left[A\left(\mathbf{x} - \mathbf{x}^A\right)\right] = C_0^+$. Since the accuracy $\epsilon < \frac{C_0^-}{C_0^+} - 1$, any $\mathbf{x} \in \epsilon\text{-}IMAC^{(*)}(g, A)$ must have

$$A\left(\mathbf{x} - \mathbf{x}^A\right) \le (1 + \epsilon)C_0^+ < \frac{C_0^-}{C_0^+}C_0^+ = C_0^-$$

whereas any $\mathbf{y} \in \epsilon\text{-}IMAC^{(*)}(f, A)$ must have $A\left(\mathbf{y} - \mathbf{x}^A\right) \geq C_0^-$. Thus, $\epsilon\text{-}IMAC^{(*)}(f, A)$ $\cap\, \epsilon\text{-}IMAC^{(*)}(g, A) = \emptyset$, and we have constructed two convex-inducing classifiers f and g, which are both consistent with the query responses with no common $\epsilon\text{-}IMAC^{(*)}$. Similarly, since $\eta < C_0^- - C_0^+$, any $\mathbf{x} \in \eta\text{-}IMAC^{(+)}(g, A)$ must have

$$A\left(\mathbf{x} - \mathbf{x}^A\right) \leq \eta + C_0^+ < C_0^- - C_0^+ + C_0^+ = C_0^-$$

whereas any $\mathbf{y} \in \eta\text{-}IMAC^{(+)}(f, A)$ must have $A\left(\mathbf{y} - \mathbf{x}^A\right) \geq C_0^-$. Thus, $\eta\text{-}IMAC^{(+)}(f, A) \cap \eta\text{-}IMAC^{(+)}(g, A) = \emptyset$, and so the two convex-inducing classifiers f and g also have no common $\eta\text{-}IMAC^{(+)}$.

Suppose instead that a query-based algorithm submits $N < L_\epsilon^{(*)}$ membership queries (or $N < L_\eta^{(+)}$ for the additive case). Recall our definitions: C_0^- is the initial upper bound on the MAC, C_0^+ is the initial lower bound on the MAC, and $G_t^{(*)} = C_t^- / C_t^+$ is the gap between the upper bound and lower bound at iteration t ($G_t^{(+)} = C_t^- - C_t^+$ for the additive case). The malicious classifier f responds with

$$f\left(\mathbf{x}^{(t)}\right) = \begin{cases} +1, & \text{if } A\left(\mathbf{x}^{(t)} - \mathbf{x}^A\right) \leq \sqrt{C_{t-1}^- \cdot C_{t-1}^+} \\ -1, & \text{otherwise} \end{cases} \tag{D.5}$$

(for additive optimality, the condition for the first case is $A\left(\mathbf{x}^{(t)} - \mathbf{x}^A\right) \leq \frac{C_{t-1}^- + C_{t-1}^+}{2}$). When the classifier responds with "+", C_t^+ increases to no more than $\sqrt{C_{t-1}^- \cdot C_{t-1}^+}$ and so $G_t \geq \sqrt{G_{t-1}}$. Similarly when this classifier responds with "−", C_t^- decreases to no less than $\sqrt{C_{t-1}^- \cdot C_{t-1}^+}$ and so again $G_t \geq \sqrt{G_{t-1}}$. Thus, these responses ensure that at each iteration $G_t \geq \sqrt{G_{t-1}}$ (or in the additive case $G_t \geq \frac{G_{t-1}}{2}$) and since the algorithm cannot terminate until $G_N \leq 1 + \epsilon$, it must be the case that $N \geq L_\epsilon^{(*)}$ because of Equation (8.6) (or in the additive case, it must be the case that $N \geq L_\eta^{(+)}$ because of Equation (8.5)). Otherwise, there are still two convex-inducing classifiers with consistent query responses but with no common $\epsilon\text{-}IMAC$. The first classifier's positive set is the smallest cost-ball enclosing all positive queries, while the second classifier's positive set is the largest cost-ball enclosing all positive queries but no negatives. The MAC values for these classifiers differ by more than a factor of $(1 + \epsilon)$ if $N < L_\epsilon^{(*)}$ (or, for the additive case, by a difference of more than η if $N < L_\eta^{(+)}$), so they have no common $\epsilon\text{-}IMAC$. $\qquad\square$

Proof of Theorem 8.12

For the proof of Theorem 8.12, we use the orthants (centered at $\mathbf{x}^A$)—i.e., an *orthant* is the D-dimensional generalization of a quadrant in 2-dimensions. There are 2^D orthants in a D-dimensional space. We represent each orthant by its *canonical representation*, which is a vector of D positive or negative ones; i.e., the orthant represented by

$\mathbf{a} = (\pm 1, \pm 1, \ldots, \pm 1)$ contains the point $\mathbf{x}^A + \mathbf{a}$ and is the set of all points $\mathbf{x}$ satisfying

$$x_i \in \begin{cases} [0, +\infty], & \text{if } a_i = +1 \\ [-\infty, 0], & \text{if } a_i = -1 \end{cases}.$$

Now based on Lemma A.2, we give the required proof of Theorem 8.12:

Proof of Theorem 8.12   Suppose a query-based algorithm submits N membership queries $\mathbf{x}^{(1)}, \ldots, \mathbf{x}^{(N)} \in \Re^D$ to the classifier. Again, for the algorithm to be ϵ-optimal, these queries must constrain all consistent classifiers in the family $\hat{\mathcal{F}}^{\text{convex},\text{"+"}}$ to have a common point among their ϵ-*IMAC* sets. The responses described above are consistent with the classifier f defined as

$$f(\mathbf{x}) = \begin{cases} +1, & \text{if } A_p\left(\mathbf{x} - \mathbf{x}^A\right) < C_0^- \\ -1, & \text{otherwise} \end{cases}.$$

For this classifier, $\mathcal{X}_f^+$ is convex since A_p is a convex function for $p \geq 1$, $\mathbb{B}^{C_0^+}\left(A_p\right) \subseteq \mathcal{X}_f^+$ since $C_0^+ < C_0^-$, and $\mathbb{B}^{C_0^-}\left(A_p\right) \not\subseteq \mathcal{X}_f^+$ since $\mathcal{X}_f^+$ is the open C_0^--ball, whereas $\mathbb{B}^{C_0^-}\left(A_p\right)$ is the closed C_0^--ball. Moreover, since $\mathcal{X}_f^+$ is the open C_0^--ball, $\nexists\, \mathbf{x} \in \mathcal{X}_f^-$ such that $A_p\left(\mathbf{x} - \mathbf{x}^A\right) < C_0^-$; therefore $MAC\left(f, A_p\right) = C_0^-$, and any ϵ-optimal points $\mathbf{x}' \in \epsilon\text{-}IMAC^{(*)}\left(f, A_p\right)$ must satisfy $C_0^- \leq A_p\left(\mathbf{x}' - \mathbf{x}^A\right) \leq (1 + \epsilon)C_0^-$.

Now consider an alternative classifier g that responds identically to f for $\mathbf{x}^{(1)}, \ldots, \mathbf{x}^{(N)}$ but has a different convex positive set $\mathcal{X}_g^+$. Without loss of generality suppose the first $M \leq N$ queries are positive and the remaining are negative. Consider a set that is the convex hull of the orthants of all M positive queries; that is,

$$\mathbb{G} = conv\left(orth\left(\mathbf{x}^{(1)}\right) \cap \mathcal{X}_f^+, orth\left(\mathbf{x}^{(2)}\right) \cap \mathcal{X}_f^+, \ldots, orth\left(\mathbf{x}^{(M)}\right) \cap \mathcal{X}_f^+\right) \quad \text{(D.6)}$$

where $orth\left(\mathbf{x}\right)$ is some orthant that $\mathbf{x}$ lies within relative to the center, $\mathbf{x}^A$ (a data point may lie within more than one orthant, but it is only necessary to select one of the orthants that contains it to cover it). By intersecting each data point's orthant with the set $\mathcal{X}_f^+$ and taking the convex hull of these regions, $\mathbb{G}$ is convex, contains $\mathbf{x}^A$, and is a subset of $\mathcal{X}_f^+$ consistent with all the query responses of f; i.e., each of the M positive queries is in $\mathcal{X}_g^+$ and all the negative queries are in $\mathcal{X}_g^-$. Moreover, $\mathbb{G}$ is a superset of the convex hull of the M positive queries. Thus, the largest enclosed ℓ_p ball within $\mathbb{G}$ is an upper bound on $MAC\left(g, A_p\right)$, so we bound the size of this ℓ_p ball instead.

We now represent each orthant as a vertex in a D-dimensional hypercube graph—the Hamming distance between any pair of orthants is the number of different coordinates in their canonical representations, and two orthants are adjacent in the graph if and only if they have a Hamming distance of one. Using this notion of Hamming distance, we find a K-K-covering of $\mathbb{X}$ of the hypercube. We refer to the orthants used to construct $\mathbb{G}$ in Equation D.6 as *covering orthants* because they cover the M positive queries. The vertexes corresponding to these covering orthants form a covering of the hypercube. Suppose the M covering orthants are sufficient for a K covering but not $K - 1$ covering; then there must be at least one vertex not in the covering that has at least a K Hamming distance to every vertex in the K-covering of $\mathbb{X}$. This vertex corresponds to an empty orthant that differs from all covered orthants in at least K coordinates of their canonical vertexes. Without loss of generality, suppose this uncovered orthant has the canonical vertex of all positive ones that is scaled to $C_0^- \mathbf{1}$. Now, consider the hyperplane with normal vector $\mathbf{w} = \mathbf{1}$ and displacement

$$
d = \begin{cases} C_0^- (D - K)^{\frac{p-1}{p}} & \text{if } 1 < p < \infty \\ C_0^- (D - K) & \text{if } p = \infty \end{cases}
$$

that specifies the discriminant function $s(\mathbf{x}) = \mathbf{x}^\top \mathbf{w} - d = \sum_{i=1}^{D} x_i - d$. For this hyperplane, the vertex $C_0^- \mathbf{1}$ yields

$$
\begin{aligned}
s\left(C_0^- \mathbf{1}\right) &= C_0^- D - d \\
&= C_0^- D - \left(C_0^- D - K\right)^{\frac{p-1}{p}} \\
&> C_0^- D - \left(C_0^- D - K\right) \\
&> 0.
\end{aligned}
$$

Also for any orthant $\mathbf{a}$ with Hamming distance at least K from this uncovered orthant, all points $\mathbf{x} \in orth(\mathbf{a}) \cap \mathcal{X}_f^+$ yield the following valuation of the function s, by definition of the orthant and $\mathcal{X}_f^+$:

$$
\begin{aligned}
s(\mathbf{x}) &= \sum_{i=1}^{D} x_i - d \\
&= \sum_{\{i \,|\, a_i=+1\}} \underbrace{x_i}_{\geq 0} + \sum_{\{i \,|\, a_i=-1\}} \underbrace{x_i}_{\leq 0} - d.
\end{aligned}
$$

Since all the terms in the second summation are nonpositive, the second sum is at most 0. Thus, maximizing the first summation upper bounds $s(\mathbf{x})$. The summation $\sum_{\{i \,|\, a_i=+1\}} x_i$ (with the constraint that $\|\mathbf{x}\|_p < C_0^-$, which is necessary for $\mathbf{x}$ to be in $\mathcal{X}_f^+$) has at most $D - K$ terms and is maximized by $x_i = C_0^- (D - K)^{-1/p}$ (or $x_i = C_0^-$ for $p = \infty$) for which the first summation is upper bounded by $C_0^- (D - K)^{\frac{p-1}{p}}$ or $C_0^- (D - K)$ for $p = \infty$; i.e., it is upper bounded by d and so $s(\mathbf{x}) \leq 0$. Thus, this hyperplane separates the scaled vertex $C_0^- \mathbf{1}$ from each set $orth(\mathbf{a}) \cap \mathcal{X}_f^+$ where $\mathbf{a}$ is the canonical representation of any orthant with a Hamming distance of at least K from the positive orthant represented by $\mathbf{1}$. This hyperplane also separates the scaled vertex from $\mathbb{G}$ by the properties of the convex hull. Since the displacement d defined above is greater than 0, by applying Lemma A.3, this separating hyperplane upper bounds the cost of the largest ℓ_p ball enclosed in $\mathbb{G}$ as

$$
MAC\left(g, A_p\right) \leq C_0^- (D - K)^{\frac{p-1}{p}} \cdot \|\mathbf{1}\|_{\frac{p}{p-1}}^{-1} = C_0^- \left(\frac{D - K}{D}\right)^{\frac{p-1}{p}}
$$

for $1 < p < \infty$ and

$$
MAC\left(g, A_p\right) \leq C_0^- (D - K) \cdot \|\mathbf{1}\|_1^{-1} = C_0^- \frac{D - K}{D}
$$

for $p = \infty$. Based on this upper bound on the *MAC* of g and the *MAC* of f (i.e., C_0^-), if there is a common ϵ-*IMAC* between these classifiers, it must satisfy

$$(1 + \epsilon) \geq \begin{cases} \left(\frac{D}{D-K}\right)^{\frac{p-1}{p}}, & \text{if } 1 < p < \infty \\ \frac{D}{D-K}, & \text{if } p = \infty \end{cases}.$$

Solving for the value of K required to achieve a desired accuracy of $1 + \epsilon$ yields

$$K \leq \begin{cases} \frac{(1+\epsilon)^{\frac{p}{p-1}} - 1}{(1+\epsilon)^{\frac{p}{p-1}}} D, & \text{if } 1 < p < \infty \\ \frac{\epsilon}{1+\epsilon} D, & \text{if } p = \infty \end{cases},$$

which bounds the size of the K-covering of $\mathbb{X}$ required to achieve the desired multiplicative accuracy ϵ.

For the case $1 < p < \infty$, Lemma A.2 shows there must be

$$M \geq \exp\left\{\ln(2) \cdot D\left(1 - H\left(1 - (1+\epsilon)^{\frac{p}{1-p}}\right)\right)\right\}$$

vertexes of the hypercube in the K-covering of $\mathbb{X}$ to achieve any desired accuracy $0 < \epsilon < 2^{\frac{p-1}{p}} - 1$, for which

$$\delta = \frac{(1+\epsilon)^{\frac{p}{p-1}} - 1}{(1+\epsilon)^{\frac{p}{p-1}}} < \frac{1}{2}$$

to satisfy the condition required by the lemma. Thus, this theorem is applicable for any $\epsilon < 2^{\frac{p-1}{p}} - 1$. For example, for $p = 2$, the theorem is applicable for any $\epsilon < \sqrt{2} - 1$. Moreover, since $H(\delta) < 1$ for any $\delta < \frac{1}{2}$,

$$\alpha_{p,\epsilon} = \exp\left\{\ln(2)\left(1 - H\left(\frac{(1+\epsilon)^{\frac{p}{p-1}} - 1}{(1+\epsilon)^{\frac{p}{p-1}}}\right)\right)\right\} > 1$$

and

$$M \geq \alpha_{p,\epsilon}^D.$$

Similarly for $p = \infty$, applying Lemma A.2 requires $M \geq 2^{D(1-H(\frac{\epsilon}{1+\epsilon}))}$ to achieve any desired accuracy $0 < \epsilon < 1$ (for which $\epsilon/(1+\epsilon) < 1/2$ as required by the lemma). Again, by the properties of entropy, the constant $\alpha_{\infty,\epsilon} = 2^{(1-H(\frac{\epsilon}{1+\epsilon}))} > 1$ for any $0 < \epsilon < 1$ and $M \geq \alpha_{\infty,\epsilon}^D$. $\square$

It is worth noting that the constants $\alpha_{p,\epsilon}$ and $\alpha_{\infty,\epsilon}$ required by Theorem 8.12 can be expressed in a more concise form by expanding the entropy function ($H(\delta) = -\delta \log_2(\delta) - (1-\delta)\log_2(1-\delta)$). For $1 < p < \infty$ the constant is given by

$$\alpha_{p,\epsilon} = 2 \cdot \left(1 - (1+\epsilon)^{\frac{p}{1-p}}\right) \cdot \exp\left(\ln\left(\frac{-1}{1 - (1+\epsilon)^{\frac{p}{p-1}}}\right) \cdot (1+\epsilon)^{\frac{p}{1-p}}\right). \tag{D.7}$$

In this form, it is difficult to directly see that $\alpha_{p,\epsilon} > 1$ for $\epsilon < 2^{\frac{p-1}{p}} - 1$, but using the entropy form in the proof above shows that this is indeed the case. Similarly, for $p = \infty$

the more concise form of the constant is given by

$$\alpha_{\infty,\epsilon} = \frac{2}{1+\epsilon} \exp\left(\ln(\epsilon) \cdot \left(\frac{\epsilon}{1+\epsilon}\right)\right). \tag{D.8}$$

Again, as shown in the proof above, $\alpha_{\infty,\epsilon} > 1$ for $\epsilon < 1$.

Proof of Theorem 8.13

For this proof, we build on previous results for K-covering of $\mathbb{X}$ hyperspheres. The proof is based on a covering number result from Wyner (1965) that first appeared in Shannon (1959). This result bounds the minimum number of spherical caps required to cover the surface of a hypersphere and is summarized in Appendix A.2.

Proof of Theorem 8.13   Suppose a query-based algorithm submits $N < D + 1$ membership queries $\mathbf{x}^{(1)}, \ldots, \mathbf{x}^{(N)} \in \mathfrak{R}^D$ to the classifier. For the algorithm to be ϵ-optimal, these queries must constrain all consistent classifiers in the family $\hat{\mathcal{F}}^{\text{convex},\text{"+"}}$ to have a common point among their ϵ-$IMAC$ sets. Suppose that all the responses are consistent with the classifier f defined as

$$f(\mathbf{x}) = \begin{cases} +1, & \text{if } A_2\left(\mathbf{x} - \mathbf{x}^A\right) < C_0^-; \\ -1, & \text{otherwise} \end{cases} \tag{D.9}$$

For this classifier, $\mathcal{X}_f^+$ is convex since A_2 is a convex function, $\mathbb{B}^{C_0^+}(A_2) \subseteq \mathcal{X}_f^+$ since $C_0^+ < C_0^-$, and $\mathbb{B}^{C_0^-}(A_2) \nsubseteq \mathcal{X}_f^+$ since $\mathcal{X}_f^+$ is the open C_0^--ball, whereas $\mathbb{B}^{C_0^-}(A_2)$ is the closed C_0^--ball. Moreover, since $\mathcal{X}_f^+$ is the open C_0^--ball, $\nexists \mathbf{x} \in \mathcal{X}_f^-$ such that $A_2\left(\mathbf{x} - \mathbf{x}^A\right) < C_0^-$ therefore $MAC\left(f, A_2\right) = C_0^-$, and any ϵ-optimal points $\mathbf{x}' \in \epsilon$-$IMAC^{(*)}\left(f, A_2\right)$ must satisfy $C_0^- \le A_2\left(\mathbf{x}' - \mathbf{x}^A\right) \le (1+\epsilon)C_0^-$.

Now consider an alternative classifier g that responds identically to f for $\mathbf{x}^{(1)}, \ldots, \mathbf{x}^{(N)}$ but has a different convex positive set $\mathcal{X}_g^+$. Without loss of generality suppose the first $M \le N$ queries are positive and the remaining are negative. Let $\mathbb{G} = conv\left(\mathbf{x}^{(1)}, \ldots, \mathbf{x}^{(M)}\right)$; that is, the convex hull of the M positive queries. We assume $\mathbf{x}^A \in \mathbb{G}$, since otherwise, the malicious classifier can construct the set $\mathcal{X}_g^+$ as in the proof for Theorems 8.7 and 8.6 and achieve $MAC\left(f, A_2\right) = C_0^+$, thereby showing the desired result. Otherwise when $\mathbf{x}^A \in \mathbb{G}$, consider the points $\mathbf{z}^{(i)} = C_0^- \frac{\mathbf{x}^{(i)}}{A_2(\mathbf{x}^{(i)} - \mathbf{x}^A)}$; i.e., the projection of each of the positive queries onto the surface of the ℓ_2 ball $\mathbb{B}^{C_0^-}(A_2)$. Since each positive query lies along the line between $\mathbf{x}^A$ and its projection $\mathbf{z}^{(i)}$, by convexity and the fact that $\mathbf{x}^A \in \mathbb{G}$, the set $\mathbb{G}$ is a subset of $conv\left(\mathbf{z}^{(1)}, \mathbf{z}^{(2)}, \ldots, \mathbf{z}^{(M)}\right)$—we refer to this enlarged hull as $\hat{\mathbb{G}}$. These M projected points $\{\mathbf{z}^{(i)}\}_{i=1}^M$ must form a K-covering of $\mathbb{X}$ of the C_0^--hypersphere as the loci of caps of half-angle $\phi_\epsilon^\star = \arccos\left(\frac{1}{1+\epsilon}\right)$. If not, then there exists some point on the surface of this hypersphere that is at least an angle $\phi_\epsilon^\star$ from all $\mathbf{z}^{(i)}$ points, and the resulting $\phi_\epsilon^\star$-cap centered at this uncovered point is not in $\hat{\mathbb{G}}$ (since a cap is defined as the intersection of the hypersphere and a halfspace). Moreover, by definition of the $\phi_\epsilon^\star$-cap, it achieves a minimal ℓ_2 cost of $C_0^- \cos\phi_\epsilon^\star$. Thus, if the adversary fails to achieve a $\phi_\epsilon^\star$-K-covering of $\mathbb{X}$ of the C_0^--hypersphere, the alternative classifier g has $MAC\,(g, A_2) < C_0^- \cos\phi_\epsilon^\star = \frac{C_0^-}{1+\epsilon}$ and any $\mathbf{x} \in \epsilon\text{-}IMAC^{(*)}\,(g, A_2)$ must have

$$A_2\,\left(\mathbf{x} - \mathbf{x}^A\right) \leq (1+\epsilon)MAC < (1+\epsilon)\frac{C_0^-}{1+\epsilon} = C_0^-$$

whereas any $\mathbf{y} \in \epsilon\text{-}IMAC^{(*)}\,(f, A)$ must have $A\,\left(\mathbf{y} - \mathbf{x}^A\right) \geq C_0^-$. Thus, there are no common points in the $\epsilon\text{-}IMAC^{(*)}$ sets of these consistent classifiers (i.e., $\epsilon\text{-}IMAC^{(*)}\,(f, A) \cap \epsilon\text{-}IMAC^{(*)}\,(g, A) = \emptyset$), and so the adversary would have failed to ensure ϵ-multiplicative optimality. Thus, an $\phi_\epsilon^\star$-K-covering of $\mathbb{X}$ is necessary for ϵ-multiplicative optimality for ℓ_2 costs. Moreover, from our definition of $\phi_\epsilon^\star$, for any $\epsilon \in (0, \infty)$, $\phi^\star \in \left(0, \frac{\pi}{2}\right)$ and thus, Lemma A.1 is applicable for all ϵ. From Lemma A.1, to achieve an $\phi_\epsilon^\star$-K-covering of $\mathbb{X}$ requires at least

$$M \geq \left(\frac{1}{\sin\phi_\epsilon^\star}\right)^{D-2}$$

queries. Using the trigonometric identity $\sin\,(\arccos(x)) = \sqrt{1 - x^2}$, and substituting for $\phi_\epsilon^\star$ yields the following bound on the number of queries required for a given multiplicative accuracy ϵ:

$$M \geq \left(\frac{1}{\sin\left(\arccos\left(\frac{1}{1+\epsilon}\right)\right)}\right)^{D-2}$$

$$\geq \left(\frac{(1+\epsilon)^2}{(1+\epsilon)^2 - 1}\right)^{\frac{D-2}{2}}.$$

$\square$

Glossary

ACRE-learnable: The original framework proposed by Lowd & Meek (2005*a*) for quantifying the query complexity of a family of classifiers; see also, near-optimal evasion problem. See 49.

action: In the context of a learning algorithm, a response or decision made by the learner based on its predicted state of the system. See 20, 21, 27.

adversarial learning: Any learning problem where the learning agent faces an adversarial opponent that wants the learner to fail according to a well-defined adversarial objective. Specifically, in this book, we consider adversarial learning in security-sensitive domains. See 18, 56, 104.

anomaly detection: The task of identifying anomalies within a set of data. See 4, 8, 18, 26, 28, 37, 41, 52, 69, 70, 134–138, 144, 200, 243.

approximate optimality: A notion of optimality in which a valid assignment achieves a value that is close to the optimal achievable value for a particular optimization problem. The notion of *closeness* can be defined in several ways.

▶ **additive gap** ($G^{(+)}$): The additive difference between the estimated optimum $\hat{C}$ and the global optimum C^* as measured by the difference between these two quantities: $\hat{C} - C^*$. When the global optimum is not known, this gap refers to the difference between the estimated optimum and a *lower bound* on the global optimum. See 207.

▶ **additive optimality**: A form of approximate optimality where the estimated optimum $\hat{C}$ is compared to the global optimum C^* using the difference $\hat{C} - C^*$; η-additive optimality is achieved when this difference is less than or equal to η. See 206–208, 212, 217, 225.

▶ **multiplicative gap** ($G^{(*)}$): The multiplicative difference between the estimated optimum $\hat{C}$ and the global optimum C^* as measured by the ratio between these two quantities: $\frac{\hat{C}}{C^*}$. When the global optimum is not known, this gap refers to the ratio between the estimated optimum and a *lower bound* on the global optimum. See 207, 213, 220.

▶ **multiplicative optimality**: A form of approximate optimality where the estimated optimum $\hat{C}$ is compared to the global optimum C^* using the ratio $\frac{\hat{C}}{C^*}$; ϵ-multiplicative optimality is achieved when this ratio is less than or equal to $1 + \epsilon$. See 206–208, 211, 212, 217, 227–230.

attacker: In the learning games introduced in Chapter 3, the attacker is the malicious player who is trying to defeat the learner. See 26, 36.

batch learning: A learning process in which all training data is examined in batch by the learning algorithm to select its hypothesis, f. See 25, 50.

beta distribution: A continuous probability distribution with support on $(0, 1)$ parameterized by $\alpha \in \Re_+$ and $\beta \in \Re_+$ that has a probability density function given by $P(x) = \frac{x^{\alpha-1}(1-x)^{\beta-1}}{B(\alpha,\beta)}$. See 109, 110.

beta function $(B(\alpha, \beta))$: A two-parameter function defined by the definite integral $B(\alpha, \beta) = \int_0^1 t^{\alpha-1}(1-t)^{\beta-1} \, dt$ for parameters $\alpha > 0$ and $\beta > 0$. See 109.

blind spot: a class of miscreant activity that fails to be correctly detected by a detector; i.e., false positives. See 18, 199.

boiling frog poisoning attack: An episodic poisoning method spanning several training iterations, which is named after the folk tale that one can boil a frog by slowly increasing the water temperature over time. In a boiling frog attack, the adversary increases the total amount of poisoned data used during each subsequent training step according to some poisoning schedule so that the detector is gradually acclimated to this malicious data and fails to adequately identify the eventually large quantity of poisoning that has been introduced. See 144, 151, 159–163.

breakdown point $(\epsilon^\star)$: Informally, it is the largest fraction of malicious data that an estimator can tolerate before the adversary can use the malicious data to arbitrarily change the estimator. The breakdown point of a procedure is one measure of its robustness. See 56, 57, 145, 147, 249.

chaff: Extraneous noise added into a data source to mislead a detector. In the case of PCA-based network anomaly detection in Chapter 6, chaff is spurious traffic sent across the network by compromised nodes to interfere with PCA's subspace estimation procedure. See 134, 136, 140.

classification: A learning problem in which the learner is tasked with predicting a response in its response space $\mathcal{Y}$ given an input x from its input space $\mathcal{X}$. In a classification problem, the learned hypothesis is referred to as a classifier. The common case when the response case is boolean or $\{0, 1\}$ is referred to as binary classification. See 23, 26.

▶ **binary classification**: A classification learning problem where the response space $\mathcal{Y}$ is a set of only two elements; e.g., $\mathcal{Y} = \{0, 1\}$ or $\mathcal{Y} = \{"+", "-"\}$. See 26, 28.

classifier (f): A function $f : \mathcal{X} \to \mathcal{Y}$ that predicts a response variable based on a data point $\mathbf{x} \in \mathcal{X}$. In classification, the classifier is selected from the space $\mathcal{F}$ based on a labeled dataset $\mathbb{D}^{(\text{train})}$; e.g., in the empirical risk minimization framework. See 26, *see also* hypothesis.

convex combination: A linear combination $\sum_i \alpha_i \cdot \mathbf{x}^{(i)}$ of the vectors $\{\mathbf{x}^{(i)}\}$ where the coefficients satisfy $\alpha_i \geq 0$ and $\sum_i \alpha_i = 1$. See 76, 108, 257.

convex function: A real-valued function $g : \mathbb{X} \to \mathfrak{R}$, whose domain $\mathbb{X}$ is a convex set in a vector space, is a convex function if for any $x^{(1)}, x^{(2)} \in \mathbb{X}$, the function satisfies the inequality

$$g\left(\alpha x^{(1)} + (1-\alpha)x^{(2)}\right) \leq \alpha g\left(x^{(1)}\right) + (1-\alpha)g\left(x^{(2)}\right) \ ,$$

for any $\alpha \in [0, 1]$. See 177, 179–182, 184, 186–189, 192, 194, 210–212, 216, 221, 231, 259.

convex hull: The smallest convex set containing the set $\mathbb{X}$, or equivalently, the intersection of all convex sets containing $\mathbb{X}$, or the set of all convex combinations of the points in $\mathbb{X}$. For a finite set $\mathbb{X} = \{x^{(i)}\}$, its convex hull is thus given by $\mathbb{C}_{\mathbb{X}} = \left\{\sum_i \alpha_i x^{(i)} \mid \sum_i \alpha_i = 1 \wedge \forall i\, \alpha_i \geq 0\right\}$. See 213, 214, 227, 228.

convex optimization: The process of minimizing a convex function over a convex set. See 94, 147, 177, 184, 195, 211, 232.

convex set: A set $\mathbb{A}$ is convex if for any pair of objects $a, b \in \mathbb{A}$, all convex combinations of a and b are also in $\mathbb{A}$; i.e., $\alpha a + (1-\alpha)b \in \mathbb{A}$ for all $\alpha \in [0, 1]$. See 200, 201, 210–212, 215, 218, 221–225, 231, 232, 257, 259.

convex-inducing classifier: A binary classifier f for which either $\mathcal{X}_f^+$ or $\mathcal{X}_f^-$ is a convex set. See 11, 18, 200–202, 206, 209–211, 218, 225, 231, 232, 244, 245, *see also* classifier.

cost function: A function that describes the cost incurred in a game by a player (the adversary or learner) for its actions. In this book, the cost for the learner is a loss function based solely on the learner's predictions whereas the cost for the adversary may also be data dependent. See 32.

K-covering of $\mathbb{X}$: A collection of K balls of size ϵ (i.e., sets $\mathbb{B}_i$) arranged such that the object represented by set $\mathbb{X}$ is completely contained within their union; i.e., $\mathbb{X} \subseteq \bigcup_i \mathbb{B}_i$.

▶ **covering number**: The minimum number of balls needed to cover an object and hence, a measure of the object's complexity. See 205, 230.

data: A set of observations about the state of a system. See 20, *see also* dataset.

data collection: The process of collecting a set of observations about the system that comprise a dataset. See 23, 45.

data point (x): An element of a dataset that is a member of $\mathcal{X}$. See 23, 26, 27.

data sanitization: The process of removing anomalous data from a dataset prior to training on it. See 18.

dataset ($\mathbb{D}$): An indexed set of data points denoted by $\mathbb{D}$. See 23, 25, 26.

deep neural network: Multilayer neural network models that use cascades of hidden layers to implicitly undertake complex tasks such as feature extraction and transformation as part of the learning process. See 44, 48.

defender: In the learning games introduced in Chapter 3, the defender is a learning agent that plays against an attacker. If the learning agent is able to achieve its security goals in the game, it has achieved secure learning. See 26, 36.

degree of security: The level of security expected against an adversary with a certain set of objectives, capabilities, and incentives based on a threat model. See 13.

denial-of-service (DoS) attack: An attack that disrupts normal activity within a system. See 9, 18, 44, 52, 134, 138, 140–144, 146, 151–153, 163, 243.

dictionary attack: A *Causative Availability* attack against SpamBayes, in which attack messages contain an entire dictionary of tokens to be corrupted. See 112, 113.

differential privacy: A formal semantic information-theoretic measure of the level of training dataset privacy preserved by a learner publicly releasing predictions. See 18, 30, 62, 64–66, 171, 173–176, 179, 182, 183, 185, 186, 197, 198.

dispersion: The notion of the spread or variance of a random variable (also known as the scale or deviation). Common estimators of dispersion include the standard deviation and the median absolute deviation. See 136, 145, 147, 148.

distributional robustness: A notion of robustness against deviations from the distribution assumed by a statistical model; e.g., outliers. See 136.

DNN: See 44, 48, *Glossary:* deep neural network.

empirical risk ($\tilde{R}_N (f)$): The average loss of a decision procedure f with respect to data from a dataset $\mathbb{D}$. See 26, 57, 176, 188, 189.

empirical risk minimization: The learning principle of selecting a hypothesis that minimizes the empirical risk over the training data. See 22, 25, 26, 57, 109, 112, 176, 197, *see also* risk.

Erlang q-distribution: A continuous probability distribution with support on $[0, \infty)$ parameterized by a shape $q \in \mathfrak{N}$ and a rate $\lambda \in \mathfrak{R}_+$ that has a probability density function given by $P(x) = \frac{x^{q-1} \exp(-x/\lambda)}{\lambda^q (q-1)!}$. See 182, 183, 188.

expert: An agent that can make predictions or give advice that is used to create a composite predictor based on the advice received from a set of experts. See 56, 58–60, 133, 249, 250, 252.

explanatory variable: An observed quantity that is used to predict an unobservable response variable. See 23, *see also* data point.

false negative: An erroneous prediction that a positive instance is negative. See 27, 31, 32, 34, 36, 51, 114, 115, 119, 134, 156, 157.

false positive: An erroneous prediction that a negative instance is positive. See 27, 32, 34, 35, 71, 114–117, 156, 157.

false-negative rate: The frequency at which a predictor makes false negatives. In machine learning and statistics, this is a common performance measure for assessing a predictor along with the false-positive rate. See 27, 52, 96, 105, 120, 134, 137, 151, 157, 162, *see also* false negative.

false-positive rate: The frequency at which a predictor makes false positives. In machine learning and statistics, this is a common performance measure for assessing a predictor along with the false-negative rate. See 27, 28, 102, 105, 109, 120, 131, 134, 151, 157, 162, 243, *see also* false positive.

feature: An element of a data point; typically a particular measurement of the overall object that the data point represents. See 22, 30, 31, 38, 46, 47, 52, 63, 113, 212, 213, 219, 234, 246.

feature deletion attack: An attack proposed by Globerson & Roweis (2006) in which the adversary first causes a learning agent to associate intrusion instances with irrelevant features and subsequently removes these spurious features from its intrusion instances to evade detection. See 41, 46.

feature selection: The second phase of data collection in which the data are mapped to an alternative space $\hat{\mathcal{X}}$ to select the most relevant representation of the data for the learning task. In this book, we do not distinguish between the feature selection and measurement phases; instead they are considered to be a single step, and $\mathcal{X}$ is used in place of $\hat{\mathcal{X}}$. See 24, 30, 31, 41, 46, 47, 246, 247.

feature selection map (ϕ): The (data-dependent) function used by feature selection to map from the original input space $\mathcal{X}$ to a second feature space $\hat{\mathcal{X}}$ of the features most relevant for the subsequent learning task. See 21, 24, 46, 72, 236, 247.

Gaussian distribution (N (μ, σ)): A (multivariate) continuous probability distribution with support on $\Re^D$ parameterized by a center $\mu \in \Re^D$ and a scale $\sigma \in \Re_+$ that has a probability density function given by $P(\mathbf{x}) = \frac{1}{\sqrt{2\pi}\sigma} \exp\left(-\frac{\|\mathbf{x}-\mu\|_2^2}{2\sigma^2}\right)$. See 25, 136, 159, 160, 235.

good word attack: A spam attack studied by Wittel & Wu (2004) and Lowd & Meek (2005b), in which the spammer adds words associated with non-spam messages to its spam to evade a spam filter. More generally, any attack where an adversary adds features to make intrusion instances appear to be normal instances. See 41, 42.

gross-error model ($\mathcal{P}_\epsilon(F_Z)$): A family of distributions about the known distribution F_Z parameterized by the fraction of contamination ϵ that combine F_Z with a fraction ϵ of contamination from distributions $H_Z \in \mathcal{P}_Z$. See 57.

gross-error sensitivity: The supremum, or smallest upper bound, on the magnitude of the influence function for an estimator; this serves as a quantitative measure of a procedure or estimator. See 58.

Hilbert space ($\mathcal{H}$): An inner-product space that is complete with respect to the metric induced by its inner product; i.e., the metric $\|x\|_{\mathcal{H}} \triangleq \sqrt{\langle x, x \rangle}$ for all $x \in \mathcal{H}$. See 102, 178, 188.

▶ **reproducing kernel Hilbert space**: A Hilbert space $\mathcal{H}$ of real-valued functions on the space $\mathcal{X}$, which includes, for each point $x \in \mathcal{X}$, a point-evaluation function $k(\,\cdot\,, x)$ having the reproducing kernel property $\langle f, k(\,\cdot\,, x)\rangle_{\mathcal{H}} = f(x)$ for all $f \in \mathcal{H}$. See 177–179, 185, 186, 188, 189, 197, 198, 233.

hypothesis (f): A function f mapping from the data space $\mathcal{X}$ to the response space $\mathcal{Y}$. The task for a learner is to select a hypothesis from its hypothesis space to best predict the response variables based on the input variables. See 21, 22, 24–27, *see also* classifier.

hypothesis space ($\mathcal{F}$): The set of all possible hypotheses, f, that are supported by the learning model. While this space is often infinite, it is indexed by a parameter θ that maps to each hypothesis in the space. See 24–26.

IDS: See 31, 40, 41, 45, 47, 53, 201, *Glossary:* intrusion detection system.

index set: A set $\mathbb{I}$ that is used as an index to the members of another set $\mathbb{X}$ such that there is a mapping from each element of $\mathbb{I}$ to a unique element of $\mathbb{X}$. See 256.

indicator function: The function $I[\,\cdot\,]$ that is 1 when its argument is true and is 0 otherwise. See 256.

inductive bias: A set of (implicit) assumptions used in inductive learning to bias generalizations from a set of observations. See 22, 24.

inductive learning: A task where the learner generalizes a pattern from training examples; e.g., finding a linear combination of features that empirically discriminates between positive and negative data points. See 22.

influence function ($IF(z; H, F_Z)$): A functional used extensively in robust statistics that quantifies the impact of an infinitesimal point contamination at z on an asymptotic estimator H on distribution F_Z; see Section 3.5.4.3. See 56, 57, 249.

input space ($\mathcal{X}$): The space of all data points. See 23, *see also* data point.

intrusion detection system: A detector that is designed to identify suspicious activity that is indicative of illegitimate intrusions. Typically these systems are either host-based or network-based detectors. See 31.

intrusion instance: A data point that corresponds to an illegitimate activity. The goal of malfeasance detection is to properly identify normal and intrusion instances and prevent the intrusion instances from achieving their intended objective. See 26.

intrusion prevention system: A system tasked with detecting intrusions and taking automatic actions to prevent detected intrusions from succeeding. See 31, *see also* intrusion detection system.

iterated game: In game theory, a game in which players choose moves in a series of repetitions of the game. See 58, 71.

kernel function (k): A bivariate real-valued function on the space $\mathcal{X} \times \mathcal{X}$, which implicitly represents an inner product in some Hilbert space so long as it is a positive semi-definite function. See 69, 102, 177–180, 182, 186, 187, 189, 191, 192, 197, 198.

▶ **RBF kernel**: A commonly used kernel function for numeric-valued data. The radial basis function (RBF) kernel is defined here as $k\left(\mathbf{x}^{(i)}, \mathbf{x}^{(j)}\right) = \exp\left(-\frac{\|\mathbf{x}^{(i)}-\mathbf{x}^{(j)}\|_2^2}{2\sigma^2}\right)$ where $\sigma > 0$ is the kernel's bandwidth parameter. See 174, 182, 197, *see also* Gaussian distribution.

label: A special aspect of the world that is to be predicted in a classification problem or past examples of this quantity associated with a set of data points that are jointly used to train the predictor. See 23, 25–28, 33, 55, 58, 59, 63, 106, 107, 109, 110, 114, 115, 120, 130, 201, 235.

labeled dataset: A dataset in which each data point has an associated label. See 23.

Laplace distribution (*Laplace*($\boldsymbol{\mu}$, λ)): A (multivariate) continuous probability distribution with support on $\Re^D$ parameterized by a center $\boldsymbol{\mu} \in \Re^D$ and a scale $\lambda \in \Re_+$ that has a probability density function given by $P(\mathbf{x}) = \frac{1}{2\lambda} \exp\left(-\frac{\|\mathbf{x}-\boldsymbol{\mu}\|_1}{\lambda}\right)$. See 173, 182.

Laplace noise: A random variable drawn from a **0**-centered Laplace distribution and added to a nonrandom quantity. Laplace noise is used extensively in Chapter 7 through the Laplace mechanism to provide privacy properties to nonprivate learners. See 173, 179, 186, 188, 198, 244, *see also* Laplace distribution.

learner: An agent or algorithm that performs actions or makes predictions based on past experiences or examples of how to properly perform its task. When presented with new examples, the learner should adapt according to a measure of its performance. See 24.

learning algorithm: Any algorithm that adapts to a task based on past experiences of the task and a performance measure to assess its mistakes. See 25.

loss function (ℓ): A function, commonly used in statistical learning, that assesses the penalty incurred by a learner for making a particular prediction/action compared to the best or correct one according to the *true* state of the world; e.g., the squared loss for real-valued prediction is given by $\ell(y, \hat{y}) \triangleq (\hat{y} - y)^2$. See 21, 25–27, 40, 50, 58, 59, 111, 112, 174, 177, 179, 180, 182–184, 186, 187, 192.

machine learning: A scientific discipline that investigates algorithms that adapt their behavior based on past experiences and observations. As stated by Mitchell (1997), "A computer program is said to learn from experience E with respect to some class of tasks T and performance measure P, if its performance at tasks in T, as measured by P, improves with experience E." See 20.

malfeasance detection: The task of detecting some particular form of illegitimate activity; e.g., virus, spam, intrusion, or fraud detection. See 4.

measurement: An object mapped from the space of real-world object to the data representation used by a learning algorithm. See 22.

measurement map: A description of the process that creates a measurement based on the observations and properties of a real-world object. See 23.

median absolute deviation: A robust estimator for dispersion defined by Equation (6.5), which attains the highest possible breakdown point of 50% and is the most robust M-estimator for dispersion. See 136.

membership query: A query sent to an oracle to determine set membership for some set defined by the oracle's responses. See 203, 231, 245.

mimicry attack: An attack where the attacker tries to disguise malicious activity to appear to be normal. See 41, 47, 54, 201.

minimal adversarial cost (*MAC*): The smallest adversarial cost A that can be obtained for instances in the negative class $\mathcal{X}_f^-$ of a deterministic classifier f. See 204.

Minkowski metric: A distance metric for the convex set $\mathbb{C}$ that is defined relative to a point $\mathbf{x}^{(c)}$ in the interior of the set. See 210.

near-isotropic: A set or body that is nearly round as defined by Equation 8.12. See 222–224, 226.

near-optimal evasion problem: A framework for measuring the difficulty for an adversary to find blind spots in a classifier using a probing attack with few queries. A family of classifiers is considered difficult to evade if there is no efficient query-based algorithm for finding near-optimal instances; see Chapter 8. See 11, 48, 200, 205.

negative class: The set of data points that are classified as negative by the classifier f (denoted by $\mathcal{X}_f^-$). See 26, 210, 211, 225, 231, 232.

norm ($\| \cdot \|$): A non-negative function on a vector space $\mathcal{X}$ that is zero only for the zero vector $\mathbf{0} \in \mathcal{X}$, is positive homogeneous, and obeys the triangle inequality. See 257.

normal instance: A data point that represents normal (allowable) activity such as a regular email message. See 26, *see also* data point.

obfuscation: Any method used by adversaries (particularly spammers) to conceal their malfeasance. See 8, 11, 40–42, 46, 112, 118.

Ockham's Razor: An assumption that the simplest hypothesis is probably the correct one. See 22.

OD flow volume anomaly: An unusual traffic pattern in an OD flow between two points-of-presence (PoPs) in a communication network; e.g., a DoS attack. See 138.

one-class support vector machine: A formulation of the support vector machine used for anomaly detection. See *see also* support vector machine.

one-shot game: In game theory, any game in which players each make only a single move. See 58.

online learning: A learning process in which data points from the training dataset arrive sequentially. Often, online learning consists of sequential prediction followed by retraining as described in Section 3.6. See 25, 59–61, 235, 249, 252.

overfitting: A phenomenon in which a learned hypothesis fails to generalize to test data; i.e., it poorly predicts new data items drawn from the same distribution. Typically this occurs because the model has too much complexity for its training data and captures random fluctuations in it rather than the underlying relationships. Note, this phenomenon is distinct from nonstationarity; e.g., distributional shift. See 27.

PCA evasion problem: A problem discussed in Chapter 6 in which the attacker attempts to send DoS attacks that evade detection by a PCA subspace-based detector as proposed by Lakhina, Crovella, and Diot (2004*b*). See 142, 143.

performance measure: A function used to assess the predictions made by or actions taken by a learning agent. See 26, *see also* loss function.

polymorphic blending attack: Attacks proposed by Fogla & Lee (2006) that use encryption techniques to make intrusion instances indistinguishable from normal instances. See 41.

positive class ($\mathcal{X}_f^+$): The set of data points that are classified as positive by the classifier f (denoted by $\mathcal{X}_f^+$). See 26, 203, 210, 211, 225, 231.

positive homogeneous function: Any function p on a vector space $\mathcal{X}$ that satisfies $p(a\mathbf{x}) = |a|\, p(\mathbf{x})$ for all $a \in \Re$ and $\mathbf{x} \in \mathcal{X}$. See 214.

positive semi-definite function: A real-valued bivariate function, $k(\,\cdot\,,\,\cdot\,)$, on the space $\mathcal{X} \times \mathcal{X}$ is positive semi-definite if and only if $k(\mathbf{x}, \mathbf{x}) \geq 0$ for all $\mathbf{x} \in \mathcal{X}$. See *see also* kernel function.

prediction: The task of predicting an unobserved quantity about the state of a system based on observable information about the system's state and past experience. See 25.

prior distribution: A distribution on the parameters of a model that reflects information or assumptions about the model formed before obtaining empirical data about it. See 24, 107–110, 112, 278–280.

probably approximately correct: A learning framework introduced by Valiant (1984) in which the goal of the learner is to select a hypothesis that achieve a low training error with high probability. See 15, 51, 55, 58, 65, 174, 176, 202.

probing attack: An attack that uses queries to discern hidden information about a system that could expose its weaknesses. See 11, 31, 40, 45, 61, 208, 227, 234, 251, *see also* near-optimal evasion problem.

query: A question posed to an oracle; in an adversarial learning setting, queries can be used to infer hidden information about a learning agent. See 10, 11, 18, 40, 42, 48, 49, 200, 201, 204, 205, 207, 209, 211, 212, 214–217, 220, 221, 225, 228, 229, 231, 232, 235–237, 244, 245, 264.

regret: The difference in loss incurred by a composite predictor and the loss of an expert used by the composite in forming its predictions. See 58, 60.

▶ **cumulative regret** $(R^{(m)})$: The total regret received for the mth expert over the course of K rounds of an iterated game. See 60.

▶ **instantaneous regret** $(r^{(k,m)})$: The difference in loss between the composite predictor and the mth expert in the kth round of the game. See 59.

▶ **worst-case regret** (R^*): The maximum cumulative regret for a set of M experts. See 60.

regret minimization procedure: A learning paradigm in which the learner dynamically reweighs advice from a set of experts based on their past performance so that the resulting combined predictor has a small worst-case regret; i.e., it predicts almost as well as the best expert in hindsight. See 60.

regularization: The process of providing additional information or constraints in a learning problem to solve an ill-posed problem or to prevent overfitting, typically by penalizing hypothesis complexity or introducing a prior distribution. Regularization techniques include smoothness constraints, bounds on the norm of the hypothesis, $\|f\|$, and prior distributions on parameters. See 27.

reject on negative impact: A defense against *Causative* attacks, which measures the empirical effect that each training instance has when training a classifier with it, identifies all instances that had a substantial negative impact on that classifier's accuracy, and removes the offending instances from the training set, $\mathbb{D}^{(train)}$, before training the final classifier. See 55, 114, 120, 128, 129, 131, 243.

residual: The error in an observation that is not accounted for by a model. Models such as PCA select a model according to the total size of their residuals for a given dataset. See 136, 145, 148–150, 152, 153, 159, 160, 163.

▶ **residual rate**: A statistic that measures the change in, the size of the residual caused by adding a single unit of traffic volume into the network along a particular

OD flow. Alternatively, it can be thought of as a measure of how closely a subspace aligns with the flow's vector. See 152–154.

▶ **residual subspace**: In subspace estimation, the residual subspace (or abnormal subspace) is the orthogonal complement to the normal subspace used by the model to describe the observed data; i.e., the error component of each data point lies in the residual subspace. See 136, 139, 152.

response space ($\mathcal{Y}$): The space of values for the response variables; in classification this is a finite set of categories and in binary classification it is {"+", "−"}. See 23, 26.

response variable: An unobserved quantity that is to be predicted based on observable explanatory variables. See 23, *see also* label.

risk ($R(P_Z, f)$): The expected loss of a decision procedure f with respect to data drawn from the distribution P_Z. See 26, 171, 176, 177, 180, 185, 188.

robust statistics: The study and design of statistical procedures that are resilient to small deviations from the assumed underlying statistical model; e.g., outliers. See 55.

RONI: See vii, 120, 128–132, 243, *Glossary:* reject on negative impact.

scale invariant: A property that does not change when the space is scaled by a constant factor. See 208.

secure learning: The ability of a learning agent to achieve its security goals in spite of the presence of an adversary that tries to prevent it from doing so. See 7.

security goal: Any objective that a system needs to achieve to ensure the security of the system and/or its users. See 31.

security-sensitive domain: A task or problem domain in which malicious entities have a motivation and a means to disrupt the normal operation of system. In the context of adversarial learning, these are problems where an adversary wants to mislead or evade a learning algorithm. See 3, 5, 6, 29, 31.

set indicator function: The function $I_{\mathbb{X}}[\,\cdot\,]$ associated with the set $\mathbb{X}$ that is 1 for any $x \in \mathbb{X}$ and is 0 otherwise. See 256.

shift invariant: A property that does not change when the space is shifted by a constant amount. See 208.

stationarity: A stochastic process in which a sequence of observations are all drawn from the *same* distribution. Also, in machine learning, it is often assumed that the training and evaluation data are both drawn from the same distribution—we refer to this as an assumption of stationarity. See 22, 31.

support vector machine: A family of (nonlinear) learning algorithms that find a maximally separating hyperplane in a high-dimensional space known as its reproducing kernel Hilbert space (RKHS). The kernel function allows the method to compute inner products in that space without explicitly mapping the data into the RKHS. See 39, 43, 46, 52, 55, 63, 171, 176.

SVM: See 55, *Glossary:* support vector machine.

threat model: A description of an adversary's incentives, capabilities, and limitations. See 13, 31.

training: The process of using a training dataset $\mathbb{D}^{(\text{train})}$ to choose a hypothesis f from among a hypothesis space, $\mathcal{F}$. See 25, 33, 34, 40, 44, 131, 134, 142–144.

training algorithm $(H^{(N)})$: An algorithm that selects a classifier to optimize a performance measure for a training dataset; also known as an estimating procedure or learning algorithm. See 24, 25, 32, 203, 234, 247.

training dataset $(\mathbb{D}^{(\text{train})})$: A dataset used by a training algorithm to construct or select a classifier. See 6, 17, 18, 21, 25, 27, 30–32, 34, 36, 39, 40, 45, 46, 49, 55, 56, 58, 61, 63, 69, 71, 72, 94, 106, 107, 114–116, 119, 120, 128, 134, 162, 171, 197, 247, 278, 281, *see also* dataset.

true-positive rate: The frequency for which a predictor correctly classifies positive instances. This is a common measure of a predictor's performance and is one minus the false-negative rate. See 151, *see also* false-negative rate.

unfavorable evaluation distribution: A distribution introduced by the adversary during the evaluation phase to defeat the learner's ability to make correct predictions; this is also referred to as *distributional drift*. See 45.

VC-dimension: The VC or Vapnik-Chervonenkis dimension is a measure of the complexity of a family of classifiers, which is defined as the cardinality of the largest set of data points that can be shattered by the classifiers. See 174, 176, 179, 205.

vector space: A set of objects (vectors) that can be added or multiplied by a scalar; i.e., the space is closed under vector addition and scalar multiplication operations that obey associativity, commutativity, and distributivity and has an additive and multiplicative identity as well as additive inverses. See 257, 259.

virus detection system: A detector tasked with identifying potential computer viruses. See 31.

References

Aldà, F. & Rubinstein, B. I. P. (2017), The Bernstein mechanism: Function release under differential privacy, *in* "Proceedings of the 31st AAAI Conference on Artificial Intelligence (AAAI'2017)."

Alfeld, S., Zhu, X., & Barford, P. (2016), Data poisoning attacks against autoregressive models, *in* "Proceedings of the 30th AAAI Conference on Artificial Intelligence (AAAI'2016)," pp. 1452–1458.

Alfeld, S., Zhu, X., & Barford, P. (2017), Explicit defense actions against test-set attacks, *in* "Proceedings of the 31st AAAI Conference on Artificial Intelligence (AAAI'2017)."

Alpcan, T., Rubinstein, B. I. P., & Leckie, C. (2016), Large-scale strategic games and adversarial machine learning, *in* "2016 IEEE 55th Conference on Decision and Control (CDC)," IEEE, pp. 4420–4426.

Amsaleg, L., Bailey, J., Erfani, S., Furon, T., Houle, M. E., Radovanović, M., & Vinh, N. X. (2016), The vulnerability of learning to adversarial perturbation increases with intrinsic dimensionality, Technical Report NII-2016-005E, National Institute of Informatics, Japan.

Angluin, D. (1988), "Queries and concept learning," *Machine Learning* **2**, 319–342.

Apa (n.d.), *Apache SpamAssassin*.

Bahl, P., Chandra, R., Greenberg, A., Kandula, S., Maltz, D. A., & Zhang, M. (2007), Towards highly reliable enterprise network services via inference of multi-level dependencies, *in* "Proceedings of the 2007 Conference on Applications, Technologies, Architectures, and Protocols for Computer Communications (SIGCOMM)," pp. 13–24.

Balfanz, D. & Staddon, J., eds (2008), *Proceedings of the 1st ACM Workshop on Security and Artificial Intelligence, AISec 2008*.

Balfanz, D. & Staddon, J., eds (2009), *Proceedings of the 2nd ACM Workshop on Security and Artificial Intelligence, AISec 2009*.

Barak, B., Chaudhuri, K., Dwork, C., Kale, S., McSherry, F., & Talwar, K. (2007), Privacy, accuracy, and consistency too: A holistic solution to contingency table release, *in* "Proceedings of the Twenty-Sixth ACM SIGMOD-SIGACT-SIGART Symposium on Principles of Database Systems," pp. 273–282.

Barbaro, M. & Zeller Jr., T. (2006), "A face is exposed for AOL searcher no. 4417749," *New York Times*.

Barreno, M. (2008), Evaluating the security of machine learning algorithms. PhD thesis, University of California, Berkeley.

Barreno, M., Nelson, B., Joseph, A. D., & Tygar, J. D. (2010), "The security of machine learning," *Machine Learning* **81**(2), 121–148.

Barreno, M., Nelson, B., Sears, R., Joseph, A. D., & Tygar, J. D. (2006), Can machine learning be secure?, *in* "Proceedings of the ACM Symposium on Information, Computer and Communications Security (ASIACCS)," pp. 16–25.

Barth, A., Rubinstein, B. I. P., Sundararajan, M., Mitchell, J. C., Song, D., & Bartlett, P. L. (2012), "A learning-based approach to reactive security," *IEEE Transactions on Dependable and Secure Computing* **9**(4), 482–493. Special Issue on Learning, Games, and Security.

Bassily, R., Smith, A., & Thakurta, A. (2014), Private empirical risk minimization: Efficient algorithms and tight error bounds, *in* "2014 IEEE 55th Annual Symposium on Foundations of Computer Science (FOCS)," pp. 464–473.

Beimel, A., Kasiviswanathan, S., & Nissim, K. (2010), Bounds on the sample complexity for private learning and private data release, *in* "Theory of Cryptography Conference," Vol. 5978 of *Lecture Notes in Computer Science*, Springer, pp. 437–454.

Bennett, J., Lanning, S., et al. (2007), The Netflix prize, *in* "Proceedings of KDD Cup and Workshop," Vol. 2007, pp. 3–6.

Bertsimas, D. & Vempala, S. (2004), "Solving convex programs by random walks," *Journal of the ACM* **51**(4), 540–556.

Biggio, B., Corona, I., Maiorca, D., Nelson, B., Srndic, N., Laskov, P., Giacinto, G., & Roli, F. (2013), Evasion attacks against machine learning at test time, *in* "Machine Learning and Knowledge Discovery in Databases - European Conference, ECML PKDD 2013," pp. 387–402.

Biggio, B., Fumera, G., & Roli, F. (2010), Multiple classifier systems under attack, *in* N. E. G. J. K. F. Roli, ed., "Proceedings of the 9th International Workshop on Multiple Classifier Systems (MCS)," Vol. 5997, Springer, pp. 74–83.

Biggio, B., Nelson, B., & Laskov, P. (2012), Poisoning attacks against support vector machines, *in* "Proceedings of the 29th International Conference on Machine Learning (ICML-12)," pp. 1807–1814.

Biggio, B., Rieck, K., Ariu, D., Wressnegger, C., Corona, I., Giacinto, G., & Roli, F. (2014), Poisoning behavioral malware clustering, *in* "Proceedings of the 2014 Workshop on Artificial Intelligent and Security Workshop, AISec 2014," pp. 27–36.

Billingsley, P. (1995), *Probability and Measure*, 3rd edn, Wiley.

Bishop, C. M. (2006), *Pattern Recognition and Machine Learning*, Springer-Verlag.

Blocki, J., Christin, N., Datta, A., & Sinha, A. (2011), Regret minimizing audits: A learning-theoretic basis for privacy protection, *in* "Proceedings of the 24th IEEE Computer Security Foundations Symposium," pp. 312–327.

Blum, A., Dwork, C., McSherry, F., & Nissim, K. (2005), Practical privacy: The SuLQ framework, *in* "Proceedings of the Twenty-Fourth ACM SIGMOD-SIGACT-SIGART Symposium on Principles of Database Systems," pp. 128–138.

Blum, A., Ligett, K., & Roth, A. (2008), A learning theory approach to non-interactive database privacy, *in* "Proceedings of the Fortieth Annual ACM Symposium on Theory of Computing (STOC)," pp. 609–618.

Bodík, P., Fox, A., Franklin, M. J., Jordan, M. I., & Patterson, D. A. (2010), Characterizing, modeling, and generating workload spikes for stateful services, *in* "Proceedings of the 1st ACM Symposium on Cloud Computing (SoCC)," pp. 241–252.

Bodík, P., Griffith, R., Sutton, C., Fox, A., Jordan, M. I., & Patterson, D. A. (2009), Statistical machine learning makes automatic control practical for internet datacenters, *in* "Proceedings of the Workshop on Hot Topics in Cloud Computing (HotCloud)," USENIX Association, pp. 12–17.

Bolton, R. J. & Hand, D. J. (2002), "Statistical fraud detection: A review," *Journal of Statistical Science* **17**(3), 235–255.

Bousquet, O. & Elisseeff, A. (2002), "Stability and generalization," *Journal of Machine Learning Research* **2**(Mar), 499–526.

Boyd, S. & Vandenberghe, L. (2004), *Convex Optimization*, Cambridge University Press.

Brauckhoff, D., Salamatian, K., & May, M. (2009), Applying PCA for traffic anomaly detection: Problems and solutions, *in* "Proceedings of the 28th IEEE International Conference on Computer Communications (INFOCOM)," pp. 2866–2870.

Brent, R. P. (1973), *Algorithms for Minimization without Derivatives*, Prentice-Hall.

Brückner, M. & Scheffer, T. (2009), Nash equilibria of static prediction games, *in* Y. Bengio, D. Schuurmans, J. Lafferty, C. K. I. Williams & A. Culotta, eds., "Advances in Neural Information Processing Systems (NIPS)," Vol. 22, MIT Press, pp. 171–179.

Burden, R. L. & Faires, J. D. (2000), *Numerical Analysis*, 7th edn, Brooks Cole.

Burges, C. J. C. (1998), "A tutorial on support vector machines for pattern recognition," *Data Mining and Knowledge Discovery* **2**(2), 121–167.

Cárdenas, A. A., Greenstadt, R., & Rubinstein, B. I. P., eds (2011), *Proceedings of the 4th ACM Workshop on Security and Artificial Intelligence, AISec 2011 Chicago, October 21, 2011*, ACM.

Cárdenas, A. A., Nelson, B., & Rubinstein, B. I., eds (2012), *Proceedings of the 5th ACM Workshop on Security and Artificial Intelligence, AISec 2012, Raleigh, North Carolina, October, 19, 2012*, ACM.

Cauwenberghs, G. & Poggio, T. (2000), "Incremental and decremental support vector machine learning," *Advances in Neural Information Processing Systems* **13**, 409–415.

Cesa-Bianchi, N. & Lugosi, G. (2006), *Prediction, Learning, and Games*, Cambridge University Press.

Chandrashekar, J., Orrin, S., Livadas, C., & Schooler, E. M. (2009), "The dark cloud: Understanding and defending against botnets and stealthy malware," *Intel Technology Journal* **13**(2), 130–145.

Chaudhuri, K. & Monteleoni, C. (2009), Privacy-preserving logistic regression, "Advances in Neural Information Processing Systems," 289–296.

Chaudhuri, K., Monteleoni, C., & Sarwate, A. D. (2011), "Differentially private empirical risk minimization," *Journal of Machine Learning Research* **12**, 1069–1109.

Chen, T. M. & Robert, J.-M. (2004), The evolution of viruses and worms, *in* W. W. Chen, ed., *Statistical Methods in Computer Security*, CRC Press, pp. 265–282.

Cheng, Y.-C., Afanasyev, M., Verkaik, P., Benkö, P., Chiang, J., Snoeren, A. C., Savage, S., & Voelker, G. M. (2007), Automating cross-layer diagnosis of enterprise wireless networks, *in* "Proceedings of the Conference on Applications, Technologies, Architectures, and Protocols for Computer Communications (SIGCOMM)," pp. 25–36.

Christmann, A. & Steinwart, I. (2004), "On robustness properties of convex risk minimization methods for pattern recognition," *Journal of Machine Learning Research* **5**, 1007–1034.

Chung, S. P. & Mok, A. K. (2006), Allergy attack against automatic signature generation, *in* D. Zamboni & C. Krügel, eds., "Proceedings of the 9th International Symposium on Recent Advances in Intrusion Detection (RAID)," Springer, pp. 61–80.

Chung, S. P. & Mok, A. K. (2007), Advanced allergy attacks: Does a corpus really help?, *in* C. Krügel, R. Lippmann & A. Clark, eds, "Proceedings of the 10th International Symposium on Recent Advances in Intrusion Detection (RAID)," Vol. 4637 of *Lecture Notes in Computer Science*, Springer, pp. 236–255.

Cormack, G. & Lynam, T. (2005), Spam corpus creation for TREC, *in* "Proceedings of the Conference on Email and Anti-Spam (CEAS)."

Cormen, T. H., Leiserson, C. E., Rivest, R. L., & Stein, C. (2001), *Introduction to Algorithms*, 2nd edn, McGraw-Hill. http://citeseerx.ist.psu.edu/viewdoc/download?doi=10.1.1.86.3539&rep=rep1&type=pdf.

Cormode, G., Procopiuc, C., Srivastava, D., Shen, E., & Yu, T. (2012), Differentially private spatial decompositions, *in* "2012 IEEE 28th International Conference on Data Engineering (ICDE)," pp. 20–31.

Cover, T. M. (1991), "Universal portfolios," *Mathematical Finance* **1**(1), 1–29.

Cristianini, N. & Shawe-Taylor, J. (2000), *An Introduction to Support Vector Machines*, Cambridge University Press.

Croux, C., Filzmoser, P., & Oliveira, M. R. (2007), "Algorithms for projection-pursuit robust principal component analysis," *Chemometrics and Intelligent Laboratory Systems* **87**(2), 218–225.

Croux, C. & Ruiz-Gazen, A. (2005), "High breakdown estimators for principal components: The projection-pursuit approach revisited," *Journal of Multivariate Analysis* **95**(1), 206–226.

Dalvi, N., Domingos, P., Mausam, Sanghai, S., & Verma, D. (2004), Adversarial classification, *in* "Proceedings of the 10th ACM International Conference on Knowledge Discovery and Data Mining (KDD)," pp. 99–108.

Dasgupta, S., Kalai, A. T., & Monteleoni, C. (2009), "Analysis of perceptron-based active learning," *Journal of Machine Learning Research* **10**, 281–299.

De, A. (2012), Lower bounds in differential privacy, *in* "Theory of Cryptography Conference," Springer, pp. 321–338.

Denning, D. E. & Denning, P. J. (1979), "Data security," *ACM Computing Surveys* **11**, 227–249.

Devlin, S. J., Gnanadesikan, R., & Kettenring, J. R. (1981), "Robust estimation of dispersion matrices and principal components," *Journal of the American Statistical Association* **76**, 354–362.

Devroye, L., Györfi, L., & Lugosi, G. (1996), *A Probabilistic Theory of Pattern Recognition*, Springer Verlag.

Devroye, L. P. & Wagner, T. J. (1979), "Distribution-free performance bounds for potential function rules," *IEEE Transactions on Information Theory* **25**(5), 601–604.

Diffie, W. & Hellman, M. E. (1976), "New directions in cryptography," *IEEE Transactions on Information Theory* **22**(6), 644–654.

Dimitrakakis, C., Gkoulalas-Divanis, A., Mitrokotsa, A., Verykios, V. S., & Saygin, Y., eds (2011), *Privacy and Security Issues in Data Mining and Machine Learning - International ECML/PKDD Workshop, PSDML 2010, Barcelona, September 24, 2010. Revised Selected Papers*, Springer.

Dimitrakakis, C., Laskov, P., Lowd, D., Rubinstein, B. I. P., & Shi, E., eds (2014), *Proceedings of the 1st ICML Workshop on Learning, Security and Privacy, Beijing, China, June 25, 2014*.

Dimitrakakis, C., Mitrokotsa, K., & Rubinstein, B. I. P., eds (2014), *Proceedings of the 7th ACM Workshop on Artificial Intelligence and Security, AISec 2014, Scottsdale, AZ, November 7, 2014*.

Dimitrakakis, C., Mitrokotsa, K., & Sinha, A., eds. (2015), *Proceedings of the 8th ACM Workshop on Artificial Intelligence and Security, AISec 2015, Denver, CO, October 16, 2015*.

Dimitrakakis, C., Nelson, B., Mitrokotsa, A., & Rubinstein, B. I. P. (2014), Robust and private Bayesian inference, *in* "Proceedings of the 25th International Conference Algorithmic Learning Theory (ALT)," pp. 291–305.

Dinur, I. & Nissim, K. (2003), Revealing information while preserving privacy, *in* "Proceedings of the Twenty-Second ACM SIGMOD-SIGACT-SIGART Symposium on Principles of Database Systems," pp. 202–210.

Dredze, M., Gevaryahu, R., & Elias-Bachrach, A. (2007), Learning fast classifiers for image spam, *in* "Proceedings of the 4th Conference on Email and Anti-Spam (CEAS)." http://citeseerx.ist.psu.edu/viewdoc/download?doi=10.1.1.102.8417&rep=rep1&type=pdf.

Duchi, J. C., Jordan, M. I., & Wainwright, M. J. (2013), Local privacy and statistical minimax rates, *in* "2013 IEEE 54th Annual Symposium on Foundations of Computer Science (FOCS)," pp. 429–438.

Dwork, C. (2006), Differential privacy, *in* "Proceedings of the 33rd International Conference on Automata, Languages and Programming," pp. 1–12.

Dwork, C. (2010), "A firm foundation for private data analysis," *Communications of the ACM* **53** (6), 705–714.

Dwork, C. & Lei, J. (2009), Differential privacy and robust statistics, *in* "Proceedings of the Forty-First Annual ACM Symposium on Theory of Computing (STOC)," pp. 371–380.

Dwork, C., McSherry, F., Nissim, K., & Smith, A. (2006), Calibrating noise to sensitivity in private data analysis, *in* "Theory of Cryptography Conference," pp. 265–284.

Dwork, C., McSherry, F., & Talwar, K. (2007), The price of privacy and the limits of LP decoding, *in* "Proceedings of the 39th Annual ACM Symposium on Theory of Computing (STOC)," pp. 85–94.

Dwork, C., Naor, M., Reingold, O., Rothblum, G. N., & Vadhan, S. (2009), On the complexity of differentially private data release: Efficient algorithms and hardness results, *in* "Proceedings of the Forty-First Annual ACM Symposium on Theory of Computing (STOC)," pp. 381–390.

Dwork, C. & Roth, A. (2014), "The algorithmic foundations of differential privacy," *Foundations and Trends in Theoretical Computer Science* **9**(3–4), 211–407.

Dwork, C. & Yekhanin, S. (2008), New efficient attacks on statistical disclosure control mechanisms, *in* "CRYPTO'08," pp. 469–480.

Erlich, Y. & Narayanan, A. (2014), "Routes for breaching and protecting genetic privacy," *Nature Reviews Genetics* **15**, 409–421.

Eskin, E., Arnold, A., Prerau, M., Portnoy, L., & Stolfo, S. J. (2002), A geometric framework for unsupervised anomaly detection: Detecting intrusions in unlabeled data, *in Data Mining for Security Applications*, Kluwer.

Feldman, V. (2009), "On the power of membership queries in agnostic learning," *Journal of Machine Learning Research* **10**, 163–182.

Fisher, R. A. (1948), "Question 14: Combining independent tests of significance," *American Statistician* **2**(5), 30–31.

Flum, J. & Grohe, M. (2006), *Parameterized Complexity Theory*, Texts in Theoretical Computer Science, Springer-Verlag.

Fogla, P. & Lee, W. (2006), Evading network anomaly detection systems: Formal reasoning and practical techniques, *in* "Proceedings of the 13th ACM Conference on Computer and Communications Security (CCS)," pp. 59–68.

Forrest, S., Hofmeyr, S. A., Somayaji, A., & Longstaff, T. A. (1996), A sense of self for Unix processes, *in* "Proceedings of the IEEE Symposium on Security and Privacy (SP)," pp. 120–128.

Freeman, D., Mitrokotsa, K., & Sinha, A., eds (2016), *Proceedings of the 9th ACM Workshop on Artificial Intelligence and Security, AISec 2016, Vienna, Austria, October 28, 2016.*

Globerson, A. & Roweis, S. (2006), Nightmare at test time: Robust learning by feature deletion, *in* "Proceedings of the 23rd International Conference on Machine Learning (ICML)," pp. 353–360.

Goldman, S. A. & Kearns, M. J. (1995), "On the complexity of teaching," *Journal of Computer and System Sciences* **50**(1), 20–31.

Goodfellow, I. J., Shlens, J., & Szegedy, C. (2015), Explaining and harnessing adversarial challenges, *in* "Proceedings of the International Conference on Learning Representations."

Goodfellow, I., Pouget-Abadie, J., Mirza, M., Xu, B., Warde-Farley, D., Ozair, S., Courville, A., & Bengio, Y. (2014), Generative adversarial nets, *in* "Advances in Neural Information Processing Systems," pp. 2672–2680.

Gottlieb, L.-A., Kontorovich, A., & Mossel, E. (2011), VC bounds on the cardinality of nearly orthogonal function classes, Technical Report arXiv:1007.4915v2 [math.CO], arXiv.

Graham, P. (2002), "A plan for spam," http://www.paulgraham.com/spam.html.

Greenstadt, R., ed. (2010), *Proceedings of the 3rd ACM Workshop on Security and Artificial Intelligence, AISec 2010, Chicago, October 8, 2010*, ACM.

Großhans, M., Sawade, C., Brückner, M., & Scheffer, T. (2013), Bayesian games for adversarial regression problems, *in* "Proceedings of the 30th International Conference on Machine Learning, ICML 2013," pp. 55–63.

Gymrek, M., McGuire, A. L., Golan, D., Halperin, E., & Erlich, Y. (2013), "Identifying personal genomes by surname inference," *Science* **339**(6117), 321–324.

Hall, J. F. (2005), "Fun with stacking blocks," *American Journal of Physics* **73**(12), 1107–1116.

Hall, R., Rinaldo, A., & Wasserman, L. (2013), "Differential privacy for functions and functional data," *Journal of Machine Learning Research* **14**(1), 703–727.

Hampel, F. R., Ronchetti, E. M., Rousseeuw, P. J., & Stahel, W. A. (1986), *Robust Statistics: The Approach Based on Influence Functions*, John Wiley.

Hardt, M., Ligett, K., & McSherry, F. (2012), A simple and practical algorithm for differentially private data release, *in* F. Pereira, C. J. C. Burges, L. Bottou, & K. Q. Weinberger, eds., "Advances in Neural Information Processing Systems 25 (NIPS)," pp. 2339–2347.

Hardt, M. & Talwar, K. (2010), On the geometry of differential privacy, *in* "Proceedings of the Forty-Second Annual ACM Symposium on Theory of Computing (STOC)," pp. 705–714.

Hastie, T., Tibshirani, R., & Friedman, J. (2003), *The Elements of Statistical Learning: Data Mining, Inference and Prediction*, Springer.

He, X., Cormode, G., Machanavajjhala, A., Procopiuc, C. M., & Srivastava, D. (2015), "Dpt: differentially private trajectory synthesis using hierarchical reference systems," *Proceedings of the VLDB Endowment* **8**(11), 1154–1165.

Helmbold, D. P., Singer, Y., Schapire, R. E., & Warmuth, M. K. (1998), "On-line portfolio selection using multiplicative updates," *Mathematical Finance* **8**, 325–347.

Hofmeyr, S. A., Forrest, S., & Somayaji, A. (1998), "Intrusion detection using sequences of system calls," *Journal of Computer Security* **6**(3), 151–180.

Hohm, T., Egli, M., Gaehwiler, S., Bleuler, S., Feller, J., Frick, D., Huber, R., Karlsson, M., Lingenhag, R., Ruetimann, T., Sasse, T., Steiner, T., Stocker, J., & Zitzler, E. (2007), An evolutionary algorithm for the block stacking problem, *in* "8th International Conference Artificial Evolution (EA 2007)," Springer, pp. 112–123.

Holz, T., Steiner, M., Dahl, F., Biersack, E., & Freiling, F. (2008), Measurements and mitigation of peer-to-peer-based botnets: A case study on storm worm, *in* "Proceedings of the 1st Usenix Workshop on Large-Scale Exploits and Emergent Threats," LEET'08, pp. 1–9.

Homer, N., Szelinger, S., Redman, M., Duggan, D., Tembe, W., Muehling, J., Pearson, J. V., Stephan, D. A., Nelson, S. F., & Craig, D. W. (2008), "Resolving individuals contributing trace amounts of DNA to highly complex mixtures using high-density SNP genotyping microarrays," *PLoS Genetics* **4**(8).

Hössjer, O. & Croux, C. (1995), "Generalizing univariate signed rank statistics for testing and estimating a multivariate location parameter," *Journal of Nonparametric Statistics* **4**(3), 293–308.

Huang, L., Nguyen, X., Garofalakis, M., Jordan, M. I., Joseph, A., & Taft, N. (2007), In-network PCA and anomaly detection, *in* B. Schölkopf, J. Platt & T. Hoffman, eds., "Advances in Neural Information Processing Systems 19 (NIPS)," MIT Press, pp. 617–624.

Huber, P. J. (1981), *Robust Statistics*, Probability and Mathematical Statistics, John Wiley.

Jackson, J. E. & Mudholkar, G. S. (1979), "Control procedures for residuals associated with principal component analysis," *Technometrics* **21**(3), 341–349.

Johnson, P. B. (1955), "Leaning tower of lire," *American Journal of Physics* **23**(4), 240.

Jones, D. R. (2001), "A taxonomy of global optimization methods based on response surfaces," *Journal of Global Optimization* **21**(4), 345–383.

Jones, D. R., Perttunen, C. D., & Stuckman, B. E. (1993), "Lipschitzian optimization without the Lipschitz constant," *Journal of Optimization Theory and Application* **79**(1), 157–181.

Joseph, A. D., Laskov, P., Roli, F., Tygar, J. D., & Nelson, B. (2013), "Machine Learning Methods for Computer Security (Dagstuhl Perspectives Workshop 12371)," *Dagstuhl Manifestos* **3**(1), 1–30. http://drops.dagstuhl.de/opus/volltexte/2013/4356.

Jurafsky, D. & Martin, J. H. (2008), *Speech and Language Processing: An Introduction to Natural Language Processing, Computational Linguistics and Speech Recognition*, 2nd edn, Prentice-Hall.

Kalai, A. & Vempala, S. (2002), "Efficient algorithms for universal portfolios," *Journal of Machine Learning Research* **3**, 423–440.

Kandula, S., Chandra, R., & Katabi, D. (2008), What's going on? Learning communication rules in edge networks, *in* "Proceedings of the Conference on Applications, Technologies, Architectures, and Protocols for Computer Communications (SIGCOMM)," pp. 87–98.

Kantarcioglu, M., Xi, B., & Clifton, C. (2009), Classifier evaluation and attribute selection against active adversaries, Technical Report 09-01, Purdue University.

Kantchelian, A., Ma, J., Huang, L., Afroz, S., Joseph, A. D., & Tygar, J. D. (2012), Robust detection of comment spam using entropy rate, *in* "Proceedings of the 5th ACM Workshop on Security and Artificial Intelligence (AISec 2012)," pp. 59–70.

Kasiviswanathan, S. P., Lee, H. K., Nissim, K., Raskhodnikova, S., & Smith, A. (2008), What can we learn privately?, *in* "Proceedings of the 49th Annual IEEE Symposium on Foundations of Computer Science (FOCS)," pp. 531–540.

Kearns, M. & Li, M. (1993), "Learning in the presence of malicious errors," *SIAM Journal on Computing* **22**(4), 807–837.

Kearns, M. & Ron, D. (1999), "Algorithmic stability and sanity-check bounds for leave-one-out cross-validation," *Neural Computation* **11**, 1427–1453.

Kerckhoffs, A. (1883), "La cryptographie militaire," *Journal des Sciences Militaires* **9**, 5–83.

Kim, H.-A. & Karp, B. (2004), Autograph: Toward automated, distributed worm signature detection, *in* "USENIX Security Symposium" available at https://www.usenix.org/legacy/publications/library/proceedings/sec04/tech/full_papers/kim/kim.pdf.

Kimeldorf, G. & Wahba, G. (1971), "Some results on Tchebycheffian spline functions," *Journal of Mathematical Analysis and Applications* **33**(1), 82–95.

Klíma, R., Lisỳ, V., & Kiekintveld, C. (2015), Combining online learning and equilibrium computation in security games, *in* "International Conference on Decision and Game Theory for Security," Springer, pp. 130–149.

Klimt, B. & Yang, Y. (2004), Introducing the Enron corpus, *in* "Proceedings of the Conference on Email and Anti-Spam (CEAS)" available at https://bklimt.com/papers/2004_klimt_ceas.pdf.

Kloft, M. & Laskov, P. (2010), Online anomaly detection under adversarial impact, *in* "Proceedings of the 13th International Conference on Artificial Intelligence and Statistics (AISTATS)," pp. 406–412.

Kloft, M. & Laskov, P. (2012), "Security analysis of online centroid anomaly detection," *Journal of Machine Learning Research* **13**, 3681–3724.

Kolda, T. G., Lewis, R. M., & Torczon, V. (2003), "Optimization by direct search: New perspectives on some classical and modern methods," *SIAM Review* **45**(3), 385–482.

Korolova, A. (2011), "Privacy violations using microtargeted ads: A case study," *Journal of Privacy and Confidentiality* **3**(1).

Kutin, S. & Niyogi, P. (2002), Almost-everywhere algorithmic stability and generalization error, Technical report TR-2002-03, Computer Science Dept., University of Chicago.

Lakhina, A., Crovella, M., & Diot, C. (2004*a*), Characterization of network-wide anomalies in traffic flows, *in* A. Lombardo & J. F. Kurose, eds., "Proceedings of the 4th ACM SIGCOMM Conference on Internet Measurement (IMC)," pp. 201–206.

Lakhina, A., Crovella, M., & Diot, C. (2004*b*), Diagnosing network-wide traffic anomalies, *in* R. Yavatkar, E. W. Zegura & J. Rexford, eds., "Proceedings of the Conference on Applications, Technologies, Architectures, and Protocols for Computer Communications (SIGCOMM)," pp. 219–230.

Lakhina, A., Crovella, M., & Diot, C. (2005*a*), Detecting distributed attacks using network-wide flow traffic, *in* "Proceedings of the FloCon 2005 Analysis Workshop" available at http://www.cs.bu.edu/~crovella/paper-archive/flocon05.pdf.

Lakhina, A., Crovella, M., & Diot, C. (2005*b*), Mining anomalies using traffic feature distributions, *in* "Proceedings of the Conference on Applications, Technologies, Architectures, and Protocols for Computer Communications (SIGCOMM)," pp. 217–228.

Laskov, P. & Kloft, M. (2009), A framework for quantitative security analysis of machine learning, *in* "Proceedings of the 2nd ACM Workshop on Security and Artificial Intelligence (AISec)," pp. 1–4.

Laskov, P. & Lippmann, R. (2010), "Machine learning in adversarial environments," *Machine Learning* **81**(2), 115–119.

Lazarevic, A., Ertöz, L., Kumar, V., Ozgur, A., & Srivastava, J. (2003), A comparative study of anomaly detection schemes in network intrusion detection, *in* D. Barbará & C. Kamath, eds., "Proceedings of the SIAM International Conference on Data Mining," pp. 25–36.

LeCun, Y., Bengio, Y., & Hinton, G. (2015), "Deep learning," *Nature* **521**(7553), 436–444.

Li, B. & Vorobeychik, Y. (2014), Feature cross-substitution in adversarial classification, *in* "Advances in Neural Information Processing Systems," pp. 2087–2095.

Li, B., Wang, Y., Singh, A., & Vorobeychik, Y. (2016), Data poisoning attacks on factorization-based collaborative filtering, *in* "Advances in Neural Information Processing Systems," pp. 1885–1893.

Li, C., Hay, M., Miklau, G., & Wang, Y. (2014), "A data-and workload-aware algorithm for range queries under differential privacy," *Proceedings of the VLDB Endowment* **7**(5), 341–352.

Li, G. & Chen, Z. (1985), "Projection-pursuit approach to robust dispersion matrices and principal components: Primary theory and Monte Carlo," *Journal of the American Statistical Association* **80**(391), 759–766.

Li, N., Li, T., & Venkatasubramanian, S. (2007), t-Closeness: Privacy beyond k-anonymity and l-diversity, *in* "IEEE 23rd International Conference on Data Engineering (ICED)," pp. 106–115.

Li, X., Bian, F., Crovella, M., Diot, C., Govindan, R., Iannaccone, G., & Lakhina, A. (2006), Detection and identification of network anomalies using sketch subspaces, *in* J. M. Almeida,

V. A. F. Almeida, & P. Barford, eds., "Proceedings of the 6th ACM SIGCOMM Conference on Internet Measurement (IMC)," pp. 147–152.

Littlestone, N. & Warmuth, M. K. (1994), "The weighted majority algorithm," *Information and Computation* **108**(2), 212–261.

Liu, C. & Stamm, S. (2007), Fighting unicode-obfuscated spam, *in* "Proceedings of the Anti-Phishing Working Groups 2nd Annual eCrime Researchers Summit," pp. 45–59.

Liu, Y., Chen, X., Liu, C., & Song, D. (2017), Delving into transferable adversarial examples and black-box attacks, *in* "Proceedings of the International Conference on Learning Representations" available at https://people.eecs.berkeley.edu/~liuchang/paper/transferability_iclr_2017.pdf.

Lovász, L. & Vempala, S. (2003), Simulated annealing in convex bodies and an $O^*(n^4)$ volume algorithm, *in* "Proceedings of the 44th Annual IEEE Symposium on Foundations of Computer Science (FOCS)," pp. 650–659.

Lovász, L. & Vempala, S. (2004), Hit-and-run from a corner, *in* "Proceedings of the 36th Annual ACM Symposium on Theory of Computing (STOC)," pp. 310–314.

Lowd, D. & Meek, C. (2005*a*), Adversarial learning, *in* "Proceedings of the 11th ACM International Conference on Knowledge Discovery and Data Mining (SIGKDD)," pp. 641–647.

Lowd, D. & Meek, C. (2005*b*), Good word attacks on statistical spam filters, *in* "Proceedings of the 2nd Conference on Email and Anti-Spam (CEAS)" available at http://citeseerx.ist.psu.edu/viewdoc/download?doi=10.1.1.130.9846&rep=rep1&type=pdf.

Machanavajjhala, A., Kifer, D., Abowd, J., Gehrke, J., & Vilhuber, L. (2008), Privacy: Theory meets practice on the map, *in* "Proceedings of the 2008 IEEE 24th International Conference on Data Engineering," IEEE Computer Society, pp. 277–286.

Machanavajjhala, A., Kifer, D., Gehrke, J., & Venkitasubramaniam, M. (2007), "ℓ-Diversity: Privacy beyond k-anonymity," *ACM Transactions on KDD* **1**(1).

Mahoney, M. V. & Chan, P. K. (2002), Learning nonstationary models of normal network traffic for detecting novel attacks, *in* "Proceedings of the 8th ACM International Conference on Knowledge Discovery and Data Mining (KDD)," pp. 376–385.

Mahoney, M. V. & Chan, P. K. (2003), An analysis of the 1999 DARPA/Lincoln Laboratory evaluation data for network anomaly detection, *in* G. Vigna, E. Jonsson, & C. Krügel, eds., "Proceedings of the 6th International Symposium on Recent Advances in Intrusion Detection (RAID)," Vol. 2820 of *Lecture Notes in Computer Science*, Springer, pp. 220–237.

Maronna, R. (2005), "Principal components and orthogonal regression based on robust scales," *Technometrics* **47**(3), 264–273.

Maronna, R. A., Martin, D. R., & Yohai, V. J. (2006), *Robust Statistics: Theory and Methods*, John Wiley.

Martinez, D. R., Streilein, W. W., Carter, K. M., & Sinha, A., eds (2016), *Proceedings of the AAAI Workshop on Artificial Intelligence for Cyber Security, AICS 2016, Phoenix, AZ, February 12, 2016*.

McSherry, F. & Mironov, I. (2009), Differentially private recommender systems: Building privacy into the net, *in* "Proceedings of the 15th ACM International Conference on Knowledge Discovery and Data Mining (KDD)," pp. 627–636.

McSherry, F. & Talwar, K. (2007), Mechanism design via differential privacy, *in* "Proceedings of the 48th Annual IEEE Symposium on Foundations of Computer Science (FOCS)," pp. 94–103.

Mei, S. & Zhu, X. (2015*a*), The security of latent Dirichlet allocation, *in* "Proceedings of the Eighteenth International Conference on Artificial Intelligence and Statistics (AISTATS)," pp. 681–689.

Mei, S. & Zhu, X. (2015*b*), Using machine teaching to identify optimal training-set attacks on machine learners, *in* "Proceedings of the Twenty-Ninth AAAI Conference on Artificial Intelligence (AAAI)," AAAI Press, pp. 2871–2877.

Meyer, T. A. & Whateley, B. (2004), SpamBayes: Effective open-source, Bayesian based, email classification system, *in* "Proceedings of the Conference on Email and Anti-Spam (CEAS)" available at http://citeseerx.ist.psu.edu/viewdoc/download?doi=10.1.1.3.9543& rep=rep1&type=pdf.

Microsoft (2009), "H1n1 swine flu response center." https://h1n1.cloudapp.net; Date accessed: March 3, 2011.

Miller, B., Kantchelian, A., Afroz, S., Bachwani, R., Dauber, E., Huang, L., Tschantz, M. C., Joseph, A. D., & Tygar, J. D. (2014), Adversarial active learning, *in* "Proceedings of the 2014 Workshop on Artificial Intelligent and Security Workshop," ACM, pp. 3–14.

Mitchell, T. (1997), *Machine Learning*, McGraw Hill.

Mitchell, T. M. (2006), The discipline of machine learning, Technical Report CMU-ML-06-108, Carnegie Mellon University.

Moore, D., Shannon, C., Brown, D. J., Voelker, G. M., & Savage, S. (2006), "Inferring internet denial-of-service activity," *ACM Transactions on Computer Systems (TOCS)* **24**(2), 115–139.

Mukkamala, S., Janoski, G., & Sung, A. (2002), Intrusion detection using neural networks and support vector machines, *in* "Proceedings of the International Joint Conference on Neural Networks (IJCNN)," Vol. 2, pp. 1702–1707.

Mutz, D., Valeur, F., Vigna, G., & Kruegel, C. (2006), "Anomalous system call detection," *ACM Transactions on Information and System Security (TISSEC)* **9**(1), 61–93.

Narayanan, A., Shi, E., & Rubinstein, B. I. P. (2011), Link prediction by de-anonymization: How we won the kaggle social network challenge, *in* "Proceedings of the 2011 International Joint Conference on Neural Networks (IJCNN)," IEEE, pp. 1825–1834.

Narayanan, A. & Shmatikov, V. (2008), Robust de-anonymization of large sparse datasets, *in* "Proceedings of the 2008 IEEE Symposium on Security and Privacy," SP '08, IEEE Computer Society, pp. 111–125.

Narayanan, A. & Shmatikov, V. (2009), De-anonymizing social networks, *in* "30th IEEE Symposium on Security and Privacy," pp. 173–187.

Nelder, J. A. & Mead, R. (1965), "A simplex method for function minimization," *Computer Journal* **7**(4), 308–313.

Nelson, B. (2005), Designing, Implementing, and Analyzing a System for Virus Detection, Master's thesis, University of California, Berkeley.

Nelson, B., Barreno, M., Chi, F. J., Joseph, A. D., Rubinstein, B. I. P., Saini, U., Sutton, C., Tygar, J. D., & Xia, K. (2008), Exploiting machine learning to subvert your spam filter, *in* "Proceedings of the 1st USENIX Workshop on Large-Scale Exploits and Emergent Threats (LEET)," USENIX Association, pp. 1–9.

Nelson, B., Barreno, M., Chi, F. J., Joseph, A. D., Rubinstein, B. I. P., Saini, U., Sutton, C., Tygar, J. D., & Xia, K. (2009), Misleading learners: Co-opting your spam filter, *in* J. J. P. Tsai & P. S. Yu, eds., *Machine Learning in Cyber Trust: Security, Privacy, Reliability*, Springer, pp. 17–51.

Nelson, B., Dimitrakakis, C., & Shi, E., eds (2013), *Proceedings of the 6th ACM Workshop on Artificial Intelligence and Security, AISec*, ACM.

Nelson, B. & Joseph, A. D. (2006), Bounding an attack's complexity for a simple learning model, *in* "Proceedings of the 1st Workshop on Tackling Computer Systems Problems with Machine Learning Techniques (SysML)" http://citeseerx.ist.psu.edu/viewdoc/download?doi =10.1.1.71.9869&rep=rep1&type=pdf.

Nelson, B., Rubinstein, B. I. P., Huang, L., Joseph, A. D., Lau, S., Lee, S., Rao, S., Tran, A., & Tygar, J. D. (2010), Near-optimal evasion of convex-inducing classifiers, *in* "Proceedings of the 13th International Conference on Artificial Intelligence and Statistics (AISTATS)," pp. 549–556.

Nelson, B., Rubinstein, B. I. P., Huang, L., Joseph, A. D., Lee, S. J., Rao, S., & Tygar, J. D., (2012), "Query strategies for evading convex-inducing classifiers," *Journal of Machine Learning Research* **13**(May), 1293–1332.

Nelson, B., Rubinstein, B. I. P., Huang, L., Joseph, A. D., & Tygar, J. D. (2010), Classifier evasion: Models and open problems (position paper), *in* "Proceedings of ECML/PKDD Workshop on Privacy and Security issues in Data Mining and Machine Learning (PSDML)," pp. 92–98.

Newsome, J., Karp, B., & Song, D. (2005), Polygraph: Automatically generating signatures for polymorphic worms, *in* "Proceedings of the IEEE Symposium on Security and Privacy (SP)," IEEE Computer Society, pp. 226–241.

Newsome, J., Karp, B., & Song, D. (2006), Paragraph: Thwarting signature learning by training maliciously, *in* D. Zamboni & C. Krügel, eds., "Proceedings of the 9th International Symposium on Recent Advances in Intrusion Detection (RAID)," Vol. 4219 of *Lecture Notes in Computer Science*, Springer, pp. 81–105.

Papernot, N., McDaniel, P., Goodfellow, I., Jha, S., Celik, Z. B., & Swami, A. (2016), "Practical black-box attacks against deep learning systems using adversarial examples," *arXiv preprint arXiv:1602.02697*.

Papernot, N., McDaniel, P., Goodfellow, I., Jha, S., Celik, Z. B., & Swami, A. (2017), Practical black-box attacks against deep learning systems using adversarial examples *in* "Proceedings of the 2017 ACM Asia Conference on Computer and Communications Security (ASIACCS)," ACM, pp. 506–519.

Paxson, V. (1999), "Bro: A system for detecting network intruders in real-time," *Computer Networks* **31**(23), 2435–2463.

Pearson, K. (1901), "On lines and planes of closest fit to systems of points in space," *Philosophical Magazine* **2**(6), 559–572.

Peressini, A. L., Sullivan, F. E., & Jerry J. Uhl, J. (1988), *The Mathematics of Nonlinear Programming*, Springer-Verlag.

Plamondon, R. & Srihari, S. N., (2000), "On-line and off-line handwriting recognition: A comprehensive survey," *IEEE Transactions on Pattern Analysis and Machine Intelligence* **22**(1), 63–84.

Rademacher, L. & Goyal, N. (2009), Learning convex bodies is hard, *in* "Proceedings of the 22nd Annual Conference on Learning Theory (COLT)," pp. 303–308.

Rahimi, A. & Recht, B. (2008), Random features for large-scale kernel machines, *in* "Advances in Neural Information Processing Systems 20 (NIPS)," pp. 1177–1184.

Ramachandran, A., Feamster, N., & Vempala, S. (2007), Filtering spam with behavioral blacklisting, *in* "Proceedings of the 14th ACM Conference on Computer and Communications Security (CCS)," pp. 342–351.

Rieck, K. & Laskov, P. (2006), Detecting unknown network attacks using language models, *in* R. Büschkes & P. Laskov, eds., "Detection of Intrusions and Malware & Vulnerability Assessment, Third International Conference (DIMVA)," Vol. 4064 of *Lecture Notes in Computer Science*, Springer, pp. 74–90.

Rieck, K. & Laskov, P. (2007), "Language models for detection of unknown attacks in network traffic," *Journal in Computer Virology* **2**(4), 243–256.

Rieck, K., Trinius, P., Willems, C., & Holz, T. (2011), "Automatic analysis of malware behavior using machine learning," *Journal of Computer Security* **19**(4), 639–668.

Ringberg, H., Soule, A., Rexford, J., & Diot, C. (2007), Sensitivity of PCA for traffic anomaly detection, *in* L. Golubchik, M. H. Ammar, & M. Harchol-Balter, eds., "Proceedings of the ACM SIGMETRICS International Conference on Measurement and Modeling of Computer Systems (SIGMETRICS)," pp. 109–120.

Rivest, R. L., Shamir, A., & Adleman, L. (1978), "A method for obtaining digital signatures and public-key cryptosystems," *Communications of the ACM* **21**(2), 120–126.

Robinson, G. (2003), "A statistical approach to the spam problem," *Linux Journal*, p. 3.

Rubinstein, B. I. P. (2010), Secure Learning and Learning for Security: Research in the Intersection, PhD thesis, University of California, Berkeley.

Rubinstein, B. I. P., Bartlett, P. L., Huang, L., & Taft, N. (2009), "Learning in a large function space: Privacy-preserving mechanisms for SVM learning," *CoRR* **abs/0911.5708**.

Rubinstein, B. I. P., Bartlett, P. L., Huang, L., & Taft, N. (2012), "Learning in a large function space: Privacy-preserving mechanisms for SVM learning," *Journal of Privacy and Confidentiality* **4**(1), 65–100. Special Issue on Statistical and Learning-Theoretic Challenges in Data Privacy.

Rubinstein, B. I. P., Nelson, B., Huang, L., Joseph, A. D., Lau, S., Rao, S., Taft, N., & Tygar, J. D. (2009*a*), ANTIDOTE: Understanding and defending against poisoning of anomaly detectors, *in* A. Feldmann & L. Mathy, eds., "Proceedings of the 9th ACM SIGCOMM Conference on Internet Measurement (IMC)," pp. 1–14.

Rubinstein, B. I. P., Nelson, B., Huang, L., Joseph, A. D., Lau, S., Rao, S., Taft, N., & Tygar, J. D. (2009*b*), "Stealthy poisoning attacks on PCA-based anomaly detectors," *SIGMETRICS Performance Evaluation Review* **37**(2), 73–74.

Rubinstein, B. I. P., Nelson, B., Huang, L., Joseph, A. D., Lau, S., Taft, N., & Tygar, J. D. (2008), Compromising PCA-based anomaly detectors for network-wide traffic, Technical Report UCB/EECS-2008-73, EECS Department, University of California, Berkeley.

Rudin, W. (1994), *Fourier Analysis on Groups*, reprint edn, Wiley-Interscience.

Russu, P., Demontis, A., Biggio, B., Fumera, G., & Roli, F. (2016), Secure kernel machines against evasion attacks, *in* "Proceedings of the 2016 ACM Workshop on Artificial Intelligence and Security, (AISec)," pp. 59–69.

Sahami, M., Dumais, S., Heckerman, D., & Horvitz, E. (1998), A Bayesian approach to filtering junk E-mail, *in* "Learning for Text Categorization: Papers from the 1998 Workshop," AAAI Technical Report WS-98-05, Madison, Wisconsin.

Saini, U. (2008), Machine Learning in the Presence of an Adversary: Attacking and Defending the SpamBayes Spam Filter, Master's thesis, University of California at Berkeley.

Schohn, G. & Cohn, D. (2000), Less is more: Active learning with support vector machines, *in* "Proceedings of the 17th International Conference on Machine Learning (ICML)," pp. 839–846.

Schölkopf, B. & Smola, A. J. (2001), *Learning with Kernels: Support Vector Machines, Regularization, Optimization, and Beyond*, MIT Press.

Sculley, D., Otey, M. E., Pohl, M., Spitznagel, B., Hainsworth, J., & Zhou, Y. (2011), Detecting adversarial advertisements in the wild, *in* "Proceedings of the 17th ACM SIGKDD International Conference on Knowledge Discovery and Data Mining (KDD)," pp. 274–282.

Sculley, D., Wachman, G. M., & Brodley, C. E. (2006), Spam filtering using inexact string matching in explicit feature space with on-line linear classifiers, *in* E. M. Voorhees & L. P. Buckland, eds., "Proceedings of the 15th Text REtrieval Conference (TREC)," Special Publication 500-272, National Institute of Standards and Technology (NIST).

Segal, R., Crawford, J., Kephart, J., & Leiba, B. (2004), SpamGuru: An enterprise anti-spam filtering system, *in* "Conference on Email and Anti-Spam (CEAS)" available at http://citeseerx.ist.psu.edu/viewdoc/download?doi=10.1.1.60.114&rep=rep1&type=pdf.

Settles, B. (2009), Active Learning Literature Survey, Computer Sciences Technical Report 1648, University of Wisconsin–Madison.

Shalev-Shwartz, S. & Srebro, N. (2008), SVM optimization: Inverse dependence on training set size, *in* "25th International Conference on Machine Learning (ICML)," pp. 928–935.

Shannon, C. E. (1949), "Communication theory of secrecy systems," *Bell System Technical Journal* **28**, 656–715.

Shannon, C. E. (1959), "Probability of error for optimal codes in a Gaussian channel," *Bell System Technical Journal* **38**(3), 611–656.

Shaoul, C. & Westbury, C. (2007), "A USENET corpus (2005–2007)." Accessed October 2007 at http://www.psych.ualberta.ca/~westburylab/downloads/usenetcorpus.download.html. A more expansive version is available at The Westbury Lab USENET Corpus, https://aws.amazon.com/datasets/the-westburylab-usenet-corpus/.

Shawe-Taylor, J. & Cristianini, N. (2004), *Kernel Methods for Pattern Analysis*, Cambridge University Press.

Smith, A. (2011), Privacy-preserving statistical estimation with optimal convergence rates, *in* "Proceedings of the Forty-Third Annual ACM Symposium on Theory of Computing (STOC)," pp. 813–822.

Smith, R. L. (1996), The hit-and-run sampler: A globally reaching Markov chain sampler for generating arbitrary multivariate distributions, *in* "Proceedings of the 28th Conference on Winter Simulation (WSC)," pp. 260–264.

Somayaji, A. & Forrest, S. (2000), Automated response using system-call delays, *in* "Proceedings of the Conference on USENIX Security Symposium (SSYM)," pp. 185–197.

Sommer, R. & Paxson, V. (2010), Outside the closed world: On using machine learning for network intrusion detection, *in* "Proceedings of the 2010 IEEE Symposium on Security and Privacy," pp. 305–316.

Soule, A., Salamatian, K., & Taft, N. (2005), Combining filtering and statistical methods for anomaly detection, *in* "Proceedings of the 5th Conference on Internet Measurement (IMC)," USENIX Association, pp. 331–344.

Srndic, N. & Laskov, P. (2014), Practical evasion of a learning-based classifier: A case study, *in* "2014 IEEE Symposium on Security and Privacy, SP 2014," pp. 197–211.

Stevens, D. & Lowd, D. (2013), On the hardness of evading combinations of linear classifiers, *in* "Proceedings of the 2013 ACM Workshop on Artificial Intelligence and Security (AISec'13)," pp. 77–86.

Stolfo, S. J., Hershkop, S., Wang, K., Nimeskern, O., & Hu, C.-W. (2003), A behavior-based approach to securing email systems, *in Mathematical Methods, Models and Architectures for Computer Networks Security*, Springer-Verlag, pp. 57–81.

Stolfo, S. J., Li, W., Hershkop, S., Wang, K., Hu, C., & Nimeskern, O. (2006), Behavior-based modeling and its application to Email analysis, *in* "ACM Transactions on Internet Technology (TOIT)," pp. 187–211.

Sweeney, L. (2002), "*k*-anonymity: A model for protecting privacy," *International Journal of Uncertainty, Fuzziness and Knowledge-Based Systems* **10**(5), 557–570.

Tan, K. M. C., Killourhy, K. S., & Maxion, R. A. (2002), Undermining an anomaly-based intrusion detection system using common exploits, *in* A. Wespi, G. Vigna, & L. Deri, eds., "Proceedings of the 5th International Symposium on Recent Advances in Intrusion Detection (RAID)," Vol. 2516 of *Lecture Notes in Computer Science*, Springer, pp. 54–73.

Tan, K. M. C., McHugh, J., & Killourhy, K. S. (2003), Hiding intrusions: From the abnormal to the normal and beyond, *in* "Revised Papers from the 5th International Workshop on Information Hiding (IH)," Springer-Verlag, pp. 1–17.

Torkamani, M. & Lowd, D. (2013), Convex adversarial collective classification, *in* "Proceedings of the 30th International Conference on Machine Learning ICML," pp. 642–650.

Torkamani, M. A. & Lowd, D. (2014), On robustness and regularization of structural support vector machines, *in* "Proceedings of the 31st International Conference on Machine Learning (ICML-14)," pp. 577–585.

Tramèr, F., Zhang, F., Juels, A., Reiter, M. K., & Ristenpart, T. (2016), Stealing machine learning models via prediction apis, *in* "Proceedings of the 25th USENIX Security Symposium," pp. 601–618.

Tukey, J. W. (1960), "A survey of sampling from contaminated distributions," *Contributions to Probability and Statistics* pp. 448–485.

Turing, A. M. (1950), "Computing machinery and intelligence," *Mind* **59**(236), 433–460.

Valiant, L. G. (1984), "A theory of the learnable," *Communications of the ACM* **27**(11), 1134–1142.

Valiant, L. G. (1985), Learning disjunctions of conjunctions, *in* "Proceedings of the International Joint Conference on Artificial Intelligence (IJCAI)," pp. 560–566.

Vapnik, V. N. (1995), *The Nature of Statistical Learning Theory*, Springer-Verlag.

Venkataraman, S., Blum, A., & Song, D. (2008), Limits of learning-based signature generation with adversaries, *in* "Proceedings of the Network and Distributed System Security Symposium (NDSS)," The Internet Society available at http://www.isoc.org/isoc/conferences/ndss/08/papers/18_limits_learning-based.pdf.

Wagner, D. (2004), Resilient aggregation in sensor networks, *in* "Proceedings of the Workshop on Security of Ad Hoc and Sensor Networks (SASN)," pp. 78–87.

Wagner, D. & Soto, P. (2002), Mimicry attacks on host-based intrusion detection systems, *in* "Proceedings of the 9th ACM Conference on Computer and Communications Security (CCS)," pp. 255–264.

Wang, K., Parekh, J. J., & Stolfo, S. J. (2006), Anagram: A content anomaly detector resistant to mimicry attack, *in* D. Zamboni & C. Krügel, eds., "Proceedings of the 9th International Symposium on Recent Advances in Intrusion Detection (RAID)," Vol. 4219 of *Lecture Notes in Computer Science*, Springer, pp. 226–248.

Wang, K. & Stolfo, S. J. (2004), Anomalous payload-based network intrusion detection, *in* E. Jonsson, A. Valdes, & M. Almgren, eds., "Proceedings of the 7th International Conference on Recent Advances in Intrusion Detection (RAID)," Vol. 3224 of *Lecture Notes in Computer Science*, Springer, pp. 203–222.

Wang, Y.-X., Fienberg, S. E., & Smola, A. J. (2015), Privacy for free: Posterior sampling and stochastic gradient Monte Carlo, *in* "ICML," pp. 2493–2502.

Wang, Y.-X., Lei, J., & Fienberg, S. E. (2016), "Learning with differential privacy: Stability, learnability and the sufficiency and necessity of ERM principle," *Journal of Machine Learning Research* **17**(183), 1–40.

Wang, Z., Fan, K., Zhang, J., & Wang, L. (2013), Efficient algorithm for privately releasing smooth queries, *in* "Advances in Neural Information Processing Systems," pp. 782–790.

Wang, Z., Josephson, W. K., Lv, Q., Charikar, M., & Li, K. (2007), Filtering image spam with near-duplicate detection, *in* "Proceedings of the 4th Conference on Email and Anti-Spam (CEAS)" available at http://citeseerx.ist.psu.edu/viewdoc/download?doi=10.1.1.94.9550&rep=rep1&type=pdf.

Warrender, C., Forrest, S., & Pearlmutter, B. (1999), Detecting intrusions using system calls: Alternative data models, *in* "Proceedings of the IEEE Symposium on Security and Privacy (SP)," IEEE Computer Society, pp. 133–145.

Wittel, G. L. & Wu, S. F. (2004), On attacking statistical spam filters, *in* "Proceedings of the 1st Conference on Email and Anti-Spam (CEAS)" available at https://pdfs.semanticscholar.org/af5f/4b5f8548e740735b6c2abc1a5ef9c5ebf2df.pdf.

Wyner, A. D. (1965), "Capabilities of bounded discrepancy decoding," *Bell System Technical Journal* **44**, 1061–1122.

Xiao, H., Biggio, B., Brown, G., Fumera, G., Eckert, C., & Roli, F. (2015), Is feature selection secure against training data poisoning?, *in* "Proceedings of the 32nd International Conference on Machine Learning, ICML 2015," pp. 1689–1698.

Xu, H., Caramanis, C., & Mannor, S. (2009), "Robustness and regularization of support vector machines," *Journal of Machine Learning Research* **10**(Jul), 1485–1510.

Xu, W., Bodík, P., & Patterson, D. A. (2004), A flexible architecture for statistical learning and data mining from system log streams, *in* "Proceedings of Workshop on Temporal Data Mining: Algorithms, Theory and Applications at the 4th IEEE International Conference on Data Mining (ICDM)" available at http://citeseerx.ist.psu.edu/viewdoc/download?doi=10.1.1.135.7897&rep=rep1&type=pdf.

Zhang, F., Chan, P. P. K., Biggio, B., Yeung, D. S., & Roli, F. (2016), "Adversarial feature selection against evasion attacks," *IEEE Transactions of Cybernetics* **46**(3), 766–777.

Zhang, J., Zhang, Z., Xiao, X., Yang, Y., & Winslett, M. (2012), "Functional mechanism: Regression analysis under differential privacy," *Proceedings of the VLDB Endowment* **5**(11), 1364–1375.

Zhang, Y., Ge, Z., Greenberg, A., & Roughan, M. (2005), Network anomography, *in* "Proceedings of the 5th ACM SIGCOMM Conference on Internet Measurement (IMC)," USENIX Association, Berkeley, CA, USA, pp. 317–330.

Zhang, Z., Rubinstein, B. I. P., & Dimitrakakis, C. (2016), On the differential privacy of Bayesian inference, *in* "Proceedings of the 30th AAAI Conference on Artificial Intelligence (AAAI'2016)," pp. 51–60.

Zhao, W.-Y., Chellappa, R., Phillips, P. J., & Rosenfeld, A. (2003), "Face recognition: A literature survey," *ACM Computing Surveys* **35**(4), 399–458.

Index